Directive (Pseudooperation)	MASM 6.0	MASM 5.1	MsQA 2.51		
.ENDIF	✓				
ENDIF	✓	✓	✓	✓	✓
ENDM	✓	✓	✓	✓	✓
ENDP	✓	✓	✓	✓	✓
ENDS	✓	✓	✓	✓	✓
.ENDW	✓				
ENUM				✓	
EQU	✓	✓	✓	✓	✓
.ERR	✓	✓	✓	✓	✓
ERR				✓	✓
.ERR1		✓	✓	✓	✓
.ERR2		✓	✓	✓	✓
.ERRB	✓	✓	✓	✓	✓
.ERRDEF	✓	✓	✓	✓	✓
.ERRDIF	✓	✓	✓	✓	✓
.ERRDIFI	✓	✓	✓	✓	✓
.ERRE	✓	✓	✓	✓	✓
.ERRIDN	✓	✓	✓	✓	✓
.ERRIDNI	✓	✓	✓	✓	✓
ERRIF, ERRIF1, ERRIF2				✓	✓
ERRIFB, ERRIFDEF, ERRIFDIF				✓	✓
ERRIFDIFI, ERRIFE, ERRIFIDN				✓	✓
ERRIFIDNI, ERRIFNB, ERRIFNDEF				✓	✓
.ERRNB	✓	✓	✓	✓	✓
.ERRNDEF	✓	✓	✓	✓	✓
.ERRNZ	✓	✓	✓	✓	✓
EVEN	✓	✓	✓	✓	✓
EVENDATA				✓	✓
.EXIT	✓				
EXITCODE				✓	
EXITM	✓	✓	✓	✓	✓
EXTERN	✓				
EXTERNDEF	✓				
EXTRN	✓	✓	✓	✓	✓
.FARDATA	✓	✓	✓	✓	✓
.FARDATA?	✓	✓	✓	✓	✓
FARDATA				✓	✓
FOR	✓				
FORC	✓				
FWORD	✓				
GLOBAL				✓	✓
GOTO	✓				
GROUP	✓	✓	✓		✓
IDEAL				✓	✓
.IF	✓				
IF	✓	✓	✓	✓	✓
IF1		✓	✓	✓	✓
IF2		✓	✓	✓	✓
IFB, IFDEF, IFDIF	✓	✓	✓	✓	✓
IFDIFI, IFE, IFIDN	✓	✓	✓	✓	✓
IFIDNI, IFNB, IFNDEF	✓	✓	✓	✓	✓
%INCL				✓	✓
INCLUDE	✓	✓	✓	✓	✓
INCLUDELIB	✓	✓	✓	✓	✓
INSTR	✓	✓	✓	✓	✓
IRP	✓	✓	✓	✓	✓
IRPC	✓	✓	✓	✓	✓
INVOKE	✓				
JUMPS				✓	✓
LABEL	✓	✓	✓	✓	✓
.LALL	✓	✓	✓	✓	✓
LARGESTACK				✓	

Continues on the inside back cover

Using Assembly Language

3rd Edition

Allen L. Wyatt, Sr.

PROGRAMMING
S E R I E S

Using Assembly Language,
3rd Edition

Library of Congress Catalog No.: 92-80083

ISBN: 0-88022-884-9

95 94 93 92   8 7 6 5 4 3 2 1

Interpretation of the printing code: the rightmost number
of the first series of numbers is the year of the book's
printing; the rightmost number of the second series of
numbers is the number of the book's printing. For
example, a printing code of 92-1 shows that the first
printing of the book occurred in 1992.

This book was written for DOS version 5.0. The examples
in this book should work with the following software,
through the versions listed:

Borland C++ 3.0	Microsoft Macro Assembler 6.0
Clipper 5.01	Microsoft Source Profiler 1.0
CodeView 3.14	NMAKE.EXE 1.13
dBASE III+ 1.1	QBasic (version with DOS 5.0)
dBASE IV 1.1	QuickBASIC 4.5
FoxPro 2.0	QuickC 2.5
GW-BASIC (version with DOS 4.01)	TLIB.EXE 3.02
LIB.EXE 3.18	TLINK.EXE 5.0
LINK.EXE 5.13	Turbo Assembler 3.0
MAKE.EXE 3.6	Turbo Debugger 3.0
Microsoft BASIC Compiler 7.1	Turbo Pascal 6.0
Microsoft C 6.0	Turbo Profiler 5.0

D edicated to Life.
In all its varied forms, it is nothing if not interesting.

Publisher	**Production Analyst**
Richard K. Swadley	Mary Beth Wakefield
Publishing Manager	**Book Design**
Joseph B. Wikert	Michele Laseau
Managing Editor	**Illustrator**
Neweleen A. Trebnik	Susan Moore
Acquisitions Editor	**Cover Art and Design**
Gregory S. Croy	Dan Armstrong
Development Editor	**Production**
Paula Northam Grady	Jeff Baker
	Keith Davenport
Production Editor	Mark Enochs
Andy Saff	Brook Farling
	Carrie Keesling
	Laurie Lee
Editors	Juli Pavey
Gail S. Burlakoff	Cindy L. Phipps
Erik Dafforn	Louise Shinault
Bryan Gambrel	Kevin Spear
	Phil Worthington
	Christine Young
Editorial Assistants	
Rosemarie Graham	
San Dee Phillips	**Indexer**
	Johnna Van Hoose
Technical Reviewer	
Greg Guntle	

*Composed in ITC Garamond and
MCP Digital by Prentice Hall Computer Publishing.*

Printed in the United States of America

*Screen reproductions in this book were created by means
of the program Collage Plus from Inner Media, Inc., Hollis, NH.*

ABOUT THE AUTHOR ▼

Allen L. Wyatt, Sr.

Allen Wyatt has been working with small computers for more than a dozen years, and has worked in virtually all facets of programming. He has written 15 books related to computing, programming, and programming languages. He is the president of Discovery Computing, Inc., a microcomputer consulting and services corporation. In his spare time, Allen likes to spend time with his wife and children doing the things that families do together.

CONTENT OVERVIEW

TABLE OF CONTENTS ▼

Part I: The Fundamentals of Assembly Language

Part II: Mixed Language Programming with Assembly Language

Part III: Applying Assembly Language Techniques

Part IV: Reference

TRADEMARK
ACKNOWLEDGMENTS

Que Corporation has made every attempt to supply trademark information about company names, products, and services mentioned in this book. Trademarks indicated below were derived from various sources. Que Corporation cannot attest to the accuracy of this information.

Ashton-Tate, dBASE III, dBASE III+, and dBASE IV are registered trademarks of Ashton-Tate Corporation.

Borland, SideKick, Turbo Assembler, Turbo C, and Turbo Pascal are registered trademarks of Borland International, Inc. Turbo Profiler is a trademark of Borland International, Inc.

Clipper is a trademark of Nantucket, Inc.

FoxBase, FoxBase+, and FoxPro are trademarks of Fox Holdings, Inc.

IBM and PS/2 are registered trademarks of International Business Machines Corporation. OS/2, PCjr, and PC XT are trademarks of International Business Machines Corporation.

Intel is a registered trademark of Intel Corporation. 386 is a trademark of Intel Corporation.

Microsoft, MS, MS-DOS, CodeView, GW-BASIC, QuickC, QuickAssembler, QuickBASIC, and XENIX are registered trademarks of Microsoft Corporation. Windows and QBasic are trademarks of Microsoft Corporation.

Motorola is a registered trademark of Motorola, Inc.

THUMB TAB INDEX

Introduction

Welcome to *Using Assembly Language*, 3rd Edition, a book written to help
you learn how to use assembly language subroutines to increase the performance of your programs. In a nutshell, this book is designed to help you put
assembly language to work in a meaningful way.

If you write programs in BASIC, Pascal, C, or C++ on the IBM family of
microcomputers and you want to make the most of your programming, you'll find
Using Assembly Language, 3rd Edition, a helpful learning aid and reference guide.
Each carefully designed chapter is packed with detailed information about the use
of assembly language subroutines in high-level language programs.

This book is written from a programmer's perspective. Precepts and examples are included to teach you the information you need to become proficient in the
use of assembly language. Also included are detailed reference materials. Building
on the framework developed in the first two editions, *Using Assembly Language*,
3rd Edition, covers more languages and more assembly language tools than any
other assembly language book available.

To help you understand *why* programming works, and what happens when
you program, I've emphasized the effects of assembly language instructions,
commands, and functions—how they are used and what they produce. There are no
"black boxes" here—nothing mysterious or questionable left unexplained. By
understanding assembly language, you will learn how to make better use of your
particular IBM environment.

The computer field changes quickly, seeming to go from simple to complex
overnight. *Using Assembly Language*, 3rd Edition, lays a firm foundation of the
precepts and underlying concepts on which the field's complex ideas are built. I've

1

tried to simplify many of the concepts the assembly language programmer must understand, so that you will lose neither your interest in nor your focus on these guiding precepts.

I've included many examples that you can try on your computer. Working through these examples on the computer (or even in your mind) should help you retain key ideas. I recommend that you use the computer as you read the book. If you want, you can also get the programming examples on disk; an order form is included at the back of the book.

Clearly, *Using Assembly Language*, 3rd Edition, is not intended as light, after-dinner reading. It is meant to provide a sound basis in the principles of developing assembly language subroutines, tapping the internal power of BIOS and DOS functions, and interfacing assembly language subroutines to high-level language programs. You can use many sections of the book as reference.

Why Use Assembly Language?

Broadly, assembly language falls into the category of a low-level language—in fact, many people consider it the *only* low-level language. As an assembly language programmer, you need to be more concerned and aware of what the computer is capable of and how it performs tasks than you are when you program in a high-level language. High-level languages such as BASIC, Pascal, C, or C++ introduce levels of abstraction that free you from needing to worry much about the hardware; many of these languages are portable to differing computers.

You may ask, "Why should I use assembly language?" There's no easy answer. The reasons for using assembly language vary, depending on the application in which you use it and the high-level language you use as the controlling program. A brief look at the development of high-level languages may help you better understand the value of assembly language.

Assembly language once was the only language available for microcomputers. But with the advent of high-level languages such as BASIC, and then Pascal, and later C, many programmers learned only these languages. Compared to assembly language, these languages were easy to learn and provided most of the functions ordinarily needed to program. Assembly language was often relegated to programmers in research labs (and padded cells).

Over time, as applications became increasingly complex, the limits of various high-level languages were tested and pushed about as far as they could go. Surely you have experienced the frustration of knowing that there must be a faster, slicker, more efficient way to do something than what you can do with the high-level language you're using. This frustration has led some programmers to change languages (hoping to find one that addressed most, if not all, of their needs) or to accept the limitations of their current high-level language.

No language is perfect. High-level languages are no exception—they all have strong points and corresponding weak points. And that's where assembly language subroutines come in: you can use them to augment the capabilities of the high-level languages in which you program.

The benefits of programming well-defined tasks in assembly language fall into four general areas: *speed*, *versatility*, *flexibility*, and *compact code*.

Assembly language is *fast*. To paraphrase an old saying, "It don't get any faster." During the assembly process, assembly language mnemonics translate directly into machine language—the native language for computers. No language is faster than machine language; its execution speed is the fastest possible on any given computer. Because assembly language is the root of all high-level programming languages, assembly language runs faster than any of these languages.

High-level languages can be *interpretive*, *compiled*, or *pseudocode*. Interpretive and pseudocode (a cross between interpretive and compiled code) languages require some translation into machine language at the time of execution. It is true that, depending on the implementation of the language, some high-level languages, once compiled, require no such translation at run-time. But assembly language source-code files, once assembled, never require translation; they have no overhead penalty of greater execution time.

Assembly language is *versatile*. Anything that can possibly be done with a computer can be done with assembly language. The only limiting factors are your imagination and the capacity of the computer system you're using.

Many high-level languages are designed to execute on a wide variety of computers, each of which has different capabilities and peripherals. These languages are designed for the "lowest common denominator" so that they cover the capabilities and peripherals likely to be on virtually every machine on which they might run. Assembly language has no such artificial limitation. Because the capabilities of your specific machine are the only limiting factor, assembly language allows great versatility in program development.

Although specifically suited only to one particular type of CPU, assembly language is *flexible*. Assembly language gives you a multitude of ways to accomplish one task. Some languages have rigid coding restraints that restrict the number of approaches to coding a particular task. Assembly language has no coding restraints. If your coding style is undisciplined, this degree of freedom may present drawbacks; you can easily end up with "spaghetti code." But if you are a disciplined, structured person (or at least write disciplined, structured code), you'll find the flexibility of assembly language refreshing. Mastering the language can be both challenging and rewarding.

Assembly language produces *compact code*. Because assembly language routines are written for a specific purpose in a language that translates directly into machine language, these routines will include code that only you, the programmer, want included.

High-level languages, on the other hand, are written for a general audience and include extraneous code. For instance, many high-level languages include intrinsic graphics functions or file-handling functions used by only a few applications. Needed or not, this irrelevant coding is included in every application.

Because assembly language mnemonic instructions translate directly into one or, at most, several bytes of data, there is no overhead unless you specifically choose to include it in your executable file.

What You Should Know

In any book, assumptions are made about what the reader knows. Those assumptions may be stated up front or may become clear after you've read the book. Before you read this book, you need to know what the assumptions are.

First, it is assumed that you know at least one high-level language—BASIC, Pascal, C, or C++—or one of the database languages such as dBASE. These are used throughout this book. (If you know more than one of these languages, you will benefit even more from *Using Assembly Language*, 3rd Edition.)

You should be familiar with ASCII, the native coding scheme used for character representation on the IBM PC family of microcomputers. Many assembly language subroutines in this book (and elsewhere) use and manipulate ASCII characters. You don't need to memorize the entire code, but you may want to keep an ASCII table within reach while you work through this book. Appendix A is an ASCII chart.

Because you're reading this book, I assume that at one time or another you have had experience programming and that you are familiar with the different numbering systems commonly used with microcomputers: binary (base 2), decimal (base 10), and hexadecimal (base 16). If you're familiar with octal (base 8), so much the better, but familiarity with octal is not necessary. If you have trouble working with any of these systems, writing assembly language code should quickly provide all the familiarity you could ever want. *Using Assembly Language*, 3rd Edition, doesn't delve into the differences between numbering systems or the reasons for using binary or hexadecimal systems.

Depending on your programming background, you may be familiar with many different notations for numbering systems. Because of the inherent possibilities for confusion when you work with binary, decimal, and hexadecimal numbers, some sort of notation is needed to differentiate between the systems.

This book's approach to notation is simple and straightforward: a lowercase *b* is appended to *binary* numbers, and a lowercase *h* to *hexadecimal* numbers; decimal numbers have no appendage (see table I.1).

Table I.1. *Number representation.*

Binary	Decimal	Hexadecimal
00001110b	14	0Eh
01101011b	107	6Bh
10111011b	187	BBh
11010101b	213	D5h
0000000110110000b	432	01B0h
0000001001010101b	597	0255h
0000001101100111b	871	0367h
0000101111111111b	3071	0BFFh
0101111111111000b	24568	5FF8h

As you can see from this table, binary and hexadecimal numbers occupy an even number of digits. Every digit in a binary number represents a *bit*. Every two digits of a hexadecimal number represent a *byte*, or eight bits, and every four digits represent a *word*, or two bytes. As an assembly language programmer, you must learn to think in groupings—bits, bytes, and words.

Speaking of words—the other kind—you should be familiar with certain rudimentary terms. You'll find a glossary at the end of this book, but the following definitions should prove helpful at this point and throughout the book:

Assembler: The software program that translates (assembles) assembly language mnemonics into machine language for direct execution by the computer. Typical assemblers include MASM from Microsoft and Turbo Assembler from Borland International.

Assembly: A process of code conversion, done by an assembler, that translates assembly language source code into machine language.

Assembly Language: The English-style language (also called *source code*) that is understandable to humans. Assembly language is not directly executable by computers. The previously listed assemblers share a common assembly language subset, but each includes some unique language elements that are missing from the others. This book concentrates on the common subset.

Linker: A program that performs the linking process. Typical linkers include LINK from Microsoft and TLINK from Borland.

Linking: The process of resolving external references and address references in object code. The resulting machine language instructions are directly executable by a computer.

Machine Language: The series of binary digits executed by a microprocessor to accomplish individual tasks. People seldom (if ever) program in machine language. Instead, they program in assembly language and use an assembler to translate their instructions into machine language.

Object Code: A half-way step between source code and executable machine language. Object code, which is not directly executable by a computer, must go through a *linking* process that resolves external references and address references.

Source Code: The assembly language instructions written by a programmer and then translated into object code by an assembler.

What Is Covered in This Book

Whenever I pick up a book, the first thing I want to know is whether the book will help me. Will it teach me what I need to know?

You can see from the table of contents that *Using Assembly Language*, 3rd Edition, covers many technical areas related to assembly language programming. For easy reference, the book is divided into four parts. The following is a quick outline of the contents of each chapter.

Part I, "The Fundamentals of Assembly Language." Chapter 1, "Understanding the Programming Environment," introduces you to the basic information you need to successfully program in assembly language on Intel microprocessors in the IBM family of computers.

Chapter 2, "An Overview of Assembly Language," introduces you to the basics of programming in assembly language. This chapter touches on the structure, main commands, and operations needed to use assembly language.

Chapter 3, "Choosing and Using Your Assembler," explains what the assembler does, describes a couple of the most popular assembler programs, and describes the common ways in which these programs operate.

Chapter 4, "Choosing and Using Your Linker," compares the most popular linker programs and explains how to link assembled programs. LINK parameters and file types are included in this chapter.

Chapter 5, "Using Microsoft's Assembly Language Products," covers the assembler and linker available from Microsoft. In this chapter you learn, through a hands-on session, how MASM 6.0 does its work.

Chapter 6, "Using Borland's Assembly Language Products," accomplishes the same tasks in relation to Borland's assembler and linker. Through a detailed hands-on example, you learn how to develop, assemble, and link a subroutine with a program developed in Borland C++.

Chapter 7, "Debugging Assembly Language Subroutines," shows how to use the DEBUG program that comes with DOS, or one of the popular symbolic debuggers, such as CodeView and Turbo Debugger. In this chapter you learn to locate, isolate, and correct errors and problems in assembly language subroutines.

Chapter 8, "Using Additional Tools," explains how to use make files and profilers to speed your work. You learn why these tools are so popular and what they can do for you.

Chapter 9, "Developing Libraries," covers the creation, use, and management of object-file libraries of assembly language subroutines.

Part II, "Mixed Language Programming with Assembly Language." Chapter 10, "Interfacing Subroutines," covers general information about interfacing assembly language subroutines with high-level language programs.

Chapter 11, "Interfacing with BASIC," provides specific information about and examples of using assembly language subroutines from both interpretive and compiled BASIC.

Chapter 12, "Interfacing with Pascal," gives you specific interfacing information for programs written in Pascal.

Chapter 13, "Interfacing with C and C++," details how to interface assembly language subroutines with these most-popular of languages.

Chapter 14, "Interfacing with dBASE III+ and FoxPro," explains how to interface assembly language subroutines with the most widely used DBMS language.

Chapter 15, "Interfacing with Clipper," shows how to create user-defined functions in assembly language for use with the Clipper database compiler.

Part III, "Applying Assembly Language Techniques." Chapter 16, "Working with Different Processors," explains how to discover what type of CPU you are using and determine whether you have a numeric coprocessor in your computer.

Chapter 17, "Video Memory," provides extremely detailed information on how to manipulate (from assembly language) the memory areas that control the display of information on a computer monitor.

Chapter 18, "Accessing Hardware Ports," covers working at the hardware level from assembly language. Examples include accessing the keyboard and speaker controllers.

Chapter 19, "Working with Disk Drives," covers low-level disk access, focusing on how to format floppy disks.

Part IV, "Reference." Chapter 20, "Accessing BIOS Services," details the BIOS interrupts and services and the tasks they perform. Corresponding information for the different DOS interrupts and services is included in Chapter 21, "The DOS Services."

Chapter 22, "Processor Instruction Set," provides detailed reference information for the Intel 8086/8088, 80286, 80386, 80486, 8087, 80287, and 80387.

Chapter 23, "Assembler Directives," covers all the extended capabilities added to MASM and TASM through directives. Through the use of directives, you can make your assembler do much of the "grunt work" of assembly language for you automatically.

Using Assembly Language, 3rd Edition, contains two useful appendixes. Appendix A presents the standard ASCII character codes, and the BIOS keyboard codes and keyboard controller codes are included in Appendix B.

Finally, *Using Assembly Language*, 3rd Edition, contains a brief glossary.

What Is Not Covered in This Book

Using Assembly Language, 3rd Edition, is packed with information but cannot possibly cover all related subjects. This book has limits.

First, this book does not teach high-level languages. In fact, it does not purport to teach any language. Its purpose is to show how to make two languages—assembly language and BASIC, Pascal, C, C++, or your database language—work together for the benefit of both the program and programmer.

As you read and work through this book, you probably will learn something about each of these languages. You'll undoubtedly learn a great deal about assembly language, but please don't feel that you've learned it all. Learning how to do things well takes *years*—and by then the rules have all changed. And don't be surprised if someday you learn from another source a quicker, easier way to do a task than what you learn here. Part of the fun of living is that people keep developing new ideas and methods.

Programming style is a big deal for many authors. Style is fine and promotes logical thinking, but I believe that coding must meet only a few criteria:

❏ *Is the code intelligible?* Adequate remarks (perhaps for every line) and appropriate line formatting help.

❏ *Will others understand the code?* Because you may not be around to decipher any sloppy, obtuse, or idiosyncratic coding when changes to the code must be made in a month or a year, you must write for those who follow. In case you are around to make the changes, don't challenge yourself to remember months or years from now what you had in mind when you wrote some cryptic gobbledygook; keep it clear and simple.

❏ *Does it work?* In my opinion, this is the single most important criterion of all.

This book does not adhere to any published or unpublished set of programming conventions or techniques. The goal for this book is to provide clear, concise, intelligent, working code to help you become more productive. You can organize and optimize your software by simply applying to assembly language programming the same logical structures and common sense encouraged by high-level languages.

Graphics programming, because of its specialized nature, is beyond the scope of this book. Entire volumes can be written about true graphics and graphic manipulation. Indeed, assembly language is well suited for writing graphics routines. For example, the sheer volume of data that must be processed to perform animation demands a level of speed available only through assembly language.

Writers, programmers, and others often misuse the word *graphics*. Text screens are frequently referred to as "graphics" screens. This confusion arises because, on the IBM, certain ASCII codes correspond to special characters that are neither textual nor numeric, but clearly graphic. Although these characters permit you to enhance an otherwise bland text screen, the screen is not a true graphics screen. Text screens deal with data on a character level; graphics screens manipulate data on a pixel level.

Using Assembly Language, 3rd Edition, *does* cover the use of textual graphics and color. Library routines that allow all sorts of snazzy screen creations (using text characters) with assembly language drivers from high-level languages are discussed and developed.

Summary

I hope that you now have a sense of what this book is, as well as what it isn't. Because I've felt the need for this type of book, writing it has been important to me. Ideally, you also have felt that need. Items missing from the earlier editions have been included in this edition, along with new information yielded by technology. If any information that you feel belongs in this book is missing, I would like to know about it. Feel free to contact me either through the publisher, at the address on the order form at the back of the book, or on CompuServe (72561,2207).

Now, if you're ready, let's begin the process. May yours be a fruitful journey.

Part I

The Fundamentals of Assembly Language

1

Understanding the Programming Environment

Before you can start using assembly language, you must understand the environment in which you will be programming. Without at least a rudimentary understanding, you may find yourself writing unnecessary code and redoing your work quite a bit. In this chapter, you learn about the programming environment of the IBM PC family of computers. This environment includes both hardware and software facets.

The hardware environment includes the structure and programming architecture of the microprocessor used in the IBM family. The IBM PC and PC XT and their clones use the Intel 8088; the IBM Personal Computer AT uses the Intel 80286; newer computers use the Intel 80386 or 80486. The new generation of DOS or OS/2 computers all use one of these four microprocessors.

All of these microprocessor chips are *upward compatible*—anything programmed for the 8086/8088 will run on the 80286, 80386, and 80486, and anything programmed for the 80286 will run on the 80386 and 80486. These processors are not *downward compatible*, however. Software written for the 80386 or 80486 will not necessarily run on the 80286, and that written for the 80286 may not run on the 8086/8088.

Each generation of microprocessor has added different instructions and operating modes to the basic set used in the 8086/8088. These improvements prevent the processors from being downward compatible. In addition, you can add even more assembly language instructions if your computer has one of three chips—usually called the 8087, 80287, or 80387 numeric coprocessors.

The software environment refers to features made available through the use of any type of controlling software. "Controlling software" refers primarily to the Basic Input/Output System (BIOS) and the Disk Operating System (DOS), but may refer to other software such as DOS extenders, memory managers, device drivers, or to programs such as Windows.

This chapter will teach you about key points of both hardware and software in the programming environment. You need a solid understanding of this environment to program successfully in assembly language. The concepts presented in later chapters build upon the foundation in this chapter and Chapter 2, "An Overview of Assembly Language."

The 25-Cent Tour of Memory

Because assembly language inherently involves working at a level that is much closer to the computer than other languages, you need to understand how your computer uses memory. (Other languages generally handle memory and memory management automatically.)

On the IBM PC, running under DOS, as much as 640K of memory is available (655,360 bytes of storage). Your specific computer system may have additional memory (called *high memory*, *extended memory*, or *expanded memory*). Under regular, plain-vanilla DOS, however, this additional memory is not directly accessible. In fact, the main memory area (the first 640K of memory) is not completely available.

Within main memory, certain areas are reserved for specific predefined uses. For instance, some of the memory is used for BIOS and DOS. Other areas are system areas that hold information enabling BIOS and DOS to function properly. Still other areas may have user-installed resident programs such as memory managers, network drivers, or utility programs like SideKick or ProKey. Figure 1.1 is a typical memory map.

Fig. 1.1. Sample memory map.

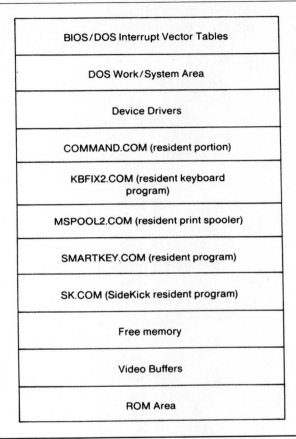

If it weren't for some of the memory-management functions built into DOS, the average programmer would have to struggle with memory conflicts among programs. DOS functions allow you to request, reserve, and manage blocks of memory for your programs. These functions are detailed in Chapter 21.

Microprocessors use an address register to keep track of memory locations at which operations should be occurring. The size of the address register usually dictates the maximum amount of memory a computer can use. Table 1.1 shows how much memory is addressable by various address register capacities.

Table 1.1. *Addressable memory by address-register size.*

Address Register Bits	Addressable Memory (bytes)	Memory Size
8	256	
9	512	
10	1,024	1K
11	2,048	2K
12	4,096	4K
13	8,192	8K
14	16,384	16K
15	32,768	32K
16	65,536	64K
17	131,072	128K
18	262,144	256K
19	524,288	512K
20	1,048,576	1M
21	2,097,152	2M
22	4,194,304	4M
23	8,388,608	8M
24	16,777,216	16M
25	33,554,432	32M
26	67,108,864	64M
27	134,217,728	128M
28	268,435,456	256M
29	536,870,912	512M
30	1,073,741,824	1G
31	2,147,483,648	2G
32	4,294,967,296	4G

Each memory location requires its own unique address. Two memory locations cannot have the same address; if they did, operations affecting the locations would become jumbled. Imagine what would happen if your house and your neighbor's house had the same address. Without additional information, the mailman wouldn't know what mail went to which house.

The Intel microprocessors use an instruction pointer (IP) to keep track of the machine-language instructions currently being executed. This pointer is simply a 16-bit address register specialized for this purpose. From table 1.1, you can determine that 16 bits can hold unsigned integers in the range of 0 to 65,535.

As mentioned earlier, the IBM PC (running under DOS) can have up to 640K of memory. If the IP can hold only 65,536 values, how can each of 655,360 possible memory locations be addressed? Holding the 655,360 values necessary for 640K of memory would require an address register of at least 20 bits. The obvious solution would be to use a larger register size, but Intel used a more indirect and potentially confusing solution.

Intel used a *segment register* to control the general area (segment) of memory being pointed to, with the IP as an offset pointer into that segment. Each segment of memory can be up to 65,536 bytes (64K) in size. This scheme was a radical departure not only from the memory addressing schemes used in earlier microprocessors but also from the schemes used by other microprocessors such as the Motorola 68000 family. Suddenly, the program could address directly a maximum of only 64K of memory.

Through segment notation, each memory location can be addressed individually in the format

SSSS:OOOO

where SSSS is the segment and OOOO is the offset. Memory locations given in this format are always in hexadecimal notation. The segment portion of the address can range from 0 to FFFFh; depending on the segment, the offset portion also can range from 0 to FFFFh.

The absolute address of any memory location can be determined by multiplying the segment value by 10h (which is the same as 16 decimal) and then adding the offset value. Thus, the absolute location of 1871:321F is determined by 18710h plus 321Fh, or 1B92Fh. Based on this addressing notation, it seems logical that the total addressable memory could range from 0000:0000 (0) to FFFF:FFFF (1,114,095)—slightly over 1M (megabyte) of memory. Remember, however, that the limit for DOS is 640K; therefore, the calculated absolute memory address cannot exceed 655,360. (The "missing" 384K is actually used by the ROM-BIOS, video RAM, and other system components; it's not really missing at all, just unavailable to your programs.)

Clearly, memory segments can overlap and any unique memory location can be addressed in many ways. Table 1.2 shows the notation of several memory addresses, all of which refer to the same absolute memory location.

Table 1.2. *Segment/offset pairs address absolute memory location 027920h.*

Segment Notation	Physical Address Calculation
17A5:FED0	17A50h + FED0h = 27920h
1A74:D1E0	1A740h + D1E0h = 27920h
1AFF:C930	1AFF0h + C930h = 27920h
1D90:A020	1D900h + A020h = 27920h
1F93:7FF0	1f930h + 7FF0h = 27920h
2292:5000	22920h + 5000h = 27920h
2515:27D0	25150h + 27D0h = 27920h
2654:13E0	26540h + 13E0h = 27920h
26D0:0C20	26D00h + 0C20h = 27920h
2777:01B0	27770h + 01B0h = 27920h
278F:0030	278F0h + 0030h = 27920h
2790:0020	27900h + 0020h = 27920h
2791:0010	27910h + 0010h = 27920h
2792:0000	27920h + 0000h = 27920h

To create figure 1.2, addresses were attached to the memory map shown in figure 1.1. The address in your system may vary (sometimes greatly) depending on your memory configuration, DOS version, program use, and other factors.

If you are using DOS 5, you can see a fairly detailed memory map for your system by using the MEM command with the /P command-line switch. The following is an example of what is displayed when you issue the MEM /P command:

```
Address    Name        Size      Type
-------    --------    ------    ------
000000                 000400    Interrupt Vector
000400                 000100    ROM Communication Area
000500                 000200    DOS Communication Area

000700     IO          000A60    System Data

001160     MSDOS       0013D0    System Data

002530     IO          002210    System Data
           QEMM386     000970      DEVICE=
```

```
              LOADHI     0000A0      DEVICE=
              LOADHI     0000A0      DEVICE=
              LOADHI     0000A0      DEVICE=
              LOADHI     0000A0      DEVICE=
              LOADHI     0000A0      DEVICE=
              LOADHI     0000A0      DEVICE=
                         000820      FILES=
                         000100      FCBS=
                         000200      BUFFERS=
                         0001C0      LASTDRIVE=
                         000740      STACKS=
    004750    MSDOS      000040      System Program

    0047A0    COMMAND    000940      Program
    0050F0    MSDOS      000040      -- Free --
    005140    COMMAND    000140      Environment
    005290    MEM        0000D0      Environment
    005370    MEM        0176F0      Program
    01CA70    MSDOS      083580      -- Free --


    655360 bytes total conventional memory
    655360 bytes available to MS-DOS
    633984 largest executable program size

   3866624 bytes total EMS memory
   1064960 bytes free EMS memory

   3145728 bytes total contiguous extended memory
         0 bytes available contiguous extended memory
   1064960 bytes available XMS memory
           MS-DOS resident in High Memory Area
```

Notice that the MEM command does not indicate some of the information shown in figure 1.2. For instance, it does not show the beginning addresses of the video buffers or the ROM area.

When you program in assembly language, you need not be concerned about the actual memory address in which your program will reside physically. The linking process, and subsequent DOS loaders, take care of positioning your program and getting it ready to execute. If you want more information about where the program will reside, you may want to refer to a more technical book about DOS, such as *DOS Programmer's Reference*, 3rd Edition, published by Que Corporation. One of the issues such books address is how programs are loaded and how they begin execution. If you find this topic interesting, you may want to pay particular attention to the differences between COM and EXE files.

Although you don't need to worry about *program* addresses, you do need to know about segment and offset notation for addressing specific *data* in memory, such as system parameters or vector addresses. That specific topic is covered shortly.

Fig. 1.2. *Sample memory map with addresses.*

00000h	BIOS/DOS Interrupt Vector Tables
00500h	DOS Work/System Area
04C00h	Device Drivers
05400h	COMMAND.COM (resident portion)
0E0A0h	KBFIX2.COM (resident keyboard program)
0E8E0h	MSPOOL2.COM (resident print spooler)
1E720h	SMARTKEY.COM (resident program)
26F70h	SK.COM (SideKick resident program)
37A80h	Free memory
A0000h	Video Buffers
C0000h	ROM Area

The Stack

A special segment of memory, called the *stack*, is reserved for the temporary storage of data. To program effectively in assembly language, you must understand the stack. Even if you are already familiar with the concepts related to a stack, take just a moment to review them. Because later sections of this book present assembly language instructions and routines that rely on the stack, the basics must be covered now.

If you have never worked with one, a stack can be confusing at first. A stack is a last-in, first-out (LIFO) *queue*; it operates much like the spring-loaded plate servers in a cafeteria line. Each plate placed on the server makes the lower plates inaccessible. Conversely, removing a plate makes the one under it immediately available. Plates can only be removed in the reverse order of their placement on the server. The last plate added is always the first to be removed.

In the conceptual representation of the stack shown in figure 1.3, each box contains one *word* (16 bits) of data. The boxes can be removed in the reverse order of their placement on the stack. Only data at the top of the stack is accessible by conventional means. Data is shown as individual bytes, even though it can be deposited or extracted from the stack only one word (two bytes) at a time.

Fig. 1.3. *Conceptual representation of the stack.*

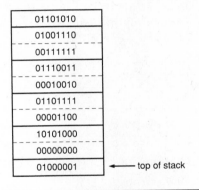

If your computer uses the 80386 or 80486 microprocessors, its stack is based on a *doubleword* (32 bits of data). Although you can use original commands that push and pop information from the stack in 16-bit increments, commands to manipulate the complete 32 bits also exist.

Throughout this book, you will see references to the stack. Some specific assembly language commands cause information to be deposited in the stack; others cause the information to be removed. This depositing and removing frequently results from another action you want to perform. As I discuss the assembly language commands, I will touch on the specific operations that affect the stack.

The stack is integral to passing information from a high-level language to an assembly language subroutine. Generally, information to be passed is pushed onto the stack, then removed as needed by the assembly language subroutine. This process is covered in detail in the discussion of passing parameters to assembly language subroutines, beginning in Chapter 10, "Interfacing Subroutines."

If you are a little confused about how the stack works and why it is important in assembly language programming, don't despair; such confusion is normal. As you work through the examples in this book, pay particular attention to how operations affect the stack. Doing so should clarify the concepts.

If you are quite confused about the stack, reread this section until you begin to grasp the concepts. Before you can understand the concepts behind assembly language programming, you must first understand the stack.

Registers and Flags

The 8086/8088 and subsequent generations of Intel microprocessors use *registers* to operate on data and to perform tasks. Registers are special storage areas built into the microprocessor. All registers are 16 bits (1 word) wide, but some operations can be performed on only one byte (8 bits) of specific registers. Table 1.3 shows the 8086/8088 register set.

Table 1.3. The 8086/8088 register set.

Name	Category	Purpose
AX	General purpose	Accumulator
BX	General purpose	Base
CX	General purpose	Counter
DX	General purpose	Data
SI	Index	Source index
DI	Index	Destination index
SP	Stack	Stack pointer
BP	Stack	Base pointer
CS	Segment	Code segment
DS	Segment	Data segment
SS	Segment	Stack segment
ES	Segment	Extra segment
IP		Instruction pointer
FLAGS		Operation flags

The four general-purpose registers (AX, BX, CX, and DX) can also be addressed by their component bytes. For instance, AH and AL are the individual bytes that make up the word register AX. The H and L indicate, respectively, the high byte or low byte. Similarly, BH and BL form BX, CH and CL make up CX, and DH and DL form DX.

The stack, segment, and instruction pointer registers are discussed in the following section. An understanding of the flag register will help you understand the 8086/8088 instruction set introduced in the next section of this chapter.

The flag register is the same size as the other registers (16 bits), but the 8086/8088 uses only 9 bits to signify status flags (see Chapter 22, "Processor Instruction Sets," for differences in later processor versions). These flags, shown in table 1.4, are set or cleared based on the results of individual operations.

Table 1.4. *Use of the 8086/8088 flag register.*

Bit	Use
0	Carry flag (CF)
1	
2	Parity flag (PF)
3	
4	Auxiliary carry flag (AF)
5	
6	Zero flag (ZF)
7	Sign flag (SF)
8	Trap flag (TF)
9	Interrupt flag (IF)
10	Direction flag (DF)
11	Overflow flag (OF)
12	
13	
14	
15	

Notice from table 1.4 that only nine flags are represented in the flag register. Bits 1, 3, 5, and 12 through 15 of this register are not used. Each of the other bits can, of course, be set to either 0 or 1. A 0 indicates that the flag is clear; a 1 indicates that the flag is set.

Certain assembly language instructions are used to set or clear individual flags. These instructions, often referred to as *flag* and *processor control* instructions, are detailed shortly. Other instructions set or clear individual flags to indicate the result of a previous operation. For instance, the zero flag (ZF) is set if the result of an arithmetic operation is zero, and cleared if the result is not zero.

A group of instructions referred to as *control transfer* instructions is used to test the value of the flags and then, based on the result, to transfer program control conditionally. To program effectively in assembly language, you must understand what the flags are and how they are used.

The Segment Registers

The processors used in the IBM family of microcomputers have four segment registers for addressing: the code, data, extra, and stack segment registers.

The code segment register (CS) contains the segment used with the instruction pointer register (IP). Thus, CS:IP contains the segment and offset of the next instruction to be executed by the processor.

The data segment register (DS) contains the segment used by general-purpose data operations. It is used also as the source segment for string operations.

The extra segment register (ES) is used as the target segment for string operations. It can be used also as a secondary segment register for general-purpose data operations.

The stack segment register (SS) is used as the reference segment for the stack and is used with the stack pointer (SP). Thus, SS:SP points to the top of the stack, the last place information was stored in the stack segment.

When you write small routines for use from high-level languages, most segment registers are set to the same addresses. In many instances, the code and data segments can be set to the same values so that the data used by the subroutines is actually part of the coding. This simplifies subroutine development. Exceptions occur when you want to use a specialized data area, in which case you can change the DS or ES registers. Typically, this is done when you need these registers to point into the data areas used by the high-level language. Many sample programs in this book use this technique.

When you write subroutines, don't change the stack segment. The controlling program usually sets the stack segment—you don't need to change it in your routines. Changing the stack segment without knowing how the stack was used prior to reaching your subroutine or without restoring the value of SP, the stack segment register, can result in undesirable side effects (usually a "system crash").

Additional Registers

The registers described so far are available in every Intel microprocessor, starting with the earliest 8088/8086. The 80286 (and the 80386 and 80486) include additional special-purpose registers.

80286 Registers

The additional registers used with the 80286 microprocessor include the global descriptor table (GDT) register, the interrupt descriptor table (IDT) register, the local descriptor table (LDT) register, the machine status word (MSW), and the task register.

These additional registers are used only when programming for *protected mode* operation. Because DOS cannot operate in protected mode (all DOS operations run in *real mode*, the other operating mode of the 80286), you are unlikely to find these registers useful. Typically, they are used in such system software as DOS extenders, which enable general programming in protected mode.

The two descriptor table registers make it possible to access 16M of memory address space rather than the 1M limit of the 8086/8088 designs, but again this capability is available only when operating in protected mode. If programmed for compatibility with DOS, the 80286 is little more than a faster version of the 8086/8088.

80386 and 80486 Registers

Unlike their 8-bit and 16-bit predecessors, the 80386 and 80486 are 32-bit microprocessors. The registers in the 80386 and 80486 reflect this enlarged structure. Both processors still use the same general-purpose registers as the 8086/8088 and the 80286 (AX, BX, CX, and DX), but the registers' full 32-bit counterparts are addressed by using the *E* (extended) prefix. EAX, EBX, ECX, and EDX are 32-bit general-purpose registers. Without the E, only the lower 16 bits of each register are accessed. Using the traditional AL, AH, BL, BH, CL, CH, DL, or DH gives you access to 8-bit chunks of the lower 16 bits of the registers.

This use of the *E* prefix to denote 32-bit register size applies also to other microprocessor registers, such as BP, SI, DI, and SP, which become EBP, ESI, EDI, and ESP, respectively.

The other segment registers—CS, DS, SS, and ES—are intact as implemented in earlier Intel microprocessors. These registers (still 16-bits wide) are joined by the FS and GS segment registers (also 16-bits wide), which operate the same as the ES register.

Interrupts

Frequently, a computer is called on to do many things at once. For instance, your computer may need to accept input from the keyboard, update the video screen, write information to disk, and print a report—all at the same time. This sort of processing is not unusual.

How does the computer do so many things simultaneously? In one method—*polling*—the operating system repeatedly checks everything it needs to check. The other method relies on *interrupts* to indicate when a task needs to be addressed. Perhaps an illustration is in order.

Suppose that you are the computer, and that you have half a dozen friends with whom you need to work. From time to time they have information to give you and you have things to tell them. If you operate by polling, you contact each friend at a set interval to see whether they need you and to give them any pending information. You may need to contact them every hour, or even every five minutes if you don't want to risk missing any information. Clearly, this can quickly become wasteful—you end up doing virtually nothing but call your friends repeatedly.

If you are operating in an interrupt-driven fashion, however, you give information to a friend only when you have some to give, and you receive information only when your friend calls you. Thus, you spend less time making repeated contacts and more time doing other tasks. This method is much more efficient.

Your computer uses interrupts in the same manner. When you press a key on the keyboard, you generate an interrupt that tells the computer a key has been pressed. The interrupt grabs the computer's attention so that the keypress can be processed.

The two types of interrupts are hardware interrupts and software interrupts. The keypress, an example of a hardware interrupt, is generated by a piece of hardware (the keyboard). A software interrupt is one meant to be called to perform a standardized task. The BIOS and DOS services are accessed by way of software interrupts.

BIOS Services

The BIOS is a collection of low-level routines used for communicating with the computer hardware. This collection is known as the *Basic Input/Output System*, or BIOS for short. Because the BIOS software usually is contained in the computer's read-only memory (ROM), BIOS is often referred to as *ROM-BIOS*.

The BIOS contains a series of functions that are easily accessible to an outside program (such as one you may develop). These functions, invoked through software interrupts, are nothing more than callable subroutines.

The interface layer that BIOS introduces between the hardware and software levels has definite benefits. The primary benefit should be immediately apparent— because software development time is greatly enhanced, programmers can develop software more efficiently. Because of the BIOS, you don't have to develop a different interface for every possible hardware combination. Other benefits include the security of knowing that your software will work on a variety of hardware configurations.

Even though the BIOS functions are rudimentary, the list of tasks performed by the BIOS is quite extensive. These services are used in examples throughout this book and are discussed completely in Chapter 20, "Using BIOS Services."

DOS Services

DOS, like BIOS, contains a series of functions that are accessible to outside programs. As with the BIOS, you use software interrupts to invoke these functions.

The range of services provided by DOS functions is much more extensive than what is provided by BIOS. In fact, the DOS functions rely extensively on the BIOS functions. For instance, if you use a DOS function, it may in turn use a BIOS function to complete a task.

The DOS services are used throughout this book and are detailed in Chapter 21, "Accessing DOS Services."

Device Drivers

DOS enables you to add capabilities that may be unique to your particular computer setup. To add such capabilities, you use *device drivers*, special programs loaded right after DOS is started. The device drivers are appended to DOS; they enable your programs to communicate with and control special devices.

For instance, many people have a mouse attached to their computer. This device is not a standard part of a computer, at least not as far as DOS is concerned. Thus, you can use a device driver called MOUSE.SYS to let DOS know that you have a mouse. Because the device driver becomes an extension to DOS, your programs can take advantage of the mouse by using additional software interrupts. Device drivers such as MOUSE.SYS typically are provided by the manufacturer of the device.

Summary

Understanding the programming environment is as important as understanding how to program. The IBM PC family of microcomputers provides a rich environment for programming. The basic concepts you need to understand to work within the environment include the following:

❑ Memory use

❑ The stack

❑ CPU registers and flags

❑ Interrupts

❑ BIOS and DOS services

Each of these items is introduced and discussed in this chapter. The foundation laid here is necessary if you are to absorb the information in the rest of the book.

The next chapter introduces you to programming in assembly language.

2

An Overview of Assembly Language

B efore you can begin to use assembly language to its fullest potential, you must start with the basics. This chapter presents a *quick* introduction to assembly language, not an exhaustive discussion of assembly language programs. It is meant to touch on the structure, main commands, and operations of the language. The information presented in this chapter will help you as you apply the concepts and examples discussed in the rest of the book.

If you have not read Chapter 1, "Understanding the Programming Environment," you probably should do so before reading this chapter. The concepts covered in that chapter are important to an understanding of the assembly language presented in this chapter.

Conceptual Guide to Assembly Language

Assembly language is similar to many other computer languages. At their root, languages provide building blocks the programmer can arrange to create programs. The building blocks in assembly language are smaller than those in high-level languages.

The building block concept should already be familiar to you. You program by using commands, variables, and words that are almost like English to instruct the computer what to do. These words are translated into machine code, a series of numbers the computer understands. But the work appears to be done with the building blocks, not with the numbers used by the computer.

Because the building blocks used in assembly language are smaller than those in high-level languages, they are individually less powerful. Because each building block, or command, does less, more commands are necessary to perform a given task.

Typically, if you program solely in a high-level language, you don't need to be directly concerned with operations that occur "behind the scenes." For instance, you usually do not need to even think about *where* and *how* your data will reside in the computer's memory. These matters are arranged by the compiler or by the *run-time system* used by your language. A run-time system is a manager that oversees program execution.

Another example of these "behind the scenes" operations is the use of what I call *compound commands*. For instance, consider the BASIC statement

```
PRINT "This is a test"
```

Pascal uses the following syntax to accomplish the same task:

```
writeln('This is a test');
```

C uses this syntax:

```
printf("This is a test\n");
```

All of these statements accomplish the same task. They print to the output device (usually the display monitor) a string of characters followed by a carriage return and line feed. Inherent in the PRINT, writeln(), and printf() commands, however, are several smaller commands that do other tasks related to the display of information. These smaller commands locate the information to be displayed, determine where to display it, decide how to display the information, and handle the carriage return and line feed at the end of the string.

With assembly language, very little happens "behind the scenes." You must specify virtually everything related to the composition, storage, and execution of your program or subroutine. For example, if you want to perform the equivalent of printing a string in assembly language, the following lines accomplish the task:

```
        MOV     DX,OFFSET MSG
        MOV     AH,09h
        INT     21h

MSG     DB      'This is a test',13,10,'$'
```

Although many other elements (covered later in this book) must be added before this code can be executed, this example clearly indicates how extremely specific you must be when working in assembly language. This need for specificity to perform even relatively simple tasks requires that you use much more source code than you would with a high-level language.

Another point may not be quite as obvious in this example: data must be declared explicitly. If you are accustomed to working in Pascal or C, you will not have to change your habits much. BASIC programmers, however, must get used to explicitly declaring data elements. Later, this chapter discusses how data is defined and manipulated in assembly language.

Conceptually, assembly language is the same as any other computer language: it enables you to instruct the computer to perform specific tasks. Depending on your background, however, you may find the application of the concepts radically different.

The assembly language development process is similar to that for many high-level languages. There are several distinct phases:

❏ Source-code generation or editing

❏ Assembly

❏ Linking

❏ Execution

If your high-level language uses a *compiler* and *linker*, this process will seem familiar. The second step (assembly) is analogous to the compilation step of high-level language development. The third step (linking) uses the linker you currently use. Thus, the assembly language development process is no different from the steps most high-level language programmers currently perform.

Assembly Language Structure

If you have been following along in the book so far, you may already have figured out the basic structure for assembly language programming lines. If not, here is the basic structure:

```
Label Operator Operands ;Comments
```

There are no hard and fast spacing rules, other than that you must separate each element of the coding line with at least one space or tab character. Also, almost every part of the program line is optional. You don't need a label (unless you want one or decide that one is necessary). Depending on the operator (instruction) being used, you may not need operands. And comments are always optional. In fact, your program line does not even need an instruction. It can consist simply of a label or comments. How you structure the line is entirely up to you.

As you work through the examples in this book, each element of an assembly language program line will become clear. Practice is the best teacher as you learn how to compose your programs. The structure of individual assembly language program lines is discussed in detail in Chapter 3, "Choosing and Using Your Assembler."

The Assembly Language Instruction Set

The instructions used by the assembler and translated into machine language depend on which microprocessor is used in the computer. Because of the diversity of possible assembly language instructions, the installed base of computers using the 8086/8088, and the upward compatibility of 8086/8088 code, the discussions of specific assembly language instructions in this book focus on the 8086 instruction set. All assembly language examples in this book are written to work on the 8086/8088; they work also on computers that use the 80286, 80386, and 80486 microprocessors.

Approximately 116 different assembly language mnemonics for the 8086/8088 can translate to 180 different machine language codes, depending on their context usage. The assembler takes care of the translation into machine language.

While this may seem a formidable number of assembly language instructions, it's not as bad as it sounds. Most of the time, only a handful of these instructions are used. Others, used less often, are still available as you need them. Other microcomputer chips include even more instructions and provide correspondingly greater power to the programmer.

Because of the sheer number of instructions, this chapter lists only those for the 8086/8088. They are listed also, with detailed instruction information, in Chapter 22, "Processor Instructions Sets," as are the corresponding instruction sets for the 80286, 80386, 80486, 8087, 80287, and 80387.

Table 2.1 lists the different classes of assembly language mnemonics for the 8086/8088. Notice that the instructions are divided into six different groups, depending on the type of operation performed. Also listed are the individual assembly language instructions that form each group.

Table 2.1. *The 8086/8088 microprocessor instruction set.*

Data-Transfer Instructions

IN	Input from port
LAHF	Load AH register with flags
LDS	Load DS register
LEA	Load effective address
LES	Load ES register
MOV	Move
OUT	Output to port
POP	Remove data from stack
POPF	Remove flags from stack
PUSH	Place data on stack
PUSHF	Place flags on stack
SAHF	Store AH into flag register
XCHG	Exchange
XLAT	Translate

Arithmetic Instructions

AAA	ASCII adjust for addition
AAD	ASCII adjust for division
AAM	ASCII adjust for multiplication
AAS	ASCII adjust for subtraction
ADC	Add with carry
ADD	Add
CBW	Convert byte to word
CMP	Compare
CWD	Convert word to doubleword
DAA	Decimal adjust for addition
DAS	Decimal adjust for subtraction
DEC	Decrement by 1
DIV	Divide, unsigned
IDIV	Integer divide
IMUL	Integer multiply
INC	Increment by 1
MUL	Multiply

continues

Table 2.1. *continued*

NEG	Negate
SBB	Subtract with carry
SUB	Subtract

Bit-Manipulation Instructions

AND	Logical AND on bits
NOT	Logical NOT on bits
OR	Logical OR on bits
RCL	Rotate left through carry
RCR	Rotate right through carry
ROL	Rotate left
ROR	Rotate right
SAL	Arithmetic shift left
SAR	Arithmetic shift right
SHL	Shift left
SHR	Shift right
TEST	Test bits
XOR	Logical exclusive-or on bits

String-Manipulation Instructions

CMPSB	Compare strings, byte for byte
CMPSW	Compare strings, word for word
LODSB	Load a byte from string into AL
LODSW	Load a word from string into AX
MOVSB	Move string, byte by byte
MOVSW	Move string, word by word
REP	Repeat
REPE	Repeat if equal
REPNE	Repeat if not equal
REPNZ	Repeat if not zero
REPZ	Repeat if zero
SCASB	Scan string for byte
SCASW	Scan string for word
STOSB	Store byte in AL at string
STOSW	Store word in AX at string

Control Transfer Instructions

CALL	Perform subroutine
INT	Software interrupt
INTO	Interrupt on overflow
IRET	Return from interrupt
JA	Jump if above
JAE	Jump if above or equal
JB	Jump if below
JBE	Jump if below or equal
JC	Jump on carry
JCXZ	Jump if CX=0
JE	Jump if equal
JG	Jump if greater than
JGE	Jump if greater than or equal
JL	Jump if less than
JLE	Jump if less than or equal
JMP	Jump
JNA	Jump if not above
JNAE	Jump if not above or equal
JNB	Jump if not below
JNBE	Jump if not below or equal
JNC	Jump on no carry
JNE	Jump if not equal
JNG	Jump if not greater than
JNGE	Jump if not greater than or equal
JNL	Jump if not less than
JNLE	Jump if not less than or equal
JNO	Jump on no overflow
JNP	Jump on no parity
JNS	Jump on not sign
JNZ	Jump on not zero
JO	Jump on overflow
JP	Jump on parity
JPE	Jump on parity even
JPO	Jump on parity odd

continues

Table 2.1. continued

JS	Jump on sign
JZ	Jump on zero
LOOP	Loop
LOOPE	Loop while equal
LOOPNE	Loop while not equal
LOOPNZ	Loop while not zero
LOOPZ	Loop while zero
RET	Return from subroutine

Flag- and Processor-Control Instructions

CLC	Clear carry flag
CLD	Clear direction flag
CLI	Clear interrupt flag
CMC	Complement carry flag
ESC	Escape
HLT	Halt
LOCK	Lock bus
NOP	No operation
STC	Set carry flag
STD	Set direction flag
STI	Set interrupt flag
WAIT	Wait

Although table 2.1 lists quite a few assembly language mnemonics, don't be overly concerned. Some mnemonics, although they appear to be different in this table, translate to the same machine-language value. For instance, JZ and JE test the same flags and make the same branching decisions based on the condition of those flags. They translate to the *same* machine code, but more than one mnemonic is provided so that you can write code that is easy to understand in the context of the task being done.

Although this chapter does not discuss these instructions in any depth, you need to understand what each instruction does and how the instructions affect the flags and registers.

Assembly Language Directives

The major assemblers use the assembly language instruction set as a beginning point only. Each assembler adds its own set of directives, whose sole function is to instruct the assembler how to go about translating and processing the source-code file.

For instance, table 2.2 shows the 154 directives available with MASM 6.0. Many of these directives have been added in version 6; alternate spellings of earlier directives also have been added. Table 2.3 shows the directives available with TASM 3.0, the assembler from Borland International. In this instance, there are 214 unique directives.

Table 2.2. *MASM 6.0 directive list.*

=	.DATA	.ERR	.IF
.186	.DATA?	.ERRB	IFDEF
.286	DB	.ERRDEF	IFDIF
.286P	DD	.ERRDIF	IFDIFI
.287	DF	.ERRDIFI	IFE
.386	.DOSSEG	.ERRE	IFIDN
.386P	DOSSEG	.ERRIDN	IFIDNI
.387	DQ	.ERRIDNI	IFIFB
.486	DT	.ERRNB	IFNB
.486P	DW	.ERRNDEF	IFNDEF
.8086	DWORD	.ERRNZ	INCLUDE
.8087	ECHO	EVEN	INCLUDELIB
ALIGN	.ELSE	.EXIT	INSTR
.ALPHA	ELSE	EXITM	INVOKE
ASSUME	.ELSEIF	EXTERN	IRP
.BREAK	ELSEIF	EXTERNDEF	IRPC
BYTE	END	EXTRN	LABEL
CATSTR	.ENDIF	.FARDATA	.LALL
.CODE	ENDIF	.FARDATA?	.LFCOND
COMM	ENDM	FOR	.LIST
COMMENT	ENDP	FORC	.LISTALL
.CONST	ENDS	FWORD	.LISTIF
.CONTINUE	.ENDW	GOTO	.LISTMACRO
.CREF	EQU	GROUP	.LISTMACROALL

continues

Table 2.2. *continued*

LOCAL	PROC	.SALL	TBYTE
MACRO	PROTO	SBYTE	TEXTEQU
.MODEL	PUBLIC	SDWORD	.TFCOND
NAME	PURGE	SEGMENT.SEQ	TITLE
.NO87	PUSHCONTEXT	.SFCOND	TYPEDEF
.NOCREF	QWORD	SIZESTR	UNION
.NOLIST	.RADIX	.STACK	.UNTIL
.NOLISTIF	REAL4	.STARTUP	.UNTILCXZ
.NOLISTMACRO	REAL8	STRUC	.WHILE
OPTION	REAL10	STRUCT	WHILE
ORG	RECORD	SUBSTR	WORD
%OUT	.REPEAT	SUBTITLE	.XALL
PAGE	REPEAT	SUBTTL	.XCREF
POPCONTEXT	REPT	SWORD	.XLIST

Table 2.3. *TASM 3.0 directive list.*

=	ARG	.DATA	ENDIF
.186	ASSUME	.DATA?	ENDM
.286	%BIN	DATASEG	ENDP
.286C	CATSTR	DB	ENDS
.286P	.CODE	DD	ENUM
.287	CODESEG	%DEPTH	EQU
.386	COMM	DF	.ERR
.386C	COMMENT	DISPLAY	ERR
.386P	%CONDS	DOSSEG	.ERR1
.387	.CONST	DP	.ERR2
.486	CONST	DQ	.ERRB
.486C	.CREF	DT	.ERRDEF
.486P	%CREF	DW	.ERRDIF
.8086	%CREFALL	ELSE	.ERRDIFI
.8087	%CREFREF	ELSEIF	.ERRE
ALIGN	%CREFUREF	EMUL	.ERRIDN
.ALPHA	%CTLS	END	.ERRIDNI

ERRIF	IFIDNI	NOMASM51	.SALL
ERRIF1	IFNB	NOMULTERRS	SEGMENT
ERRIF2	IFNDEF	NOSMART	.SEQ
ERRIFB	%INCL	%NOSYMS	SEQ
ERRIFDEF	INCLUDE	%NOTRUNC	.SFCOND
ERRIFDIF	INCLUDELIB	NOWARN	SIZESTR
ERRIFDIFI	INSTR	ORG	SMALLSTACK
ERRIFE	IRP	%OUT	SMART
ERRIFIDN	IRPC	P186	.STACK
ERRIFIDNI	JUMPS	P286	STACK
ERRIFNB	LABEL	P286N	.STARTUP
ERRIFNDEF	.LALL	P286P	STARTUPCODE
.ERRNB	LARGESTACK	P287	STRUC
.ERRNDEF	.LFCOND	P386	SUBSTR
.ERRNZ	%LINUM	P386N	SUBTTL
EVEN	%LIST	P386P	%SUBTTL
EVENDATA	.LIST	P387	%SYMS
.EXIT	LOCAL	P486	TABLE
EXITCODE	LOCALS	P486N	%TABSIZE
EXITM	MACRO	P8086	TBLPTR
EXTRN	%MACS	P8087	%TEXT
.FARDATA	MASM	PAGE	.TFCOND
.FARDATA?	MASM51	%PAGESIZE	TITLE
FARDATA	.MODEL	%PCNT	%TITLE
GLOBAL	MODEL	PNO87	%TRUNC
GOTO	MULTERRS	%POPLCTL	TYPEDEF
GROUP	NAME	PROC	UDATASEG
IDEAL	%NEWPAGE	PUBLIC	UFARDATA
IF	%NOCONDS	PUBLICDLL	UNION
IF1	%NOCREF	PURGE	USES
IF2	%NOCTLS	%PUSHLCTL	VERSION
IFB	NOEMUL	QUIRKS	WARN
IFDEF	%NOINCL	.RADIX	WHILE
IFDIF	NOJUMPS	RADIX	.XALL
IFDIFI	%NOLIST	RECORD	.XCREF
IFE	NOLOCALS	REPT	.XLIST
IFIDN	%NOMACS		

A directive does not translate into machine code the microprocessor can execute. Rather, when an assembler encounters a directive, the assembler changes the way in which it does its job. This chapter shows you how to use some of these directives, particularly those used for defining data. Each directive shown in table 2.2 and 2.3 is explained in detail also in Chapter 23, "Assembler Directives."

Data Storage in Memory

Data is stored in the computer's memory as a series of bytes. In Chapter 1, "Understanding the Programming Environment," you learned that the IBM PC operating under DOS normally can address up to 640K of memory. This work area has 655,360 individual bytes, each of which can store a specific, individual value. Because each byte is made up of 8 bits, and each bit can have a value of 0 or 1, each byte can store a value in the range of 0 through 255.

As you program in assembly language and then assemble and link the programs you create, your instructions (if syntactically correct) are translated into individual bytes of information that the microprocessor later uses to perform tasks. To the computer, no physical difference exists between *machine language program instruction bytes* and *data bytes*. To the programmer, a distinction is vital to ensure that data bytes do not overwrite coding bytes while the program is executing.

Several methods are available for setting aside data areas in an assembly language program. Typically, the task is done with special assembler directives, such as those introduced in the preceding section of this chapter. The most common methods involve the use of *equates* and the data-allocation directives. Let's take a look at each of these methods, focusing first on equates.

Equates

Equates do not set aside a physical memory area for data. Rather, the assembler uses equates as substitute values later in the program. For instance, the following set of equates can be used to define the IBM color set:

```
; --------------------------------------------------------------
BLACK           EQU         0
BLUE            EQU         1
GREEN           EQU         2
CYAN            EQU         3
RED             EQU         4
MAGENTA         EQU         5
```

```
BROWN           EQU       6
WHITE           EQU       7
GRAY            EQU       8
LT_BLUE         EQU       9
LT_GREEN        EQU       10
LT_CYAN         EQU       11
LT_RED          EQU       12
LT_MAGENTA      EQU       13
YELLOW          EQU       14
BR_WHITE        EQU       15
; - - - - - - - - - - - - - - - - - - - - - - - - - - - - - - - - - - - - - - - -
```

Equates are helpful because remembering RED is much easier than remembering that four is equal to the color red. For example, although the following commands are functionally the same, the first one is considerably easier for humans to understand:

```
MOV     AH,LT_BLUE
MOV     AH,9
```

Both commands result in the value nine being placed in the AH register. In the following section, other uses for the EQU directive become apparent.

Data-Allocation Directives

In assembly language programs, data is defined and storage space for that data is allocated through the use of several directives. These directives instruct the assembler to set aside specific amounts of memory for the program to use later. Optionally, you can direct the memory to be filled with specific values. Table 2.4 lists the data-allocation directives for assembly language programs.

Table 2.4. *Data-allocation directives and their meanings.*

Directive	*Meaning*
BYTE *or* DB	Define an unsigned byte (1 byte)
WORD *or* DW	Define an unsigned word (2 bytes)
DWORD *or* DD	Define an unsigned doubleword (4 bytes)
QWORD *or* DQ	Define an unsigned quadword (8 bytes)
TBYTE *or* DT	Define 10 bytes (10 bytes)
SBYTE	Define a signed byte (1 byte)
SWORD	Define a signed word (2 bytes)

continues

Table 2.4. *continued*

Directive	Meaning
SDWORD	Define a signed doubleword (4 bytes)
FWORD	Define six bytes (6 bytes)
REAL4	Define a single-precision floating-point number (4 bytes)
REAL8	Define a double-precision floating-point number (8 bytes)
REAL10	Define a 10-byte floating-point number (10 bytes)

Note that not all the data-allocation directives shown in table 2.4 are available in all assemblers. For instance, the SBYTE, SWORD, and SDWORD directives are new to MASM 6.0; they are not available in previous versions. Similarly, previous versions of MASM did not allow you to use the alternate directives for DB, DW, DD, DQ, or DT. Although the examples in this book use the more universal nomenclature of DB, DW, DD, DQ, and DT, you should be aware that if you have MASM 6.0 you can use the alternate directives.

Each data-allocation directive sets aside memory for subsequent use by your program. These directives can be further modified and made more powerful through the use of the DUP and OFFSET operators. Understanding how these directives function may be easier if you see how they are used in a program. Look at the following selected data declarations in a program:

```
; ------------------------------------------------------------
ORIG_DRIVE        DB      00
ORIG_PATH         DB      64 DUP(0)
PRE_PATH          DB      '\'
PATH              DB      64 DUP(0)

ANY_FILE          DB      '*.*',0

DIR_TABLE         DB      256 DUP(19 DUP(0))

BREAK_INT_OFF     DW      00
BREAK_INT_SEG     DW      00
CMD_TABLE         EQU     THIS BYTE
                  DW      OFFSET ACTION_CMD
                  DW      OFFSET DOIT_CMD
                  DW      OFFSET DRIVE_CMD
```

```
                    DW      OFFSET PATH_CMD
                    DW      OFFSET EXIT_CMD

ACTION_CMD          DB      'SELECT',0
DOIT_CMD            DB      'DELETE',0
DRIVE_CMD           DB      'DRIVE',0
PATH_CMD            DB      'PATH',0
EXIT_CMD            DB      'EXIT',0
ONE-MOMENT          DB      'Examining diskette ... One moment please!',0


; -------------------------------------------------------------------
```

Notice that directives DB, DW, and EQU are used here. If you are using MASM 6.0, you can just as easily use BYTE in place of DB, and WORD in place of DW. There is no difference in the generated program.

These few lines set aside and define a data area 5,084 bytes long. Further, they provide a means by which data can later be referenced. Referring to each line by its label, I'll describe what the data-allocation directives accomplish in this example.

ORIG_DRIVE is defined as a variable one byte long, initially set to 0. ORIG_PATH also is set to an initial value of 0; through use of the DUP operator, however, ORIG_PATH is defined as 64 consecutive zeros. ORIG_PATH can be referenced directly only as a byte value. For instance, the command

```
MOV     AH,ORIG_PATH
```

works because a byte value (the first of the 64 bytes of ORIG_PATH) is being loaded into a byte register. The line

```
MOV     AX,ORIG_PATH
```

does not work, however, because the assembler does not allow 8 bits to be loaded directly into 16.

The following example shows how to override this declared reference to ORIG_PATH as byte values only:

```
MOV     AX,WORD PTR ORIG_PATH
```

The use of WORD PTR tells the assembler that even though the label ORIG_PATH is a reference to a byte value, you want to reference the word that begins at the address associated with ORIG_PATH.

PRE_PATH is similar to ORIG_DRIVE, except that here the byte is being set to 92, the ASCII value of the backslash character. ANY_FILE translates directly to the following four individual bytes:

```
42      46      42      00
 *       .       *
```

DIR_TABLE becomes an area of zeros 256 * 19 (or 4,864 bytes) long. You can use the DUP operator multiple times in the same declaration to make it more readable.

BREAK_INT_OFF and BREAK_INT_SEG set aside one word each and initially set the contents of those memory locations to zero. Later, the contents of these named memory locations can be loaded directly into a register by a line similar to the following:

```
MOV     AX,BREAK_INT_SEG
```

Through the use of EQU and THIS BYTE, CMD_TABLE is set up to reference the first byte of an area to be used later as an offset table to other values. For this example, the five words beginning at CMD_TABLE are set equal to the offset addresses of other variables. In this way, the messages ACTION_CMD, DOIT_CMD, DRIVE_CMD, PATH_CMD, and EXIT_CMD can all be accessed by address, even though the length of each message is different.

Finally, ONE_MOMENT is a series of bytes that spells the message Examining diskette ... One moment please!, followed by a zero, or null byte.

The preceding example illustrates the most commonly used data-allocation directives. (At least, they are the most common when you are writing assembly language subroutines or small utilities.) The concepts illustrated in the example, however, are equally applicable when you work with the other data-allocation directives.

Addressing

The 8086/8088 offers a multitude of ways to address data: register-to-register, immediate addressing, direct addressing, and several types of indirect addressing. Because you will use each of these modes as you program, you need to understand them now.

Each addressing mode always has a source and a destination. The destination is always to the left of the comma; the source is always to the right. In addition, both direct and indirect addressing assume an implied addressing segment. Let's take a look at each type of addressing and any applicable segment-addressing assumptions.

Register Addressing

Register addressing is the fastest mode of data addressing. These instructions take fewer physical bytes and are executed entirely in the CPU. If your data needs are small within certain subroutines, always perform manipulations within registers. Some examples of this type of addressing are

```
MOV     AX,BX
MOV     DX,CX
MOV     DI,SI
```

These instructions result in the contents of the register to the right of the comma being *copied* into the register to the left of the comma. Thus the contents of BX, CX, and SI are copied into AX, DX, and DI, respectively. Notice that the contents are *copied*, not simply *moved*. Therefore, after the first instruction is completed, AX and BX contain the same values.

Immediate Addressing

Immediate addressing causes a constant numeric value to be placed into a register or a memory location. Consider the following instructions:

```
RED     EQU     4
LOC_1   DB      00
LOC_2   DW      0000

        MOV     AX,5
        MOV     BL,RED
        MOV     LOC_1,RED
        MOV     LOC_2,5
```

In all instances, a constant value (right of the comma) is being placed at the specified destination (left of the comma). The specified destination is either a register or a memory location. Although several of these instructions use equates instead of specific numbers, the correct numbers will replace the equates when the coding is assembled. Thus, all occurrences of RED will be replaced by 4 to provide the constant numeric value required by immediate addressing.

Direct Addressing

Whereas immediate addressing places data at either a register or a memory location, direct addressing moves data from a memory location to a register, or from a register to a memory location, as the following instructions illustrate:

```
LOC_1       DB      00
LOC_2       DW      0000

            MOV     AL,LOC_1
            MOV     BX,LOC_2
            MOV     LOC_1,AH
            MOV     LOC_2,CX
```

As with the other addressing modes, the values contained in the memory location or register to the right of the comma are copied into the memory location or register to the left of the comma.

Indirect Addressing

Indirect addressing is not only the most difficult addressing mode to master but also the most powerful. The three methods of indirect addressing are *register indirect*, *indexed* (or *based*), and *based and indexed with displacement*. Instead of considering each of these methods individually, this section covers the general category of indirect addressing as a whole.

To illustrate the different indirect addressing methods, consider the following code fragments:

```
CMD_TABLE         EQU         THIS BYTE
                  DW          OFFSET ACTION_CMD
                  DW          OFFSET DOIT_CMD
                  DW          OFFSET DRIVE_CMD
                  DW          OFFSET PATH_CMD
                  DW          OFFSET EXIT_CMD


ACTION_CMD        DB          'SELECT',0
DOIT_CMD          DB          'DELETE',0
DRIVE_CMD         DB          'DRIVE',0
PATH_CMD          DB          'PATH',0
EXIT_CMD          DB          'EXIT',0
CMD_NUM           DW          0003

                  MOV         AX,CMD_NUM
                  MOV         BX,OFFSET CMD_TABLE
                  SHL         AX,1
                  ADD         BX,AX
                  MOV         SI,[BX]
```

Suppose that the variable CMD_NUM contains the value 3. The first instruction in this fragment uses direct addressing to copy the contents of CMD_NUM (3) into AX. Then immediate addressing is used to load BX with the offset address of CMD_TABLE. Remember that when this code is assembled, the directive OFFSET CMD_TABLE is replaced with a literal number that represents the desired offset address. Then the contents of AX are multiplied by 2 (which *always* happens when you shift the bits one position to the left), and this value is added to what is already in BX. At this point, BX contains a value 6 greater than the address of the start of CMD_TABLE, which is the address of the table entry for PATH_CMD.

The final statement in this code fragment is an example of indirect addressing. This statement results in SI being loaded with the contents of the location addressed by BX, which is the address for the string PATH_CMD. This indirect addressing usage always assumes that BX contains an address. The brackets (as used in this example) instruct the assembler to use the *content* of the memory location pointed to by the register within the brackets. Only the registers BX, BP, SI, or DI may be used within brackets.

Don't let the preceding paragraph mislead you into believing that the brackets *always* indicate indirect addressing; the Microsoft assembler lets them be used also for other purposes; in some versions, the assembler even requires their use under certain circumstances to obtain special forms of direct addressing! This topic is covered in greater detail in Chapter 3, when the differences between the most popular assemblers are examined.

Clearly, indirect addressing is inherently powerful. As indirect addressing is used in the sample routine, a different address can be loaded into SI simply by changing the number in CMD_NUM. In this instance, because it contains an address used as a base (or starting point), BX is referred to as the *base register*.

Variations on this basic indirect-addressing method provide even greater flexibility in addressing:

```
MOV        SI,[BX]
MOV        SI,[BP+2]
MOV        AX,[BX+SI+2]
```

The first instruction shows the indirect-addressing method already described. The second and third examples, however, show some variations. The second example uses the base register and a *displacement value* which is added to the contents of the base register, producing a value that is assumed to be the address of the source value to be copied to the destination.

The third example uses the base register, an *index register*, and a displacement value, all of which are added together, resulting in a value that again is assumed to be the address of the source value from which the destination is loaded.

In all of these indirect-addressing methods, the specifications of the source and destination can be reversed, as with each of the other addressing schemes. Thus:

```
MOV        [BX],SI
MOV        [BP+2],SI
MOV        [BX+SI+2],AX
```

are all perfectly acceptable as destinations for data.

Segment Assumptions

When addressing data, the destination and source are always assumed to be in the data segment or relative to the DS register. The exception to this assumption is when the base pointer, BP, is used as the base register in indirect addressing; in this instance the stack segment, SS, is used.

The default segment can be overridden by explicit use of the desired segment, as follows:

```
MOV        CS:LOC_2,5
MOV        AL,CS:LOC_1
MOV        CS:LOC_2,CX
MOV        SI,ES:[BX]
MOV        DS:[BP+2],SI
MOV        ES:[BX+SI+2],AX
```

Notice that in the fifth line of these examples, DS must be stated explicitly as an override segment because the BP register is being used as the base register. Normally, SS would be assumed, but in this case DS is used.

Looping and Branching

A programming language's most powerful capability may be that of repeating a series of instructions a specific number of times. Assembly language is no different than other languages in this regard. Specific commands enable you to *branch* (transfer execution to a new location) and to *loop* (repeat a task in a controlled manner).

If you look back at table 2.1, notice the section labeled *Control Transfer Instructions*. These are the individual assembly language instructions that control the flow of the program.

In the basic 8086/8088 instruction set, 42 instructions control the order in which a program is executed. Each of these instructions (except CALL, INT, IRET, JMP, and RET) is conditional. That is, the instructions branch only if a certain condition is met. Consider the following program fragment:

```
MOV    AH,03h        ; get current cursor position
INT    10h
CMP    DH,5          ; on row 5?
JNE    NOT_THERE     ; no, so skip following code
MOV    DH,6          ; set to row 6
MOV    AH,02h        ; set current cursor position
```

```
            INT    10h
            MOV    CX,03h      ; loop control
ALARM:      MOV    AH,02h      ; output character
            MOV    DL,7        ; sending BEL character
            INT    21h
            LOOP   ALARM       ; do it again  Till CX = ∅
NOT_THERE:  JMP    DONE
```

This example uses four control transfer instructions. Two of them (INT and JMP) are nonconditional—the action is taken right away. The other two instructions (JNE and LOOP) are conditional. In the case of JNE, the branch is taken only if the result of the previous comparison is nonzero. The second conditional instruction, LOOP, is a compound instruction. It results in the value in CX being decremented, after which execution is transferred to the address represented by the label ALARM.

Throughout the examples in this book, looping and branching commands are used extensively. How you use them is up to your imagination, but you should try for the simplest possible method of program execution. If you include many loops and branches, your program may be difficult to understand and maintain later.

Segments and Classes

As you learned in Chapter 1, the IBM family of microcomputers uses processors that address memory by using segment addresses and offset addresses. When you program in assembly language, segment addresses are set either explicitly, by loading the segment registers, or implicitly, through assembler directives to the linker.

But there are segment addresses—and then there are segments. So far, I have talked about segment addresses and how they are used. This definition is the logical use of the word *segment* for the Intel family of microprocessors. To program effectively in assembly language, you must understand these segments and their use.

Another definition of the word *segment*, however, is used in reference to the macro assembler and linker developed by Microsoft. Because many (if not most) assemblers and linkers are based on standards established by Microsoft, you need to be familiar with this alternate (and potentially confusing) use of the word *segment*.

When you write assembly language source code, a *segment* is simply a group of instructions that operate relative to the same segment address. Although it is difficult not to confuse such *program segments* with *memory segments*, they are not directly related. A program segment is just a block of code delineated by explicit starting and ending points. To avoid confusion, some assemblers call these coding sections PSECTs (for *program sections*) rather than SEGMENTs.

At the beginning of any group of instructions (usually at the beginning of the code in the file), the assembler directive SEGMENT is used to signify the start of a segment. At the close of the group of instructions, the ENDS directive is used. The assembler and linker then use these directives to delineate the explicit start and end of groups of assembly language code.

The following example shows how the SEGMENT and ENDS directives might be used in an assembly language file:

```
TEXT              SEGMENT BYTE PUBLIC 'CODE'
     assembly language coding goes in this area
TEXT              ENDS
```

Let's look at each part of this example. The word TEXT is the name of the segment (this is a completely arbitrary name). Notice also the corresponding appearance of the name TEXT with the ENDS directive.

The word BYTE directs the assembler to place this segment at the next available byte in the object file. In the example, BYTE is the *align type* of the segment. A segment can be aligned to a byte, word, paragraph, or page. BYTE starts the segment at the byte following the end of the preceding segment. WORD begins the segment at the next even address. PARAgraph begins the segment at the next hexadecimal address that ends in a 0. PAGE begins the segment at the next hexadecimal address that ends in 00. Table 2.5 summarizes these align types.

Table 2.5. *Align types available with the Microsoft Assembler.*

Type	Description
BYTE	Segment is placed at next available byte in object file.
WORD	Segment is placed at next available even byte in object file.
DWORD	Segment is placed at next available doubleword address in object file.
PARAGRAPH	Segment is placed at next available paragraph boundary in object file; address of segment will end in a 0.
PAGE	Segment is placed at next available page boundary in object file; address of segment will end in a 00.

The word PUBLIC is a declaration of the segment's *combine type*. The combine type, which is optional, denotes how a segment will be combined with other segments that have the same name. Several different combine types are available (see table 2.6). The default combine type is PRIVATE.

Table 2.6. *Combine types available with the Microsoft Assembler and Linker.*

Type	Description
PRIVATE	Results in no combining of segments, even if segments in other modules have the same name.
PUBLIC	Joins all segments with the same name into one segment when linked. All addresses and offsets in the resulting segment are relative to a single segment register.
STACK	Joins all segments with this combine type to form one segment when linked. All addresses and offsets in the resulting segment are relative to the stack segment register. The stack pointer (SP) register is initialized to the ending address of the segment. This combine type normally is used to define the stack area for a program. The linker requires that exactly one stack segment be defined for an EXE program.
COMMON	Same as PUBLIC, except that the segments are not joined to form a new, large segment. All COMMON segments with the same name begin at the same point; the resulting segment is equal in length to the longest individual segment.
MEMORY	Works exactly like the PUBLIC combine type.
AT	Used to prepare a template that will be used for accessing fixed location data. In the format AT *XXXX* (where *XXXX* is a memory address), AT signifies that addresses and offsets are to be calculated relative to the specified memory address.

The word 'CODE' is the segment's *class type*. This name, which must be enclosed in single quotation marks, signifies the groupings to be used when the different segments are linked. All segments of a given class type are loaded contiguously in memory before another class type is begun. In the directives example, the segment belongs to the 'CODE' class type and will be grouped with other segments of the same class type.

Normally, you use only one class type when you prepare assembly language subroutines for use from high-level languages. Sometimes this class type is specified by the high-level language you are using, as you will see in examples in later chapters.

Subroutines and Procedures

Subroutines are essential to programs of any magnitude. They enable a programmer to break a task into smaller tasks, continuing to do so as necessary to complete a project. Using subroutines is much like outlining. You start with the main idea and break it down further and further until the entire topic is covered.

A subroutine is basically the same as a procedure or function. Although some technical distinction may exist between subroutines, procedures, and functions, this book assumes that they are essentially the same. All of these terms describe coding developed to perform a specialized task or set of tasks, and called (either singularly or repetitively) from a higher-level controlling program. Because assembly language uses the terms *procedure* and *proc* to identify such an entity, so have I.

In high-level languages, you can easily define procedures that other programs can call. BASIC uses the GOSUB command to invoke a subroutine and the RETURN command to signal its end. Pascal, C, C++, and compiled BASIC enable you to call a procedure or function by using a user-defined name. In Pascal, control is subsequently returned to the calling program by use of the end marker; and in C or C++, the closing brace (or optional return statement) marks the end of the function.

Because assembly language requires much more interaction on the programmer's part to accomplish a given task, and because the amount of source code written to accomplish the task can be prodigious, using procedures becomes even more important than with other languages. Two types of procedures (NEAR and FAR) are used in assembly language. They are procedurally the same, differing only in how a CALL to and RETurn from each affects the stack and CS:IP registers.

NEAR procedures are contained in the same code segment as the program invoking the procedure. The declaration of a NEAR procedure is accomplished with the PROC NEAR directives. The following example shows a subroutine to load the AX register with the contents of the word to which DS:SI points, after which SI is incremented to point to the next word:

```
GET_WORD        PROC    NEAR
                MOV     AX,[SI]
                INC     SI
                INC     SI
                RET
GET_WORD        ENDP
```

This example is declared as a NEAR procedure because it will reside in the same segment as the routine from which it is called. The only change necessary to make this routine a FAR procedure is to change NEAR to FAR.

The following line executes either a NEAR or FAR procedure:

```
CALL     GET_WORD
```

In the case of a NEAR procedure, this invocation results in the offset address of the instruction *following* the CALL being pushed on the stack, and the address of CS:GET_WORD being loaded into the IP (thus, execution begins at GET_WORD). When the subsequent RET is encountered, the value of the IP is retrieved from the stack, and execution continues from the point following the original CALL.

Because this is a NEAR routine, only offset addresses one word long are pushed on and subsequently popped from the stack.

A FAR procedure operates exactly the same way, except that two address words (the value of the code segment and the offset address) are pushed on and later popped from the stack. Also, both the CS and IP registers are set to point to the beginning of the subroutine.

The vast majority of procedures you use will be of the NEAR persuasion. FAR procedures ordinarily are used for controlling programs, for extremely large programs, and for interrupt-handler routines. When you write routines to use with certain high-level languages, however, these languages require that your routines be defined as FAR procedures.

The Assembly Language Subroutine Skeleton

By this point, programmers who have done most of their work with high-level languages are usually shaking their heads in amazement and starting to visualize assembly language programmers in padded cells with small, barred windows.

Don't despair! All this information about memory usage, program organization, data storage, and procedures is necessary so that you can see the structure and power of assembly language. The following statement may help simplify everything discussed on the last several pages: Virtually all assembly language programs and subroutines can be written using a standard program skeleton. Through the use of a program skeleton, you can concentrate on task completion rather than administrative overhead.

A program skeleton is a template that gives a bare-bones (pardon the pun) outline of the program header, data declaration areas, and other "overhead" information. For example, most subroutines and COM files have data and code in the same memory segment. Thus, the following program skeleton can be entered, saved as a file, and used as a starting point for future assembly language programs or subroutines:

```
Page 60,132
Comment ¦
**********************************************************************


File:     [file name goes here]
Author:   [your name goes here]
Date:     [date program written]

Purpose:  [description of program or routine]

Format:   [syntax of calling statement]


**********************************************************************¦

; *** Public declaration of subroutines and data

              PUBLIC  [list entry points and data here]

; *** External data needed by these subroutines

              EXTRN   [data and its type goes here]

; *** External subroutines called by these subroutines

              EXTRN   [routine and its type goes here]

              .MODEL  [model information goes here]

; *** Declaration of equates

FALSE         EQU     -1          ;These are sample equates.
TRUE          EQU     0           ;Yours will vary according to
                                  ;your needs.

; *** Declaration of data
              .DATA

DATA1         DW      0000        ;These are sample data
DATA2         DW      0000        ;definitions. Yours will vary.
DATA3         DW      0000        ;

; ----------------------------------------------------------------
; START OF MAIN CODING
```

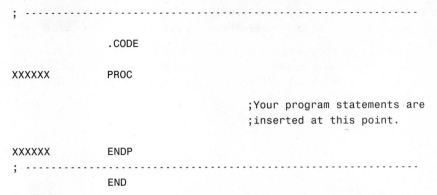

```
; -------------------------------------------------------------

                .CODE

XXXXXX          PROC

                                    ;Your program statements are
                                    ;inserted at this point.

XXXXXX          ENDP
; -------------------------------------------------------------
                END
```

Notice the liberal use of comments. Getting into the habit of documenting your programs will help make your job much easier. In assembly language, there are two ways to denote comments. You can use a semicolon to start a comment, or you can define a block of comments by using the COMMENT directive. When the program is assembled, everything between a semicolon and the end of a line, or everything in a comment block, is disregarded. Thus, the comments you place in a source file do not make your program longer or slower; they just increase the size of the source file and make it easier to understand later.

To define a block of comments, as is done near the beginning of this program skeleton, use the COMMENT directive followed by any character you choose. You should use a character that is not used elsewhere in your comment block; I have used the vertical bar (¦). Everything between this character and the next occurrence of this character is treated as a comment and disregarded by the assembler.

In this program skeleton, information enclosed in brackets is to be supplied when the skeleton is developed into a real program. Also, the locations indicated by *XXXXXX* are to be replaced with the name of the routine or program. This is the name used to call this routine from other programs; it is also the name the linker uses when the program modules are put together.

How you use a program skeleton is up to you; your individual programming habits and needs necessarily differ from everyone else's. If you do not have a skeleton developed already, develop one and store it in a file. Then you can copy the file and edit the skeleton each time you start a new program.

Summary

Assembly language is quick, compact, and powerful. Because the "building blocks" provided by the language are small, to create a program you will need quite a few more blocks than with a high-level language. Resulting programs, however, can yield benefits—such as speed and compact code—not possible with other languages. Other benefits are outlined in the introduction to this book.

This chapter is a quick overview of some features and basic tenets of the language. Detailed information on the use of individual instructions can be gleaned from studying the examples through the rest of this book or by referring to Part IV, "Reference."

3

Choosing and Using
Your Assembler

To do any serious work with assembly language, you must have an assembler. Microsoft's MASM (Macro ASseMbler) is probably the most widely known, but several available alternatives provide essentially complete compatibility with it. Still other assemblers are quite different from the Microsoft version.

To help you choose an assembler, this chapter lists brief summaries of the advantages and disadvantages of each. But before getting into the specifics of how any one assembler operates, let's look at what all assemblers do.

What an Assembler Does

As the Introduction points out, an *assembler* is a program that translates assembly language instructions into machine language. In concept, the assembler's job is simple. Its translation process simply converts assembly language mnemonics into a numeric equivalent that represents the proper machine language code. This sounds straightforward enough, but frequently it is not; determining what the programmer wants can be tedious and tricky. This translation or *parsing* process is what the assembler program spends the most time doing.

In the strictest sense of the word, an assembler does not fully translate source code into machine language. Rather, it creates an object code file, which by itself is not executable. Although the assembler program parses and translates virtually every instruction, some instructions cannot be encoded at this point. Rather, a separate pass is required to translate the object file into an executable file. (This step, called *linking*, is covered in Chapter 4, "Choosing and Using Your Linker.")

To translate code, an assembler must read the source file at least once. Each complete read of the source file, with its associated processing, is called a *pass*. Most assemblers require two passes to create the object code file. Some do it all in one pass, however, and others need even more than two. For instance, MASM 6.0 is a single-pass assembler (previous versions were two-pass), TASM 2.5 is a two-pass assembler, and OptAsm (a competing assembler from SLR, Inc., that is not discussed in this book) is an *n*-pass assembler (it has no limit on the number of passes).

During the first pass, the assembler does the following:

❑ Parses the source code, calculating the offset for each line

❑ Makes assumptions about undefined values

❑ Does elementary error checking, displaying error messages if necessary

❑ Generates a preliminary listing file, if requested (not all assemblers provide this action)

During the final pass, which *may* also be the first pass, the assembler does the following:

❑ Attempts to reconcile the value assumptions made during previous passes

❑ Generates the final assembly listing (LST) file, if specified

❑ Generates the object code, storing it in the object (OBJ) file

❑ Generates the cross-reference (CRF) file, if specified

❑ Completes the error-checking process, displaying error messages if necessary

The Leading Contenders

The two leading assembler products come, understandably, from the two leading programming language companies: Microsoft and Borland. Although MASM sets the industry's standard for PC-oriented assemblers, it has stiff competition from Borland's Turbo Assembler. Another product from Microsoft, QuickAssembler, is available only with the QuickC package. It uses a subset of the MASM capabilities.

Let's compare these three products and see how they differ. Each has a few advantages and each has a few problems; all are capable of excellent results. Your final choice, of course, must be based on the features that are most important to you.

One way of comparing the products is to note which features are common to two or more of them and which features are unique. For instance, table 3.1, a list of directives supported by the various assemblers, indicates where you can expect major differences between the assemblers. Notice that the table includes two MASM and two TASM columns that indicate the two most recent versions of each product. Major differences exist between these latest versions.

Table 3.1. *Directives supported by major assemblers.*

Directive (Pseudooperation)	MASM 6.0	MASM 5.1	MsQA 2.51	TASM 3.0	TASM 2.0
=	Y	Y	Y	Y	Y
.186	Y	Y	Y	Y	Y
.286	Y	Y	Y	Y	Y
.286C			Y	Y	Y
.286P	Y			Y	Y
.287	Y	Y	Y	Y	Y
.386	Y	Y		Y	Y
.386C				Y	Y
.386P	Y			Y	Y
.387	Y			Y	Y
.486	Y			Y	
.486C				Y	
.486P	Y			Y	
.8086	Y	Y	Y	Y	Y
.8087	Y	Y	Y	Y	Y
ALIGN	Y	Y	Y	Y	Y
.ALPHA	Y	Y	Y	Y	Y
ARG		Y		Y	Y
ASSUME	Y	Y	Y	Y	Y
%BIN		Y		Y	Y
.BREAK	Y				
BYTE	Y				
CATSTR	Y	Y	Y	Y	Y
.CODE	Y		Y	Y	Y
CODESEG				Y	Y

continues

Table 3.1. *continued*

Directive (Pseudooperation)	MASM 6.0	MASM 5.1	MsQA 2.51	TASM 3.0	TASM 2.0
COMM	Y	Y	Y	Y	Y
COMMENT	Y	Y	Y	Y	Y
%CONDS				Y	Y
.CONST	Y	Y	Y	Y	Y
CONST				Y	Y
.CONTINUE	Y				
.CREF	Y	Y		Y	Y
%CREF				Y	Y
%CREFALL				Y	Y
%CREFREF				Y	Y
%CREFUREF				Y	Y
%CTLS				Y	Y
.DATA	Y	Y	Y	Y	Y
.DATA?	Y	Y	Y	Y	Y
DATASEG				Y	Y
DB	Y	Y	Y	Y	Y
DD	Y	Y	Y	Y	Y
%DEPTH				Y	Y
DF	Y	Y		Y	Y
DISPLAY				Y	Y
.DOSSEG	Y				
DOSSEG	Y	Y	Y	Y	Y
DP		Y		Y	Y
DQ	Y	Y	Y	Y	Y
DT	Y	Y	Y	Y	Y
DW	Y	Y	Y	Y	Y
DWORD	Y				
ECHO	Y				
.ELSE	Y				
ELSE	Y	Y	Y	Y	Y
.ELSEIF	Y				

Directive (Pseudooperation)	MASM 6.0	MASM 5.1	MsQA 2.51	TASM 3.0	TASM 2.0
ELSEIF	Y		Y	Y	Y
EMUL				Y	Y
END	Y	Y	Y	Y	Y
.ENDIF			Y		
ENDIF	Y	Y	Y	Y	Y
ENDM	Y	Y	Y	Y	Y
ENDP	Y	Y	Y	Y	Y
ENDS	Y	Y	Y	Y	Y
.ENDW	Y				
ENUM				Y	
EQU	Y	Y	Y	Y	Y
.ERR	Y	Y	Y	Y	Y
ERR				Y	Y
.ERR1		Y	Y	Y	Y
.ERR2		Y	Y	Y	Y
.ERRB	Y	Y	Y	Y	Y
.ERRDEF	Y	Y	Y	Y	Y
.ERRDIF	Y	Y	Y	Y	Y
.ERRDIFI	Y	Y	Y	Y	Y
.ERRE	Y	Y	Y	Y	Y
.ERRIDN	Y	Y	Y	Y	Y
.ERRIDNI	Y	Y	Y	Y	Y
ERRIF				Y	Y
ERRIF1				Y	Y
ERRIF2				Y	Y
ERRIFB				Y	Y
ERRIFDEF				Y	Y
ERRIFDIF				Y	Y
ERRIFDIFI				Y	Y
ERRIFE				Y	Y
ERRIFIDN				Y	Y
ERRIFIDNI				Y	Y

continues

Table 3.1. *continued*

Directive (Pseudooperation)	MASM 6.0	MASM 5.1	MsQA 2.51	TASM 3.0	TASM 2.0
ERRIFNB				Y	Y
ERRIFNDEF				Y	Y
.ERRNB	Y	Y	Y	Y	Y
.ERRNDEF	Y	Y	Y	Y	Y
.ERRNZ	Y	Y	Y	Y	Y
EVEN	Y	Y	Y	Y	Y
EVENDATA				Y	Y
.EXIT			Y		
EXITCODE				Y	
EXITM	Y	Y	Y	Y	Y
EXTERN	Y				
EXTERNDEF	Y				
EXTRN	Y	Y	Y	Y	Y
.FARDATA	Y	Y	Y	Y	Y
.FARDATA?	Y	Y	Y	Y	Y
FARDATA				Y	Y
FOR	Y				
FORC	Y				
FWORD	Y				
GLOBAL				Y	Y
GOTO	Y			Y	
GROUP	Y	Y	Y	Y	Y
IDEAL				Y	Y
.IF	Y				
IF	Y	Y	Y	Y	Y
IF1		Y	Y	Y	Y
IF2		Y	Y	Y	Y
IFB	Y	Y	Y	Y	Y
IFDEF	Y	Y	Y	Y	Y
IFDIF	Y	Y	Y	Y	Y
IFDIFI	Y	Y	Y	Y	Y

Directive (Pseudooperation)	MASM 6.0	MASM 5.1	MsQA 2.51	TASM 3.0	TASM 2.0
IFE	Y	Y	Y	Y	Y
IFIDN	Y	Y	Y	Y	Y
IFIDNI	Y	Y	Y	Y	Y
IFNB	Y	Y	Y	Y	Y
IFNDEF	Y	Y	Y	Y	Y
%INCL				Y	Y
INCLUDE	Y	Y	Y	Y	Y
INCLUDELIB	Y	Y	Y	Y	Y
INSTR	Y	Y	Y	Y	Y
IRP	Y	Y	Y	Y	Y
IRPC	Y	Y	Y	Y	Y
INVOKE	Y				
JUMPS				Y	Y
LABEL	Y	Y	Y	Y	Y
.LALL	Y	Y	Y	Y	Y
LARGESTACK				Y	
.LFCOND	Y	Y	Y	Y	Y
%LINUM				Y	Y
%LIST				Y	Y
.LIST	Y	Y	Y	Y	Y
.LISTALL	Y				
.LISTIF	Y				
.LISTMACRO	Y				
.LISTMACROALL	Y				
LOCAL	Y	Y	Y	Y	Y
LOCALS				Y	Y
MACRO	Y	Y	Y	Y	Y
%MACS				Y	Y
MASM				Y	Y
MASM51				Y	Y
.MODEL	Y	Y	Y	Y	Y
MODEL				Y	Y

continues

Table 3.1. *continued*

Directive (Pseudooperation)	MASM 6.0	MASM 5.1	MsQA 2.51	TASM 3.0	TASM 2.0
.MSFLOAT			Y		
MULTERRS				Y	Y
NAME	Y	Y	Y	Y	Y
%NEWPAGE				Y	Y
.NO87	Y				
%NOCONDS				Y	Y
%NOCREF				Y	Y
.NOCREF	Y				
%NOCTLS				Y	Y
NOEMUL				Y	Y
%NOINCL				Y	Y
NOJUMPS				Y	Y
%NOLIST				Y	Y
.NOLIST	Y				
.NOLISTIF	Y				
.NOLISTMACRO	Y				
NOLOCALS				Y	Y
%NOMACS				Y	Y
NOMASM51				Y	Y
NOMULTERRS				Y	Y
NOSMART				Y	
%NOSYMS				Y	Y
%NOTRUNC				Y	Y
NOWARN				Y	Y
OPTION		Y			
ORG	Y	Y	Y	Y	Y
%OUT	Y	Y	Y	Y	Y
P186				Y	Y
P286				Y	Y
P286N				Y	Y
P286P				Y	Y

Directive (Pseudooperation)	MASM 6.0	MASM 5.1	MsQA 2.51	TASM 3.0	TASM 2.0
P287				Y	Y
P386				Y	Y
P386N				Y	Y
P386P				Y	Y
P387				Y	Y
P486				Y	Y
P486N				Y	Y
P8086				Y	Y
P8087				Y	Y
PAGE	Y	Y	Y	Y	Y
%PAGESIZE				Y	Y
%PCNT				Y	Y
PNO87				Y	Y
POPCONTEXT	Y				
%POPLCTL				Y	Y
PROC	Y	Y	Y	Y	Y
PROTO	Y				
PUBLIC	Y	Y	Y	Y	Y
PUBLICDLL				Y	Y
PURGE	Y	Y	Y	Y	Y
PUSHCONTEXT	Y				
%PUSHLCTL				Y	Y
QUIRKS				Y	Y
QWORD	Y				
.RADIX	Y	Y	Y	Y	Y
RADIX				Y	Y
REAL4	Y				
REAL8	Y				
REAL10	Y				
RECORD	Y	Y	Y	Y	Y
.REPEAT	Y				
REPEAT	Y				

continues

Table 3.1. continued

Directive (Pseudooperation)	MASM 6.0	MASM 5.1	MsQA 2.51	TASM 3.0	TASM 2.0
REPT	Y	Y	Y	Y	Y
.SALL	Y	Y	Y	Y	Y
SBYTE	Y				
SDWORD	Y				
SEGMENT	Y	Y	Y	Y	Y
.SEQ	Y	Y	Y	Y	Y
SEQ				Y	
.SFCOND	Y	Y	Y	Y	Y
SIZESTR	Y		Y	Y	Y
SMALLSTACK				Y	
SMART				Y	
.STACK	Y	Y	Y	Y	Y
STACK				Y	Y
.STARTUP	Y	Y	Y	Y	Y
STARTUPCODE				Y	
STRUC	Y	Y	Y	Y	Y
STRUCT	Y				
SUBSTR	Y		Y	Y	Y
SUBTITLE	Y				
SUBTTL	Y	Y	Y	Y	Y
%SUBTTL				Y	Y
%SYMS				Y	Y
SWORD	Y				
TABLE				Y	
%TABSIZE				Y	Y
TBLPTR				Y	
TBYTE			Y		
%TEXT				Y	Y
TEXTEQU	Y				
.TFCOND	Y	Y	Y	Y	Y
TITLE	Y	Y	Y	Y	Y

Directive (Pseudooperation)	MASM 6.0	MASM 5.1	MsQA 2.51	TASM 3.0	TASM 2.0
%TITLE				Y	Y
%TRUNC				Y	Y
TYPEDEF	Y			Y	
UDATASEG				Y	Y
UFARDATA				Y	Y
UNION	Y			Y	Y
.UNTIL	Y				
.UNTILCXZ	Y				
USES				Y	Y
VERSION				Y	
WARN			Y	Y	Y
.WHILE	Y				
WHILE	Y			Y	
WORD	Y				
.XALL	Y	Y	Y	Y	Y
.XCREF	Y	Y		Y	Y
.XLIST	Y	Y	Y	Y	Y

As this table shows, many directives are supported by all four contenders (two versions of MASM are listed), but Turbo Assembler has the largest number of unique, added directives. In most cases these are simply *aliases* for names of other existing, nonunique directives, such as FARDATA for .FARDATA. Such aliases are needed because in Turbo Assembler's *ideal* mode no directive can begin with a period, and in the MASM standard world nearly half of the available directives do so.

MASM from Microsoft

Microsoft's MASM is one of the most popular assemblers for assembly language. (Some other assemblers, such as the one with the IBM name on it, are actually the MASM Microsoft publishes.)

MASM 6.0 is a single-pass assembler that creates relocatable object code, which can subsequently be linked and executed. Optionally ,it can create listing files and collect cross-reference data to be processed by a separate program. Prior to version 6, MASM was a two-pass assembler.

Because MASM was effectively the first assembler to achieve wide distribution and was distributed by IBM, it has become the standard against which all others are measured. This is not to say that MASM is perfect; from its earliest days MASM has borne a reputation for harboring strange bugs. Even in the latest version (6.0), some of MASM's actions seem a bit bizarre to many users.

Most of the true bugs in earlier versions, such as failure of some of the directives to do anything at all, have been corrected in later releases, but in doing so Microsoft has made one MASM version incompatible with the next. MASM 6.0 represents a large departure from previous versions of MASM. Many directives and design structures reminiscent of features of the C language were added. Indeed, programmers familiar with C (particularly Microsoft's C products) should have little trouble adapting to using MASM 6.0.

Prior to MASM 6.0, one of the biggest disadvantages of MASM was its susceptibility to "phase error" problems. MASM used this term to describe a situation where it failed to assign memory space properly during the first pass, so that address references changed between the first pass and the second. What made this bug so puzzling is that it usually went undetected at the point at which it occured, showing up only at the first memory location that changed, which may have been many lines of code past the real error.

If you do not have MASM 6.0, the only practical way to find this kind of error is to generate listings for *both* passes, then compare the two listings line-by-line to discover the point at which the assigned memory addresses fail to match. Careful examination of the code generated by the instruction immediately preceding the first mismatch usually shows what's wrong.

In MASM 6.0, there is no such thing as a phase error, because MASM is no longer a two-pass compiler.

Possibly the greatest advantage MASM has over its competitors is that it *does* set the standard and therefore usually includes at least a few new features the other products lack. Another advantage is that it's the only assembler that offers full support for OS/2.

QuickAssembler from Microsoft

Microsoft's latest verion of QuickAssembler is version 2.51. It is available only as a part of the QuickC version 2.5 package, and runs only as part of QuickC.

QuickAssembler, a full implementation of 8086 assembly language, omits all support of the 80386, 80387, and OS/2 protected-mode features in MASM. Although the QuickAssembler manual claims that QuickAssembler can use the "full set" of

MASM 5.1 directives and operations, the manual itself describes only the directives listed in table 3.1. If you cannot find out what a directive is supposed to do, using it is a bit difficult.

QuickAssembler's greatest advantage is that it comes at no extra cost when you buy the latest version of the QuickC compiler. This advantage is counterbalanced by QuickAssembler's lack of adequate documentation, however. (The documentation problem is a flaw shared by all the Quick implementations, which depend a bit too much on their hypertext help system and thus fail to provide adequate printed reference data for serious users.) Another potentially serious drawback is QuickAssembler's lack of support for 80386, 80486, 80387, and protected mode OS/2 features.

By default, QuickAssembler is a single-pass assembler. This makes it faster than it otherwise would be (its speed on moderate-sized source files is astounding) but prevents features such as program-listing generation from working. You can configure QuickAssembler to operate as a two-pass system; it then works much like MASM 5.1, but with a few added directives MASM 5.1 lacks.

Because QuickAssembler normally is used only from inside the QuickC environment, and because it is so similar to MASM in all other respects, it is not discussed separately in the rest of this chapter.

If you use QuickC, QuickAssembler is arguably the simplest way to ease into the world of assembly language; otherwise, you would do better with one of the separate products, if only because they offer better documentation than QuickAssembler.

Turbo Assembler from Borland

The other major competitor among assemblers is Borland's Turbo Assembler (TASM). Turbo Assembler claims "100 percent" compatibility with full MASM; since the different versions of MASM are not compatible with each other, TASM is a useful tool when you must support several MASM versions.

The unique Turbo Assembler feature that makes supporting several MASM versions possible is the availability of different assembly modes for existing assembly programs. To retain MASM compatibility, you have the option of using MASM, MASM51, or QUIRKS modes, either individually or in combination.

For new programs in which you prefer that the assembler not duplicate the sometimes bizarre actions of MASM but that it instead be completely consistent, you can set the mode to IDEAL. Because ideal mode is not compatible with the mainstream of assembly language programming, this book does not discuss the mode in detail. Although this capability certainly is a plus for Turbo Assembler, it should not be the deciding factor unless weighing other more critical advantages and disadvantages leaves you undecided.

Table 3.2 lists the conditions that determine which MASM-compatible mode you should use and when. Note that the default operating mode is MASM.

Table 3.2. *Turbo Assembler's conditions for selecting a MASM-compatible mode.*

Mode	Conditions for Use
Normal (MASM)	Assembles under MASM 4.00 or MASM 5.00
QUIRKS	Assembles under MASM 4.00 or MASM 5.00; will not assemble under TASM without MASM51 or QUIRKS
MASM51	Requires MASM 5.1 for assembly
MASM51 and QUIRKS	Requires MASM 5.1 for assembly but will not assemble under TASM with only the MASM51 switch set

The following paragraphs detail the differences in operation offered by each of these modes.

When used by itself, QUIRKS mode provides the following capabilities:

❑ FAR jumps can be generated as NEAR or SHORT if ASSUME directives for CS permit it.

❑ If present, one register can determine all instruction sizes in a binary operation.

❑ OFFSET, segment override, and other such information on = or numeric EQU assignments are destroyed.

❑ EQU assignments are forced to expressions with PTR or :, which will appear as text.

When used by itself, MASM51 mode provides the following capabilities:

❑ Instr, Catstr, Substr, Sizestr, and \ line continuation can all be used.

❑ EQUs to keywords are made TEXT instead of ALIASes.

❑ Leading whitespace is not discarded on %textmacro in macro arguments.

When used together, MASM51 and QUIRKS modes provide the following capabilities:

❑ Each capability listed under QUIRKS is available.

❑ Each capability listed under MASM51 is available.

❑ The @@, @F, and @B local labels can be used.

❑ Procedure names are made PUBLIC automatically in extended MODELs.

❏ Near labels in PROCs can be redefined in other PROCs.

❏ The :: operator can define symbols accessible outside the current PROC.

This versatility is one of the greatest advantages provided by Turbo Assembler. IDEAL mode's extended syntax is an option none of its competitors offer.

Like MASM, Turbo Assembler supports the 80386 and 80387 special instructions and provides simplified segment-management directives that can greatly ease the chore of setting up the "right" interface conventions for your high-level language. If you use Turbo Pascal, Turbo Assembler's special .MODEL TPASCAL directive automatically sets up the correct segment definitions for TP compatibility. No other assembler provides this advantageous option.

Turbo Assembler also has some disadvantages, however. Because it is a single-pass assembler (version 2 can be configured to take as many as five passes), it can be confused by undeclared forward references that a multipass assembler would resolve automatically. Unlike MASM, Turbo Assembler cannot be configured by the DOS environment; however, Turbo Assembler can be configured by using its special TASM.CFG file (described in the on-line help files).

The Files Involved

No matter which assembler you choose, you will be dealing with at least two kinds of files, and probably more. The two that are always involved are the input file (the source code), which bears the file extension ASM by default, and the output file (the object code), identified by the default extension OBJ.

Other files you may work with include MAC, INC, LST, CRF, and XRF files. The MAC and INC files can be included as part of your input data if you use INCLUDE statements in the ASM file. You also can (and usually should) request that the assembler generate the LST listing file for you and that the CRF or XRF files generate a cross-reference of all the symbol names you use.

Let's look at these different kinds of files in more detail.

The ASM Source File

Every assembly language program originally exists as an ASM source file, because these files are what all the assemblers use as their primary input. In addition to the normal ASM file, a program can also have MAC or INC files. But before looking at other files, let's see what makes up the normal ASM file. The following file descriptions apply to each of the assemblers introduced earlier in this chapter.

Format for an ASM file is relatively simple. The file must be a pure ASCII "text" file rather than a word processor document, which has embedded control characters that confuse the assembler. Each line of the file is considered a separate record, and each line normally is divided into four fields.

These four fields contain the label, the operator, the operand(s), and any comments. Any or all of the fields may be blank; if all are blank, the record is ignored.

The label field extends from the front of the line to the first blank space (a space character or a tab). If the line begins with a blank space, the label field is considered empty. If the label field is not empty but does not contain a directive, its content is entered into the symbol table by the assembler and eventually will be translated into an address.

The operator field, which is the next field in the record, begins with the first nonblank character after the label field and extends to the next blank or to the end of the line, whichever comes first. It contains either an assembly language operator (also called an *instruction*), such as MOV or RET, or a directive.

As you may recall, directives are discussed in Chapter 2, "An Overview of Assembly Language." A directive, sometimes called a *pseudooperator* (or just a *pseudo*, for short), is an instruction to the assembler. It can appear in either the label or the operator field of a line (unless it requires a label; in that case it can appear only in the operator field). The assembler responds to a directive by performing some action, such as reserving memory in the case of the DB directive or noting the limits of a procedure in the case of PROC or ENDP. An operator, on the other hand, causes the generation of machine code that will perform a particular operation.

Following the operator field is the operand field, which begins with the first nonblank character after the operator field and extends to the first semicolon (;) or the end of the line, whichever comes first. This field specifies what the operator or the directive is to operate on. For example, a MOV operator has no purpose until you tell it what to move. The line MOV AX,1234 has no label, but contains the operator MOV and the operands AX,1234.

The final field is the comment field, which includes everything from the semicolon (if present) to the end of the line. Extended comments also can be created by using the COMMENT directive, which takes one character (any nonblank character) as its operand and then ignores all fields of all records until that character occurs again. The following example shows a comment at the end of a line of code:

```
MAIN:    MOV    AX,0              ; set AX to initial value
```

where MAIN is the label, MOV is the operator, AX,0 is the operand, and everything beginning with the semicolon is the comment field.

The following shows an example of a multiline comment, using the COMMENT directive:

```
COMMENT @
    This routine is used to clear the entire
    video buffer area.  It initializes each memory
    location to a specific value. @
```

The operator after the directive (in this case, the at sign @) indicates what character should be interpreted by the assembler as the end of the comments. In this case, everything is assumed to be a comment and ignored up through the final at sign (@).

With some assemblers, an asterisk as the first character of a record marks the entire record as a comment. Because this is not true of all assemblers, using the semicolon is safer than relying on this method.

The normal assembler ASM file forces the MAC and INC types of files (if used) into it by naming them as operands for the INCLUDE directive. The MAC extension usually identifies a macro library, which is a method for speeding up coding of repetitive tasks; the INC extension usually denotes any other type of INCLUDE file such as one containing a collection of frequently needed data. Because they become part of the ASM file at assembly time, both types of files must follow the standard ASM-file formatting rules.

The OBJ Output File

This file, the most important file created by the assembler (in fact, the assembler *exists* to create this file), is basically a machine language file. But because the linking pass must be performed to resolve external references, these files are not executable. Chapter 4, "Choosing and Using Your Linker," discusses object files in greater detail.

The LST Listing File

You decide whether a listing file is created; if created, it normally has the file extension LST. This file is the assembler's "report of operations" and contains the source statements as well as the machine language instructions into which they translate. A LST file may contain other information also, such as a symbol table or, in some cases, cross-reference data.

This file and listing can be a useful tool. With it you can generate the hard copy you need to debug a program efficiently, and the listing is great for hard-copy archiving.

Here's the output from a typical listing file, generated by MASM from a sample file you learn about in Chapter 5, "Using Microsoft's Assembly Language Products":

```
Microsoft (R) Macro Assembler Version 6.00              08/25/91 18:51:42
sums.asm                                                Page 1 - 1


                        Page 60,132
                        Comment ¦
                        ***********************************************************************

                        File:    SUMS.ASM for Microsoft Macro Assembler 6.0
                        Author:  Allen L. Wyatt
                        Date:    8/3/91

                        Purpose: Given an integer number X, find the sum of
                                 X + (X-1) + (X-2) + (X-3) + (X-4) ... + 2 + 1
                                 Designed to be called from Microsoft C.

                        Format:  SUMS(X)


                        ***********************************************************************¦

                        PUBLIC      sums

                        .MODEL      small, C
0000                    .CODE

0000                    sums    PROC C Value:SWORD
0003  B8 0000                   MOV   AX,0            ;Initialize to zero
0006  8B 4E 04                  MOV   CX,Value        ;Get actual value
0009  E3 0B                     JCXZ S3              ;Num=0, no need to do
000B  13 C1             S1:     ADC   AX,CX           ;Add row value
000D  72 04                     JC    S2             ;Quit if AX overflowed
000F  E2 FA                     LOOP S1              ;Repeat process
0011  EB 03                     JMP   S3             ;Successful completion
0013  B8 0000           S2:     MOV   AX,0            ;Force a zero
0016                    S3:     RET                  ;Return to C
0018                    sums    ENDP

                        END
```

Microsoft (R) Macro Assembler Version 6.00   08/25/91 18:51:42
sums.asm   Symbols 2 - 1

Segments and Groups:

N a m e	Size	Length	Align	Combine	Class
DGROUP	GROUP				
_DATA	16 Bit	0000	Word	Public	'DATA'
_TEXT	16 Bit	0018	Word	Public	'CODE'

Microsoft (R) Macro Assembler Version 6.00   08/25/91 18:51:42
sums.asm   Symbols 3 - 1

Procedures, parameters and locals:

N a m e	Type	Value	Attr
sums	P Near	0000	_TEXT Length= 0018 Public **C**
Value	Word	bp + 0004	
S1	L Near	000B	_TEXT
S2	L Near	0013	_TEXT
S3	L Near	0016	_TEXT

Microsoft (R) Macro Assembler Version 6.00   08/25/91 18:51:42
sums.asm   Symbols 4 - 1

Symbols:

N a m e	Type	Value	Attr

```
@CodeSize  . . . . . . . . . .        Number    0000h
@DataSize  . . . . . . . . . .        Number    0000h
@Interface . . . . . . . . . .        Number    0001h
@Model . . . . . . . . . . . .        Number    0002h
@code  . . . . . . . . . . . .        Text      _TEXT
@data  . . . . . . . . . . . .        Text      DGROUP
@fardata?  . . . . . . . . . .        Text      FAR_BSS
@fardata . . . . . . . . . . .        Text      FAR_DATA
@stack . . . . . . . . . . . .        Text      DGROUP


       0 Warnings
       0 Errors
```

The LST file created by Turbo Assembler is similar to MASM's. The following is the listing file from Turbo Assembler:

```
Turbo Assembler  Version 3.0        08/25/91 18:54:28       Page 1
sums.asm



  1                            Page 60,132
  2                            Comment ¦
  3
********************************************************************
  4
  5                            File:    SUMS.ASM for Turbo Assembler 3.0
  6                            Author:  Allen L. Wyatt
  7                            Date:    8/17/91
  8
  9                            Purpose: Given an integer number X, find the sum of
 10                                     X + (X-1) + (X-2) + (X-3) + (X-4) ... + 2 + 1
 11                                     Designed to be called from Turbo Pascal 6.0.
 12
 13                            Format:  SUMS(X)
 14
 15
********************************************************************¦
 16
 17                            PUBLIC    sums
 18
 19 0000                       .MODEL    small, Pascal
 20 0000                       .CODE
 21
 22 0000            sums       PROC Value:WORD RETURNS Sum:WORD
```

```
1    23 0000  55                        PUSH    BP
1    24 0001  8B EC                     MOV     BP,SP
1    25 0003  B8 0000                   MOV     AX,0          ;Initialize to zero
     26 0006  8B 4E 04                  MOV     CX,Value      ;Get actual value
     27 0009  E3 0C                     JCXZ    S3            ;Num=0, no need to do
     28 000B  13 C1          S1:        ADC     AX,CX         ;Add row value
     29 000D  72 05                     JC      S2            ;Quit if AX
                                                                overflowed
     30 000F  E2 FA                     LOOP    S1            ;Repeat process
     31 0011  EB 04 90                  JMP     S3            ;Successful
                                                                completion
     32 0014  B8 0000        S2:        MOV     AX,0          ;Force a zero
1    33 0017  5D                        POP     BP
1    34 0018  C2 0002                   RET     00002h
     35 001B                 sums       ENDP
     36
     37                                 END
```

Turbo Assembler   Version 3.0   08/25/91 18:54:28   Page 2
Symbol Table


```
Symbol Name                    Type    Value

??DATE                         Text    "08/25/91"
??FILENAME                     Text    "sums       "
??TIME                         Text    "18:54:28"
??VERSION                      Number  0300
@32BIT                         Text    0
@CODE                          Text    _TEXT
@CODESIZE                      Text    0
@CPU                           Text    0101H
@CURSEG                        Text    _TEXT
@DATA                          Text    DGROUP
@DATASIZE                      Text    0
@FILENAME                      Text    SUMS
@INTERFACE                     Text    4H
@MODEL                         Text    2
@STACK                         Text    DGROUP
```

```
@WORDSIZE                      Text   2
S1                             Near   _TEXT:000B
S2                             Near   _TEXT:0014
S3                             Near   _TEXT:0017
SUM                            Number [DGROUP:BP+0006]
SUMS                           Near   _TEXT:0000
VALUE                          Number [DGROUP:BP+0004]


Groups & Segments              Bit Size Align  Combine Class

DGROUP                         Group
  _DATA                        16  0000 Word    Public  DATA
_TEXT                          16  001B Word    Public  CODE
```

Notice that the listing file produced by TASM 3.0 includes the code created by the compiler (lines 23, 24, 33, and 34), but the one for MASM 6.0 does not. Aside from this rather small difference, the major variations in the listings produced by the two assemblers are in the symbol-table and error reports. I have presented these pages complete so that you can compare them. You can suppress the information by using special command-line options when you assemble the file. These command-line options are covered in detail in Chapters 5 and 6 ("Using Microsoft's Assembly Language Products" and "Using Borland's Assembly Language Products," respectively).

Not all printers print the same number of characters per line. These listing files were all formatted for 60-line pages, with 132 characters per line. The PAGE directive at the top of the ASM file controls this format. If your printer handles only 80 characters per line, you easily can change the line to

PAGE 60,80

for a LST file formatted for 80 characters per line. How you change the line is up to you.

More about Assembler Directives

This chapter has made frequent mention of assembler directives (introduced in Chapter 2, "An Overview of Assembly Language") without fully describing what they do. A full list of directives appears earlier in the chapter. Although many directives exist for each assembler, only a few of them are used often. The easiest way to learn those directives is to see how they are used in the sample programs and to study your assembler's reference manual. For a complete description of the assembler directives, see Chapter 23, "Assembler Directives."

Two groups of directives—those that control conditional assembly of code sequences, and those involved with the definition and control of macro operations—are especially important and deserve additional emphasis here. Both groups function the same, regardless of your assembler.

Conditional Assembly

The conditional assembly capability is one of the powerful features common to both MASM and TASM. *Conditional assembly* means that the assembler can decide, based on the values of certain symbols (or flags), whether to include specific blocks of code. This capability can greatly simplify the development process.

Table 3.4 lists a few of the more common conditional assembly directives. These directives are not direct assembly language commands; rather, they are commands to the assembler that control how the source-code file is processed.

Table 3.4. *Common conditional assembly directives.*

Directive	Meaning
IF	Assemble if true
IFB	Assemble if blank
IFDEF	Assemble if defined
IFDIF	Assemble if different
IFDIFI	Assemble if different, ignoring case
IFE	Assemble if false
IFIDN	Assemble if identical
IFIDNI	Assemble if identical, ignoring case
IFNB	Assemble if not blank
IFNDEF	Assemble if not defined
ELSE	Used with any of the above
ENDIF	End of conditional block

Each of the conditional assembly directives listed in table 3.4 requires an expression or argument. The assembler evaluates the expression or argument and, based on that evaluation, takes appropriate action.

For instance, consider the following code segment:

```
ifdef debug
                INCLUDE DEBUG.ASM
endif
```

When this segment is coupled with a command-line switch that defines the debug variable, the file DEBUG.ASM will be included in the object code. If you do not define debug, the code will not be included. This usage lets you include debugging code easily and flexibly to facilitate the development process. Command-line switches are discussed fully in later chapters devoted solely to the major assemblers.

Conditional assembly statements can be used in numerous ways. Used wisely, they can make the development process faster and less painful. Just remember that conditional assembly statements control only the assembler.

Macro Operations

If you're familiar with C, the easiest way to understand what an assembly language *macro operation* does is to think of it as the equivalent of the #define statement. Unfortunately, if your chosen language is BASIC or Pascal, that won't tell you much!

A macro operation, usually shortened to just *macro*, is a sequence of assembly language statements that has been assigned a symbolic name. Once a macro has been defined in an ASM file, you can include the entire sequence of statements simply by using the macro name as an operator. If you defined the macro to have parameters, you can also pass operands to it at each call.

In effect, the macro gives you the capability of redefining assembly language to be what you need most. Theoretically, you can redefine assembly language until your final program is nothing but a series of macro calls, and is unreadable to any skilled assembly language programmer without the matching set of macro definitions, which are often hidden away in a separate MAC or INC file and are hardly ever printed out on the listing.

Table 3.5 lists the significant macro directives common to all the assemblers described in this chapter.

Table 3.5. *Assembler macro directives.*

Directive	Meaning
MACRO	Begin definition of macro
IRP	Repeat for each parameter
IRPC	Repeat for each character
REPT	Repeat sequence *n* times
ENDM	End sequence for all of above
LOCAL	Establish local-label list
PURGE	Remove listed definitions

The first four directives listed in table 3.5 establish the start of a macro sequence; each sequence is ended by the ENDM directive, and sequences can be nested. Each sequence requires its own ENDM. Only the MACRO directive establishes a named sequence that can be called elsewhere; the three "repeat" directives provide an internal loop structure that can be used either in the main program or in a MACRO definition.

The syntax used by all the assemblers for the MACRO...ENDM definition sequence is

```
name MACRO list
       .
       .
       .
   ENDM
```

where *name* is the name by which the macro will be called subsequently, and *list* is an optional group of "formal parameters" that define what information can be passed into the macro when it is called.

The LOCAL directive may be used inside a MACRO...ENDM sequence to specify a list of labels to be replaced with unique symbols each time the macro is expanded. This use of LOCAL in macros prevents problems caused when a macro defines the same symbol to mean two different addresses.

The IRP, IRPC, and REPT directives follow a syntax similar to that used by MACRO but do not use a *name* field. Each also uses a different kind of parameter *list*.

REPT uses a single expression that must evaluate to a numeric constant and repeats that many times the code contained in the REPT...ENDM sequence.

IRP takes exactly one formal parameter, followed by an argument list enclosed in angle brackets. The assembler repeats the IRP...ENDM sequence once for each argument in the list, substituting that argument for the formal parameter wherever it occurs within the sequence. If you are using MASM 6.0, you can use the FOR directive instead of IRP.

IRPC is like IRP, but instead of the angle-bracket-enclosed list of arguments, IRPC requires a single text string. IRPC repeats the IRPC...ENDM sequence once for each character in that string, each time substituting that character for the formal parameter. If you are using MASM 6.0, you can use the FORC directive instead of IRPC.

The PURGE directive takes as its operand a list of macro names and removes each macro from memory. Normally, PURGE is not required; if, however, you have dozens of lengthy definitions, each of which is used only once or twice, you may need this directive to free memory for the assembler. PURGE does *not* generate any code, nor does it have any effect on your system; all it does is free some RAM for the assembler.

To illustrate how macros can be helpful and how to define them, here's an example. Let's suppose that you want to use the BIOS functions to set the cursor type or to position the cursor. The following macros can be defined to do much of the detail work, and you have fewer lines of code to type:

```
SETCUR     MACRO
           MOV   AH,1        ;; set cursor type from CX
           INT   10h
           ENDM


MOVCUR     MACRO     R,C
           MOV   DH,BYTE PTR R
           MOV   DL,BYTE PTR C
           MOV   AH,2        ;; set cursor to row R, col C
           INT   10h
           ENDM
```

Once these two macros are defined, simply use SETCUR to set the cursor (you must make sure that CX contains the cursor type you want).

MOVCUR, however, is a bit more complicated. This sequence illustrates the use of formal parameters in macro definitions. Because the parameter list is R,C, each time MOVCUR is called, the R in the MOV DH,BYTE PTR R line is replaced with the first argument you provided as part of the call, and the second argument you provide similarly affects the C in the next line. If you have stored the desired row and column values in the low bytes of 16-bit variables named ROW_WORD and COL_WORD, you can call MOVCUR with the following single line:

```
MOVCUR   ROW_WORD,COL_WORD
```

The assembler will replace this with the code sequence

```
MOV   DH,BYTE PTR ROW_WORD
MOV   DL,BYTE PTR COL_WORD
MOV   AH,2                    ; set cursor to row R, col C
INT   10h
```

The BYTE and PTR operators are specifically included in this example so that you can use *any* type or size of variable without generating an assembler error. You can omit these operators if the only locations you use when calling MOVCUR are those defined with the DB or BYTE directives.

All the assemblers have files containing collections of useful macros as a part of the distribution packages. A few hours spent mastering macros will save you much more time eventually by making your programming faster.

Summary

This chapter covered concepts, files, and procedures common to the use of the major assembler programs: MASM from Microsoft, Turbo Assembler from Borland, and QuickAssembler, also by Microsoft.

Using the assembler properly is essential to your success in using assembly language. The next chapter discusses commonalities of the various linking programs. Then Chapters 5, "Using Microsoft's Assembly Language Products," and 6, "Using Borland's Assembly Language Products," discuss the major assemblers in detail.

4

Choosing and Using
Your Linker

In Chapter 3, "Choosing and Using Your Assembler," you learned how to use the assembler. You learned also that an assembler does not produce executable machine code. Instead, the OBJ file that the assembler creates must be *linked* successfully to work properly.

The program you use to do this task is called, curiously enough, a *linker*. You need a copy of such a program to complete the examples in this chapter. Each of the assemblers discussed in Chapter 3 has a matching linker, but most of these linkers work properly on OBJ files produced by any of the assemblers (or any other OBJ file that meets standard format specifications).

You should note that some assemblers hide the actions taken by the linker. For instance, the linking phase of creating an executable file is done automatically if you use any of the following systems:

❑ Programmer's Workbench (comes with MASM 6.0)

❑ ML command-line program for MASM 6.0

❑ QuickAssembler

❑ Turbo Assembler

This does not mean that linking is not done, it simply means that linking is done every time you assemble a source code-file. Nevertheless, you need to understand the process of linking.

Unfortunately, OBJ files produced by some of the newer compilers do *not* follow the standard format specification; they go beyond it. Such OBJ files can be linked only by linkers designed to recognize the extensions. QuickC is one such language; its manual tells you to use only the linker furnished with it, although some other versions of the Microsoft linker also work.

This chapter covers how to choose and use a linker program. Most likely, you'll simply use the program that came with your assembler or high-level language, but you may find that differences in performance from one linker to another are significant enough to warrant a special purchase.

Before comparing the linkers that come with each of the assemblers, let's look at what a linker does.

What the Linker Does

A *linker* is a program that translates relocatable object code (produced by an assembler or compiler) into executable machine code. The linker performs the following three main tasks:

❑ Combines separate object modules into one executable file

❑ Attempts to resolve references to external variables

❑ Produces a listing (if you ask for one) showing how the object files were linked

Most people refer to these programs as linkers (as I have); others call them *linkage editors*. Whatever they are called, they do these three basic tasks. Many different linkers are available.

Choosing Your Linker

To help you decide whether to use the linker furnished with your assembler or high-level language or to purchase one elsewhere, here's a quick overview of the similarities and differences of two major linkers: LINK from Microsoft and TLINK from Borland.

Until recently, you had to use the Microsoft linker if you wanted to do source-level debugging (described in Chapter 7). This requirement no longer applies, however, because both linkers can now provide debugging information in their output EXE files.

LINK from Microsoft

Microsoft's LINK.EXE program is available from many sources, most noticeably Microsoft and IBM. For many years, a copy of LINK.EXE was even included (with DOS) with any MS- or PC DOS computer system (but it has not been included for the past few versions of DOS). LINK.EXE is always included with every Microsoft language product.

As a result, several copies of LINK.EXE probably are available to you; the major question is which one to use. Ordinarily, the rule is to always use the most recent copy (the one with the highest version number) because Microsoft has attempted to maintain downward compatibility from one release to the next. The exception to this rule is that QuickC requires that you use the linker furnished with it, even though that version number may be lower than the version number for the linker that came with MASM. (You only see the version numbers when you run the LINK program.)

Like its companion assembler, and for the same reasons, LINK sets the industry standard against which other linkers are compared. It is not the fastest linker available, nor is it the slowest. The current version supports overlays but does not include an overlay manager that enables you to use them; for this reason, overlays can be used only when the high-level language provides such a manager. (Although third-party overlay managers are available as shareware, they are beyond the scope of this book.) The term *overlay* is used for portions of program code stored on disk. These portions are loaded into memory only when they are needed, and they "overlay" other unused portions of code. An overlay manager takes care of loading these code blocks, as necessary.

The major advantages of LINK can be summed up easily: it's acceptably fast, it's accurate, and it's free when you buy any Microsoft language product.

The disadvantages aren't as obvious. If you frequently link large programs (such as EXE files greater than 200K), LINK seems to drag on forever. If you are generating COM or BIN files rather than directly executable programs, LINK requires that you perform some additional steps. If your requirements call for consistent use of the option switches, other linkers (such as TLINK) can be configured to your needs, but LINK cannot. And finally, LINK will let some of your programming errors slip by without detection (opinion is divided among professionals as to whether this is a bug or a feature).

TLINK from Borland

Borland's TLINK program is furnished with all its high-level languages but is not available as a separate product. Unlike LINK, TLINK operates only from the command line and has no interactive mode. Although you may consider this a disadvantage initially, with practice you probably will stop using interactive mode anyway, and this difference eventually will lose its significance.

Borland's own description of TLINK is "lean and mean." Features of other linkers that Borland considered superfluous were dropped to create a fast, compact utility. Thus it has the shortest list of options as well as the smallest size.

The major advantages of TLINK are its small size and speed. TLINK can also generate a COM, SYS, or BIN file directly without requiring any subsequent conversion of its output. The major disadvantage of TLINK is that it cannot be purchased separately (it comes only with a Borland language).

If you are using Borland's high-level languages, TLINK is probably your linker of choice because it is tailored to work efficiently with other Borland products. For use with other languages, it does not offer enough unique advantages to warrant buying it.

The Files Involved

Throughout this chapter I refer to the file types the linker creates: the *executable* and *listing* files.

Whether these files actually are created depends on how you invoke the assembler or answer the assembler's prompts. Assuming that you assembled SUMS.ASM (from Chapter 3) using MASM, and that you requested all files, you should find the following files when you use DIR after assembly and linking. Also shown are the TEST files referred to in this chapter, but described fully in Chapter 5, "Using Microsoft's Assembly Language Products." If you are working with Borland's products, you will not be working with TEST.C. Rather, in Chapter 6 ("Using Borland's Assembly Language Products"), you will produce TEST.CPP for use with Borland C++.

```
C>DIR

 Volume in drive C is DCI
 Volume Serial Number is 16B2-BB87
 Directory of C:\TEST


 .             <DIR>      10-16-91   10:38a
 ..            <DIR>      10-16-91   10:38a
 SUMS    ASM      1137    10-16-91   10:37a
 SUMS    OBJ       379    10-16-91   10:37a
 SUMS    LST      3075    10-16-91   10:37a
 TEST    C         672    08-20-91    7:10a
```

```
TEST    OBJ      1387 10-16-91  10:43a
TEST    COD      4079 10-16-91  10:43a
TEST    EXE      9075 10-16-91  10:44a
TEST    MAP      1915 10-16-91  10:44a
       10 file(s)     21719 bytes
                    1626112 bytes free
```

You may remember from Chapter 3 that SUMS.ASM is the assembly language source code file. SUMS.LST and SUMS.OBJ were created by MASM. TEST.C is the C source code (described in Chapter 5), or you may use TEST.CPP (described in Chapter 6). In either case, TEST.OBJ is the object code file generated by the C or C++ compiler. The remaining files, TEST.MAP and TEST.EXE, were created by the linker. Sometimes the linker also creates a temporary file, VM.TMP.

Don't pay much attention to the file sizes. Had you used one of the other assemblers or linkers, the sizes might be slightly different but the final results would be much the same. Before we take a look at the files created by the linker, let's recap what the OBJ file does.

The Input File (OBJ)

The OBJ file is the output from the assembler or high-level language (except Turbo Pascal; when you create programs with Turbo Pascal, the OBJ stage is skipped and an EXE file is created directly). This example has two OBJ files: SUMS.OBJ, produced by assembling SUMS.ASM, and TEST.OBJ, created by compiling TEST.C or TEST.CPP. In actual practice you may have dozens of OBJ files, all to be combined into a single executable program. These OBJ files serve as the input files for your linker.

Each OBJ file contains all the machine language code necessary to perform the corresponding portion of your program; the bytes where memory address information must appear are left blank, to be filled in by the linker when it determines what the address will be. This depends on where the OBJ module fits into the total program and can be determined only at link time.

In addition to the machine language data, the OBJ file contains "housekeeping" information that lets it relate names (defined in one OBJ file) and references to these names (from other OBJ files) so that everything comes together. This information is used by the linker but does not become part of the final executable program; it can easily take more space in the OBJ file than the machine code itself. For this reason, the size of an OBJ file cannot be used as a reliable estimate of the size of the EXE file that is produced from the OBJ file.

The Executable File (EXE)

The EXE file usually is the end result of the development process: an executable file. If the source files' logic and construction are correct, and no debugging or further development is needed, the EXE file is the finished program that you can invoke from DOS.

The List File (MAP)

The MAP file is the listing the linker produced as it processed each object code file. The MAP file contains at least the beginning and ending addresses of the segments the linker processed to create TEST.EXE, and may contain even more information. LINK.EXE produces the following file, TEST.MAP:

```
Start   Stop    Length  Name            Class
00000H  01C5FH  01C60H  _TEXT           CODE
01C60H  01C61H  00002H  EMULATOR_TEXT   CODE
01C62H  01C62H  00000H  C_ETEXT         ENDCODE
01C70H  01C70H  00000H  EMULATOR_DATA   FAR_DATA
01C70H  01CB1H  00042H  NULL            BEGDATA
01CB2H  02071H  003C0H  _DATA           DATA
02072H  02073H  00002H  XIQC            DATA
02074H  02081H  0000EH  DBDATA          DATA
02082H  0208FH  0000EH  CDATA           DATA
02090H  02090H  00000H  XIFB            DATA
02090H  02090H  00000H  XIF             DATA
02090H  02090H  00000H  XIFE            DATA
02090H  02090H  00000H  XIB             DATA
02090H  02090H  00000H  XI              DATA
02090H  02090H  00000H  XIE             DATA
02090H  02090H  00000H  XPB             DATA
02090H  02091H  00002H  XP              DATA
02092H  02092H  00000H  XPE             DATA
02092H  02092H  00000H  XCB             DATA
02092H  02092H  00000H  XC              DATA
02092H  02092H  00000H  XCE             DATA
02092H  02092H  00000H  XCFB            DATA
02092H  02092H  00000H  XCF             DATA
02092H  02092H  00000H  XCFE            DATA
02092H  02092H  00000H  CONST           CONST
02092H  02099H  00008H  HDR             MSG
```

```
0209AH 0216FH 000D6H MSG                        MSG
02170H 02171H 00002H PAD                        MSG
02172H 02172H 00001H EPAD                       MSG
02174H 02174H 00000H _BSS                       BSS
02174H 02174H 00000H XOB                        BSS
02174H 02174H 00000H XO                         BSS
02174H 02174H 00000H XOE                        BSS
02180H 0237FH 00200H c_common                   BSS
02380H 02B7FH 00800H STACK                      STACK


Origin   Group
01C7:0   DGROUP


Program entry point at 0000:00DC
```

If you compiled TEST.CPP with the Borland C++ compiler and then used TLINK to link the sample files, the following map file, TEST.MAP, is created:

```
Start  Stop   Length Name               Class

00000H 027E4H 027E5H _TEXT              CODE
027F0H 027F0H 00000H _FARDATA           FAR_DATA
027F0H 027F0H 00000H _FARBSS            FAR_BSS
027F0H 027F0H 00000H _OVERLAY_          OVRINFO
027F0H 027F0H 00000H _1STUB_            STUBSEG
027F0H 02D3BH 0054CH _DATA              DATA
02D3CH 02D3CH 00000H _CVTSEG            DATA
02D3CH 02D3CH 00000H _SCNSEG            DATA
02D3CH 02D3CH 00000H _CONST             CONST
02D3CH 02D4DH 00012H _INIT_             INITDATA
02D4EH 02D4EH 00000H _INITEND_          INITDATA
02D4EH 02D59H 0000CH _EXIT_             EXITDATA
02D5AH 02D5AH 00000H _EXITEND_          EXITDATA
02D5AH 02DA1H 00048H _BSS               BSS
02DA2H 02DA2H 00000H _BSSEND            BSSEND
02DB0H 02E2FH 00080H _STACK             STACK


Program entry point at 0000:0000
```

In each example, you will notice that the compiler automatically included a number of segments beyond those you explicitly requested. As your programs grow, you will find this map file increasingly more valuable in your debugging efforts.

The Temporary File (VM.TMP)

Notice that nothing in your disk directory looks like a temporary (TMP) file. The linker creates this type of file only if necessary.

The linker normally attempts to perform all operations in memory. If this is not possible (because the program is large or because a large amount of data is being processed), the linker creates a temporary file on the DOS default drive and uses this intermediate work file to store the linked portions of the final program. With older DOS versions, this file was always named VM.TMP; with DOS 3.1 and later versions, which provide facilities for automatic creation of temporary file names, the file name will be a strange blend of numbers and letters derived from the date and time.

If LINK needs to create a virtual memory file, a message similar to the following is displayed, where drive B is the default drive:

```
VM.TMP has been created
Do not change diskette in drive B:
```

If you are using floppy disks or working in a networked environment, deleting or moving the VM.TMP file while LINK is working can have unpredictable results. When LINK is finished, it automatically deletes the temporary file. Other linkers treat the temporary file the same way, although the exact messages may differ slightly.

For most practical development purposes, you will never see LINK create this temporary file; most operations can be done in memory. I have used LINK routinely with object files of 54K and libraries of 30K to create a 41K EXE file, and all operations were still performed in memory (using an older system with 640K of RAM).

Using Linker Options

All linkers have several parameters that alter how the linkers function. These parameters are known as *options* or *switches*. You can enter them directly from the command line or when you are running the linker interactively. Table 4.1 lists alphabetically the linker options and their meanings.

***Table 4.1.** Linker options.*

Option	LINK	TLINK	Meaning
/?	X	X	Display help information.
/3		X	Enable 32-bit processing.
/A:*size*	X	X	Align segment data along boundaries of *size* bytes, where *size* is a power of 2.

Option	LINK	TLINK	Meaning
/BA	X		Operate in batch mode; do not prompt for LIBs.
/C		X	Make lowercase significant in exports and imports.
/c		X	Make lowercase significant in symbols (same as /NOI in LINK).
/CO	X		Create CodeView-compatible file.
/CP:*para*	X		Set maximum allocation space.
/d		X	Warn if libraries have duplicate symbols.
/DO	X		Use MS-DOS segment ordering.
/DS	X		Place DGROUP (a program's data group) data at high end of group.
/E	X		Pack the EXE file created by LINK.
/e		X	Ignore extended dictionary (same as /NOE in LINK).
/F	X		Convert FAR calls to NEAR where possible.
/h		X	Display TLINK help information.
/HE	X		Extended LINK help information.
/HI	X		Load program in high memory.
/i		X	Initialize all segments.
/INC	X		Prepare for incremental linking.
/INF	X		Display what link process is doing.
/l		X	Include line numbers in map file (same as /LI in LINK).
/L*path*		X	Specify library search path.
/LI	X		Include line numbers in map file (same as /l in TLINK).
/m	X	X	Include global symbol table in map file.
/n		X	Exclude default libraries (similar to /NOD in LINK).
/NOD:*name*	X		Exclude default libraries (similar to /n in TLINK). If you specify *name*, only the specified default library is excluded.

continues

Table 4.1. *continued*

Option	LINK	TLINK	Meaning
/NOE	X		Ignore extended dictionary (same as /e in TLINK).
/NOF	X		Do not translate FAR calls.
/NOG	X		Do not associate groups.
/NOI	X		Do not ignore case differences (same as /c in TLINK).
/NOL	X		Do not display copyright information.
/NON	X		Same as /DO, but excludes additional bytes at start of _TEXT segment.
/NOP	X		Do not pack code segments.
/o		X	Create overlays.
/O:*int*	X		Set overlay loader interrupt number.
/P=*size*		X	Pack code segments up to the optional segment *size* (same as /PACKC in MASM).
/PACKC:*size*	X		Pack code segments up to the optional segment *size* (same as /P in TLINK).
/PACKD:*size*	X		Pack data segments up to the optional segment *size*.
/PADC:*size*	X		Add filler bytes to the end of code segments for later incremental linking.
/PADD:*size*	X		Add filler bytes to the end of data segments for later incremental linking.
/PAU	X		Pause for disk change.
/PM:*type*	X		Used to specify the type of OS/2 or Windows application being linked.
/Q	X		Produce Quick Library QLB file.
/s		X	Generate detailed segment map.
/SE:*seg*	X		Specify maximum program segments.
/ST:*size*	X		Override stack size.
/t	X	X	Create COM/SYS/BIN image file.
/Td*?*		X	Create executable DOS file (third letter can be *c*=COM or *e*=EXE).
/Tw*?*		X	Create executable Windows file (third letter can be *e*=EXE or *d*=DLL).

Option	LINK	TLINK	Meaning
/Tx?		X	Specify output file type (third letter can be *c*=COM, *e*=EXE, or *d*=DLL).
/v		X	Include debugger data in EXE file (same as /CO in LINK).
/W	X		Issue warnings when using displacement fixup values.
/x	X		Do not produce any MAP file.
/ye		X	Expanded memory swapping.
/yx		X	Extended memory swapping.

Some of the options shown may not be available in your linker version. Note also that some of the options are in uppercase, and others in lowercase; the point to remember is that TLINK is sensitive to the case of options, whereas LINK is not.

You can include linker options at any point in the LINK command or during the interactive format. Regardless of the inclusion point, options affect all the relevant files. Usually, you include the options at the end of the command line or at the end of your response to the last LINK prompt.

You must include a delimiter before the option letter. Table 4.1 shows this delimiter as a slash, but with LINK you can also use a hyphen (-) as an equivalent delimiter.

Let's look at each of the listed options.

Display Help Information (/? or /h)

If you forget what the syntax or command-line options are for your linker, this is a quick way to get help. When you use this option with LINK, the following is displayed on the screen:

```
C:\MASM60>LINK /?


Microsoft (R) Segmented-Executable Linker  Version 5.13
Copyright (C) Microsoft Corp 1984-1991.  All rights reserved.


Usage:


LINK
LINK @<response file>
LINK <objs>,<exefile>,<mapfile>,<libs>,<deffile>
```

```
Valid options are:
  /?                          /ALIGNMENT
  /BATCH                      /CODEVIEW
  /CPARMAXALLOC               /DOSSEG
  /DSALLOCATE                 /EXEPACK
  /FARCALLTRANSLATION         /HELP
  /HIGH                       /INCREMENTAL
  /INFORMATION                /LINENUMBERS
  /MAP                        /NODEFAULTLIBRARYSEARCH
  /NOEXTDICTIONARY            /NOFARCALLTRANSLATION
  /NOGROUPASSOCIATION         /NOIGNORECASE
  /NOLOGO                     /NONULLSDOSSEG
  /NOPACKCODE                 /OVERLAYINTERRUPT
  /PACKCODE                   /PACKDATA
  /PADCODE                    /PADDATA
  /PAUSE                      /PMTYPE
  /QUICKLIBRARY               /SEGMENTS
  /STACK                      /TINY
  /WARNFIXUP
```

Notice that the long forms of the option names are listed. You need to enter only enough characters to differentiate the option you want from the others.

When you use this option with TLINK, the following screen is displayed:

```
C:\TASM30>TLINK /?

Turbo Link  Version 5.0 Copyright (c) 1991 Borland International
Syntax: TLINK objfiles, exefile, mapfile, libfiles, deffile
@xxxx indicates use response file xxxx
/m  Map file with publics        /x  No map file at all
/i  Initialize all segments      /l  Include source line numbers
/L  Specify library search paths /s  Detailed map of segments
/n  No default libraries         /d  Warn if duplicate symbols in libraries
/c  Case significant in symbols  /3  Enable 32-bit processing
/o  Overlay switch               /v  Full symbolic debug information
/P[=NNNNN]  Pack code segments   /A=NNNN  Set NewExe segment alignment
/ye Expanded memory swapping     /yx Extended memory swapping
/e  Ignore Extended Dictionary
/t  Create COM file (same as /Tdc)
/C  Case sensitive exports and imports
/Txx  Specify output file type
```

```
/Tdx  DOS image (default)
/Twx  Windows image
 (third letter can be c=COM, e=EXE, d=DLL)
```

Enable 32-Bit Processing (/3)

This option enables TLINK to handle properly 32-bit code for the 80386 processor. You should use this option only when you have generated code that explicitly uses 32-bit addressing, as it slows down the work TLINK does.

Align Segment Data (/A:*size*)

This option is used primarily to reduce the size of the physical gaps between segments in a disk file. Both LINK and TLINK use a default segment boundary of 512 bytes. If a segment takes less space than 512 bytes or some multiple of 512 bytes, the linker pads out to the next 512-byte boundary.

With this option you can specify a smaller segment boundary, provided that the boundary size (in bytes) is a power of two (2, 4, 8, 16, 32, etc.). If your program has many segments, this option may make your linked file much smaller. It does not affect the memory your program occupies while executing.

Operate Linker in Batch Mode (/BA)

This option causes LINK to not prompt for a library or path name if a required library or object file cannot be located, and may result in unresolved externals in your files. It is included to facilitate use of the linker with batch files and make programs.

Do Not Ignore Case Differences in Exports and Imports (/C)

The /C option causes TLINK to differentiate between upper- and lowercase letters in the exports and imports section of the module. Using /C or /C+ turns on case sensitivity, whereas /C- turns off case sensitivity (the default).

Do Not Ignore Case Differences
(/c or /NOI)

The /c option causes TLINK to differentiate between upper- and lowercase letters. The /NOI option does the same thing with LINK.

Create Debugger-compatible File
(/CO or /V)

This special option, available to LINK as /CO and to TLINK as /V, instructs the linker to create an EXE file that is compatible with high-level debuggers such as CodeView and Turbo Debugger. For more information on using these products, see Chapter 7, "Debugging Assembly Language Subroutines."

Set Allocation Space (/CP:*para*)

With this option, you can specify to LINK how much memory (in paragraphs) the program is to use. MS-DOS requires that programs request a block of memory for program use so that there are no memory conflicts. Usually, the linker requests all memory, 65,535 paragraphs. Because this much memory is never available, MS-DOS returns the largest contiguous block of memory for program use.

Using this option lets you state explicitly how much memory should be requested. *para* is the number of paragraphs (16-byte memory blocks) your program's code and data need. Because the amount of memory you designate probably will be smaller than the amount the linker normally allocates, memory will be freed for other purposes.

If *para* is smaller than the amount of memory the program needs, the linker ignores the *para* parameter and requests the maximum memory area.

Warn about Duplicate LIB Symbols (/d)

This option forces TLINK to list all duplicate symbols encountered in the library files it searches. /d is used when you have identical symbols in different LIB files for different code and want to know which file TLINK encounters first, because the code in that file will be the code TLINK uses.

Use MS-DOS Segment Ordering (/DO)

This option instructs LINK to process files using the MS-DOS segment ordering rules. These rules are as follows:

1. Segments with a class name of CODE are placed at the start of the linked file.

2. All segments outside the DGROUP are placed next.

3. DGROUP segments are in the following order:

   Any segment with the class name BEGDATA
   Any segment not of class BEGDATA, BSS, or STACK
   BSS segments
   STACK segments

Normally, the linker copies segments to the file in the order they occur in the object files.

Place DGROUP at High End (/DS)

The linker normally assigns data in DGROUP (a program's data group) to a low address, starting at an offset of 0. This option causes the linker to start data assignments so that the last byte in DGROUP is at an offset of FFFFh, or the top of memory. Usually, this option is used with the /HI option.

Pack EXE File (/E)

The /E option causes LINK to create an EXE file that is optimized for size. Use of this option may result in a more compact EXE file. How much, if any, space this option will save through packing the executable file depends on how many repeated bytes are used in the file. If your program requires much relocation upon loading, this option causes the relocation table to be optimized for size. If the resulting EXE file is smaller, it logically will load faster than a file linked without this option.

If you plan to convert your EXE file to a COM file, do not use this option. If you pack your EXE file, you cannot convert it to a COM file.

Ignore Extended Dictionary (/e or /NOE)

All newer versions of the library-manager utilities (discussed in Chapter 9, "Developing Libraries") can create *extended dictionaries* that the linker normally will use to complete the linking process more rapidly. This option, known to TLINK as /e and to LINK as /NOE, prevents the linker from using any extended dictionary that may be available. Ordinarily, this would be done only if you need every byte of memory you can get to link your program.

Translate FAR Calls where Possible (/F)

This option causes CALL instructions to FAR procedures to be converted into a PUSH CS followed by a NEAR call instruction, which takes fewer bytes in the program and executes more rapidly.

List Linker Options (/HE)

The /HE option causes LINK to load the QuickHelp utility program and display extended help information in an interactive format.

To view the available options for TLINK, simply omit all command-line parameters, as follows:

```
TLINK
```

Load Program in High Memory (/HI)

Normally, the linker assumes that a program is to be loaded at the lowest free memory address. The /HI option instructs LINK to load the linked program as high in memory as possible. This option typically is used with the /DS option.

Initialize All Segments (/i)

This option causes TLINK to output all segments named in the OBJ files, even if some of them do not contain any bytes. Without this option, TLINK will not output empty segments (inserted by some high-level languages to establish segment sequence). LINK, which always outputs all segments, does not need this option.

Prepare for Incremental Linking (/INC)

If you plan to do incremental linking to speed the development process, use this option. Incremental linking is done with both LINK and a program called ILINK. This option causes the linker to produce a SYM and an ILK file, each of which contains information needed by ILINK.

Display Progress of Linking Process (/INF)

This option causes LINK to display a running account of what it is doing. The display is used primarily to debug problems that show up as an inability to link your OBJ files successfully.

Include Line Numbers in List File (/l or /LI)

If you specified a listing file, you can use the /1 (TASM) or /LI (MASM) option to include a list of all source-code-line memory addresses in the list file. Such a list is helpful when you are debugging.

This option is useful only if the OBJ file includes a line number, which depends on how the OBJ file was created. MASM does not include line numbers in the OBJ file, but many high-level languages do. If the OBJ file does not include line-number information, no extra information is generated in the MAP file.

Specify Library Search Path (/L*path*)

This option is used to tell TLINK where (in addition to the current directory) library files can be found. You can specify multiple paths if you separate them with semicolons.

Include Global Symbol Table in List File (/m)

When you include the /M option, the linker creates a public symbol listing. This option forces a listing file to be created. The listing file has the name of the first OBJ file and the extension MAP, unless you provide a different name on the command line or at the interactive prompt.

Note that if you are using LINK, this option does not have to be lowercase.

Do Not Use Default Libraries (/n or /NOD:*name*)

Some high-level languages include in the OBJ file the names of default libraries for the linker to search when linking the file. This option, known to TLINK as /n and to LINK as /NOD, overrides such specifications so that the linker ignores any libraries the language specified in the OBJ files.

MASM gives you the option of including the name of a specific library to be ignored. All default libraries except the one named will be used.

Do Not Translate FAR Calls (/NOF)

This option prevents LINK from converting FAR calls into NEAR calls. Unless this option is used, LINK's default condition is to insert a PUSH CS machine instruction, then emit a NEAR call using only the CS offset. This saves both time and space but confuses debugging efforts.

Do Not Associate Groups (/NOG)

The /NOG option instructs LINK to ignore GROUP associations when it assigns memory addresses for data and program code. The option is intended specifically for use with object code generated by old versions of the Microsoft FORTRAN and Pascal compilers.

Suppress Copyright Message (/NOL)

This option causes LINK to suppress the copyright information normally displayed. If included, this option must be the first one on the command line.

Use MS-DOS Segment Ordering without Nulls (/NON)

This option instructs LINK to process files in the same manner as the /DO option, but no null characters are placed at the beginning of the _TEXT segment, if it is defined.

Do Not Pack Code Segments (/NOP)

This option prevents LINK from packing contiguous code segments that have different names into a single segment for loading. Because this is the default condition, /NOP usually is not needed. If LINK is switched by an environment variable to the /PAC condition, however, /NOP at the command line restores nonpacking mode.

Create Overlays (/o)

The /o option is used to turn on overlay handling, and /o- is used to turn it off. All files between this option and the next comma or the /o- option are treated as overlays.

If you specify /o#*int*, where *int* is an interrupt number, TLINK will use *int* as the overlay-loader interrupt number (similar to LINK's /O option).

Set Overlay-Loader Interrupt Number (/O:*int*)

The /O:*int* option enables you to specify the interrupt number used by an overlay loader. Use this option with object code generated by compilers that support overlays. *int* is the number (between 0 and 255) of the MS-DOS interrupt to use for the overlay loader. Normally, interrupt 63 is used, but it may already be reserved for some other use on your system.

Pack Contiguous Code Segments (/P=*size* or /PACKC:*size*)

This option instructs the linker to pack adjacent code segments bearing different names into a single segment and adjust offset addresses accordingly. The resulting code segment cannot be larger than *size*; if it is, a new code segment is begun.

Used with the /F option, this option can significantly reduce code size and increase operating speed for programs that have multiple code segments.

Pack Contiguous Code Segments (/PACKD:*size*)

This option instructs LINK to pack adjacent data segments bearing different names into a single segment and adjust offset addresses accordingly. The resulting data segment cannot be larger than *size*; if it is, a new data segment is begun.

This option is valid for Windows and OS/2 programs only.

Pad Code Segments (/PADC:*size*)

In preparation for later incremental linking, this option causes LINK to add a specific number of filler bytes to the end of each code segment. The default is 0 added bytes, but you can specify a particular *size*.

This option must be used with the /INC option.

Pad Data Segments (/PADD:*size*)

In preparation for later incremental linking, this option causes LINK to add a specific number of filler bytes to the end of each data segment. The default is 16 added bytes, but you can specify a particular *size*.

This option must be used with the /INC option.

Pause for Disk Change (/PAU)

Using this option causes LINK to display a message and wait for you to switch disks before the linker writes the EXE file. This option is particularly useful if you have a limited number of disk drives or disk space. When the linker has written the EXE file completely, the linker prompts you to return the original disk.

Specify Application Type (/PM:*type*)

This is the option to use when linking programs for Windows or OS/2. It allows you to specify the type of application program being linked, where *type* is a specific value from table 4.2.

Table 4.2. *Windows and OS/2 application program types.*

Value	Meaning
PM	Presentation Manager or Windows application
VIO	Character-mode PM or Windows application, designed to be run in a text window
NOVIO	Full-screen character-mode application (default value)

Produce QuickLibrary QLB File (/Q)

This option instructs LINK to generate as its output a QLB file rather than a normal executable EXE file. The QLB file is suitable for use with the Microsoft Quick languages.

Generate Detailed Segment Map (/s)

This option directs TLINK to generate a detailed segment map as part of the listing file.

Specify Maximum Segments (/SE:*seg*)

This option directs LINK to process no more than a specific number of segments. Typically, this option is used if the program being linked has many segments. By default, LINK handles only up to 128 segments. *seg* can be any number between 1 and 1024.

Override Stack Size (/ST:*size*)

Normally, LINK determines the stack size in the finished program based on any stack declarations in the OBJ file. The /ST:*size* option overrides this value. To use this option you must substitute for *size* a number between 1 and 65,535, representing the desired stack size in bytes.

Produce Binary Image File (/t)

Directs the linker to produce a binary image file (COM or SYS style) rather than an EXE file. This is the same as using the /Tdc option.

Specify Executable File Type (/Td? or /Tw?)

These options allow you to specify how you want TLINK to create the target executable file. The following are valid choices:

Option	Meaning
/Td	Create a DOS EXE file (the default)
/Tdc	Create a DOS COM file
/Tde	Create a DOS EXE file (the default)
/Tw	Create a Windows EXE file
/Twd	Create a Windows DLL file
/Twe	Create a Windows EXE file

Issue Fixup Warnings (/W)

Normally, when LINK is creating a segmented executable file, it does not issue any message when it uses a displacement from the beginning of a group to determine fixup values. Fixup values are stored in the EXE file and used by the DOS loader when the file is later loaded preparatory to execution. This option directs LINK to issue a warning every time such a fixup occurs.

Do Not Generate Any Listing File (/x)

This option, available only to TLINK, directs the linker not to generate a listing file. Unlike the other linkers, TLINK generates a MAP file by default and must be directed not to do so if you do not want one.

Use Memory Swapping (/ye and /yx)

By default, TLINK swaps data to expanded memory as necessary to improve linker performance. If your system does not have expanded memory, you may want to use the /yx or /yx+ option to enable swapping to extended memory, or use /ye- to turn off swapping to expanded memory. You can also use /ye or /ye+ to enable swapping to expanded memory, although this would be redundant because it is the default condition.

Summary

The linking step is vital to completion of any program. Using a linker is easy because during ordinary use, you don't need to worry about using options or other complicating factors.

In this chapter, you have compared the characteristics of the two major linkers. In the next few chapters you learn how to use each linker with its associated assembler to create a finished program.

Using Microsoft's Assembly Language Products

Y ou have already learned many of the differences between the two major assemblers and linkers. In this chapter, you learn more about MASM and LINK, the assembler and linker from Microsoft; Chapter 6 focuses on Borland's assembly language products. This chapter and Chapter 6 are similar in construction and content; they differ only in the specific details that apply to the environments provided by Microsoft and Borland.

MASM, a contraction for Macro Assembler, has been around a long time. The current version, MASM 6.0, has been out since the second quarter of 1991. It offers more capabilities and features than previous versions, as well as many changes that affect how you program and use the assembler itself.

LINK has been around as long as MASM. In the early days of MS-DOS and PC DOS, LINK.EXE was distributed free with every copy of DOS (it was on the utilties disk). Although LINK no longer comes with DOS, it is shipped with every Microsoft language product. The version shipped with MASM 6.0 is LINK 5.13.

A Sample Program

To proceed through this chapter, you need a sample subroutine to assemble. This subroutine will be neither large nor complex, nor will it exemplify the best reasons for using assembly language. Although writing this routine in C would be easier than writing it in assembly language, I will use it to demonstrate how to assemble (and later link and debug) a subroutine.

Let's assume that you need to determine the total number of blocks in a pyramid where each ascending row contains one less block than the row beneath it, and the top row is only one block (see fig. 5.1).

Fig. 5.1. *A sample pyramid.*

The bottom row contains 15 blocks, the next row contains 14, and so on, with only one block in the top row. Your job is to calculate the total number of blocks needed, given only the number of blocks in the bottom row. You'll use the sample program to do the job.

The program (SUMS.ASM) is designed to be called from C. When passed a signed 16-bit integer, the program calculates and returns the result as a signed integer. The assembly language subroutine, written for MASM 6.0, is as follows:

```
Page 60,132
Comment ¦
**********************************************************************


File:     SUMS.ASM
Author:   Allen L. Wyatt
Date:     8/3/91

Purpose:  Given an integer number X, find the sum of
          X + (X-1) + (X-2) + (X-3) + (X-4) ... + 2 + 1
          Designed to be called from Microsoft C.


Format:   SUMS(X)


**********************************************************************¦

          PUBLIC    sums

          .MODEL    small, C
          .CODE

sums      PROC C Value:SWORD
          MOV  AX,0              ;Initialize to zero
          MOV  CX,Value          ;Get actual value
          JCXZ S3                ;Num=0, no need to do
          CLC                    ;Initialize for start
S1:       ADC  AX,CX             ;Add row value
          JC   S2                ;Quit if AX overflowed
          LOOP S1                ;Repeat process
          JMP  S3                ;Successful completion
S2:       MOV  AX,0              ;Force a zero
S3:       RET                    ;Return to C
sums      ENDP

          END
```

If the entered number results in a sum greater than 65,535 (the largest unsigned integer number that can be held in 16 bits), the subroutine sets the result to 0.

Go ahead and enter this program. When you are done, save it as SUMS.ASM. You are now ready to assemble the program.

Using MASM 6.0

Before beginning the assembly process, make sure that you have installed MASM 6.0 according to the instructions that came with the software. If you install the full language system, you can assemble in one of three ways. The first way is to use the Programmer's Workbench shell. This is perhaps the easiest way, especially if you already are familiar with other Microsoft products, such as QuickC and QuickAssembler.

The other two ways to assemble the program are closely related. In earlier versions of MASM, the program that did the assembly was called MASM.EXE; in the latest version, it is called ML.EXE. Actually, ML.EXE does more than just assemble a program. After assembly is completed, ML.EXE also calls the linker (LINK.EXE), and totally bypasses creating an OBJ file.

Although MASM.EXE is still available with version 6.0, all it does is translate the older MASM command-line switches to the ones appropriate for ML.EXE. Then control is passed to ML.EXE for assembly. Whether you use ML.EXE or MASM.EXE, you do the assembly from the DOS command line.

Many things determine whether you use the Programmer's Workbench interface or work strictly from the DOS command line. Perhaps the biggest deciding factor is habit. If you have been using MASM for a while, or are used to working with other languages from the command line, you probably will want to do the same with MASM 6.0. After all, you probably are familiar with your favorite editor, and have a series of batch files prepared to help in the development process.

If you are new to assembly language, however, or have used the Programmer's Workbench shell with other Microsoft languages, you probably will feel comfortable doing the same here.

This chapter provides instructions for assembling a file using both the Programmer's Workbench and command-line methods. You choose the one you are most comfortable with.

Using MASM 6.0 in Programmer's Workbench

If you have MASM 6.0 fully installed, make sure that SUMS.ASM (the subroutine file) is in your current disk directory. At the DOS prompt, type

PWB

to load and enter the Programmer's Workbench. A few messages will flash quickly on the screen, indicating that PWB is opening files it needs. When the Programmer's Workbench is fully loaded, your screen will look similar to figure 5.2.

Fig. 5.2. Programmer's Workbench screen.

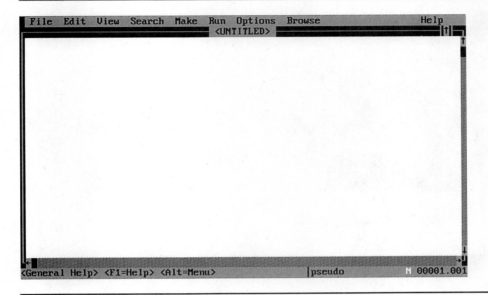

Very possibly, if you have used the Programmer's Workbench before, the file you previously were working on may be loaded already (instead of a blank workspace). If this is the case, close the file so that you are beginning fresh.

Notice the series of pull-down menus across the top of the screen. These menus are used to issue commands within the Programmer's Workbench. You may want to take a moment to familiarize yourself with each of the menus. If you are using the keyboard, you can access a menu or command by pressing the Alt key and then pressing the highlighted letter. For instance, to access the File menu, you would press Alt-F. If you are using a mouse, simply position the mouse cursor on the menu or command name and click on the left mouse button.

Before you can assemble a file, you must load it into the workspace. To do this, pull down the File menu. When you do, your screen will look like figure 5.3.

Select the Open command. From the displayed list of files in the current directory, select SUMS.ASM to load it into the workspace. Once the file is loaded, your screen should look like figure 5.4.

Fig. 5.3. *The File pull-down menu.*

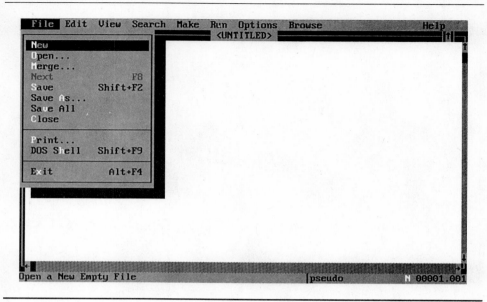

Fig. 5.4. *Programmer's Workbench with SUMS.ASM loaded in the workspace.*

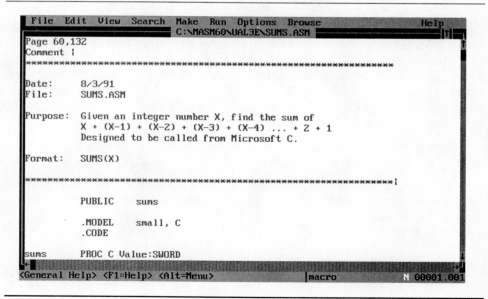

Now you are ready to assemble the file. Select the Make menu and choose the first option, Compile File. Because the Programmer's Workbench is meant to work across all of Microsoft's languages, the term *compile*, although not really applicable to assembly language programming, is the proper choice to DOS a program.

As it completes your task, the Programmer's Workbench keeps you informed of what it is doing. If any errors were encountered during assembly of the file, you are notified and given a chance to correct them; correct any errors and reassemble the file.

When you finish assembling the program, you can exit the Programmer's Workbench (from the File menu). If you look at your subdirectory and see the file SUMS.OBJ, you have assembled a file successfully.

Using MASM 6.0 from the Command Line

The way to use MASM from the command line is through use of the ML.EXE program. Make sure that SUMS.ASM (the subroutine file) is in your current disk directory and, at the DOS prompt, type

```
ML
```

to invoke ML.EXE. The following appears on-screen:

```
Microsoft (R) Macro Assembler Version 6.00
Copyright (C) Microsoft Corp 1981-1991.  All rights reserved.

usage: ML [ options ] filelist [ /link linkoptions]
Run "ML /help" or "ML -?" for more info
```

This terse help information lets you know what you need to enter from the command line to make ML.EXE work properly. If you are familiar with older versions of MASM, notice that you no longer can work interactively with the assembler. You must enter a complete command line that ML can work with right away.

Examine the help line again. Because everything enclosed in brackets is optional, at a minimum you need to enter a list of files to process. Remember that if you do this, ML will assemble the file first and then try to link it. Since SUMS.ASM is only a subroutine, meant to be called from a C program, there is no point to linking it now. Thus, in addition to the name of the file to be assembled, you must enter also a few command-line options that instruct ML to assemble the file only, and to do it properly so that it will work later with a program written in C.

To do this, enter the following command line at the DOS prompt:

```
ML /c /Cx /FoSUMS.OBJ /Fl SUMS.ASM
```

You should enter the command line exactly as it is shown here. Although upper- and lowercase don't matter in some instances, case *does* matter for command-line options (they must be entered exactly as shown).

The command options you have just entered are covered in detail in the next section. Basically, this is what they mean:

/c	Compile only, do not link
/Cx	Maintain case of labels in source file
/FoSUMS.OBJ	Save object file in SUMS.OBJ
/Fl	Create a listing file

When you enter the command line and press Enter, ML starts its work. You see a single line stating that the file is being assembled. If there are no errors, you are returned shortly to the DOS prompt. If the assembly was successful, you see no other messages, and the file SUMS.OBJ is in your subdirectory.

If there are errors, you see a message indicating the type of error and where it is located. If you receive any error messages, you must correct the errors before continuing. Check your source file (SUMS.ASM) against the listing file (SUMS.LST), correct any errors, and try the assembly process again. When you have corrected all the errors, you can proceed with this chapter.

Assembler Options

You can use a number of parameters (referred to as *options* or *switches* in the documentation) with ML to alter the way the program functions. You enter these options directly from the command line.

Remember the following syntax line

```
usage: ML [ options ] filelist [ /link linkoptions]
```

that appeared when you entered only the ML command at the DOS prompt?

With previous versions of MASM, you could enter command line options at any point on the command line. Now, however, because the ML program is used also to control the linker, you must place all your assembler command options before the files they will affect. If you plan to assemble several source files with the same command line, and you have different options you want used with each file, you can enter them in the following manner:

```
ML [options] filelist [options] filelist [options] filelist
```

The individual options apply only to the files that follow them.

The 46 command-line options possible for ML are listed in table 5.1, and detailed in the following sections.

Table 5.1. *ML command-line options.*

Option	Meaning
/?	Display help information.
/AT	Assemble as a COM file.
/Bl*filename*	Specify alternate *filename* as linker.
/c	Do not link; assemble only.
/Cp	Do not ignore case differences of user identifiers.
/Cu	Convert all user identifiers to uppercase.
/Cx	Do not ignore case differences in PUBLIC and EXTERN symbols.
/D*name=text*	Define an identifier, assigning *text* to *name*.
/EP	Output first-pass listing to STDOUT.
/F *size*	Override stack size.
/Fb*filename*	Create bound executable file.
/Fe*filename*	Use *filename* for the executable file.
/Fl*filename*	Create a source listing file using *filename*.LST.
/Fm*filename*	Create a linker map listing file using *filename*.MAP.
/Fo*filename*	Create an object file using *filename*.OBJ.
/FPi	Generate math emulator fixups.
/Fr*filename*	Create a source browser file using *filename*.SBR.
/FR*filename*	Create an extended source browser file using *filename*.SBR.
/Gc	Use FORTRAN/Pascal/BASIC calling and naming conventions.
/Gd	Use C calling and naming conventions.
/H*max*	Limit number of significant characters in EXTERN symbols.
/help	Extended ML help information.
/I*pathname*	Override default include-file path.
/link	Pass options to the linker.
/nologo	Do not display copyright message.
/Sa	Generate complete listings.
/Sf	Generate optional first-pass listings.
/Sg	Generate listing of assembler-generated code.

continues

Table 5.1. *continued*

Option	Meaning
/Sl*width*	Set line width for listings.
/Sn	Exclude symbol table from listings.
/Sp*lines*	Set page depth for listings.
/Ss*text*	Set listing subtitle to *text*.
/St*text*	Set listing title to *text*.
/Sx	Include false conditionals in listings.
/Ta*filename*	Assemble file without ASM extension.
/VM	Enable virtual memory.
/w	Set warning level 0.
/W*level*	Set warning level to *level* (0, 1, 2, or 3).
/WX	Treat warnings as errors.
/X	Ignore the INCLUDE environment variable.
/Zd	Include line numbers in object file.
/Zf	Make all symbols PUBLIC.
/Zi	Create CodeView-compatible file.
/Zm	Force compatibility with MASM 5.1.
/Zp*boundary*	Pack structures to byte *boundary* (1, 2, or 4).
/Zs	Check syntax only.

You must include a delimiter before the first letter of each option. This delimiter can be either a slash (/), as shown in table 5.1, or a dash (-). MASM does not differentiate between the two symbols.

As you can see from table 5.1, many command-line options have variables you can specify (*width*, *lines*, and *filename*, for example). One way that specifying options for ML differs from specifying them for other programs, such as LINK, is that with ML there are no colons between the option and the variable for the option. Instead, the variable immediately follows the option. The only exception to this is the /F option, in which a space between the option and the numeric variable is mandatory.

Let's look at each ML option in greater detail.

Display Help Information (/?)

If, while you are using ML, you forget what the syntax or command-line options are, this is the quickest way to get help. When you use this option, the following is displayed on-screen:

```
C:\MASM60>ML /?

        ML [ /options ] filelist [ /link linkoptions ]
```

/AT Enable tiny model (.COM file)	/nologo Suppress copyright message
/Bl<linker> Use alternate linker	/Sa Maximize source listing
/c Assemble without linking	/Sf Generate first pass listing
/Cp Preserve case of user identifiers	/Sl<width> Set line width
/Cu Map all identifiers to upper case	/Sn Suppress symbol-table listing
/Cx Preserve case in publics, externs	/Sp<length> Set page length
/D<name>[=text] Define text macro	/Ss<string> Set subtitle
/EP Output preprocessed listing to stdout	/St<string> Set title
/F <hex> Set stack size (bytes)	/Sx List false conditionals
/Fb[file] Generate bound executable	/Ta<file> Assemble non-.ASM file
/Fe<file> Name executable	/VM Enable virtual memory
/Fl[file] Generate listing	/w Same as /W0 /WX
/Fm[file] Generate map	/WX Treat warnings as errors
/Fo<file> Name object file	/W<number> Set warning level
/FPi Generate 80x87 emulator encoding	/X Ignore INCLUDE environment path
/Fr[file] Generate limited browser info	/Zd Add line number debug info
/FR[file] Generate full browser info	/Zf Make all symbols public
/G<c¦d> Generate Pascal or C calls	/Zi Add symbolic debug info
/H<number> Set max external name length	/Zm Enable MASM 5.10 compatibility
/I<name> Add include path	/Zp[n] Set structure alignment
/link <linker options and libraries>	/Zs Perform syntax check only

On this help screen, items such as <file> are mandatory, whereas those like [file] are optional.

Assemble as a COM File (/AT)

This option causes assembler to make sure that you have not programmed inconsistently with a program designed to be a COM file. For instance, the entire program (code and data) must reside in a single segment. The effect of this option is the same as that of using the .MODEL TINY directive in your program.

If you do not use the /c option, /AT causes the linker to be invoked with the /T option.

Specify Alternate Linker (/Bl*filename*)

ML automatically invokes the linker after the assembly process is complete. If you do not want to use the LINK program as your linker, this option allows you to specify a different program.

Assemble Only (/c)

If you do not want to link your file, use this option, which causes ML to assemble only. This option does not result in the creation of an OBJ file on disk, however; you must use the /Fo option for that.

Do Not Ignore Case Differences of User Identifiers (/Cp)

Normally, ML treats all identifiers (names of variables and procedures) the same, converting them all to uppercase. Some high-level languages are not insensitive to case; they treat an *A* differently than an *a*. If this is the case (no pun intended), you can use this option to direct ML to maintain the original case of your identifiers.

Convert All User Identifiers to Uppercase (/Cu)

This is the default setting for ML. It is included for those instances in which you are assembling several files and the first may require the use of /Cp, whereas the second can be set back to the default case identification.

Do Not Ignore Case Differences in Public and Extern Symbols (/Cx)

This modified version of the /Cp option results in special treatment only for identifiers that will be seen by other programs. An identifier private to a particular procedure is still converted to uppercase.

This option should cause your routines to work with most high-level languages.

Define an Identifier (/D*name*=*text*)

If you use conditional assembly directives in your program, this option really can come in handy. It allows you to define an identifier at the time you use ML. Thus, you can assign a specific value to a label that controls how the program will be assembled.

For example, assume that some special code included in your program has meaning only when the program is being debugged. If these instructions are conditional, being included only when the identifier debug is set to yes, including the option /Ddebug=yes will cause the code to be included.

Output First-Pass Listing to STDOUT (/Ep)

This option can be a bit confusing. As you may recall, MASM 6.0 processes files differently than previous versions of the assembler. Because it is now a single-pass compiler, references to "first pass" or "second pass" lose their meaning. This option does nothing more than provide an elemental listing of the assembled file before final resolution of all source-file elements. It does not give as detailed a listing as the /Fl option used with the /S options.

If you choose this option, a listing that has macros and most identifiers expanded, and the original macro definitions removed, is sent to STDOUT (usually the screen). This listing can be helpful in determining how to fix some pesky errors that can crop up during the assembly process.

This option is not the same as other listing options such as /Fl. If you want to save the output of this listing, you must use redirection to capture output to a disk file or send it to the printer.

Override Stack Size (/F *size*)

This option does nothing in ML itself. It causes the linker to be invoked with the /ST option set to the stack size (in bytes) you specify. The space between the option and the size is mandatory.

Normally, LINK determines the stack size in the finished program based on any stack declarations in the OBJ file. The /ST:*size* option overrides this value.

Create Bound Executable File (/Fb*filename*)

If you are using ML to create OS/2 programs, this option causes ML to create and link an OS/2-compatible program and then invoke the BIND utility. This utility modifies the executable file so that it will work under OS/2 as well as DOS.

Specify Executable File (/Fe*filename*)

The file name specified with this option is passed to the linker as the name of the final EXE or COM file. ML does nothing except pass it on.

Create a Source Listing File (/Fl*filename*)

This option enables listing capabilities in ML. It causes a listing file to be created, appending the .LST extension to the name you supply.

Several other options affect the way ML creates the listing enabled by this option. For more information on this topic, see the options /Sa, /Sf, /Sg, /Sl, /Sn, /Sp, /Ss, /St, and /Sx.

Create a Map Listing File (/Fm*filename*)

This option is passed on to the linker so that the linker can create a listing file (referred to as a *MAP* file) while linking. For more information about map files, see Chapter 4, "Choosing and Using Your Linker."

Create an Object File (/Fo*filename*)

Unless you specify this option, ML does not save the work done in the assembly process. If you plan to use ML and to go directly to an EXE or COM file, you probably won't want to use this option. But if you are creating subroutines to link later, or if you are building a library, you will use this option quite a bit.

You must provide a file extension when you use this option. The .OBJ extension is not used automatically.

Generate Math-Emulator Fixups (/Fpi)

Use this option to direct ML to emulate the floating-point capabilities of the different NPX chips. The assembler does not contain the emulation routines; they are included when the object code is linked and a math-emulation library is used. Your high-level language (Microsoft C, for example) includes a library of this type.

When you use the /E option, the code that results can be executed on any compatible computer, regardless of whether you have an NPX.

Create a Source Browser File (/Fr*filename*)

This option directs ML to create a file with the extension .SBR, which is used in the Programmer's Workbench to browse through the source file and view detailed development information (such as cross references for variables).

Create an Extended Source Browser File (/FR*filename*)

This option creates an extended version of the .SBR file for use with Programmer's Workbench. See the information provided for the /Fr option.

Use FORTRAN/Pascal/BASIC Calling and Naming Conventions (/Gc)

This option sets the parameter-passing conventions used by ML when assembling a program. You can use this option to specify not only how parameters are passed to your routine but also how they are returned to the calling high-level language program.

This option is equivalent to the following directives:

```
OPTION LANGUAGE:PASCAL
OPTION LANGUAGE:BASIC
OPTION LANGUAGE:FORTRAN
```

Use C Calling and Naming Conventions (/Gd)

This option sets the parameter-passing conventions used by ML when assembling a program. You can use this option to specify not only how parameters are passed to your routine but also how they are returned to the calling high-level language program.

This option is equivalent to the OPTION LANGUAGE:C directive.

Limit Significant External Symbol Characters (/H*max*)

Some high-level languages limit the number of significant characters in procedure names or variables. This option tells ML to set a limit on how many characters are significant. Valid lengths are anywhere from 1 to 255 characters.

With this option set, ML disregards anything longer than the maximum you set. Therefore, ML checks to see that there are no duplicate symbols (the first *max* characters are the same, where *max* is the maximum significant length).

Extended ML Help Information (/help)

This option causes ML to load the QuickHelp utility program and display extended help information in an interactive format.

Override Default Include-File Path (/I*pathname*)

This option instructs ML where to search for include files in the source file. These are files pulled in during assembly through use of the INCLUDE directive. Typically, these include files are stored in a single directory that is specified with an environment variable. For instance, if your include files are stored in the subdirectory \MASM60\INCS, you can use the DOS command

    SET INCLUDE=\MASM60\INCS

to instruct ML where to look for the files. The /I option overrides this environment variable and tells ML where to look first for include files.

If your include files are spread among several directories, you can use multiple /I options to specify different directories. Each directory is searched in turn until the necessary include file is located. If, after each directory has been searched, the required include file is not found, an error is generated.

See also the /X option.

Pass Options to the Linker (/link)

This should be the very last ML option on the command line. ML assumes that anything to the right of this option should be passed directly to the linker. You use this option to pass linker commands at the time you start ML.

Clearly, this option has no meaning if used with such options as /c or /Zs.

Do Not Display Copyright Message (/nologo)

Normally, a copyright message displays when ML first starts. Including this option on the command line suppresses the copyright message. Unlike the corresponding option in LINK, this option does not have to be the first on the command line.

Generate Complete Listings (/Sa)

This option, which instructs ML to include (in the listing file) everything it can, is equivalent to using /Fl with all the other enabling options such as /Sg and /Sx.

This option has no effect on output produced with the /EP option; additionally, you must use /Fl for this option to have any effect.

Generate Optional First-Pass Listings (/Sf)

This option causes the first-pass listing information to be included at the beginning of the listing file. (The same information is displayed when the /EP option is used).

This option has no effect if the /Fl option is not used.

Generate Listing of Assembler-Generated Code (/Sg)

Normally, ML does not include assembler-generated code in a listing file. This assembler-generated code includes code generated with the `.IF`, `.WHILE`, `.STARTUP`, and `INVOKE` directives. This option causes the code to be included in the listing.

Set Line Width for Listings (/Sl*width*)

Using this option is the same as using the `PAGE` directive in your source files. Whereas the `PAGE` directive allows you to specify both the length and width of your listings, this option allows you to set a line width only. (See also the section about the `/Sp` option.)

This option has no effect on output produced with the `/EP` option, and has no effect if the `/Fl` option is not used.

Exclude Symbol Table from Listings (/Sn)

When creating a listing file, ML normally includes a complete symbol table. This option causes the symbol table to be excluded.

This option has no effect if the `/Fl` option is not used.

Set Page Depth for Listings (/Sp*lines*)

Using this option is the same as using the `PAGE` directive in your source files. Whereas the `PAGE` directive allows you to specify both the length and width of listings, this option allows you to set a page length only. See also the section about the `/Sl` option.

This option has no effect on output produced with the `/EP` option, and has no effect if the `/Fl` option is not used.

Set Listing Subtitle (/Ss*text*)

Using this option is the same as using the `SUBTITLE` directive in your source file. It allows you to specify a string that will be included as the subtitle on listings (file or printed). If the string contains spaces, you must enclose the text string in quotation marks. See also the section about the /St option.

This option has no effect on output produced with the /EP option, and has no effect if the /Fl option is not used.

Set Listing Title (/St*text*)

This option has the same effect as using the TITLE directive in your source file. You specify a string, and that string will appear at the head of every page in a listing (file or printed). If the string contains spaces, you must enclose it in quotation marks. See also the section on the /Ss option.

This option has no effect on output produced with the /EP option, and has no effect if the /Fl option is not used.

Include False Conditionals in Listings (/Sx)

This option has the same effect as the .LISTIF directive. It causes source-file lines that were not conditionally assembled to be included in the listing file.

Assemble File without ASM Extension (/Ta*filename*)

Normally, ML expects source files to have the ASM extension. If you provide a different extension, ML tries to invoke a different compiler to handle the file.

This option lets ML know that you really intend it to work with a file whose extension is not ASM. This option can be used several times on a command line because it applies only to the file name immediately following the option.

Enable Virtual Memory (/VM)

If you run out of memory when assembling a large program, use this option. It instructs ML to use virtual-memory techniques while assembling. These techniques allow ML to use EMS, XMS, and disk space (in that order) to store information needed for successful assembly of the program.

Set Warning Level 0 (/w)

Issuing this option is the same as issuing the /W0 option; it suppresses all warning messages during assembly.

Set Warning Level (/W*level*)

ML uses /W0, /W1, or /W2 to provide control over which warning messages are displayed during assembly. The /W0 option suppresses all warning messages, the /W1 option suppresses advisory messages but displays serious messages, and the /W2 option displays all messages.

Treat Warnings as Errors (/WX)

Typically, the difference between warnings and errors is only a matter of degree. With warnings, however, ML can still generate an OBJ file and proceed with linking; with errors, it cannot. This option instructs ML to treat each warning as if it were an error; /WX will stop an OBJ file from being created and stop linking from occurring.

Ignore the INCLUDE Environment Variable (/X)

Typically, you set an environment variable to specify where ML should look for include files. For instance, if your include files are stored in the subdirectory \MASM60\INCS, you can use the DOS command

SET INCLUDE=\MASM60\INCS

to tell ML where to look for the files. The /X option overrides this environment variable and tells ML not to look in the subdirectory set by the SET command. Rather, ML looks in the current directory only. If the required include file is not found, an error is generated.

If you want to specify other directories where the include files are located, see the /I option.

Include Line Numbers in Object File (/Zd)

If you are working with a large program, and running out of memory when you subsequently use CodeView, this option may help. It limits the amount of CodeView-specific information stored in the OBJ file. Thus, less memory is required when you use CodeView.

Make All Symbols Public (/Zf)

This option tells ML to pass all symbols that specify memory addresses into the OBJ file as PUBLIC symbols. Its use simplifies debugging with programs such as CodeView and Turbo Debugger, which can identify any PUBLIC symbols by name. Without this option, only identifiers declared explicitly as PUBLIC are considered public.

Create CodeView-compatible File (/Zi)

This option causes line-number information and symbolic data about all labels and variable names to be included in the OBJ file. Including this data allows for full operation of the symbolic debuggers, such as CodeView or Turbo Debugger.

Force Compatibility with MASM 5.1 (/Zm)

This option is the same as using the OPTION M510 directive in your source file. It instructs ML to assume that your program uses the same structures allowed in MASM 5.1. Because these structures were more limited, you probably will not use this option unless you encounter errors when you try to assemble your program.

Pack Structures to Byte Boundary (/Zp*boundary*)

When creating structures you have defined in your program, ML typically places adjacent source-code fields immediately next to each other in the OBJ file. This option allows you to specify a byte boundary ML should use when aligning fields in your structures.

The only proper alignment values are 1, 2, and 4; in effect, these values specify the minimum field length for structures. Fields shorter than the minimum specified length are padded (from left to right) with zeros to the necessary boundary.

Check Syntax Only (/Zs)

If all you want to check is whether you have coded your program correctly from a syntactical standpoint, use this option. It results in no OBJ file being created, and does not invoke the linker. Messages are displayed only if errors exist.

Compatibility with MASM 5.1 Options

Another way to assemble programs with MASM 6.0 is to use the MASM program. Invoking the assembler this way should be familiar to programmers who have used older versions of MASM.

When you use MASM, all that happens is that the older-syntax command-line options are translated into the appropriate options for ML, and the ML command is issued. Table 5.2 shows how these options are translated.

Table 5.2. MASM 5.1 options and equivalent options in MASM 6.0. (Options with no equivalent are ignored in MASM 6.0.)

MASM 5.1 Option	MASM 6.0 Option
/A	
/Bblocks	
/C	/FR
/D	/Fl /Sf
/Dx	/D
/E	/FPi
/H	/help
/Ipath	/Ipath
/L	/Fl
/LA	/Fl /Sa

MASM 5.1 Option	MASM 6.0 Option
/ML	/Cp
/MU	/Cu
/MX	/Cx
/N	/Sn
/P	
/S	
/T	/nologo
/V	
/Wn	/Wn
/X	/Sx
/Z	
/ZD	/Zd
/ZI	/Zi

To determine the result of using options with the MASM command line, look up the description of the ML option into which the original option is translated. The following sections describe the older MASM options that have no equivalent in MASM 6.0 and are no longer supported.

Change from Alphabetic Segment Order (/A)

In MASM 5.1, this option controlled the way the assembler wrote segments into the OBJ file. Older assemblers wrote segments into the OBJ file in either alphabetical order or the order in which they occurred in the source file. ML orders segments alphabetically within group, and offers no way to change this.

Set Buffer Size (/B*blocks*)

This option controlled the way MASM 5.1 allocated and used memory while it assembled a source file. This option is no longer needed, because ML allocates memory dynamically. If memory outside conventional memory is needed, you can use the /VM option also.

Check Purity of 286/386 Code (/P)

In MASM 5.1, this option was used to check whether the source code was "pure" (that it would work in protected mode). In ML, this function is handled by the .286P, .386P, and .486P directives, which can be included in your source file.

Order Segments by Occurrence in Source Code (/S)

This option, the opposite of /A, controlled ordering of segments within the OBJ file. Again, ML orders segments alphabetically within group and offers no way to specify a different ordering scheme.

Show Extra Assembly Statistics (/V)

In MASM 5.1, this option turned on the assembler's *verbose* mode, which caused additional statistics to be generated when the file was assembled. MASM 6.0 has no equivalent command.

Display Error Lines (/Z)

This option was used in MASM 5.1 to display the source-code line that contained an error, whenever an error occurred during assembly. MASM 6.0 has no equivalent command. You can, however, use the various listings files to determine errors by specific source-code line.

Using ML through a Batch File

To make the assembly process easier, you can set up a batch file (as you can with many other development commands and programs). The first step in this process is to determine which command-line options you want to use regularly when you assemble your files.

The following batch file (called ASM.BAT) is one I routinely use to assemble, using the ML command line:

```
ECHO OFF
CLS

:LOOP
 REM - CHECK IF NO FILES AVAILABLE ON COMMAND LINE
 IF %1/ == / GOTO DONE

 REM - CHECK IF EXTENSION (.ASM) WAS ENTERED
 IF NOT EXIST %1 GOTO CHKEXT
    ECHO Could not assemble %1 -- it contained an extension
    GOTO NEXT

:CHKEXT
 REM - CHECK FOR ROOT PLUS ASSUMED EXTENSION
 IF NOT EXIST %1.ASM GOTO NOT-FOUND
    ECHO Assembling ... %1.ASM
    ML /c /Cx /Fo%1.obj /Fl %1.asm >NUL
    IF ERRORLEVEL 1 GOTO ERROR
    GOTO NEXT

:NOT-FOUND
 REM - FILE NOT LOCATED
 ECHO File %1 Not Located or Found in Current Directory !
 GOTO NEXT

:ERROR
 ECHO Error detected while assembling %1

:NEXT
 REM - CONTINUE WITH NEXT FILE - END OF LOOP
 SHIFT
 GOTO LOOP

:DONE
 ECHO All Files have been Assembled !
```

With this file, the assumption is that you will enter the command line as

```
ASM file1 file2 file3 ...
```

where *file1*, *file2*, *file3*, and so on are the names of the source-code files to be assembled. Do not enter the ASM extension, because ML can generate an object file only if you specify a file name to use for that file. Thus, if you enter a file name with the .ASM extension, such as FILE.ASM, the batch file tries to create an object file with the name FILE.ASM.obj, thereby generating a DOS error.

If ASM.BAT can be located in the current search path, you can use it from any subdirectory. The source-code file should be in the current directory, however, and the OBJ file will remain in the current directory.

Notice the line in the batch file that does all the work:

```
ML /c /Cx /Fo%1.obj /Fl %1.asm >NUL
```

This line must be entered in the batch file exactly as you see it, because ML is case-sensitive on command options.

The benefit of using ML from a batch file is that you don't have to worry about entering the command-line options every time you want to use the assembler. I use a few options (such as /c, /Fo, and /Fl) regularly, and would quickly tire of entering them manually. This batch file overcomes that problem.

If you find that you routinely use other command-line options, change the batch file to reflect your needs.

Using ML with Error Codes

In earlier versions of MASM, the assembler returned an error level when completed. This was handy for use with batch files, where the error level could be tested and acted upon. Table 5.3 lists the exit codes (and their meanings) possible for MASM version 5.1.

Table 5.3. *MASM 5.1 exit codes.*

Code	Meaning
0	No errors detected
1	Argument error
2	Cannot open source file
3	Cannot open LST file
4	Cannot open OBJ file
5	Cannot open CRF file
6	Cannot open INCLUDE file
7	Assembly error
8	Memory-allocation error
9	Unused
10	/D option error
11	Interrupted by user

Although the ML assembler in MASM 6.0 returns an error level, the functionality of this error level is much less than in previous MASM incarnations. Basically, only two significant error levels are returned: if a 0 is returned, no errors were encountered during assembly; if a nonzero value is returned, an error took place.

This low level of error indication still allows you to use rudimentary control methods in your batch files. You can use this exit code to control how the batch file will function. This exit code is used in a simple manner (through the ERRORLEVEL batch command) in the sample batch file, which checks whether an exit code of at least 1 was returned and, if it was, displays a message indicating the status. But you can be quite elaborate in your implementation of an assembler batch file.

MASM 6.0 and Turbo Assembler are now strongly oriented toward the use of MAKE files (described in Chapter 8, "Using Additional Tools") instead of batch files to control their operation; both provide "configurable" options to halt the MAKE operation when an error is encountered.

Meanwhile, Back at the Program...

Having digressed a bit so that you could learn about all the ML command-line options, it is time to return to the sample program. You should have entered and assembled SUMS.ASM earlier in this chapter. If you haven't already done so, do so now.

Remember that SUMS.ASM is designed to be called from a C program. Take a moment to enter the following C program (called TEST.C, since you simply are doing some testing). After you enter the program, compile it to produce an object-code file called TEST.OBJ. It should compile with any Microsoft C compiler.

```
/* File:     TEST.C
 * Author:   Allen L. Wyatt
 * Date:     8/3/91
 *
 * Purpose:  Program to test the calling of SUMS()
 */

#include <stdio.h>

extern short sums(short);
short status(short);
```

```
short status(short orig)
{ unsigned short new;
  new=sums(orig);
  if (orig>0 && new==0)
  {printf("Sorry, the sum has exceeded capacity (%u rows is too many)\n",orig);
  }
  else
  {printf("The sum of %u rows is %u\n",orig,new);
  }
  return (new);
}

void main()
{ unsigned short j, x;
  j=0;
  while (j!=999)
  { printf("Initial Value: ");
 scanf("%u",&j);
 if (j!=999)
 { x=status(j);
 }
 }
  for (j=1, x=1; x!=0; x=status(j++))
 ;
}
```

This simple program performs two basic tasks. First, it enables you to enter a number that is used as a value for calling SUMS(). Both the original and derived number are displayed. Second, if you enter the number 999, the program exits the interactive portion and proceeds through a loop, starting at 1, that displays values and derived values until it reaches the limit of SUMS(). You may remember from earlier in the chapter that this limit is reached when the derived value is greater than 65,535. When this limit is exceeded, SUMS() returns a 0 and terminates execution of the controlling C program.

Linking TEST.OBJ and SUMS.ASM

The linker can be used in several ways, the principal ways being interactively or with just a command line. Let's look first at using the linker interactively.

Using LINK Interactively

Once you have the two object-code files, TEST.OBJ and SUMS.OBJ, you are ready to link the files. Make sure that these files are in the current directory. You should have access also to LINK.EXE, either in the current directory or in the search path. To start the linking process, enter the following at the DOS prompt:

```
LINK
```

When you press Enter, you will see a notice and prompt similar to the following:

```
Microsoft (R) Segmented-Executable Linker  Version 5.13
Copyright (C) Microsoft Corp 1984-1991.  All rights reserved.

Object Modules [.OBJ]:
```

The linker is waiting for you to specify the files to be linked. The default answer is shown in brackets; the linker accepts this answer if you simply press the Enter key. Enter the root names of the files to be linked, separated by either a space or a plus sign (+). Because the linker assumes an extension of OBJ (unless you override it), you need to specify only the root names. When you make the proper entries, the following message should appear:

```
Object Modules [.OBJ]: test sums
Run File [test.exe]: _
```

Notice that the linker now prompts you for the name of the EXE file to create. (The EXE file is the executable run file LINK.EXE creates.) Use the default, `test.exe`. When you press Enter to signify that you accept the default, the linker asks the following:

```
Run File [test.exe]:
List File [NUL.MAP]:
```

A list file is optional, as the default (NUL.MAP) indicates. List files for the linker have the extension MAP because they provide a "map" showing how the linker did its work. For now, enter `test` to indicate that you want a list file named TEST.MAP. When you do, the following prompt is displayed:

```
List File [NUL.MAP]: test
Libraries [.LIB]: _
```

LINK needs to know which library files to use for external references that cannot be resolved from within the object-code files. (Libraries are covered in Chapter 9, "Developing Libraries.") Although there are no assembly language libraries for this example, LINK will look for a C library it needs to complete the linking process.

If you just finished compiling your C program, chances are that LINK will search and find the appropriate C library automatically. If you did not just finish compiling the C program, you may want to make sure that the library environment variable (typically LIB) is set to the proper search path for the C libraries. To do this, you have to abort the linking process, change the environment variable, and start linking all over again.

When you are ready, simply press Enter to indicate that no explicit libraries are to be used. The following prompt is displayed:

```
Libraries [.LIB]:
Definitions File [NUL.DEF]: _
```

LINK is asking for a module-definition file. This file—used only when creating programs for OS/2 or Windows—is used to describe the name, attributes, system requirements, and other characteristics of an application program. Because you are creating a simple DOS-based program, just press Enter.

Now LINK has asked (and you have responded to) its five questions. Notice that your disk drive is active for a short time, and then the DOS prompt returns. The return of the DOS prompt indicates that the linking process is complete, and that no errors occurred. Had an error occurred, an error message would have appeared during linking, indicating the type of error and the source file for the error.

If you receive any error messages, you must correct the errors before continuing. Check your files against the listings in this chapter; then try to assemble, compile, and link again. After you have corrected the errors, you can proceed with this chapter.

Using the LINK Command Line

As mentioned earlier, you can use LINK also from the DOS command line. You can enter any or all of the responses to individual prompts directly after the LINK command. For instance, entering either of the following lines produces the same results as those achieved in the last section:

```
LINK TEST SUMS,,TEST,;
```

```
LINK TEST+SUMS,,,;
```

Remember that LINK asks five questions during an interactive session. The parameters in either of these command lines provide answers to the questions. The parameters are separated by commas, and the line ends with a semicolon.

As the three consecutive commas indicate, some parameters are left blank. In this case, LINK uses the first parameter (TEST) as the implied parameter.

The following syntax is used to enter parameters directly from the command line:

```
LINK obj,exe,map,lib,def
```

Here, *obj*, *exe*, *map*, *lib*, and *def* indicate the file type each parameter designates. These file types were touched on earlier in this chapter.

How do you indicate that you do not want a particular type of file? Simply by using NUL as the parameter for that file type. For instance, both of the following commands instruct LINK to create an EXE file but no MAP file:

```
LINK TEST SUMS,,NUL;
```

```
LINK TEST+SUMS,;
```

Notice that the second command line, although shorter than the first, is effectively the same. The semicolon instructs LINK to begin processing without expecting any more parameters.

Using the LINK Response File

You can respond to the four LINK questions in a file, logically called a *response file*. This is a good way to use LINK when you know that you will be linking the same program over and over again during development; repeatedly typing answers to each question can be tiresome.

To use this method of providing input to LINK, create a normal ASCII text file, with any name you want, that has the answers to each question. Each question's answer should be on a separate line. For instance, using our sample programs, the response file would have only four lines:

```
TEST SUMS

TEST
;
```

LINK uses this response file to link TEST.OBJ and SUMS.OBJ, producing the default output file, TEST.EXE. Also, the list file TEST.MAP is created, and no libraries are specified.

To use a response file with LINK, simply invoke LINK by using the following command syntax:

```
LINK @filename.ext
```

filename.ext is the name of the response file LINK is to use. Notice the @ symbol directly before the file name. This symbol is the signal that LINK needs to differentiate between a response file and a source file.

If the sample response file is named TEST.LNK, the following command will run LINK and provide input to LINK from the response file:

```
LINK @TEST.LNK
```

The more you use LINK, the better you will understand the value of using response files.

Testing the Finished TEST.EXE

Now that your linker has created TEST.EXE, you can try your program to see whether it works. Enter the following at the DOS prompt to start execution of the program:

```
TEST
```

The result should be a prompt asking you for an initial value. Enter an integer number, such as 7. You have just asked TEST to calculate the number of blocks in a seven-level pyramid, similar to the one in figure 5.5.

Fig. 5.5. *A seven-level pyramid.*

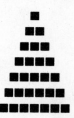

The program dialogue and results should look like this:

```
C:\>TEST
Initial Value: 7
The sum of 7 rows is 28
Initial Value:
```

When you press Enter after entering the initial value, the response indicates that there are 28 blocks in the pyramid (7 + 6 + 5 + 4 + 3 + 2 + 1 = 28). This program is designed to continue asking for values and returning results until you enter a value of 999. Then the program will generate a list showing the initial values and resulting values for pyramids between one row high and the maximum number of rows the program can handle. A partial program dialogue follows:

```
C:\>TEST
Initial Value: 7
The sum of 7 rows is 28
Initial Value: 5
The sum of 5 rows is 15
Initial Value: 22
The sum of 22 rows is 253
Initial Value: 103
The sum of 103 rows is 5356
Initial Value: 999
The sum of 1 rows is 1
The sum of 2 rows is 3
The sum of 3 rows is 6
The sum of 4 rows is 10
The sum of 5 rows is 15
The sum of 6 rows is 21
The sum of 7 rows is 28
The sum of 8 rows is 36
The sum of 9 rows is 45
The sum of 10 rows is 55
```

(Intermediate values have been deleted to conserve space.)

```
The sum of 353 rows is 62481
The sum of 354 rows is 62835
The sum of 355 rows is 63190
The sum of 356 rows is 63546
The sum of 357 rows is 63903
The sum of 358 rows is 64261
The sum of 359 rows is 64620
The sum of 360 rows is 64980
The sum of 361 rows is 65341
Sorry, the sum has exceeded capacity (362 rows is too many)

C:\>_
```

Notice that the upper limit the routine can handle represents a 361-row pyramid. A 362-row pyramid contains 65,703 blocks, a number too large to be stored in the unsigned integer used to return values from the assembly language subroutine.

Summary

This chapter covered the use of the major assembly language products from Microsoft: MASM 6.0 and LINK. These products represent the lion's share of the assembler marketplace. You have used the assembler and linker to create a functioning subroutine called from a C program.

Using an assembler properly is essential to your success in using assembly language. Even though ML (the command-line assembler within MASM 6.0) has a rich variety of command-line options available, it is not difficult to use in a basic manner. You probably will use the options only in special situations.

In the next chapter, you learn how to program using Borland's assembly language products. If you do not plan to use Turbo Assembler (TASM) or TLINK, you can skip to Chapter 7, "Debugging Assembly Language Subroutines."

6

Using Borland's Assembly Language Products

You have already learned many of the differences between the two major assemblers and linkers. In this chapter you will learn more about TASM and TLINK, the assembler and linker from Borland. This chapter and Chapter 5, "Using Microsoft's Assembly Language Products," are very similar in construction and content; they differ only in the specific details that apply to the environments provided by Microsoft and Borland.

TASM, a contraction for Turbo Assembler, has been around for several years. The current version, TASM 3.0, was introduced in December, 1991. It offers more capabilities and features than earlier versions, as well as many changes that affect how you program and use the assembler itself.

TLINK has been around a little longer than TASM. It is shipped with the professional versions of Borland's C and C++ products, which also include TASM.

A Sample Program

To proceed through this chapter, you need a sample subroutine to assemble. This subroutine will be neither large nor complex, nor will it exemplify the best reasons for using assembly language. Although writing this routine in a high-level

143

language is easier than writing it in assembly language, I will use it to demonstrate how to assemble (and later debug) a subroutine.

Let's assume that you need to determine the total number of blocks in a pyramid where each ascending row contains one less block than the row beneath it, and the top row contains only one block (see fig. 6.1).

Fig. 6.1. *A sample pyramid.*

The bottom row contains 15 blocks, the next row contains 14, and so on, with only one block in the top row. Your job is to calculate the total number of blocks needed, given only the number of blocks in the bottom row. You will use the sample program to do the job.

The program (SUMS.ASM) is designed to be called from Borland C++. When passed an unsigned 16-bit integer, this program calculates and returns the result as an unsigned integer. The assembly language subroutine, written for TASM 3.0, follows:

```
Page 60,132
Comment |
*********************************************************************

File:    SUMS.ASM for Turbo Assembler 3.0
Author:  Allen L. Wyatt
Date:    10/15/91
```

```
Purpose:  Given an integer number X, find the sum of
          X + (X-1) + (X-2) + (X-3) + (X-4) ... + 2 + 1
          Designed to be called from Borland C++.

Format:   SUMS(X)


********************************************************************

          PUBLIC    _sums

          .MODEL    small
          .CODE

_sums     PROC Value:WORD
          MOV   AX,0              ;Initialize to zero
          MOV   CX,Value          ;Get actual value
          JCXZ S3                 ;Num=0, no need to do
          CLC                     ;Initialize for start
S1:       ADC   AX,CX             ;Add row value
          JC    S2                ;Quit if AX overflowed
          LOOP S1                 ;Repeat process
          JMP   S3                ;Successful completion
S2:       MOV   AX,0              ;Force a zero
S3:       RET                     ;Return to C
_sums     ENDP

          END
```

If the number entered results in a sum that is greater than 65,535 (the largest unsigned integer number that can be held in 16 bits), the subroutine sets the result to 0.

Go ahead and enter this program. After you finish, save it as SUMS.ASM. You are now ready to assemble the program.

Using TASM 3.0

Before beginning the assembly process, make sure that you have installed TASM 3.0 according to the instructions that came with the software. Make sure that SUMS.ASM (the subroutine file) is in the current disk directory. At the DOS prompt, enter

TASM

to invoke Turbo Assembler. The following information is displayed:

```
Turbo Assembler  Version 3.0  Copyright (c) 1988, 1991 Borland International
Syntax:  TASM [options] source [,object] [,listing] [,xref]
/a,/s          Alphabetic or Source-code segment ordering
/c             Generate cross-reference in listing
/dSYM[=VAL]    Define symbol SYM = 0, or = value VAL
/e,/r          Emulated or Real floating-point instructions
/h,/?          Display this help screen
/iPATH         Search PATH for include files
/jCMD          Jam in an assembler directive CMD (eg. /jIDEAL)
/kh#           Hash table capacity # symbols
/l,/la         Generate listing: l=normal listing, la=expanded listing
/ml,/mx,/mu    Case sensitivity on symbols: ml=all, mx=globals, mu=none
/mv#           Set maximum valid length for symbols
/m#            Allow # multiple passes to resolve forward references
/n             Suppress symbol tables in listing
/o,/op         Generate overlay object code, Phar Lap-style 32-bit fixups
/p             Check for code segment overrides in protected mode
/q             Suppress OBJ records not needed for linking
/t             Suppress messages if successful assembly
/uxxxx         Set version emulation, version xxxx
/w0,/w1,/w2    Set warning level: w0=none, w1=w2=warnings on
/w-xxx,/w+xxx  Disable (-) or enable (+) warning xxx
/x             Include false conditionals in listing
/z             Display source line with error message
/zi,/zd,/zn    Debug info: zi=full, zd=line numbers only, zn=none
```

This terse help information tells you what you need to enter from the command line to make TASM.EXE work properly. You must enter a complete command line that TASM can work with right away.

Examine the help information again. Everything enclosed in brackets is optional; the least you need to enter is the name of a source file to be processed. Thus, if you enter the following command line:

```
TASM SUMS
```

Turbo Assembler will dutifully assemble SUMS.ASM and create an object (OBJ) file. You can enter other file specifications, if you want, to create the other types of files discussed in detail in Chapter 3, "Choosing and Using Your Assembler." For instance, if you want to create a listing (LST) file and also a cross-reference (XRF) file, you can enter the following:

```
TASM SUMS,,SUMS,SUMS
```

Notice the two consecutive commas, which indicate the presence of a blank parameter. The blank parameter indicates that Turbo Assembler should accept the default for the specific file. In this case, it uses SUMS as the default name for the OBJ file. If any of the other parameters had been left blank, defaults for those files would have been used (the default being that no file is created).

For now, let's assemble the file you entered at the beginning of this chapter. At the DOS prompt, enter the following line:

```
TASM SUMS,,SUMS
```

When you enter the command line and press Enter, TASM starts its work. You see a message indicating that the file is being assembled. If there are no errors, you are returned shortly to the DOS prompt. If the assembly was successful, your screen will be similar to the following:

```
Turbo Assembler  Version 3.0  Copyright (c) 1988, 1991 Borland International

Assembling file:    SUMS.ASM
Error messages:     None
Warning messages:   None
Passes:             1
Remaining memory:   457k
```

Turbo Assembler is done, and the file SUMS.OBJ should be in your sub-directory.

If there were errors, you see a message indicating the type of error and where it was located. If you receive any error messages, you must correct the errors before continuing. Check your source file (SUMS.ASM) against the listing file (SUMS.LST), correct any errors, and try the assembly process again. After you have corrected all the errors, you can proceed with this chapter.

Assembler Options

You can use several parameters (referred to as *options* or *switches* in the documentation) with TASM to alter the way the program functions. You enter these options directly from the command line.

Remember the help screen that appeared when you entered only the TASM command at the DOS prompt? It listed the command-line options you can use with TASM. The available command-line options are listed in table 6.1 and detailed in the following sections.

Table 6.1. *TASM command-line options.*

Option	Meaning
/?	Display help information.
/A	Order segments in alphabetic sequence.
/C	Include cross-references in the listing file.
/Dname[=text]	Define an identifier, optionally assigning *text* to *name*.
/E	Emulate floating-point instructions.
/H	Display help information.
/Ipathname	Search *pathname* for include files.
/Jname	Jam directive into effect.
/KHsize	Set hash table capacity.
/L	Create a listing file.
/LA	Create an expanded listing file.
/Mpasses	Set number of passes.
/ML	Make case of names significant.
/MU	Make all names uppercase.
/MVlength	Set maximum valid length for symbols.
/MX	Make case of global symbols significant.
/N	Exclude tables from the listing file.
/O	Generate overlay code.
/OP	Generate overlay code with Phar-Lap-style fixups.
/P	Check purity of 286/386 code.
/Q	Suppress OBJ records not needed for linking.
/R	Create code for numeric coprocessors.
/S	Order segments by occurrence in source code.
/T	Suppress assembly completion messages.
/Uversion	Set assembler emulation version.
/W0	Suppress all warning messages.
/W1	Enable all warning messages.
/W2	Enable all warning messages.
/W-xxx	Disable warning class *xxx*.
/W+xxx	Enable warning class *xxx*.
/X	List false conditional statements.
/Z	Display source lines with errors.

Option	Meaning
/ZD	Add only line numbers to OBJ file.
/ZI	Add full debugging data to OBJ file.
/ZN	Add no debugging data to OBJ file.

Notice that many of the command-line options listed in table 6.1 have variables that you can specify, such as *version*, *passes*, or *size*. When specifying these variables, note that there are no colons or spaces between the option and the variable for the option. Rather, the variable immediately follows the option.

Let's look at each TASM option in greater detail.

Display Help Information (/? or /H)

If you are using TASM and you forget what the syntax or command-line options are, this option displays the quick help screen (you saw this screen earlier in the chapter, when you entered TASM with no parameters).

Alphabetic Segment Ordering (/A)

This option controls the way the assembler writes segments into the object (OBJ) file. Ordinarily, the assembler writes segments in the order in which they occur in the source file. Some linkers, however, expect segments to be arranged alphabetically. If you are using such a linker, you should use this command-line option.

Include Cross-References in the Listing File (/C)

If you have directed TASM to create a listing file, this option will create a cross-reference in the listing file. For instance, in Chapter 3, if the listing file for SUMS.ASM had included a cross-reference, the symbol-table page would have appeared as follows:

```
Turbo Assembler  Version 3.0        12/18/91 17:39:44       Page 2
Symbol Table


Symbol Name              Type   Value                     Cref (defined at #)

??DATE                   Text   "12/18/91"
??FILENAME               Text   "sums     "
??TIME                   Text   "17:39:44"
??VERSION                Number 0300
@32BIT                   Text   0                         #17
@CODE                    Text   _TEXT                     #17  #17  #18
@CODESIZE                Text   0                         #17
@CPU                     Text   0101H
@CURSEG                  Text   _TEXT                     #18
@DATA                    Text   DGROUP                    #17
@DATASIZE                Text   0                         #17
@FILENAME                Text   SUMS
@INTERFACE               Text   4H                        #17
@MODEL                   Text   2                         #17
@STACK                   Text   DGROUP                    #17
@WORDSIZE                Text   2                         #18
S1                       Near   _TEXT:000B                #26  28
S2                       Near   _TEXT:0014                27   #30
S3                       Near   _TEXT:0017                25   29  #31
SUM                      Number [DGROUP:BP+0006]          #20
SUMS                     Near   _TEXT:0000                15   #20
VALUE                    Number [DGROUP:BP+0004]          #20  24


Groups & Segments        Bit Size Align  Combine Class    Cref (defined at #)

DGROUP                   Group                             #17  17
  _DATA                  16  0000 Word   Public  DATA     #17
_TEXT                    16  001B Word   Public  CODE     #17  17  #18  18
```

Define an Identifier (/D*name[=text]*)

If you use conditional assembly directives in your program, this option can come in handy. It allows you to define an identifier when you use ML. Thus, you can assign a specific value to a label that controls how the program will be assembled.

For example, assume that your program includes some special code that has meaning only when the program is being debugged. If these instructions are conditional, being included only when the identifier debug is set to yes, including the option /Ddebug=yes will cause the code to be included.

Notice that you can specify just a label, with no value assigned to the label. If you do this, the label will be set equal to 0.

Emulate Floating-Point Instructions (/E)

The /E option (the opposite of the /R option) directs TASM to emulate the floating-point capabilities of the 8087, 80287, 80387, or 80486 chips. The assembler does not contain the actual emulation routines; they are included when the object code is linked and a math-emulation library is used. Your high-level language may include a library of this type because such libraries generally come from a third-party source.

The code that results from use of the /E option can be executed on any compatible computer, regardless of whether you have an numeric coprocessor.

Override Default Include-File Path (/I*pathname*)

This option tells ML where to search for include files in the source file. (These files are pulled in during assembly through use of the INCLUDE directive.)

If your include files are spread among several directories, you can use multiple /I options to specify different directories. Each directory is searched in turn until the necessary include file is located. If, after searching each directory, the required include file is not found, an error is generated.

Jam Directive into Effect (/J*name*)

This option puts any desired Turbo Assembler directive into effect from the command line. Its major use is to establish processing modes.

Set Hash Table Capacity (/KH*size*)

This option sets the maximum number of symbols your program can use. Without this option, Turbo Assembler is limited to 8,192 symbols; with it, you can specify as many as 32,768 symbols. And if you have trouble fitting everything into your available RAM, this option can reduce the amount of space needed.

Create a Listing File (/L)

This option controls creation of an assembly listing (LST) file. When invoked, the /L option creates a file with the same root name as the source file and an LST extension. (This file is detailed in Chapter 3.)

Create an Expanded Listing File (/LA)

This option not only causes a listing file to be generated (like the /L option) but also includes in the listing file all code generated by the simplified segment directive and high-level-language support features.

Set Number of Passes (/M*passes*)

By default, TASM is a single-pass assembler. This option is used to specify the number of passes you want the assembler to make. This option comes in handy if you are using conditional assembly or conditional error directives that rely on there being at least two passes.

Make Case of Names Significant (/ML)

Normally, TASM treats all identifiers (names of variables and procedures) the same, converting them all to uppercase. Some high-level languages are sensitive to case, however, treating *A* differently than *a*. If this is the case (no pun intended), you can use this option to direct TASM to maintain the original case of your identifiers.

Make All Names Uppercase (/MU)

The default setting for TASM, this option causes all names, labels, and symbols to be converted to uppercase.

Set Maximum Valid Length for Symbols (/MV*length*)

Some high-level languages limit the number of significant characters in procedure names or variables. This option tells TASM to set a limit on how many characters are significant. Valid lengths are anywhere from 1 to 255 characters. With this option set, TASM disregards anything longer than the maximum you set.

Make Case of Global Symbols Significant (/MX)

This modified version of the /ML option results in special treatment of only those identifiers that are seen by other programs. An identifier private to a particular procedure is still converted to uppercase.

This option should cause your routines to work with most high-level languages.

Exclude Tables from the Listing File (/N)

Normally, the assembler includes (at the end of an assembly listing LST file) several tables that recap the source file's structure. You can use /N to exclude those tables without changing the rest of the listing. Using /N causes the assembler to function slightly faster.

Generate Overlay Code (/O)

This command-line option causes the assembler to generate fixups that will work with overlays. These fixups are then resolved by the linker so that your program can use overlays correctly. If you use this option, you should not use any directives in your source code that instruct the assembler to use 32-bit addresses.

Generate Overlay Code with Phar-Lap-Style Fixups (/OP)

This option is similar to the /O option, except that a different type of fixup is generated. Because these fixups work with the Phar Lap linker only , you will not be able to use TLINK to link your program if you use this option.

Check Purity of 286/386 Code (/P)

Turbo Assembler can create protected-mode coding for the 80286, 80386, or 80486 microprocessors if the proper assembler directives are present in the source file. The /P option specifies that the assembler should check whether the source code is "pure" (that it contains no data accessed in the code segment with a CS: override). If you use this option, an additional check is done and an additional error code may be generated.

Suppress OBJ Records Not Needed for Linking (/Q)

Normally, information that is not technically necessary for linking is included in the OBJ file for legal or other reasons. Using this option causes Turbo Assembler to exclude the typical copyright information written into the OBJ file, as well as any file-dependency records. Because these records are used by programs such as MAKE, you shouldn't use the /Q option if you use MAKE. If you do, MAKE will not work properly.

Create Code for Numeric Coprocessors (/R)

Using this option causes the assembler to generate coding compatible with the numeric capabilities of the 8087, 80287, 80387, or 80486 chips. This generation of code affects only floating-point operations. Code created with the /R option can run only on computers that use one of these chips.

Order Segments by Occurrence in Source Code (/S)

This option, which is the opposite of /A, is the default option. It specifies that segments be written in the order they occur in the source code.

Suppress Assembly Completion Messages (/T)

The /T (for *terse*) option suppresses all assembler messages if the assembly is successful. If at least one error occurs, the normal assembler copyright and version information is displayed before the error is listed.

Set Assembler Emulation Version (/U*version*)

This option is equivalent to using the VERSION directive in your source-code file. It allows you to specify which version of MASM or TASM should be emulated while Turbo Assembler is doing its work. The *version* may be one of the following:

Assembler	*Version*
MASM 4.0	M400
MASM 5.0	M500
MASM 5.1	M510
Quick Assembler	M520
TASM 1.0	T100
TASM 1.01	T101
TASM 2.0	T200
TASM 2.5	T250
TASM 3.0	T300

Control Warning Messages (/W, /W0, /W1, /W2, /W-*xxx*, and /W+*xxx*)

Turbo Assembler gives you full control over the number and type of warning messages you receive when problems are found during assembly. This control is implemented with different variations of the /W option.

You can turn off warning messages with the /W0 option, whereas both /W1 and /W2 enable their display. Turbo Assembler also classifies messages into groups and uses /W- and /W+, followed by a three-letter class code, to individually disable or enable each group. By default, all serious and most advisory warnings are enabled. The warning classes are

Class	*Meaning*
ALN	Segment alignment
ASS	Assume segment is 16-bit
BRK	Brackets needed
ICG	Inefficient code
LCO	Location counter overflow
OPI	Unterminated (open) IF condition
OPP	Unclosed (open) procedure
OPS	Unclosed (open) segment
OVF	Arithmetic overflow
PDC	Pass-dependent coding
PQK	Assumes constant for warning
PRO	Incorrect protected-mode memory write
RES	Reserved word infraction
TPI	Illegal Turbo Pascal operation

List False Conditional Statements (/X)

If you request a listing file, and your source file includes conditional assembly directives, this option controls the listing of the code not normally included in the LST file. If code were omitted from the OBJ file because the conditional assembly directives controlling that code's inclusion were FALSE, that code normally would be excluded also from the assembly listing file. Using the /X option, however, enables such source code lines to be included in the listing even though no machine language code is generated.

Display Source Lines with Errors (/Z)

The assembler ordinarily indicates assembly errors by displaying an error message and the line number at which the error(s) occurred. To display also the source-code line that contains the error, use the /Z option.

Include Line Numbers in Object File (/ZD)

If you are working with a large program and running out of memory when you subsequently use CodeView or Turbo Debugger, this option may help. It limits the amount of debugger-specific information stored in the OBJ file. Thus, you need less memory later when you use a high-level debugger.

Add Full Debugging Data to OBJ File (/ZI)

This option causes line-number information and symbolic data about all labels and variable names to be included in the OBJ file. This provides full operation of the symbolic debuggers (such as CodeView or Turbo Debugger), including evaluation of values at run-time and replacement with new values.

Add No Debugging Data to OBJ File (/ZN)

This option is the opposite of the /ZI option. If you use it, no debugging information is written to the OBJ file. Although your code will be smaller, it will not work as fully with symbolic debuggers such as CodeView and Turbo Debugger. (You will not be able to take full advantage of all of the debugger's features.)

Using TASM through a Batch File

To make the assembly process easier, you can set up a batch file (as you can with many other development commands and programs). To do so, you must first determine which command-line options you want to use as a matter of course when you assemble your files.

The following batch file (ASM.BAT) is one I routinely use to assemble with the TASM command line:

```
      ECHO OFF
      CLS

      :LOOP
       REM - CHECK IF NO FILES AVAILABLE ON COMMAND LINE
       IF %1/ == / GOTO DONE

       REM - CHECK IF EXTENSION (.ASM) WAS ENTERED
       IF NOT EXIST %1 GOTO CHKEXT
          ECHO Could not assemble %1 -- it contained an extension
          GOTO NEXT

      :CHKEXT
       REM - CHECK FOR ROOT PLUS ASSUMED EXTENSION
       IF NOT EXIST %1.ASM GOTO NOT-FOUND
          ECHO Assembling ... %1.ASM
          TASM /C /ML %1,,%1 >NUL
          IF ERRORLEVEL 1 GOTO ERROR
          GOTO NEXT

      :NOT-FOUND
       REM - FILE NOT LOCATED
       ECHO File %1 Not Located or Found in Current Directory !
       GOTO NEXT

      :ERROR
       ECHO Error detected while assembling %1

      :NEXT
       REM - CONTINUE WITH NEXT FILE - END OF LOOP
       SHIFT
       GOTO LOOP

      :DONE
       ECHO All Files have been Assembled !
```

In this file, the assumption is that you will enter the command line as

```
ASM file1 file2 file3 ...
```

where file1, file2, file3, and so on are the names of the source-code files to be assembled. If ASM.BAT can be located in the current search path, you can use it from any subdirectory. The source-code file should be in the current directory, however, and the OBJ file will remain in the current directory.

The benefit of using TASM from a batch file is that you don't have to worry about entering the command-line options every time you want to use the assembler. I regularly use a few options (such as /C and /ML) that I would quickly tire of entering manually. This batch file overcomes that problem.

If you use other command-line options routinely, you can change the batch file to fill your needs.

Meanwhile, Back at the Program...

Having digressed a bit so that you could learn about all the TASM command-line options, it is time to return to the sample program. You should have entered and assembled SUMS.ASM earlier in this chapter. If you didn't, go back and do so now.

Remember that SUMS.ASM is designed to be called from a C++ program. Take a moment to enter the following program. Since you are simply doing some testing, the name of this program is TEST.CPP. After entering the program, use the Borland C++ compiler to compile it to an OBJ file.

```
/* File:     TEST.CPP
 * Author:   Allen L. Wyatt
 * Date:     10/15/91
 *
 * Purpose:  Program to test the calling of SUMS()
 */

#include <iostream.h>

extern "C" {short sums(unsigned short);}
short status(unsigned short);

void main()
{
  unsigned short j, x;
  j=0;
  while (j!=999)
  { cout << "Initial Value: ";
 cin >> j;
 if (j!=999)
 { x=status(j);
 }
```

```
  }
  for (j=1, x=1; x!=0; x=status(j++))
 ;
}

short status(unsigned short orig)
{
  unsigned short result;
  result = sums(orig);
  if (orig>0 && result==0)
    cout << "Sorry, the sum has exceeded capacity ("
    cout << orig << " rows is too many)\n";
  else
    cout << "The sum of " << orig << " rows is "
    cout << result << "\n";
  return result;
}
```

This simple program performs two basic tasks. First, it enables you to enter a number that is used as a value for calling SUMS(). Both the original and derived numbers are displayed. Second, if you enter the number 999, the program exits the interactive portion and proceeds through a loop, starting at 1, that displays values and derived values until it reaches the limit of SUMS(). You may remember from earlier in the chapter that this limit is reached when the derived value is greater than 65,535. When this limit is exceeded, SUMS() returns a 0 and terminates execution of the controlling C program.

Linking TEST.OBJ and SUMS.ASM

Unlike Microsoft's linking program, TLINK from Borland does not have an interactive mode. All linking is done from the command line or from a response file. Let's look first at the command-line method.

Using the TLINK Command Line

Used from the command line, TLINK has the following general syntax:

TLINK *obj*, *exe*, *map*, *lib*, *options*

where *obj* is the name of the OBJ files, separated by spaces, *exe* is the name of the final executeable file, *map* is the linker's listing file, *lib* is the name of any library files, and *options* are the TLINK command-line options discussed in Chapter 4.

In the case of our program, the correct command line for the linker is as follows:

```
TLINK c0s test sums,test,,cs
```

This line links the three necessary OBJ files. You should already be familiar with two, but C0S.OBJ may be new to you. This is the start-up code needed for Borland C++ to operate properly. Also, CS.LIB is the library for the Borland C++ functions. In both files (C0S and CS) the *S* indicates that you are creating a program using the small memory model. You may want to look at the source code for SUMS.ASM to confirm this.

Using the TLINK Response File

Anything that comes after the TLINK command at the DOS prompt can be placed in a response file. This method of using TLINK is beneficial when you know that you will be linking the same program over and over again during development; repeatedly typing answers to each question can be tiresome.

To use this method of providing input to TLINK, create a normal ASCII text file, with any name you want, that has the input for the command line. Putting each element of the command line (*OBJ*, *EXE*, *MAP*, *LIB*, and *options*) on individual lines is particularly useful. For instance, using the sample programs, the response file would have only four lines:

```
c0s test sums
test
nul
cs
```

TLINK uses this response file to link C0S.OBJ, TEST.OBJ, and SUMS.OBJ, producing the default output file TEST.EXE. Notice the third line of the file, however. The response here indicates that a map file is not wanted. Nul is the name of a standard DOS device—anything sent out to the nul device is simply thrown away.

To use a response file with TLINK, simply invoke TLINK using the following command syntax:

```
TLINK @filename.ext
```

filename.ext is the name of the response file TLINK is to use. Notice the @ symbol that directly precedes the file name. This symbol is the signal that TLINK needs to differentiate between a response file and a source file.

If the sample response file is named TEST.LNK, the following command will run TLINK and provide input to TLINK from the response file:

```
TLINK @TEST.LNK
```

The more you use TLINK, the better you will understand the value of using response files.

Testing the Finished TEST.EXE

Now that your linker has created TEST.EXE, you can try your program to see whether it works. To start execution of the program, enter the following at the DOS prompt:

```
TEST
```

The result should be a prompt asking you for an initial value. Enter an integer number, such as 7. You have just asked TEST to calculate the number of blocks in a seven-level pyramid, such as the one shown in figure 6.2.

Fig. 6.2. *A seven-level pyramid.*

The program dialog and results should look like this:

```
C:\>TEST
Initial Value: 7
The sum of 7 rows is 28
Initial Value:
```

When you press return after entering the initial value, the response indicates that there are 28 blocks in the pyramid (7 + 6 + 5 + 4 + 3 + 2 + 1 = 28). This program is designed to continue asking for values and returning results until you enter a value of 999. Then the program generates a list showing both the initial and resulting values for pyramids between one row high and the maximum number of rows the program can handle. A partial program dialog follows:

```
C:\>TEST
Initial Value: 7
The sum of 7 rows is 28
Initial Value: 5
The sum of 5 rows is 15
Initial Value: 22
The sum of 22 rows is 253
Initial Value: 103
The sum of 103 rows is 5356
Initial Value: 999
The sum of 1 rows is 1
The sum of 2 rows is 3
The sum of 3 rows is 6
The sum of 4 rows is 10
The sum of 5 rows is 15
The sum of 6 rows is 21
The sum of 7 rows is 28
The sum of 8 rows is 36
The sum of 9 rows is 45
The sum of 10 rows is 55
```

(Intermediate values have been deleted to conserve space.)

```
The sum of 353 rows is 62481
The sum of 354 rows is 62835
The sum of 355 rows is 63190
The sum of 356 rows is 63546
The sum of 357 rows is 63903
The sum of 358 rows is 64261
The sum of 359 rows is 64620
The sum of 360 rows is 64980
The sum of 361 rows is 65341
Sorry, the sum has exceeded capacity (362 rows is too many)
```

```
C:\>_
```

Notice that the upper limit the routine can handle is a 361-row pyramid. A 362-row pyramid contains 65,703 blocks, a number too large to be stored in the unsigned integer used to return values from the assembly language subroutine.

Summary

This chapter covered the use of the major assembly language products from Borland: TASM 3.0 and TLINK. These products are formidable challengers to the marketplace traditionally dominated by Microsoft products. You have used the assembler and linker to create a functioning subroutine called from a Borland C++ program.

Using an assembler properly is essential to your success in using assembly language. Even though TASM 3.0 has a rich variety of command-line options available, it is not difficult to use in a basic manner. You probably will use the options only in special situations.

In the next chapter, you learn how to debug assembly language programs using DEBUG, CodeView, and Turbo Debugger.

Debugging Assembly Language Subroutines

We all know what *bugs* are. The bane of programmers everywhere, bugs seem to crop up at the most inopportune times (such as when the program you are working on is supposed to be shipped out the door) and have been known to keep frustrated programmers from sleeping at night. The term *debugging* refers to removal of these pesky problems from your programs.

Debugging as an Art Form

If you have been programming for any length of time, you are already familiar with debugging tools for high-level languages. Anyone who has stared at program listings for hours on end knows that debugging software can make the job of debugging much faster and easier.

Assembly language programmers can benefit from this software as much as high-level-language programmers. The type and amount of programming you do are important factors in determining the type (and price) of the debugging tool you need. Hundreds of debugging tools, which run the gamut of features and prices, are available.

165

No debugging tool will, in itself, make the task of finding and removing bugs really easy. To do that, you must learn the *art* of debugging, and the only way to do that is the hard way, through experience.

You may question my statement that debugging is an art; most other programming activity is usually considered to be either a science or a craft. However, there's a true art to a good debugger's work; it's much like comparing the detective exploits of Sherlock Holmes with tedious beat-pounding police work.

Sometimes, of course, it takes the boring step-by-step trace through a program to pin down a really subtle problem. More often, though, the debug artist will absorb clues from the way the bug manifests itself. Often, the things that *don't* happen reveal more than the things that *do* happen, as Sherlock Holmes observed in *Hound of the Baskervilles* about the dog's failure to bark at night. The debug artist then leaps directly to the root cause by what looks to others as either a feat of magic or an uncommonly good guess.

To learn the art of debugging, you'll need to choose a set of debugging tools that fits the way you personally prefer to work. Yet before you can make that choice, you must learn at least the beginnings of the art. Although this may seem to be a catch-22 situation, it's just typical of everything that happens in the wacky world of debugging!

I can show you enough of the art so that you can wisely select your first set of tools. But first let's take a quick look at the tools that are available.

The Two General Classes of Tools

Software and hardware *debuggers* are development tools that simplify the task of tracking and exterminating software bugs. Software debuggers (such as DEBUG, CodeView, and Turbo Debugger) are memory-resident and work from within memory. Hardware debuggers usually combine a hardware computer card with software to provide external debugging capabilities.

Which group of debuggers is *better* depends on the type of bugs you anticipate. If you are an applications programmer, software debuggers usually fill the bill. But for system-level programmers as well as for applications programmers who develop software designed to operate in real-time using interrupts, hardware debuggers can make life much easier. The types of glitches that crop up in such programs can easily lock up a computer, rendering software debuggers useless.

Software Debuggers

Software debuggers range in price from free (DEBUG) to more than $500. Higher-priced debuggers usually offer advanced features that may make the investment worthwhile. For example, if your programming time is worth $40 an hour, just a few hours lost to manual debugging (using a free debugger) would justify the cost of a higher-priced commercial system. Many programmers have found that the time saved locating a single bug more than offsets the cost of the debugger.

Typically, software debuggers are written to monitor (in a controlled way) the operation of the target program. These debuggers load themselves in RAM and then load the program to be debugged into a work area where the debugger can control execution of the program.

Benign observers, software debuggers ignorantly follow instructions. If you instruct the debugger to execute a section of code, it will attempt to do so, sometimes destroying itself in the process. For example, if an errant program causes a sector to be loaded from disk into RAM at the place where the debugging software resides, the debugging session will come to a screeching halt, and the debugger will do nothing to stop the error. Totally isolating a software-only debugger is impossible.

Hardware Debuggers

Hardware debuggers come in a variety of shapes, sizes, and capabilities. They typically consist of both hardware and software components. Usually, the hardware component is either a card that fits in an expansion slot of the computer, or a device that is placed between the microprocessor and the system board. The software component may be similar to the previously described software debuggers, or it may reside in ROM on the hardware board.

Hardware debuggers, which are much more expensive than software debuggers, can range in price from $200 to almost $8,000. The prices vary according to the type of hardware debugger, the types of options added, and the type of computer you will use.

The more expensive systems usually require a second computer to monitor the functioning of the first. These systems are called *in-circuit emulators* or *in-circuit devices*. With systems such as these, you can come as close as possible to total system isolation.

As with software debuggers, the time saved in the development process may justify the cost of a hardware debugger. Hardware debuggers are best suited for systems-level or interrupt-driven software programs, which are prone to bugs that are virtually impossible to ferret out with software debuggers only.

And hardware debuggers offer greater control over the program environment than their software-only counterparts. By using the *nonmaskable interrupt* (NMI) line of the processor, hardware debuggers usually provide a way for you to recover system control at virtually any time, even if the computer has "hung." Such a brute-force method of seizing control of the computer seldom fails to work.

Some Software Debuggers Compared

To help you get a feel for how software debuggers compare, I'll describe the commands and general usage of half a dozen. These programs should be available at no extra cost as parts of the assembler and high-level language packages. Although you are unlikely to have all of them on hand, you should have two or three from this group available, no matter what assembler and language you choose.

Built-In, High-Level Language Debuggers

If you are using any of the Quick languages, the Programmer's WorkBench from Microsoft, or the Turbo languages from Borland, your language's Integrated Development Environment (the full-screen editor and compiler combo normally used for program development) has a built-in debugging tool. This tool tracks each high-level language source statement so that you can *watch* any variable you specify.

These debuggers are quite useful for finding problems in the high-level language code itself; they are much less useful for attempting to find problems in assembly language modules called from the high-level language. The reason for this is that these debuggers make it difficult or impossible to see what is going on in the CPU registers while stepping through your assembly language modules, and the register contents provide many of the clues about what is going wrong.

With Microsoft's Quick languages, you can set watch variables with the register names and see those variables change; Borland's Turbo languages, however, require that you set the pseudovariables (_AX for AX, and so forth) in the watch window so that you can see what is happening. Apparently, neither language can enable you to view the result in the FLAGS register.

The major use I have found for the built-in debuggers in this situation is to verify that the problem really *is* in the assembly language module and not elsewhere in the high-level program. However, once the trouble has been isolated to the assembly language area, you have to switch to a tool that can show you everything that is happening there. For this, you need one of the separate debugging utilities.

DEBUG, the Standard

You probably already have a copy of DEBUG on your DOS distribution disk. Only a few versions of DOS omit it, although the documentation for the program was moved over to the extra-cost *Technical Reference Manual* at version 3.3.

Although the axiom "you get what you pay for" is often true, DEBUG is a notable exception. This "free" program (free in the sense that most DOS users don't even know it's part of the package they pay for—it comes at no extra cost) has most of the capability of any other software debugger. It can be used for just about anything except tracing the operation of DOS itself; that requires a hardware debugger and a separate system connected to it!

Once you know how to handle DEBUG, you can quickly learn just about any other software debugger. DEBUG's only serious shortcoming is that it does not provide source-program display and tracking.

DEBUG recognizes two special file extensions, EXE and HEX, and treats files that have them differently from all others. The program loads any EXE file into memory just as the DOS loader would, using the file's relocation information to do the loading, and then discarding the information from the file. For this reason EXE files cannot be written back to disk; they're not all there by the time you see the first DEBUG prompt.

The other special file extension, HEX, is seldom used today except with embedded systems, although in the days of CP/M, HEX files were the standard output of assemblers. Files with the HEX extension undergo a conversion similar to that of EXE files, and, like EXE files, cannot be written back to disk from DEBUG.

All other files are treated as memory images, like COM files, and are loaded at an offset of 0100h; if you debug BIN files or device drivers, both of which begin at offset 0000h, all assigned addresses will be 0100h too high.

DEBUG provides the 24 commands listed in table 7.1. The commands discussed in this chapter reflect the version of DEBUG distributed with DOS 5; your version may provide fewer commands. Normally, only about half these commands are used during a debugging session. The most frequently used commands are indicated by an asterisk (*) after the command letter.

Table 7.1. *The DEBUG command set.*

Command	Meaning
?	Display help screen
A *	Assemble
C	Compare
D *	Dump
E *	Enter
F	Fill
G *	Go
H *	Hexadecimal arithmetic
I	Input
L	Load
M	Move
N	Name
O	Output
P *	Proceed through operation
Q *	Quit
R *	Register
S *	Search
T *	Trace into operation
U *	Unassemble
W	Write
XA	Allocate expanded memory
XD	Deallocate expanded memory
XM	Map expanded memory
XS	Expanded memory status

To invoke any of these commands, enter the command character in either upper- or lowercase, and then enter any parameters that the command may require. In this chapter's examples of DEBUG commands, the command and any required parameters are shown in this typeface, with optional parameters in *this one*.

DEBUG does not require any delimiters between commands and parameters, except when two hexadecimal numbers are entered as separate parameters. In all other instances, delimiters are optional, although you may find that using them makes the commands you enter more readable. A delimiter can be either a space or a comma; use a colon as the delimiter between the segment and offset of a hexadecimal address.

Commands are executed when you press Enter, not as you type them. You can change a line by pressing the backspace key to delete what you have typed and then type the correct characters. When the command line is as you want it, press Enter to execute the entire line.

DEBUG does not detect errors until you have pressed Enter. If you make a syntax error in an entry, the command line is redisplayed with the word error added at the point at which the error was detected. If a command line contains more than one error, only the first error is detected and indicated, and execution ceases at that point.

Let's examine each of the DEBUG commands. (Discussions in later sections of this chapter about the more advanced, source-level debuggers describe only the commands needed to get through a sample debugging session.)

Display Help Screen (?)

Once you are within DEBUG, using the question mark produces a screen of information that briefly recaps the syntax for DEBUG commands. Using this command with the DOS 5 version of DEBUG produces the following:

```
-?
assemble     A [address]
compare      C range address
dump         D [range]
enter        E address [list]
fill         F range list
go           G [=address] [addresses]
hex          H value1 value2
input        I port
load         L [address] [drive] [firstsector] [number]
move         M range address
name         N [pathname] [arglist]
output       O port byte
proceed      P [=address] [number]
quit         Q
register     R [register]
search       S range list
trace        T [=address] [value]
unassemble   U [range]
write        W [address] [drive] [firstsector] [number]
```

```
allocate expanded memory        XA [#pages]
deallocate expanded memory      XD [handle]
map expanded memory pages       XM [Lpage] [Ppage] [handle]
display expanded memory status  XS
```

Assemble (A)

The Assemble command is used for entering assembly language mnemonics and for having them translated directly into machine language instructions in memory. This capability is extremely helpful for making on-the-fly changes to a program and for entering short test programs. The syntax for this command is

A *address*

address is an optional beginning address (hexadecimal) at which the assembled machine language instructions are placed. If you do not specify an address, DEBUG starts placing the instructions either at CS:0100 or after the last machine language instruction entered through Assemble.

Virtually every assembly language mnemonic, including segment override specifiers (CS:, DS:, ES:, SS:), is supported. There are one or two differences, however, between the standard mnemonics and DEBUG's implementation of them. First, because DEBUG cannot differentiate between NEAR and FAR returns, RET is assumed to be a near return, and RETF to be a far return.

Also, when a command line you enter refers to memory locations, DEBUG cannot always determine whether you want to act on a byte or on a word at that location. In the following example:

DEC [42B]

it is not clear whether a byte or a word should be decremented at that location. To overcome this ambiguity, you must indicate explicitly which you intend. To do so, use BYTE PTR or WORD PTR, as in the following amended example:

DEC BYTE PTR [42B]

Clearly, such explicitness is not always necessary, as in this example:

MOV AL,[42B]

Because only a byte can be moved into AL, using BYTE PTR here would be redundant.

The Assemble command lets you use DB and DW (in addition to the regular 8088 and 8087 assembly language mnemonics) to define data areas.

Each line is assembled after you press Enter. If DEBUG cannot determine what you want when you enter a certain mnemonic, it flags the error and does not assemble that line.

When you have finished using the Assemble command, press Enter to return to the DEBUG dash prompt.

Compare (C)

The Compare command compares and reports on any differences between the contents of two memory blocks. The syntax for this command is

```
C block1 address
```

block1 is either both the beginning and ending addresses or, if preceded by an *l*, the beginning address and length of the first memory block. *address* is the start of the second memory block. The length of the second block is assumed to be equal to the length of the first. The memory blocks can overlap, and the second block can lie physically before the first.

The command compares the two blocks, byte-by-byte, and reports any differences in the following format:

```
address1    value1      value2    address2
```

Dump (D)

The Dump command is one you will use often. It displays the contents of a series of memory locations. The syntax for the command is

```
D address1 address2
```

You must specify *address1*, an optional starting address for the display, before you can specify *address2*, an optional ending address.

If no addresses are specified, DEBUG starts displaying memory locations with DS:0100 or, if Dump already has been used, with the byte following the last byte displayed by the most recent Dump command.

Dump always displays 16 bytes per line, beginning with the nearest paragraph (16-byte) boundary. This display rule may differ with the first and last lines displayed, because you may have asked DEBUG to start the dump with a memory location that was not on a paragraph boundary.

If you do not specify an ending address, DEBUG always displays 128 bytes of memory. Each byte is shown in both hexadecimal and ASCII representation, as in the following example:

```
-D 2C5
126F:02C0                   0F 00 03-D1 52 57 36 FF 2E AC 04      ....RW6....
126F:02D0  58 5F 07 8B DE BE 00 05-8B 0E 40 05 3D 53 59 74   X_........@.=SYt
126F:02E0  4F 3D 48 50 74 4A 3D 49-4E 74 45 BE 54 04 8B 0E   O=HPtJ=INtE.T...
126F:02F0  51 04 3D 42 4F 74 39 26-80 3D 00 74 16 26 80 7D   Q.=BOt9&.=.t.&.}
126F:0300  01 3A 75 0F 26 8A 15 80-CA 20 80 EA 60 8A C2 FE   :u.&.... ..'...
126F:0310  C8 EB 06 B4 19 CD 21 32-D2 04 41 AA B8 3A 5C AB   ......!2..A..:\.
126F:0320  8C C0 8E D8 87 FE B4 47-CD 21 87 FE 73 12 EB 0D   .......G.!..s...
126F:0330  83 F9 03 74 01 49 D1 E9-73 01 A4 F3 A5 32 C0 AA   ...t.I..s....2..
126F:0340  8B F3 36 FF 2E                                     ..6..
```

Reading from left to right, notice that each line shows the address of the first byte, followed by eight bytes, a hyphen, and the remaining eight bytes of the paragraph. The rightmost characters on each line are the ASCII representation of the hexadecimal values in the paragraph. Note also that if a specific hexadecimal value has no corresponding ASCII character, a period is used as a placeholder.

Enter (E)

To try temporary fixes during a session, you frequently need to use the Enter command. It enables you to change the contents of specific memory locations. The syntax for this command is

E *address changes*

address is the beginning address for entering changes, and *changes* is an optional list of the changes to be made.

You can specify *changes* on the command line in any combination of hexadecimal numbers or ASCII characters. (ASCII characters must be enclosed in quotation marks.)

If you do not specify changes on the command line, DEBUG enters a special entry mode in which the values of memory locations, beginning at *address*, are displayed. You can change these values one byte at a time. (Be sure to enter the changes as hexadecimal numbers.) After each entry, press the space bar to effect the change. The next byte is then displayed so that you can make any necessary changes. To exit entry mode and return to DEBUG command mode, press Enter.

If you enter a minus sign or hyphen as part of a change to a byte, DEBUG goes back one byte to the preceding memory location. You can then make additional changes to that byte.

If you have not made any changes to a byte, press the space bar to proceed to the next byte. The unchanged byte retains its original value.

Fill (F)

Use this command to fill a block of memory with a specific value or series of values. The syntax for this command is

```
F block fillvalue
```

block is either both the beginning and ending addresses or, if preceded by an *l*, the beginning address and length of the memory block. *fillvalue* is the byte value(s) that should be used to fill the memory block. If *fillvalue* represents fewer bytes than are needed to fill the *block*, the series is repeated until the *block* is completed.

fillvalue may be any combination of hexadecimal numbers or ASCII characters. (Any ASCII characters must be enclosed in quotation marks.)

As an example, either of the following command lines fills (with a null value) the memory block DS:0000 through DS:00FF:

```
F DS:0000 00FF 0
F DS:0000 LFF 0
```

To fill the same area with the hexadecimal equivalents of the ASCII characters "ALW", followed by a carriage return and a line feed, you would use either of the following command lines:

```
F DS:0000 00FF "ALW"D A
F DS:0000 LFF "ALW"D A
```

Remember that the five values (41, 4C, 57, 0D, and 0A) are repeated again and again until all 256 bytes have been filled.

Go (G)

The Go command, which causes machine language statements to be executed, is one of the most frequently used DEBUG commands. If you are debugging a program, this command executes the program you have loaded. It also lets you specify optional *breakpoints*, which are addresses at which program execution will stop. The syntax for the Go command is

```
G =start break1 break2 ... break10
```

=*start* is an optional starting address, and *break1* through *break10* are optional breakpoint addresses. If the starting address is not specified, Go begins program execution with the current address contained in CS:IP.

If the breakpoints are not reached, execution continues until the program ends. If you specify only an offset for a breakpoint address, CS is assumed to be the segment.

To facilitate a breakpoint, DEBUG replaces the code at the breakpoint address with the hexadecimal value CC, which is the code for an interrupt. If DEBUG reaches the interrupt (the breakpoint), all breakpoints are returned to their original values, the registers are displayed (as though by the R command), and program execution stops. If DEBUG never reaches the breakpoint, the values at the breakpoints remain in their changed state.

Hexadecimal Arithmetic (H)

This convenience command does simple hexadecimal addition and subtraction. If you are using a hexadecimal calculator, you may never need to issue this command. The syntax for this command is

H *value1* *value2*

value1 and *value2* are hexadecimal numbers. This command returns a result line that shows two values: the sum of *value1* and *value2*, and the difference between *value1* and *value2*. This command does not alter any registers or flags.

The following examples show how the H command is used. In the first example, AHh and BFh are added, which results in 016Dh, and then subtracted, resulting in FFEFh:

```
-H AE BF
016D  FFEF
```

The second example performs the same operations with 96h and C2h:

```
-H 96 C2
0158  FFD4
```

Input (I)

The Input command (the opposite of the Output command) fetches a byte from a port. The syntax is

I *port*

port is the address of the specified port to read. The Input command fetches a byte from the desired port and then displays it as a hexadecimal value. This command does not change any registers or flags.

Load (L)

The Load command (the opposite of the Write command) is used to load a file or disk sectors into memory. The syntax is

```
L buffer drivenum startsector numsector
```

buffer is the destination memory address for the information to be loaded. *drivenum* is an optional numeric disk-drive designator. *startsector* is the absolute disk sector (a hexadecimal number) with which to begin reading, and *numsector* is the total number of disk sectors (a hexadecimal number) to read.

drivenum, the drive specification, is such that 0=A, 1=B, 2=C, and so on. In *numsector*, no more than 128 (80h) sectors can be loaded.

If you do not provide the *drivenum startsector numsector* combination, DEBUG assumes that you want to load a file, in which case the *buffer* address is optional. If you do not specify an address, DEBUG loads the file at CS:0100. Use the Name command (described shortly) to specify the name of the file.

After a file has been loaded, BX:CX contains the number of bytes successfully read, provided that the file does not have an EXE extension. If the file has an EXE extension, BX:CX is set to the size of the program.

Move (M)

The Move command moves a block of memory from one location to another. The syntax is

```
M block1 address
```

block1 is either both the beginning and ending addresses or, if preceded by an *l*, the beginning address and length of the first memory block. *address* is the destination address for the move. The destination address and the source block can overlap. The bytes from the source block are moved, one at a time, to the destination address.

Name (N)

The Name command is used to specify a file name to be used either by the Load and Write commands or by the program you are debugging. The syntax of this command is

N *filename1 filename2*

filename1 is the complete file specification that is parsed and placed in a file control block at CS:005C. *filename2* is the complete file specification that is parsed and placed in a file control block at CS:006C.

In addition to parsing the file specifications, DEBUG places them (as entered) at CS:0081, preceded by a byte indicating the number of bytes entered. DEBUG then sets AX to indicate the parsing status (validity) of the file specifications, with AL corresponding to the first file and AH to the second. If either file name is invalid, its corresponding byte is set to 1; otherwise, it is set to 0.

Output (O)

The Output command (the opposite of the Input command) outputs a byte to a specified port. The syntax is

O *port value*

port is the address of the specified port, and *value* is the hexadecimal byte to write. This command does not change any registers or flags.

Proceed (P)

The Proceed command is available only with DEBUG programs distributed with DOS 3.0 or later versions. Using this command, you can execute machine language instructions in a single step, treating a CALL or an INT as a single instruction and performing the entire action with no pause, after which the register status is displayed (as with the Register command). The syntax of the Proceed command is

P =*start count*

Both of these parameters are optional; =*start* is a starting address and *count* is a hexadecimal number that signifies how many individual instructions must be traced through to execute the command. If =*start* is not specified, execution begins with the current address contained in CS:IP. If *count* is excluded, only one machine language instruction is executed.

The P command differs from T only in its handling of the CALL and INT instructions; P executes the entire called routine before pausing, whereas T executes only the transfer of control and then pauses at the first instruction of the called routine.

Quit (Q)

The Quit command is used to quit DEBUG and return control of the computer to DOS. You simply press *Q*. There are no parameters for this command, which does not save the programs on which you were working.

Register (R)

The Register command displays the microprocessor's register and flag values, and enables you to change individual register values. The command's syntax is

R *register*

register, the optional name of the register to modify, may be any of the following: AX, BX, CX, DX, SP, BP, SI, DI, DS, ES, SS, CS, IP, PC, or F. IP and PC are synonymous; both refer to the instruction pointer register. F refers to the flags register.

If you enter the Register command with no parameters, DEBUG responds by displaying a register summary similar to the following:

```
-r
AX=0000  BX=0000  CX=0000  DX=0000  SP=FFEE  BP=0000  SI=0000  DI=0000
DS=1206  ES=1206  SS=1206  CS=1206  IP=0100   NV UP EI PL NZ NA PO NC
1206:0100 FB            STI
-
```

If you enter a register name as a parameter, DEBUG displays the current register value and waits for you to enter a new value. If you enter a value, it is assumed to be in hexadecimal. If you do not enter a value, no change is made to the register value.

(For more information on the Register command, refer to this chapter's "Using DEBUG" section.)

Search (S)

With the Search command, you can search a block of memory for a specific sequence of values. The syntax is

S *block searchvalue*

block is either both the beginning and ending addresses or, if preceded by an *l*, the beginning address and length of the first memory block. *searchvalue* is the byte value(s) you want to search for in the memory block.

The values that DEBUG searches for can be any combination of hexadecimal numbers and ASCII characters. (ASCII characters must be enclosed in quotation marks.)

If DEBUG locates any exact matches, it displays the address of the beginning of the match. If no matches are found, no message is displayed.

Trace (T)

Using the Trace command, you can execute machine language instructions in a single step, after which the register status is displayed (as with the Register command). The syntax of the Trace command is

```
T =start count
```

Both of these parameters are optional; =start is a starting address, and count is a hexadecimal number that signifies how many individual instructions must be traced through to execute the command. If =start is not specified, execution begins with the current address contained in CS:IP. If count is excluded, only one machine language instruction will be executed.

The T command differs from P only in its handling of the CALL and INT instructions; T executes only the transfer of control and then pauses at the first instruction of the called routine, but P executes the entire called routine before pausing.

Unassemble (U)

The Unassemble command decodes the values of a group of memory locations into 8088 mnemonics. One of the most frequently used DEBUG commands, Unassemble enables you to view the instructions that are executed during the DEBUG operation. The syntax is as follows:

```
U address range
```

address, which is optional, is the beginning address of the area to be unassembled. range, which is optional if address is specified, is either the ending address of the area or, if preceded by an l, the length of the area. If you specify an address but no range, approximately one screenful of data is displayed.

If you do not specify an address or range, unassembly begins with the memory location indicated by CS:IP or (if Unassemble has already been used) with the byte following the last byte displayed by the most recent Unassemble command. The unassembly proceeds for 16 bytes. The number of instruction lines this process represents depends on the number of bytes used in each instruction line. If you specify an address and a range, all bytes within that block are unassembled.

(The Unassemble command is used extensively in this chapter's "Debugging TEST.EXE" section.)

Write (W)

The Write command (the opposite of the Load command) is used to write a file or individual disk sectors to a disk. The syntax is

```
W buffer drivenum startsector numsector
```

buffer is the memory address of the information to be written; *drivenum* is an optional numeric disk-drive designator; *startsector* is the absolute disk sector (a hexadecimal number) at which writing is to begin; and *numsector* is the total number of disk sectors (a hexadecimal number) to be written.

The drive specification, *drivenum*, is such that 0=A, 1=B, 2=C, and so on. In *numsector*, the number of sectors loaded cannot exceed 128, or 80h.

If you do not provide the *drivenum startsector numsector* combination, DEBUG assumes that you want to write a file; the buffer address is then optional. If you do not specify an address, DEBUG assumes that the start of the file is CS:0100. (Use the Name command to specify the name of the file.)

Before a file is written, BX:CX must be set to the number of bytes to be written.

As noted previously, two types of files cannot be written back to disk: those with an extension of EXE and those with an extension of HEX. The distinction is made solely on the file name's extension; if necessary, you could use the N command to change the name and then write the file. However, the file that is written will be significantly different from the one that DEBUG read into memory. What is written will be a straight memory image. Thus, an EXE file will not be able to be properly loaded by DOS because it is no longer relocatable. Similarly, a HEX file is saved in ASCII text format by DEBUG.

Allocate Expanded Memory (XA)

This command was added beginning with DOS 5. If your system has expanded memory and an expanded-memory driver installed that conforms to the 4.0 LIM standard, this command allows you to allocate pages of expanded memory.

The syntax for this command is

```
XA pages
```

where *pages* is the number of EMS pages desired. Each page is equivalent to 16K of expanded memory. DEBUG displays an error message if the requested memory is not available or if you omit the *pages* parameter.

Deallocate Expanded Memory (XD)

This command was added beginning with DOS 5. If your system has expanded memory and an expanded-memory driver installed that conforms to the 4.0 LIM standard, this command allows you to deallocate pages of expanded memory.

The syntax for this command is

```
XD handle
```

where *handle* is the EMS handle number for a specific block of EMS. If you previously used the XA command, this is the number returned when memory was allocated.

Be careful not to inadvertently deallocate memory allocated to other programs that may be in memory. If you do, the results are unpredictable.

Map Expanded Memory (XM)

This command was added beginning with DOS 5. If your system has expanded memory and an expanded-memory driver installed that conforms to the 4.0 LIM standard, this command allows you to specify a relationship between logical and physical pages of expanded memory. The syntax for this command is

```
XM logical physical handle
```

The relationship between each parameter is as follows: *logical* page of expanded memory, using a specific *handle*, is mapped to the *physical* page you also specify.

Expanded Memory Status (XS)

This command was added beginning with DOS 5. If your system has expanded memory and an expanded-memory driver installed that conforms to the 4.0 LIM standard, this command allows you to view information about how expanded memory is being used in your system.

There are no parameters for this command. When you enter it, DEBUG responds with a list of EMS handles and the number of pages allocated to each handle. Following that is a list of physical EMS pages and associated frame segments.

For instance, the following is a typical expanded-memory status display provided by this command:

```
-xs
Handle 0000 has 0024 pages allocated
Handle 0001 has 0004 pages allocated
Handle 0002 has 0080 pages allocated
Handle 0003 has 0003 pages allocated

Physical page 04 = Frame segment 1000
Physical page 05 = Frame segment 1400
Physical page 06 = Frame segment 1800
Physical page 07 = Frame segment 1C00
Physical page 08 = Frame segment 2000
Physical page 09 = Frame segment 2400
Physical page 0A = Frame segment 2800
Physical page 0B = Frame segment 2C00
Physical page 0C = Frame segment 3000
Physical page 0D = Frame segment 3400
Physical page 0E = Frame segment 3800
Physical page 0F = Frame segment 3C00
Physical page 10 = Frame segment 4000
Physical page 11 = Frame segment 4400
Physical page 12 = Frame segment 4800
Physical page 13 = Frame segment 4C00
Physical page 14 = Frame segment 5000
Physical page 15 = Frame segment 5400
Physical page 16 = Frame segment 5800
Physical page 17 = Frame segment 5C00
Physical page 18 = Frame segment 6000
Physical page 19 = Frame segment 6400
Physical page 1A = Frame segment 6800
Physical page 1B = Frame segment 6C00
Physical page 1C = Frame segment 7000
Physical page 1D = Frame segment 7400
Physical page 1E = Frame segment 7800
Physical page 1F = Frame segment 7C00
Physical page 20 = Frame segment 8000
Physical page 21 = Frame segment 8400
Physical page 22 = Frame segment 8800
Physical page 23 = Frame segment 8C00
Physical page 24 = Frame segment 9000
Physical page 25 = Frame segment 9400
Physical page 26 = Frame segment 9800
```

continues

```
Physical page 27 = Frame segment 9C00
Physical page 00 = Frame segment E000
Physical page 01 = Frame segment E400
Physical page 02 = Frame segment E800
Physical page 03 = Frame segment EC00

 AB of a total   EC EMS pages have been allocated
  4 of a total   40 EMS handles have been allocated
```

Clearly, this is more than one screenful of information. Because it scrolls by quickly, you may need to use Ctrl-S or the Pause key to halt the display temporarily.

CodeView from Microsoft

As you will see a bit later when you go through the debugging technique with TEST.EXE (created in Chapter 5), making effective use of DEBUG with programs generated by a high-level language requires some extra effort to get past the "invisible" start-up code that all high-level languages include in their output programs.

Because of this, *source-level debuggers* have become popular. One of the first of these utilities was Microsoft's CodeView. First distributed with the Microsoft C Compiler version 4.0, it is now packed with all the upper-echelon Microsoft language products. The version used for these examples came as part of the MASM 6.0 package.

Microsoft's manual describes CodeView as "a powerful, window-oriented tool that enables you to track down logical errors in programs." That's an accurate description. Like DEBUG, CodeView enables you to step through the execution of your program one operation at a time. Unlike DEBUG, it can also show you your source program in the language in which you wrote it, and perform entire statements without pause; yet when you need the single-step capability, that's present also.

You can use CodeView with any executable program, either COM or EXE. To take full advantage of the debugger's capabilities, however, you must create an EXE file, using the special CodeView options during all steps of its creation, to get all the symbolic information from your source programs to a place where CodeView can use it.

This means that your high-level language code and your assembly language modules should all be compiled or assembled, using the /Zi or /Zd options, to put the information into the OBJ files. Then when you do the linking, you should use the /CO option to move this information to the EXE file.

Only when you do all this can CodeView show you your source program, line-by-line, and replace the hex memory addresses in the register window with the names of your variables. Because these options are available only in Microsoft products, you will not be able to take full advantage of CodeView if you're a Turbo user. But as you will soon see, you're not left out in the cold, either.

Unlike DEBUG, whose 24 simple commands mainly follow the same syntax as CodeView's commands, CodeView offers an extensive list of command variations. The entries for "Commands" fill 1 1/2 pages in the CodeView manual's index (and those are the major references only).

For routine debugging, however, you need only a few of the available commands. Those that I have found essential are listed in table 7.2. Notice that, unlike DEBUG, many of these "commands" are actually "hot-key" operations; that is, all you do is press the function key, and the command executes. You need to press Enter only for the Q (quit) action.

***Table* 7.2.** *Essential CodeView commands.*

Key	Action
F1	Display on-line help screens
F2	Open Registers window (display registers)
F5	Go (same as DEBUG's G)
F8	Trace (same as DEBUG's T)
F9	Set breakpoint at cursor location
F10	Proceed (same as DEBUG's P)
P	Proceed (same as DEBUG)
Q	Quit
R	Register (same as DEBUG)
T	Trace (same as DEBUG)

When you call CodeView with a program file, as explained later in this chapter, CodeView automatically brings in the program's source code if that code is available in the current directory. If the source code is not available, or the program file does not contain debugging information, the debugger automatically goes into "machine language" mode, which provides a display much like that of DEBUG.

You can move the screen cursor by using the arrow keys or a mouse. As you step through a program, using either F8 or F10, the highlight bar moves with you. When you get to the assembly language module, if you use F8 so that you do not step right over the module, the display changes to show the ASM source code.

That characteristic makes CodeView much simpler to use than DEBUG, as you will see when you step through a session with DEBUG. If you have CodeView available, you may choose to use DEBUG only when you cannot spare the memory that CodeView requires.

Turbo Debugger from Borland

Borland describes Turbo Debugger as a state-of-the-art source-level debugger designed for Turbo language programmers and those using other languages who want a more powerful debugging environment. Turbo Debugger *does* offer several features not present in the other programs discussed in this chapter. Among the most notable are its ability to take advantage of the 80386 chip's capability to run multiple virtual machines, and its provisions for remote debugging.

For the average DOS user, however, Turbo Debugger's major advantage is that it's designed especially for compatibility with the Turbo programming-language packages, and meshes with them more easily than CodeView. For example, the screen layout and menu choices are similar to those found in the integrated development environments of Borland's Turbo and C++ languages.

Similarly, where possible the command and function keys serve the same purposes: F3 calls up the pick list, Alt-X exits, and so forth. The essential keys and commands needed for using Turbo Debugger are listed in table 7.3. As in all the Turbo environments, a context-sensitive reminder bar across the bottom of the screen shows you the most essential items at all times.

Table 7.3. Essential commands for Turbo Debugger.

Key	Action
F1	Display help screen
Alt-F1	Display last help used
F2	Set breakpoint at cursor
F7	Trace (like DEBUG's T)
F8	Proceed (like DEBUG's P)
F9	Go (like DEBUG's G)
F10	Use top-of-screen menu
Alt-X	Quit to DOS

Upon entering an assembly language module, Turbo Debugger (like CodeView) can automatically display the source file for each module and switch between source files, provided that the program is compiled, assembled, and linked with all the appropriate options. These options are different for Turbo Debugger than they are for CodeView, however, and EXE files prepared for CodeView debugging must be processed through a TDCONVRT utility to change them to the TD format. Then they are no longer compatible with CodeView.

This incompatibility with CodeView is not likely to be a major factor. You probably will choose (and stick with) either CodeView or Turbo Debugger. Only in most unusual circumstances would you find it useful to convert repeatedly between the two debugger-data EXE-file formats.

The General Techniques

This section will give you enough experience with the art of debugging to make informed decisions about which debugging tool best fits your own ways of working. An example of a debugging session leads you through a problem that, although somewhat artificial, is typical of many real-life bugs: those accidentally caused by a typing error, which result in a subtle code flaw so similar to the intended code that it slips by proofreading.

The initial, step-by-step description of how to debug this error uses a tool you most likely already have, DEBUG. Then I'll go through the same exercise much more briefly using the other three debugging tools to show you how they differ from DEBUG and from each other.

Using DEBUG

You should already have DEBUG because it is normally supplied with DOS. This section describes the basics of using DEBUG and takes you step-by-step through a sample debugging session.

Loading DEBUG by Itself

You can begin a DEBUG session with or without a file. The simplest way to start is without a file. At the DOS prompt, enter

DEBUG

After you enter this command, a dash appears on-screen at the left edge of the next line. This dash, which is DEBUG's prompt character, tells you that DEBUG is awaiting your command. If you see any other message, chances are that you have misspelled DEBUG or that DEBUG.COM is not available on the current disk drive.

At the DEBUG prompt, type the letter R in either upper- or lowercase, and press Enter. The screen display should be similar to the following:

```
C>debug
-r
AX=0000  BX=0000  CX=0000  DX=0000  SP=FFEE  BP=0000  SI=0000  DI=0000
DS=1206  ES=1206  SS=1206  CS=1206  IP=0100    NV UP EI PL NZ NA PO NC
1206:0100 FB            STI
-
```

This entire display is the basic DEBUG "status line." (On your screen, the numbers and letters on the line that starts with DS= may be different from those shown here.) The R you entered is DEBUG's Register command, which causes DEBUG to display the contents of the CPU registers.

As you learned in Chapter 1, AX, BX, CX, and DX are general-purpose registers. Ordinarily, they are the ones used for direct data manipulation. The other registers (SP, BP, SI, DI, DS, ES, SS, CS, and IP) are specialized registers. When you start DEBUG, the registers AX, BX, CX, DX, BP, SI, and DI are all set to zero.

The characters NV, UP, EI, PL, NZ, NA, PO, and NC are the settings of each of the bits in the flags register. Table 7.4 shows the possible display values for each flag, depending on the flag setting. Note that in the Condition column, *set* denotes a value of 1 in the corresponding register bit, and *clear* denotes a value of 0.

The current disassembled values of the code segment and the offset are displayed in the bottom line. 1206, the value of the code segment (CS) register, is used as the segment; 0100, the value of the instruction pointer (IP) register, is used as the offset.

When you enter DEBUG without a file, the value shown for disassembly could be almost anything because you have not instructed DEBUG to initialize the memory area. In this instance, the byte at 1206:0100 contains the value FBh, which is the numeric value for the mnemonic instruction STI.

To end the DEBUG session and return to DOS, press Q (for Quit) and then press Enter.

Now let's look at the other way to start DEBUG.

Table 7.4. *Status-flag display characteristics for DEBUG.*

Status flag	Condition	Meaning	Display
Overflow	Set	Yes	OV
	Clear	No	NV
Direction	Set	Decrement	DN
	Clear	Increment	UP
Interrupt	Set	Enabled	EI
	Clear	Disabled	DI
Sign	Set	Negative	NG
	Clear	Positive	PL
Zero	Set	Yes	ZR
	Clear	No	NZ
Auxiliary carry	Set	Yes	AC
	Clear	No	NA
Parity	Set	Even	PE
	Clear	Odd	PO
Carry	Set	Yes	CY
	Clear	No	NC

Loading DEBUG with a File

The other way to begin a DEBUG session is to specify the file you want to debug. Suppose, for example, that you want to debug a file called TEST.COM. To load DEBUG and then TEST.COM, enter the following line at the DOS prompt:

```
DEBUG TEST.COM
```

If DEBUG cannot find the specified file, you see an error message, and DEBUG continues as though you had not entered a file name. Should this happen, you must do either of the following:

❏ Use the Q command to exit DEBUG and then, using the proper file specification, start over. (I prefer this option because it lets me verify the file specification.)

❏ Use the N command to correct the file name, followed by the L command to load the correct file. (These commands are described earlier in the chapter.)

If the program you are debugging requires command-line parameters to function, simply add the parameters to the line invoking DEBUG. For instance, if TEST.COM needed a drive specification as a parameter, you would enter:

```
DEBUG TEST.COM B:
```

After DEBUG has loaded TEST.COM, you see the dash prompt—DEBUG is ready and waiting for a command. If you enter the Register command, the status display is similar to the one shown in the preceding section. But this time the BX:CX register pair equal the number of bytes loaded from the file TEST.COM. All other registers and flags should be equivalent to the default settings DEBUG uses when no file has been loaded.

Debugging TEST.EXE

Now that you are familiar with starting and quitting DEBUG and with the DEBUG commands, let's see how DEBUG functions in a real-life debugging session. First, you put a bug in the assembly language subroutine of the TEST.EXE program (developed in Chapter 5) so that there's a reason for the search. Then, using DEBUG, you step through the faulty program to find out why it isn't working.

The bug to be introduced is a common typing error: reversing the two register names in an ADC command. To create it, modify SUMS.ASM by changing the line labeled S1. The modified listing follows:

```
Page 60,132
Comment ¦
*********************************************************************

File:     SUMS.ASM for Microsoft Macro Assembler 6.0
Author:   Allen L. Wyatt
Date:     8/3/91

Purpose:  Given an integer number X, find the sum of
          X + (X-1) + (X-2) + (X-3) + (X-4) ... + 2 + 1
          Designed to be called from Microsoft C.

Format:   SUMS(X)


*********************************************************************¦

          PUBLIC    sums

          .MODEL    small, C
          .CODE
```

```
sums      PROC C Value:SWORD
          MOV  AX,0              ;Initialize to zero
          MOV  CX,Value          ;Get actual value
          JCXZ S3                ;Num=0, no need to do
S1:       ADC  CX,AX             ;Add row value
          JC   S2                ;Quit if AX overflowed
          LOOP S1                ;Repeat process
          JMP  S3                ;Successful completion
S2:       MOV  AX,0              ;Force a zero
S3:       RET                    ;Return to C
sums      ENDP

          END
```

The change you've made will cause the routine to always return an answer of 0. From this point on, pretend that you do not know what is causing this error. Put yourself in the place of a programmer who has discovered an honest-to-goodness bug in a program.

Assemble the modified routine, and then link it to TEST.OBJ to form a new TEST.EXE. Next, test this version of TEST.EXE to see what happens. If you use the inputs shown in Chapter 5, the following results occur:

```
C:\MASM>TEST
Initial Value: 7
Sorry, the sum has exceeded capacity (7 rows is too many)
Initial Value: 5
Sorry, the sum has exceeded capacity (5 rows is too many)
Initial Value: 22
Sorry, the sum has exceeded capacity (22 rows is too many)
Initial Value: 103
Sorry, the sum has exceeded capacity (103 rows is too many)
Initial Value: 999
Sorry, the sum has exceeded capacity (1 rows is too many)

C:\MASM>_
```

This is not the intent of the program! Clearly, a problem exists. But where in the program or routine is it occurring? We need to start looking. Deductively, we can determine that the SUMS routine, where the returned value always appears to be 0, is a good place to begin the search.

To begin using DEBUG with TEST.EXE, enter

```
DEBUG  TEST.EXE
```

DEBUG should respond with the dash prompt, signaling that it is ready and awaiting a command. To get an idea of where you are in the program, enter the Register command (press R).

```
DEBUG TEST.EXE
-r
AX=0000  BX=0000  CX=2163  DX=0000  SP=0800  BP=0000  SI=0000  DI=0000
DS=0B14  ES=0B14  SS=0D5B  CS=0B24  IP=00C8   NV UP EI PL NZ NA PO NC
0B24:00D4 B430          MOV  AH,30
-
```

This display tells you that TEST.EXE has been loaded, the segment registers have been set properly, and the IP register is loaded correctly with the address of the first program instruction to be executed. Notice that the offset entry address is 00D4h, which is the entry address noted in the MAP file produced by LINK.EXE (refer to Chapter 5). Notice also the values of the segment registers, particularly CS and DS. (The values in your segment registers may be different from those shown here, depending on where in your computer's memory DEBUG has loaded the program.)

Next, use the Unassemble command so that you can look at the first portions of program code:

```
-u
0B24:00C8 B430          MOV   AH,30
0B24:00CA CD21          INT   21
0B24:00CC 3C02          CMP   AL,02
0B24:00CE 7305          JNB   00D5
0B24:00D0 33C0          XOR   AX,AX
0B24:00D2 06            PUSH  ES
0B24:00D3 50            PUSH  AX
0B24:00D4 CB            RETF
0B24:00D5 BFA65A        MOV   DI,0CEA
0B24:00D8 8B360200      MOV   SI,[0002]
0B24:00DC 2BF7          SUB   SI,DI
0B24:00DE 81FE0010      CMP   SI,1000
0B24:00E2 7203          JB    00E7
0B24:00E4 BE0010        MOV   SI,1000
0B24:00E7 FA            CLI
-u
0B24:00E8 8ED7          MOV   SS,DI
0B24:00EA 81C40E07      ADD   SP,070E
0B24:00EE FB            STI
0B24:00EF 7310          JNB   0101
0B24:00F1 16            PUSH  SS
0B24:00F2 1F            POP   DS
```

```
0B24:00F3 E85A02        CALL    0350
0B24:00F6 33C0          XOR     AX,AX
0B24:00F8 50            PUSH    AX
0B24:00F9 E8EB04        CALL    05E7
0B24:00FC B8FF4C        MOV     AX,4CFF
0B24:00FF CD21          INT     21
0B24:0101 8BC6          MOV     AX,SI
0B24:0103 B104          MOV     CL,04
0B24:0105 D3E0          SHL     AX,CL
0B24:0107 48            DEC     AX
-
```

This code is the assembly language translation of the machine language to which the C program (TEST.C) was converted. However, you have deduced that the bug probably is not in the C program; it is in the assembly language subroutine. How do you find it?

One way to find the right subroutine is to use the Search command. But first you must determine what to search for. To do so, you need to look at the contents of the file TEST.LST (shown in Chapter 3) to see what the first several bytes of machine language *should* be. The appropriate code follows:

```
                            .MODEL      small, C
0000                        .CODE

0000              sums       PROC C Value:SWORD
0003  B8 0000               MOV  AX,0            ;Initialize to zero
0006  8B 4E 04              MOV  CX,Value        ;Get actual value
```

Notice that the first machine code bytes generated by the assembler were B8, 00, 00, 8B, 4E, and 04. You will search for these six bytes—a combination unique enough to pinpoint the start of the SUMS subroutine.

Using the Search command, search for these bytes from the beginning of the code segment. Be sure to search an area at least equal to the length of the file.

When you enter

```
-S CS:00 L2163 B8 00 00 8B 4E 04
```

the computer responds

```
0B24:00B3
-
```

Sure enough, this series of bytes occurs at only one point in memory: at offset 00B3h, the entry point for the SUMS subroutine. To view the code, use the Unassemble command. When you enter U B3, the following code is displayed:

```
-u b3
0B24:00B3 B80000        MOV     AX,0000
0B24:00B6 8B4E04        MOV     CX,[BP+04]
0B24:00B9 E30B          JCXZ    00C6
0B24:00BB 13C8          ADC     CX,AX
0B24:00BD 7204          JB      00C3
0B24:00BF E2FA          LOOP    00BB
0B24:00C1 EB03          JMP     00C6
0B24:00C3 B80000        MOV     AX,0000
0B24:00C6 5D            POP     BP
0B24:00C7 C3            RET
0B24:00C8 B430          MOV     AH,30
0B24:00CA CD21          INT     21
0B24:00CC 3C02          CMP     AL,02
0B24:00CE 7305          JNB     00D5
0B24:00D0 33C0          XOR     AX,AX
0B24:00D2 06            PUSH    ES
-
```

This code is the unassembled SUMS routine, beginning at offset 00B3h and continuing through offset 00C7h. It is not the entire routine, as the few bytes preceding offset 00B3h represent code generated automatically by the assembler to save information on the stack. But the important part of the routine begins at 00B3h.

Following this routine, a different one begins at offset 00C8h. (The routine at 00C8h happens to be the startup code for the C program, as Unassembled earlier.)

As you probably have guessed, the search technique can quickly become tedious if you have not one but a dozen or so assembly language modules. Finding just the right one can take quite a while and divert your attention from the more essential task of finding the bug inside it.

A quick way to get to the start of a specific assembly language routine is to go back and edit its source file, inserting the statement INT 3 as the first line after the PROC directive in the module to be located. Then reassemble and relink the file, and bring it into DEBUG. Instead of searching for its first few bytes, however, just press G to let the program begin executing.

INT 3 is referred to as the debugging interrupt, or breakpoint interrupt. When the program gets to your INT 3 operation, it automatically pops back to the DEBUG status line displaying the INT 3 as the current operation. In the present case, the screen would look like this:

```
-g
Initial Value: 5

AX=0002  BX=0EE2  CX=0019  DX=0000  SP=0EDC  BP=0EDC  SI=0420  DI=0420
DS=0CED  ES=0CED  SS=0CED  CS=0B27  IP=00B3   NV UP EI PL NZ NA PE NC
0B27:00B3 CC            INT     3
-
```

To get past this instruction and into the routine itself, use the RIP (*Register Instruction Pointer*) command

```
-rip
IP 00B3
:_
```

and reply with the next address, B4. This command achieves the same effect attained by following the search with a breakpoint.

The RIP command works because the INT 3 instruction is the way that all debuggers make the breakpoint happen. By placing the command right in your source program, you automatically have put a breakpoint exactly where it needs to be.

Because using the INT 3 instruction does require that you take the time to reassemble and relink your program, however, let's use the search technique for this sample session. Remember that we found the one and only occurrence of the target string of bytes at location 00B3.

Now, because you want to see what happens in this routine, simply use the Go command to execute the program through the beginning of SUMS. Because the program runs normally until it reaches the breakpoint, you must answer the question asked by TEST.EXE—for test purposes, enter a 5 at the prompt for an initial value:

```
-g b3
Initial Value: 5

AX=0002  BX=0EE2  CX=0019  DX=0000  SP=0EDC  BP=0EDC  SI=0420  DI=0420
DS=0CEA  ES=0CEA  SS=0CEA  CS=0B24  IP=00B3   NV UP EI PL NZ NA PE NC
0B24:00B3 B80000        MOV     AX,0000
-
```

When DEBUG reaches the specified breakpoint of CS:00B3 (the CS is assumed), program execution stops and the register values are displayed. Now, using the Trace command to step through the routine, you can examine what is happening to the number being passed from C.

```
-t

AX=0000  BX=0EE2  CX=0019  DX=0000  SP=0EDC  BP=0EDC  SI=0420  DI=0420
DS=0CEA  ES=0CEA  SS=0CEA  CS=0B24  IP=00B6   NV UP EI PL NZ NA PE NC
0B24:00B6 8B4E04        MOV     CX,[BP+04]                    SS:0EE0=0005
-
```

After each Trace command is entered, DEBUG executes the previously displayed instruction, which is shown on the unassembled status line, and displays the registers again, as in the following code:

```
-t

AX=0000  BX=0EE2  CX=0005  DX=0000  SP=0EDC  BP=0EDC  SI=0420  DI=0420
DS=0CEA  ES=0CEA  SS=0CEA  CS=0B24  IP=00B9   NV UP EI PL NZ NA PE NC
0B24:00B9 E30B           JCXZ    00C6
-
```

In this display, the CX register has been loaded with the integer value (5) being passed from the controlling program. The next Trace instruction results in execution of the JCXZ 00C6 instruction, which bypasses the entire subroutine if the value being passed from C is a 0. Go ahead and Trace through the next step:

```
-t

AX=0000  BX=0EE2  CX=0005  DX=0000  SP=0EDC  BP=0EDC  SI=0420  DI=0420
DS=0CEA  ES=0CEA  SS=0CEA  CS=0B24  IP=00BB   NV UP EI PL NZ NA PE NC
0B24:00BB 13C8           ADC     CX,AX
-
```

The instruction to be executed next (ADC CX,AX) is supposed to add the row value (5, which also represents the number of blocks on the row) to the value in AX (which is currently 0). But in the following display:

```
-t

AX=0000  BX=0EE2  CX=0005  DX=0000  SP=0EDC  BP=0EDC  SI=0420  DI=0420
DS=0CEA  ES=0CEA  SS=0CEA  CS=0B24  IP=00BD   NV UP EI PL NZ NA PE NC
0B24:00BD 7204           JB      00C3
-
```

the value in AX did not change. The problem must be occurring here; the value is not being added to AX. As written, the program results in the sum of AX and CX being deposited in the wrong register, CX.

To test this hypothesis, change the coding here by using the Assemble command to enter the following code at address CS:00BB:

```
-a bb
0B24:00BB ADC AX,CX
0B24:00BD
-
```

Now the corrected coding is in place, but the instruction pointer register still points to the wrong location. You need to have the computer execute this newly entered instruction. The following dialogue shows how to use the Register command to change the IP register and then use the command again to view the register contents:

```
-rip
IP 00BD
:bb
-r
AX=0000  BX=0EE2  CX=0005  DX=0000  SP=0EDC  BP=0EDC  SI=0420  DI=0420
DS=0CEA  ES=0CEA  SS=0CEA  CS=0B24  IP=00BB   NV UP EI PL NZ NA PE NC
0B24:00BB 11C8          ADC     AX,CX
-
```

RIP enabled the IP register to be changed to BB, the memory offset of the instructions just entered. Finally, the Register command causes DEBUG to display the registers so that you can verify that the computer is indeed ready to execute the proper instruction. Now you will trace through this step (ADC AX,CX) to verify its effect on the AX register.

In the following display, the AX register has been updated to the correct value:

```
-t

AX=0005  BX=0EE2  CX=0005  DX=0000  SP=0EDC  BP=0EDC  SI=0420  DI=0420
DS=0CEA  ES=0CEA  SS=0CEA  CS=0B24  IP=00BD   NV UP EI PL NZ NA PE NC
0B24:00BD 7205          JB      00B7
-
```

Now, so that you can quit DEBUG, execute the rest of the program by using the Go command:

```
-g
The sum of 5 rows is 15
Initial Value: 3
The sum of 3 rows is 6
Initial Value: 7
The sum of 7 rows is 28
Initial Value: 999
The sum of 1 rows is 1
The sum of 2 rows is 3
The sum of 3 rows is 6
The sum of 4 rows is 10
The sum of 5 rows is 15
```

(Portion of output is deleted to save space.)

```
The sum of 358 rows is 64261
The sum of 359 rows is 64620
The sum of 360 rows is 64980
The sum of 361 rows is 65341
Sorry, the sum has exceeded capacity (362 rows is too many)

Program terminated normally
-q

C>_
```

Well, you've done it! You have just used DEBUG to track down a bug in a program. This example may be simple, but the precepts are the same regardless of the complexity of the problem. Whatever the task, you must step through the coding to make sure that all is going as expected.

By the way, DEBUG did not change the source or executable files. Now that you have discovered what the problem was, you need to change SUMS.ASM, reassemble, and then link to produce a corrected version of TEST.EXE.

Using CodeView

Now that you have seen how to locate the bug using DEBUG, let's look at how it's done with CodeView. The same bug will be used, but the OBJ files and the EXE file must be rebuilt to include the necessary debugging data. You can do this by following these steps:

1. Reassemble SUMS.ASM as shown in Chapter 5, but include the /Zd option on the command line.

2. Recompile TEST.C as before, but include the /Zd option on the command line.

3. Relink TEST.OBJ and SUMS.OBJ as shown in Chapter 5, but include the /CO option on the command line.

After completing these three steps, you are ready to use CodeView fully with TEST.EXE. You can now invoke CodeView with the following command line:

```
CV TEST.EXE
```

Be sure that both TEST.C and SUMS.ASM are in the current directory so that CodeView can find them. The debugger will load, and the first screen will look like figure 7.1.

Fig. 7.1. The initial CodeView screen.

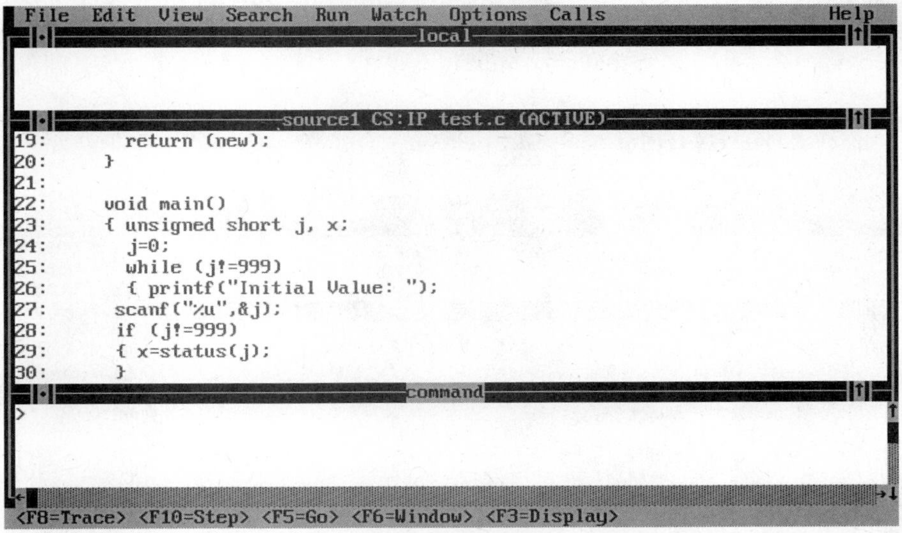

```
 File   Edit   View   Search   Run   Watch   Options   Calls                Help
                                   local
                          source1 CS:IP test.c (ACTIVE)
19:       return (new);
20:     }
21:
22:     void main()
23:     { unsigned short j, x;
24:       j=0;
25:       while (j!=999)
26:       { printf("Initial Value: ");
27:       scanf("%u",&j);
28:       if (j!=999)
29:       { x=status(j);
30:       }
                                  command

>

<F8=Trace> <F10=Step> <F5=Go> <F6=Window> <F3=Display>
```

If you have used CodeView before, your screen may look a little different. You see, CodeView remembers how it was configured from last time it was used, and starts using that same configuration. The important thing, however, is that TEST.EXE is loaded, along with the source-code file, which is shown in the center source-code window.

At this point the debugger is awaiting your instructions. What you see on-screen is not the machine code that DEBUG displays, but rather a portion of the source file TEST.C. Notice also that you get no indication of what the CPU registers contain (refer to fig. 7.1).

To see what is in the registers, you can enable the register-display window by pressing F2. When you do, the screen changes so that it looks like figure 7.2.

Now you can step through the program, one C statement at a time, by pressing F10 once for each line. This is the same as using the P command in DEBUG and fully executes any lower-level function without pausing. When you get to the line containing the scanf() function, CodeView switches to the DOS screen and allows you to respond to the program's prompt. Enter 5 as the initial value, and press Enter. At this point, the CodeView screen should be displayed again.

Continue pressing F10 until the following C source-code line is highlighted:

```
{ x=status(j);
```

Now, instead of using F10, use the F8 function key so that CodeView traces into the status() function. Once in status(), you can continue to use F8 because it calls no lower-level functions except your machine language routine, sums(), and that's the one you want to examine. When you reach line 15 of TEST.C and press F8, the screen display changes to that shown in figure 7.3.

Fig. 7.2. CodeView C screen with register window.

```
 File   Edit   View   Search   Run   Watch   Options   Calls              Help
 ·                              local                        ·  reg
                                                              AX = 0000
                                                              BX = 0000
                                                              CX = 0000
         ·         source1 CS:IP test.c (ACTIVE)             DX = 0000
19:        return (new);                                     SP =
20:      }                                                   BP = 0000
21:                                                          SI = 0000
22:      void main()                                         DI = 0000
23:      { unsigned short j, x;                              DS =
24:        j=0;                                              ES =
25:        while (j!=999)                                    SS =
26:        { printf("Initial Value: ");                      CS =
27:      scanf("%u",&j);                                     IP =
28:      if (j!=999)                                         FL =
29:      { x=status(j);
30:      }                                                   NV UP    PL
 ·                            command                        NZ NA PO NC
>
 <F8=Trace> <F10=Step> <F5=Go> <F6=Window> <F3=Display>
```

Notice how much simpler it was to reach the assembly language routine with CodeView than with DEBUG. As you continue to press F8, operation steps through the SUMS module; when control returns to status(), the display changes back to the C source code.

You should have noticed, as with the earlier DEBUG session, that the subroutine obviously contained an error. When you have determined that the instruction at label S1 in figure 7.3 is at fault, use the F10 and F8 function keys to get back to that line (so that it is highlighted). Then, use the A command as you would have in DEBUG. Press A and then press Enter. Now you can input assembly language code to correct the error, as shown in figure 7.4.

Fig. 7.3. CodeView MASM screen.

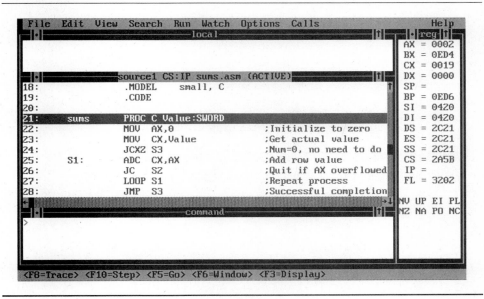

Fig. 7.4. After using the A command and entering the assembly language correction.

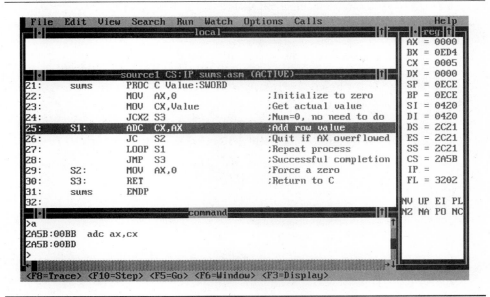

Notice that the code in the center source-code window is not changed. That is because you have not changed the source-code file; you have only changed the assembly language instructions stored in memory by CodeView. If you press F3, the display in the center source-code window changes to that shown in figure 7.5.

Fig. 7.5. *Mixed source code and assembly language instructions.*

```
 File   Edit  View   Search  Run  Watch  Options  Calls          Help
|·|                           local                   |↑| |·|reg|↑|
                                                          AX = 0000
                                                          BX = 0ED4
                                                          CX = 0005
|·|         source1 CS:IP sums.asm (ACTIVE)          |↑| DX = 0000
25:     S1:     ADC  CX,AX            ;Add row value      SP = 0ECE
2A5B:00BB 11C8          ADC      AX,CX                    BP = 0ECE
26:             JC   S2               ;Quit if AX overflowed  SI = 0420
2A5B:00BD 7204          JB       00C3                     DI = 0420
27:             LOOP S1               ;Repeat process     DS = 2C21
2A5B:00BF E2FA          LOOP     00BB                     ES = 2C21
28:             JMP  S3               ;Successful completion  SS = 2C21
2A5B:00C1 EB03          JMP      00C6                     CS = 2A5B
29:     S2:     MOV  AX,0             ;Force a zero       IP =
2A5B:00C3 B80000        MOV      AX,0000                  FL = 3202
30:     S3:     RET                   ;Return to C
2A5B:00C6 5D            POP      BP                       NV UP EI PL
|·|                         command                  |↑| NZ NA PO NC
>a
2A5B:00BB  adc ax,cx
2A5B:00BD
>
```
```
<F8=Trace> <F10=Step> <F5=Go> <F6=Window> <F3=Display>
```

Notice line 25 at the top of the source-code window. Immediately after this line is the real assembly language statement that CodeView will execute. This line reflects the patch you made to the code. Press F8 to execute the changed line. Now your screen should resemble figure 7.6.

Notice that the value of AX (displayed at the top of the register-display window) has changed. Now you can press F5; the program will run unhindered.

When you finally enter 999 as an initial value, and your program completes execution, CodeView again takes control and displays the screen shown in figure 7.7.

Fig. 7.6. The CodeView screen after executing the changed instruction.

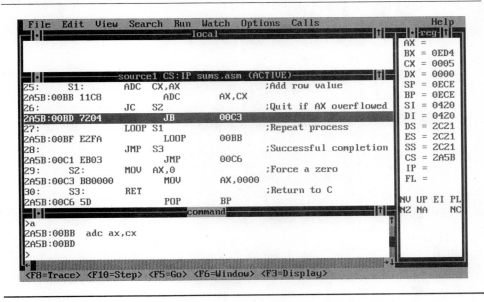

Fig. 7.7. The CodeView program completion screen.

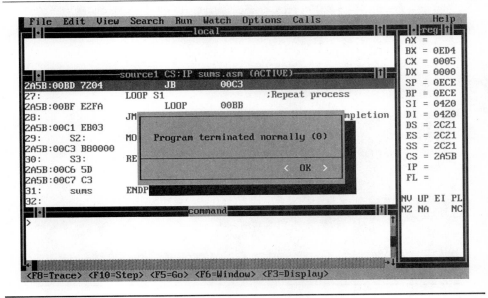

Press Enter to acknowledge the message. Now you are free to exit CodeView. It is important to remember that, as with DEBUG, you have done nothing to make a permanent fix. After using the CodeView debugger to identify the problem and verify a fix that will work, you still have to put the fix into the source files.

Using Turbo Debugger

Turbo Debugger also requires that the EXE file contain appropriate debugging data but cannot use directly the data from the CodeView-linked EXE file. A utility (TDCONVRT.EXE) for converting CodeView files is included with the package. To use it, first type

```
TDCONVRT TEST.EXE TDTEST.EXE
```

to convert the CodeView-linked TEST.EXE file into a TD-linked file, TDTEST.EXE. Then type

```
TD TDTEST
```

to invoke Turbo Debugger for TDTEST.EXE. The first screen displayed will look something like figure 7.8.

Fig. 7.8. First screen of Turbo Debugger.

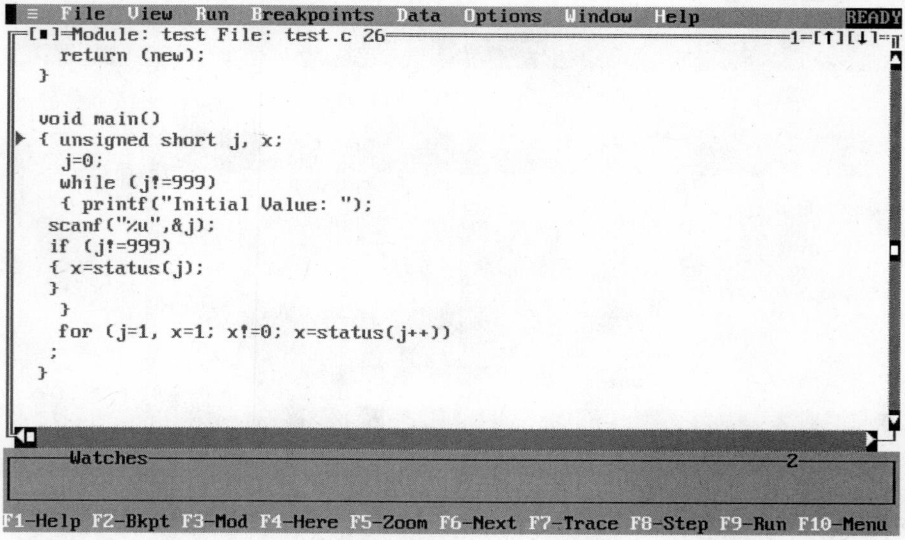

Notice that, unlike other source-level debuggers, Turbo Debugger shows you a one-line help reference across the bottom of the screen. This reminds you that F7 is the key for tracing into a routine and that F8 is the key for stepping over a low-level routine without pausing (what I have called *Proceed* in the other descriptions).

Just like CodeView, Turbo Debugger automatically switches to the appropriate source file when you trace into a new module and enables you to try various corrective actions once you have spotted the bug you are hunting. Figure 7.9 shows the result. The exact commands differ slightly, but the capabilities of Turbo Debugger are essentially equivalent to those of CodeView. The differences between them are related more to their general look and feel than their capabilities for ordinary use.

Fig. 7.9. *Turbo Debugger ASM screen.*

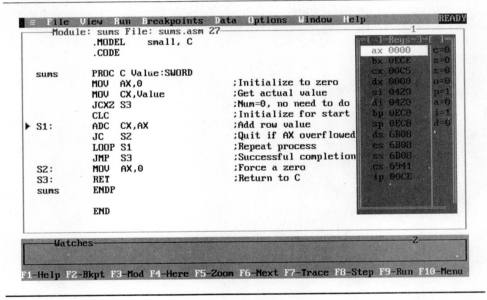

Summary

In this chapter you learned the differences between software debuggers and hardware debuggers, and saw some of the characteristics of a few popular software debuggers.

You learned also what the DEBUG commands are and how to use them to help uncover errors in your subroutines. As you work with DEBUG, try to become familiar with all the available commands so that you can make your debugging sessions as efficient and productive as possible.

Although DEBUG is helpful, it is not the answer to every debugging need. You may discover errors that completely lock up your computer, so that your only alternative for regaining control is to turn off the computer. In these instances, software debuggers such as DEBUG are virtually useless because they assume that you will always have some control, such as the ability to enter keyboard commands.

Professional debuggers that combine hardware and software also are available. These debuggers provide a virtually independent way to monitor and debug programs. Professional debuggers may be expensive but in many development environments are the only viable option for effective debugging.

The ideal debugging system, regardless of type, performs as a benign observer until you instruct it to perform a task. A debugger that interferes with the operation of the program is of little use because there is no way to examine how the program operates without the debugger.

Using Additional Tools

So far in this book I have focused only on the primary development tools for assembly language programming: the assembler, linker, and debugger. Numerous other tools, however, are available to assist you in developing software. These tools are available from a variety of sources, including Microsoft, Borland, and a number of third parties. This chapter and the next cover a few of these tools: makefiles and profilers are discussed in this chapter, whereas Chapter 9 discusses creating and maintaining libraries.

Working with Makefiles

In earlier chapters you learned ways to simplify the management of a project by creating BAT files that enter all the necessary keystrokes to completely compile, assemble, and link an application. But what do you do when you have an application that's made up of a dozen C files and twice that many assembly language modules, and you make a change to just *one* of those pieces?

Of course, you *could* just run the BAT file that recompiles and reassembles everything, but professional system developers came up with a better way over a decade ago. Now that same technique is available to anyone who buys a copy of MASM, Quick-C, or Turbo Assembler.

The technique is known as *MAKE*, from the name of the first such program developed (as part of the UNIX system). In many ways it resembles the use of BAT files, but with a twist: when you execute a BAT file, almost all the commands it contains are executed—but when you run MAKE or one of its descendants, only the necessary commands get done; the rest are bypassed.

How can MAKE know which commands are necessary and which should be bypassed at any specific run time? That's the secret of the technique, and that's the next subject.

What Does MAKE Do?

What the various implementations of MAKE do, specifically, is cycle through a file you provide that describes how the different parts of your application depend on each other. Such a file is called a *dependency file* in most MAKE documentation. The original system's default file name, *MAKEFILE*, also is widely used in cases where a dependency file name is not specified.

A dependency file consists of several parts. Because most of these parts are optional, the various brands of available MAKE programs differ significantly. All dependency files share one common key part, however: a list of *description blocks*.

Each description block begins with an *outfile-infile* relationship. Such a statement is easy to identify because it starts at the first column of the line and does not begin with a # character (the # denotes a comment line). This relationship statement contains at least two file names, separated by a colon (:). The first file name is that of the outfile, the output file for this block. The second is that of the input file. You can have multiple input files, but only one outfile per block.

This relationship line specifically says that outfile depends on all the listed infiles; thus, if the date-time stamp of any infile is later than that of the outfile, you will have to correct the situation, usually by rebuilding the outfile.

The remaining lines of the description block, each of which starts with a blank space or a tab character, are called *command lines*. They specify exactly what actions are to be performed if action is indicated by the date-time comparison.

The command lines are exactly like the individual lines in a BAT file except that the command lines are indented. If MAKE determines that the actions of this description block must be performed, the command lines are fed in strict sequence to the computer just as though they had been typed in from the keyboard.

One of the major differences between the available MAKE programs involves the sequence in which the description blocks are evaluated. Some of them go through the dependency file in strict sequence—the first block in the file is the first one evaluated, and its actions are performed, if necessary, before the second one is examined. With this approach, the final application file must be the one described by the final description block.

Other MAKE programs, however, evaluate only the first description block in the file (unless another target is specified on the command line). Any actions the block calls for may, in turn, require subsequent blocks to be evaluated (this process is similar to the way a linker searches a library file). For this approach, the final application file must be the *first* one described rather than the last.

Because of the present lack of standardization, evaluation sequencing varies among MAKE programs. A dependency file that works well with one MAKE program may not work at all with another.

Microsoft's Program-Maintenance Utility

MASM 6.0 comes with a copy of NMAKE.EXE, the Microsoft program-maintenance utility. Although not representative of mainstream MAKE programs, this utility is described first because it is probably the simplest to comprehend.

In its documentation, Microsoft refers to the dependency file for NMAKE simply as a *description file*. NMAKE enables one or more description blocks to be entered in the description file, and either a specific target file is evaluated, or the first target file in the description file is evaluated (as a default).

You can place comment lines anywhere you want in the description file. Whenever the program encounters the # character—which indicates the start of a comment—all subsequent characters to the end of that line are ignored. Thus, comments may be added at the end of any line, embedded within a description block, or used for headers.

A dependency line always marks the beginning of a description block in NMAKE. If you like, you can use empty lines to separate description blocks. The dependency line begins with the name of the output or *target* file, including its extension but without a path. This need not be an actual file name. For example, the *pseudo-target* ALL (or any other string you like) can be used if you want to force the *command list* to be executed every time this dependency file is processed.

The target-file name is followed by a colon (:) and the *infile* list, a list of one or more file names (again, without a path). Either a comma or a blank space may be used to separate the names in the infile list.

When the dependency line is evaluated, the date-time stamp maintained by DOS for each file in the infile list is compared to that of the target. If any infile has a more recent time or date than that of the target, the command list is executed; if the target is more recent than any infile, the command list is skipped over and the next dependency block, if any, is evaluated.

The command list consists of one or more DOS commands to be executed, just as in a conventional batch (BAT) file. To distinguish the command-list lines from the rest of the dependency file's contents, however, each of the lines must begin with at least one blank space or tab character. Most dependency blocks contain at least one line in their command list, although this is not mandatory. If no commands follow the dependency line, a default mechanism called the *inference rule* list takes over. If the dependency line fits any inference rule, the command list for that rule is executed. If not, nothing is executed (but no error is declared).

The full syntax for an NMAKE dependency block is

```
target : infile[[,] infile][# comment]
    [command [# comment]]
```

where the items shown within brackets are optional.

Inference Rules

The inference-rule list consists of one or more rules that tell NMAKE which commands to execute when a dependency block contains no command list of its own. Each rule, like a dependency block, begins with a relationship statement, but instead of dealing with specific files by name, an inference rule applies to groups of files distinguished by their extensions. The syntax is

```
[# comment]
.inext.outext:
    command
    [command]
```

Notice that in the inference rule, both the `inext` and the `outext` appear in the "target" position, to the left of the colon, and nothing appears to the right of the colon. When a rule is to be applied, the time relationships have already been determined; the purpose of this line in the rule list is to let NMAKE find the specific rule to apply. For instance, a typical inference-rule list for assembly language programs might be the following:

```
# default actions when assembly required, keep CODEVIEW info
.ASM.OBJ:
    ML /C /Cx /Zi /Fo$@ /Fl $*.asm


# default linker actions
.OBJ.EXE:
    LINK /MAP /CO $**,$@;
```

The dependency line, `test.obj : test.asm`, with no associated command list, would match the first of these rules, executing the command `ML /C /Cx /Zi /Fotest.obj /Fl test.asm` as a result of the match. A subsequent dependency line, `test.exe : test.obj mine.obj` (again, with no command list) would match the second rule and, as a result, execute `LINK /MAP /CO test.obj mine.obj,test.exe;`.

Command Modifiers

Dependency blocks and inference rules both enable you to specify commands to be executed by NMAKE. You can modify the way NMAKE executes commands through the use of *command modifiers* (see table 8.1). When command modifiers are prefixed to commands, NMAKE changes the way the prefixed commands are executed.

Table 8.1. *Command modifiers for Microsoft NMAKE.*

Modifier	Meaning
-	Disables error checking for command it modifies. If - is followed by a number, NMAKE halts only when exit code returned by command is greater than the specified number.
@	Prevents NMAKE from displaying command as it executes; modifier's action is identical to that of similar modifier for BAT files in DOS version 3.3 and later versions.
!	Causes command to be repeated for each listed file represented by special macro if modified command uses one of the special macros $? or $**; on each repetition, special macro is replaced by next file name in list.

In all three cases, the command modifier must immediately precede the command to which it applies.

Macro Definitions

Those strange expressions ($*, $**, and $@) in the preceding inference-rule list are references to *macro definitions* built into NMAKE and defined in table 8.2. The program provides also for user-defined macros in its dependency files.

Table 8.2. *Built-in macros.*

Macro	Meaning
$$@	Target currently being evaluated
$(AFLAGS)	Options to pass to Macro Assembler
$(AS)	Command to invoke Macro Assembler; preset to ml
$(BC)	Command to invoke BASIC compiler; preset to bc

continues

Table 8.2. continued

Macro	Meaning
$(BFLAGS)	Options to pass to BASIC compiler
$(CC)	Command to invoke C compiler; preset to cl
$(CFLAGS)	Options to pass to C compiler
$(COBFLAGS)	Options to pass to COBOL compiler
$(COBOL)	Command to invoke COBOL compiler; preset to cobol
$(FFLAGS)	Options to pass to FORTRAN compiler
$(FOR)	Command to invoke FORTRAN compiler; preset to fl
$(MAKE)	Name with which NMAKE was invoked, used to call program recursively; causes line in which it appears to be executed even if /N option is in effect
$(MAKEDIR)	Directory from which NMAKE was invoked
$(MAKEFLAGS)	List of NMAKE options currently in effect; cannot be redefined, but is used with $(MAKE) to pass current option list to recursive call—for example: $(MAKE) $(MAKEFLAGS)
$(PASCAL)	Command to invoke Pascal compiler; preset to pl
$(PFLAGS)	Options to pass to Pascal compiler
$(RC)	Command to invoke Microsoft Resource Compiler; preset to rc
$(RFLAGS)	Options to pass to Microsoft Resource Compiler
$*	Target name without extension
$**	Complete list of infiles
$<	Name of infile that triggered execution of command list (evaluated only for inference rules)
$?	List of infiles newer than target; useful for updating LIB files and executing similar actions
$@	Complete target name

When NMAKE is processing any command list, whether from an inference rule or from a dependency block, these macros expand into the corresponding file reference as shown in the example ($(MAKE) $(MAKEFLAGS)). The macro capability is not limited to file-name references, however. Macros are commonly used also to modify the options passed to the assembler, the linker, or the library manager.

The syntax for creating a user-defined macro is similar to that used at the DOS level to SET an environment string:

```
[# comment]
name[ ]=[ ]["]text["]
```

NMAKE ignores any blank space on either side of the equals sign (=) character. If the text string that will replace the macro name when referenced contains any blank spaces or "special" characters, the string must be enclosed in quotation marks. Including the quotation marks never hurts and can prevent problems caused by "special" characters (that is, characters other than letters and numbers).

To indicate where NMAKE should replace a macro with a text string, just reference the macro as follows:

```
$(name)
```

This entire string is then replaced by the text associated with *name*. For example, if the command line for the LINK inference rule in the previous example had been LINK $(LOPT) $**,$@; instead of LINK /MAP /CO $**,$@;, and the macro definition LOPT="/MAP /CO" had preceded the inference rule in the file, the results would have been the same as those shown in the example.

To remove the CodeView information from the output file, however, all you need to do is redefine LOPT as /MAP and that, as you will see shortly, can be done from the command line when NMAKE is invoked. Thus, the macro capability gives you an added dimension of freedom (and consequently a greater possibility for complications) in the use of the file.

You can also refer to environment variables as if they were macro definitions in the file. For instance, to use the environment variable PATH as part of a command line, you simply insert $(PATH) in that command line of the dependency file. If the file has a macro named PATH, it is used; if not, the content of the environment variable PATH is used.

Be careful not to overuse the macro feature. Excessive use of macros is the major reason most sample dependency files supplied with the different language products are incomprehensible at first glance. NMAKE itself never requires such complexity.

NMAKE Directives

NMAKE enables you also to control the flow of actions in a dependency file by using *directives*. These directives, also called *preprocessing directives*, are used in dependency files much as directives are used in the assemblers themselves—as commands directed primarily toward controlling the NMAKE program's actions rather than toward generating output. Using the NMAKE directives listed and described in table 8.3, you can change the commands that are executed, based on the presence or absence of a defined macro name, or on the value of an expression. Directives also let you use include files, output an error message, or alter the settings of the option switches.

Table 8.3. *Directives for Microsoft NMAKE.*

Directive	Description
!CMDSWITCHES:	This directive, which may be followed by a plus sign (+) or a minus sign (-); must then specify one of four option indicators: /D, /I, /N, or /S. If the plus sign (+) is used, the named option is turned on; if the minus sign (-) is used, the option is turned off; if neither one is used, the option is returned to the condition specified by the command line used to invoke this NMAKE. This directive changes the MAKEFLAGS macro, which cannot be altered directly.
!ELSE	Used only between !IF and !ENDIF statements, !ELSE indicates end of a statement list to be executed if !IF is true (nonzero), and beginning of a list to be executed if condition is false (zero).
!ENDIF	Marks end of an !IF sequence. !IF…!ENDIF sequences can be nested because each !IF extends to its matching !ENDIF.
!ERROR *text*	Causes message *text* to be printed, then halting execution of NMAKE.
!IF *expr*	If value of *expr* is nonzero, statements in the file between this directive and next matching !ELSE or !ENDIF are executed; otherwise, such a sequence of statements is not executed. If an !ELSE statement is the next matching directive, statements between it and the matching !ENDIF are executed; otherwise no statements before the matching !ENDIF are executed.
!IFDEF *macro*	Similar to the !IF directive, but instead of basing its decision on the value of an expression, !IFDEF executes subsequent statements only if *macro* has been defined, although the value of *macro* is immaterial. !ELSE and !ENDIF statements are executed as they were with !IF.

Directive	Description
!IFNDEF *macro*	Exactly like !IFDEF, but with reversed meaning; statements are executed if *macro* has *not* been defined.
!INCLUDE	Followed by a file name, causes named file to be read and evaluated before continuing processing of current makefile. If file name is enclosed in angle brackets (<>), paths specified by an INCLUDE macro or an environment variable are searched for the file; otherwise, only current directory is searched.
!UNDEF *macro*	Used to undefine *macro*; after execution of this directive, *macro* is no longer defined.

Using the directives greatly complicates the design of a dependency file but does make it possible to introduce powerful capabilities, based on choices specified by the presence or absence of only a few command-line-defined macros. Until you are completely comfortable with the simpler ways of dealing with dependency files, however, you are better off avoiding these directives.

Invoking NMAKE

To use NMAKE, invoke it from the DOS prompt with the following syntax:

```
NMAKE[ options][ macrodefs][ targets][ filename]
```

The options recognized by NMAKE are listed and described in table 8.4. You can use any noncontradictory options simultaneously.

Table 8.4. *Command-line options for Microsoft's NMAKE.*

Option	Meaning
/?	Display quick help screen
/A	Force execution of all commands, regardless of date of last update
/C	Suppress nonfatal error or warning messages and the NMAKE copyright message
/D	As file is processed, display date each file was last modified

continues

Table 8.4. *continued*

Option	Meaning
/E	Use environment variables instead of macro definitions in description file
/F *filename*	Specify description file to use instead of MAKEFILE
/HELP	Invoke expanded help system
/I	Ignore exit codes returned by command-line programs
/N	Display (but do not execute) commands that would otherwise be executed; useful for debugging
/NO	Suppress NMAKE copyright message
/P	Display macros, inference rules, and target descriptions during processing
/Q	Quick execution; checks update time of files and returns an error code if target file should be updated
/R	Ignore predefined macros and inference rules
/S	"Silent" mode; does not display command lines as they are executed
/T	Execute preprocessing commands only, and change modification times for command-line targets
/X *filename*	Redirect all error output to *filename*

Notice that when you invoke NMAKE, all the parameters on the command line are optional. If they are all omitted, NMAKE looks (by default) for a file named MAKEFILE and processes it as the dependency file. In fact, unless the /F *filename* option is used to specify the dependency file's name as part of the option list, MAKEFILE is used if it exists. The file name passed by itself on the command line is used only if MAKEFILE cannot be found.

You can define macros in the command line just as you would in a dependency file. Any definition given in the command line overrides internal definitions in the dependency file itself (which, in turn, override environment variables of the same name). Thus, to change the definition of the LOPT macro (in the previous example) so that no CodeView information is put into the EXE file (and assuming that the dependency file is named sample.mak), simply type

```
NMAKE LOPT="/MAP" sample.mak
```

For a full example of the use of NMAKE, see the "Creating and Using a Makefile" section later in this chapter.

Borland's Version of MAKE

The MAKE.EXE file supplied with Borland's Turbo Assembler operates very much like NMAKE.EXE. In fact, Borland's MAKE is so similar to NMAKE that I will discuss only those features in which the two programs differ.

The command-line syntax for the program is similar to NMAKE's, but shorter:

```
MAKE[ options][ targets]
```

Notice that this version treats all file names on the command line as targets and does not provide for macro definitions as a separate kind of command-line parameter; the macro definitions are still there, but as options.

The option list for MAKE is much shorter than that for NMAKE. And MAKE, unlike the Microsoft programs, treats as significant the case of the option character: -Dmac defines a macro named mac, but -dmac is not recognized and results in a fatal error. Valid options and their meanings are listed in table 8.5.

Table 8.5. *Options recognized by Borland's MAKE.*

Option	Meaning
-a	Causes MAKE to perform an autodependency check (unfortunately, neither the manuals nor the on-line help give any clue as to what this autodependency check might be!)
/B	Builds all targets regardless of file dates
-D*macro*	Defines a macro with no content
-D*macro=string*	Defines a macro containing a string; both -D options provide for command-line redefinition of macros
-f*filename*	Tells MAKE to use *filename* as its input dependency file; if *filename* cannot be found and does not contain an extension, MAKE then searches for *filename*.MAK
-i	Does not check exit status of all programs run
-I*directory*	Specifies the directory to be searched (in addition to the current directory) for files to be INCLUDEd
-K	Keeps temporary files created by MAKE
-n	Does not execute commands (same as Microsoft program's /N option)
-s	Does not display command lines as they are executed (same as Microsoft program's "silent" mode)

continues

Table 8.5. *continued*

Option	Meaning
-S	Swaps MAKE out of memory while executing commands
-Umacro	Undefines any existing definitions of *macro*
-? or -h	Provides on-line help
-W	Writes the current specified nonstring options

Like NMAKE, MAKE evaluates the dependency blocks for all files named on the command line as targets and, if no -f option is used, takes MAKEFILE as the default name for the dependency file to process.

Also like NMAKE, if no target files are designated on the command line, the first dependency block encountered is the only one evaluated automatically. All other blocks are evaluated *only* if their target files are in the infiles list for that first dependency block or for some subsequent block that was evaluated because its target was involved in the first block.

The list of built-in macros for MAKE is much shorter than the corresponding list for NMAKE; table 8.6 lists and describes all of them. In addition to the seven macros listed in the table, all existing environment variables automatically are loaded as macros.

Table 8.6. *Built-in macros for Borland's MAKE.*

Macro	Meaning
$d(macro)	Expands to 1 if *macro* is defined, and to 0 if not; valid only when used in !if and !elif directives to achieve the same results as NMAKE's !IFDEF and !IFNDEF directives
$*	Expands to the base name (including the path but without the extension) of the target file
$<	Expands to the full name (including path and extension) of the target file when used in a dependency block, or to the base name plus source-file extension when used in an inference rule
$:	Expands to the path name (without the file name or extension) of the target file
$.	Expands to the file name (without the path but including extension) of the target file

Macro	Meaning
$&	Expands to the base name only (without the path or extension) of target file
MAKE	Expands to 1

Like NMAKE, Borland's MAKE implements directives that serve the same purpose as those used in assembly language. The seven directives for MAKE are described next.

As in NMAKE, the !if directive begins an !if...!endif sequence that optionally may include !elif and !else directives. The directive must be followed by an expression (using any of the standard C operators), which may include the $d() macro. If the expression evaluates to a nonzero value, all statements up to the next matching !elif, !else, or !endif statement are executed; then statements are ignored until the matching !endif is reached. If the expression evaluates to zero, statements up to the next matching !elif or !else are ignored.

The !elif directive, unique to Borland's MAKE, performs another test similar to !if when previous tests have failed. Like !if, !elif is always followed by an expression. If !elif is reached by skipping over previous statements because a zero resulted earlier, the expression is evaluated in the same way as for the !if, and has the same result (executing or skipping over subsequent statements). If reached after execution of statements because of an earlier nonzero !if or !elif, the expression is not evaluated; all subsequent statements up to the next matching !endif are skipped. As many !elif tests as you like may be placed between an !if directive and the !else directive to perform multiple, mutually exclusive tests and conditional execution.

The !else directive can appear only between an !if or !elif and the matching !endif, and (unlike !elif) can appear only once during the sequence. If reached after execution of statements because of a nonzero test result, !else causes all following statements, up to the matching !endif, to be skipped. If reached while skipping over statements because of a zero test result, !else causes execution of subsequent statements (up to the matching !endif).

The !endif directive ends an !if...!elif...!else...!endif sequence.

The !undef directive, which must be followed by the name of a macro, causes MAKE to forget the named macro. If no such macro exists, !undef has no effect.

!include, which must be followed by the name of a file enclosed in quotation marks ("*name*"), causes MAKE to evaluate and execute the entire contents of the named file before proceeding with evaluation of the current file.

The !error directive, which must be followed by a text string, causes the text string to be displayed and then halts execution of MAKE.

This version of MAKE has no built-in inference rules; you can define your own standard set, however, and store them in a file named BUILTINS.MAK. MAKE automatically loads the contents of such a file before any processing for a dependency file begins.

Only two of the three command modifiers used by NMAKE are valid for MAKE; the ! modifier is not recognized. Table 8.7 lists and describes the valid modifier characters. In both cases, these characters appear as prefixes to the command being modified.

Table 8.7. *Command modifiers for Borland's MAKE.*

Modifier	Meaning
-	Disables error checking for the command it modifies; if modifier is followed by a number, MAKE halts only when exit code returned by command is greater than the specified number
@	Prevents MAKE from displaying the command as it executes; identical in action with similar modifier for batch files in DOS version 3.3 and later

Except for the differences noted in this section, Borland's MAKE operates almost exactly like NMAKE.

Creating and Using a Makefile with Microsoft NMAKE

To create a dependency file, you must first decide which modules you want it to include. All modules related to a single project should be handled by the same dependency file; if the name you assign to that file indicates a specific project, you can update everything by simply typing

```
NMAKE project
```

after you make any source-file changes. If your dependency blocks are accurately written, all processes necessary for the update will be executed.

As an example of the way MAKE typically is used, the following dependency file for VIDEO.LIB (a program developed in Chapter 17, "Video Memory") can be used with NMAKE:

```
# Makefile for VIDEO.LIB - 9/29/91

.asm.obj:
  ml /c /Cx /Zi /Fo$@ $**

video.lib : findcard.obj pchar.obj pstring.obj \
            pchara.obj pstringa.obj box.obj \
            setdi.obj scrn.obj
  if exist video.lib del video.lib
  lib @videolib
```

This file, which I named VIDEO, shows the essentials of classic dependency-file construction. The file uses one inference rule to define a desired invocation of ML to process ASM files. Here's how the file works.

When NMAKE is executed, and VIDEO is specified as the dependency file, NMAKE examines the first (and only) dependency block in the file. This is the one that says that VIDEO.LIB is the target and is composed of all the OBJ files to the right of the colon.

Then NMAKE checks to make sure that every OBJ file was created before VIDEO.LIB. If so, no action is taken; if not, the OBJ file is created by using the inference rule to create OBJ files from ASM files.

Finally, the commands in the dependency block are executed. If an old copy of VIDEO.LIB exists, it is deleted. Then LIB.EXE is invoked to create the new VIDEO.LIB. LIB.EXE is invoked using a response file, VIDEOLIB, which contains the following:

```
video
y
+ findcard.obj &
+ pchar.obj &
+ pstring.obj &
+ pchara.obj &
+ pstringa.obj &
+ box.obj &
+ setdi.obj &
+ scrn.obj
video.lst
```

To illustrate how this dependency file works, I deleted one OBJ file from the directory (to force rebuilding of that file) and then ran NMAKE. Here's the result:

```
C:\>nmake /f video

Microsoft (R) Program Maintenance Utility   Version 1.13
Copyright (c) Microsoft Corp 1988-91. All rights reserved.

    ml /c /Cx /Zi /Fopchar.obj pchar.asm
Microsoft (R) Macro Assembler Version 6.00
Copyright (C) Microsoft Corp 1981-1991.  All rights reserved.

Assembling: pchar.asm
    if exist video.lib del video.lib
    lib @videolib

Microsoft (R) Library Manager  Version 3.18
Copyright (C) Microsoft Corp 1983-1991.  All rights reserved.

Library name: video
Library does not exist.  Create? (y/n) y
Operations: + findcard.obj &
Operations: + pchar.obj &
Operations: + pstring.obj &
Operations: + pchara.obj &
Operations: + pstringa.obj &
Operations: + box.obj &
Operations: + setdi.obj &
Operations: + scrn.obj
List file: video.lst


C:\>_
```

Note that you can override the effects of the inference rule by stating an explict command to use for any of the OBJ files. For example, in the following dependency file:

```
# Makefile for VIDEO.LIB - 9/29/91

.asm.obj:
  ml /c /Cx /Zi /Fo$@ $**

video.lib : findcard.obj pchar.obj pstring.obj \
    pchara.obj pstringa.obj box.obj \
    setdi.obj scrn.obj
```

```
if exist video.lib del video.lib
lib @videolib

findcard.obj : findcard.asm
  ml /c /Cx /Fofindcard.obj /Fl findcard.asm
```

the inference rule is used to create all the OBJ files except FINDCARD.OBJ—the specific command under the second dependency block is used for it. In this way, you can tailor your dependency files to do virtually anything you want for creating and maintaining your program files.

Working with Profilers

Another tool available to programmers is called a *profiler*. Because this tool generally is used to determine the overall performance of a program, it can be used to determine which part of your program requires the most time and is therefore a candidate for translation to assembly language.

Profilers are available from both Borland and Microsoft. Borland's Turbo Profiler is available as part of the professional language packages (Turbo C/C++ Professional or Turbo Pascal Professional) or as a part of Borland C++. Turbo Profiler has been available for several years. The Microsoft Source Profiler, on the other hand, comes as a separate product (you pay more for it) and first became available in 1991.

Let's look at both profilers—first the Microsoft product and then the product from Borland.

Using the Microsoft Source Profiler

As with all Microsoft language products, you can run the Source Profiler from inside the Programmer's Work Bench environment, or you can run it from the DOS prompt. Once installed on your hard disk, the product is available from the PWB menus. Instead of looking at how the Source Profiler works in the PWB, this section focuses on using it from DOS.

To use the profiler, you need to compile, assemble, and link your programs using the CodeView options. After you have done this, the profiler enables you to analyze programs in any of four ways:

❑ Coverage analysis

❑ Sampling analysis

❏ Counting analysis

❏ Timing analysis

Each type of analysis can be done at either a function or individual-line level. The profiler comes complete with a series of batch files that enable you to quickly use the programs from the DOS prompt.

Coverage analysis simply tells you which functions or lines in a program are used during a session. This type of analysis is most useful when you want to discover whether any section of your code is not used (you'd be surprised how often this happens in large programs). Using the batch files provided, you can perform coverage analysis by using the following command lines:

```
LCOVER filename [options]
FCOVER filename [options]
```

The first line, using LCOVER, does a line-by-line coverage analysis; the second does a function-level analysis.

Sampling analysis ignores your program most of the time, but at periodic intervals (you set the interval) peeks at your program to determine where (in the execution process) the program is, and then records this information. Since full-scale profiling can slow down a program considerably, sampling can be valuable; because it interrupts your program only occasionally, your program will run faster. (Just be aware that the results of this type of profiling can be less than complete.) Using the provided batch files, you can perform sampling analysis with the following command lines:

```
LSAMPLE filename [options]
FSAMPLE filename [options]
```

The first line, using LSAMPLE, does a line-by-line sample analysis; the second does a function-level analysis.

Counting and timing, the analysis methods most useful to most programmers, deserve more in-depth examination.

Counting Analysis

This type of analysis simply counts how many times each function or line of your program is executed. This information may be helpful in determining the "load" borne by each portion of your program.

As an example of this type of analysis, I ran the FCOUNT and LCOUNT batch files on TEST.EXE, the program developed in Chapter 5 for testing the SUMS routine. The results of the function-level analysis (FCOUNT) were stored in the file TEST.OUT, and appeared as follows:

```
Microsoft PLIST Version 1.00

Profile: Function counting, sorted by counts.
Date:    Tue Oct 01 07:32:25 1991


Program Statistics
- - - - - - - - - - - - - - - - - -
   Total functions: 3
   Total hits: 731
   Function coverage: 100.0%

Module Statistics for c:\test.exe
- - - - - - - - - - - - - - - - - - - - - - - - - - - - - - - - - - - - -
   Functions in module: 3
   Hits in module: 731
   Module function coverage: 100.0%


 Hit
count   %   Function
- - - - - - - - - - - - - - - - - - - -
    365  49.9 status (test.c:14)
    365  49.9 sums (sums.asm:22)
    1    0.1 main (test.c:26)
```

Because TEST.EXE contains only a few functions, the information provided may be of limited use. But on larger programs, this information can be quite helpful in determining how often certain routines get called.

Using the same type of analysis on a line-by-line level yields the following information in TEST.OUT:

```
Microsoft PLIST Version 1.00

Profile: Line counting, sorted by line.
Date:    Tue Oct 01 07:38:57 1991


Program Statistics
- - - - - - - - - - - - - - - - - -
   Total lines: 29
   Total hits: 201823
   Line coverage:  96.6%
```

```
Module Statistics for c:\test.exe
------------------------------------------
     Lines in module: 29
     Hits in module: 201823
     Module line coverage:  96.6%


Source file: test.c


        Hit
   Line count   %   Source
---------------------------
     1:                 /* File:    TEST.C
     2:                  * Author:   Allen L. Wyatt
     3:                  * Date:     8/3/91
     4:                  *
     5:                  * Purpose:  Program to test the calling of SUMS()
     6:                  */
     7:
     8:                 #include <stdio.h>
     9:
    10:                 extern short sums(short);
    11:                 short status(short);
    12:
    13:                 short status(short orig)
    14:    365   0.2 { unsigned short new;
    15:    365   0.2   new=sums(orig);
    16:    365   0.2   if (orig>0 && new==0)
    17:      1   0.0   {printf("Sorry, the sum has exceeded capacity
                          (%u rows is too many)\n",orig);
    18:                  }
    19:      1   0.0   else
    20:    364   0.2   {printf("The sum of %u rows is %u\n",orig,new);
    21:                  }
    22:    365   0.2   return (new);
    23:      0   0.0 }
    24:
    25:                 void main()
    26:      1   0.0 { unsigned short j, x;
    27:      1   0.0   j=0;
    28:      5   0.0   while (j!=999)
    29:      4   0.0   { printf("Initial Value: ");
    30:      4   0.0   scanf("%u",&j);
    31:      4   0.0   if (j!=999)
    32:      3   0.0   { x=status(j);
```

```
33:                     }
34:      4    0.0   }
35:      1    0.0   for (j=1, x=1; x!=0; x=status(j++))
36:    362    0.2   ;
37:      1    0.0 }
```

Source file: sums.asm

```
        Hit
Line   count   %   Source
- - - - - - - - - - - - - - - - - - - - - - - - -
   1:                   Page 60,132
   2:                   Comment |
   3:***********************************************************************
   4:
   5:                   File:     SUMS.ASM for Microsoft Macro Assembler 6.0
   6:                   Author:   Allen L. Wyatt
   7:                   Date:     8/3/91
   8:
   9:                   Purpose:  Given an integer number X, find the sum of
  10:                             X + (X-1) + (X-2) + (X-3) + (X-4) ... + 2 + 1
  11:                             Designed to be called from Microsoft C.
  12:
  13:                   Format:   SUMS(X)
  14:
  15:***********************************************************************|
  16:
  17:                   PUBLIC    sums
  18:
  19:                   .MODEL    small, C
  20:                   .CODE
  21:
  22:    365   0.2 sums    PROC C Value:SWORD
  23:    365   0.2         MOV  AX,0             ;Initialize to zero
  24:    365   0.2         MOV  CX,Value         ;Get actual value
  25:    365   0.2         JCXZ S3               ;Num=0, no need to do
  26:  65806  32.6 S1:     ADC  AX,CX            ;Add row value
  27:  65806  32.6         JC   S2               ;Quit if AX overflowed
  28:  65805  32.6         LOOP S1               ;Repeat process
  29:    364   0.2         JMP  S3               ;Successful completion
  30:      1   0.0 S2:     MOV  AX,0             ;Force a zero
  31:    365   0.2 S3:     RET                   ;Return to C
  32:              sums    ENDP
  33:
  34:                      END
```

This information shows a line-by-line profile of your program, which can be even more useful as you are attempting to fine-tune your programs.

Timing Analysis

Timing analysis is particularly useful in determining which portions of a program are taking the most time. Then the functions that require the most time can be converted to assembly language to increase the speed and efficiency of your programs.

To illustrate the output of the profiler for timing results, I ran the FTIME and LTIME batch files on TEST.EXE, the program developed in Chapter 5 for testing the SUMS routine. The results of the function-level analysis (FTIME) stored in TEST.OUT follow:

```
Microsoft PLIST Version 1.00

Profile: Function timing, sorted by time.
Date:    Tue Oct 01 07:30:12 1991


Program Statistics
------------------
    Total time: 7003.032 milliseconds
    Time outside of functions: 2.912 milliseconds
    Call depth: 3
    Total functions: 3
    Total hits: 731
    Function coverage: 100.0%

Module Statistics for c:\test.exe
-----------------------------------------
    Time in module: 7000.120 milliseconds
    Percent of time in module: 100.0%
    Functions in module: 3
    Hits in module: 731
    Module function coverage: 100.0%

        Func          Func+Child       Hit
        Time    %      Time      %     count Function
    ------------------------------------------------
     3984.531  56.9   4017.217  57.4    365 status (test.c:14)
     2982.903  42.6   7000.120 100.0      1 main (test.c:26)
       32.686   0.5     32.686   0.5    365 sums (sums.asm:22)
```

This analysis tells you that well over half the time (56.9 percent) was spent in the status function—a routine that does processing only and (unlike the main function) does not wait for user input. Thus, if this were a time-critical program that needed improvement, the status function would be a candidate for conversion.

Examining the same information on a line-by-line basis is informative. The results of doing this (with the LTIME batch file) are stored in TEST.OUT, as follows:

```
Microsoft PLIST Version 1.00


Profile: Line timing, sorted by line.
Date:    Tue Oct 01 07:41:43 1991



Program Statistics
------------------
    Total time: 7713.861 milliseconds
    Time before any line: 1.167 milliseconds
    Total lines: 29
    Total hits: 201823
    Line coverage:  96.6%

Module Statistics for c:\test.exe
-----------------------------------------
    Time in module: 7712.695 milliseconds
    Percent of time in module: 100.0%
    Lines in module: 29
    Hits in module: 201823
    Module line coverage:  96.6%


Source file: test.c


          Line      Hit
  Line    Time   %  count Source
-----------------------------------------
    1:                    /* File:    TEST.C
    2:                     * Author:  Allen L. Wyatt
    3:                     * Date:    8/3/91
    4:                     *
    5:                     * Purpose: Program to test the calling of SUMS()
    6:                     */
    7:
    8:                    #include <stdio.h>
    9:
```

```
10:                            extern short sums(short);
11:                            short status(short);
12:
13:                            short status(short orig)
14:        1.442    0.0    365 { unsigned short new;
15:        0.892    0.0    365   new=sums(orig);
16:        0.762    0.0    365   if (orig>0 && new==0)
17:       16.599    0.2      1   {printf("Sorry, the sum has exceeded capacity
                                      (%u rows is too many)\n",orig);
18:                                }
19:        0.003    0.0      1   else
20:     3966.631   51.4    364   {printf("The sum of %u rows is %u\n",orig,new);
21:                                }
22:        1.500    0.0    365   return (new);
23:        0.000    0.0      0 }
24:
25:                            void main()
26:        0.006    0.0      1 { unsigned short j, x;
27:        0.003    0.0      1   j=0;
28:        0.004    0.0      5   while (j!=999)
29:       11.763    0.2      4   { printf("Initial Value: ");
30:     3576.825   46.4      4   scanf("%u",&j);
31:        0.022    0.0      4   if (j!=999)
32:        0.005    0.0      3   { x=status(j);
33:                                }
34:        0.004    0.0      4   }
35:        0.003    0.0      1   for (j=1, x=1; x!=0; x=status(j++))
36:        0.774    0.0    362   ;
37:        1.737    0.0      1 }
```

Source file: sums.asm

```
          Line        Hit
  Line    Time    %   count Source
----------------------------------------
    1:                      Page 60,132
    2:                      Comment ¦
    3:
********************************************************************
    4:
    5:                      File:    SUMS.ASM for Microsoft Macro Assembler 6.0
    6:                      Author:  Allen L. Wyatt
    7:                      Date:    8/3/91
    8:
    9:                      Purpose: Given an integer number X, find the sum of
```

```
10:                                    X + (X-1) + (X-2) + (X-3) + (X-4) ... + 2 + 1
11:                                    Designed to be called from Microsoft C.
12:
13:                        Format:     SUMS(X)
14:
15:
 ***************************************************************|
16:
17:                                    PUBLIC      sums
18:
19:                                    .MODEL      small, C
20:                                    .CODE
21:
22:    0.406    0.0    365 sums        PROC C Value:SWORD
23:    0.300    0.0    365             MOV  AX,0              ;Initialize to zero
24:    0.308    0.0    365             MOV  CX,Value          ;Get actual value
25:    0.137    0.0    365             JCXZ S3                ;Num=0, no need to do
26:   30.488    0.4  65806 S1:         ADC  AX,CX             ;Add row value
27:   58.790    0.8  65806             JC   S2                ;Quit if AX overflowed
28:   42.462    0.6  65805             LOOP S1                ;Repeat process
29:    0.443    0.0    364             JMP  S3                ;Successful completion
30:    0.000    0.0      1 S2:         MOV  AX,0              ;Force a zero
31:    0.387    0.0    365 S3:         RET                   ;Return to C
32:                        sums        ENDP
33:
34:                                    END
```

Notice that the original source code (if available in the current directory) is included in the report. Notice in the C source code that the output (printf) and input (scanf) lines account for 97.8 percent of the program's time. Thus, instead of replacing the entire status routine, you may decide to simply improve input and output performance.

One thing to keep in mind with a timing analysis, particularly at a line-by-line level, is that it dramatically slows down your program. Thus, completing the profiling process can take quite a while. The rewards, however, can be well worth the wait.

Using Borland's Turbo Profiler

Borland's profiler has been available for some time (much longer, in fact, than the Microsoft profiler has been available). And Borland's Turbo Profiler is much more compatible with their IDE (integrated development environment) concept.

When you load Turbo Profiler, the look and feel of the product is similar to the interactive modes of Borland's other language products.

Turbo Profiler is available with Turbo Debugger and Tools (the stand-alone package that included Turbo Assembler 2.5) or with professional versions of Borland's high-level languages, such as Borland C++ or Turbo Pascal 6.0.

Turbo Profiler enables you to perform a wide array of tests on your programs. You can test not only how often or how long files, modules, routines, or program lines execute, but also which computer resources—such as the disk, the keyboard, and the printer—are used.

Interestingly, Turbo Profiler also gives you complete flexibility to totally control what you monitor and how you monitor it. This capability is much more powerful (and potentially confusing) than Microsoft's profiler.

This chapter focuses only on doing a quick profiling session to see how long each line of our program takes to execute. Before you can use Turbo Profiler, you need to compile, assemble, and link your programs, making sure that you include all debugger information wherever possible. (This example assumes that you have compiled, assembled, and linked the files detailed in Chapter 6.)

Having prepared the files in this way, you can start Turbo Profiler with the following command:

```
TPROF TEST.EXE
```

which instructs Turbo Profiler to start and then load TEST.EXE. When this process is completed, your screen will look like the one shown in figure 8.1.

The top portion of the screen shows the source code for the current module (in this case, the main C++ program). The bottom portion, known as the Execution Profile window, displays statistics about any profiling tests already conducted.

To start profiling, you must tell Turbo Profiler what you want it to check. You do this by specifying *areas* to analyze. These areas can include files, modules, interrupts, overlays, or individual program lines. To specify which areas to profile, you can press Alt-F10, the standard key combination Turbo Profiler uses to bring up a *local* menu. The local menu differs according to which main window is active.

Assuming that the source-code window (the screen's top window) is active, press Alt-F10. Now your screen should resemble the one shown in figure 8.2.

Fig. 8.1. *The Turbo Profiler startup screen, with TEST.EXE loaded.*

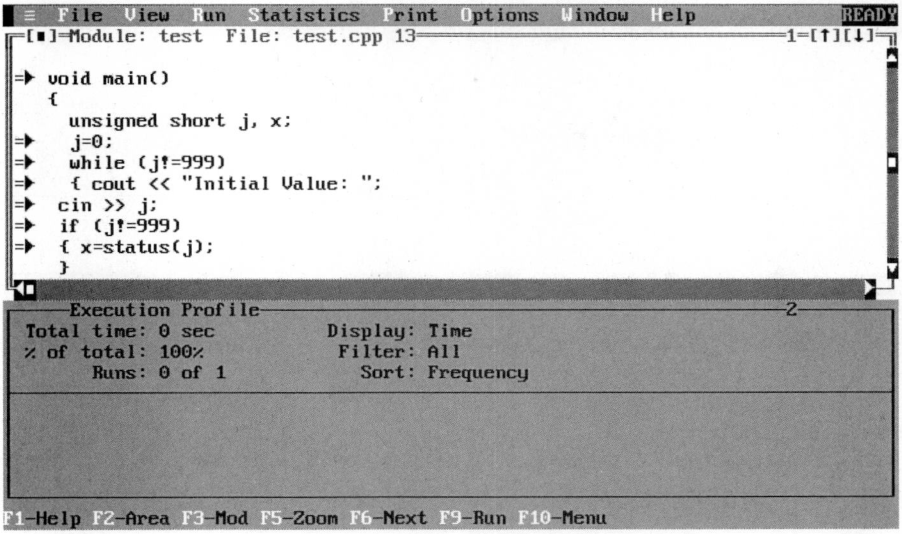

Fig. 8.2. *The local menu for the source-code window.*

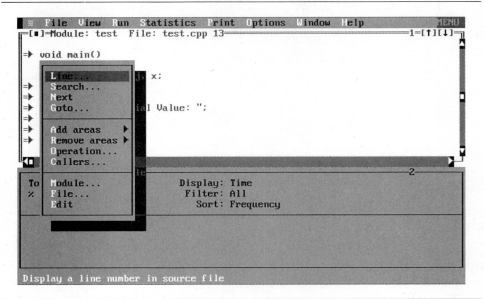

With the local menu displayed, you want to select Add areas. Then select Every line in module, thus instructing Turbo Profiler to monitor and profile every source-code line in the C++ program. If you want Turbo profiler to monitor and profile every line in the assembly language subroutine, you must select a different module for display in the source-code window.

To do so, press Alt-F10 again to bring up the local menu. Now select the Module option. Your screen will look like the one shown in figure 8.3.

Fig. 8.3. *The module selection menu.*

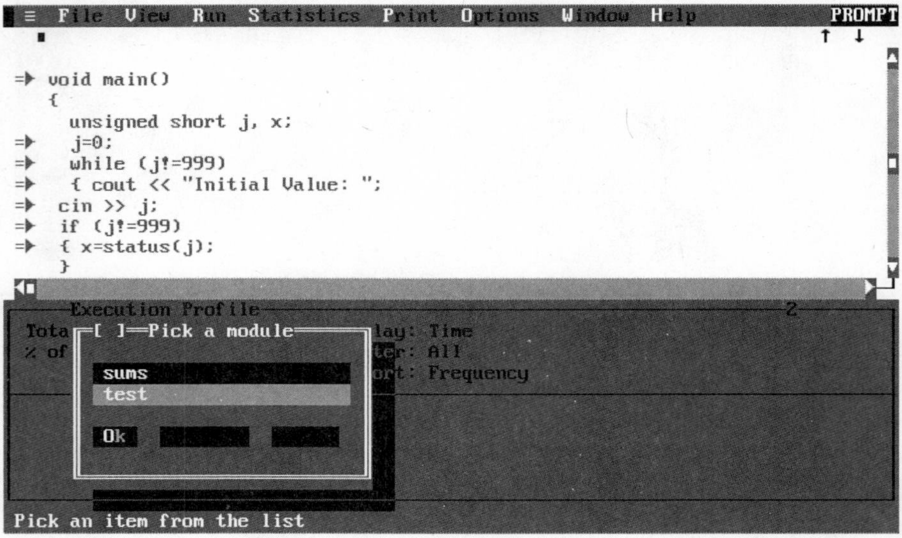

From this menu you can select which module, sums or test, you want to work with. Because you have already done your work with test, simply press Enter to select the sums module. When you do, the source code for SUMS.ASM should appear in the source-code window.

Now you can select all the source-code lines in this module. As you did with the C++ module, simply press Alt-F10 and then press **A** and **E**. Now you have informed Turbo Profiler that you want to monitor every line of the sums module, in addition to every line of the test module.

You are now ready to profile the program. Do this by pressing F9. The program runs normally, albeit much slower than it does from the DOS prompt. You should provide a few input numbers when prompted. Enter the number 999 to complete the program.

After TEST.EXE runs, you see the Turbo Profiler screen again. Your screen should resemble the one in figure 8.4.

Fig. 8.4. *The completed profiler screen.*

```
 ≡ File View Run Statistics Print Options Window Help          READY
  ─Module: sums  File: sums.asm 1──────────────────────────1──
   Page 60,132
   Comment ¦
   ***********************************************************************

   File:      SUMS.ASM for Turbo Assembler 3.0
   Author:    Allen L. Wyatt
   Date:      10/15/91

   Purpose:   Given an integer number X, find the sum of
              X + (X-1) + (X-2) + (X-3) + (X-4) ... + 2 + 1
              Designed to be called from Borland C++.

   ▪                                                         ↑ ↓
   Total time: 14.851 sec    Display: Time
   % of total: 99 %           Filter: All
          Runs: 1 of 1          Sort: Frequency

  #test#c:\lang\bc 5.9658 sec  40% |==============================
  #test#19         4.1619 sec  27% |=========================
  ostream::operato 1.3645 sec   8% |========
  #sums#29         1.0696 sec   7% |======
  F1-Help F2-Area F3-Mod F5-Zoom F6-Next F9-Run F10-Menu
```

Notice that the Execution Profile window is active and that the first item is highlighted. This highlighted item is the source-code line that took the longest to execute (about 40 percent of total execution time). You can see exactly which line it is by simply pressing Enter. When you do, the source-code window becomes active and displays the source-code line that took 40 percent of execution time. Notice that this line is in the C++ streams library, which has to do with COUT and CIN in this program. It is not unusual that these portions of the program should take the greatest percentage of time.

Activate the Execution Profile window again, and press the down arrow a few times. Notice that the highest percentage of time taken by a line from SUMS.ASM was about 7 percent. If you press Enter with this statistic highlighted, you will notice that this line is the LOOP directive in SUMS.ASM.

You can continue to work with the various displays and options in Turbo Profiler. Having had a glimpse of what it can do, you should realize that using it can be advantageous to your programs.

Summary

In this chapter, you have learned about makefiles and profilers. You have learned not only that judicious use of these makefiles can greatly simplify the task of maintaining your assembly language programs, but also how profilers can help you optimize your code.

You have seen also the significant differences between the major make and profiler utilities. Which flavor you use depends, in large part, on which assembler, high-level language, and linker you use.

Of the tools presented in this chapter, you probably will work most with makefiles, which can simplify your day-to-day programming tasks. But profilers should not be overlooked. You can use them toward the end of the development process to refine and sharpen your programs so that they are the best they can be.

CHAPTER 9

Developing Libraries

W hen it's time to link your assembly language subroutines, the process of specifying each file name can be unwieldy if you use an increasingly large number of routines. Consider, for example, the following external declaration section from one (and *only* one) subroutine, keeping in mind that these external subroutines call other subroutines, which may call still other subroutines:

```
; ****    OUTSIDE SUBROUTINES CALLED    ****
            EXTRN      SET_DI:NEAR
            EXTRN      CURSOR_ON:NEAR
            EXTRN      CURSOR_OFF:NEAR
            EXTRN      HORIZ_LINE:NEAR
            EXTRN      PRINT_CHAR:NEAR
            EXTRN      PRINT_STRING:NEAR
            EXTRN      ERASE_LINE:NEAR
            EXTRN      BOOP:NEAR
            EXTRN      CALC_LEN:NEAR
```

As you can imagine, the list of possible subroutines can become extensive. To solve this problem, you can place your assembly language OBJ files into a *library*, a special file that is searched when you go through the linking process.

The Advantages of Libraries

When the linker finds an external declaration, it looks for the external reference in the explicit OBJ file names you entered. If one of those files does not contain the external reference, the linker searches for the reference in any libraries

237

you named. If the reference is located, the linker extracts the OBJ module and combines it into the executable file being created.

This library concept relieves the programmer of several potential headaches (and errors) in the program-development process. If you change a source file, you can simply update the library and recompile or reassemble all files that use that routine—quick, simple, and effective.

In addition, the library greatly simplifies the task of distributing all the necessary routines. In fact, without the library concept, you would not have the high-level languages as you know them today. They all depend on their library routines to support input, output, and housekeeping requirements.

But all these advantages that libraries provide are not restricted to software publishers; you also can create libraries that contain your own customized routines. All you need is a library-maintenance program, and most assembler packages include a library utility as part of the package.

Library-Maintenance Programs

Both Microsoft's MASM and Borland's TASM provide library-maintenance programs as part of the package sold with the assembler. Other library-management software is available from various vendors.

Many library-maintenance programs are available, but to simplify our discussion this book focuses on a single system: a program (LIB.EXE) distributed with the Microsoft and IBM assembler packages. To show you how similar the other library programs are, I've also summarized the commands and operations of TLIB from Borland.

Don't be concerned if the descriptions that follow seem somewhat confusing; when you review them after you finish the chapter, they should be much clearer. The actions controlled by the program options involve details with which you are not yet familiar.

LIB from Microsoft

The LIB program has only seven options (listed in table 9.1), and three operation codes that can in some cases be combined for a total of five functional operations. The options can be given either on the command line (immediately following the word LIB and preceding the first OBJ file name), or in response to the first prompt.

Table 9.1. *LIB options.*

Option	Meaning
/?	Display quick help screen
/Help	Start extended help system
/Ignorecase	Force all symbols to uppercase
/NOIgnorecase	Do not change case of any symbols
/NOExtdict	Do not create extended dictionary for library
/NOLogo	Do not display the LIB introductory information
/PAgesize:	Set increment of storage space used (normally 16 bytes)

The operation codes are the plus sign (+) to add a module, the minus sign (-) to delete a module, and the asterisk (*) to copy a module to an OBJ file. The allowable combinations are minus-plus (-+) to replace an entry by deleting the old and adding the new, and minus-asterisk (-*) or asterisk-minus (*-) to move an entry by copying and relocating the entry and then deleting the entry at its original location).

For details of the use of these options and operations, read this chapter's sections on creating a library and maintaining a library.

TLIB from Borland

Borland's TLIB program has the same three operation codes as LIB and uses them identically. TLIB offers even fewer options than LIB, however, providing only the following pair:

❑ /C flags case (when used, TLIB becomes case-sensitive).

❑ /E creates an extended dictionary.

❑ /Psize sets storage space page size.

TLIB's /C option is the same as LIB's /NOI option, and TLIB's /E option is the opposite of LIB's /NOE option. If neither option is used, TLIB converts all public symbols to uppercase and does not create extended dictionaries.

Creating a Library

You create a library by using one of the library-maintenance programs. If you enter the examples in this book, you will have created several assembly language subroutines that can be joined together into a library (see table 9.2). Be sure that the OBJ files created for these routines are available; you will use them in this session.

Table 9.2. *Available files to be placed in a library file.*

File Name	Chapter	Function
CEX3.ASM	13	C cursor switch
CLREOL2.ASM	11	BASIC clear to end of line
READSCRN.ASM	12	Pascal screen read
SUMS.ASM	5	Linker example for C

Using LIB

Let's look first at how to use the software from Microsoft and IBM to create and modify libraries. Like MASM and LINK, LIB has several ways of getting its input data. Only the interactive method is discussed in this section; I explain the others later.

Make sure that you have the Microsoft LIB.EXE program on a floppy disk, either in the current directory or accessible through a search path. Then, at the DOS prompt, type the following command:

```
LIB
```

to execute the LIB.EXE program. You will see on your screen a notice and prompt similar to the following:

```
C:\>LIB

Microsoft (R) Library Manager  Version 3.18
Copyright (C) Microsoft Corp 1983-1991.  All rights reserved.

Library name: _
```

If you are using the IBM version of LIB.EXE, or a version of LIB which came with something other than MASM 6.0, your screen will look a little different. Because the prompts are similar, you should be able to follow this session.

Now type TEST, the name of the library file you want to create. Because the standard library extension (LIB) is appended automatically unless another extension is entered, the full name of this library is TEST.LIB. When you press Enter, the following prompt is displayed:

```
Library name: TEST
Library does not exist.  Create? (y/n) _
```

This prompt is just a precaution, in case you misspelled the name of the library. Because you are creating a new library, press Y. After you press Enter, your screen looks like this:

```
Library does not exist.  Create? (y/n) Y
Operations: _
```

LIB is requesting information about the operations you want to perform with TEST.LIB. The three basic operations are adding, deleting, and copying. By combining these basic commands, you can perform two additional operations. For instance, you can replace a library entry by deleting the old and then adding the new, or you can move the entry by deleting it at its original location and then copying the entry at a new location. Table 9.3 lists the available LIB operations.

Table 9.3. LIB operations.

Operation	Function
+	Add an OBJ file as a library entry
-	Delete a library entry
*	Copy a library entry
-+	Replace a library entry
-*	Move a library entry

Because you are creating a new library, you don't need to delete, copy, replace, or move an entry. You want to add OBJ files to the new library; to do so, enter the following at the Operations: prompt:

```
+CEX3 +CLREOL2 +READSCRN +SUMS
```

This entry instructs LIB to add to the newly created and still empty library the object-code files (CEX3.OBJ, CLREOL2.OBJ, READSCRN.OBJ, and SUMS.OBJ) you created in the chapters listed in table 9.2. (OBJ is the default file extension).

If you want to add any of the other OBJ files created in this book, you can. Just add a plus sign and include the name of the OBJ file. You may not want to add some of the examples from Chapter 11, "Interfacing with BASIC," however. The examples in that chapter which apply only to interpretive BASIC are not suitable for inclusion in a library.

If the operation commands you give to LIB run long, you can enter the commands on individual lines as follows:

```
Operations: +CEX3 +CLREOL2 &
Operations: +READSCRN +SUMS
```

The ampersand (&) at the end of the first line signifies that more follows. Use it if you cannot fit all the desired operations onto one command line.

Finally, the following prompt appears on the screen:

```
Operations: +CEX3 +CLREOL2 +READSCRN +SUMS
List file: _
```

A *list file*, which is optional, contains reference information you may find interesting and helpful. If you do not want a list file, simply press Enter; but here, for the sake of illustration, enter TEST.LST as a file name. Be sure to specify the LST file extension because LIB does not provide a default extension for list files.

After a few moments, the DOS prompt returns to the screen, signifying that LIB has created the library TEST.LIB. If any errors occur during the process of creating a library, an error message is displayed. (In some instances, notification of the action taken by LIB is displayed also.)

To get an idea of what happened during the process of creating the library, look at the list file that was created. If you type TEST.LST, you should see the following display:

```
C>TYPE TEST.LST

CLREOL...........clreol2         READSCRN..........readscrn
_CurSw...........cex3            _sums.............sums


cex3            Offset: 00000010H  Code and data size: 7bH
  _CurSw

clreol2         Offset: 000001c0H  Code and data size: 6dH
  CLREOL

readscrn        Offset: 00000360H  Code and data size: 62H
  READSCRN

sums            Offset: 000004a0H  Code and data size: 72H
  _sums

C:\>_
```

The list file (in this case, TEST.LST) contains information about the newly created library: the names of the modules in the library, as well as information about where each module begins and the length of each module. From this TEST.LST file, you can see that the file SUMS (the OBJ extension is assumed) contains the public label _SUMS, that the module begins at a file offset of 4A0h, and that its length is 72h. Note that a leading underscore precedes the module name of modules prepared for use with C programs. The linker requires C programs to have this underscore; the assembler adds it automatically because you indicated in the source file that you want to use the C language model.

Using TLIB

Because TLIB has no interactive capability, you must pass all its input data either on the command line or in a response file. The response-file method is identical to that used by LIB and explained later in this chapter; this section describes only the use of the command line.

Make sure you have the TLIB.EXE program on a floppy disk, in the current directory, or accessible through a search path. Then, at the DOS prompt, enter the following command:

```
TLIB TEST +CEX3 +CLREOL2 +READSCRN +SUMS, TEST.LST
```

This tells TLIB to create or update the library TEST.LIB, adding the four OBJ modules (CEX3.OBJ, CLREOL2.OBJ, READSCRN.OBJ, and SUMS.OBJ), and to create a listing file, TEST.LST.

After you enter the command, the following is displayed on-screen:

```
TLIB 3.01   Copyright (c) 1991 Borland International

C:\>_
```

That's all there is to it! Your library file is now created. If you had entered the command line incorrectly, or an error had occurred, an error message would have been displayed. If no problems occur during library creation, no messages are shown.

Here is the listing file (TEST.LST) you asked TLIB to create:

```
Publics by module

CEX3     size = 123
    CurSw

CLREOL2  size = 109
    CLREOL
```

```
READSCRN  size = 98
     READSCRN

SUMS       size = 114
    _sums
```

Although TLIB's listing file is much less wordy than the one provided by LIB, it gives you all the essential information: the module names, the symbol names, and the size of each module. Unlike LIB, which lists sizes in hexadecimal, the TLIB report is in decimal, which makes it much more comprehensible to the average reader.

Using a Library

Now that you have learned how to create a library using LIB or TLIB, let's see how the result can be used. Again, although I mostly use Microsoft products in my examples, the following explanations apply to both LIB and TLIB, except for a few specific details that I point out as appropriate.

Linking with a Library

As you may recall from Chapters 5 and 6, one of the LINK prompts asked which libraries to use in the linking process. Because libraries had not yet been discussed, the discussion of linking libraries was deferred to this chapter. Now that you have created a library (TEST.LIB), you can perform the linking process again to see how TEST.LIB affects the process.

When you enter the LINK command at the DOS prompt, your screen should look like this:

```
C:\>LINK
Microsoft (R) Segmented-Executable Linker  Version 5.13
Copyright (C) Microsoft Corp 1984-1991.  All rights reserved.

Object Modules [.OBJ]: _
```

Type TEST (the name of the object file used in Chapter 5), and then, to signify that the run file will be the default file, press Enter. Your screen should look like this:

```
Object Modules [.OBJ]: test
Run File [test.exe]:
List File [NUL.MAP]: _
```

Because you do not need a list file for this example, simply press Enter. Now comes the important question:

```
List File [NUL.MAP]:
Libraries [.LIB]: _
```

In response to this prompt, enter the name of the library (or libraries) you want to use to link this file. If you enter several library names, use spaces to separate them. You don't have to include a file extension (LIB is assumed).

To continue with the sample library (TEST.LIB), simply type TEST and press Enter. LINK asks no further questions but goes to work on the tasks you specified. First, all the specified object files are linked together (in this case, there is only one: TEST.OBJ). Then, if any unresolved external references remain, the library files are searched to see whether the references are included as public symbol declarations. Thus, when _SUMS cannot be located in TEST.OBJ, TEST.LIB is examined to ascertain whether it contains the symbol. If (as in this case) the library file contains the symbol, the module containing the symbol is extracted from TEST.LIB and linked to TEST.OBJ.

If any other unresolved external references remain (in other words, if the _SUMS routine contains any references that cannot be satisfied internally to _SUMS or in the TEST.OBJ file), the library is searched again. This search-and-include cycle continues until all possible references have been resolved. If some references cannot be resolved, LINK generates an error message and the linkage process stops.

If an error message such as the following occurs:

```
C:\>LINK
Microsoft (R) Segmented-Executable Linker  Version 5.13
Copyright (C) Microsoft Corp 1984-1991.  All rights reserved.

Object Modules [.OBJ]: test
Run File [test.exe]:
List File [NUL.MAP]: _
Libraries [.LIB]: test

Unresolved externals:

_sums in file(s):
TEST.OBJ(test.C)

There was 1 error detected

C:\>_
```

you know that LINK could not find the subroutine in the object file (TEST.OBJ) or in the library (TEST.LIB). Usually, this means that you have forgotten to include all necessary files in the library. Check your work again and try the linking procedure one more time.

Creating and Using Library Response Files

With LIB, as with LINK, you can provide a file (cleverly called a *response file*) of responses to questions. Because repeatedly typing answers to each question is tiresome, this method of using LIB is beneficial when you know that you will be adjusting a library time and again during development.

To use this method of providing input to LIB, create an ASCII text file that contains the answers to each question. You can give this file whatever name you want. Just be sure to place the answer to each question on a separate line. For instance, I regularly create a new library of all my assembly language subroutines by using the following LIB response file:

```
\assemble\huge.lib
Y
+ \assemble\obj\asciibin &
+ \assemble\obj\box &
+ \assemble\obj\boxita &
+ \assemble\obj\calclen &
+ \assemble\obj\cdir &
+ \assemble\obj\clrwndow &
+ \assemble\obj\cls &
+ \assemble\obj\conascii &
+ \assemble\obj\conhex &
+ \assemble\obj\concase &
+ \assemble\obj\crc &
+ \assemble\obj\cursoff &
+ \assemble\obj\curson &
+ \assemble\obj\dait &
+ \assemble\obj\dayt &
+ \assemble\obj\direct &
+ \assemble\obj\eraselne &
+ \assemble\obj\findcard &
+ \assemble\obj\fmenu &
+ \assemble\obj\fsize &
+ \assemble\obj\getkey &
+ \assemble\obj\getline &
```

```
+ \assemble\obj\getlinea &
+ \assemble\obj\getyn &
+ \assemble\obj\horiz &
+ \assemble\obj\invert &
+ \assemble\obj\mbindiv &
+ \assemble\obj\mencom &
+ \assemble\obj\menuar &
+ \assemble\obj\menubox &
+ \assemble\obj\message &
+ \assemble\obj\motr &
+ \assemble\obj\pauztick &
+ \assemble\obj\pauztime &
+ \assemble\obj\pchar &
+ \assemble\obj\pmsg &
+ \assemble\obj\pnum &
+ \assemble\obj\pstrng &
+ \assemble\obj\pstrng2 &
+ \assemble\obj\qscreen &
+ \assemble\obj\sbox &
+ \assemble\obj\scrn &
+ \assemble\obj\scrnbas &
+ \assemble\obj\seekey &
+ \assemble\obj\setcolor &
+ \assemble\obj\setdi &
+ \assemble\obj\soundasm &
+ \assemble\obj\soundbas &
+ \assemble\obj\tbox &
+ \assemble\obj\timer &
+ \assemble\obj\vidbas &
+ \assemble\obj\viddata
\assemble\huge.lst
;
```

Notice the response on the second line of this file, the letter Y, which is there to answer the following question:

```
Library does not exist. Create? (y/n): _
```

LIB asks this question if it cannot find HUGE.LIB. The construction of this response file presupposes that the original library (if any) has been deleted. The Y response causes LIB to combine into HUGE.LIB the 52 specified object-code files. The ampersand (&) at the end of each line (except the final file-specification line) tells LIB that additional commands follow. Finally, LIB is directed to create a list file called HUGE.LST.

If you are using TLIB, omit the Y line from a TLIB response file because TLIB does not ask the Create? question. Otherwise, TLIB works exactly the same way as LIB, even though it has no interactive mode to imitate.

To use a response with LIB, simply invoke LIB with the following command syntax:

```
LIB @filename.ext
```

or, if you are using TLIB, use the following syntax:

```
TLIB @filename.ext
```

where *filename.ext* is the name of the response file to be used. Notice the @ symbol immediately preceding the file name. LIB needs this key symbol to differentiate between a response file and a library name.

If the sample response file were called HUGE.LRF, you could use it by issuing the following command:

```
LIB @HUGE.LRF
```

As you repeatedly use LIB, you will appreciate being able to use response files.

Maintaining a Library

After you become accustomed to the idea of creating libraries to keep collections of similar assembly language routines together in one place, and to using libraries when you create programs, you come face-to-face with the need to maintain your libraries. You need to add new routines or change old ones, and you may even want to extract routines from one library and add them to another.

This is all made simple by the library-managing programs. First I'll show you how it's done, by correcting the conflict that showed up earlier as TEST.LIB was created. Then I'll discuss some techniques to help make the entire library-management task easier.

Making Changes to a Library

Changing a library file is as easy as creating one. By using the commands to delete, add, copy, replace, or move, you can update an existing library to meet current needs. For example, let's assume that you have made some changes to the file CLREOL2.ASM. You reassembled the file, and now you need to add the new OBJ file to TEST.LIB to replace the old CLREOL2 module. You can update TEST.LIB by using the following dialog:

```
C:\>LIB

Microsoft (R) Library Manager  Version 3.18
Copyright (C) Microsoft Corp 1983-1991.  All rights reserved.

Operations: -+clreol2
List file: test.lst
Output library:

C:\>_
```

The key to this entire dialog is the -+ operation code, which told the library-manager program to delete (-) the existing copy from the library file and then append (+) a new copy from CLREOL2.OBJ. This process updates TEST.LIB with the new version of the CLREOL2 module.

Notice the final question asked by LIB in this dialog (Output library:). It gives you the opportunity to give a different name to the library created as a result of the operations you are requesting. If TEST.LIB were a brand new file, this question would not be displayed. If you simply press Enter in response to this question, the output library is assumed to have the same name as the original library. The original library is saved as a backup (in this instance, as TEST.BAK).

What if a module you want to add is in another directory or on another disk? You simply provide the necessary information at the Operations: prompt, as in the following dialog:

```
C:\>LIB

Microsoft (R) Library Manager  Version 3.18
Copyright (C) Microsoft Corp 1983-1991.  All rights reserved.

Operations: -clreol2 +d:\obj\clreol2
List file: test.lst
Output library:

C:\>_
```

Notice that you indicate the deletion and addition as two separate steps. The result, however, is the same as in the previous example.

To modify the library in other ways, simply specify the operation you want performed (refer to table 9.3) and the name of the file module you want to modify.

Managing a Library

As you add files to your library, you can follow either of two avenues usually taken by programmers: you can create one large library containing (in one convenient location) all your subroutines, or you can create several smaller libraries, each representing a specialized category of subroutine.

Let's assume that you want to manage only one large library and that, from time to time, you would like to be able to update one of the subroutines in the library. Updating the library is simple if you combine the procedures you have learned in this chapter with the capabilities of DOS batch files. You can apply the same techniques to smaller libraries, as well.

The usual process for updating a library is as follows:

1. Assemble the source file.

2. Delete the original OBJ file from the library.

3. Add the new OBJ file to the library.

Let's assume that your library is called HUGE.LIB and that, to make matters more complicated, you need to update several files. You can update your library by using the following batch file (UPDATE.BAT) to perform the three steps:

```
@echo off
 cls
 del *.obj >nul
 del \assemble\hugelib.txt
 :loop
     if %1\ == \ goto exit
         echo Working on %1.asm
         echo Assembling %1.asm >>\assemble\hugelib.txt
         ml /c /Cx /Fo%1.obj /Fl %1.asm >>\assemble\hugelib.txt
         echo Adding %1.obj to HUGE.LIB >>\assemble\hugelib.txt
         lib \assemble\huge -+%1; >>\assemble\hugelib.txt
         shift
         goto loop
:exit
del *.obj >nul
```

This batch file assumes that MASM and LIB are in the current directory or the search path, that the source file (ASM) is in the current directory, and that you want HUGE.LIB to be in the subdirectory ASSEMBLE.

The proper syntax for this batch file is

```
UPDATE file1 file2 file3 file4 ....
```

where *file1* is the root file name of the ASM file to be updated in the library. *file2*, *file3*, *file4*, and so on are the optional names of other source files that you want updated to the library.

After this batch file has completed its job, the dialog normally presented by MASM and LIB is saved (in the ASSEMBLE subdirectory) in a file called HUGELIB.TXT. Any errors are noted in this file. Notice the use of the >> redirection symbol, rather than the usual >; this forces each stage of the process to append its messages to the end of the file. If you use the > symbol instead, only the report from the last LIB run will be in HUGELIB.TXT.

Summary

This chapter has shown you how to create, change, and manage libraries and how libraries fit into the linking process.

Libraries, which are intended to make the programmer's life easier, can be a headache if they are not managed properly or logically. Take time to think through your library needs. Consider how to fit library use into your normal methods for program development. Then develop some batch files (such as the one described in this chapter) to help you make the most of libraries.

As you become adept at using libraries, you will find that they can make your tasks much easier.

Part II

Mixed Language Programming with Assembly Language

10

Interfacing Subroutines

W hen you interface assembly language subroutines with a high-level language, you must address the following:

❏ How the subroutine is invoked

❏ How parameters are passed

❏ How values are returned

This chapter does not attempt to address the specifics of all these points. The nitty-gritty details of each of these considerations are covered in Part II: Mixed Language Programming (Chapters 10 through 15). The way you invoke an assembly language subroutine, for example, largely depends on the high-level language from which that subroutine is called. The information in this chapter is more or less common to the process of interfacing assembly language subroutines, no matter which high-level language you may be using.

Let's look first at how parameters are passed to assembly language subroutines. Later in this chapter you will see how values are returned to a high-level language.

Passing Parameters

Generally, the stack is used to pass parameters to subroutines. As you learned from Chapter 1, "Understanding the Programming Environment," the stack is a general-purpose work area; using it correctly is critical to successful program execution.

Not all languages pass parameters on the stack. Parameters can be passed also in the CPU registers or in some other memory area (usually called a *parameter block*). Neither of these methods is widely used, however; you probably will use them only when you work with DBMS languages. Chapters 14 and 15 discuss these methods in more detail.

Because each high-level language uses memory in different ways, a common area is needed for subroutine interfacing. The accepted standard for this area is the stack. If you push the parameters on the stack before you call a subroutine, the subroutine can access and modify the data. To prepare for the discussion of how parameters are accessed on the stack, let's look at how the data is placed on the stack and how parameters are formatted.

How Parameters Are Placed on the Stack

Although the specifics of how parameters are pushed on the stack are determined by the type of data the parameter represents and which high-level language you use, individual parameters usually are passed either as data values or as pointers to the values.

Normally, if the parameter is a short numeric integer (16 bits or less), its data value is pushed on the stack. If the parameter is an alphanumeric string, a pointer to the string is passed. A parameter that is a large numeric integer or a floating-point number can be passed by either method.

Because parameter placement differs from language to language, later chapters cover the specifics for each language.

How Parameters Are Formatted

Individual parameter format may vary from language to language. For instance, if the data value of a floating-point number is being passed on the stack, the high-level language you are using determines the way in which the number is encoded.

Parameters must occupy at least one complete word (16 bits) on the stack, although, depending on the high-level language, additional words can be used. If that one word is a pointer to the variable in the high-level language's data segment, the translation of the data at that memory location will differ from language to language. The number of bytes each data element uses is particularly open to variation. Again, later chapters cover specifics for parameter format.

Accessing Parameters on the Stack

Two methods can be used to access information passed through the stack (these methods translate to the same method when your assembly language programs are assembled). The routines in this book use simplified segment- and language-specification directives found in both MASM and TASM. These directives enable you to specify in plain English the type of language you are interfacing with. Then the assembler takes care of accessing the parameters on the stack.

Note that the simplified language directives are available only for such general-purpose programming languages as BASIC, C, Pascal, and FORTRAN. They are not available for specific-purpose languages such as database languages. If a specific database passes parameters through the stack, they must be accessed using the older, nonsimplified methods, by direct coding access using the BP register (the base pointer, introduced in Chapter 1).

In older incarnations of MASM and TASM, the BP register was used for accessing information on the stack. This register is used as a secondary stack pointer, primarily for accessing data on the stack relative to a given location. The simplified directives referred to a short time ago actually translate into instructions that use BP to access the stack.

The specific way you use the BP register depends largely on the type of subroutine being called. Let's look at the contents of the stack when the assembly language subroutine is a NEAR procedure. Even if you are using the language directives, an understanding of how the assembler accesses parameters on the stack is important.

When the subroutine is invoked, each individual parameter is pushed on the stack, followed by the calling program's return address. In a NEAR procedure, this return address is the segment offset—technically, the incremented contents of the instruction pointer (IP) register. Thus, at the start of the assembly language subroutine to which three 16-bit parameters are being passed, the stack would look like the one shown in figure 10.1.

If the routine being called were a FAR procedure, the stack contents would look like those in figure 10.2.

Fig. 10.1. Stack at beginning of execution of a NEAR procedure.

????
????
????
????
high byte of return address offset
low byte of return address offset

←——stack pointer (SP) is here

Fig. 10.2. Stack at beginning of execution of a FAR procedure.

????
????
high byte of return address segment
low byte of return address segment
high byte of return address offset
low byte of return address offset

←——stack pointer (SP) is here

Notice that invoking a FAR procedure involves pushing one additional word of data. This word is the segment of the calling program, technically the contents of the code segment (CS) register.

Other than the number of bytes pushed for the return address, the information for both procedures is in the same format and in a predictable position on the stack. To access the information, you simply set the BP register and use offsets to retrieve values from the stack. The following code segment shows the proper way to do this in a NEAR procedure, assuming that the parameters have been placed on the stack by a C compiler and that each occupies 16 bits; the code segment would be slightly different for other languages:

```
PARM_A      EQU     4
PARM_B      EQU     6
PARM_C      EQU     8

TEST        PROC    NEAR
            PUSH    BP
            MOV     BP,SP
```

```
           MOV     AX,[BP]+PARM_A
           MOV     BX,[BP]+PARM_B
           MOV     CX,[BP]+PARM_C

; REST OF PROGRAM GOES HERE

           POP     BP
           RET
TEST       ENDP
```

Notice that the three parameters are called PARM_A, PARM_B, and PARM_C in this subroutine. PARM_A, PARM_B, and PARM_C are equated with a specific offset value at the beginning of the program. When the subroutine executes, the first commands encountered set the base pointer so that it can be used with the offset values to access the parameters. Let's follow what happens in this coding segment step by step.

Remember that, on entry, the stack looks like the one shown in figure 2.1. At this point, the return address occupies the two bytes at stack offset 0, and the parameters begin with the byte at offset 2. To save the contents of the BP register, however, you must push the register on the stack. After you push BP on the stack, the value of BP occupies the two bytes at stack offset 0, followed by the two-byte return address; the parameters then begin at an offset of 4.

The next instruction sets BP equal to the current stack pointer (SP), which means that BP contains the stack offset address of the old BP value. Because you know that the parameters begin at offset 4, you can access them through indirect addressing, using BP and an offset.

At the end of the subroutine, you must pop BP off the stack. Doing so leaves the stack clean and restores BP (BP must be restored because it is almost always used in the calling program).

Because a call to a FAR procedure results in an additional word on the stack, the only change necessary to the preceding coding segment is that of changing the equates (EQU) to

```
PARM_A     EQU     6
PARM_B     EQU     8
PARM_C     EQU     10
```

This change compensates for the additional word placed on the stack when the FAR procedure is called.

Now that you understand how BP is used to access parameter information on the stack, you should understand also that using the simplified language directives is a much easier way to access parameters. The same code segment just discussed would look like this if you used the simplified directives:

```
TEST        PROC     NEAR C PARM_A:WORD, PARM_B:WORD, PARM_C:WORD

            MOV      AX,PARM_A
            MOV      BX,PARM_B
            MOV      CX,PARM_C

; REST OF PROGRAM GOES HERE

            RET
TEST        ENDP
```

Notice how much shorter the code is. The assembler takes care of the routine work; since you have declared at the beginning of the procedure that you will use the assembler to pass information from C, it knows how to translate the three MOV instructions in the body of the procedure. Your job as programmer is made simpler.

Returning Values

Values usually are returned from an assembly language subroutine in one of the following ways:

❏ Through the stack

❏ Through a register

❏ Through memory

None of these methods is automatic; you must predetermine how you will return values. The high-level language with which you are interfacing is the major determinant for selecting which method to use. Some languages require that you use a certain method; others, such as C, allow some programming flexibility.

Let's take a look at each method.

Returning Values through the Stack

The stack can be used not only for passing parameters but also for returning values. For example, if the calling program pushes four unsigned integer numbers on the stack before calling an assembly language subroutine, the subroutine can use and even modify these four words of data. On return to the controlling program, the four values remain on the stack. The controlling program can retrieve and use these values, which may have been altered by the subroutine. In some languages, this is a common way to pass information to and from a subroutine.

Returning Values through a Register

In some languages, such as C, you can provide a return value in a register. Because the expected register varies from language to language and possibly from version to version, be sure to verify which registers to use for your particular language.

As an example of this method of returning values, assume that a calling program uses the following command line to invoke an assembly language subroutine:

```
x=whizbang();
```

Clearly, whatever the purpose of the whizbang subroutine, a return value is expected and will be assigned to the variable x. The format of x determines the value's expected format. If we assume that x is a 16-bit integer, a value can be returned in a register, such as AX, and then the high-level language will assign the contents of AX to the variable x. This is how 16-bit values are returned in C.

Returning Values through Memory

If your high-level language passes pointers to data instead of passing data values, you can modify high-level language variables directly.

When passing string variables to a subroutine, many high-level languages pass only a pointer to the string's memory location. Because the length of the string may vary, passing the entire string on the stack is unrealistic. Using the pointer, however, you can access the string directly and even make changes to it (the changes are then available to the high-level language).

This method has powerful possibilities but also has a drawback. For example, an assembly language subroutine cannot readily change the length of a string. Changing memory allocation is dangerous when that allocation is under the control of a high-level language. Many pointers and assumptions that affect the high-level language's use of the variable may be in play and, by changing the data length, you may overwrite other data or invalidate other pointers. Either of these possibilities is dangerous to successful program execution.

You can prevent most potential problems by making sure that you pass a string long enough for any reasonable amount of data you might need to return. For instance, dBASE permits strings to be as many as 255 bytes long; therefore, passing a string of 255 blanks to your routine provides buffer space big enough to handle *any* string the language permits. If you know that you will never need more than 64 bytes in the return value, however, passing a 64-byte string will be adequate.

Other Considerations

In addition to the observations already made about the stack and its use, I want to point out several other considerations. Mainly, these are tips for you to keep in mind when you do any programming that manipulates the stack.

As you've learned, additional data (I call it *overhead data*) is pushed on the stack when a procedure is invoked. One item of this data—the return address for the calling program—is common to all high-level languages.

Inadvertently changing this overhead data can, and usually does, have disastrous effects. For example, if the return address is modified, program execution does not resume at the proper point in the calling program. If you are lucky, the entire system may "hang" and require rebooting; if you are extremely unlucky, control could accidentally drop into the DOS routine that reformats your hard disk!

A more common error is failure to remove information that was pushed on the stack or failure to restore the stack pointer properly after using the stack for temporary storage. This leaves the stack "dirty." Figure 10.3 illustrates what may happen if you inadvertently leave an extra word of data on the stack.

Fig. 10.3. Corrupted stack; too much data left at end of procedure.

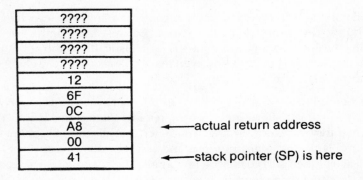

When a RET (return) instruction is executed, execution resumes at 0CA8:0041 instead of at 126F:0CA8 (the proper return address). The return address varies according to what is left on the stack. And the results of this error vary, depending on the memory contents beginning at the erroneous return address. This address may be in the program or, as in figure 10.3, it may be somewhere outside the program area. To solve the problem of program execution that does not continue as you want it to, make sure that everything pushed on the stack is subsequently popped off. Then execute the return.

A similar error occurs if you pop too much data from the stack; execution continues at an unintended memory address.

These two errors bring up an interesting (and potentially devastating) possibility, which has already been mentioned. Many hard disk manufacturers include a set of low-level routines in ROM. These routines, which include low-level hard disk formatting and other preparation software, lie quietly in wait until you call them—either purposely or inadvertently. It is possible, although unlikely, that an erroneous return address on the stack could cause program execution to resume at a memory address located at the start of the formatting code for the hard disk (or other dangerous code). The results could be devastating. To guard against such a possibility, back up your hard disk at regular intervals, and make sure that your routines leave the proper return address undisturbed.

Data Manipulation Tips

When working with data passed to assembly language subroutines, you should follow several safety guidelines:

1. Never manipulate data values unless you need to.

2. Use intermediate working variables or registers during execution of assembly language subroutines.

3. *Always* remember to leave the stack as it was when the routine was called. The stack should be free of extraneous data. (Simplified language directives handle much of this for you in the latest assembler versions.)

4. Make sure not to pop too much data from the stack.

5. Determine your subroutine procedure ahead of time, and make allowance for it. Is it NEAR or FAR? The type of subroutine affects how data is accessed.

6. Take special care to preserve the calling program's return address unchanged.

Summary

Because different high-level languages use memory in different ways, a common way to pass information to assembly language subroutines is mandatory.

The accepted method is to pass information on the stack, where that data can be accessed by the assembly language subroutines.

This chapter introduced and explained some general concepts, but did not cover language-specific information. In the following five chapters, you will discover how to interface specific high-level languages with assembly language subroutines.

CHAPTER 11

Interfacing with BASIC

B ASIC (Beginner's All-purpose Symbolic Instruction Code) is perhaps the most popular of all computer languages. Its free-form structure, easy English-like vocabulary, and low cost make it the most widely distributed language in the world of microcomputers.

Although BASIC is popular, it has several shortcomings that have caused some people to disdain the language and other people to adopt apparently unorthodox methods of circumventing the problem areas.

BASIC's slowness is its most serious and memorable legacy. I use the word *legacy* because many newer implementations of BASIC, most notably QuickBASIC, are compiled languages that have overcome the slowness of yesteryear. Yet the bad reputation for slowness persists with many programmers.

BASIC began as an interpretive language; indeed, many interpretive versions of BASIC are still available. In these versions, every line of source code is parsed to its machine language equivalent when the code is executed, a process that ultimately slows down BASIC programs. The only reliable way to get around this problem is to use a BASIC compiler, which translates the BASIC source code into machine language for subsequent execution. Using a compiler greatly increases speed but also increases development time and destroys the interactive nature of the language. The frustration of this dilemma was somewhat alleviated after Microsoft's QuickBASIC and Borland's TurboBASIC (now called PowerBASIC) were introduced, however. In environments like these, you get both the interactive advantages of interpretive BASIC and the increased power and speed of a compiled language.

To overcome the slowness of interpretive BASIC (and some compiled BASIC routines), many programmers have resorted to the technique of reducing time-consuming procedures to their assembly language equivalent, and then combining

265

them with the BASIC program. This technique, which is certainly not without perils, is the type of assembly language interfacing covered in this chapter.

Those who turned to compiled BASIC seemed to solve the speed problem—for a while. IBM's BASIC compiler (introduced in the early 1980s and made to work with DOS versions prior to 2.0) did not support such features as hierarchical directories and path names, but programmers could use assembly language subroutines to sidestep these deficiencies. Many programmers converted other routines to assembly language; execution time for those routines was noticeably faster. The newer compilers such as QuickBASIC, TurboBASIC (now called PowerBASIC), and the Professional Development System (PDS) from Microsoft removed many of the barriers to compiler use.

This chapter examines both interpretive and compiled BASIC. First, let's look at the process of interfacing with interpretive BASIC. The next couple of sections deal with GW-BASIC and BASICA, the BASIC interpreters distributed with every version of DOS through 4.01. Shortly, QBasic, the interpretive BASIC that comes with DOS 5.0, also is discussed.

Working with GW-BASIC or BASICA

Shielded from the computer's day-to-day, machine-level intricacies, most interpretive BASIC programmers do not have to concern themselves with where code or data reside, or how peripherals are interfaced with the computer. The BASIC interpreter takes care of all these matters behind the scenes. A limited number of commands enable you to examine BASIC's internal workings more closely, however. These commands, which include VARPTR and DEF SEG, are not used frequently in the course of normal, BASIC-only programming.

You can use several methods to interface assembly language subroutines with BASIC. This chapter focuses on two methods: storing short routines in string variables, and storing long routines in a set position in memory. Each method is well-suited for different types of subroutines, depending on their length.

Interfacing Short Subroutines

You can enter short subroutines directly into memory by placing them in the variable space used by BASIC strings. These subroutines must (by definition) be short because, under interpretive BASIC, strings cannot be longer than 255 characters.

To place an assembly language subroutine into a string, follow these steps:

1. Determine the length (in bytes) of the machine language subroutine.

2. Set aside a string variable equal in length to the number of bytes determined in Step 1.

3. Move the subroutine, byte by byte, into the memory space occupied by the string variable.

After completing these steps, you can call the subroutine at any time by simply calling the address associated with the string variable.

To understand this method of interfacing an assembly language subroutine, let's look at a practical example; because interpretive BASIC has CLS but no "clear to end of line" capability, let's create a subroutine that provides it. First comes the actual assembly language coding:

```
Page 60,132
Comment ¦
*****************************************************************


File:    CLREOL.ASM
Author:  Allen L. Wyatt
Date:    8/17/91

Purpose: Subroutine to clear screen from current cursor position to end
         of line.  Designed to be called from interpretive BASIC.

Format:  CALL D      <--- D is the address of the subroutine


*****************************************************************¦

               PUBLIC  CLREOL

               .MODEL  large,BASIC
               .CODE

CLREOL         PROC

               MOV     AH,0Fh          ; get video mode data
               INT     10h             ; using BIOS function
               XCHG    AH,AL           ; set up COLS data
               XOR     AH,AH
               PUSH    AX              ; and save it
```

```
                    MOV      AH,03h              ; get current cursor pos
                    INT      10h
                    XOR      DH,DH               ; ignore row
                    POP      CX                  ; get width back
                    SUB      CX,DX               ; calc number left on line
                    MOV      AX,0A20h            ; write char only, blank
                    INT      10h

                    RET
CLREOL              ENDP

                    END
```

This simple little subroutine first checks how many character positions are on a line (since BASIC can have either 40 or 80 columns), then finds out which column the cursor is currently in, calculates how many characters are needed to reach the end of the line, and finally writes that many blank spaces, starting at the current position, without moving the cursor. All of this magic is done by three calls to the video BIOS routine.

After completing the three steps outlined at the beginning of this section, you must then determine the number of bytes required by the preceding routine. To make this simpler, you can use the following BASIC program after you have assembled the assembler source program into an OBJ file:

```
10 ' ****************************************************************
15 ' *                                                              *
20 ' * File:     OBJREAD.BAS                                        *
25 ' * Author:   Allen L. Wyatt                                     *
30 ' * Date:     8/17/91                                            *
35 ' *                                                              *
40 ' * Purpose:  Analyzes an OBJ file created by MASM or TASM,      *
45 ' *           displaying the data values necessary to poke       *
50 ' *           short assembly language subroutines into           *
55 ' *           string space.                                      *
60 ' *                                                              *
65 ' ****************************************************************
70 '
100 CLS
110 LINE INPUT "Name of OBJ file to analyze: ";FI$
120 IF FI$="" THEN END
130 IF INSTR(FI$,".")=0 THEN FI$=FI$+".OBJ"
140 OPEN FI$ FOR RANDOM AS #1 LEN = 1
150 FIELD #1, 1 AS A$
160 P = 1
```

```
170 GET #1, P : P = P + 1
180 IF ASC(A$) = 160 THEN 220
190 GET #1, P
200 P = P + 2 + ASC(A$)
210 GOTO 170
220 CLS
230 PRINT "Use the following data statements in your program:" : PRINT
240 GET #1, P : P = P + 5
250 N = ASC(A$) - 4
260 PRINT "1000 DATA"; N;
270 L = 1010
280 FOR J = N TO 1 STEP -1
290 IF Z = 0 THEN PRINT : PRINT USING "#### DATA "; L;
300 IF Z > 0 THEN PRINT ", ";
310 Z = Z + 1 : IF Z = 10 THEN Z = 0 : L = L + 10
320 GET #1, P : P = P + 1
330 PRINT RIGHT$("0"+HEX$(ASC(A$)),2);
340 NEXT J
350 PRINT
360 CLOSE
```

This program runs in GW-BASIC, BASICA, or QBasic. It reads your OBJ file and displays on-screen the appropriate DATA statements to be used later. Translated to machine language by means of the assembler-OBJREAD route, the CLREOL routine consists of the following 24 bytes:

```
B4 0F CD 10 86 E0 32 E4 50 B4 03 CD 10 32 F6 59 2B CA B8 20 0A CD 10 CB
```

Knowing this, you can create a string 24 bytes long for this routine. Of the many ways available for creating a string, one is as good as another; pick the method you find most comfortable. In the following sample BASIC program, I have used the SPACE instruction:

```
10 ' ****************************************************************
15 ' *                                                             *
20 ' * File:      CH11A.BAS                                        *
25 ' * Author:    Allen L. Wyatt                                   *
30 ' * Date:      8/18/91                                          *
35 ' *                                                             *
40 ' * Purpose:   Sample program to show poking an assembly        *
45 ' *            language subroutine into BASIC's string variable *
50 ' *            space.  Designed to work with GW-BASIC.          *
55 ' *                                                             *
60 ' ****************************************************************
65 '
100 CLS
```

```
110 DEF FN ADR(X$)=256*PEEK(VARPTR(X$)+2)+PEEK(VARPTR(X$)+1)
120 RESTORE 1000
130 READ NUMBYTES
140 MODULE$=SPACE$(NUMBYTES)
150 FOR J=1 TO NUMBYTES
160 READ VALUE$
170 MID$(MODULE$,J,1)=CHR$(VAL("&H"+VALUE$))
180 NEXT J
190 LOCATE 10,1
200 PRINT "This line will be cleared from HERE on to the end;";
210 PRINT " press any key now.";
220 WHILE INKEY$="":WEND
230 LOCATE 10,36
240 D=FN ADR(MODULE$)
250 CALL D
260 END
1000 DATA 24
1010 DATA B4,0F,CD,10,86,E0,32,E4,50,B4
1020 DATA 03,CD,10,32,F6,59,2B,CA,B8,20
1030 DATA 0A,CD,10,CB
```

Notice that the byte values which make up the subroutine are contained in DATA statements at the end of the program. The first DATA statement (in line 1000) indicates the number of bytes in the subroutine. These lines were created using OBJREAD.BAS.

Lines 120 through 180 read and act on the DATA statements. Line 170 stores the values into the variable space of MODULE$. These lines can be used, unchanged, to load any assembly language module into string space.

Lines 190 through 260 test the routine to show that it works. The two LOCATE statements position the cursor appropriately, and the WHILE...WEND loop in line 220 provides the time delay so that you can see what is happening.

Notice line 240, which is used to determine the physical address of MODULE$. Through the use of the function definition at line 110, the address is determined by using the string descriptor (maintained by BASIC) that specifies the length and location of variables. Look again at line 110:

```
110 DEF FN ADR(X$)=256*PEEK(VARPTR(X$)+2)+PEEK(VARPTR(X$)+1)
```

VARPTR returns the address of MODULE$. In this case, because we are working with a string, the address of the string descriptor is returned. This descriptor consists of three bytes that give the string's length and address. Because the length is unimportant in this case, you need to use the first and second offset bytes at the descriptor address.

These offset bytes specify the address in memory of the first byte of MODULE$. The address is assigned (in line 240) to the numeric variable D. Because MODULE$ contains the machine language subroutine that should be called, line 250 passes control to that routine, starting at the first byte of MODULE$ (whose address is in D).

Sometimes you may want to clear a portion of the screen in a different color without using the BASIC color-setting capabilities. By slightly rewriting the routine, you can pass to assembly language a variable that specifies the color attribute to use, as in the following assembly language program:

```
Page 60,132
Comment ¦
********************************************************************


File:     CLREOL2.ASM
Author:   Allen L. Wyatt
Date:     8/18/91

Purpose:  Subroutine to clear screen from current cursor position to end
          of line.  Designed to be called from interpretive BASIC.

Format:   CALL D(A%)
              D  = Address of subroutine
              A% = Attribute to use when clearing


********************************************************************¦

                PUBLIC  CLREOL

                .MODEL  large,BASIC
                .CODE

CLREOL          PROC Attribute_Address:WORD

                MOV     AH,0Fh          ; get video mode data
                INT     10h             ; using BIOS function
                XCHG    AH,AL           ; set up COLS data
                XOR     AH,AH
                PUSH    AX              ; and save it

                MOV     AH,03h          ; get current cursor pos
                INT     10h
                XOR     DH,DH           ; ignore row
                POP     CX              ; get width back
                SUB     CX,DX           ; calc number left on line
```

```
            MOV     SI,Attribute_Address
            MOV     BL,[SI]
            MOV     AX,0920h        ; write char + attr, blank
            INT     10h

            RET
CLREOL      ENDP

            END
```

The two versions of the assembly language routine are noticeably different. This rewritten version is 11 bytes longer, and all the added bytes of code are used to obtain the attribute value from the calling BASIC program.

The variable is passed through the stack. When the CALL statement is executed, BASIC pushes the variable's *address* on the stack. Thus, to access the parameter value, you must first retrieve the pointer from the stack and then use the pointer to load BL with the parameter value itself.

Not quite so obvious is the change in the BIOS function call that writes the blanks to the screen. This call now tells the screen to use the attribute value in the BL register instead of the one already on-screen. Without this change, all the rest would be wasted.

You also must change the BASIC program that uses this routine for passing a value. The modified routine follows:

```
10  ' ****************************************************************
15  ' *                                                             *
20  ' * File:    CH11B.BAS                                          *
25  ' * Author:  Allen L. Wyatt                                     *
30  ' * Date:    8/18/91                                            *
35  ' *                                                             *
40  ' * Purpose: Sample program to show poking an assembly          *
45  ' *          language subroutine into BASIC's string variable   *
50  ' *          space.  Designed to work with GW-BASIC.            *
55  ' *                                                             *
60  ' ****************************************************************
65  '
100 CLS
110 DEF FN ADR(X$)=256*PEEK(VARPTR(X$)+2)+PEEK(VARPTR(X$)+1)
120 RESTORE 1000
130 READ NUMBYTES
140 MODULE$=SPACE$(NUMBYTES)
150 FOR J=1 TO NUMBYTES
160 READ VALUE$
```

```
170 MID$(MODULE$,J,1)=CHR$(VAL("&H"+VALUE$))
180 NEXT J
190 LOCATE 10,1
200 PRINT "This line will be cleared from HERE on to the end;";
210 PRINT " press any key now.";
220 WHILE INKEY$="":WEND
230 LOCATE 10,36
240 A%=&H10
250 D=FN ADR(MODULE$)
260 CALL D(A%)
270 PRINT
280 PRINT "The clearing will be UNDERLINE if mono, or BLUE if color."
290 END
1000 DATA 35
1010 DATA 55, 8B, EC, B4, 0F, CD, 10, 86, C4, 32
1020 DATA E4, 50, B4, 03, CD, 10, 32, F6, 59, 2B
1030 DATA CA, 8B, 76, 06, 8A, 1C, B8, 20, 09, CD
1040 DATA 10, 5D, CA, 02, 00
```

Notice that the only modifications to the routine are in the invocation (lines 240 and 260) and in the DATA statements that begin at line 1000 (after all, this assembly language routine is longer than the first).

Some new lines are added (lines 270 and 280) to verify that control returns to BASIC properly after the routine is CALLed.

In line 260, note especially that the variable being passed to the routine (A%) is an integer variable. Integer variables are extremely easy to work with in assembly language. They require only two bytes in the BASIC variable area and can be accessed as word values in assembly language. This routine would have been far more complicated had the % integer flag been left out!

Interfacing Longer Subroutines

If a subroutine is more than 255 bytes long, or if you are not comfortable placing the subroutine into a string variable, you can place it directly into memory by following these steps:

1. Determine how much space to reserve for the assembly language subroutine.

2. Use the CLEAR command to set aside the necessary memory space.

3. Poke the subroutine into the reserved area of memory.

Even though this process is particularly well-suited to subroutines longer than 255 bytes, I use the same routine as the previous example to demonstrate the process. This routine has no coding that would render it static, and it is *"relocatable,"* which means that it will function properly no matter where it is placed in memory. Interfacing is relatively easy. This type of routine gives programmers few headaches and little trouble.

To reserve memory for this routine, you use the CLEAR command with a designation specifying the highest memory address that BASIC can access. BASIC ordinarily uses a full 64K segment. (64K is essentially equivalent to FFFFh.) By subtracting (from this unlimited amount) the amount of space you want to reserve for your assembly language routines, you can determine a new ceiling limit to use in the CLEAR statement.

For example, this subroutine, which occupies 35 bytes of memory, and an additional 10 similar routines would need perhaps one full K of memory. Subtracting 400h (1K) from FFFFh results in FBFFh—the address (FBFFh, or 64511) to use with the CLEAR statement in the BASIC program. The process is shown in the following routine:

```
10  ' ********************************************************************
15  ' *                                                                  *
20  ' * File:      CH11C.BAS                                             *
25  ' * Author:    Allen L. Wyatt                                        *
30  ' * Date:      8/18/91                                               *
35  ' *                                                                  *
40  ' * Purpose:   Sample program to show poking an assembly             *
45  ' *            language subroutine into BASIC's high memory          *
50  ' *            area.  Designed to work with GW-BASIC.                *
55  ' *                                                                  *
60  ' ********************************************************************
65  '
100 CLEAR ,64511!
110 D=64512!
120 CLS
130 RESTORE 1000
140 READ NUMBYTES
150 FOR J=1 TO NUMBYTES
160 READ VALUE$
170 POKE 64511!+J,VAL("&H"+VALUE$)
180 NEXT
190 LOCATE 10,1
200 PRINT "This line will be cleared from HERE on to the end;";
210 PRINT " press any key now.";
220 WHILE INKEY$="":WEND
```

```
230 LOCATE 10,36
240 A%=&H10
250 CALL D(A%)
260 PRINT
270 PRINT "The clearing will be UNDERLINE if mono, or BLUE if color."
280 END
1000 DATA 35
1010 DATA 55, 8B, EC, B4, 0F, CD, 10, 86, C4, 32
1020 DATA E4, 50, B4, 03, CD, 10, 32, F6, 59, 2B
1030 DATA CA, 8B, 76, 06, 8A, 1C, B8, 20, 09, CD
1040 DATA 10, 5D, CA, 02, 00
```

Notice the program coding at line 170. In this method of using an assembly language routine, the POKE statement is used to transfer the routine to the appropriate memory area. Note also that the function definition is omitted because the routine's address will never change.

This type of usage has clear advantages, the greatest of which is that BASIC can access long assembly language subroutines. The other advantage is that the subroutine resides at one static location. In this example, the assembly language subroutine will always reside at FC00h (64512). Clearly, this is preferable to having to calculate the beginning address whenever you want to invoke the routine.

Working with QBasic

QBasic is the interpretive version of BASIC distributed with DOS 5.0. If you have installed DOS 5 on your machine, you may have noticed that GW-BASIC is gone—it is no longer part of the DOS package Microsoft distributes. If for some reason you prefer GW-BASIC to QBasic, you can always copy GW-BASIC from the disk set of an older version of DOS; it should work properly.

If you want to work with QBasic, however, you must realize that some things have changed when interfacing assembly language subroutines. The syntax and internal structure of the language are now more closely akin to QuickBASIC than to GW-BASIC.

Because it is closely akin to QuickBASIC, one of QBasic's features is that it handles longer strings than earlier interpreted BASICs. As you may recall, string length in GW-BASIC and BASICA is limited to 255 characters. QBasic's length limit is 32,767 characters. This means, first, that you can store longer routines in a string and second, that you must change the way you call those routines.

Remember that regardless of the implementation, BASIC stores strings using a string descriptor. In the BASICs discussed thus far, this string descriptor was three bytes long. The first byte was used for the length, and the next two bytes for the offset string address. Since longer strings are a feature of QBasic, there is no way the length can be held in a single byte. The string descriptors are now four bytes long: two bytes for the length and two for the offset address.

This means that changing the assembly language programs used so far is not necessary, but changing the BASIC programs is necessary. The QBasic version of the CH11A.BAS, presented earlier in this chapter, follows:

```
' ****************************************************************
' *                                                              *
' * File:     CH11D.BAS                                          *
' * Author:   Allen L. Wyatt                                     *
' * Date:     8/18/91                                            *
' *                                                              *
' * Purpose:  Sample program to show poking an assembly          *
' *           language subroutine into BASIC's string variable  *
' *           space.  Designed to work with QBasic.             *
' *                                                              *
' ****************************************************************

DEFINT A-Z

CLS
RESTORE 1000
READ NumBytes
Module$ = SPACE$(NumBytes)
FOR j = 1 TO NumBytes
    READ Value$
    MID$(Module$, j, 1) = CHR$(VAL("&H" + Value$))
NEXT j

LOCATE 10, 1
PRINT "This line will be cleared from HERE on to the end;";
PRINT " press any key now.";
WHILE INKEY$ = "": WEND

DEF SEG = VARSEG(Module$)
Address& = 256 * PEEK(VARPTR(Module$) + 3) + PEEK(VARPTR(Module$) + 2)
LOCATE 10, 36
CALL ABSOLUTE(Address&)
END
```

```
1000 DATA 24
     DATA B4,0F,CD,10,86,E0,32,E4,50,B4
     DATA 03,CD,10,32,F6,59,2B,CA,B8,20
     DATA 0A,CD,10,CB
```

Several differences exist, some obvious and others subtle. First, as you probably noticed right away, there are no line numbers. This similarity to compiled versions of BASIC is discussed shortly.

Second, notice the block of calling code, as shown here:

```
DEF SEG = VARSEG(Module$)
Address& = 256 * PEEK(VARPTR(Module$) + 3) + PEEK(VARPTR(Module$) + 2)
LOCATE 10, 36
CALL ABSOLUTE(Address&)
```

The VARSEG and VARPTR functions are still used, but then the actual string address is calculated by looking at the third and fourth bytes of the string descriptor. Only the address of the descriptor is returned by VARSEG and VARPTR.

Once the address is calculated, the old CALL statement is changed to CALL ABSOLUTE, which tells QBasic that a memory address is being called, rather than a named subroutine in the BASIC program.

The changes in the program for passing parameters are similar to those just discussed. The QBasic program for use with the enhanced version of CLREOL appears as follows:

```
' ******************************************************************
' *                                                                *
' * File:     CH11E.BAS                                            *
' * Author:   Allen L. Wyatt                                       *
' * Date:     8/20/91                                              *
' *                                                                *
' * Purpose:  Sample program to show poking an assembly            *
' *           language subroutine into BASIC's string variable     *
' *           space.  Designed to work with QBasic.                *
' *                                                                *
' ******************************************************************

    DEFINT A-Z

    CLS
    RESTORE 1000
    READ NumBytes
    Module$ = SPACE$(NumBytes)
```

```
    FOR j = 1 TO NumBytes
        READ Value$
        MID$(Module$, j, 1) = CHR$(VAL("&H" + Value$))
    NEXT j

    LOCATE 10, 1
    PRINT "This line will be cleared from HERE on to the end;";
    PRINT " press any key now.";
    WHILE INKEY$ = "": WEND

    A = &H10
    DEF SEG = VARSEG(Module$)
    Address& = 256 * PEEK(VARPTR(Module$) + 3) + PEEK(VARPTR(Module$) + 2)
    LOCATE 10, 36
    CALL ABSOLUTE(A, Address&)
    PRINT
    PRINT "The clearing will be UNDERLINE if mono, or BLUE if color."
    END

1000 DATA 35
    DATA 55, 8B, EC, B4, 0F, CD, 10, 86, C4, 32
    DATA E4, 50, B4, 03, CD, 10, 32, F6, 59, 2B
    DATA CA, 8B, 76, 06, 8A, 1C, B8, 20, 09, CD
    DATA 10, 5D, CA, 02, 00
```

The only change here worth mentioning is in the use of CALL ABSOLUTE. Notice that the parameter being passed is placed *before* the address of the subroutine. This differs from the older BASICs, in which the parameters effectively followed the address.

Compiled BASIC

Several compilers for BASIC exist, but the least expensive and apparently most popular is Microsoft's QuickBASIC, which is now at version 4.5. All the compilers vary slightly from each other; the examples in this chapter were written and tested with QuickBASIC 4.5.

Although normal interpretive BASIC offers quick development time, compiled BASIC programs require a few extra steps. With earlier compilers, you had to run the source programs through the compiler and linker. QuickBASIC gives you the option of doing program development in an integrated environment or of using a command-line compiler. With either option, program development takes place in an environment that makes the compiling and linking steps essentially invisible.

Compiled and interpretive BASIC differ in several ways. One of the most noticeable distinctions—already mentioned in relation to QBasic—is that strings may be as many as 32,767 bytes long. Another difference is that instead of poking assembly language routines into memory, you can call them by their names. In the QuickBASIC environment, the routines must exist in a Quick Library QLB file before you can call them; with the command-line compiler, they can be linked to the BASIC program by using the LINK program provided with QuickBASIC.

As in QBasic, QuickBASIC uses string descriptors four bytes long. During the CALL, the address of a string descriptor is passed to the subroutine on the stack.

By taking into account this consideration for the string descriptors, you can handle assembly language subroutines as you would handle them under interpretive BASIC. They can be stored in a string variable. A simpler, more straightforward method, however, involves using just the name of the assembly language subroutine. The LINK process takes care of the rest of the details.

As an example of how to interface assembly language subroutines with compiled BASIC programs, consider the enhanced version of CLREOL presented earlier in the chapter. To use this routine in the QuickBASIC environment, all that's necessary is to put it into a QLB file. No change to the routine is required.

To create a QLB file containing just the CLREOL routine, use LINK with the /QUICKLIB option switch as follows. The CLREOL routine is assumed to be in the current directory; the LINK operation creates Quick Library MINE.QLB.

```
C:\QB>link /q clreol2,mine,,bqlb45;

Microsoft (R) Segmented-Executable Linker  Version 5.13
Copyright (C) Microsoft Corp 1984-1981.  All rights reserved.

LINK : warning L4045: name of output file is 'mine.qlb'
```

Notice that LINK provides a warning message to let you know that the library name differs from that of the OBJ file. This message can be ignored; it does not indicate any kind of true error. The BQLB45 library must be specified to create a QLB file.

Once the QLB file exists, you can cause QuickBASIC to use it during a development session by typing the following:

```
C:\QB>QB /LMINE
```

This brings the QuickBASIC environment into action, loading library file MINE.QLB into memory. Inside the environment, you can type in the following QuickBASIC program:

```
' ****************************************************************
' *                                                              *
' * File:     CH11F.BAS                                          *
' * Author:   Allen L. Wyatt                                     *
' * Date:     8/20/91                                            *
' *                                                              *
' * Purpose:  Sample program to demonstrate using an assembly    *
' *           language subroutine with a QuickBASIC 4.5          *
' *           program.                                           *
' *                                                              *
' ****************************************************************

DEFINT A-Z
CLS
LOCATE 10, 1
PRINT "This line will be cleared from HERE on to the end;";
PRINT " press any key now."
WHILE INKEY$ = "" : WEND
LOCATE 10, 36
a = 16
CALL clreol(a)
PRINT
PRINT "The clearing will be UNDERLINE if mono, or BLUE if color."
```

Note the total lack of any setup routine or DATA statements—the only difference between the programs.

If you want to verify that the attribute value is actually being passed through and used, you can change the value assigned to a just before the CALL statement. On a color monitor, a value of 32 produces a green background, 48 creates cyan, 64 results in red, and so on up to 112, which specifies white. The code is simply 16 times the normal color value, but color values must be from 0 through 7; higher values are handled mod 8.

As you may have noticed, the procedure for calling assembly language subroutines in this program is a good deal simpler than the corresponding procedure for interpretive BASIC (because you don't need to worry about poking or addresses).

If you use the command-line compiler rather than the environment, you don't even need to create the QLB file. In this case, combining the assembly language subroutine with the BASIC program is accomplished through the LINK process (as described in Chapter 4, "Choosing and Using Your Linker").

Summary

Although BASIC is a readily available and extremely popular computer language, it has several shortcomings that make assembly language subroutines attractive and, in some instances, necessary to the viability of a program.

The process of interfacing assembly language subroutines depends largely on whether the BASIC program is written in interpretive or compiled BASIC. Each type and version of BASIC has differences that affect how the language interacts with and passes variables to assembly language subroutines.

In the next chapter you learn how to interface assembly language subroutines with Pascal.

12

Interfacing with Pascal

P ascal, a programming language that first appeared in 1970, has a loyal following
of users who enjoy the language's structured approach to programming. Pascal
is readily available for most computer systems at a moderate cost, with Borland
owning the lion's share of the market with their Turbo Pascal compiler. Such
availability has added to the language's popularity.

Like any other computer language, Pascal "bogs down" in certain areas. I don't
mean to imply that Pascal is unacceptable; it's just slower than assembly language in
certain areas. As a result, many programmers have developed assembly language
subroutines to interface with their Pascal programs.

General Interfacing Guidelines

The way you interface your assembly language subroutines with Pascal programs is determined largely by your personal programming style, and to a lesser
extent by the Pascal compiler you are using. For example, using either Microsoft's
QuickPascal or Borland's Turbo Pascal, you can include machine language code by
means of the `inline()` statement or by automatic inclusion of OBJ files through the
`{$L filename}` compiler directive (before version 4.0, Turbo Pascal provided only the
`inline()` capability). The choice of methods to use is left to you.

As an example of how the compiler itself affects the interfacing technique, many
older Pascal compilers use a two-step approach to program development. Once
complete, the source code is *compiled* and then, in the second step, *linked*. If your
Pascal compiler uses this two-step approach, you can incorporate assembly language
subroutines into your programs only by assembling the subroutines separately and
including them at the link step.

Inline Routines

When you use the `inline()` capability to include assembly language subroutines in Pascal programs, the subroutines must be completely "relocatable" and fully self-contained. In other words, the subroutine can hold no external references, and all branching must be short. Although this type of structure is possible in assembly language coding, it is severely limiting.

External Procedures

If you compile the assembly language subroutine separately, whether you use the `{$L filename}` directive to associate the subroutine with your Pascal program or use the two-phase development process of compiling and linking, there usually is only one stipulation for interfacing with assembly language subroutines: you must use the `PROCEDURE` statement to define the subroutine name and the variables to be passed. The format of this statement is

```
PROCEDURE function_name(arg1,arg2,arg3, ... ,argn: dtype); EXTERNAL;
```

In this syntax, `function_name` is the publicly declared name of the assembly language subroutine. The arguments (1 through n) are the names of the variables whose values or pointers will be passed to the subroutine. For simplicity's sake, the parameters' data type (`dtype`) usually is `INTEGER`. (Although all parameters in the example are of the same type, these parameter types can often be mixed; see your compiler's reference manual for details.)

To indicate that pointers rather than values should be passed, the variable names can be modified with `VAR` prefixes. `VAR` indicates that only the offset address of the variable will be passed.

The Interrupt Attribute

Beginning with Turbo Pascal 4.0, and under all versions of QuickPascal, you can write interrupt procedures in addition to the usual procedures and functions. When you choose the `inline()` technique for associating your assembly language module with your Pascal program, you can add the `Interrupt;` attribute to the declaration to specify that this procedure is made suitable for servicing a machine interrupt.

Because it affects *only* the code generated automatically by the compiler, this attribute does not apply to external procedures. You have always had the ability to make external procedures suitable for interrupt servicing, however, because you must provide all of their code.

When you add the `Interrupt;` attribute to the declaration of a procedure that uses `inline()` coding, extra code is generated automatically at the procedure's entry point to save all the CPU registers and to change the DS register so that it points to your procedure's own DATA area. In addition, the normal RET instruction is replaced by an IRET, and all registers are restored before exit.

The extra code generated corresponds to the following typical declaration:

```
PROCEDURE intsvc( Flags,CS,IP,AX,BX,CX,DX,SI,DI,DS,ES,BP : word );
INTERRUPT;
BEGIN
.
.
.
END;
```

Your procedure can modify any of these parameters on the stack; the changes will affect the registers upon return from the interrupt. Because predicting what the system will be doing at the instant the interrupt occurs is usually impossible, however, hardware interrupt procedures should leave the saved register values alone.

Using this feature requires relatively advanced knowledge of your system's architecture. Any simplified examples of such a procedure's use would be misleading.

Note that the `Interrupt;` attribute is not limited solely to assembly language routines; any Pascal code can be used in such a procedure. One of the most frequent applications of this feature is in the creation of serial-communications programs capable of keeping up with data rates of 1,200 bps and higher. To communicate with the serial-port hardware, these routines often mix inline assembly language and Pascal code that deals with memory use.

Interfacing Subroutines without Variable Passing

To help you better understand how an assembly language subroutine is interfaced with Pascal, let's look at a sample subroutine that does not require parameter passing. Consider the following assembly language program:

```
        Page 60,132
        Comment |
        *********************************************************************

        File:     CUROFF.ASM
        Author:   Allen L. Wyatt
        Date:     8/24/91

        Purpose:  Subroutine to turn the cursor off.  Designed to be
                  called from Turbo Pascal 6.0.

        Format:   CUROFF()


        *********************************************************************!

                PUBLIC  curoff

                .MODEL  small, Pascal
                .CODE

        curoff  PROC
                MOV     AH,3            ; get current cursor
                XOR     BX,BX
                INT     10h
                OR      CH,20h          ; force to OFF condition
                MOV     AH,1            ; set new cursor values
                INT     10h
                RET

        curoff  ENDP

                END
```

This short routine turns off the video cursor, using the BIOS functions that first get the current cursor type and then set a new cursor type after forcing the cursor-off control bit to a value of 1 by means of the OR CH,20h instruction. A notable omission from both the QuickPascal and Turbo Pascal libraries is a method for controlling the cursor's visibility; thus, this routine is not only a simple example but also serves a useful purpose.

To include CurOff in a program by means of the inline() facility, assemble CUROFF.ASM. Then you can use the following Pascal program to determine the bytes you should use in your inline statements:

```
{ *************************************************************
  *                                                         *
  * File:      OBJREAD.PAS                                  *
  * Author:    Allen L. Wyatt                               *
  * Date:      8/21/91                                      *
  *                                                         *
  * Purpose:   Analyzes an OBJ file created by MASM or TASM, *
  *            displaying the data values necessary to use  *
  *            with inline assembly language routines in    *
  *            Turbo Pascal.                                *
  *                                                         *
  *************************************************************}

program ObjRead;
  uses Crt;

  var Good, Rpt:Boolean;
      N, Z:Integer;
      FileName:String;
      Fptr:Longint;
      FromFile:Byte;
      FN:File of Byte;

function OpenFile:boolean;
  var Flen, Loop:Integer;
      Ext:Boolean;

  begin
    Write ('Name of OBJ file to analyze: ');
    Readln (FileName);
    if (FileName = '') then Halt(1);
    FLen := Length(FileName);
    Ext := False;
    for Loop := 1 to Flen do
    begin
      if FileName[Loop] = '.' then Ext := True;
    end;
    if not Ext then FileName := FileName + '.OBJ';

    Assign(FN, FileName);
    {$I-}
    Reset(FN);
    {$I+}
    OpenFile := IOResult = 0;
  end {OpenFile};
```

```
function GetByte(var RecNum:Longint):Byte;
  var Raw:Byte;
  begin
    Seek(FN, RecNum);
    Read(FN, Raw);
    GetByte := Raw;
  end {GetByte};

function HexByte(var X:Byte):String;
  var I, J: Integer;
      Con: String;
  begin
    Con := '0123456789ABCDEF';
    I := (X Div 16) + 1;
    J := (X Mod 16) + 1;
    HexByte := '$'+Con[I]+Con[J]
  end {Hex};

begin
  ClrScr;
  Good := False;
  while not Good do Good := OpenFile;
  Fptr := 0;
  Rpt := True;

  while Rpt do
  begin
    FromFile := GetByte(Fptr);
    Fptr := Fptr + 1;
    if FromFile <> 160 then
    begin
      FromFile := GetByte(Fptr);
      Fptr := Fptr + 2 + FromFile;
    end
    else
      Rpt := False;
  end;

  ClrScr;
  Writeln ('Use the following statements in your program:');
  Writeln ('');
  FromFile := GetByte(Fptr);
  Fptr := Fptr + 5;
```

```
  N := FromFile - 4;
  Z := N Mod 5;
  Write ('inline(');
  while N > 1 do       {Ignore final byte; assume it is RET}
  begin
    if N Mod 5 = Z then
    begin
      Writeln ('');
      Write ('  ');
    end;

    FromFile := GetByte(Fptr);
    Fptr := Fptr + 1;
    Write (HexByte(FromFile));
    N := N - 1;
    if N > 1 then Write ('/');
  end;
  Writeln (');');
  Close(FN);
end.
```

If you worked through Chapter 11, this program may seem familiar. It provides the same function for Turbo Pascal programmers that OBJREAD.BAS provides for BASIC programmers. The program works with OBJ files created for assembly language subroutines that do not use parameter passing.

When you run this program and supply the name of the OBJ file (CUROFF), you will see the correct inline statements to use in your program. The following shows a Turbo Pascal program with the inline statements in place:

```
{ PEX1.PAS }
{ Written by Allen L. Wyatt }
{ Date 8/27/91 }
{ Program to test calling of CurOff() }

procedure CurOff;
begin
inline(
    $B4/$03/$33/$DB/$CD/
    $10/$80/$CD/$20/$B4/
    $01/$CD/$10);
end;
```

```
begin
  Writeln('The cursor is now turning OFF');
  CurOff;
  ReadLn;
end.
```

This program works, but two things are wrong. First, the program is not well commented. This may not be a big issue while the program is fresh in your mind, but it may be a problem a few weeks or months from now.

Second, the program turns off the cursor completely—it is still off when the program is done and you return to DOS. Both problems can be solved by taking a slightly different approach to including the inline statements in the Turbo Pascal program.

If you created a LST file when you assembled CUROFF.ASM, you can use your text editor's cut-and-paste facilities to move the hex code bytes from the LST file into a Pascal source program. Note how this is done in the following program:

```
{ PEX2.PAS }
{ Written by Allen L. Wyatt }
{ Date 8/27/91 }
{ Program to test calling of CurOff() }

procedure CurOff;
begin
inline(
    $B4/$03/       { MOV     AH,3     ; get current cursor       }
    $33/$DB/       { XOR     BX,BX                               }
    $CD/$10/       { INT     10h                                 }
    $80/$CD/$20/ { OR     CH,20h    ; force to OFF condition }
    $B4/$01/       { MOV     AH,1     ; set new cursor values   }
    $CD/$10);     { INT     10h                                 }
end;

procedure CurOn;
begin
inline(
    $B4/$03/       { MOV     AH,3     ; get current cursor       }
    $33/$DB/       { XOR     BX,BX                               }
    $CD/$10/       { INT     10h                                 }
    $80/$E5/$1F/ { AND     CH,1Fh    ; force to ON condition }
    $B4/$01/       { MOV     AH,1     ; set new cursor values   }
    $CD/$10);     { INT     10h                                 }
end;
```

```
begin
  Writeln('The cursor is now turning OFF');
  CurOff;
  ReadLn;
  Writeln('Now going back ON');
  CurOn;
end.
```

The program is much more readable now, as the original assembly language statements have been included as comments. Note that I have also included CurOn, which differs in only one statement (two bytes), so that the test can turn the cursor back on before returning to DOS).

You probably noticed that the final RET statement in the assembly language file was not included in the inline statements of the Turbo Pascal program. Including this statement is not necessary, as it is handled automatically by the Pascal compiler and the begin and end keywords that bracket the procedure definition.

If you are using any version of Turbo Pascal earlier than 4.0, this technique is the *only* method available for including assembly language in your programs. Although you can use this method with later versions also, the following option is available as well. This program is somewhat simpler to type but requires that you assemble your subroutines separately so that OBJ files are available when you compile the main program.

```
{ PEX3.PAS }
{ Written by Allen L. Wyatt
{ Date 8/27/91 }
{ Program to test calling of CurOff() }

{$L CUROFF.OBJ}
procedure CurOff; external;

{$L CURON.OBJ}
procedure CurOn; external;

begin
  Writeln('The cursor is now turning OFF');
  CurOff;
  ReadLn;
  Writeln('Now going back ON');
  CurOn;
end.
```

When this technique is used, the OBJ files must contain all the program statements necessary to protect the stack and return to Pascal properly; the Turbo

Pascal compiler does not add anything to a procedure defined as external. The only difference in this technique and that used by older compilers that require a separate link step is the presence of the {$L} compiler directives. The {$L} directives cause the OBJ file to be linked in the final program.

Both CUROFF and CURON were created as NEAR routines. If you are creating routines that are FAR, you need to use an additional directive in your Turbo Pascal source file. For instance, if CUROFF and CURON had been created as FAR routines, the Turbo Pascal program would have been changed in the following manner:

```
{$L CUROFF.OBJ}
{$F+}procedure CurOff; external{$F-};

{$L CURON.OBJ}
{$F+}procedure CurOn; external{$F-};
```

The $F directives tell Turbo Pascal to switch between NEAR and FAR addressing. If the OBJ files are created using FAR procedures, it is absolutely essential that the procedure statements be bracketed by the {$F+} and {$F-} switches. Otherwise, although no error will be detected during compilation, the program will cause your system to lock up when it executes because it will not return properly from the first such procedure called.

Notice that there is nothing mystical or magical about the way this routine is called. The compiler or the linker makes sure that the proper routines are linked to create the executable (EXE) file. Invocation of the assembly language subroutine presupposes that the external procedures have been declared in the program header. Without the procedure statements, an error would be generated during the compilation process.

Interfacing Subroutines with Variable Passing

Pascal uses the stack for passing variables to assembly language. Values, short pointers, and long pointers can be passed.

Because the preceding subroutines (CurOff and CurOn) differ in only one instruction, combining them into a single routine that can do both jobs is a more efficient use of space. You can easily modify the routine so that a flag value specifies whether to turn the cursor off or on. The following assembly language program includes this modification:

```
Page 60,132
Comment ¦
********************************************************************

File:     CURSW.ASM
Author:   Allen L. Wyatt
Date:     8/27/91

Purpose:  Subroutine to turn the cursor on or off.  Designed
          to be called from Turbo Pascal 6.0.

Format:   CurSw(0) to turn the cursor off
          CurSw(1) to turn the cursor on
          The variable passed to CurSw() should be an
          integer value.


********************************************************************¦

        PUBLIC  CurSw

        .MODEL  small, Pascal
        .CODE

CurSw   PROC    NEAR Switch:WORD
        MOV     AX,Switch       ; get flag value
        OR      AX,AX           ; test zero/nonzero
        JNZ     CS1
        MOV     AX,20h          ; zero means OFF
        JMP     SHORT CS2
CS1:    MOV     AX,0            ; else turn ON
CS2:    PUSH    AX              ; either way, save it
        MOV     AH,3            ; get current cursor
        XOR     BX,BX
        INT     10H
        POP     AX              ; retrieve saved control
        AND     CH,1Fh          ; clear previous bit
        OR      CH,AL           ; and set in new one
        MOV     AH,1            ; set new cursor values
        INT     10H
        RET
CurSw   ENDP

        END
```

This version of the assembly language routine differs noticeably from its predecessors. CURSW tests an input value and turns the cursor off for zero (or on for any other value).

Notice that the variable is passed through the stack as described in Chapter 2, "An Overview of Assembly Language." On entry to this routine, Pascal pushes the variable's *value* on the stack. Because the variable is an integer (it must be declared as such in the Pascal program), it can be accessed as a word on the stack.

This routine is written as a NEAR routine so that it will work properly as a series of inline statements in a Turbo Pascal program. You must change the Pascal programs that use this routine to pass a value. The modified routine using inline statements is as follows:

```
{ PEX4.PAS }
{ Written by Allen L. Wyatt }
{ Date 8/27/91 }
{ Program to test calling of CurSw() }

procedure CurSw( switch : integer );
begin
inline(
    $8B/$46/$04/ {        MOV  AX,Switch  ; get flag value        }
    $0B/$C0/     {        OR   AX,AX      ; test zero/nonzero     }
    $75/$05/     {        JNZ  CS1                                }
    $B8/$20/$00/ {        MOV  AX,20h     ; zero means OFF        }
    $EB/$03/     {        JMP  SHORT CS2                          }
    $B8/$00/$00/ { CS1:   MOV  AX,0       ; else turn ON          }
    $50/         { CS2:   PUSH AX         ; either way, save it   }
    $B4/$03/     {        MOV  AH,3       ; get current cursor    }
    $33/$DB/     {        XOR  BX,BX                              }
    $CD/$10/     {        INT  10H                                }
    $58/         {        POP  AX         ; retrieve saved control }
    $80/$E5/$1F/ {        AND  CH,1Fh     ; clear previous bit    }
    $0A/$E8/     {        OR   CH,AL      ; and set in new one    }
    $B4/$01/     {        MOV  AH,1       ; set new cursor values }
    $CD/$10);    {        INT  10H                                }
end;

begin
  Writeln('The cursor is now turning OFF');
  CurSw(0);
  ReadLn;
  Writeln('Now going back ON');
  CurSw(1);
end.
```

For the external procedure version, the Pascal program is modified as follows:

```
{ PEX5.PAS }
{ Written by Allen L. Wyatt }
{ Date 8/27/91 }
{ Program to test calling of CurSw() }

{$L CURSW.OBJ}
procedure CurSw( switch : integer ); external;

begin
  Writeln('The cursor is now turning OFF');
  CurSw(0);
  ReadLn;
  Writeln('Now going back ON');
  CurSw(1);
end.
```

Notice that only a few modifications are made to the routine. The line that declares the procedure uses a name enclosed in parentheses, and the lines that invoke the name enclose in parentheses a constant value to control the routine's actions.

Because it fills a void in the provided video-control libraries, the CurSw() routine can become a useful item in your Pascal toolbox.

Passing Variable Pointers

The preceding routine works well if the variable being passed on the stack is a value. But a pointer to a variable would cause problems for the assembly language subroutine, which is not designed to pass a pointer.

Why would passing a variable's address pointer be valuable, as opposed to passing only a value? Because if you know the variable's location in memory, you can make direct changes to the variable's value in the assembly language subroutine. This capability can be invaluable if you need to pass information back to the calling program.

One feature notably absent from most Pascal run-time libraries is a capability for reading data directly from the screen. To do so, you must pass the data being read back to the calling program. One way of doing this is to use a pointer to a string variable that is available also to the calling program. Here's the assembly language for such a module; it must be assembled with TASM 3.0. (Note that it is much more complex than any example shown so far.)

```
Page 60,132
Comment ¦
********************************************************************


File:     READSCRN.ASM
Author:   Allen L. Wyatt
Date:     8/27/91

Purpose:  Subroutine designed to read data directly from
          screen to Pascal string.

Format:   READSCRN(ROW,COL,NUM:word;BFR:string);
              ROW: Row at which to start, 0-24
              COL: Column at which to start, 0-79
              NUM: number of characters to read, 1 through 80-COL
              BFR: pointer to string where data will be put.


********************************************************************¦


          PUBLIC    ReadScrn

          .MODEL    small, Pascal
          .CODE

ReadScrn  PROC      NEAR Row, Col, Num:WORD, Bptr:DWORD
          USES      ES, DI

          LES       DI,Bptr               ;Get string address

          MOV       AH,0Fh                ;Get video page in BH
          INT       10h
          MOV       AH,03                 ;Get current cursor location
          INT       10h
          PUSH      DX                    ;Save it to restore later

          MOV       AX,Row                ;Get row number
          CMP       AX,25
          JAE       ERROR                 ;Too big, get out
          MOV       DH,AL                 ;Okay, set into DH
          MOV       AX,Col                ;Get col number
          CMP       AX,80
          JB        OKAY                  ;Not too big so proceed
ERROR:    XOR       AL,AL                 ;Too big, set string to zero
          STOSB
          JMP       SHORT EXIT
```

```
OKAY:       MOV     DL,AL           ;Now set in column
            PUSH    DX              ;Store column for later
            MOV     AH,2            ;Change cursor location
            INT     10h
            POP     DX              ;Get column back
            MOV     CX,Num          ;Get length of string
            JCXZ    ERROR           ;No length for string, so error
            MOV     AX,80           ;Maximum string length
            SUB     AX,DX           ;Adjust maximum for starting column
            CMP     CX,AX           ;Is it longer than allowed?
            JA      ERROR           ;Yes, so exit with an error
            MOV     AL,CL           ;Otherwise, store it as string length
            STOSB


READEM:     MOV     AH,8            ;Get char from BIOS
            INT     10h
            STOSB                   ;Put down in string
            INC     DL              ;Advance cursor
            CMP     DL,80           ;If off end of row, do wrap
            JB      R1              ;Still on row, okay
            INC     DH              ;Off end, go to next row
            XOR     DL,DL           ;at column zero
R1:         MOV     AH,2            ;Set new cursor location
            INT     10h
            LOOP    READEM          ;and go back for next


EXIT:       POP     DX              ;Restore original cursor
            MOV     AH,2
            INT     10h
            RET
READSCRN    ENDP

            END
```

In this routine, the calling program passes the row and column where the reading action is to begin and the number of characters to be read, as well as a pointer to the string variable where the data is to be placed. The assembly language code then saves the original cursor position, moves the cursor to the position where the read is to begin, and copies characters from the screen to the string until the desired number of characters have been read. The routine then restores the original cursor position and returns.

If any of the values passed to the routine are outside the limits of the screen, no characters are read, and the length of the string is set to zero to indicate that an error occurred.

To use this routine from Turbo Pascal, enter the following program. Since the OBJ file would be quite lengthy, converting the file to inline statements doesn't make much sense. Using the linking directives instead saves time and space.

```
{ RDSCRN.PAS }
{ Written by Allen L. Wyatt }
{ Date 8/27/91 }
{ Program to test calling of ReadScrn() }

program RdScrn;
  uses Crt;

{$L READSCRN.OBJ}
procedure ReadScrn(Row, Col, Num: Integer; var Bfr: String ); external;

var
  Inputbuf: String;
  R, C, W: Integer;

begin
  ClrScr;
  Writeln('The following line will be read, beginning with the 5th column:');
  Writeln('----This is a test line, to see how many characters will be read');
  ReadScrn(1,4,20,Inputbuf);
  Writeln('');
  Writeln('The following are the 20 characters read by the routine:');
  Writeln(Inputbuf);
  Writeln('');
  Writeln('Remember that the top left corner is 0,0.');
  Writeln('To exit this demo program, enter a row of 0 and a column of 0.');
  repeat
    R := 90;
    while R > 24 do
    begin
      Write('Row: ');
      Readln(R);
    end;
    C := 90;
    while C > 79 do
    begin
      Write('Column: ');
      Readln(C);
    end;
```

```
    if R+C > 0 then
    begin
      W := 0;
      while (W < 1) or (W > (80 - C)) do
      begin
        Write('Width: ');
        Readln(W);
      end;
      ReadScrn(R,C,W,Inputbuf);
      Writeln(Inputbuf);
      Writeln('');
    end;
  until R+C = 0;
end.
```

In this test program, the string `Inputbuf`, declared at the global level, accumulates the data read from the screen. The single word `var` in the declaration of the external procedure, preceding the reference to `Inputbuf`, is what makes Pascal pass the *address* of the string, rather than the string itself, to the procedure.

Pointers can also be useful when you work with strings, as you can see from the following program:

```
Page 60,132
Comment ¦
*******************************************************************


File:    ULCASE.ASM for Turbo Assembler 3.0
Author:  Allen L. Wyatt
Date:    8/27/91


Purpose: Subroutine designed to convert a string to upper-
         or lowercase.  Designed to be called from Turbo Pascal.


Format:  ULCase(S,X)
             S:  Pointer to string to be converted
             X:  Controls conversion
                 0 = Convert to uppercase
                 ?   Any other value signifies convert to lowercase


*******************************************************************¦
```

```
        PUBLIC   ULCase

        .MODEL   small, Pascal
        .CODE

ULCase  PROC     NEAR Sptr:DWORD, Case:WORD
        USES     ES, DI

        LES      DI,Sptr            ;Get string address
        INC      DI                 ;Point past length
        MOV      AX,Case            ;Get action variable
        CMP      AX,0               ;Converting to uppercase?
        JZ       UPPER              ;Yes, so go handle

LOWER:  CMP      BYTE PTR [DI],0    ;Is this end of string?
        JE       EXIT               ;Yes, so exit
        CMP      BYTE PTR [DI],'A'  ;Is it < A ?
        JB       L1                 ;Yes, so skip character
        CMP      BYTE PTR [DI],'Z'  ;Is it > Z ?
        JA       L1                 ;Yes, so skip character
        OR       BYTE PTR [DI],20h  ;Make lowercase (00100000b)
L1:     INC      DI                 ;Next character
        JMP      LOWER              ;Do it again

UPPER:  CMP      BYTE PTR [DI],0    ;Is this end of string?
        JE       EXIT               ;Yes, so exit
        CMP      BYTE PTR [DI],'a'  ;Is it < a ?
        JB       U1                 ;Yes, so skip character
        CMP      BYTE PTR [DI],'z'  ;Is it > z ?
        JA       U1                 ;Yes, so skip character
        AND      BYTE PTR [DI],05Fh ;Make uppercase (01011111b)
U1:     INC      DI                 ;Next character
        JMP      UPPER              ;Do it again

EXIT:   RET
ULCase  ENDP

        END
```

This simple program, which converts a string to either all upper- or all lowercase, expects two parameters to be passed from Pascal: a pointer to the string to be converted, and an integer value indicating whether the string is to be converted to upper- or lowercase.

As you study this routine, notice that the conversion process begins at the string's second character, not its first. This happens because the first position of a string variable always contains the number of characters in the string.

The Pascal program that will use this subroutine follows:

```pascal
{ TESTCASE.PAS }
{ Written by Allen L. Wyatt }
{ Date 8/27/91 }
{ Program to test calling of ULCase() }

program TestCase;
  uses Crt;

var
  s: String;

{$L ULCASE.OBJ}
procedure ULCase(var s:String; x:Integer); external;

begin
  ClrScr;
  s:='Original string value';
  While length(s)>0 do
    begin
    Write('String to convert: ');
    Readln(s);
    If length(s)>0 then
      begin
        Writeln('UPPERCASE:    ');
        ULCase(s,0);
        Writeln(s);
        Writeln('');
        Writeln('lowercase:    ');
        ULCase(s,1);
        Writeln(S);
        Writeln('');
      end;
  end;
end.
```

Using Function Subprograms

When you want an assembly language routine to return a value to your Pascal program, you don't have to pass in a pointer to a variable for the routine to use. Instead, you can make the routine itself return a value to the calling program. Although doing so is a little more trouble for the programmer, it can greatly simplify the calling program.

To return a value, your assembly language routine must be declared as a *function* rather than a *procedure*, and the type of value the routine will return must be specified. Then, in the routine, you can use the new RETURNS modifier to specify the value to be returned to the calling program.

The following assembly language program for a function version of READSCRN.ASM shows the differences between using a pointer and creating a function. Again, it should be assembled with TASM 3.0.

```
Page 60,132
Comment ¦
***********************************************************************


File:      RSFUNC.ASM
Author:    Allen L. Wyatt
Date:      8/27/91

Purpose:   Subroutine designed to read data directly from
           screen to Pascal string.

Format:    READSCRN(ROW,COL,NUM:word):string);
             ROW: Row at which to start, 0-24
             COL: Column at which to start, 0-79
             NUM: number of characters to read, 1 through 80-COL


***********************************************************************¦


           PUBLIC    RSFunc

           .MODEL    small, Pascal
           .CODE

RSFunc     PROC      NEAR Row, Col, Num:WORD RETURNS Bptr:DWORD
           USES      ES, DI

           LES       DI,Bptr                  ;Get return value address
```

```
                MOV       AH,0Fh              ;Get video page in BH
                INT       10h
                MOV       AH,03               ;Get current cursor location
                INT       10h
                PUSH      DX                  ;Save it to restore later

                MOV       AX,Row              ;Get row number
                CMP       AX,25
                JAE       ERROR               ;Too big, get out
                MOV       DH,AL               ;Okay, set into DH
                MOV       AX,Col              ;Get col number
                CMP       AX,80
                JB        OKAY                ;Not too big so proceed
ERROR:          XOR       AL,AL               ;Too big, set retval to zero
                STOSB
                JMP       SHORT EXIT


OKAY:           MOV       DL,AL               ;Now set in column
                PUSH      DX                  ;Store column for later
                MOV       AH,2                ;and change cursor location
                INT       10h
                POP       DX                  ;Get column back
                MOV       CX,Num              ;Get length of retval
                JCXZ      ERROR               ;No length for string, so error
                MOV       AX,80               ;Maximum string length
                SUB       AX,DX               ;Adjust maximum for starting column
                CMP       CX,AX               ;Is it longer than allowed?
                JA        ERROR               ;Yes, so exit with an error
                MOV       AL,CL               ;and store it as string length
                STOSB


READEM:         MOV       AH,8                ;Get char from BIOS
                INT       10h
                STOSB                         ;Put down in retval
                INC       DL                  ;Advance cursor
                CMP       DL,80               ;If off end of row, do wrap
                JB        R1                  ;Still on row, okay
                INC       DH                  ;Off end, go to next row
                XOR       DL,DL               ;At column zero
R1:             MOV       AH,2                ;Set new cursor location
                INT       10h
                LOOP      READEM              ;and go back for next
```

```
EXIT:          POP     DX                    ;Restore original cursor
               MOV     AH,2
               INT     10h
               RET
RSFunc         ENDP                          ;Leave temp pointer on stack!

               END
```

To use this function version, the Pascal program must be changed somewhat, as follows:

```
{ RSFUNC.PAS }
{ Written by Allen L. Wyatt }
{ Date 8/27/91 }
{ Program to test calling of RSFunc() }

program RSFuncTest;
  uses Crt;

{$L RSFUNC.OBJ}
function RSFunc(Row, Col, Num: Integer): String; external;

var
  X: String;
  R, C, W: Integer;

begin
  ClrScr;
  Writeln('The following line will be read, beginning with the 5th column:');
  Writeln('----This is a test line, to see how many characters will be read');
  X := RSFunc(1, 4, 20);
  Writeln('');
  Writeln('The following are the 20 characters read by the routine:');
  Writeln(X);
  Writeln('');
  Writeln('Remember that the top left corner is 0,0.');
  Writeln('To exit this demo program, enter a row of 0 and a column of 0.');
  repeat
    R := 90;
    while R > 24 do
    begin
      Write('Row: ');
      Readln(R);
    end;
```

```
    C := 90;
    while C > 79 do
    begin
      Write('Column: ');
      Readln(C);
    end;
    if R+C > 0 then
    begin
      W := 0;
      while (W < 1) or (W > (80 - C)) do
      begin
        Write('Width: ');
        Readln(W);
      end;
      X := RSFunc(R,C,W);
      Writeln(X);
      Writeln('');
    end;
  until R+C = 0;
end.
```

Notice that the external declaration, which is for a function rather than a procedure, does not mention the string pointer. A type declaration follows the closing parenthesis of the external declaration.

The major difference in the program is that RSFunc() is invoked by assigning its value to a string variable instead of just calling it by name. Not having to include the buffer name as a parameter to each call clarifies the program's operation a bit, however; this way, all the parameters are information passed *into* the routine.

Summary

Pascal is a popular language among many programmers. The ease with which you can combine assembly language subroutines with Pascal programs depends, however, on the way you use your Pascal compiler.

Until Turbo Pascal version 4.0 became available, only the high-powered "professional" Pascal compilers that required a separate linking phase were easy to augment with assembly language modules. Turbo Pascal now offers a choice of several simple interfacing methods, however.

No matter which method you choose, you will find that the performance of your Pascal programs can be improved significantly if you make the small effort necessary for mastering the assembly language interface.

13

Interfacing with C and C++

C and C++ are two of the fastest-growing high-level languages available, in terms of market share. It has been said that over 75 percent of all commercial programs for personal computers are written in C—quite a plaudit for the popularity of the language. And C++ is gaining in popularity because of its object-oriented nature and the release of Borland's C++ products.

Why are these languages so popular? Although the reasons vary from programmer to programmer, for most people C seems to provide the right mix of ease of use, access to system-level functions, and transportability. C++ provides not only the full benefits of C, but also the flexibility of objects. These benefits combine to make either language attractive for development.

Eventually, most serious C or C++ programmers must face the task of interfacing assembly language subroutines with the language. Because C and C++ are compiled languages, assembly language subroutines can be linked as the final step in program development. The trick is to make sure that the interface between assembly language and C or C++ is followed strictly, to allow proper passage of variables. Since C++ is an evolutionary step of the C language, the interface between C++ and assembly language is identical to the interface between C and assembly language.

The popularity of C compilers comes and goes, and it is probable that C++ compilers will follow this same cycle. In recent years, several C compilers (including Microsoft C, Lattice C, Aztec C, and Turbo C) have been popular. The list of C++ compilers has been more rarified; the most notable are Turbo C++ (and the variant

307

Borland C++) and Zortech C++. In the C arena, most of the popular compilers have similar functions and implementations of the language. C++ compilers are somewhat more disparate, but not completely incompatible. Any notable differences between versions are mentioned as the examples in this chapter are developed.

Watching what Borland is doing in the area of object-oriented programming, as exemplified in their C++ compilers, is particularly interesting. In the latest version of TASM, Borland has even brought object-oriented programming to assembly language. Such a move, unthinkable a few years ago, seems to be the direction in which Borland wants to lead the market. It will be interesting to see what happens in the coming years.

Because the object-oriented applications of assembly language are brand new and have no wide-spread practical use as of this writing, their specific development is not covered here. Rather, this chapter focuses on general-purpose assembly language routines that can easily be interfaced with any version of either C or C++. Thus, references to C in this chapter can be assumed to apply to C++ as well.

Memory Models

Before any general guidelines for interfacing with C programs can be developed, memory models must be discussed because they have significant impact on all guidelines.

Chapter 1 discussed how the Intel CPU chip design forces memory management to be done in segments and how each segment can address a maximum of 65,636 (64K) bytes. That's the basis of the memory model concept; it simply specifies how the segments are to be managed.

Originally, C compilers for MS-DOS addressed only one memory model, the one now known as *small*. All code procedures shared a single 64K-maximum code segment and all data had to fit into another 64K-maximum data segment. Programmers found this far too limiting, however, and today's compilers support four to six memory models. The usual definitions for these models are listed in table 13.1.

The *tiny* model may be familiar to you as the format used by COM files in which data, code, and stack must all fit into a single 64K segment. The *small* model breaks code and data into separate segments of 64K each. In both of these models, all pointers for both procedures and data are NEAR.

In the *medium* model, each separate module of code has its own segment and each may be as many as 64K, but all data is confined to a single segment. In this model, procedure pointers usually are FAR but data pointers remain NEAR.

Table 13.1. *Memory model definitions.*

Model	Code Segments	Data Segments
Tiny	One, also containing data	Shared with code
Small	One for all procedures	One for all data
Medium	Many	One
Compact	One	Many
Large	Many	Many (64K static)
Huge	Many	Many (>64K static)

The reverse of the medium model is the *compact* model, where each major data structure has its own segment, but code is all contained within 64K; pointers are NEAR and data pointers are FAR. This model is seldom encountered.

The *large* model uses FAR pointers for both code and data, although it still confines static data storage to 64K. This model often is used when dealing with complex systems of programs; it combines the advantages of the medium and compact models.

Finally, the *huge* model removes the 64K limit on static data and enables a single data structure to span more than one segment. When you use the huge model, internal address calculations rapidly become complicated; therefore, you should avoid using this model unless it is necessary for writing your program.

Most C programs are written using either the small or the large memory models. Most C and C++ compilers are configured for the small model by default, but their options can be changed to default to any desired model. When you use these compilers' command-line versions rather than the integrated development environments, the desired model is selected by an option switch.

General Interface Guidelines

There are two ways to interface with C or C++. The easier method is to specify a language, using the new simplified model directives for the assemblers. This feature is available with both MASM and TASM. The older and somewhat more arcane method is to do manually what is now done automatically by the simplified directives. To give you a firm footing in how interfacing occurs, I'll discuss this older method first.

To interface assembly language subroutines with C or C++, you must follow a few general guidelines. First, you must give a specific segment name to the code segment of your assembly language subroutine. The name varies, depending on which compiler you use. For example, Microsoft C, QuickC, and Turbo C require either the segment name _TEXT (for tiny, small, or compact memory-model programs; Microsoft C does not support the tiny model) or a segment name with the suffix _TEXT (for other memory models). Aztec C requires the segment name CODESEG.

Second, your C compiler may require specific names for data segments (if the data is being referenced outside the code segment). Microsoft C, QuickC, and Turbo C require that the segment be named _DATA, whereas you must use the segment name DATASEG with Aztec C. You must use these segment names, which are specific to C, to properly link and then execute the programs.

Third, you must understand how variables are passed to assembly language subroutines through the stack. In the function-calling syntax of

```
function_name(arg1,arg2,arg3,...,argn);
```

the values of each argument are pushed on the stack in reverse order. Thus, argument n (argn) is pushed on the stack first, and argument 1 (arg1) is pushed last. A value, or a pointer to a variable, can be passed on the stack. Although most values and pointers are passed as word-length stack elements, the longer data elements such as long or unsigned long-type variables require 32 bits (2 words) of stack space.

If the memory model being used is compact, large, or huge, or if the data item has a segment override, data pointers also require 32 bits of stack space. Float-type variables use 64 bits (4 words) of stack space. Remember this distinction of stack usage by variable type; failure to do so can produce undesired results.

Fourth, in the assembly language source file, the assembly language routines to be called from C must begin (for Microsoft C, QuickC, or Turbo C if using its default options) or end (for Aztec C) with an underline character. The underline is not included when the routines are invoked in C, however. The examples in this chapter reflect this distinction; Turbo C's option for this (the underscore) was left set at its default ON condition to obtain maximum compatibility in the code while testing, but can be set to OFF if you want to eliminate the need for the underline prefix.

Fifth, remember to save any special-purpose registers (such as CS, DS, SS, BP, SI, and DI) your assembly language subroutine may disturb. Failure to save them may have undesired consequences when control is returned to the C program. Saving registers is especially important with Turbo C because Turbo C defaults to the automatic use of register variables. You do not have to save the contents of AX, BX, CX, or DX because these registers are considered to be volatile by C; that is, the language assumes that you will change them and even requires you to do so in order to return a value.

The examples in this chapter were designed to work with C compilers from Microsoft and Borland, or C++ compilers from Borland. If you are using another compiler, the only differences you need to deal with should be in the required segment names for code and data or in the naming of the subroutines.

Simpler Interfacing

Over the years, assemblers have evolved to the point where the interface to high-level languages is quite well developed. In earlier chapters in this book, you may have noticed this with the use of the simplified model directives that enable you to specify the language type you are interfacing with. For instance, you can specify C (your programs will also work with C++); then the assembler automatically takes care of such issues as whether to use NEAR or FAR pointers, what segment names to use, how to access variables on the stack, and whether to use a leading underscore on labels.

For instance, the following is a sample (from a program used in the next section) of the correct assembly language coding, using the older interfacing methods:

```
        PUBLIC  _CURON,_CUROFF

_TEXT   SEGMENT WORD PUBLIC 'CODE'
        ASSUME  CS:_TEXT

_CURON  PROC    NEAR            ; for small model
```

If you use the newer simplified directives, this same information is coded as follows:

```
        PUBLIC  CURON, CUROFF

        .MODEL  small, C
        .CODE
CURON   PROC
```

This source code is much cleaner and easier to read. The directives .MODEL and .CODE instruct the assembler to make the necessary assumptions and adjustments so that the routine will work with a small-model C program. The assembler also adds the necessary underscores before the label names.

Which method you use to write your assembly language programs is up to you. Either works well, and both result in basically the same code being generated by the assembler.

Interfacing Subroutines with No Variable Passing

To help you understand how an assembly language subroutine is interfaced with C, let's look at a sample subroutine that requires no parameter passing. Consider the following assembly language program:

```
Page 60,132
Comment ¦
*********************************************************************


File:      CEX1.ASM
Author:    Allen L. Wyatt
Date:      8/26/91

Purpose:   Subroutine designed to turn the cursor on and off.

Format:    CurOn()
           CurOff()


*********************************************************************¦

        PUBLIC  CurOn, CurOff

        .MODEL  small, C
        .CODE

CurOn   PROC
        MOV     AH,3            ; get current cursor
        XOR     BX,BX
        INT     10h
        AND     CH,1Fh          ; force to ON condition
        MOV     AH,1            ; set new cursor values
        INT     10h
        RET
CurOn   ENDP

CurOff  PROC
        MOV     AH,3            ; get current cursor
        XOR     BX,BX
        INT     10h
        OR      CH,20h          ; force to OFF condition
```

```
        MOV     AH,1            ; set new cursor values
        INT     10h
        RET
CurOff  ENDP

        END
```

You may remember this example from Chapter 12; note that in this version of the example, both procedures have been included in a single ASM file so that only one OBJ file is necessary. This is possible because most C programs that use assembly language do so by means of OBJ files that are incorporated at link time. Pascal's methods of dealing with assembly language modules make such manipulation more difficult.

The C program to test this routine is as follows:

```
/* File:     CEX1S.C
 * Author:   Allen L. Wyatt
 * Date:     8/26/91
 *
 * Purpose:  Example of using curon() and curoff()
 */

#include <stdio.h>

void CurOn(void);
void CurOff(void);

void main()
{ printf( "%s\n", "The cursor is now turning OFF");
  CurOff();
  getchar();
  printf( "%s\n", "Now going back ON");
  CurOn();
}
```

After you have assembled and compiled these examples, link them together and try them out.

Had the older method of interfacing to assembly language been used, it would have been important to make sure that CurOn and CurOff were preceded by underscores (_CurOn and _CurOff) in the assembly language source file. If you choose to use this older method, remembering the leading underscore is critical.

Using QuickAssembler with QuickC

You can create this entire program, both the ASM and C portions of it, without leaving the integrated development environment, if you are using QuickC version 2.51 (which includes QuickAssembler).

The program was tested initially using exactly that combination. To make everything work, the option settings for all steps (the assembler, the compiler, and the linker) had to be modified. The key change was to turn off all debugging options and incremental linking and to make the link step insensitive to case. This was necessary because the ASM file uses all-uppercase procedure names, whereas the C program uses mixed-case names.

Using Inline ASM Coding with Borland C or C++ Products

If you use Turbo C, Turbo C++, or Borland C++, you can include your assembly language routines as inline statements in much the same way you can with Turbo Pascal. Because doing so involves many extra restrictions, however, this is probably not worth the effort. Here's what the previous CurOn()/CurOff() example looks like when you use Turbo C's inline-assembler capability:

```
/* File:     CEX2S.C
 * Author:   Allen L. Wyatt
 * Date:     8/29/91
 *
 * Purpose:  Example of using curon() and curoff()
 */


#include <stdio.h>

void CurOn()
{ asm MOV AH,3;         /* get current cursor     */
  asm XOR BX,BX;
  asm INT 0x10;
  asm AND CH,0x1F       /* force to ON condition  */
  asm MOV AH,1;         /* set new cursor values  */
  asm INT 0x10;
}
```

```
void CurOff()
{ asm MOV AH,3;          /* get current cursor     */
  asm XOR BX,BX;
  asm INT 0x10;
  asm OR  CH,0x20;        /* force to OFF condition */
  asm MOV AH,1;           /* set new cursor values  */
  asm INT 0x10;
}

void main()
{ printf( "%s\n", "The cursor is now turning OFF");
  CurOff();
  getchar();
  printf( "%s\n", "Now going back ON");
  CurOn();
}
```

This example is named CEX2S.C; if you are using Turbo C++ or Borland C++, change the name to CEX2S.CPP. No other changes are necessary; the file will compile regardless of your variation of the Borland C/C++ family.

Notice that every line of ASM code requires its own asm keyword and that the comments follow C standards rather than those of normal assembly language.

What this example does *not* show is that the inline coding cannot be used from Turbo C's integrated environment; it works *only* with the command-line compiler. Furthermore, inline coding requires that a version of C0.ASM (contained in Borland's STARTUP.ARC package) appropriate to the memory model in use be available. Without it, the linker cannot complete its work.

About the only advantage you gain by using this inline capability is that the program itself needs no changes if you decide to switch from one memory model to another. The C0?.OBJ file for the desired memory model must exist, however. Because Borland's C/C++ products are the only compilers that support inline assembly language, and this support adds several layers of complication, you probably will find that doing everything through OBJ files and link-time inclusion is much easier.

Interfacing Subroutines with Variable Passing

As you probably remember from the discussions earlier in this chapter and in Chapter 10, variables are passed on the stack in C and C++. This is the normal method of variable passing.

You can easily combine the preceding subroutines and eliminate much of the extensive duplication of code by passing a variable that specifies whether to turn the cursor on or off. The following assembly language program includes this modification:

```
Page 60,132
Comment ¦
**********************************************************************


File:      CEX3.ASM
Author:    Allen L. Wyatt
Date:      9/17/91

Purpose:   Subroutine designed to turn the cursor on and off by
           passing a variable on the stack.

Format:    void CurSw(integer switch)
                switch = 0; turn cursor off
                switch <> 0; turn cursor on


**********************************************************************¦


        PUBLIC  CurSw

        .MODEL  small, C
        .CODE

CurSw   PROC    Switch:WORD
        MOV     AX,Switch       ; get flag value
        OR      AX,AX           ; test zero/nonzero
        JNZ     CS1
        MOV     AX,20h          ; zero means OFF
        JMP     SHORT CS2

CS1:    MOV     AX,0            ; else turn ON
CS2:    PUSH    AX              ; either way, save it
        MOV     AH,3            ; get current cursor
        XOR     BX,BX
        INT     10H
        POP     AX              ; retrieve saved control
        AND     CH,1Fh          ; clear previous bit
        OR      CH,AL           ; and set in new one
        MOV     AH,1            ; set new cursor values
```

```
        INT     10H
        RET
CurSw   ENDP

        END
```

Notice that the variable is passed through the stack, as described earlier in this chapter and in Chapter 2. On entry to this routine, C pushes the variable's *value* on the stack. Because the variable is an integer (it must be declared as such in the C program), it can be accessed as a word on the stack.

The C program that uses this routine was also changed to pass a value. The modified routine (based on the previous example, CEX2S.C) follows:

```
/* File:     CEX3S.C
 * Author:   Allen L. Wyatt
 * Date:     9/17/91
 *
 * Purpose:  Example of using CurSw()
 */

#include <stdio.h>

void CurSw( int );

void main()
{ printf( "%s\n", "The cursor is now turning OFF");
  CurSw(0);
  getchar();
  printf( "%s\n", "Now going back ON");
  CurSw(1);
}
```

Notice that both the prototype and the invocations of the function now include material enclosed in parentheses. The prototype declaration specifies that the parameter passed must be an integer, and the invocations specify integer constant values: 0 to turn the cursor off and 1 to turn it back on.

When you are developing from the integrated environments of QuickC and Turbo C, certain tricks are necessary to force the linker to consider the assembler module's OBJ file. Both tricks are based on the idea of the MAKE file (discussed in detail in Chapter 12).

In QuickC, you must add the OBJ file by name to the program list for your C file, using the MAKE menu (if you have not already established a program list, you must do so first from the same menu). The MAKE file that drives the link process is generated automatically from this program list.

In Turbo C, you must create a PRJ file for your program. This is merely a text file that lists names of the files to be included. For the previous example, CEX3.PRJ contained

```
cex3s
cex3.obj
```

The file extension is not necessary for a C source file but is required for OBJ or LIB files. The PRJ file can be created by any text editor and should bear the file name you want assigned to the final EXE file, with the extension PRJ.

Passing Variable Pointers

Simply passing information into your assembly language routines is not always enough—you need to be able to get data back from them as well. Unlike Pascal and BASIC, C keeps the calling program in full control of things; thus, one of the standard techniques for returning information is to pass in a pointer that contains the address of a storage area in the main program.

Returning Data via Pointers

To understand how pointers are handled, consider first this assembly language program, which was designed to read a specified number of characters from the screen:

```
Page 60,132
Comment ¦
**********************************************************************

File:     CEX4.ASM
Author:   Allen L. Wyatt
Date:     9/17/91

Purpose:  Subroutine designed to read data directly from the
          screen to a C char array.

Format:   void ReadScrn(unsigned ROW,
                         unsigned COL,
                         unsigned NUM,
                         char * BFR);
             ROW: Row at which to start, 0-24
```

```
                COL: Column at which to start, 0-79
                NUM: number of characters to read, 1-255
                BFR: pointer to array where data will be put.


    ****************************************************************|

                PUBLIC   ReadScrn

                .MODEL   small, C
                .CODE

ReadScrn        PROC USES ES DI, Row, Col, Num, BFR:WORD

                PUSH     DS
                POP      ES
                MOV      DI,BFR              ;Get string address

                MOV      AH,0Fh              ;Get video page in BH
                INT      10h
                MOV      AH,03               ;Get current cursor location
                INT      10h
                PUSH     DX                  ;Save it to restore later

                MOV      AX,Row              ;Get row number
                CMP      AX,25
                JAE      Exit                ;Too big, get out
                MOV      DH,AL               ;Okay, set into DH
                MOV      AX,Col              ;Get col number
                CMP      AX,80
                JAE      Exit                ;Too big, get out
                MOV      DL,AL               ;Okay, so set column
                PUSH     DX                  ;Store column for later
                MOV      AH,2                ;and change cursor location
                INT      10h
                POP      DX                  ;Get column back
                MOV      CX,Num              ;Get length of string
                JCXZ     Exit                ;No length, get out
                MOV      AX,80               ;Maximum string length
                SUB      AX,DX               ;Adjust maximum for starting column
                CMP      CX,AX               ;Is it longer than allowed?
                JA       Exit                ;Yes, so get out
```

```
READEM:    MOV      AH,8                  ;Get char from BIOS
           INT      10h
           STOSB                          ;Put down in string
           INC      DL                    ;Advance cursor
           CMP      DL,80                 ;If off end of row, do wrap
           JB       R1                    ;Still on row, okay
           INC      DH                    ;Off end, go to next row
           XOR      DL,DL                 ;at column zero
R1:        MOV      AH,2                  ;Set new cursor location
           INT      10h
           LOOP     READEM                ;and go back for next

Exit:      XOR      AL,AL                 ;Mark end of string
           STOSB
           POP      DX                    ;Restore original cursor
           MOV      AH,2
           INT      10h
           RET
ReadScrn   ENDP

           END
```

This routine is the C version of the one, described in the last chapter, for use with Pascal. Comparing the two to see what changes were required is instructive. The biggest change results from the way that Pascal and C store strings—Pascal requires the first byte of the stored string to be the length, whereas C requires only that the ending byte to be a null (0).

The following program demonstrates how ReadScrn() can be used:

```
/* File:     CEX4S.C
 * Author:   Allen L. Wyatt
 * Date:     9/17/91
 *
 * Purpose:  Example of using ReadScrn()
 */

#include <stdio.h>

void ReadScrn( int r, int c, int w, char * b );
void ClrHome();

char Buf[81];
int r, c, w;
```

```
void main()
{ ClrHome();
  printf("The following line will be read, beginning with the 5th column:\n");
  printf("----This is a test line, to see how many characters will be read\n");
  ReadScrn(1,4,20,&Buf[0]);
  printf("\nThe following is the 20 charcters read by the routine\n%s\n",Buf);
  printf("\nRemember that the top left corner is 0,0.\n");
  printf("To exit this demo program, enter a row of 0 and a column of 0.\n");
  do
  { r = 90;
    do
    { printf("Row: ");
      scanf( "%d", &r );
    } while (r > 24);

    c = 90;
    do
    { printf("Column: ");
      scanf( "%d", &c );
    } while (c > 79);

    if ((r + c) > 0)
    { w = 0;
      do
      { printf("Width: ");
        scanf( "%d", &w );
      } while ((w < 1) || (w > (80 - c)));

      ReadScrn(r,c,w,&Buf[0]);
      printf("%s\n\n",Buf);
    }
  } while (r+c != 0);

}
```

Notice that another external function is in this program—one that clears the screen and homes the cursor through the use of the ClrHome function. The listing for this function is as follows:

```
Page 60,132
Comment ¦
*********************************************************************

File:    CLRHOME.ASM
Author:  Allen L. Wyatt
Date:    9/17/91

Purpose: Subroutine designed to clear the screen and home the
         cursor.  Works with C.

Format:  ClrHome()

*********************************************************************¦


         PUBLIC  ClrHome

         .MODEL  small, C
         .CODE

ClrHome  PROC
         MOV     AH,0Fh              ;Discover display state
         INT     10h
         PUSH    AX                  ;Save mode/width
         PUSH    BX                  ;Save page

         MOV     DX,0                ;Position 0,0
         MOV     AH,2                ;Set cursor position
         INT     10h

         POP     BX                  ;Get back page
         POP     AX                  ;Get back mode/width
         MOV     CX,0                ;Upper left is 0,0
         MOV     DH,24               ;Bottom row
         MOV     DL,AH               ;Set column width
         DEC     DL                  ;Actual column number
         MOV     BH,07h              ;Attribute
         MOV     AL,DH               ;Lines to scroll
         INC     AL                  ;Full screen
         MOV     AH,6                ;Scroll window up
         INT     10h

         RET
ClrHome  ENDP

         END
```

This routine works on any text page you may be using. It positions the cursor at the upper left corner of the screen and then blanks the screen to white-on-black attribute.

Take a look at the C program to test ReadScrn(). This program simply asks you for a row and a column at which to begin reading the screen. If the sum of the row and column are greater than 0, you are asked for the width of the string you want to read. The string is dutifully read and then displayed from inside C. The procedure continues until you enter a row of 0 and a column of 0, at which time the program ends.

Admittedly, this example is a bit simplistic. In practice, ReadScrn() would be used with other functions. For example, a mouse driver could position the mouse pointer over some data on the screen, and then a click of the left button would cause the data there to be copied by ReadScrn() into a buffer from which a later click of the right button could stuff the data into the keyboard buffer as simulated keyboard input.

Using Pointers to Process Strings

Another reason to pass a pointer to a variable's address instead of simply passing the value is that if you know the variable's location in memory, you can directly change the value in your assembly language subroutine. This capability can be invaluable when you are working with strings, as in the following example:

```
Page 60,132
Comment |
********************************************************************


File:     ULCASEC.ASM for MASM 6.0
Author:   Allen L. Wyatt
Date:     9/25/91

Purpose:  Subroutine designed to convert a string to upper- or
          lowercase.  Designed to be called from C.

Format:   ULCase(s,x)
               s:  Pointer to string to be converted
               x:  Controls conversion
                   0 = Convert to uppercase
                   ?   Any other value signifies convert to lowercase


********************************************************************|
```

```
                PUBLIC    ULCase

                .MODEL    small, C
                .CODE

ULCase          PROC   USES DS DI, Sptr, Case:WORD
                MOV       DI,Sptr             ;Get string address
                MOV       AX,Case             ;Get action variable
                CMP       AX,0                ;Converting to uppercase?
                JZ        UPPER               ;Yes, so go handle

LOWER:          CMP       BYTE PTR [DI],0     ;Is this end of string?
                JE        EXIT                ;Yes, so exit
                CMP       BYTE PTR [DI],'A'   ;Is it < A ?
                JB        L1                  ;Yes, so skip character
                CMP       BYTE PTR [DI],'Z'   ;Is it > Z ?
                JA        L1                  ;Yes, so skip character
                OR        BYTE PTR [DI],20h   ;Make lowercase (00100000b)
L1:             INC       DI                  ;Next character
                JMP       LOWER               ;Do it again

UPPER:          CMP       BYTE PTR [DI],0     ;Is this end of string?
                JE        EXIT                ;Yes, so exit
                CMP       BYTE PTR [DI],'a'   ;Is it < a ?
                JB        U1                  ;Yes, so skip character
                CMP       BYTE PTR [DI],'z'   ;Is it > z ?
                JA        U1                  ;Yes, so skip character
                AND       BYTE PTR [DI],05Fh  ;Make uppercase (01011111b)
U1:             INC       DI                  ;Next character
                JMP       UPPER               ;Do it again

EXIT:           RET
ULCase          ENDP

                END
```

This simple program converts a string to all upper- or all lowercase. The program expects two parameters to be passed from C: a pointer to the string to be converted and an integer value indicating whether the string is to be converted to upper- or lowercase.

Notice the calling syntax for the subroutine: ULCase(s,x). Unlike some other languages, C places the function parameters onto the stack in reverse order, from right to left. Thus, the first item pushed is the value for x and the second item pushed is the pointer to s.

The C program that uses this subroutine follows:

```
/* File:      CEX5S.C
 * Author:    Allen L. Wyatt
 * Date:      9/25/91
 *
 * Purpose:   Example of using ULCase()
 */


#include <stdio.h>
#include <string.h>

void ulcase( char *, int );    /* function prototype */

unsigned char s[]="This is the original string";

void main()
{ while (strlen(s) != 0)
  { printf("String to convert: ");
    gets(s);
    if (strlen(s) != 0)
      { printf("\nUPPERCASE:\n");
        ulcase(s,0);
        printf("   %s\nlowercase:\n",s);
        ulcase(s,1);
        printf("   %s\n\n",s);
      }
  }
}
```

Summary

C is a popular language to which assembly language programs are easily interfaced, and C++ is quickly becoming more popular than it used to be. Although the specific interfacing syntax may vary from one compiler to another, the general guidelines are the same for all compilers.

Variables can be passed in C in many ways. You can pass variables on the stack as values or as pointers. Variables can be returned to C either by changing the variable value in the C data segment or by returning a variable in the AX register. (This second method for returning a variable is not covered in this chapter but is shown in examples elsewhere in this book.)

14

Interfacing with dBASE III+ and FoxPro

O ne of the most widely used high-level languages for business applications of MS-DOS computers has no official name. The language originated as the command set for one of the first popular database management systems, Ashton-Tate's dBASE II. As dBASE II evolved through versions III and III+ into the current dBASE IV, other firms found a market for enhanced dBASE clones, and as a result the language and the product began to lead separate lives.

Recently, Ashton-Tate dropped their copyright claims to the language, which means that they have recognized what their competitors have been saying for some time—that dBASE is a full language in its own right.

The many different implementations of the dBASE language are referred to collectively as *xBase*. Most of these implementations feature among their core attractions a strict compatibility with the Ashton-Tate version. One result is that most of them need a bit of help, via assembly language routines, to do such common actions as turning the cursor on and off, or saving a screen while displaying help data.

Fortunately, the xBase language provides commands that work together to provide such assistance:

❑ LOAD brings a separately assembled support procedure into memory and makes it available to the xBase program.

❑ CALL invokes execution of the LOADed program, in much the same way that the GOSUB statement operates in BASIC.

327

❏ RELEASE MODULE can be used to remove from memory any LOADed program that is no longer needed, freeing space for other modules. Its use is optional; LOAD and CALL must be used together.

In dBASE III+ a maximum of 5 separate support files, each up to 32K in size, can be LOADed into memory at the same time. Any or all of them can then be CALLed as required. Both LOAD and CALL commands can be included in PRG program files or issued interactively from the dot prompt. If you use FoxPro or dBASE IV, the number of loadable files increases to 16, with a maximum size of 64K each.

If you're an old hand at xBase, you can skip the rest of this section and go directly to the section titled "General Interfacing Guidelines." If you're a newcomer to the world of xBase, however, you may find these terms confusing. Here's a brief explanation.

All of the conventional implementations of the xBase language (such as dBASE III+ and IV, or FoxPro 2.0) operate primarily as *interpreters* in an interactive mode. That's the way DOS itself works. Just as DOS issues the C> prompt to let you know it's ready for a new command, the xBase program issues a dot prompt, consisting of a single period at the left margin, to let you know when it's ready for another instruction. And just as DOS enables you to string a sequence of commands together into a BAT file and then execute the entire stream of actions without individually typing each at the command prompt, the xBase program provides command files with the same capability. Because the command file is indicated by the extension PRG in xBase, such files commonly are called PRG files.

Other special file extensions used by xBase include MEM for files of saved memory variables (memvars) and BIN for the assembly language support routines this chapter discusses. There are many more, but these are the only ones you need to know about in this chapter.

General Interfacing Guidelines

Certain restrictions are imposed on BIN files to ensure that they are completely compatible with the xBase interpreters:

❏ The file must be a pure memory image, like a COM file, instead of being in the relocatable EXE format usually produced by most linker programs.

❏ All memory addresses in the file must be relative to zero. That is, the assembly language source must contain an implicit or explicit ORG 0 statement; this differs from conventional COM-file usage, which requires an ORG 0100h starting point.

❑ Because the file is accessed by a FAR call from the interpreter, it must use the far version of RET to return to its caller.

❑ The CS and SS registers must both be returned to the caller holding the same values they had at entry. This means that if your procedure changes the registers, it must save the original values and restore them before returning. No other registers need be preserved by your routine.

❑ All code and working data storage must be contained within a single 64K segment (32K for dBASE III+). The procedure must not attempt to access any data maintained by the xBase program, except through the parameter-passing mechanism provided. This restriction, however, does not apply to accessing data outside the xBase program, such as the BIOS data area, the video RAM, and so forth.

❑ Your assembly language program must not change the size or length of any variables passed to it.

❑ The BIN file must not contain a STACK segment or make any reference to other segments that would have to be resolved when the file is linked. Failure to observe this restriction may make converting the file to the required memory-image format impossible.

To prevent confusion, the file name used for the BIN file and the procedure name used for the internal procedure should be identical. Thus, the procedure name must follow DOS file-naming conventions—most notably, the procedure name can be only as many as eight characters long. The xBase program uses only one lookup table. This table, which is set up to refer to the file name when you LOAD the file, is used later to find the procedure when you CALL it. Thus, only one callable procedure can be contained in each BIN file.

The procedure name is unimportant to the system itself because that name never gets through to the xBase interpreter; only the file name is ever known to xBase. Keeping track of things is much easier, however, when your ASM files and your PRG files use the same names for procedures.

Interfacing Subroutines without Variable Passing

To understand how the restrictions on BIN files apply in practice, consider first the simplest types of BIN files—those that simply perform a procedure without needing data from the calling program or passing any values back to it.

One such procedure, which fills a real need in dBASE III+, is a routine that turns off the cursor when it is called. Although FoxPro and other competitors added special capabilities for cursor control, dBASE III+ lacks such a feature. Let's look first at turning off the cursor and then at turning the cursor back on.

Turning Off the Cursor

The video BIOS turns the cursor on and off. The assembly language procedures call BIOS to get the current cursor condition, change it, and call BIOS again to put it back. Here's how to turn off the cursor:

```
Page 60,132
Comment |
**********************************************************************


File:      CUROFF.ASM
Author:    Allen L. Wyatt
Date:      10/1/91

Purpose:   Turn the cursor off from an xBase program. Requires
           no parameter passing. Particularly of use from a
           dBASE III+ program.

Format:    LOAD curoff
           CALL curoff          && to turn cursor OFF


**********************************************************************|

CODE       SEGMENT BYTE PUBLIC 'CODE'
           ASSUME  CS:CODE
           ORG     0

CurOff     PROC    FAR
           MOV     AH,03           ; Read cursor information
           INT     10h             ;    using BIOS
           OR      CH,20h          ; Set cursor off bit
           MOV     AH,01           ; Set cursor type
           INT     10h             ;    using BIOS
           RET
CurOff     ENDP

CODE       ENDS
           END
```

This file, when assembled and linked as described later in this chapter, creates a 12-byte BIN file. If the file is named CUROFF.BIN, the command LOAD CUROFF will bring it into memory and make it available to xBase, and a subsequent command, CALL CUROFF, will make the cursor vanish.

Although this example is indeed tiny, it does illustrate all the major requirements of an assembly language source file for any BIN-file routine. Everything is contained in a single segment (CODE), the program begins at zero (ORG 0), and the code is declared as PROC FAR, which ensures that the proper type of RET opcode is generated.

The cursor is turned off by the single line OR CH,20h; this bit instructs the CRT controller on the video card to shut off the cursor until further notice. The code before that ensures that the CX register contains the proper cursor-size information when the second call sends the data back to BIOS.

Turning On the Cursor

Now that you can turn off the cursor, you need a corresponding capability to turn the cursor back on the next time you want it to show up on-screen. The following code provides this capability:

```
Page 60,132
Comment ¦
***********************************************************************


File:     CURON.ASM
Author:   Allen L. Wyatt
Date:     10/1/91

Purpose:  Turn the cursor on from an xBase program. Requires
          no parameter passing. Particularly of use from a
          dBASE III+ program.

Format:   LOAD curon
          CALL curon            && to turn cursor ON


***********************************************************************¦

CODE        SEGMENT BYTE PUBLIC 'CODE'
            ASSUME  CS:CODE
            ORG     0
```

```
CurOn      PROC    FAR
           MOV     AH,03         ; Read cursor information
           INT     10h           ;   using BIOS
           AND     CH,1Fh        ; Clear cursor off bit
           MOV     AH,01         ; Set cursor type
           INT     10h           ;   using BIOS
           RET
CurOn      ENDP

CODE       ENDS
           END
```

The only difference between this routine and that shown in the preceding section is the line AND CH,1Fh. Where that example set the cursor-off bit to 1 by ORing in a value of 20h, this routine uses the inverse operation to force that same bit to zero so that the CRT controller can enable the cursor to show once again.

Because you can LOAD several BIN files at once with xBase, you can LOAD both CUROFF and CURON and, then alternate CALLs to them for full cursor control.

And even though FoxPro provides a special SYS() function that can be used to do the same thing, many developers who support several implementations of xBase prefer to use identical code for all of them, to keep the maintenance job simpler. These routines work not only with dBASE but also with FoxPro.

Interfacing Subroutines with Variable Passing

While the two preceding examples describe the techniques for creating and using BIN files, most assembly language routines you write will probably require that information be passed in from or back to the caller. Although the xBase language provides the capability to pass information, the capability is somewhat restricted, compared to C or Pascal.

In addition to the simple CALL statement used with the preceding examples, you can use the statement

CALL *procedure* WITH *parameter*

to pass a single parameter to your procedure. The procedure can then return any results in that same parameter.

Unfortunately, usually only one parameter can be passed (dBASE IV can pass more, as is explained later). When your routine is entered, the segment address of that single parameter is in the DS register and its offset is in BX. (If no parameter is passed in, BX contains 0.)

Although the official language definitions all agree that a character expression, or a memory variable of *any* type, can be passed in the CALL statement, the practice of using a memvar of type "character" as the parameter is almost universal. You can use such a memvar as a buffer to pass data that is not necessarily in character format.

The following additional restrictions are imposed on a parameter when it is passed:

❏ The size of the parameter may not be changed by your routine; if the result takes less space than the parameter passed in, your routine must handle it by some method *other* than changing the parameter's length.

❏ If a character (or string) variable is involved, never try to save its address from one call of your routine to the next. Some implementations of xBase move data in memory as much as BASIC does. Always get addresses immediately before they are to be used to ensure that they are correct.

The limit of only one parameter makes it necessary to pass multiple arguments as a string, which may include several fields in ASCII with commas as delimiters. Such a string cannot contain bytes that are all zeroes, and its maximum size is 254 bytes.

Saving and Restoring the Screen

To understand how data is passed into a procedure, consider the program SCRUTL.ASM. This procedure can save and restore up to three screens. FoxPro provides this capability in its implementation, but dBASE III+ does not. SCRUTL.BIN works with both dBASE III+ and FoxPro, and can easily be expanded to save up to 12 screens of information. Several similar programs have been published; this example combines the best features of all:

```
Page 60,132
Comment ¦
*******************************************************************


File:     SCRUTL.ASM
Author:   Allen L. Wyatt
Date:     10/1/91

Purpose:  Save and restore the screen from an xBase program.
          Requires one parameter, as shown in the Format section.
          This routine allows for three screen save areas, but
          more could be added if desired. If called from FoxPro,
          you should use the SAVE keyword with the call function.
```

```
Format:     LOAD scrutl
            OpCode = 'S1'            && to save screen area 1
            CALL scrutl WITH OpCode  && call routine
            OpCode = 'R1'            && to restore screen area 1
            CALL scrutl WITH OpCode  && call routine


*********************************************************************|


CODE        SEGMENT BYTE PUBLIC 'CODE'
            ASSUME  CS:CODE
            ORG     0


Scrutl      PROC    FAR
            PUSH    BX
            MOV     AH,0Fh          ; Get video state
            INT     10h
            CMP     AL,7            ; Is it monochrome display mode?
            MOV     AX,0B000h       ; Preset video segment for monochrome
            JE      Mono            ; Flags still set from CMP operation
            ADD     AH,8            ; Adjust video segment for color
Mono:       POP     BX
            MOV     DX,[BX]         ; Get 2-byte variable from xBase      DL = code, DH = area

            PUSH    CS              ; Set data segment properly
            POP     DS
            SUB     DH,'1'          ; Make area number 0-based
            CMP     DH,2            ; Is it out of 0-2 range?
            JA      WindUp          ; Yes, so ignore invalid parameter
            SHL     DH,1            ; Multiply by 2
            MOV     BX,OFFSET AreaTable
            ADD     BL,DH           ; Adjust for area pointer

            AND     DL,5Fh          ; Force code to uppercase
            CMP     DL,'S'          ; Want to save the screen?
            JE      Save            ; Yes, so go handle
            CMP     DL,'R'          ; Want to restore the screen?
            JE      Restor          ; Yes, so go handle
            JMP     SHORT WindUp    ; Invalid code, so ignore it

Save:       PUSH    CS
            POP     ES              ; Set destination segment
            MOV     DI,[BX]         ; Get address from table pointed to by BX
            MOV     DS,AX           ; Move segment address for video RAM
            MOV     SI,0
```

```
            JMP      SHORT Xfer        ; Go do actual transfer

Restor:     MOV      SI,[BX]           ; Get address from table pointed to by BX
            MOV      ES,AX             ; Move segment address for video RAM
            MOV      DI,0

Xfer:       MOV      CX,25*80          ; Want to move full screen
            CLD                        ; Be sure of transfer direction
            REP      MOVSW             ; Perform block move

WindUp:     RET
Scrutl      ENDP


; -------------------------------------------------------------------------
AreaTable   DW       OFFSET Area1
            DW       OFFSET Area2
            DW       OFFSET Area3

Area1       DW       2000 DUP (0)      ; screen save areas
Area2       DW       2000 DUP (0)      ; (in SEG but not PROC)
Area3       DW       2000 DUP (0)

CODE        ENDS
            END
```

Although much larger than the previous examples in this chapter, SCRUTL.BIN is not much more complex. It begins by determining whether it is running with a monochrome or a color monitor and placing the appropriate segment address (B000h for mono or B800h for color) of the video RAM in the AX register.

The program then uses the parameter address in BX to load the first two bytes of the parameter string into the DX register. The first byte goes into DL and the second into DH. This is all done by a single instruction to move a 16-bit value.

Because accessing the calling program's data area is complete, the data segment can now be set equal to the current code segment in order to access the data built into the routine.

The next step is to determine what screen area the user wants to save or restore. This is done by converting the number in DH into a number between 0 and 2. If the number is out of this range, the routine is exited with no action taken. If the number is in range, it is multiplied by 2 and added to the offset of the screen-area table that has been loaded into the BX register. The value in BX now points to the correct table entry for the address of the appropriate memory area.

The byte in DL should be either S (for *save*) or R (for *restore*). The byte in DL is masked against 5Fh to convert it from lowercase to uppercase if necessary. If the byte is not a letter or is already uppercase, this step doesn't change anything. If the resulting byte is S, control jumps to the label Save; if it is R, control goes to Restor. If the byte is neither S nor R, control goes to WindUp, which returns to the caller without doing anything else.

At either Save or Restor, the source and destination addresses are set and control is transferred to Xfer.

At Xfer, CX is loaded with the proper number of words to transfer. Note the use of assembly-time arithmetic to calculate this number in terms of rows and columns. This use of assembly-time arithmetic makes modifying the routine to support other display sizes simpler. Next, a CLD instruction ensures that the move will be made in the correct direction (see Chapter 22, "Processor Instruction Sets," for details of why this is needed), and a REP MOVSW instruction causes a block move of data from DS:SI to ES:DI, continuing for the number of words specified by the value in CX.

Finally, control goes to WindUp, which returns to the caller. The specified area now contains an exact copy of the current content of the video RAM.

Interfacing for dBASE IV

Interfacing to a BIN file with dBASE IV is a bit more complex and flexible than with dBASE III+. The main difference is that up to seven arguments can be passed rather than just one. As in the other xBase implementations, the address of the first parameter is passed in DS:BX. The number of values being passed is in the CX register, however, and the addresses are placed in a table of FAR (four-byte) pointers. This table begins at the address in ES:DI.

Any BIN file created to work with the older xBase implementations will work with dBASE IV, but dBASE IV BIN files will not necessarily work with the older xBase implementations. If you want maximum portability of your routines from one version of xBase to another, you must avoid using the multiparameter capability. For this reason, no example of this capability is provided.

Assembling and Linking the BIN Files

Every assembly language program used with the LOAD and CALL capability must be assembled, linked, and converted to a BIN file. The details of doing this differ according to the assembler and linker you use. The major differences are among the link steps.

No matter which assembler you use, the technique for assembling your BIN-file routine is the same. To create an OBJ file that the linker can use, you should invoke the assembler as described in Chapters 5 ("Using Microsoft's Assembly Language Products") and 6 ("Using Borland's Assembly Language Products").

If the assembler reports warning messages or errors, study them carefully and correct their causes before proceeding. You may need to reassemble the program and specify that a LST file be output to find the exact spots at which the errors occur. Only when the assembly step reports no problems should you proceed to the linking action.

When your routine is successfully assembled into an OBJ file, you must convert that OBJ file into the final BIN file by using your linker program and, in some cases, other utilities.

If you use Borland's TLINK, you can create the final file in a single step by using the following command line:

```
C>TLINK /t scrutl,scrutl.bin;
```

which automatically forces the output file to meet the BIN-file requirements. The /t option switch is necessary. (If you are linking the other files—CURON and CUROFF—you should substitute their names for SCRUTL in this example.)

If you are using Microsoft's LINK, the procedure is slightly more complex. You need to follow these three steps:

1. Link the OBJ file into EXE format as follows (you can safely ignore the one or two warning messages, which are normal in this case):

   ```
   C>LINK scrutl;
   ```

2. Convert the EXE file into BIN format:

   ```
   C>EXE2BIN scrutl
   ```

3. Delete the intermediate file:

   ```
   C>DEL scrutl.exe
   ```

Again, if you are working with CURON or CUROFF, use those file names in the appropriate places.

Using the BIN Files

Once you have created your BIN files, you can use them in PRG files to be executed by either dBASE or FoxPro, or you can use them directly from the dot prompt in an interactive mode.

The following program, SCRUTL.PRG, is designed to be used from dBASE or FoxPro. It demonstrates the proper use of BIN files.

```
SET STATUS OFF
SET SCOREBOARD OFF
SET TALK OFF

LOAD scrutl
LOAD curoff
LOAD curon

SET COLOR TO W/B
CALL curoff
CLEAR

i = 2
DO WHILE i < 22
   @ i, i SAY 'Test screen for Using Assembly Language, 3rd Edition'
   i = i+1
ENDDO

SET COLOR TO W*/N
@ 1,21 SAY " Using Assembly Language, 3rd Edition "
SET COLOR TO W/N

@ 22,0 SAY SPACE(75)
@ 21,0 SAY ""
WAIT
@ 22,0 SAY SPACE(75)
CALL scrutl WITH "S1"
@ 5,5 CLEAR TO 10,20
@ 5,5 TO 10,20 DOUBLE
@ 6,6 SAY "This is Area 1"

CALL scrutl WITH "S2"
@ 21,0 SAY ""
WAIT

@ 22,0 SAY SPACE(75)
SET COLOR TO N/W
@ 7,8 CLEAR TO 20,70
@ 7,8 TO 20,70
@ 8,9 SAY "Here's Area 2"
SET COLOR TO W/N
@ 21,0 SAY ""
WAIT
```

```
@ 22,0 SAY SPACE(75)
CALL scrutl WITH "S3"
SET COLOR TO N/N
@ 13,25 CLEAR TO 20,61         && create the shadow
SET COLOR TO W+/B
@ 12,24 CLEAR TO 19,60         && create the window
@ 12,24 TO 19,60 DOUBLE        && draw the border
@ 13,25 SAY "And in Area 3 a shadowed display"
@ 15,25 SAY "(By the way; notice that the cursor"
@ 16,25 SAY " has been turned off up to this"
@ 17,25 SAY " point. It will be turned on in the"
@ 18,25 SAY " next screen.)"
SET COLOR TO W/N
@ 21,1 SAY ""
WAIT "Press any key to begin removing windows"

CALL scrutl WITH "R3"
@ 21,1 SAY ""
CALL curon
WAIT "Restored from area 3"

CALL scrutl WITH "R2"
@ 21,1 SAY ""
WAIT "Restored from area 2"

CALL scrutl WITH "R1"
@ 21,1 SAY ""
WAIT "Demo complete, press any key to return to DOS"

QUIT
```

Note that to use this program successfully from FoxPro, you should change the CALL statements for restoring the screen, as follows:

```
CALL scrutl WITH "R3" SAVE
CALL scrutl WITH "R2" SAVE
CALL scrutl WITH "R1" SAVE
```

This alteration causes the program to work properly with the way FoxPro handles video screens.

Although this demonstration program performs a fairly worthless task, the program structure itself demonstrates a number of techniques made possible by the BIN files described in this chapter. These techniques can be used in your production programs to add a more professional touch to the screen displays.

Summary

The xBase language may be the most popular high-level language used today for business applications in the MS-DOS environment. This chapter showed you how to create assembly language modules to extend the capabilities of that language and how to use those modules in your programs.

15

Interfacing with Clipper

The Clipper package from Nantucket, Inc., compiles a superset of the DBMS language used by dBASE and FoxPro into stand-alone programs. The Clipper programs do not require that a run-time module be furnished to the end user.

A major feature available with Clipper is that you can code just about anything you need, using either C or assembler, and then link it with the Clipper-generated OBJ file. With this capability, you can extend the language almost any way you want.

The only drawback to this feature is that it has changed at each major update to Clipper. The techniques described in this chapter are those used with Clipper 5.0 or 5.01. These versions changed slightly from the previous (Summer '87) version, which was a drastic change from earlier versions.

Before getting into a detailed discussion of interfacing with Clipper, a definition of terms may be in order. If you already are familiar with Clipper terminology, you can skip the next two paragraphs.

Clipper source files, like source files in dBASE, are stored in ASCII program files with the extension PRG. These PRG files are nothing mysterious; they just hold the program source code written with the xBase language and any Clipper extensions to the language.

UDF is an acronym for *user-defined function*. These are the external functions—written either in Clipper or in a non-xBase language—that are linked to your Clipper application when it is compiled. UDFs are created and linked with Clipper through the *Extend System*, Clipper's interface for assembly language and C programmers.

General Interfacing Guidelines

When interfacing assembly language routines to Clipper, you must follow a few well-defined rules. It's absolutely essential that between entry to your routine and return to Clipper you preserve unchanged the values of the DS, SS, BP, SI, and DI registers. All other registers can be modified as needed.

Clipper, unlike compiled BASIC, Pascal, and C, does not generate true native machine code. An EXE file generated by Clipper consists of one call to Clipper's internal run-time interpreter for each PRG file contained in the EXE file. These calls are followed by a sequence of bytes in Clipper's own proprietary internal "tokenization." The run-time interpreter translates these tokens into calls to the native-code library routines.

Because of this translation, when you write a UDF in assembly language (or in C), you must always use the subroutines furnished with Clipper (as part of the CLIPPER.LIB file) to communicate with your UDF. If your function doesn't pass information, you do not need to use CLIPPER.LIB; one example of such a UDF would be a function that changes the cursor shape.

Most useful functions either pass information from the calling program or return data to the calling program, however. Because Clipper's data-storage structure is not directly accessible to your assembly language code, such functions require routines from CLIPPER.LIB to perform either of these tasks.

The techniques described in this chapter work equally well with either MASM or TASM. One thing you should note, however, is that you should not assemble your program with the options to include CodeView or Turbo Debugger information. The extra debugging data embedded in the OBJ file prevents Clipper from properly using your code.

Interfacing Subroutines

Many of the examples in earlier chapters deal with cursor control. The examples in this chapter do as well, although Clipper provides a cursor-control function. Instead of pursuing capabilities that only duplicate built-in Clipper functions, however, the sample code in this chapter shows how to do something Clipper will not do. Although many languages change the shape of the cursor to indicate whether you are operating in insert or overtype mode, Clipper does not provide this capability.

Three examples—each a bit more advanced (and therefore a little more complicated) than its predecessor—are presented.

The first example shows how to interface without passing any parameters or returning any values. The code consists of three different functions, each of which first uses BIOS to read the current cursor information, then modifies it and puts it back. One function turns the cursor into a regular line, one into a half block, and one into a full block.

The second example shows how you can use the parameters to make just one procedure do the entire job. The sizes are specified by a code number passed into the function from Clipper; a code of 1 makes the cursor a line, 2 is a half block, and 3 is a full block.

Because both of these examples go directly to BIOS to change the cursor size, Clipper's internal record does not reflect the actual cursor condition. This makes the built-in SET CURSOR function unreliable, and makes it difficult for your program to determine the previous condition of the cursor. Therefore, the third example adds a value-return capability to the second example, so that it tells your program what the cursor condition *was* before you changed it. This is exactly like (and is modeled from) the existing Clipper SETCOLOR() function action.

In all three examples, the same basic plan is followed: first, ask BIOS what type of cursor is presently displayed; then go to BIOS again to change the cursor type.

Interfacing Subroutines without Variable Passing

First, let's look at an example of code that does not require variable passing. The following assembly language subroutine requires a separate function to perform each action:

```
Page 60,132
Comment ¦
******************************************************************


File:     CLIPEX1.ASM
Author:   Allen L. Wyatt
Date:     10/29/91

Purpose:  Clipper example programs, 1st pass: cursor sizing
          with no parameter passing.

Format:   CurLine()
          CurHalf()
          CurBlock()


******************************************************************¦
```

```
            PUBLIC  CurLine, CurBlock, CurHalf

            .MODEL  large
            .CODE

CurLine     PROC    FAR
            MOV     AH,3            ; Get current cursor
            XOR     BX,BX           ; Clipper uses Page 0 only
            INT     10h             ; Start in CH, end in CL
            AND     CL,1Fh          ; Be sure it's ON
            MOV     CH,CL           ; Copy endline to startline
            DEC     CH              ; And back up by 1
            MOV     AH,1            ; Set new cursor values
            INT     10h
            RET
CurLine     ENDP

CurHalf     PROC    FAR
            MOV     AH,3            ; Get current cursor
            XOR     BX,BX           ; Clipper uses Page 0 only
            INT     10h             ; Start in CH, end in CL
            AND     CL,1Fh          ; Be sure it's ON
            MOV     CH,CL           ; Copy endline to startline
            SHR     CH,1            ; And divide start by 2
            MOV     AH,1            ; Set new cursor values
            INT     10h
            RET
CurHalf     ENDP

CurBlock    PROC    FAR
            MOV     AH,3            ; Get current cursor
            XOR     BX,BX           ; Clipper uses Page 0 only
            INT     10h             ; Start in CH, end in CL
            AND     CL,1Fh          ; Be sure it's ON
            XOR     CH,CH           ; Force start to scanline 0
            MOV     AH,1            ; Set new cursor values
            INT     10h
            RET
CurBlock    ENDP

            END
```

Although this looks like a great deal of code, remember that it's essentially four copies of the same procedure. These procedures vary only in the values set in the CL register just before the second INT 10h call. Everything else remains unchanged from one procedure to the next.

Notice the following items about this routine:

❑ The large memory model is used

❑ Each procedure is declared as FAR

❑ All entry ports (in this case, the four procedure names) are declared PUBLIC

Each of these items is essential for all assembly language routines you interface with Clipper.

In each of these procedures, BIOS function Interrupt 10/03 was used to read the cursor position and size. Upon returning, CH holds the startline value and CL holds the endline value; these two values together define the cursor shape. These values can then be modified and, by using the BIOS function to set the cursor size (Interrupt 10/01), the shape of the cursor can be changed. The trick is to adjust appropriately the values in CH and CL.

To make sure that the cursor is on, AND the bits in CH with 1Fh. To create a line cursor, set the startline (in CH) to one less than the endline value (in CL). This is the same type of cursor normally used in Clipper. For a half-block cursor, set the startline value (CH) to be half the value of the endline value (CL). Finally, for a block cursor, force the startline value (CH) to zero.

Now that the values have been modified, they are used to set the cursor size with the proper BIOS function, and control is passed back to the caller—in this case, the Clipper program. The following short Clipper program, CLTEST1.PRG, can be used to test the routines:

```
SET STATUS OFF
SET SCOREBOARD OFF
SET TALK OFF

CLS
@ 0, 0 SAY 'This is a test of the CurLine, CurHalf, and CurBlock functions'

@ 3, 0 SAY 'This is regular cursor'
INKEY(0)
@ 6, 0 SAY 'This is with the cursor as a line'
CurLine()
INKEY(0)
@ 9, 0 SAY 'This is with the cursor as a half block'
CurHalf()
```

```
INKEY(0)
@ 12, 0 SAY 'This is with the cursor as a block'
CurBlock()
INKEY(0)

QUIT
```

Interfacing Subroutines with Variable Passing

The routines in the preceding example illustrate the simplest possible interface of assembly language and Clipper programs, but it would be better if just one routine could do all three jobs. This can be done by adding a few lines of code to pass a numeric parameter from the Clipper program, as follows:

```
Page 60,132
Comment ¦
*********************************************************************


File:     CLIPEX2.ASM
Author:   Allen L. Wyatt
Date:     10/29/91

Purpose:  Clipper example programs, 2nd pass: cursor sizing
          with parameter passing. Routine accepts a value that
          indicates how to set cursor.

Format:   CurSet(x)
                  1 = Line cursor
                  2 = Half-block cursor
                  3 = Block cursor


*********************************************************************¦


          EXTRN    __PARNI:FAR      ;Clipper routines

          PUBLIC  CurSet

          .MODEL  large
          .CODE
```

```
CurSet     PROC    FAR
           MOV     AX,1              ;Get number passed in
           PUSH    AX
           CALL    _ _PARNI          ;Using EXTEND facility
           POP     BX               ;Throw away original stack value
           AND     AX,3             ;Force to a valid value

           PUSH    AX               ;Save the value
           MOV     AH,3             ;Read cursor position and size
           XOR     BX,BX            ;Clipper uses page 0 only
           INT     10h              ;BIOS services
           AND     CL,1Fh           ;Make sure cursor is on
           MOV     CH,CL            ;Copy endline to startline
           POP     AX               ;Retrieve saved number

           CMP     AX,1             ;Do we want to set to a line?
           JNE     CS1              ;No, go to next check
           DEC     CH               ;And back up by 1
           JMP     SHORT SetIt

CS1:       CMP     AX,2             ;Do we want to set to a half block?
           JNE     CS2              ;No, go to next check
           SHR     CH,1             ;And divide start by 2
           JMP     SHORT SetIt

CS2:       CMP     AX,3             ;Do we want to set to a full block?
           JNE     Exit             ;No, so exit
           XOR     CH,CH            ;Force start to scanline 0

SetIt:     MOV     AH,1             ;Set new cursor values
           INT     10h

Exit:      RET
CurSet     ENDP

           END
```

One of the first major differences you see here (besides the fact that it's only one function rather than three) is the external declaration of the _ _PARNI procedure. This standard Extend-System routine retrieves a numeric integer-format parameter passed from Clipper, and returns it in the AX register. To tell _ _PARNI which parameter to get, push a value on the stack before calling _ _PARNI. Here, the program pushes the value 1 to tell _ _PARNI to return the *first* parameter being passed.

The Extend System provides routines that accomplish the following:

❏ Determine how many parameters were passed in the call

❏ Identify the type of each parameter

❏ Retrieve the value in each of the valid types

❏ Return values in each valid type

These Extend-System routines are described in more detail later in the chapter. For now, let's look at the other features added to this example.

The value returned by _ _PARNI is ANDed with 3 to force the value to an acceptable range. The routine then preserves this value by pushing it onto the stack, and goes to the BIOS to find the current cursor type (as is done earlier in the chapter). Here, only one such sequence suffices for all four actions. After returning, the cursor type is in the CX register. In preparation for one of three operations that will set the final cursor shape, the routine ensures that the cursor is turned on, and makes the starting and ending scan lines the same. The routine then retrieves the value of AX from the stack.

The value in AX is tested to determine what should be done to the cursor. Based on that value, the starting cursor scan line is set to the proper value, and the BIOS functions are used to set the new cursor shape. The procedure then returns to the Clipper program that called it.

The following Clipper program, CLTEST2.PRG, can be used to test this subroutine:

```
SET STATUS OFF
SET SCOREBOARD OFF
SET TALK OFF

CLS
@ 0, 0 SAY 'This is a test of the CurSet() function'

@ 3, 0 SAY 'This is regular cursor'
INKEY(0)
@ 6, 0 SAY 'This is with the cursor as a line'
CurSet(1)
INKEY(0)
@ 9, 0 SAY 'This is with the cursor as a half block'
CurSet(2)
INKEY(0)
@ 12, 0 SAY 'This is with the cursor as a block'
CurSet(3)
INKEY(0)

QUIT
```

Interfacing Subroutines that Return Values

To return a value to the Clipper program that indicates what the previous cursor condition was, all that's necessary is to add one byte of storage and a few lines of code:

```
Page 60,132
Comment ¦
******************************************************************


File:      CLIPEX3.ASM
Author:    Allen L. Wyatt
Date:      10/29/91


Purpose:   Clipper example programs, 3rd pass: cursor sizing
           with parameter passing in both directions. Routine
           accepts a value that indicates how to set cursor,
           and returns a value indicating how the cursor was
           set before the call.


Format:    EXTERNAL CurSet
           OldCurVal = CurSet(x)
               1 = Line cursor
               2 = Half-block cursor
               3 = Block cursor


******************************************************************¦


           EXTRN    __PARNI:FAR      ; Using Clipper routines
           EXTRN    __RETNI:FAR

           PUBLIC   CURSET

           .MODEL   large
           .DATA
OldVal     DB       1                ; Stores last value

           .CODE
CurSet     PROC     FAR
           MOV      AL,OldVal        ;Get current value
           PUSH     AX               ;and save it for now

           MOV      AX,1             ;Get number passed in
           PUSH     AX
```

```
              CALL      __PARNI          ;Using EXTEND facility
              POP       BX               ;Throw away original stack value
              AND       AX,3             ;Force to a valid value

              MOV       OldVal,AL        ;Save for next call
              PUSH      AX               ;Save the value
              MOV       AH,3             ;Get cursor position and size
              XOR       BX,BX            ;Clipper uses Page 0 only
              INT       10h              ;BIOS services
              AND       CL,1Fh           ;Make sure cursor is on
              MOV       CH,CL            ;Copy endline to startline
              POP       AX               ;Retrieve saved number

              CMP       AX,1             ;Do we want to set to a line?
              JNE       CS1              ;No, go to next check
              DEC       CH               ;And back up by 1
              JMP       SHORT SetIt

CS1:          CMP       AX,2             ;Do we want to set to a half block?
              JNE       CS2              ;No, go to next check
              SHR       CH,1             ;And divide start by 2
              JMP       SHORT SetIt

CS2:          CMP       AX,3             ;Do we want to set to a full block?
              JNE       Exit             ;No, so exit
              XOR       CH,CH            ;Force start to scanline 0

SetIt:        MOV       AH,1             ;Set new cursor values
              INT       10h

Exit:         POP       AX               ;get original OldVal back
              CBW                        ;extend the sign bit
              PUSH      AX               ;push down for __RETNI
              CALL      __RETNI          ;using EXTEND facility
              POP       AX               ;Throw away value on stack
              RET
CurSet        ENDP

              END
```

The added byte of storage, OldVal, is initialized to 1 because all Clipper applications start with the cursor set to a line.

At each call to CurSet, the current content of OldVal is first pushed onto the stack to save it. Then the routine is free to store the new cursor-shape code into OldVal for use on the next call.

Finally, after the new cursor condition has been set, the original value of OldVal is brought back from the stack, converted from a byte to a word, and returned to the calling procedure as the value of the function by the second Extend-System function, __RETNI.

The following Clipper program, CLTEST3.PRG, enables you to test this latest subroutine:

```
SET STATUS OFF
SET SCOREBOARD OFF
SET TALK OFF

CLS
@ 0, 0 SAY 'This is a test of the CurSet() function, returns a value'

@ 3, 0 SAY 'This is regular cursor'
INKEY(0)

OldVal := CurSet(1)
@ 5, 0 SAY 'The original cursor value was ' + TRANSFORM (OldVal, "@B")
@ 6, 0 SAY 'This is with the cursor as a line'
INKEY(0)

OldVal := CurSet(2)
@ 8, 0 SAY 'The cursor value was ' + TRANSFORM (OldVal, "@B")
@ 9, 0 SAY 'This is with the cursor as a half block'
INKEY(0)

OldVal := CurSet(3)
@ 11, 0 SAY 'The cursor value was ' + TRANSFORM (OldVal, "@B")
@ 12, 0 SAY 'This is with the cursor as a block'
INKEY(0)

QUIT
```

The Extend System Functions

With the 27 Extend-System functions Clipper provides in CLIPPER.LIB, you can easily interface between Clipper programs and assembly language UDFs. The following are declarations for the 27 functions:

```
EXTRN     _ _PARC:FAR          ;Receive a character parameter
EXTRN     _ _PARCLEN:FAR       ;Get length of a character parameter
EXTRN     _ _PARDS:FAR         ;Receive a date parameter
EXTRN     _ _PARINFA:FAR       ;Get length of an element or array parameter
EXTRN     _ _PARINFO:FAR       ;Get parameter count or data type
EXTRN     _ _PARL:FAR          ;Receive a logical parameter
EXTRN     _ _PARND:FAR         ;Receive a double-precision floating-point parameter
EXTRN     _ _PARNI:FAR         ;Receive an integer parameter (one byte)
EXTRN     _ _PARNL:FAR         ;Receive a long integer parameter (one word)

EXTRN     _ _RET:FAR           ;Return a NIL value
EXTRN     _ _RETC:FAR          ;Return an ASCIIZ string (null-terminated)
EXTRN     _ _RETCLEN:FAR       ;Return a string of specific length
EXTRN     _ _RETDS:FAR         ;Return a date value
EXTRN     _ _RETL:FAR          ;Return a logical value
EXTRN     _ _RETND:FAR         ;Return a double-precision floating-point value
EXTRN     _ _RETNI:FAR         ;Return an integer value
EXTRN     _ _RETNL:FAR         ;Return a long integer value

EXTRN     _ _STORC:FAR         ;Assign an ASCIIZ string (null-terminated)
                               ;  to a parameter pointer
EXTRN     _ _STORCLEN:FAR      ;Store a string of specific length
                               ;  to a parameter pointer
EXTRN     _ _STORDS:FAR        ;Store a date value to a parameter pointer
EXTRN     _ _STORL:FAR         ;Store a logical value to a parameter pointer
EXTRN     _ _STORND:FAR        ;Store a double-precision floating-point value
                               ;  to a parameter pointer
EXTRN     _ _STORNI:FAR        ;Store an integer value to a parameter pointer
EXTRN     _ _STORNL:FAR        ;Store a long integer value to a parameter pointer

EXTRN     _ _XALLOC:FAR        ;Allocate Clipper memory
EXTRN     _ _XFREE:FAR         ;Release Clipper memory previously allocated
EXTRN     _ _XGRAB:FAR         ;Allocate Clipper memory with error generation
```

These functions are used to pass values, return values (either directly or by storing in memory), and control memory allocation. The storing functions are designed primarily for storing data in predefined Clipper data arrays, elements of which have been passed as parameters to your assembly language subroutine.

If you have been using Clipper through several versions, you probably noticed that the number of available Extend-System functions has increased significantly in Clipper 5.0 and 5.01. For most assembly language subroutines, you probably will use only a few of the functions, such as the functions to pass and return an integer (used earlier in the chapter).

After you get past the simple data structures (those that can be passed or returned in a single register), Clipper gives and expects to receive pointers to data. This is not unlike other high-level languages that expect data structures to be passed as pointers.

The full description of what each of these functions does, and how you should use them, is beyond the scope of this book. Your Clipper 5.0 or 5.01 *Programming and Utilities* manual contains all the information you should need, however.

Summary

Although the language Clipper uses is largely compatible with dBASE and FoxBase, Clipper operates differently; assembly language routines used in Clipper programs must be designed with the differences in mind.

One distinction is that in Clipper, assembly language routines can be used anywhere in the main program that an expression is acceptable. The interpretive languages require that your routines be loaded and then called. Another major feature is that the CLIPPER.LIB facilities Clipper provides *must* be used to pass information into or out of your assembly language modules.

Learning to interface with Clipper is much like learning to do so with C or with Pascal. After the first few practice runs, it's easy to do. And the results are definitely worth the effort.

Part III

Applying Assembly Language Techniques

16

Working with Different Processors

If you are writing programs for the 8088/8086 CPU, you normally don't need to worry about your processor environment. All the programs in this book work on any member of the Intel 80x86 family.

Each processor in the Intel family differs from the others, however. Chapter 22, "Processor Instruction Sets," lists these differences in detail. You may want to write a program for a specific processor—perhaps a program that requires, at minimum, an 80286—or you may require the presence of a numeric coprocessor (NPX).

This chapter covers how you detect which CPU is in the computer, as well as whether an NPX is present.

Detecting the CPU Type

Unfortunately, no special directive or instruction indicates which CPU model is being used. Instead, the programmer is left to examine the behavior of the CPU under known conditions. This means that you can determine the CPU type only by the process of elimination; you must see how the CPU reacts to instructions known to have different effects on different models.

The assembly language routine presented in this section can be used to determine the type of CPU being used. It is designed to be called from C, and will return one of the values shown in table 16.1.

Table 16.1. *Values returned by the CPU.ASM function.*

Value	CPU Type
86	8086
88	8088
186	80186
188	80188
286	80288
386	80386
486	80486

The listing for CPU.ASM is as follows:

```
Page 60,132
Comment ¦
********************************************************************


File:      CPU.ASM
Author:    Allen L. Wyatt
Date:      10/26/91

Purpose:   Return a value indicating the CPU on which the program
           is operating. Designed to be called from C.

Format:    CPU()


********************************************************************¦


           PUBLIC  cpu

           .MODEL  small, C

           .DATA
CPUType    DW      0000

           .CODE
cpu        PROC
```

```
; This first part checks for the setting of bits 14-15. Intel documentation
; actually indicates that bits 12-15 act differently on pre-80286 machines,
; but it seems that some operating systems may set the general protection
; level, which causes the IOPL flag (bits 12-13) to always remain set. The
; solution is to test only bits 14-15.
```

```
        PUSHF                        ;Original flags
        POP     AX                   ;Into a workable register
        AND     AX,3FFFh             ;Turn off bits 14-15
        PUSH    AX

        POPF                         ;Put in proper register
        PUSHF                        ;Store flags
        POP     AX                   ;Get flags back to examine
        AND     AX,0C000h            ;Only interested in bits 14-15
        CMP     AX,0                 ;Have the bits been cleared?
        JE      I286_1               ;Yes, so at least a 286

        MOV     CL,21h
        MOV     AL,0FFh
        SHR     AL,CL                ;If AL is not cleared, then 80186 or 80188
        CMP     AL,0
        MOV     AX,188               ;Assume running 80188
        JNE     DoBus                ;Flag still set from previous CMP
        MOV     AX,88                ;Assume running 8088
DoBus:  CALL    TestQueue            ;Go check bus width
        SUB     AX,BX                ;BX is 0 if 188, otherwise 2
        MOV     CPUType,AX
        JMP     Exit

; Processor is a 286, 386, or 486

I286_1: PUSHF
        POP     AX
        OR      AX,4000h             ;Set bit 14 (NT flag)
        PUSH    AX
        POPF                         ;Flag bit 14 now set
        PUSHF                        ;Store flags
        POP     AX                   ;Get flags back to examine
        AND     AX,4000h             ;Only care about bit 14
        CMP     AX,4000h             ;Still set?
        JE      I386_1               ;Yes, so at least a 386
        MOV     CPUType,286          ;No, so this is a 286
        JMP     Exit
```

; By the time this part is reached, we know we are working with a 32-bit
; processor. This part kicks into 32-bit mode to test whether the AC bit
; in the extended flags register can be set. If it can, we are running on
; an 80486.

```
                .386                            ;Enable 386 assembly
I386_1:         PUSHFD                          ;Push the extended flags register
                POP       EAX                   ;Get it back to work with
                MOV       EBX,EAX               ;Store a copy of it
                AND       EBX,40000h            ;Only care about bit 18 (AC flag)
                XOR       EAX,40000h            ;Toggle AC flag (bit 18), rest stay as is
                PUSH      EAX                   ;Stuff adjusted flags register
                POPFD                           ;And put it in the proper place
                PUSHFD                          ;Push it again
                POP       EAX                   ;And back where it can be examined
                AND       EAX,40000h            ;Only want to look at bit 18 (AC flag)
                MOV       CPUType,386           ;Assume working on 386
                CMP       EAX,EBX               ;If same, then we're on a 386
                JE        Exit                  ;Go away now

                PUSHFD                          ;Working on 486; push flags once more
                POP       EAX                   ;Work with them again
                XOR       EAX,40000h            ;Toggle AC flag (bit 18) to original state
                PUSH      EAX                   ;Stuff adjusted flags register
                POPFD                           ;And put it in the proper place
                MOV       CPUType,486           ;And put CPU type in its place

                .8086                           ;Back to default code
Exit:           MOV       AX,CPUType            ;Ready to return
                RET                             ;Return to C
cpu             ENDP
```

```
; The following routine will return with BX set to either 0 or 2.
; If it is set to 0, then the processor has an 8-bit data bus.
; If it is set to 2, then the processor has a 16-bit data bus.
```

```
TestQueue       PROC      USES AX
                MOV       BX,1
                MOV       AL,TestInst           ;Load opcode for INC BX
                XOR       AL,8                  ;Change INC BX to DEC BX
                MOV       TestInst,AL           ;Move it back to proper place
                NOP                             ;If using an 8-bit data bus,
                NOP                             ;   these 4 NOP instructions will
                NOP                             ;   fill the queue, allowing the
                NOP                             ;   next byte to be changed
TestInst        DB        43h                   ;This is opcode for INC BX
                RET
TestQueue       ENDP


                END
```

The comments included in the program listing should explain most of the operations, but they bear closer examination.

As you can see from table 16.1, testing is done for seven processors. The first step in the program basically divides the group in half. It examines how the CPU treats the flags register to determine whether the CPU is of the pre- or post-80286 genre. According to Intel documentation, the high-order nibble (bits 12-15) of the flags register is always set on the 8086/8088, 80186, and 80188 chips. The 80286, 80386, and 80486 basically leave these settings as originally set (at least in bits 12-14).

Because of this behavior, you should be able to clear bits 12-15, push them on the stack, and then—if they are set when you pop them again—you can assume that you are operating on one of the older processors.

In practice, however, this may not happen. Depending on your operating system, or on any protected-mode programs you may have been running, bits 12 and 13 may always be set. These bits, collectively known as the *IOPL flag*, indicate the privilege level at which the program is currently operating.

To overcome the IOPL flag always being set, it is best to examine only bits 14 and 15. If when you clear them, push the flags, and pop them, bits 14 and 15 are set, you can assume that you are operating on the older processors. If they are still clear, you are on one of the newer processors.

The next step differentiates between the 8086/8088 and the 80186/80188. These two groups behave differently when they execute the SHR instruction. On the 8086/8088, you can shift by any value up to 255; the instruction will operate as expected. On the 80186/81088, however, you can shift by a value up to 31 only. This change was introduced because if you shift 16 bits by 31 bits, you still have only 0 left as a result. Thus, shifting more than 31 times is redundant and slows the operation of the processor.

To limit the SHR value to 31, the 80186/80188 simply masks off the top three bits of the shift register by ANDing the value in CL with 31. This masking is done before the actual SHR instruction is executed. Thus, when the test shifts by 21h (33 decimal), the result is as follows:

```
0 0 1 0 0 0 0 1     <— 21h, 33 decimal
0 0 0 1 1 1 1 1     <— 1Fh, 31 decimal
_____

0 0 0 0 0 0 0 1     <— 01h, 1 decimal
```

Remember that on the 8086/8088, the code simply shifts 33 times; the result in AL is 0. But on the 80186/80188, because the value in CL is ANDed with 1Fh, the value in AL is shifted only one place to the right. Thus, a 0 value in AL would indicate that the CPU was either an 8086 or an 8088.

The next test is done by calling the routine at TestQueue. This routine is used to determine the difference between the 8086 and the 8088, or between the 80186 and the 80188. The only difference between these chips (the ones ending in 6 and the ones ending in 8) is the size of their data bus. The 8086 and the 80186 have a 16-bit data bus, whereas the others have an 8-bit bus.

Take a look at the TestQueue routine. It works correctly because it is known that the 16-bit machines have a 6-byte prefetch queue, whereas the 8-bit machines have only a 4-byte queue. This queue is used to hold the bytes following the currently executing instruction. Thus, if you change either byte 5 or 6 (after the current instruction), then you can determine whether you are using a 16-bit or an 8-bit CPU.

Notice the odd coding in TestQueue. The byte at TestInst is the opcode for the INC BX instruction. But earlier in the routine, this byte is loaded into AX and modified into the DEC BX instruction by XORing the byte with 08h.

The instruction MOV TestInst,AL is used to store the modified instruction. But on an 8-bit CPU, while this instruction is being executed the next 4 bytes (all the NOPs) are in the prefetch queue. Thus, the modified instruction can be placed in memory before it is fetched, and BX will be decremented to 0.

On a 16-bit CPU, however, the prefetch queue consists of not only the NOP instructions, but also the original INC BX and the RET instruction. The bytes representing these instructions have already been fetched, pending execution, and any changes to memory will not affect operation. Thus, BX will be incremented to 2.

When the routine returns, the value in BX is subtracted from the CPU value in AX; AX then contains 86, 88, 186, or 188.

So far, the routine has accounted for 4 processors. The code beginning at I286_1 is used to differentiate between the 80286, 80386, and 80486 chips.

The first test, which weeds out the 80286, is a flags test similar to the one at the beginning of the routine. It works because you can set the NT flag (bit 14) in real mode on the 80386 and 80486 but not on the 80286. On that chip, the NT flag is always set to 0 in real mode. If you can set the bit and maintain it while pushing and popping the flags, you can assume that it is not an 80286 chip.

Finally, some 32-bit instructions are used to differentiate between the 80386 and 80486. This differentiation is accomplished by checking how bit 18 of the extended flags is handled. This is the AC (alignment check) flag; it is implemented on the 80486, but not on the 80386. If this bit position holds a setting, you can assume that you are using the 80486.

That concludes the routine. All that remains is the C program (TESTCPU.C) used to call it.

```
/* File:     TESTCPU.C
 * Author:   Allen L. Wyatt
 * Date:     8/26/91
 *
 * Purpose:  Program to test the calling of CPU()
 */

#include <stdio.h>

extern short cpu();

void main()
{ unsigned short CPUType;
  CPUType = cpu();
  printf ("\nThis is running on a %u chip\n",CPUType);
}
```

As you can see, this short program simply executes the function and prints the value returned.

Now let's see how to determine whether a numeric coprocessor is in your system.

Detecting the Presence of an NPX

As you have already learned from this book, there are many names for what is commonly called a numeric coprocessor. Intel and many other sources refer to this chip also as the NPX (numeric-processor extension) or the FPU (floating-point unit).

Regardless of what it is called, the NPX is the chip responsible for performing fast floating-point calculations and higher-math functions. Many programs require the use of an NPX to run. How do you determine the presence of an NPX? The following routine, designed to be called from C, does the trick:

```
Page 60,132
Comment |
*******************************************************************

File:     NPX.ASM
Author:   Allen L. Wyatt
Date:     10/26/91
```

```
Purpose:   Returns a value indicating whether there is a numeric
           coprocessor in the system. Returns 0 if none, 1 if
           present. Designed to be called from C.

Format:    NPX()

*********************************************************************

           PUBLIC  npx

           .MODEL  small, C

           .DATA
Scratch    DW      0000                    ;Place to store status word

           .CODE
npx        PROC
           MOV     SI,OFFSET Scratch
           MOV     WORD PTR [SI],4321h  ;Initialize to non-zero
           FNINIT                       ;Initialize NPX without checking for error
           FNSTSW  [SI]                 ;Get the status word
           MOV     AX,0                 ;Assume no NPX chip
           CMP     BYTE PTR [SI],0      ;Was a status value returned?
           JNE     Exit                 ;No, so exit
           MOV     AX,1                 ;NPX is present
Exit:      RET                          ;Return to C
npx        ENDP

           END
```

The way this routine operates is very simple: it uses two floating-point instructions to determine whether the NPX is present. The FNINIT instruction initializes the NPX but does not check to see whether an error occurred. (The FINIT instruction is the variation that checks for an error.) You do not want the routine to check for an error, because an error will always occur if there is no NPX.

The next instruction stores the NPX status word at the memory location pointed to by SI. Again, this version of the FSTSW instruction does not wait to see whether any errors occurred. If no NPX is present, no action takes place and the information at SI is not changed.

If an NPX is present, the value at SI is overwritten with the NPX status word. The high-order byte of this status word is always 0 immediately following an initialization. Thus, if the byte at SI is 0, an NPX is present.

Note also that if you are using the 80486 chip in your system, this routine will indicate the presence of the numeric coprocessor because the functionality of the NPX is built into the 80486.

To test this routine, use the following C program:

```
/* File:      TESTNPX.C
 * Author:    Allen L. Wyatt
 * Date:      8/26/91
 *
 * Purpose:   Program to test the calling of NPX()
 */

#include <stdio.h>

extern short npx();

void main()
{ unsigned short GotNPX;
  GotNPX = npx();
  switch (GotNPX)
     { case 0:
          printf("\nA numeric coprocessor is missing\n");
          break;
       case 1:
          printf("\nA numeric coprocessor is present\n");
          break;
       default:
          printf("\nUnknown value returned: %u\n",GotNPX);
     }
}
```

This program calls the assembly language routine and, based on the value returned, indicates whether an NPX is present.

Summary

This chapter has presented some short but very useful subroutines that can help you understand your processing environment. With these routines, you can determine what type of CPU you are using and find out whether there is a numeric coprocessor.

Once you have this information, you can alter your program's execution accordingly or issue warnings or errors to the user to indicate that the environment is not satisfactory.

In the next chapter, you will learn how to take advantage of your computer's video system.

CHAPTER 17

Video Memory

Writing information to a video display monitor is perhaps the biggest bottleneck in most high-level languages. The sad thing is, most programmers do not even realize that it is a bottleneck.

The video display is simply a representation of what is contained in a specific area of memory. This type of display is referred to as a *memory-mapped* display; the display memory area is called a *video buffer* because it holds what will be displayed on the monitor. Changes occur constantly in the video buffer, and affect what is seen on the video display. The buffer's location in memory depends on the type of display adapter being used. A discussion of the buffer's location is included in this chapter's description of each display-adapter type.

The original displays for the PC used an 80-column, 25-line screen. Each text screen's video buffer occupied 4,000 bytes (0FA0h) of data. How was this number derived? Each character position on the screen uses two bytes of memory—one for the character and one for the character's attribute. The *attribute byte* controls how the character will be displayed (in color, with underlining, blinking, and so on). Thus, one text screen required 4,000 bytes (80 x 25 x 2) of memory.

With the introduction of the EGA, and later the MCGA and VGA, display capabilities became a bit more complex. With these advanced video adapter cards, you can extend the number of columns on each line to 132, and the number of lines per screen to 60. Doing so raises the buffer size requirement from 4,000 to 15,840 bytes.

You can display individual characters or strings by using certain BIOS and DOS interrupts, but they tend to be rather slow. You can use BIOS and DOS functions to gain some (but not much) speed advantage over high-level language display techniques. You do not gain much of an advantage because, to guarantee portability

367

and compatibility, most high-level languages ordinarily use the BIOS and DOS interrupts in their display library routines.

Because of the way BIOS, and subsequently DOS, routines were written, they repeat several tasks during a display operation. This repetition may be necessary to maintain the general-purpose design of the BIOS routines, but it can slow down display operations so much that they become almost unacceptable. For example, in more than one instance in the BIOS video routines, the individual routines that make up INT 10h call themselves to determine necessary information for completing the current task. This results in much more pushing, popping, and overhead than if the video routines had been written for a specific purpose. On newer PC models, with clock speeds of 16 MHz and up instead of the original 4.77 MHz speed, the delays become much less noticeable but are nonetheless time consuming.

Because a video display is simply a representation of a special memory area, you can alter the display by altering that memory area directly. As you know, you can transfer large blocks of memory quickly from one location to another. By using the string-manipulation mnemonics, you can use the following subroutine to transfer an entire video screen in approximately 80,100 clock cycles. (The actual number of clock cycles depends on your CPU version.)

```
MOVE_BLOCK    PROC    NEAR
              USES    CX, SI, DI, ES        ;Save all used registers

              MOV     SI,OFFSET SOURCE_DAT  ;Image data to be moved
              MOV     ES,VIDEO_BUFFER       ;Segment of video buffer
              MOV     DI,0                  ;Start at beginning of buffer
              MOV     CX,0FA0h              ;Size of video screen
              REP     MOVSB                 ;Move it

              RET
MOVE_BLOCK    ENDP
```

Stated in clock cycles, this may sound like a long time for transferring data. However, you must remember that on a standard IBM PC running at 4.772727 MHz, one clock cycle is only 0.0000002095238 seconds; therefore, the entire process takes approximately 0.01678307 seconds. The speed increases significantly on faster machines.

No matter which machine you use, an entire screen can be displayed in less than 1/50 of a second, which is virtually instantaneous. (Refresh times on television screens are only 1/60 of a second.) Compare that to a high-level language and the way you have to clear the screen and then move data elements individually to the screen!

For those of us who use high-level languages, the capability of displaying things instantaneously on-screen is one of the attractions of using assembly language.

Because the physical location of the video memory depends on which display adapter is used, let's take just a moment to examine the display adapters commonly used on IBM microcomputers.

Differences between Display Adapters

The IBM family of personal computers (and major clones) uses a variety of display devices. Several have been around for years, and new ones crop up periodically. In this section, I discuss the methods and conventions used to display information on the six most popular display devices:

❑ The IBM Monochrome Display Adapter (MDA)

❑ The Hercules Graphics Adapter (HGA), which includes a monochrome graphics capability

❑ The IBM Color Graphics Adapter (CGA)

❑ The IBM Enhanced Graphics Adapter (EGA)

❑ The IBM Multi-Color Graphics Array (MCGA)

❑ The IBM Video Graphics Array (VGA)

I also mention briefly the newer super VGA (SVGA) cards, although there is no clear standard among them.

The way you program your application depends largely on which display device you use. You should do some advance research to ensure that you know which device(s) you will use. If several display types are likely to be used, you can program your software to make intelligent choices about which type of display is currently in use. You will learn about one such method later in this chapter.

All these display adapters (except the MDA) can display true graphics data. As I stated in the introduction, I will not delve into specific graphics routines. Rather, I will discuss the way in which each type of display adapter stores and displays textual data.

The Monochrome Display Adapter (MDA)

The IBM Monochrome Display Adapter made its debut when the IBM Personal Computer was introduced in 1981. As the name implies, the MDA displays information in monochrome (one color). Which color depends on the type of monitor you have. Most monochrome monitors display data in either green or amber, although other colors can be displayed.

The MDA offers a resolution of 720 by 350 pixels—a total of 252,000 picture elements. This total is segmented into 2,000 character cells (each with a resolution of 9 by 14 pixels) arranged in 25 rows of 80 cells each.

The contents of each character cell are stored in memory as a single byte of information. Each character cell has a corresponding attribute byte that controls the way in which the character is displayed. The composition and use of the attribute byte are discussed later in this chapter.

The video buffer used by the MDA holds a single text screen and consists of 4K of RAM, beginning at B0000h (segment address B000:0000). The characters and their attribute bytes are interlaced so that the video memory is mapped beginning at the upper left corner of the screen and proceeding across and down the display (see table 17.1).

Table 17.1. Memory locations for MDA display data.

Segment Address	Character/Attribute
B000:0000	Character for row 1, column 1
B000:0001	Attribute for row 1, column 1
B000:0002	Character for row 1, column 2
B000:0003	Attribute for row 1, column 2
B000:0004	Character for row 1, column 3
B000:0005	Attribute for row 1, column 3
B000:009C	Character for row 1, column 79
B000:009D	Attribute for row 1, column 79
B000:009E	Character for row 1, column 80
B000:009F	Attribute for row 1, column 80
B000:00A0	Character for row 2, column 1
B000:00A1	Attribute for row 2, column 1
B000:00A2	Character for row 2, column 2
B000:00A3	Attribute for row 2, column 2
B000:0EFC	Character for row 24, column 79
B000:0EFD	Attribute for row 24, column 79
B000:0EFE	Character for row 24, column 80
B000:0EFF	Attribute for row 24, column 80
B000:0F00	Character for row 25, column 1

Segment Address	Character/Attribute
B000:0F01	Attribute for row 25, column 1
B000:0F02	Character for row 25, column 2
B000:0F03	Attribute for row 25, column 2
B000:0F9C	Character for row 25, column 79
B000:0F9D	Attribute for row 25, column 79
B000:0F9E	Character for row 25, column 80
B000:0F9F	Attribute for row 25, column 80

Each character-display position can contain a value of 1 through 256, with each value equivalent to a specific character code. The character code used by the MDA is a superset of ASCII (see fig. 17.1).

Fig. 17.1. *ASCII character code for MDA.*

0=	32=	64=@	96=`	128=Ç	160=á	192=└	224=α
1=☺	33=!	65=A	97=a	129=ü	161=í	193=┴	225=β
2=☻	34="	66=B	98=b	130=é	162=ó	194=┬	226=Γ
3=♥	35=#	67=C	99=c	131=â	163=ú	195=├	227=π
4=♦	36=$	68=D	100=d	132=ä	164=ñ	196=─	228=Σ
5=♣	37=%	69=E	101=e	133=à	165=Ñ	197=┼	229=σ
6=♠	38=&	70=F	102=f	134=å	166=ª	198=╞	230=µ
7=•	39='	71=G	103=g	135=ç	167=º	199=╟	231=τ
8=◘	40=(	72=H	104=h	136=ê	168=¿	200=╚	232=Φ
9=○	41=)	73=I	105=i	137=ë	169=⌐	201=╔	233=Θ
10=◙	42=*	74=J	106=j	138=è	170=¬	202=╩	234=Ω
11=♂	43=+	75=K	107=k	139=ï	171=½	203=╦	235=δ
12=♀	44=,	76=L	108=l	140=î	172=¼	204=╠	236=∞
13=♪	45=-	77=M	109=m	141=ì	173=¡	205==	237=φ
14=♫	46=.	78=N	110=n	142=Ä	174=«	206=╬	238=ε
15=☼	47=/	79=O	111=o	143=Å	175=»	207=╧	239=∩
16=►	48=0	80=P	112=p	144=É	176=░	208=╨	240=≡
17=◄	49=1	81=Q	113=q	145=æ	177=▒	209=╤	241=±
18=↕	50=2	82=R	114=r	146=Æ	178=▓	210=╥	242=≥
19=‼	51=3	83=S	115=s	147=ô	179=│	211=╙	243=≤
20=¶	52=4	84=T	116=t	148=ö	180=┤	212=╘	244=⌠
21=§	53=5	85=U	117=u	149=ò	181=╡	213=╒	245=⌡
22=▬	54=6	86=W	118=v	150=û	182=╢	214=╓	246=÷
23=↨	55=7	87=W	119=w	151=ù	183=╖	215=╫	247=≈
24=↑	56=8	88=X	120=x	152=ÿ	184=╕	216=╪	248=°
25=↓	57=9	89=Y	121=y	153=Ö	185=╣	217=┘	249=∙
26=→	58=:	90=Z	122=z	154=Ü	186=║	218=┌	250=·
27=←	59=;	91=[	123={	155=¢	187=╗	219=█	251=√
28=∟	60=<	92=\	124=|	156=£	188=╝	220=▄	252=ⁿ
29=↔	61==	93=]	125=}	157=¥	189=╜	221=▌	253=²
30=▲	62=>	94=^	126=~	158=₧	190=╛	222=▐	254=■
31=▼	63=?	95=_	127=⌂	159=ƒ	191=┐	223=▀	255=

The character codes shown in figure 17.1 are created by an 8K character generator on the MDA interface board. To generate a character, simply place the character in the proper memory location in the MDA buffer. The internal hardware of the MDA takes care of the rest.

The Hercules Graphics Adapter (HGA)

The Hercules Graphics Adapter, which is similar to the MDA, comes from a company called Hercules Computer Technology. This display adapter has been around for many years. It is supported by a great deal of software and is the standard for monochrome graphics.

Ordinarily, the HGA behaves exactly like the MDA, except that the HGA includes a monochrome graphics capability. In bit-mapped graphics mode, the HGA provides a resolution of 720 by 348 pixels. In text mode, the HGA operates exactly like the MDA. (For additional information, refer to the section on the MDA.)

The Color Graphics Adapter (CGA)

IBM's first offering for color graphics capability on the IBM family of microcomputers, the Color Graphics Adapter, can operate in text mode (like the MDA) or in a bit-mapped graphics mode. I focus on the display of textual data because, as I stated in the introduction, the bit-mapped graphics mode is beyond the scope of this book.

The high resolution offered by the CGA is 640 by 200 pixels, a total of 128,000 picture elements. As with the MDA, this total can be segmented into 2,000 character cells, arranged in 25 rows of either 40 or 80 cells each. But the resolution of each cell is significantly less with the CGA—only 8 by 8 pixels, which renders characters less readable and crisp than those on the MDA.

In text mode, the CGA functions much like the MDA. This is understandable— the CGA and MDA both use the Motorola 6845 CRT Controller chip. With the CGA as with the MDA, the contents of each character cell are stored in memory as a single byte of information. Each character cell has a corresponding attribute byte that controls how the character is displayed. The composition and use of the attribute byte is different in the CGA and the MDA, as you will learn later in this chapter.

The video buffer used by the CGA consists of 16K of RAM, beginning at B8000h (segment address B800:0000). Because a 40 by 25 text screen requires only 2K of memory, the video buffer can hold as many as 8 text screens, or pages. With an 80 by 25 text screen, which requires 4K of memory, as many as 4 video pages can be contained in the video buffer.

The currently displayed video page can be changed easily; to do so, you modify the buffer start address used by the 6845 CRTC. Normally, this address is set to point to the memory block starting at B8000h. The current video page is changed through the use of BIOS function calls (see Chapter 20, "Accessing BIOS Services").

As with the MDA, the characters and their attribute bytes are interlaced, beginning at the upper left corner of the screen and proceeding across and down the display. Table 17.2 shows how the video memory for the first page of an 80 by 25 screen is mapped.

Table 17.2. *Memory locations for first page of an 80 by 25 CGA.*

Segment Address	Character/Attribute
B800:0000	Character for row 1, column 1
B800:0001	Attribute for row 1, column 1
B800:0002	Character for row 1, column 2
B800:0003	Attribute for row 1, column 2
B800:0004	Character for row 1, column 3
B800:0005	Attribute for row 1, column 3
B800:009C	Character for row 1, column 79
B800:009D	Attribute for row 1, column 79
B800:009E	Character for row 1, column 80
B800:009F	Attribute for row 1, column 80
B800:00A0	Character for row 2, column 1
B800:00A1	Attribute for row 2, column 1
B800:00A2	Character for row 2, column 2
B800:00A3	Attribute for row 2, column 2
B800:0EFC	Character for row 24, column 79
B800:0EFD	Attribute for row 24, column 79
B800:0EFE	Character for row 24, column 80
B800:0EFF	Attribute for row 24, column 80
B800:0F00	Character for row 25, column 1
B800:0F01	Attribute for row 25, column 1
B800:0F02	Character for row 25, column 2
B800:0F03	Attribute for row 25, column 2
B800:0F9C	Character for row 25, column 79
B800:0F9D	Attribute for row 25, column 79
B800:0F9E	Character for row 25, column 80
B800:0F9F	Attribute for row 25, column 80

Each character-display position can contain a value of 1 through 256, with each value equivalent to a specific character code. The character codes used by the CGA are the same as those used by the MDA, and are a superset of ASCII. The CGA uses a ROM character generator also.

The Enhanced Graphics Adapter (EGA)

IBM introduced the Enhanced Graphics Adapter in late 1984. In text mode, there are several noticeable differences between the EGA and the Color Graphics Adapter. The following advantages are available with an EGA card:

- ❏ More colors can be displayed
- ❏ Text information, displayed in color, can blink
- ❏ Resolution is improved
- ❏ More display modes are available
- ❏ User-defined character sets are available

Before proceeding, let's examine this last point. As you can see from table 17.3, the EGA offers 12 display modes.

Notice that the resolution offered by the EGA is not quite as good as that offered by the MDA and HGA boards. EGA resolution is 640 by 350 pixels—a total of 224,000 picture elements.

The possibilities of using this resolution in a color graphics mode are quite impressive, but these capabilities are beyond the scope of this book. Because describing how to use the EGA effectively would fill an entire book, I focus only on using the EGA in text mode.

Like the other video adapters, the EGA normally segments the text screen into 2,000 character cells, each with a resolution of 8 by 14 pixels. These character cells are arranged in 25 rows of 80 cells each. The contents of each character cell are stored in memory as a single byte of information. Each character cell has a corresponding attribute byte that controls how the character is displayed. (The composition and use of the attribute byte are discussed later in this chapter.)

The EGA provides a capability for loading user-specified character sets, however, and when you load the 8-by-8-pixel ROM set normally used only with 40-column graphics modes, the number of rows of text rises from 25 to 43! This in turn increases the size of the video buffer to 6,880 bytes (3,440 characters, plus the same number of attribute bytes).

Table 17.3. *EGA display modes.*

Mode Number	Mode Type	Display Type	Pixel Resolution	Characters	Box Size	Colors
0	Text	Color	320 x 200	40 x 25	8 x 8	16
	Enhanced	320 x 350	40 x 25	8 x 14	16/64	
1	—————— Same as mode 0 ——————					
2	Text	Color	640 x 200	80 x 25	8 x 8	16
	Enhanced	640 x 350	80 x 25	8 x 14	16/64	
3	—————— Same as mode 2 ——————					
4	Graph	Clr/Enh	320 x 200	40 x 25	8 x 8	4
5	—————— Same as mode 4 ——————					
6	Graph	Clr/Enh	640 x 200	80 x 25	8 x 14	2
7	Text	Mono	720 x 350	80 x 25	9 x 14	4
13	Graph	Clr/Enh	320 x 200	40 x 25	8 x 8	16
14	Graph	Clr/Enh	640 x 200	80 x 25	8 x 8	16
15	Graph	Mono	640 x 350	80 x 25	8 x 14	4
16	Graph	Enhanced	640 x 350	80 x 25	8 x 14	varies

Which video buffer is used by the EGA depends on the amount of memory available on the card. Most of the higher memory capabilities are used only in multipage graphics software or in animation. In text mode, however, the EGA is capable of emulating either the MDA or CGA in memory usage. If connected to a monochrome monitor, the video buffer begins at absolute address B0000h (segment address B000:0000), as does the MDA. If connected to a color monitor, the video buffer begins at absolute address B8000h (segment address B800:0000), as does the CGA.

As with other text screens, the characters and their attribute bytes are interlaced so that, beginning at the upper left corner of the screen and proceeding across and down the display, the video memory is mapped as shown in table 17.4. The question mark is replaced by 0 if the EGA is connected to a monochrome monitor, and by 8 if connected to a color monitor.

The EGA can display the same character set that each of the other display adapters can display, but the characters are displayed differently. The EGA uses a RAM character generator, not one that is ROM-based. This means that you can design and download custom fonts based on your own needs. As many as four fonts of 256 characters each can be developed and subsequently used by the EGA, but only two of the fonts can be used at any given time. Detailed information on the development and use of alternate fonts is beyond the scope of this book.

Table 17.4. *Memory locations for EGA display data.*

Segment Address	Character/Attribute
B?00:0000	Character for row 1, column 1
B?00:0001	Attribute for row 1, column 1
B?00:0002	Character for row 1, column 2
B?00:0003	Attribute for row 1, column 2
B?00:0004	Character for row 1, column 3
B?00:0005	Attribute for row 1, column 3
B?00:009C	Character for row 1, column 79
B?00:009D	Attribute for row 1, column 79
B?00:009E	Character for row 1, column 80
B?00:009F	Attribute for row 1, column 80
B?00:00A0	Character for row 2, column 1
B?00:00A1	Attribute for row 2, column 1
B?00:00A2	Character for row 2, column 2
B?00:00A3	Attribute for row 2, column 2
B?00:0EFC	Character for row 24, column 79
B?00:0EFD	Attribute for row 24, column 79
B?00:0EFE	Character for row 24, column 80
B?00:0EFF	Attribute for row 24, column 80
B?00:0F00	Character for row 25, column 1
B?00:0F01	Attribute for row 25, column 1
B?00:0F02	Character for row 25, column 2
B?00:0F03	Attribute for row 25, column 2
B?00:0F9C	Character for row 25, column 79
B?00:0F9D	Attribute for row 25, column 79
B?00:0F9E	Character for row 25, column 80
B?00:0F9F	Attribute for row 25, column 80

The Multi-Color Graphics Array (MCGA)

When the PS/2 line was introduced, IBM moved the video-adapter functions from the traditional separate card onto the system motherboard and changed the name from "adapter" to "array."

IBM also produced two different kinds of graphics arrays, one for the "low end" of the line (Models 25 and 30) and another for the rest of the PS/2 line.

The "low-end" device is the Multi-Color Graphics Array, which replaces the CGA and offers vastly improved performance. Resolution was increased to 640 by 480 pixels, and the number of colors MCGA can display is limited only by the quality of the attached monitor. In graphics mode, MCGA can display any 256 colors from a range of more than 262,000 hues, in 320 by 200 resolution. In text mode, MCGA's performance is similar to that of the high-end device, the VGA (discussed in the next section), except that MCGA's vertical resolution is limited to 350 scan lines.

The Video Graphics Array (VGA)

The Video Graphics Array—the "high-end" device for the PS/2 line of IBM systems—is available also as an adapter card for other IBM-compatible PCs and clones. The prices of VGA adapters have decreased so much that the VGA has become the default card-of-choice for color graphics systems.

The VGA offers all the capabilities of the MCGA (and more) in graphics modes, but increases resolution up to 720 by 400 pixels in text modes, whereas the MCGA goes only to 640 by 350.

Like the EGA, both the MCGA and the VGA can be loaded with user-defined fonts. The VGA also gives you the choice of 200-line, 350-line, or 400-line vertical resolution, a choice that gives you an even wider range of possible buffer sizes because you can have as many as 60 rows of text on a single screen. The most common choices, however, are either 25 rows (the conventional 8-by-16-character box at 400 lines) or 50 rows (an 8-by-8 box at 400 lines).

If you will be using an MCGA or VGA with a screen that is not the conventional 25-line size, you may not be able to use the exact code developed in this chapter; you can easily modify the code to work properly with any screen size you choose, however, by changing the portions that convert row and column counts.

Like the EGA, both the MCGA and the VGA automatically map their text-buffer memory addresses to either the B000h or B800h range, depending on whether a monochrome or color monitor is connected. As long as you stick to the 80-by-25 screen dimensions, you can use the same assembly language routines to deal with all the displays available.

Super VGA Cards (SVGA)

The newest entries in the mass-market video-card arena are members of the *super VGA* classification. These cards offer much higher resolution and color capabilities than VGA cards, and can really enhance the use of certain programs.

The only problem with these cards is that no clear standard as to what constitutes super VGA exists. Rather, super VGA is simply a classification for any video card that exceeds the capabilities of the VGA cards. Although these cards may be compatible individually with the VGA (they allow the same video modes as the VGA), there is no clear plan on how to use the "super modes."

How do the card manufacturers overcome this problem? Easy—they simply create video drivers for such popular software as Windows or AutoCAD and bundle the drivers with their product.

Unfortunately, the programmer who wants to take advantage of these cards must program to the individual product. Thus, programs you write for one super VGA card may not work with a different super VGA card.

Determining the Type of Display Installed

Because the type of display adapter installed determines the way text is displayed, your first task is to have your program determine what type of adapter is installed in the computer. To communicate with the peripherals attached to it, the computer must know what those peripherals are—including the display adapters.

BIOS cannot display information unless it knows what type of display adapter currently is being used. BIOS keeps a list of video-related information, beginning at memory locations 0449h through 0489h (see table 17.5).

Currently, two of the memory locations shown in table 17.5 are of interest. The byte at 0410h tells what the system-board switch settings were when the POST (Power-On Self Test) was performed at booting. Each bit of the word denotes a different setting. Table 17.6 shows the bit meanings of the value at 0410h.

The value of bits 5-4 tells you what type of card (color or monochrome) is installed, according to the system-board dip-switch settings. But you can't tell whether the monochrome board is an MDA or HGA or whether the color board is a CGA or EGA. (The distinction is not germane to this discussion, however, because we are dealing only with textual display of data.) A monochrome adapter, such as the MDA, the HGA, or the EGA, MCGA, or VGA in monochrome mode, uses a video buffer starting at B0000h; a color adapter, such as the CGA, or EGA, MCGA, or VGA in a text color mode, uses a video buffer starting at B8000h.

Table 17.5. *BIOS video-related data.*

Memory Location	Length	Purpose
0410h	Byte	POST equipment list 1
0411h	Byte	POST equipment list 2
0449h	Byte	BIOS video mode
044Ah	Word	Columns
044Ch	Word	Page length
044Eh	Word	Page beginning
0460h	Word	Cursor start/end
0462h	Byte	Page number
0463h	Word	Current adapter base port
0465h	Byte	Mode selection
0466h	Byte	Palette
0484h	Byte	Rows (EGA/MCGA/VGA only)
0485h	Byte	Points (EGA/MCGA/VGA only)

Table 17.6. *Meaning of bits at memory location 0410b.*

Bits 76543210	Meaning of Bits
00	1 disk drive installed, if bit 0=1
01	2 disk drives installed, if bit 0=1
10	3 disk drives installed, if bit 0=1
11	4 disk drives installed, if bit 0=1
01	Initial video mode is color, 40 by 25
10	Initial video mode is color, 80 by 25
11	Initial video mode is monochrome, 80 by 25
00	64K system board RAM installed
01	128K system board RAM installed
10	192K system board RAM installed
11	256K system board RAM installed
0	Math coprocessor not installed (AT only)
1	Math coprocessor installed (AT only)
0	No disk drives installed
1	Disk drives installed, see bits 7-6

The other memory location of interest is 0463h, which provides the adapter's base-port address, which can be either of two values (see table 17.7).

Table 17.7. Adapter base-port values stored at 0463h.

Adapter	Base Port
MDA	03B4h
HGA	03B4h
CGA	03D4h
EGA	03D4h
MCGA	03D4h
VGA	03D4h

Notice that the same values are stored at 0463h for the MDA/HGA and the CGA/EGA/MCGA/VGA. This information tells you which class of adapter is being used. Color-capable adapters have a base-port address of 03D4h, whereas monochrome adapters have a base-port address of 03B4h. Coupled with the data obtained from memory location 0410h (whether the computer is in monochrome or color mode), you easily and safely can assume which type of monitor the computer is using. It may seem that you need only one of these items to tell the monitor type; but what if you are using a monochrome monitor connected to a VGA? For some peripherals, you need to know the type of card as well as the type of monitor.

Now, let's use this information in a subroutine to determine the segment address that should be used for display of textual information. This routine is a "building block" that will be called by other (still to be developed) assembly language subroutines:

```
Page 60,132
Comment ¦
********************************************************************


File:     FINDCARD.ASM
Author:   Allen L. Wyatt
Date:     9/6/91

Purpose:  Determine the type of video card installed, and save info.
          This routine is designed to be called from other assembly
          language routines, but also needs to work within the BASIC
          memory model.


********************************************************************¦
```

```
                PUBLIC  FindCard            ;This routine
                PUBLIC  Monitor_Addr        ;Data for other routines
                PUBLIC  Status_Port         ;

                .MODEL  medium,BASIC

MONO            EQU     0B000h              ;Mono video buffer start
COLOR           EQU     0B800h              ;Color video buffer start

                .DATA

Monitor_Addr DW         0000                ;Offset of video buffer
Status_Port  DW         0000                ;Address of card status port
; ----------------------------------------------------------------

                .CODE

FindCard        PROC USES BX DX ES          ;Store registers used in this routine

                MOV     BX,0040h            ;Look at base-port value
                MOV     ES,BX               ;     03B4h = monochrome
                MOV     DX,ES:63h           ;     03D4h = color
                ADD     DX,6                ;Point to card's status port
                MOV     Status_Port,DX      ;Save the status port

                MOV     Monitor_Addr,COLOR  ;Default to color card
                MOV     BX,ES:10h           ;Get equipment list
                AND     BX,30h              ;Only want bits 5-4
                CMP     BX,30h              ;Is it monochrome (bits=11)?
                JNE     NotMono             ;No, so keep as color
                MOV     Monitor_Addr,MONO   ;Yes, set for monochrome

NotMono:        RET                         ;Return to caller
FindCard        ENDP

                END
```

At the conclusion of this routine, the address of the display adapter's status port is saved in STATUS_PORT, and the segment offset for the video buffer is stored in MONITOR_ADDR. These variables are declared PUBLIC so that they can be used by the routine that actually moves a character of data to the video buffer. (Soon you will find out why determining the adapter's status-port location is important.)

Displaying a Character in Video Memory

The next task is to develop a routine to move a character directly into video memory. You may remember that the IBM family of computers uses a memory-mapped video display. Consequently, changing the video memory results in a display change.

You can move data directly into the video buffer area, but doing so may result in an undesirable side effect of "snow" or glitches on the screen. This effect, particularly objectionable on the original IBM CGA design in text color mode and in all truly faithful clones of that adapter, is caused by accessing the video memory at a time that conflicts with other demands placed on it.

All the IBM display adapters are based on the Motorola 6845 CRT Controller chip. The chip used in the EGA is different, but is also based on the 6845. This chip controls the video RAM buffer area. When conventional memory chips make up the video buffer, they can be accessed by only one other device at a time. If you try to read from or write to them at the same time that the 6845 is trying to read them for display, you will momentarily block the 6845 from accessing the RAM. That interference is visible on the CRT as multicolored snow.

Because the effect was well known by the time the EGA was designed, the EGA's controller prevents snow from occurring. The MCGA and VGA also are snow-free. Even a few CGA designs avoided the problem by including more expensive dual-ported memory chips. But most CGA designs faithfully mimic the original version, including its susceptibility to interference and snow.

To compensate for this potential conflict, a routine must verify that a character is deposited only when the 6845 is not reading video memory. This "safe" time occurs during what is referred to as a *horizontal retrace condition* (HRC). While this condition is in effect, depositing a character in a video memory location does not result in interference.

The adapter card's status port contains information about the current state of the 6845. One factor that can be determined by reading this port is whether the adapter is currently in a horizontal retrace condition. If bit 0 is set to 0, the 6845 has video enabled and is accessing memory. If bit 0 is set to 1, a horizontal retrace condition exists and video memory is not being accessed.

The time available is extremely short; you can move only one 16-bit word—one character and its accompanying attribute—into the buffer during a single HRC time.

To display a single character without causing a conflict, you must write a low-level routine such as PCHAR. Remember that the following is a low-level routine, designed to be called from other assembly language routines:

```
Page 60,132
Comment ¦
*********************************************************************


File:     PCHAR.ASM
Author:   Allen L. Wyatt
Date:     9/11/91

Purpose:  To print a character on the video screen.

Format:   AL = ASCII value of character to print
          DI = video buffer offset at which to place AL


*********************************************************************¦


          PUBLIC   PCHAR

          EXTRN    Monitor_Addr:WORD
          EXTRN    Status_Port:WORD


          .MODEL medium, BASIC
          .CODE

PCHAR        PROC USES DX ES              ;Store registers used in this routine

             MOV      ES,Monitor_Addr
             MOV      DX,Status_Port

             CLI                          ;Don't allow interrupts
             PUSH     AX                  ;Store the character
Retrace:     IN       AL,DX              ;Get card status
             TEST     AL,1               ;Are we in a retrace state?
             JNZ      Retrace             ;Yes, so check again
                                          ;On fall-through, just
                                          ;   exited retrace state

No_Retrace:  IN       AL,DX              ;Get card status
             TEST     AL,1               ;Are we in a retrace state?
             JZ       No_Retrace          ;No, so check again
                                          ;On fall-through, just
                                          ;   entered retrace state

             POP      AX                  ;Yes, get character back
             MOV      ES:[DI],AL          ;OK to write it now
             STI                          ;OK to have interrupts now
```

```
        INC     DI                      ;Point to attribute
        INC     DI                      ;Next screen location

        RET
PCHAR   ENDP

        END
```

Notice that the 6845 status port is read in two separate loops. The first, Retrace, tests bit 0 to determine whether an HRC currently exists. If bit 0 is equal to 1, the zero flag will be clear, and the JNZ is executed to check again for an HRC. The loop is exited only when the HRC does not exist. This may sound backwards, because I pointed out earlier that accessing video memory during the retrace is safe. It *is* safe, but the instructions to pop the character from the stack and deposit it in video memory take time—the HRC could be over by the time the character is deposited.

When this routine is entered, you have no idea how long the HRC has been in effect or when it will end. Thus, the first loop waits until any existing HRC is completed. The second loop waits for an HRC and then accesses the memory at the start of the HRC. The result is the least possible snow.

Hardware interrupts are disabled (CLI) at entry to this routine and then enabled again (STI) just after storing the byte in video RAM. This is necessary; without these instructions, a lengthy hardware interrupt might occur just as the routine decided that accessing the video buffer was safe, and the HRC would be over long before the interrupt returned control to PCHAR. After the character has been stored, interrupts can be tolerated. Whenever you need to disable hardware interrupts to meet strict time requirements, be sure to enable the interrupts as soon as you can safely do so.

After verifying that an HRC has begun, PCHAR places a character at the video-buffer offset position determined by DI. The following section shows how to determine the value of DI from simple X-Y coordinates.

PCHAR returns with all registers (except DI) intact. DI is incremented to point at the next character position in the video buffer. After completion of this routine, you can develop a routine (that can be called from a high-level language) to display a string of ASCII characters instantly at any position on the screen.

Displaying an ASCII String

You now know what type of display adapter is installed, you have saved the segment address of the video buffer, and you know how to display a single character. All that remains is to determine the correct offset address so that you know where to begin displaying information.

From the details presented earlier in this chapter, you can easily derive a formula for determining the offset for displaying a character at any given location on the screen. This formula can be expressed as

$$[(ROW-1) * 80 + (COLUMN-1)] * 2$$

In this equation, ROW is assumed to be in the range of 1 through 25, and COLUMN is assumed to be in the range of 1 through 80. (If you change the number of rows when using an EGA, MCGA, or VGA, these formulas must change accordingly!) The offset for the attribute of any given character can be located by the formula

$$[(ROW-1) * 80 + (COLUMN-1)] * 2 + 1$$

Notice that the character addresses are always even, whereas the attribute addresses are always odd.

All you need to calculate the memory offset are the X (COLUMN) and Y (ROW) coordinates. Using this equation and the routines developed in the two preceding sections, you can write a routine that displays a string at any given position on the text screen. The following routine, which is called from QuickBASIC, will perform this task:

```
Page 60,132
Comment ¦
******************************************************************


File:      PSTRING.ASM
Author:    Allen L. Wyatt
Date:      9/11/91

Purpose:   To display a string directly to video memory from
           QuickBASIC.

Format:    CALL PString(A$,X%,Y%)
           A$: The BASIC string to be displayed.
           X%: The integer column value.
           Y%: The integer row value.


******************************************************************¦


        PUBLIC  PString

        EXTRN   FindCard:FAR
        EXTRN   PCHAR:FAR
```

```
        .MODEL  medium, BASIC
        .CODE

PString PROC String, Column, Row:WORD

        CALL    FindCard            ;Locate the video buffer
        MOV     BX,String           ;Get BASIC's string pointer
        MOV     CX,[BX]             ;Get the string's length
        JCXZ    Exit                ;No length, so don't print
        MOV     SI,[BX+2]           ;SI points to string

        MOV     BX,Row              ;Get address for row
        MOV     AX,[BX]             ;Get row value
        DEC     AX                  ;Put as a zero offset
        MOV     BX,Column           ;Get address for column
        MOV     DI,[BX]             ;Get column value
        DEC     DI                  ;Put as zero offset
        MOV     BX,80               ;80 characters/row
        MUL     BX                  ;Now have rows in AX
        ADD     DI,AX               ;Add to column number
        SHL     DI,1                ;Multiply by 2, DI=offset

PSLOOP: MOV     AL,[SI]             ;Get the string character
        INC     SI                  ;Point to the next character
        CALL    PCHAR               ;No, so print the character
        LOOP    PSLOOP              ;Redo for length of string

Exit:   RET
PString ENDP

        END
```

When you pass parameters from QuickBASIC to this routine, remember that the X-Y coordinates must be integer values. If integers are not used, unpredictable results may occur.

Using the Attribute Byte

You may recall that each displayed character in the video buffer requires two bytes of information—the ASCII value of the character and the character's display attribute.

This attribute byte controls how the character is displayed. Each bit of the attribute byte has a different function. Regardless of the type of display adapter you are using, the purpose of each bit is the same, but the *effect* produced by different settings varies according to the type of adapter.

Usually, bits 0-3 and 7 control the foreground, whereas bits 4-6 control the background. The foreground is the character itself. The background is the area of the character cell surrounding the character. Although these bits are used in the same way on both color and monochrome adapters, their effect on the adapters differs. Table 17.8 lists the meanings and possible settings of the bits in each character's attribute byte on a monochrome monitor. Table 17.9 shows the same information for attribute bytes on a color monitor.

Table 17.8. *Meaning of the bits in a monochrome attribute byte.*

Bits 76543210	Meaning of Bit Setting
0	Nonblinking character
1	Blinking character
000	Black background (normal)
111	White foreground (inverse)
0	Normal intensity
1	High intensity
001	Underlined white foreground
111	White foreground (normal)
000	Black foreground (inverse)

Table 17.9. *Meaning of the bits in a color attribute byte.*

Bits 76543210	Meaning of Bit Setting
0	Normal foreground
1	Blinking foreground
bbb	Background (see table 17.10)
ffff	Foreground (see table 17.10)

You can see from table 17.10 that, with the color attribute, only the first 8 colors (0-7) can be used for background values, whereas all 16 colors can be used for foreground. When you use both the monochrome and color attributes, certain combinations of foreground and background result in invisible characters. (Although invisible characters are useless to humans, they are valid to the computer.) You can test for different color combinations that you find pleasing for different applications.

You can have bright backgrounds, as well as bright foregrounds, if you are willing to give up the capability of making the foreground color blink. The method used to change bit 7 from foreground blink control to background intensity control varies with the different types of video cards, however.

If you are using an MDA, a Hercules adapter, or a CGA, just flip the value of one bit in the CRT controller's mode-control register. The values contained in this register are stored in the BIOS RAM byte at 0465h (refer to table 17.5), and the following code can be called from almost any language to flip the control bit from BLINK to BRIGHT and then called again to flip back to BLINK:

```
        .CODE

Flip    PROC USES ES
        MOV     AX,0040h
        MOV     ES,AX           ; point it to BIOS RAM
        MOV     DX,ES:[0063h]   ; CRTC base port address
        ADD     DX,4            ; offset to control port
        MOV     AL,ES:[0065h]   ; image of current content
        XOR     AL,20h          ; flip blink-enable bit
        MOV     ES:[0065h],AL   ; put it back
        OUT     DX,AL           ; and send to CRTC too
        RET                     ; to caller
FLIP    ENDP

        END
```

If you are using an EGA, MCGA, or VGA, you must go through the video BIOS routines to switch this bit; refer to Chapter 20, "Accessing BIOS Services," for details and a code example.

Table 17.10 lists the colors built into the CGA; if you use an EGA, MCGA, or VGA, you can modify the exact colors that correspond to each bit setting. With an EGA, you can select any 16 of 64 different shades; these are composed from the three primary colors (red, blue, and green) and four levels of each color (none, 1/3, 2/3, and 3/3 brightness). Thus, black is obtained by having all three colors off; bright white, by having all three at 3/3 brightness. The MCGA/VGA cards are similar.

Table 17.10. *Background and foreground colors for color attribute byte.*

Bit Setting	Decimal Value	Color
0000	0	Black
0001	1	Blue
0010	2	Green
0011	3	Cyan
0100	4	Red
0101	5	Magenta
0110	6	Brown
0111	7	White
1000	8	Gray
1001	9	Light blue
1010	10	Light green
1011	11	Light cyan
1100	12	Light red
1101	13	Light magenta
1110	14	Yellow
1111	15	White (high intensity)

How can you apply this information to enhance the routines developed in this chapter? You do not need to change the FindCard routine, which simply locates the type of card and sets two variables for use in the other routines. But PCHAR and PString can be changed so that they use a specified attribute value.

PCHAR is written to display a character on either a monochrome or color monitor. If the original routine were modified so that it could make an intelligent decision about converting attribute values, the high-level program could be written to take advantage of a color monitor, but PCHAR would translate the character attribute to a display format appropriate for a monochrome display. This new implementation, PCHARA (meaning *print character with attribute*), is as follows:

```
Page 60,132
Comment ¦
******************************************************************

File:     PCHARA.ASM
Author:   Allen L. Wyatt
Date:     9/11/91
```

```
Purpose:  To print a character on the video screen, setting the
          video attribute according to the color table values if
          using a monochrome display.

Format:   AL = ASCII value of character to print
          DI = video buffer offset at which to place AL
          Attribute should be initialized by calling routine


*********************************************************************!


          PUBLIC  PCHARA
          PUBLIC  Attribute

          EXTRN   Monitor_Addr:WORD
          EXTRN   Status_Port:WORD


          .MODEL medium,BASIC

MONO      EQU     0B000h                  ;Mono video buffer start
COLOR     EQU     0B800h                  ;Color video buffer start

          .DATA

Attribute    DB     00
Attr_Test    DB     00
Color_Table EQU     THIS BYTE
BWT_BLK      DB     0Fh,0Fh               ;Black background
BLU_BLK      DB     01h,01h
YEL_BLU      DB     1Eh,70h
BLU_WHT      DB     71h,70h
GRN_WHT      DB     72h,70h
CYN_WHT      DB     73h,70h
RED_WHT      DB     74h,70h
MAG_WHT      DB     75h,70h
BRN_WHT      DB     76h,70h
GRY_WHT      DB     78h,70h
LBL_WHT      DB     79h,70h
LGR_WHT      DB     7Ah,70h
LCY_WHT      DB     7Bh,70h
LRD_WHT      DB     7Ch,70h
LMG_WHT      DB     7Dh,70h
YEL_WHT      DB     7Eh,70h
BWT_WHT      DB     7Fh,70h
TABLE_END    DB     00h,07h               ;End of table
;   ------------------------------------------------------------------
```

```
            .CODE

PCHARA      PROC USES BX DX SI ES       ;Store registers used in this routine

            MOV     ES,Monitor_Addr
            MOV     DX,Status_Port


; Handle translation for monochrome monitors


            MOV     AH,Attribute        ;Get video attribute
            CMP     Monitor_Addr,COLOR  ;Is it a color monitor?
            JE      No_Trans            ;Yes, assume correct
            CMP     AH,Attr_Test        ;Is it the same as before?
            JE      No_Trans            ;Yes, so keep going
            MOV     SI,OFFSET Color_Table
Color_Loop: MOV     BH,[SI]             ;Get the first color
            INC     SI                  ;Point to mono equivalent
            CMP     BH,0                ;End of table?
            JE      Set_Color           ;Yes, so use default
            CMP     AH,BH               ;Should we translate?
            JE      Set_Color           ;Yes, so set new color
            INC     SI                  ;Skip the mono equivalent
            JMP     Color_Loop
Set_Color:  MOV     AH,[SI]             ;Get mono equivalent
            MOV     Attr_Test,AH        ;Reset the test byte


No_Trans:   CLI                         ;Don't allow interrupts
            PUSH    AX                  ;Store the character
Retrace:    IN      AL,DX               ;Get card status
            TEST    AL,1                ;Are we in a retrace state?
            JNZ     Retrace             ;Yes, so check again
                                        ;On fall-through, just
                                        ;   exited retrace state
No_Retrace: IN      AL,DX               ;Get card status
            TEST    AL,1                ;Are we in a retrace state?
            JZ      No_Retrace          ;No, so check again
                                        ;On fall-through, just
                                        ;   entered retrace state
            POP     AX                  ;Yes, get character back
            MOV     ES:[DI],AX          ;OK to write it now
            STI                         ;OK to have interrupts now
```

```
        INC     DI                      ;Point to attribute
        INC     DI                      ;Next screen location

        RET
PCHARA  ENDP

        END
```

This new version of the routine is only slightly different from the earlier PCHAR. The modified routine has the additional data areas needed for the attribute and the attribute translation.

The translation table begins at the label COLOR_TABLE. Each color attribute to be translated is listed, followed by the monochrome equivalent of the attribute. For instance, the color attribute for a yellow foreground on a blue background (YEL_BLU) translates to an inverse (black-on-white) attribute in monochrome.

A 0 in the color-attribute position signifies the end of the table. Any translation that has not been caught specifically in the table is translated to normal monochrome white-on-black.

This translation process is handled in PCHARA by the coding beginning at the line

```
; Handle translation for monochrome monitors
```

First, PCHARA checks whether a monochrome monitor is in use. If not, no translation is needed, and processing continues. If a monochrome monitor is in use, the old attribute (Attr_Test) is checked against the new one. If the two attributes are the same, no translation is needed, and processing continues.

If a translation is indicated, PCHARA loads the offset of Color_Table into SI. Next, the attribute byte at that location (SI) is loaded, and SI is incremented to point at the monochrome equivalent of the color attribute. Then PCHARA checks for the end-of-table flag. If the end has been reached, the routine is exited, the default attribute (white-on-black) is loaded, and the character is displayed. If a valid translation is needed, the new attribute is loaded from the table and the character is displayed.

Notice that in this version of PCHARA an entire word (both the ASCII value and its attribute) is moved into the video buffer; in the earlier version of the routine, only the ASCII character was moved to memory.

The overhead associated with the changes to this routine is a small price to pay for the added value received. Now you can control not only *which* character is displayed but also *how* a character is displayed.

Notice that Attribute is assumed to have been set before entry into PCHARA. Attribute is a video attribute that can be set in PString with a value passed from a high-level language. You can set Attribute using the following new version, PStringa, which is written for compiled BASIC:

```
Page 60,132
Comment ¦
*********************************************************************


File:     PSTRINGA.ASM
Author:   Allen L. Wyatt
Date:     9/11/91

Purpose:  To display a string directly to video memory from
          compiled BASIC, including the video attribute.

Format:   CALL PStringa(A$,X%,Y%,Z%)
          A$: The BASIC string to be displayed.
          X%: The integer column value.
          Y%: The integer row value.
          Z%: The integer video attribute.


*********************************************************************¦


          PUBLIC  PStringa

          EXTRN   FindCard:FAR
          EXTRN   PCHARA:FAR
          EXTRN   Attribute:BYTE

          .MODEL  medium, BASIC
          .CODE

PStringa  PROC String, Column, Row, Video_Attr:WORD

          CALL    FindCard            ;Locate the video buffer
          MOV     BX,Video_Attr       ;Address of attribute value
          MOV     AX,[BX]             ;Get attribute value
          MOV     Attribute,AL        ;Only working with a byte

          MOV     BX,String           ;Get BASIC's string pointer
          MOV     CX,[BX]             ;Get the string's length
          JCXZ    Exit                ;No length, so don't print
          MOV     SI,[BX+2]           ;SI points to string
```

```
        MOV     BX,Row              ;Get address for row
        MOV     AX,[BX]             ;Get row value
        DEC     AX                  ;Put as a zero offset
        MOV     BX,Column           ;Get address for column
        MOV     DI,[BX]             ;Get column value
        DEC     DI                  ;Put AS zero offset
        MOV     BX,80               ;80 characters/row
        MUL     BX                  ;Now have rows in AX
        ADD     DI,AX               ;Add to column number
        SHL     DI,1                ;Multiply by 2, DI=offset

PSLOOP: MOV     AL,[SI]             ;Get the string character
        INC     SI                  ;Point to the next character
        CALL    PCHARA              ;Print the character
        LOOP    PSLOOP              ;Redo for length of string

Exit:   RET
PStringa ENDP

        END
```

There is only one difference between this and the earlier version of PString. With this version you can pass an additional variable by BASIC to specify the attribute of the string being printed. This attribute is placed in the variable Attribute for subsequent use by PCHARA.

Notice that even though a word (16-bit integer) is passed from BASIC, only the lower byte of the word is used for the attribute. As you may recall from the memory-mapped display of the IBM computer family, only one byte is used to specify a character's attribute.

Creating Text-Based Graphics Routines

Now that you know how information is stored on the screen and how the appearance of the information is controlled, you can use these building blocks to create routines for handling text-based graphics. Such routines are helpful when you create attractive menus or data-input screens. Using assembly language, you can paint appealing screens and display them instantaneously to enhance the image of your program. In addition, you can create the screens and menus with one call from your high-level language.

In the ASCII character set of the IBM family of microcomputers, several characters are well suited for ASCII graphics. These characters were designed specifically for creating screen forms and display outlines. Figure 17.2 shows the different groups of ASCII graphics characters.

Fig. 17.2. ASCII graphics characters.

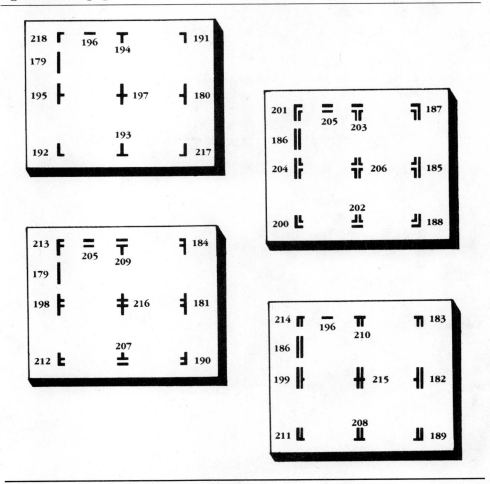

Let's create a routine that uses some of these ASCII graphics characters to display a double-lined box anywhere on the screen. All you have to do is pass the coordinates for the upper left and lower right corners of the box, along with the display attribute to use when creating the box. This routine, appropriately named Box, is coded as follows when called from compiled BASIC:

```
                Page 60,132
                Comment ¦
                ***********************************************************************


                File:     BOX.ASM
                Author:   Allen L. Wyatt
                Date:     9/13/91


                Purpose:  To display a double-lined box from QuickBASIC.


                Format:   CALL Box(TLC%,BRC%,Z%)
                          TLC%: The top left screen coordinate.
                          BRC%: The bottom right screen coordinate.
                          Z%:   The integer video attribute.


                ***********************************************************************¦


                          PUBLIC  Box

                          EXTRN   FindCard:FAR
                          EXTRN   Set_DI:FAR
                          EXTRN   PCHARA:FAR
                          EXTRN   Attribute:BYTE

                          .MODEL medium, BASIC
                          .DATA

                BoxChar   DB        ⌐ ╚╝ ╠
                BoxULC    EQU     THIS WORD
                UL_Col    DB      00
                UL_Row    DB      00
                BoxLRC    EQU     THIS WORD
                LR_Col    DB      00
                LR_Row    DB      00
                ; -------------------------------------------------------------------


                          .CODE

                Box       PROC TLC, BRC, Video_Attr:WORD

                          MOV     BX,Video_Attr       ;Get address of attribute
                          MOV     AX,[BX]             ;Get value of attribute
                          MOV     Attribute,AL        ;Store the attribute
                          MOV     BX,BRC              ;Get address of BRC
```

```
                MOV     AX,[BX]             ;Get value of BRC
                MOV     BoxLRC,AX           ;Store the value
                MOV     BX,TLC              ;Get address of TLC
                MOV     AX,[BX]             ;Get value of TLC
                MOV     BoxULC,AX           ;Store the value

                CALL    FindCard            ;Locate the monitor info

; Print sides of box, top to bottom

                MOV     BH,UL_Row           ;Get upper left (row only)
                INC     BH                  ;Start next row down
                MOV     AL,BoxChar+4        ;Character for side of box
                MOV     CH,UL_Row           ;Top row
                MOV     CL,LR_Row           ;Bottom row
                SUB     CL,CH               ;Height is left in CL
                SUB     CH,CH               ;Zero out CH
                DEC     CX                  ;Adjust for actual height
V1:             MOV     BL,UL_Col           ;Set left column
                CALL    Set_DI              ;Position offset
                CALL    PCHARA
                MOV     BL,LR_COL           ;Set right column
                CALL    Set_DI              ;Position offset
                CALL    PCHARA
                INC     BH                  ;Next row
                LOOP    V1

; Print top of box

                MOV     BX,BoxULC           ;Get upper left column
                INC     BX                  ;Next space right
                CALL    Set_DI              ;Position offset
                MOV     AL,BoxChar+5        ;Top/bottom character
                MOV     CL,LR_Col           ;Left column
                MOV     CH,UL_Col           ;Right column
                SUB     CL,CH
                SUB     CH,CH               ;Zero out
                DEC     CX                  ;Width of box is in CX
                PUSH    CX                  ;Store width for later
TB1:            CALL    PCHARA
                LOOP    TB1                 ;Do it again

; Print bottom of box
```

```
                MOV      BH,LR_Row
                MOV      BL,UL_Col            ;Now have bottom left corner
                INC      BX                   ;Next space right
                CALL     Set_DI               ;Position offset
                POP      CX                   ;Get width back
                MOV      AL,BoxChar+5         ;Top/bottom character
TB2:            CALL     PCHARA
                LOOP     TB2                  ;Do it again

; Print corners

                MOV      BX,BoxULC            ;Upper left
                CALL     Set_DI               ;Position offset
                MOV      AL,BoxChar+2         ;Upper left character
                CALL     PCHARA


                MOV      BX,BoxLRC            ;Upper right
                CALL     Set_DI               ;Position offset
                MOV      AL,BoxChar+3         ;Lower right character
                CALL     PCHARA
                MOV      BH,UL_Row
                MOV      BL,LR_Col            ;Upper right
                CALL     Set_DI               ;Position offset
                MOV      AL,BoxChar           ;Upper right character
                CALL     PCHARA


                MOV      BH,LR_Row
                MOV      BL,UL_Col            ;Lower left
                CALL     Set_DI               ;Position offset
                MOV      AL,BoxChar+1         ;Lower left character
                CALL     PCHARA

                RET
Box             ENDP

                END
```

This routine displays a double-lined box at the specified location on the video screen without erasing the area inside the box. Using the following equation, the controlling program—in QuickBASIC—passes the coordinates through an integer variable that contains the row/column coordinates:

COORD% = ROW * 256 + COLUMN

Because the controlling program uses this equation, numbers need to be manipulated less during the execution of this routine. Using this equation, the coordinates are passed in a format that places the row in the upper byte of the integer parameter, and the column in the lower byte.

This routine is designed so that you can easily change the type of border used for the box. To draw a different type of box, you simply change the contents of BOX_CHAR to the six appropriate drawing bytes.

The FindCard and PCHARA subroutines are both used in this routine, as well as another subroutine, Set_DI. The Set_DI subroutine converts a row/column coordinate, which is held in BX, into an offset into the video buffer. The code for Set_DI follows:

```
Page 60,132
Comment ¦
******************************************************************


File:     SETDI.ASM
Author:   Allen L. Wyatt
Date:     9/13/91

Purpose:  To set DI from BX. On entry, BX contains the desired
          screen row/column. On exit, DI contains the screen memory
          offset. All other registers are unchanged.


******************************************************************¦

          PUBLIC  Set_DI

          .MODEL medium, BASIC
          .CODE


; -----------------------------------------------------------------
Set_DI    PROC USES AX BX DX

          MOV     AH,0            ;Don't need AH now
          MOV     AL,BH           ;Move the row
          MOV     BH,0            ;And zero it out
          MOV     DI,BX           ;Move the column
          MOV     BX,80           ;columns per row
          MUL     BX              ;AX = row * 80
          ADD     DI,AX           ;Add to column
          SHL     DI,1            ;Multiply by 2
```

```
              RET
Set_DI        ENDP

              END
```

By studying BOX, you can see how easily you can place graphics on the video screen. Using ASCII characters, you can change the routine to create any type of screen graphics you want. The speed with which assembly language paints entire screens may surprise you.

Using Window Techniques: Saving and Restoring Windows

Now that you know how to create boxes, you can take the next logical step—creating routines that can generate pop-up windows from compiled BASIC.

To create pop-up windows, you need to follow these steps:

1. Determine the rectangular coordinates of the area to contain the window.

2. Save the current screen contents in that area.

3. Clear the defined area.

4. Draw a box around the area.

Perhaps the most important step is that of saving the video information under the pop-up window, Step 2. A complete routine must not only save this information but also be able to restore previous video information. Recreating the entire screen after the user is finished with the window is unacceptable and, in many cases, impossible.

The routines described in this section will perform all these tasks. With these routines you can use a "window stack" to save and create multiple windows. Using this stack concept, you can remove the windows from the screen in reverse order.

The following listing includes two callable routines. SAVSCRN, which is similar to the process used in BOX, requires the passing of the upper left corner and lower right corner of the window area; GETSCRN removes the previously created window. The listing is as follows:

```
                Page 60,132
                Comment ¦
                ***********************************************************************


                File:       SCRN.ASM
                Author:     Allen L. Wyatt
                Date:       9/13/91

                Purpose:    To save and restore a portion of the screen to a buffer
                            from QuickBASIC.

                Format:     CALL SaveScrn(TLC%,BRC%,B%,C%)
                            TLC%: The top left screen coordinate
                            BRC%: The bottom right screen coordinate
                            B%:   The integer video attribute to use for the box outline
                            C%:   The integer video attribute to use for inside the box

                            CALL GetScrn
                ***********************************************************************¦


                        PUBLIC   SaveScrn
                        PUBLIC   GetScrn

                        EXTRN    Set_DI:FAR
                        EXTRN    PCHARA:FAR
                        EXTRN    Monitor_Addr:WORD
                        EXTRN    Status_Port:WORD
                        EXTRN    Attribute:BYTE

                        .MODEL   medium, BASIC
                        .DATA

Temp                    DW       0000
Window_Width            DW       0000

BoxChar                 DB       ┐ └┘ ╠
BoxULC                  EQU      THIS WORD
UL_Col                  DB       00
UL_Row                  DB       00
BoxLRC                  EQU      THIS WORD
LR_Col                  DB       00
LR_Row                  DB       00
```

```
Screens          DB      4 DUP(1024 DUP(0))   ;Screen stack space
EndScreens       DB      00                   ;End of screen stack space
; ------------------------------------------------------------------

                 .CODE

SaveScrn         PROC TLC, BRC, Box_Attr, Field_Attr:WORD

                 MOV     BX,Box_Attr          ;Get address of attribute
                 MOV     AX,[BX]              ;Get value of attribute
                 MOV     Attribute,AL         ;Store the attribute
                 MOV     BX,BRC               ;Get address of BRC
                 MOV     AX,[BX]              ;Get BRC value
                 MOV     BoxLRC,AX            ;Save it
                 MOV     BX,TLC               ;Get address of TLC
                 MOV     AX,[BX]              ;Get TLC value
                 MOV     BoxULC,AX            ;Save it
                 CALL    CalcSize             ;Calculate space for save
                 CALL    FindFree             ;Find free space in screen
                                              ;  stack area
                 JNC     SS_CONT              ;Continue
                 JMP     SS_EXIT              ;Sorry, no space left

SS_CONT:         PUSH    SI                   ;Save area
                 ADD     SI,6                 ;Set past pointer area
                 MOV     AX,BoxULC            ;Move upper left corner
                 MOV     Temp,AX              ;  into work area
SS_LOOP:         MOV     BX,Temp
                 CALL    Set_DI               ;Set offset
                 MOV     ES,Monitor_Addr
                 MOV     CX,Window_Width
SS_L2:           MOV     AX,ES:[DI]           ;Get character/attribute
                 MOV     [SI],AX              ;Place into screen stack
                 INC     DI                   ;Point to next display set
                 INC     DI
                 INC     SI                   ;Increment stack pointer
                 INC     SI
                 LOOP    SS_L2                ;Do for entire line
                 ADD     Temp,0100h           ;Proceed to next line
                 MOV     AX,Temp
                 MOV     BX,BoxLRC
                 CMP     AH,BH                ;Are we too far down?
                 JLE     SS_LOOP              ;No, so continue
```

```
            MOV     BX,SI              ;Get end of screen in stack
            POP     SI                 ;Get start of area
            MOV     AX,BoxULC          ;Store upper left corner
            MOV     [SI],AX            ;   coordinates
            INC     SI                 ;Point to next coordinate
            INC     SI                 ;   location
            MOV     AX,BoxLRC          ;Store lower right corner
            MOV     [SI],AX            ;   coordinates
            INC     SI                 ;Point to next coordinate
            INC     SI                 ;   location
            MOV     [SI],BX            ;Store pointer to start of
                                       ;   stack free space

; Print sides of box, top to bottom

            MOV     BH,UL_Row          ;Get upper left (row only)
            INC     BH                 ;Start next row down
            MOV     AL,BoxChar+4       ;Character for side of box
            MOV     CH,UL_Row          ;Top row
            MOV     CL,LR_Row          ;Bottom row
            SUB     CL,CH              ;Height is left in CL
            SUB     CH,CH              ;Zero out CH
            DEC     CX                 ;Adjust for actual height
V1:         MOV     BL,UL_Col          ;Set left column
            CALL    Set_DI             ;Position offset
            CALL    PCHARA
            MOV     BL,LR_Col          ;Set right column
            CALL    Set_DI             ;Position offset
            CALL    PCHARA
            INC     BH                 ;Next row
            LOOP    V1

; Print top of box

            MOV     BX,BoxULC          ;Get upper left column
            INC     BX                 ;Next space right
            CALL    Set_DI             ;Position offset
            MOV     AL,BoxChar+5       ;Top/bottom character
            MOV     CL,LR_Col          ;Left column
            MOV     CH,UL_Col          ;Right column
            SUB     CL,CH
            SUB     CH,CH              ;Zero out
            DEC     CX                 ;Width of box is in CX
            PUSH    CX                 ;Store width for later
```

```
TB1:            CALL    PCHARA
                LOOP    TB1                     ;Do it again

; Print bottom of box

                MOV     BH,LR_Row
                MOV     BL,UL_Col               ;Now have bottom left corner
                INC     BX                      ;Next space right
                CALL    Set_DI                  ;Position offset
                POP     CX                      ;Get width back
                MOV     AL,BoxChar+5            ;Top/bottom character
TB2:            CALL    PCHARA
                LOOP    TB2                     ;Do it again

; Print corners

                MOV     BX,BoxULC               ;Upper left
                CALL    Set_DI                  ;Position offset
                MOV     AL,BoxChar+2           ;Upper left character
                CALL    PCHARA

                MOV     BX,BoxLRC               ;Upper right
                CALL    Set_DI                  ;Position offset
                MOV     AL,BoxChar+3           ;Lower right character
                CALL    PCHARA

                MOV     BH,UL_Row
                MOV     BL,LR_Col               ;Upper right
                CALL    Set_DI                  ;Position offset
                MOV     AL,BoxChar             ;Upper right character
                CALL    PCHARA
                MOV     BH,LR_Row
                MOV     BL,UL_Col               ;Lower left
                CALL    Set_DI                  ;Position offset
                MOV     AL,BoxChar+1           ;Lower left character
                CALL    PCHARA

                MOV     CX,BoxULC               ;Upper left corner
                ADD     CX,0101h                ;Don't erase box
                MOV     DX,BoxLRC               ;Bottom right corner
                SUB     DX,0101h                ;Don't erase box

                MOV     BX,Field_Attr           ;Get address of attribute
                MOV     AX,[BX]                 ;Get value of attribute
```

```
                MOV     BH,AL               ;Store the attribute
                MOV     AH,6                ;Clear upwards
                MOV     AL,0                ;Clear the window
                INT     10h                 ;Call BIOS interrupt

                CLC                         ;No errors

SS_EXIT:        RET
SaveScrn        ENDP
; --------------------------------------------------------------------

GetScrn         PROC

                CALL    FindLast            ;Find last saved screen
                JC      GS_EXIT             ;Sorry, none there

                PUSH    SI
                MOV     AX,[SI]             ;Get upper left corner
                MOV     BoxULC,AX           ;Store in this area
                MOV     Temp,AX             ;Store in work area
                INC     SI                  ;Point to next coordinate
                INC     SI                  ;  location

                MOV     AX,[SI]             ;Get lower right corner
                MOV     BoxLRC,AX           ;  and store it
                INC     SI                  ;Point to next coordinate
                INC     SI                  ;  location

                MOV     AX,[SI]             ;Get pointer to next area
                PUSH    AX                  ;Save temporarily
                INC     SI                  ;Point to next coordinate
                INC     SI                  ;  location

                CALL    CalcSize            ;This will set the width
GS_LOOP:        MOV     BX,Temp
                CALL    Set_DI              ;Position cursor there
                MOV     CX,Window_Width
GS_L2:          MOV     AX,[SI]             ;Get from stack area
                CALL    MoveChar            ;Move the character
                INC     SI                  ;Point to next character
                INC     SI                  ;  group
                LOOP    GS_L2               ;Repeat for entire line
                ADD     Temp,0100h          ;Point to next line
                MOV     AX,Temp
```

```
                    MOV     BX,BoxLRC
                    CMP     AH,BH                   ;Are we too far down?
                    JLE     GS_LOOP                 ;No, so continue

                    POP     BX                      ;Get back next area pointer
                    POP     SI                      ;Get back start
                    SUB     BX,SI                   ;Size of area
                    INC     BX
                    MOV     AX,0                    ;Zero out entire area
                    MOV     CX,BX
FL:                 MOV     [SI],AL
                    INC     SI
                    LOOP    FL
                    CLC                             ;Set for no errors

GS_EXIT:            RET
GetScrn             ENDP


; ----------------------------------------------------------------
; Subroutines for SaveScrn and GetScrn
; ----------------------------------------------------------------


; ----------------------------------------------------------------
; FindFree - Find a block on screen stack large enough to hold window
;            Enter with CX set to size needed, in bytes
; ----------------------------------------------------------------


FindFree            PROC
                    LEA     SI,Screens              ;Start of screen stack
FF_LOOP:            MOV     BX,[SI+4]               ;Get pointer to next area
                    CMP     BX,0                    ;Is there anything here?
                                                    ;  BX equal to 1 past end
                                                    ;  of saved screen if so
                    JE      FoundFree               ;Nothing here
                    MOV     SI,BX                   ;Point to next screen set
                    JMP     FF_LOOP                 ;Keep looking

FoundFree:          MOV     AX,SI                   ;Set to beginning of entry
                    ADD     AX,12                   ;Add enough for two sets of
                                                    ;  pointers
                    ADD     AX,CX                   ;Add length of save
                    LEA     DX,EndScreens           ;End of screen stack
                    CMP     AX,DX                   ;Are we past end of stack?
```

```
                JGE     FF_NOPE             ;Yes, too big (can't save)
                CLC                         ;Return without error
                JNC     FF_EXIT
FF_NOPE:        STC
FF_EXIT:        RET                         ;Return to caller
FindFree        ENDP


; -------------------------------------------------------------------
; CalcSize - Calculate the space needed for the window area
;            Returns with CX set to number of bytes
; -------------------------------------------------------------------
CalcSize        PROC
                MOV     AX,BoxULC           ;Get upper left corner
                MOV     BX,BoxLRC           ;Lower right corner
                SUB     BX,AX               ;Absolute rows/columns

                ADD     BX,0101h            ;Set to actual numbers
                MOV     AX,0
                MOV     AL,BH               ;Number of rows in AX
                MOV     BH,0                ;Number of columns in BX
                MOV     Window_Width,BX     ;Save width for later use
                MUL     BX                  ;Character positions in AX
                SHL     AX,1                ;Number of bytes in block
                MOV     CX,AX               ;Put in proper register
                RET                         ;Return to caller
CalcSize        ENDP


; -------------------------------------------------------------------
; FindLast - Locates the last saved screen on the screen stack
; -------------------------------------------------------------------
FindLast        PROC
                LEA     SI,Screens
                MOV     AX,0
                PUSH    AX                  ;Save original pointer
FL_LOOP:        MOV     BX,[SI+4]           ;Get pointer to next area
                CMP     BX,0                ;Is there anything here?
                                            ;  BX equal to 1 past end
                                            ;  of saved screen if so

                JE      FoundLast           ;Nothing here, at end
                POP     AX                  ;Get back old pointer
                PUSH    SI                  ;Save where we are now
                MOV     SI,BX               ;Point to next screen set
                JMP     FL_LOOP             ;Keep looking
```

```
FoundLast:      POP     SI                      ;Get back the good pointer
                CMP     SI,0                    ;Was it zero (nothing to
                                                ;   restore)?
                JE      FL_NOPE                 ;Yes, so error
                CLC                             ;Return without error
                JNC     FL_EXIT
FL_NOPE:        STC
FL_EXIT:        RET
FindLast        ENDP


; ------------------------------------------------------------------
; MoveChar - Move a character into the video buffer (similar to PCHAR)
; ------------------------------------------------------------------
MoveChar        PROC USES DX ES

                MOV     ES,Monitor_Addr
                MOV     DX,Status_Port

                CLI                             ;Don't allow interrupts
                PUSH    AX                      ;Store the character
Retrace:        IN      AL,DX                   ;Get card status
                TEST    AL,1                    ;Are we in a retrace state?
                JNZ     Retrace                 ;Yes, so check again
                                                ;On fall-through, just
                                                ;   exited retrace state

NoRetrace:      IN      AL,DX                   ;Get card status
                TEST    AL,1                    ;Are we in a retrace state?
                JZ      NoRetrace               ;No, so check again
                                                ;On fall-through, just
                                                ;   entered retrace state

                POP     AX                      ;Yes, get character back
                MOV     ES:[DI],AX              ;OK to write it now
                STI                             ;OK to have interrupts now

                INC     DI                      ;Point to attribute
                INC     DI                      ;Next screen location

                RET
MoveChar        ENDP
; ------------------------------------------------------------------

                END
```

This set of routines is an example of the point made at the beginning of this book—that source code for assembly language routines takes a great deal of space. When assembled, however, the resulting object code is significantly smaller than similar routines written entirely in BASIC.

Notice that these routines, particularly SaveScrn, do not use the SI and DI registers in the usual manner; in these routines, DI points to the source, whereas SI points to the destination. I did this so that maximum use could be made of existing routines, such as Set_DI. I hope that the purists among you will not become incensed.

As much as 4K of screen data (the size of the entire screen) can be saved by using SaveScrn. Because most pop-up windows do not use the whole screen, you can save several windows. If you find that you need a larger screen-stack area, you can increase the area by changing the number of bytes defined by Screens.

Notice that GetScrn uses a subroutine called MoveChar. You will find, on examination, that MoveChar seems similar to PCHAR, the routine developed earlier in this chapter. Right you are! The routines are similar because they do almost the same thing: they store information into the video buffer. A new routine was warranted because, instead of using the default Attribute (as PCHARA does), you are retrieving data one word at a time.

If you want to collect these routines into a library for use with QuickBASIC's command-line compiler capability, you can use the makefile VIDEO shown in Chapter 8 to do so. The following QuickBASIC program demonstrates most of the library's functions:

```
' ****************************************************************
' *                                                            *
' * File:     VIDTEST.BAS                                       *
' * Author:   Allen L. Wyatt                                    *
' * Date:     9/14/91                                           *
' *                                                            *
' * Purpose:  Sample program to demonstrate use of video       *
' *           subroutines. Designed to run under compiled      *
' *           BASIC.                                            *
' *                                                            *
' ****************************************************************

DEFINT A-Z

CLS
r = 4
c = 1
FOR a = 1 TO 255
```

```
      a$ = RIGHT$("     "+STR$(a)+" ",5)
      r = r + 1
      IF r > 24 THEN
         r = 5
         c = c + LEN(a$) + 1
      ENDIF
      CALL PStringa(a$, c, r, a)
NEXT a

LOCATE 1,1
PRINT "First test completed, screen painted with PStringa"
PRINT "Second test ready to start: screen saving"
LINE INPUT "Press ENTER to begin";a$
tlc = 5 * 256 + 5
brc = 20 * 256 + 75
ba = 30
fa = 30
CALL SaveScrn(tlc, brc, ba, fa)

LOCATE 1,1
PRINT "Second test completed, screen saved with SaveScrn "
PRINT "Third test ready to start: box drawing    "
LINE INPUT "Press ENTER to begin";a$
tlc = 10 * 256 + 20
brc = 15 * 256 + 60
a = 58
CALL Box(tlc, brc, a)

LOCATE 1,1
PRINT "Third test completed, box drawn with Box          "
PRINT "Fourth test ready to start: screen restoring"
LINE INPUT "Press ENTER to begin";a$
CALL GetScrn

LOCATE 1,1
PRINT "Fourth test completed, screen restored with GetScrn"
PRINT "All tests completed                     "
PRINT "                               "
```

Summary

The wide range of display adapters and monitors available for the IBM family of microcomputers can all be classified in one of two categories—monochrome or color. Because the classification of display devices can be determined by software, you can write routines that quickly display video data on either category of display adapter.

Video-display routines written in assembly language execute faster and take less object code space than those written in high-level languages. Adding assembly language display subroutines to a high-level language program increases the overall speed of the program, especially one that is heavily screen-dependent.

The routines in this chapter were all written for compiled BASIC but could have been written just as easily for any other high-level language. If you change the parameter-passing coding, the routines should work with C and Pascal as well as with compiled BASIC.

18

Accessing Hardware Ports

To communicate with peripheral devices, your PC's CPU uses *hardware ports*. These ports are areas that the 8086/8088 (or any descendant CPUs) accesses by using special assembly language instructions. This chapter discusses specific hardware ports and the assembly language instructions that apply to them. In addition, the chapter covers several significant hardware-port addresses, addresses important because they are used for direct control of such computer devices as the keyboard, the video monitor, and the speaker.

The 8086/8088 chip family can address as many as 65,536 hardware ports. Because of the way the IBM PC microcomputers were implemented, however, the microprocessor uses only the first 1K of I/O addresses (hardware I/O port addresses 0 through 3FFh).

As the designs progressed through the XT, the IBM Personal Computer AT, and the PS/2 models, the same group of port addresses was retained although some usage details changed.

These addresses (memory locations) are accessible to both the microprocessor and the I/O device. Before examining how the I/O ports are used, let's look at the specific manner in which the ports are accessed.

The *IN* and *OUT* Assembly Language Instructions

The IN and OUT assembly language instructions handle the transfer of data to and from hardware ports. By using these mnemonics, you can transfer a single byte of information to or from a port address.

Because the I/O ports greatly resemble specialized memory locations, you may wonder why you cannot use the MOV instruction to transfer the appropriate information. There is a good reason: the architecture of the Intel CPU designs does not mix these two kinds of addresses—RAM and I/O port memory are kept separate. The IN and OUT instructions cause different pins of the microprocessor to be activated for the data transfer. Therefore, when the 8086/8088 microprocessor executes the instructions, it "knows" to access the specialized I/O hardware.

If the peripheral device were designed to interface through main RAM, the IN and OUT instructions would not be needed. (Several other manufacturers produce popular microprocessor chips, not used in the IBM line or its clones, that do in fact use such a "memory-mapped" approach to dealing with hardware ports; as you saw in Chapter 17, "Video Memory," even the IBM designs mix the approaches when dealing with video displays.)

How, then, do you access these individual I/O ports? If the address of the port you are accessing is less than 256, you can code the address explicitly into the instruction, as in the following example:

```
IN          AL,50               ;Get a byte from the port
```

Notice that the byte is read from the port address specified by the source operand (50) and placed in the destination operand, or AL register. All IN and OUT instructions assume that the data transfer will be between the port address and the AL register. Attempting to transfer data to a different register results in an error during the assembly process because the CPU cannot perform such a transfer to or from any other register.

Because the IBM can access directly more than 256 I/O addresses, there must be a way to access these other ports. That method is to use the DX register to specify the port address. For example, the following code facilitates writing a byte to a port with a higher address:

```
          MOV          DX,CS:Status_Port

          CLI                             ;Don't allow interrupts
          PUSH          AX                ;Store the character
Retrace:  IN            AL,DX             ;Get card status
```

You may recognize this code as a section from the listings in Chapter 17. The I/O port address, which is assumed to be larger than 255, is loaded into DX and then used (in the Retrace line) to fetch a byte from that port and place the byte into the AL register.

OUT works the same way as IN except that the data flows in the other direction; data is transferred from the source operand (AL) to the destination operand (the I/O port address). As you can see from the following examples, port addresses lower than 256 can be coded explicitly; those that are higher than 255 must be specified in the DX register:

```
OUT        50,AL
OUT        DX,AL
```

The IN and OUT statements are analogous to the MOV statement; they all transfer information. The main difference is that the MOV statement works on RAM memory, whereas the IN and OUT statements work with I/O addresses.

IN and OUT attempt to transfer information, regardless of the meaning of the port address supplied. Even if no device is using the port address, IN places a byte of information in AL, and OUT writes a byte of information from AL. The statements do not check whether a device is at the port address or whether the specified information was written successfully to a device. Because a peripheral device ordinarily uses more than one port address (perhaps one for input, one for output, one for status, and one for line control), you can check different ports to verify the success of any interfacing. (A tip: because the IBM PC data bus *pulls up* to binary 1 when no hardware is enabled, an attempt to IN data from an address that has no device connected usually returns a value of 0FFh.)

There is no standard among devices to stipulate how the interfacing will occur. For instance, the procedure for communicating with the monochrome display adapter is different from the procedure for communicating with the asynchronous communications adapter. Each adapter or device uses different combinations of ports and addresses for different purposes.

When transferring data to or from a port, remember that not all external port devices can respond fast enough to keep pace with modern processor chips; this problem will continue to grow as processor speeds increase and port hardware becomes more complicated. To safeguard against problems caused by slow port devices, always follow any IN or OUT instruction with a do-nothing JMP $+2 statement.

For a modern high-speed processor such as the 80286 or 80386, the effect of such a statement is much greater than you might think. Because RAM access is usually the limiting factor for CPU speed, these chips use a *lookahead queue*, built into the chip itself, which contains the next several bytes of program code. The chips "cheat" by reading more than one byte per memory access. This lets the CPU decode the next instruction at the same time that it is executing the present one and possibly fetching the second, third, or fourth into the queue.

Clearly, execution of any JMP instruction makes all the data in the queue meaningless; because the next instruction has to come from somewhere else, the CPU flushes out and ignores everything in the lookahead area. It does so even if "somewhere else" is the exact same memory location from which the queue was loaded, as it is for JMP $+2. Thus, in addition to the time it takes to perform the JMP itself, this instruction slows down the CPU by the time required to reload the queue.

Buying a high-speed CPU and then deliberately slowing it down by such coding tricks may seem wasteful. Keep in mind, however, that you need to do this only for the relatively few statements that move data to or from a hardware port. And if you are *certain* that the port can respond rapidly enough (as was the case with the video routines in Chapter 17) you need not do it at all. As a general rule, however, it's the best policy to follow.

The I/O Port Map

IBM has defined some of the I/O port addresses for specific I/O purposes. The first 256 I/O ports (0-FFh) are reserved for use by the system board. Peripheral devices that control such areas as memory refresh, timers, interrupt controllers, and coprocessor utilization are linked to the main system at these ports.

The remaining I/O ports (100h-3FFh) are used for other general-purpose I/O, with some areas set aside for specialized usage. Table 18.1 details the currently defined hardware I/O addresses.

Table 18.1. Hardware I/O port addresses and their usage.

I/O Port Range	Use/Purpose
0-0Fh	8237—A direct memory-access (DMA) controller
10h	Manufacturing test point (10h-1Fh are additional DMA controllers in PS/2)
20h-23h	8259 interrupt controller (controller 1 in AT and PS/2)
30h-3Fh	8259 interrupt controller 1 in AT
40h-43h	8253 timer (AT uses 8254, PS/2 uses 40h, 42h-44h, and 47h)
50h-5Fh	8253 timer (AT uses 8254)
60h-6Fh	8255 programmable peripheral interface on PC and XT, 8042 keyboard interface on AT and PS/2
70h-71h	Real-time clock and NMI mask on AT and PS/2

I/O Port Range	Use/Purpose
80h-8Fh	DMA page registers (all models)
90h-97h	DMA page registers (PC, XT, and AT) I/O channel (PS/2)
A0h-AFh	Nonmaskable interrupt registers (PC and XT); 8259 interrupt controller 2 (AT and PS/2)
B0h-BFh	8259 interrupt controller 2 (AT only)
C0h-DFh	8237 DMA controller 2 (AT and PS/2)
E0h-EFh	Reserved for system use
F0h-FFh	Numeric coprocessor usage
100h-1EFh	AT I/O channel, PS/2 uses 100-107 for programmable option select registers
1F0h-1F8h	AT fixed disk interface
200h-20Fh	Game controller (PC, XT, and AT only)
210h-217h	Expansion unit (PC and XT only)
220h-26Fh	Reserved (available for I/O on AT)
278h-27Fh	LPT2: (PC, XT, and AT); LPT3: (PS/2)
280h-2AFh	Reserved (available for I/O on AT)
2B0h-2DFh	Alternate EGA (PC, XT, and AT only)
2E0h-2E3h	GPIB 0 (AT only)
2E8h-2EFh	COM4:
2F0h-2F7h	Reserved
2F8h-2FFh	COM2:
300h-31Fh	Prototype cards (PC, XT, and AT only)
320h-32Fh	XT fixed disk interface
360h-377h	AT network (low address)
378h-37Fh	LPT2: (not on video card; PC, XT, and AT)
380h-38Ch	SDLC/secondary bi-sync interface (PC, XT, and AT)
390h-39Fh	AT cluster adapter
3A0h-3A9h	Primary bi-sync interface (PC, XT, and AT)
3B0h-3BBh	Monochrome display or PS/2 video
3BCh-3BFh	LPT1: (on video card)
3C0h-3CFh	EGA display control or PS/2 video
3D0h-3DFh	Color/graphics display or PS/2 video
3E8h-3EFh	COM3:
3F0h-3F7h	Floppy disk controller
3F8h-3FFh	COM1:

Areas not shown as defined or in use in table 18.1 are available for other I/O devices. Some third-party interface devices may use other I/O addresses that are not shown. Port addresses below 256 (FFh) are reserved for exclusive use by the system board, however.

Because there is no real standard for communicating with external devices, and because such interfacing varies according to the type of device, the use of most I/O ports is not well documented in the IBM literature. In some cases, specialized books or manuals from either Intel or the specific peripheral manufacturer may contain relevant information. In the next few sections, I give you a brief look at some specific ports.

Some Significant Hardware Ports

Several hardware-port addresses are significant to assembly language programmers—those for the ports most often accessed through assembly language programs.

Some hardware ports are used predominantly by the internal workings of BIOS and DOS routines (see Chapters 20 and 21). Other ports are available for different interface devices. Although the exact way in which all these ports may interact with your program is beyond the scope of this book, a quick look at some of the hardware-port addresses may be helpful.

The 8259 Interrupt Controller

The computer uses the 8259 programmable interrupt controller to control interrupts. The interrupt controller handles as many as eight interrupts, according to their priority sequence, presenting them to the microprocessor in prioritized order.

As you can see from table 18.1, the 8259 interrupt controller uses four port addresses (20h through 23h). Although IBM documentation indicates that these four port addresses are reserved for the 8259, only the two lower ports (20h and 21h) are documented as usable by programmers. The other two ports (22h and 23h) are used only when reprogramming the 8259 for special dedicated systems that operate in modes not compatible with normal IBM PC operation.

I/O address 20h is referred to as the *8259 command port* because it is used to send commands to the 8259. Programmers most commonly use this port with *interrupt handlers*—assembly language routines that control how the computer will react when presented with a system interrupt. Before issuing an IRET, the programmer is responsible for informing the system that it can process other interrupts. To do so, a 20h is sent to I/O address 20h in the following manner:

```
MOV      AL,20h                  ;Signal other interrupts OK
OUT      20h,AL
```

Port 21h is the interrupt-mask register for the 8259. Specific interrupts can be either enabled or disabled, depending on the settings of the bits in this register. Table 18.2 lists the meaning of the bits at the port.

Table 18.2. Meaning of 8259 interrupt-mask register bits for I/O port 21h.

Bits 76543210	Meaning
0	IRQ 7 (parallel printer) interrupt enabled
1	IRQ 7 (parallel printer) interrupt disabled
0	IRQ 6 (floppy disk controller) interrupt enabled
1	IRQ 6 (floppy disk controller) interrupt disabled
0	IRQ 5 (XT fixed disk controller) interrupt enabled
1	IRQ 5 (XT fixed disk controller) interrupt disabled
0	IRQ 4 (COM1:) interrupt enabled
1	IRQ 4 (COM1:) interrupt disabled
0	IRQ 3 (COM2:) interrupt enabled
1	IRQ 3 (COM2:) interrupt disabled
0	IRQ 2 Reserved interrupt enabled
1	IRQ 2 Reserved interrupt disabled
0	IRQ 1 (keyboard) interrupt enabled
1	IRQ 1 (keyboard) interrupt disabled
0	IRQ 0 (system timer) interrupt enabled
1	IRQ 0 (system timer) interrupt disabled

The 8253 Timer

The IBM PC family of microcomputers uses an 8253 timer chip to control certain system functions. This chip, which operates at a frequency of 1.19318 MHz, provides for three independent timer channels and six separate operation modes.

The 8253 is interfaced through I/O port addresses 40h through 43h. Port 40h is used for timer channel 0 I/O, port 41h for timer channel 1 I/O, and port 42h for timer channel 2 I/O. Port 43h is used for mode control (see table 18.3).

Table 18.3. *Meaning of 8253 mode-control bits for I/O port 43b.*

Bits 76543210	Meaning
00	Channel 0
01	Channel 1
10	Channel 2
00	Latch present counter value
01	Read/write only MSB
10	Read/write only LSB
11	Read/write LSB followed by MSB
000	Operation mode 0
001	Operation mode 1
010	Operation mode 2
011	Operation mode 3
100	Operation mode 4
101	Operation mode 5
0	Binary counter operation
1	BCD counter operation

The 8253's three timer channels are used for different purposes in the computer. Each channel has an associated divisor (one word long) that indicates how often the channel generates an interrupt. This divisor may range from 1 to 65,536. A divisor of 0 is equivalent to 65,536. To derive the channel interrupt frequency, you divide 1,193,180 (the chip operating frequency) by the divisor.

Channel 0, which is used for the system timer, uses a divisor of 0. The resulting interrupt (INT 8, IRQ0) frequency of 1,193,180/65,536 is approximately 18.2065 times per second, or once every 54.9 milliseconds. This channel is used to update the BIOS clock counter and the controls that turn off the floppy disk drive motor. This channel operates in mode 3, which signifies that the timer generates a square wave.

Channel 1 is used for DMA memory-refresh operations. It uses a divisor of 18, resulting in a frequency of 1,193,180/18, or approximately 66,287.7778 times per second. This is equivalent to a DMA interrupt being generated approximately once every 15.086 microseconds. Operation of this channel is in mode 2, which signifies that a pulse is generated once every period.

Channel 2, which is available for general use, is used most often with the speaker port. A specific example of this type of use is covered in the following section.

The 8255A Programmable Peripheral Interface (PPI)

The 8255A programmable peripheral interface (PPI) is used to control the keyboard, the speaker, and the configuration switches. Four port addresses, 60h through 63h, (or more, depending on the computer) are associated with this device.

Because the use of each of these port addresses varies by computer, be sure to check your computer's technical documentation if you plan to program the addresses directly. This section provides some general information and direction but should not be accepted as "the gospel truth."

I/O port 60h is used for keyboard input and (on some versions of the IBM) for reading the configuration switches from the system board. If port 60h is used for reading the configuration switches, bit 7 of I/O port 61h should be set. If this bit is cleared, port 60h is used strictly for keyboard input. This port and port 61h are used in the examples shown later in this section.

I/O port 61h is used for configuration information for various devices, most notably the keyboard. Table 18.4 lists the meaning of the bit settings for this port.

Table 18.4. *Meaning of I/O port 61h bit settings.*

Bits 76543210	Meaning
0	Keyboard enabled
1	PC—Read configuration switches
1	XT—Keyboard acknowledge
0	Keyboard click off
1	Keyboard click on
0	Parity errors from expansion ports enabled
1	Parity errors from expansion ports disabled
0	RAM parity errors enabled (used for speed control on some Turbo clones)
1	RAM parity errors disabled (used for speed control on some Turbo clones)
0	PC—Cassette motor on (used for speed control on some Turbo clones)
1	PC—Cassette motor off (used for speed control on some Turbo clones)
0	XT—Read high nibble, configuration switches, port 62h
1	XT—Read low nibble, configuration switches, port 62h
0	PC—Read spare switches, port 62h
1	PC—Read RAM size switches, port 62h
x	XT—Unused
0	Speaker off
1	Speaker on
0	Direct speaker control through bit 1
1	Speaker control through 8253 timer (channel 2)

You use I/O port 62h to input a variety of system information (see table 18.5).

Table 18.5. *Meaning of I/O port 62h bit settings.*

Bits 76543210	Meaning
1	RAM parity error
1	Expansion slot error
?	8253 timer channel 2 output
?	PC—Cassette data input
x	XT—Unused
????	PC—Input according to bit 2, port 61h
????	XT—Input according to bit 3, port 61h

I/O port 63h is used as a mode-control register to control the other three I/O ports for this device. Table 18.6 details the individual bit settings and their meaning.

Table 18.6. *Meaning of I/O port 63h bit settings.*

Bits 76543210	Meaning
0	Port active
1	Port inactive
00	Port 60h mode 0
01	Port 60h mode 1
10	Port 60h mode 2
0	Port 60h used for output
1	Port 60h used for input
0	Port 62h, bits 7-4 used for output
1	Port 62h, bits 7-4 used for input
0	Port 61h mode 0
1	Port 61h mode 1
0	Port 61h used for output
1	Port 61h used for input
0	Port 62h, bits 3-0 used for output
1	Port 62h, bits 3-0 used for input

I/O port 64h is used as a status port for the keyboard on the IBM Personal Computer AT, as you will learn in the following section.

Controlling the Keyboard

Controlling hardware devices directly (through I/O ports) is possible. Because the process generally entails more work than most programmers choose to tackle, programmers usually elect to use either BIOS or DOS functions to control standard devices (see Chapters 20 and 21). Nevertheless, you should be aware that direct control of hardware devices is possible. Some programmers may even need to use direct-control programming for specific applications.

This section includes an example of such programming—a program that directly controls the keyboard. I chose this particular device because not every reader may have a speaker or a video monitor, but you're sure to be able to get your hands on a keyboard.

The following sample program reads the information presented by the keyboard and then outputs the information as a decimal scan code (originally contained in the AL register).

Although this particular example is written as a stand-alone assembly language program, you can convert and modify it easily if you want to run it as a subroutine of a high-level language.

```
Page 60,132
Comment |
*********************************************************************

File:      KEYHARD.ASM
Author:    Allen L. Wyatt
Date:      9/14/91

Purpose:   Intercepts and prints the value returned by the
           keyboard each time a key is pressed.  Once installed,
           the only way out of this program is to turn off
           the computer.


*********************************************************************|

CODE            SEGMENT BYTE PUBLIC 'CODE'
                ORG     100H
; -----------------------------------------------------------------
KEYHARD         PROC    FAR
```

```
                ASSUME  CS:CODE,DS:CODE
                JMP     KEY_BEGIN           ;Starts the program


KB_DATA         EQU     60h
STATUS_PORT     EQU     64h
INPT_BUF_FULL   EQU     02h
DIS_KBD         EQU     0ADh
ENA_KBD         EQU     0AEh


KEY_NORMAL      DD      0                   ;Holds the normal keyboard
                                            ;  interrupt vector address
OK_MSG          DB      'Program is installed$'


; -----------------------------------------------------------------
PNUM            PROC    NEAR
                PUSH    AX
                PUSH    BX
                PUSH    CX
                PUSH    DX

                MOV     CX,0FFFFh           ;Push our ending flag
                PUSH    CX
                MOV     CX,10               ;Always dividing by 10
DIVLP:          MOV     DX,0
                DIV     CX
                ADD     DX,30h              ;Change to ASCII character
                PUSH    DX                  ;Save remainder
                CMP     AX,0
                JA      DIVLP

NPLOOP:         POP     AX                  ;Get number back
                CMP     AX,0FFFFh           ;Is it our ending flag?
                JE      PNUM_EXIT           ;Yes, so go on our way
                CALL    PCHAR               ;Go print the character
                JMP     NPLOOP              ;Do next one

PNUM_EXIT:      POP     DX
                POP     CX
                POP     BX
                POP     AX
                RET
PNUM            ENDP

; -----------------------------------------------------------------
```

```
PCHAR           PROC    NEAR
                PUSH    AX
                PUSH    BX

                MOV     BH,0
                MOV     AH,0Eh              ;Display character
                INT     10h                ;BIOS interrupt

                POP     BX
                POP     AX
                RET
PCHAR           ENDP


; --------------------------------------------------------------
SEND_IT         PROC    NEAR
                PUSH    AX                 ;Save byte to send
                CLI                        ;Disable interrupts
SIO:            IN      AL,STATUS_PORT     ;Get keyboard status
                TEST    AL,INPT_BUF_FULL   ;Is the coding complete?
                LOOPNZ  SIO                ;No, so continue waiting
                POP     AX                 ;Retrieve byte to send
                OUT     STATUS_PORT,AL     ;Send the byte
                STI                        ;Enable interrupts
                RET
SEND_IT         ENDP


; --------------------------------------------------------------
NEW_KBD_INT:    PUSHF                      ;Save the flags
                PUSH    AX                 ;Only messing with AX

                MOV     AL,DIS_KBD
                CALL    SEND_IT            ;Go disable keyboard

                CLI                        ;Disable interrupts
GET_KB_STAT:    IN      AL,STATUS_PORT     ;Get keyboard status
                TEST    AL,INPT_BUF_FULL   ;Is the coding complete?
                LOOPNZ  GET_KB_STAT        ;No, so continue waiting
                IN      AL,KB_DATA         ;Yes, so get code
                STI                        ;Enable interrupts

                TEST    AL,80h             ;Is it an acknowledgment?
                JNZ     END_IT             ;Yes, so ignore it
```

```
                PUSH    AX                      ;Save code
                MOV     AL,'A'                  ;Print 'AL='
                CALL    PCHAR
                MOV     AL,'L'
                CALL    PCHAR
                MOV     AL,'='
                CALL    PCHAR
                POP     AX                      ;Retrieve code

                MOV     AH,0                    ;Only want AL
                CALL    PNUM                    ;Print decimal value
                MOV     AL,13                   ;Print carriage return
                CALL    PCHAR
                MOV     AL,10                   ;Print line feed
                CALL    PCHAR

END_IT:         MOV     AL,20h                  ;Signify end of interrupt
                OUT     20h,AL

                MOV     AL,ENA_KBD
                CALL    SEND_IT                 ;Go enable keyboard again

                POP     AX                      ;Restore AX register
                POPF                            ;  and the flags
                IRET

; --------------------------------------------------------------------
KEY_BEGIN:      MOV     AL,9h                   ;Get keyboard interrupt
                MOV     AH,35h
                INT     21h
                MOV     SI,OFFSET KEY_NORMAL     ;Store it here
                MOV     [SI],BX                  ;Offset address
                MOV     [SI+2],ES                ;Segment address
                MOV     AX,CS                    ;New segment address
                MOV     DS,AX
                MOV     DX,OFFSET NEW_KBD_INT    ;New offset address
                MOV     AL,9h                    ;Change keyboard vector
                MOV     AH,25h                   ;  to point to NEW_KBD_INT
                INT     21h

                MOV     DX,OFFSET OK_MSG         ;Installation complete
                MOV     AH,9                     ;Print message at DS:DX
                INT     21h
                MOV     DX,OFFSET KEY_BEGIN      ;End of resident portion
                INT     27h                      ;Terminate but stay resident
```

```
KEYHARD         ENDP
; -------------------------------------------------------------------
CODE            ENDS
                END     KEYHARD
```

After it has been entered, assembled, and executed, this program takes control of the keyboard by redirecting the keyboard interrupt vector to the new interrupt handler, NEW_KBD_INT. This handler intercepts and prints the decimal value of every keystroke; thus, every key on the keyboard returns a code, with no intervening translation by BIOS.

Because this routine prints the keyboard scan code for *every* key without exception, the only way to disable the program is to turn off the computer. This routine, although of limited value and usefulness, does give you a rudimentary way to control the keyboard.

Notice that this program directly reads and interprets signals from I/O ports 60h and 64h. Because the program was designed to work on an IBM Personal Computer AT (including 386 machines), the address values may be different if you are using a different type of computer.

Controlling the Speaker

This example, which shows how you can control the speaker directly, uses both the 8253 timer and the 8255A PPI. The Warble subroutine provides a good sound for error routines; Boop provides a gentle sound when the wrong key is pressed.

You can call these routines directly from C. To modify them so that they work with compiled BASIC or Pascal, simply change the language specification in the .MODEL declaration.

```
Page 60,132
Comment ¦
********************************************************************


File:       SOUND.ASM
Author:     Allen L. Wyatt
Date:       9/14/91

Purpose:    Provides common error sounds from C.

Format:     Warble()
            Boop()


********************************************************************¦
                                                                   ¦
```

```
                PUBLIC  Warble
                PUBLIC  Boop

                .MODEL  small, C
                .CODE


; -------------------------------------------------------------------
Warble          PROC

                IN      AL,61h              ;Save speaker port contents
                PUSH    AX

                MOV     DX,0Bh
MAIN:           PUSH    DX
                MOV     BX,477              ;1,193,180 / 2500
                CALL    Warbcom
                MOV     CX,0                ;High-order wait value
                MOV     DX,61A8h            ;Low-order wait value
                MOV     AH,86h              ;Wait service
                INT     15h

                MOV     BX,36               ;1,193,180 / 32767
                CALL    Warbcom
                MOV     CX,0                ;High-order wait value
                MOV     DX,61A8h            ;Low-order wait value
                MOV     AH,86h              ;Wait service
                INT     15h

                POP     DX
                DEC     DX
                JNZ     MAIN

                POP     AX                  ;Restore speaker port
                OUT     61h,AL              ;  contents (turn it off)

                RET
Warble          ENDP
; -------------------------------------------------------------------
Boop            PROC USES AX BX CX

                IN      AL,61h              ;Save speaker port contents
                PUSH    AX
```

```
              MOV     BX,6818              ;1,193,180 / 175
              CALL    Warbcom
              MOV     CX,03h               ;High-order wait value
              MOV     DX,0D04h             ;Low-order wait value
              MOV     AH,86h               ;Wait service
              INT     15h


              POP     AX                   ;Restore speaker port
              OUT     61h,AL               ;   contents (turn it off)


              RET
Boop          ENDP
; - - - - - - - - - - - - - - - - - - - - - - - - - - - - - - - - - - - - -
Warbcom       PROC
              MOV     AL,10110110b         ;Channel 2, write LSB/MSB,
              OUT     43h,AL               ;   operation mode 3, binary
              MOV     AX,BX                ;Send counter LSB
              OUT     42h,AL
              MOV     AL,AH                ;Send counter MSB
              OUT     42h,AL
              IN      AL,61h               ;Get 8255 port contents
              OR      AL,00000011b         ;Enable speaker and use
              OUT     61h,AL               ;   clock channel 2 for input
              RET
Warbcom       ENDP
; - - - - - - - - - - - - - - - - - - - - - - - - - - - - - - - - - - - - -


              END
```

The root of these subroutines is the procedure Warbcom, which turns on the speaker at a specific frequency, specified in BX. The procedure sets channel 2 of the 8253 timer chip (ports 42h and 43h) and then ties timer output to speaker input through the 8255 PPI (port 61h).

Unlike many other port addresses (which may change with succeeding generations of computers), the port addresses used in SOUND.ASM have been left unchanged by IBM. Because of this, the routines should work on any IBM PC or true compatible.

One part of this routine—the BIOS service used to introduce a delay in the routine—may cause problems on older versions of the PC. If some sort of delay were not present, the routine would finish so quickly that you would not be able to hear any sound at all. This delay service is only available beginning with the PC AT, however (see Chapter 20, "Accessing BIOS Services"). If you are using an older model of computer, you will have to make changes in the delay coding.

To test these routines, use the following C program:

```
/* File:      TESTSND.C
 * Author:    Allen L. Wyatt
 * Date:      9/14/91
 *
 * Purpose:   Program to test the calling of sound routines
 */


#include <stdio.h>

extern void Warble();
extern void Boop();

void main()
{ unsigned char a;
  printf ("Press any key to test Boop");
  a = getchar();
  Boop();
  printf ("Press any key to test Warble");
  a = getchar();
  Warble();
}
```

Video Controller Ports

The addresses of the video controller ports vary, depending on the adapter card you are using (see table 18.7).

Table 18.7. *Port address ranges for adapter cards.*

Adapter Card	Port Address Range
Monochrome	3B0h-3BBh
CGA	3D0h-3DCh
EGA or VGA	3B0h-3DFh

Your programs can determine which card is in use and modify their behavior accordingly. This section simply outlines some of the specific port uses—monochrome and color. (For an in-depth discussion of this process, refer to Chapter 17.)

The Monochrome Adapter

Although IBM lists the port addresses from 3B0h to 3BBh as being reserved for the monochrome adapter, the only ports used to control the monochrome display adapter are 3B4h, 3B5h, 3B8h, and 3BAh. The adapter does not use 3B0h through 3B3h, 3B6h, and 3B7h, and ports 3B9h and 3BBh are reserved.

Port 3B4h, the index register, is used to specify the register to be accessed through port 3B5h. You use the OUT instruction to output the desired register (0 through 17) to this port.

Port 3B5h, the data register, is used for communication with the adapter's internal registers. The desired register is specified through port 3B4h. Table 18.8 details the individual adapter registers.

Table 18.8. *The internal monochrome display-adapter registers.*

Register	Use/Meaning
0	Total horizontal characters
1	Total displayed horizontal characters
2	Horizontal sync position
3	Horizontal sync width
4	Total vertical rows
5	Vertical scan line adjust value
6	Total displayed vertical rows
7	Vertical sync position
8	Interlace mode
9	Maximum scan line address
10	Scan line at which cursor starts
11	Scan line at which cursor ends
12	High-byte start address
13	Low-byte start address
14	High-byte cursor address
15	Low-byte cursor address
16	Light pen (high byte)
17	Light pen (low byte)

Port 3B8h, the CRT control port, is set during power-up and should never be changed. Only three bits in the byte are significant (see table 18.9).

Table 18.9. *Bit meanings in monochrome adapter mode-control register, port 3B8h.*

Bits 76543210	Meaning
xx	Not used
0	Disable blink
1	Enable blink
x	Not used
0	Video disable
1	Video enable
xx	Not used
1	80 x 25 display mode

Port 3BAh, the CRT status port, is a read-only address. This byte has only two significant bits, with bit 0 (when clear) indicating that video is enabled. Bit 3 is set when a vertical retrace condition exists.

The Color/Graphics Adapter

IBM lists the port addresses from 3D0h to 3DFh as being reserved for the color/graphics adapter. But, as with the monochrome adapter, the color/graphics adapter uses only some of these ports; 3D4h, 3D5h, and 3D8h through 3DCh are the only ports used to control the color/graphics adapter.

Port 3D4h, the index register, is used to specify the register to be accessed through port 3D5h. The desired register (0 through 17) is output to this port.

Port 3D5h, the data register, is used for communication with the adapter's internal registers. The desired register is specified through port 3D4h.

Because both adapters use the same chip for display control, the register meanings for the color/graphics adapter are identical to those for the monochrome display adapter (refer to table 18.8).

Port 3D8h is the mode-control register. Only six bits in the byte are significant (see table 18.10).

Table 18.10. *Bit meanings in color/graphics adapter mode-control register, port 3D8h.*

Bits 76543210	Meaning
xx	Not used
0	Disable blink
1	Enable blink
0	Normal resolution
1	High resolution (640 x 200)
0	Video disabled
1	Video enabled
0	Color mode
1	Black-and-white mode
0	Alphanumeric mode
1	320 x 200 graphics mode
0	40 x 25 alphanumeric-display mode
1	80 x 25 alphanumeric-display mode

Port 3D9h, the color-select register, is used to specify the colors used in various display modes. Only the lower six bits are significant (see table 18.11).

Port 3DAh, a read-only address, is the CRT status port. This byte has only four significant bits, which are shown in table 18.12.

Port 3DBh, a strobe, is used to clear the light-pen latch; any writing to this port clears bit 1 at port 3DAh. Port 3DCh is a strobe used to preset the light-pen latch.

Table 18.11. *Bit meanings in color/graphics adapter color-select register, port 3D9h.*

Bits 76543210	Meaning
xx	Not used
1	Selects cyan/magenta/white color set
0	Selects green/red/brown color set
1	Selects intensified color set in graphics modes, or background colors in alphanumeric-display mode
1	Selects intensified border color in 40 x 25 alpha-numeric-display mode, intensified background color in 320 x 200 graphics mode, or red foreground color in 640 x 200 graphics mode
1	Selects red border color in 40 x 25 alphanumeric-display mode, red background color in 320 x 200 graphics mode, or red foreground color in 640 x 200 graphics mode
1	Selects green border color in 40 x 25 alphanumeric-display mode, green background color in 320 x 200 graphics mode, or green foreground color in 640 x 200 graphics mode
1	Selects blue border color in 40 x 25 alphanumeric-display mode, blue background color in 320 x 200 graphics mode, or blue foreground color in 640 x 200 graphics mode

Table 18.12. *Bit meanings in color/graphics adapter status register, port 3DAh.*

Bits 76543210	Meaning
xxxx	Not used
1	Vertical retrace condition
0	Light pen triggered
1	Light pen not triggered
1	Light pen trigger set
0	Video disabled
1	Video enabled

The EGA and VGA Adapters

Although IBM lists the port addresses from 3B0h to 3DFh as being reserved for the EGA and VGA adapters, only a few of the ports are actually used to control the adapters. The actual ports used will vary, depending on whether you are using the adapters in monochrome or color mode. Tables 18.13 through 18.17 show the various port addressing and meanings for this class of adapter.

Table 18.13. *The port address for EGA and VGA adapters.*

Address	Meaning
3B2h	Input status register 1 (monochrome mode)
3B4h	CRT controller address register (for monochrome mode; see table 18.14)
3B5h	CRT controller data register (for monochrome mode; see table 18.14)
3BAh	Feature control register (monochrome mode)
3C0h	Attribute address register (see table 18.15)
3C2h	Miscellaneous output register or input-status register 0
C4h	Sequencer address register (see table 18.16)
3C5h	Sequencer data register (see table 18.16)
3CAh	Graphics 2 position register
3CCh	Graphics 1 position register
3CEh	Graphics-control address register (see table 18.17)
3CFh	Graphics-control data register (see table 18.17)
3D2h	Input-status register 1 (color modes)
3D4h	CRT controller address register (for color modes; see table 18.14)
3D5h	CRT controller data register (for color modes; see table 18.14)
3DAh	Feature control register (color modes)

Table 18.14. *CRT controller data-register index settings for port 3B5h (monochrome) or port 3D5h (color). These registers are accessed by writing the index value to the CRT controller address register at 3B4h (monochrome) or 3D4h (color).*

Index	Use/Meaning
0	Total horizontal characters
1	Total displayed horizontal characters
2	Horizontal sync position
3	Horizontal sync width
4	Total vertical rows
5	Vertical scan line adjust value
6	Total displayed vertical rows
7	Controller overflow
8	Interlace control
9	Maximum scan line address
10	Scan line at which cursor starts
11	Scan line at which cursor ends
12	High-byte start address
13	Low-byte start address
14	High-byte cursor address
15	Low-byte cursor address
16	Vertical retrace start or light-pen high byte
17	Vertical retrace end or light-pen low byte
18	Vertical display enable end
19	Logical screen line width
20	Underline scan row
21	Scan line at which vertical blanking starts
22	Scan line at which vertical blanking ends
23	Mode control
24	Scrolling line compare value

Table 18.15. *Index settings for attribute-control register at port 3C0h.*

Index	Use/meaning
0-15	Color palette to use
16	Display-mode control
17	Border-color selection
18	Color-plane control
19	Horizontal-shift control

Table 18.16. *Sequencer data-register index settings for port 3C5h. These registers are accessed by writing the index value to the sequencer address register at 3C4h.*

Index	Use/Meaning
0	Reset
1	Clocking mode
2	Map mask
3	Character-map select
4	Memory mode

Table 18.17. *Graphics-control data-register index settings for port 3CFh. These registers are accessed by writing the index value to the graphics-control address register at 3CEh.*

Index	Use/Meaning
0	Set/reset
1	Enable set/reset
2	Color compare
3	Data rotate value
4	Memory plane to read
5	Mode register 1
6	Mode register 2
7	Ignore color compare
8	Bit mask for plane changes

As you can probably imagine, the overall use and programming of the EGA /VGA registers can become extremely complex. IBM produces an EGA technical reference that is worth getting if you plan on doing any register-level programming of these adapters.

Printer Ports

The line-printer interface ports vary according to the number of printer interface cards installed in the system. Normally, the three printer ports are addressed as indicated in table 18.18.

Table 18.18. *Normal printer-port addressing.*

Designation	Port Address Range
LPT1:	3BCh-3BFh
LPT2:	378h-37Fh
LPT3:	278h-27Fh

The addresses shown in table 18.18 are general guidelines, and will vary from installation to installation. For example, if instead of installing a printer interface that uses the addresses normally assigned to LPT1:, you install an interface card that uses one of the other port ranges, that card becomes known to the system as LPT1:.

The first port in each address range (3BCh, 378h, or 278h) is used to output information to the printer. The bits of information are output directly on the parallel port. Bit 0 corresponds to pin 2, bit 1 to pin 3, and so on through bit 7, which corresponds to pin 9 of the parallel connector.

Port 3BDh (or 379h, or 279h) is the printer-status register. The bits at this port indicate the status of various line signals for the parallel connector. The meaning of each bit is indicated in table 18.19.

Table 18.19. *Bit meanings for parallel-printer adapter status register, port 3BDh/379h/279h.*

Bits 76543210	Meaning
0	Printer busy
0	Acknowledged
1	Out of paper
1	On-line (printer selected)
1	Printer error
xx	Not used
1	Time out

Port 3BEh (or 37Ah, or 27Ah) is the printer-control register. The bits at this port are used to control the printer, as indicated in table 18.20.

Table 18.20. *Bit meanings for parallel-printer adapter control register, port 3BEh/37Ah/27Ah.*

Bits 76543210	Meaning
xxx	Not used
1	Enable IRQ7 interrupt for printer acknowledge
1	Printer reads output
1	Initialize printer
1	Enable auto-linefeed
1	Output data to printer (strobe)

The remaining ports (3BFh, 37Bh through 37Fh, and 27Bh through 27Fh) are not used by the parallel interface.

Asynchronous Communications Ports

The serial communications interface ports vary according to the number of asynchronous interface cards installed in the system. Ordinarily, BIOS and DOS allow no more than two communications ports to be used (see table 18.21).

Table 18.21*. Normal printer-port addressing.*

Designation	Port Address Range
COM1:	3F8h-3FFh
COM2:	2F8h-2FFh
COM3:	3E8h-3EFh
COM4:	2E8h-2EFh

Notice that table 18.21 lists the addresses for four communications ports. Although neither BIOS nor DOS supports the addresses for COM3: and COM4:, many communications devices do support four communications ports; software can be written to enable use of the two additional ports.

Because the intricacies and complexities of programming for asynchronous communications are astounding, a detailed explanation of the communications ports, their use, programming, and functions is best left for another book. The balance of this section simply details the meanings of the ports used by asynchronous communications devices.

Port 3F8h, ordinarily used to transmit and receive data, can be used also (if bit 7 of port 3FBh is set) to specify the low-order byte of the baud-rate divisor.

The baud-rate divisor is used to specify the baud rate of the communications device; the divisor is a number that, divided into the clock speed of a specific device, results in the proper number of bits-per-second for the baud rate of that device.

Port 3F9h also is used for different purposes. If bit 7 of port 3FBh is set, this port is used to specify the high-order byte of the baud-rate divisor.

Table 18.22 details several popular baud rates and their proper baud-rate divisor settings. The port addresses shown are for COM1:. Other communications ports should use the corresponding port addresses of 2F9h/2F8h, 3E9h/3E8h, or 2E9h/2E8h.

Table 18.22. *Baud-rate divisor settings for standard 1.8432 MHz clock speed.*

Baud-Rate Divisor MSB 3F9h	LSB 3F8h	Resulting Baud Rate (bps)
4	17h	110
1	80h	300
0	60h	1,200
0	30h	2,400
0	18h	4,800
0	0Ch	9,600
0	06h	19,200
0	01h	115,200 (maximum possible)

The proper procedure for setting the baud rate is to set bit 7 of port 3FBh, output the proper divisors to the appropriate ports, and then clear bit 7 of port 3FBh.

If bit 7 of port 3FBh is clear, port 3F9h serves as the interrupt-enable register. The interrupt-enable register lets you specify which communications events will generate interrupts to the microprocessor. The bit meanings for this register are indicated in table 18.23.

Table 18.23. *Bit meanings for the interrupt-enable register, port 3F9h (or 2F9h, 3E9h, or 2E9h).*

Bits 76543210	Meaning
0000	Not used, set to 0
1	Enable interrupt on modem status change
1	Enable interrupt on receive line status change
1	Enable interrupt on transmit holding register empty
1	Enable interrupt on data available

Port 3FAh is the interrupt-identification register. When the microprocessor receives an interrupt generated by the communications device, the program reads this register to determine exactly what caused the interrupt. Only the three least significant bits are meaningful (see table 18.24).

Table 18.24. *Bit meanings for the interrupt-identification register, port 3FAh (or 2FAh, 3EAh, or 2EAh).*

Bits 76543210	Meaning
00000	Not used, set to 0
11	Receive line status interrupt
10	Received data available
01	Transmit holding register empty
00	Modem status change
1	Interrupt not pending
0	Interrupt pending

Port 3FBh, the line-control register, is used to specify the format of the data transmitted and received through the communications port. Table 18.25 lists the meanings of the bit settings for this register.

Table 18.25. *Bit meanings for the line-control register, port 3FBh (or 2FBh, 3EBh, or 2EBh).*

Bits 76543210	Meaning
0	Normal access to ports 3F8h/3F9h
1	Use ports 3F8h/3F9h to specify baud-rate divisor
0	Normal operation
1	Transmit break condition (constant SPACE)
0	Parity held at value in bit 4
1	Parity operates normally
0	Odd parity
1	Even parity
0	Parity disabled
1	Parity enabled
0	1 stop bit
1	2 stop bits (1.5 if bits 0-1 are clear)
00	5-bit data length
01	6-bit data length
10	7-bit data length
11	8-bit data length

Port 3FCh, the modem-control register, is used for controlling the modem interface. The bit meanings for this register are detailed in table 18.26.

Table 18.26. *Bit meanings for the modem-control register, port 3FCh (or 2FCh, 3ECh, or 2ECh).*

Bits 76543210	Meaning
000	Not used, set to 0
0	Normal modem functioning
1	Operate in loop-back test mode
1	"User 2" bit, must be "1" for operation of 8250 interrupt signals
0	"User 1" bit, forces modem reset if "1"
0	RTS clear
1	RTS set
0	DTR clear
1	DTR set

Port 3FDh, the line-status register, is used to indicate the condition of data transfer. The meanings of the bits in this register are detailed in table 18.27.

Table 18.27. *Bit meanings for the line-status register, port 3FDh (or 2FDh, 3EDh, or 2DCh).*

Bits 76543210	Meaning
0	Not used, set to 0
0	Transmitter shift register full
1	Transmitter shift register empty
0	Transmitter holding register full
1	Transmitter holding register empty
1	Break condition detected
1	Framing error detected
1	Parity error detected
1	Overrun error detected
0	No character ready
1	Received character ready

Port 3FEh, the modem-status register, is used to reflect the state of the modem-control lines. Table 18.28 shows its bit meanings.

Table 18.28. *Bit meanings for the modem-status register, port 3FEh (or 2FEh, 3EEh, or 2DEh).*

Bits 76543210	Meaning
1	Receive line signal detected
1	Ring detected
1	DSR set
1	CTS set
1	Change in receive line signal detect state
1	Change in ring indicator state
1	Change in DSR state
1	Change in CTS state

Ordinarily, the communications device uses port 3FFh internally as a "scratch pad."

Summary

This chapter discussed the organization and use of hardware ports. Hardware ports are necessary for computers to be able to communicate with such outside devices as video monitors, keyboards, printers, mice, and so on. By writing software, you can access these hardware devices directly (through the IN and OUT mnemonic instructions).

To use hardware ports properly, you must know which ports are used by the device you want to control. Certain devices, such as the keyboard, speaker, and video monitors, use standardized hardware-port addresses that can be readily accessed and programmed through assembly language.

Such intimate control of the individual device has drawbacks, however. Future releases of DOS or future generations of computers may abandon the currently accepted standard I/O addresses in favor of a different standard. In that event, software that directly controls devices through I/O ports would have to be changed. The BIOS and DOS services in Chapters 20 and 21 insulate programmers from such vagaries of change.

19

Working with Disk Drives

Most programming tasks of any importance seem to do at least some work with disk drives. You either need to store information there, or you need to read information, or you need to format a disk.

The first two of these tasks are done most efficiently from high-level languages. Most high-level languages either have intrinsic functions or library routines to handle working with disk files. The third chore, formatting disks, cannot be done easily from high-level languages.

In this chapter you learn specifically how to format floppy disks from assembly language. These routines can then be adapted to work with your high-level languages to provide the formatting capability your programs currently may lack.

DOS Functions for Disk Access

If you refer to chapters 20 and 21, you will see that there are many disk-related BIOS and DOS functions. There are functions to handle both subdirectories and files. The functions of particular interest here, however, are the ones dealing with formatting disks. These are the BIOS functions:

❏ Interrupt 13h, service 17h

❏ Interrupt 13h, service 18h

❏ Interrupt 13h, service 5

The first function enables you to set the type of disk you want to format, the second specifies the type of media being used, and the third allows you to format a track. With a program built around these services, you can format any floppy disk you want.

Specifying the Disk or Media Type

The first task is to let BIOS know what type of disk you want to format so that it can set internal parameters that allow proper processing of the disk.

Two functions do this task: Interrupt 13/17h and Interrupt 13/18h. Many computers may not support this latter function, the most recent addition to the BIOS. Specifically, this function is used to specify the number of sectors per track in the disk you are about to format. If your computer does not fully support this function, you will have to access the disk base table directly to change the number of sectors. (The disk base table is covered in the next section.)

Most computers in use today should support Interrupt 13/17h, which enables you to set the DASD type properly. DASD is IBM-talk for *direct-access storage device* (in other words, a disk drive). The DASD type can be any of the values shown in table 19.1.

Table 19.1. *DASD types for BIOS service 13/17.*

Type	Meaning
1	360K disk in a 360K drive
2	360K disk in a 1.2M drive
3	1.2M disk in a 1.2M drive
4	720K disk in either a 720K or 1.44M drive

Notice that there is no DASD type for formatting a 1.44M disk. There is much uncertainty on this issue. Most books on the subject say that you can use DASD type 4, but it is still not clear. Because of this uncertainty, the routines in this chapter do not allow formatting of 1.44M disks.

The Disk Base Table

If your system does not support Interrupt 13/18h for setting the number of sectors per track, you will need to change the disk base table directly.

The disk base table is a set of parameters that controls the operation of a disk drive. Most of these parameters help directly govern the drive controller.

The location of the disk base table can be determined from the vector at Interrupt 1Eh. This vector points to the RAM address where the table begins. In the early days of DOS (Version 1.0), the disk base table was contained in ROM. Now, this table is constructed and vectored when you load DOS so that system changes in DOS can be reflected in the disk operation.

Table 19.2 details the makeup of the disk base table. The values in this table will differ according to the needs of your particular version of DOS or the disk drives you use in your computer.

Table 19.2. *The disk base table for controlling disk drives.*

Byte	Meaning
0	Step rate/head unload time in milliseconds
1	Head load time, DMA mode in milliseconds
2	Motor turn-off delay in clock ticks
3	Bytes/sector code
	0 = 128 bytes/sector
	1 = 256 bytes/sector
	2 = 512 bytes/sector
	3 = 1024 bytes/sector
4	Sectors per track
5	Intersector gap length for read/write operations
6	Data length (if sector length not specified)
7	Intersector gap length for formatting
8	Initial data value for newly formatted sectors
9	Head settle time in milliseconds
10	Motor start-up time in 1/8 second increments

Most of the values in the disk base table never have to be changed. Changing them is possible, however, if you want to copy-protect a disk by using some nonstandard formatting on the disk.

If you are formatting a disk and Interrupt 13/18h does not work on your machine, the value that needs to be changed is the value at byte 4. This specifies the number of sectors on a track, and is referenced by the BIOS track-formatting function, Interrupt 13/05h. Table 19.3 indicates the proper settings for this field, depending on the type of disk you are working with.

Table 19.3. Sectors per track for various disk sizes.

Capacity	Sectors/Track
360K	9
1.2M	15
720K	9
1.44M	18

Formatting a Track

Interrupt 13/05h is the BIOS function that allows you to format a track on a floppy disk. When you call this function, the registers must be set as shown in table 19.4. Notice that there is no allowance for setting a specific sector number. The function formats entire tracks only, not individual sectors in a given track.

Table 19.4. Register settings for Interrupt 13/05h.

Register	Setting
AH	5
CH	Track (0-based)
DH	Head or side number (0-based)
DL	Drive number (A=0, B=1)
ES:BX	Address of track address fields

You should note also that some BIOS vary the register settings shown in table 19.4. For instance, documentation for the BIOS from Phoenix Technologies (the primary supplier of BIOS chips for IBM clones) indicates that you can also set AL to the number of sectors on the track. Since you cannot always count on being able to set AL to the number of sectors on the track, however, you should stick with the method of using Interrupt 13/18h or modifying the disk base table.

Notice from table 19.4 that ES:BX contains the address of an area referred to as the *track address fields*, a collection of fields that indicate specific information about each sector on the track. Some of this information is written to the sector header so that the sector being formatted can subsequently be located with read, write, or verify operations.

The track address fields consist of four bytes for each sector on the track. These four bytes detail the following information in the following order:

Cylinder (track)
Head (side)
Record (sector number)
Size code

In common computerese, the *cylinder*, *head*, and *record* information are the track, side, and sector numbers, respectively. Clearly, the sector number will vary. But the track and side numbers are the same for all of the track address fields. These sector numbers do not have to be in sequential order, either; they can be interleaved to enhance disk performance or for some other special purpose. Regardless of the order denoted by this entry (the record or sector-number field) into the track address fields, the sectors are placed physically on the disk in the order indicated by the position of the address field. Although this description may sound confusing, it corresponds to physical and logical placement of sectors on the disk.

Physically, the sectors are always arranged in sequential order (for example, from 1 through 9 for a 360K DS/DD disk). Logically, however, physical sector 1 may have a sector address mark that is not 1. The following example shows two typical interleave schemes in which consecutive logical sectors are placed physically either two or five sectors apart. The logical numbers are those entered in the address fields.

Physical order	1	2	3	4	5	6	7	8	9
Logical order	1	6	2	7	3	8	4	9	5
Logical order	1	3	5	7	9	2	4	6	8

IBM microcomputers read sectors from the disk logically (by their sector address), not physically (by their placement on the disk).

The *size code* is nothing more than an indicator of the number of bytes the sector will contain. The size code may vary from 0 to 3 (see table 19.5).

Table 19.5. *Valid size codes for use in Interrupt 13/05h track address fields.*

Size Code	Bytes per Sector
0	128
1	256
2	512
3	1024

If you understand the makeup of the track address fields, you easily can compose the bytes necessary for formatting any disk. For instance, if you were formatting a 360K disk, writing the sectors in sequential order on side 0 of track 5, the bytes would appear as follows (for clarity, an extra space has been inserted between every four bytes):

5012 5022 5032 5042 5052 5062 5072 5082 5092

If you were constructing the same track address fields for an interleaved track with an interleave factor of 5, the bytes would appear as follows:

5012 5032 5052 5072 5092 5022 5042 5062 5082

Notice that if you want to format an entire disk, you must write the code to step through the disk, one track at a time. But that is not all—you must remember that DOS needs more than just tracks and sectors to be able to use a disk properly. You must also write the information for the boot sector, the FAT, and the directory.

The boot sector is used by the BIOS in case you try to boot the floppy disk. If you are creating a system disk, this code can get rather complex and is best left to the FORMAT program supplied with DOS. If you are creating a data disk, however, the boot sector is quite a bit simpler.

The FAT and the directory simply need to be set up so that DOS can track files stored on the disk.

A Formatting Routine

Now that you understand what goes into formatting a disk, it is time to give an example of the code necessary to format an entire disk. Consider the following subroutine, which is designed to be called from a C program. It correctly formats a 360K, 720K, or 1.2M disk, including writing the boot sector, FAT, and directory.

Don't let the length of this routine scare you away. Although it may be the longest subroutine presented in this book, it is not untypical of many assembly-language subroutines you may develop or encounter during your programming.

One caveat—the routine may not work on all machines. Why include it, then? Because it is instructional, showing the proper way to format diskettes according to available BIOS information. But the differences between DOS and BIOS from machine to machine, and the differences among disk drives, may mean that the routine will not work on all computers. I wrote, tested, and verified it to work on as many computers as I could get my hands on—but I could not get my hands on all machines.

If the routine does not work on your machine, and you feel inclined to let me know, I am interested. I am interested also in knowing what changes (if any) you institute to make it work. I'll even be glad to send you a copy of one of my other books if you do this. (Ahh—I love the free exchange of knowledge!)

That said, here is the routine to format a disk:

```
Page 60,132
Comment ¦
*********************************************************************


File:     DISKFMT.ASM
Author:   Allen L. Wyatt
Date:     10/25/91


Purpose:  To format a floppy disk. Designed to work with C.


Format:   int DiskFmt (unsigned DriveWtd, DType);
            DriveWtd: 0 if A:, 1 if B:
            DType: Type of disk to format, as follows:
                    1=360K in 360K drive
                    2=360K in 1.2M drive
                    3=1.2M in 1.2M drive
                    4=720K in 720K drive
                    5=720K in 1.44M drive


            Returned value is one of the following:
                    0=No error
                    1=Invalid parameter
                    2=Bad sector address mark
                    3=Write-protect error
                    4=Bad sector or sector not found
                    8=DMA overrun
                    9=DMA error
```

```
                         10=Bad CRC on disk read
                         20=Controller error
                         40=Seek failure
                         80=Timeout


*********************************************************************|

                PUBLIC   DiskFmt
                .MODEL   small, C

                .DATA
TRUE            EQU      -1
FALSE           EQU      0

BIOSflag        DB       00
CurDisk         DB       00
CurTrack        DB       00
RetryCount      DB       00

FmtType         DB       00                    ;This info is set from the
Heads           DB       00                    ;  tables immediately following
TtlTracks       DB       00
TtlSectors      DB       00
SecPerClust     DB       00
FATSectors      DB       00
DIRSectors      DB       00
FATid           DB       00

FmtMsg          DB       'Formatting track '
TrackMsg        DW       '00'
                DB       '$'

ConfigTable     DW       OFFSET D360in360      ;360K in 360K drive
                DW       OFFSET D360in120      ;360K in 1.2M drive
                DW       OFFSET D120in120      ;1.2M in 1.2M drive
                DW       OFFSET D720in720      ;720K in 720K drive
                DW       OFFSET D720in144      ;720K in 1.44M drive

D360in360       DB       01                    ;Format type
                DB       02                    ;Number of heads
                DB       40                    ;Number of tracks
                DB       09                    ;Number of sectors
                DB       02                    ;Sectors per cluster
```

```
                DB      04              ;Total FAT sectors
                DB      07              ;Root directory sectors
                DB      0FDh            ;FAT id

D360in120       DB      02              ;Format type
                DB      02              ;Number of heads
                DB      40              ;Number of tracks
                DB      09              ;Number of sectors
                DB      02              ;Sectors per cluster
                DB      04              ;Total FAT sectors
                DB      07              ;Root directory sectors
                DB      0FDh            ;FAT id

D120in120       DB      03              ;Format type
                DB      02              ;Number of heads
                DB      80              ;Number of tracks
                DB      15              ;Number of sectors
                DB      01              ;Sectors per cluster
                DB      14              ;Total FAT sectors
                DB      14              ;Root directory sectors
                DB      0F9h            ;FAT id

D720in720       DB      04              ;Format type
                DB      02              ;Number of heads
                DB      80              ;Number of tracks
                DB      09              ;Number of sectors
                DB      02              ;Sectors per cluster
                DB      06              ;Total FAT sectors
                DB      07              ;Root directory sectors
                DB      0FCh            ;FAT id

D720in144       DB      04              ;Format type
                DB      02              ;Number of heads
                DB      80              ;Number of tracks
                DB      09              ;Number of sectors
                DB      02              ;Sectors per cluster
                DB      06              ;Total FAT sectors
                DB      07              ;Root directory sectors
                DB      0FCh            ;FAT id

Recoverable     DB      00              ;Flag: TRUE=recoverable
                                        ;      FALSE=not recoverable

BadSpot         DB      00              ;Flag: TRUE=bad spots
                                        ;      FALSE=none bad
```

```
ErrorCode      DB      00                      ;Storage for error code

AddrField      DW      0000                    ;Track/side
               DB      01                      ;Sector number
               DB      02                      ;Size code=512 bytes/sector

               DW      0000                    ;Track/side
               DB      02                      ;Sector number
               DB      02                      ;Size code=512 bytes/sector

               DW      0000                    ;Track/side
               DB      03                      ;Sector number
               DB      02                      ;Size code=512 bytes/sector

               DW      0000                    ;Track/side
               DB      04                      ;Sector number
               DB      02                      ;Size code=512 bytes/sector

               DW      0000                    ;Track/side
               DB      05                      ;Sector number
               DB      02                      ;Size code=512 bytes/sector

               DW      0000                    ;Track/side
               DB      06                      ;Sector number
               DB      02                      ;Size code=512 bytes/sector

               DW      0000                    ;Track/side
               DB      07                      ;Sector number
               DB      02                      ;Size code=512 bytes/sector

               DW      0000                    ;Track/side
               DB      08                      ;Sector number
               DB      02                      ;Size code=512 bytes/sector

               DW      0000                    ;Track/side
               DB      09                      ;Sector number
               DB      02                      ;Size code=512 bytes/sector

               DW      0000                    ;Track/side
               DB      10                      ;Sector number
               DB      02                      ;Size code=512 bytes/sector

               DW      0000                    ;Track/side
```

```
                DB      11                      ;Sector number
                DB      02                      ;Size code=512 bytes/sector

                DW      0000                    ;Track/side
                DB      12                      ;Sector number
                DB      02                      ;Size code=512 bytes/sector

                DW      0000                    ;Track/side
                DB      13                      ;Sector number
                DB      02                      ;Size code=512 bytes/sector

                DW      0000                    ;Track/side
                DB      14                      ;Sector number
                DB      02                      ;Size code=512 bytes/sector

                DW      0000                    ;Track/side
                DB      15                      ;Sector number
                DB      02                      ;Size code=512 bytes/sector

; --------------------------------------------------------------
                .CODE

DiskFmt         PROC    USES ES DI SI, DriveWtd, DType:WORD
                PUSH    DS
                POP     ES

                MOV     BIOSflag,0FFh           ;Assume INT 13/18 is supported
                MOV     AX,DriveWtd
                MOV     ErrorCode,1             ;Assume bad drive passed
                CMP     AX,3                    ;Is it in range?
                JAE     Exit                    ;No, so exit with error
                MOV     CurDisk,AL              ;Store drive number
                MOV     AX,DType                ;Get the type wanted
                DEC     AX                      ;Make it zero-based
                CMP     AX,5                    ;Is it in range?
                JAE     Exit                    ;No, so exit with error
                MOV     BX,OFFSET ConfigTable   ;Point to start of table
                SHL     AX,1                    ;Multiply by 2 (table is composed of words)
                ADD     BX,AX                   ;Adjust offset into table
                MOV     SI,[BX]                 ;Put address in source register
                MOV     DI,OFFSET FmtType       ;This is where it goes
                MOV     CX,8                    ;Only need to move 8 bytes
                REP     MOVSB                   ;And move it
```

```
                MOV     CH,TtlTracks
                MOV     CL,TtlSectors
                MOV     DL,CurDisk
                MOV     AH,18h          ;Set media type for format
                INT     13h             ;BIOS services
                JNC     DF1             ;This service was supported; no error
                CMP     AH,0Ch          ;Unknown media error?
                JNE     Exit            ;No, so exit with error

; Since the INT 13/18 is not supported on this machine, must set the number of
; sectors directly in the disk base table.

                MOV     AH,35h          ;Get interrupt vector
                MOV     AL,1Eh          ;Disk base table vector
                INT     21h             ;DOS service to get vector
                ADD     BX,4            ;Offset to sectors per track
                MOV     AL,ES:[BX]      ;Get current last sector
                MOV     BIOSflag,AL     ;Store for later
                MOV     AL,TtlSectors
                MOV     BYTE PTR ES:[BX],AL ;Set for proper sectors/track
                MOV     AH,0            ;Reset drive
                MOV     DL,CurDisk
                INT     13h             ;BIOS services

DF1:            MOV     CurTrack,1      ;Start at beginning

FmtLoop:        MOV     BH,0            ;Video page 0
                MOV     AH,3            ;Read cursor position & size
                INT     10h             ;BIOS services
                MOV     DL,0            ;Set for column 0
                MOV     AH,2            ;Set cursor position
                INT     10h             ;BIOS services
                MOV     AH,0
                MOV     AL,CurTrack
                CALL    ToAsc           ;Convert to ASCII
                MOV     TrackMsg,AX     ;Store ASCII value
                MOV     DX,OFFSET FmtMsg ;Point at message to print
                MOV     AH,9            ;Output character string
                INT     21h             ;Go print the string

                CALL    FmtTrack        ;Go format the track
                CMP     ErrorCode,0     ;Was there an error?
```

```
          JNE     Exit                  ;Yes, so exit early
          INC     CurTrack              ;Set for next track
          MOV     AL,CurTrack           ;Get track just finished
          CMP     AL,TtlTracks          ;Has the end been reached
          JLE     FmtLoop

Exit:     CMP     BIOSflag,0FFh         ;Need to reset disk base table?
          JE      E1                    ;No, so continue
          MOV     AH,35h                ;Get interrupt vector
          MOV     AL,1Eh                ;Disk base table vector
          INT     21h                   ;DOS service to get vector
          ADD     BX,4                  ;Offset to sectors per track
          MOV     AL,BIOSflag           ;Get old sector value
          MOV     BYTE PTR ES:[BX],AL   ;Set for proper sectors/track

          MOV     AH,0                  ;Reset drive
          MOV     DL,CurDisk
          INT     13h                   ;BIOS services

E1:       MOV     AL,ErrorCode
          XOR     AH,AH                 ;Leave error code in AX for return
          CMP     AX,0                  ;Any error?
          JNE     E2                    ;Yes, so don't write prelim stuff

          CALL    WriteBoot             ;Go write the boot record
          CALL    WriteFAT              ;Go write the FAT
          CALL    WriteDIR              ;Go write the directory

E2:       RET
DiskFmt   ENDP


; --------------------------------------------------------------
; Handle formatting a single track
; --------------------------------------------------------------

FmtTrack  PROC    USES AX BX CX DX ES
          PUSH    DS                    ;Data and extra segments
          POP     ES                    ;  are the same

          MOV     AL,CurTrack           ;Move track number
          DEC     AL                    ;Allow for 0 offset
          MOV     AH,1                  ;Counter for heads done
```

```
FD_A:           MOV     RetryCount,3            ;Allow 3 retries/track
                MOV     CL,TtlSectors           ;Want to do all fields
                XOR     CH,CH
                MOV     BX,OFFSET AddrField     ;Starting here
FD_B:           MOV     [BX],AX
                ADD     BX,4                    ;Point at next field
                LOOP    FD_B


FD_C:           MOV     AL,FmtType
                MOV     DL,CurDisk
                MOV     AH,17h                  ;Set disk type for format
                INT     13h                     ;BIOS services
                JC      FmtError                ;If error, go handle

                MOV     ErrorCode,0             ;Assume no error on this track
                MOV     BX,OFFSET AddrField     ;Data area for formatting
                MOV     DX,AddrField            ;Set DH to head
                MOV     DL,CurDisk              ;Set for drive
                MOV     CH,CurTrack             ;Move track number
                DEC     CH                      ;Track here is 0 based
                MOV     AL,TtlSectors           ;Number of sectors
                MOV     AH,5                    ;Want to format a track
                INT     13h                     ;ROM BIOS diskette services
                JC      FmtError                ;If error, go handle

                MOV     AX,AddrField            ;Get current track/head
                DEC     AH                      ;Decrement head
                JZ      FD_A                    ;If zero, loop
                JNZ     FD_Exit                 ;If not, done with track

FmtError:       CALL    DoError
                CMP     Recoverable,TRUE        ;Was the error recoverable?
                JE      FD_C                    ;Yes, do it again
                DEC     RetryCount
                JNZ     FD_C
                MOV     BadSpot,TRUE            ;Set flag for bad spots
FD_Exit:        RET
FmtTrack        ENDP


; ----------------------------------------------------------------
; Handle errors that occur during formatting a track
; ----------------------------------------------------------------
```

```
DoError          PROC     USES DX
                 MOV      Recoverable,FALSE     ;Assume non-recoverable
                 MOV      ErrorCode,AH          ;Save error code
                 PUSH     AX                    ;Save for a moment
                 XOR      AX,AX                 ;Zero out, reset disk system
                 MOV      DL,CurDisk            ;For the disk in question
                 INT      13h                   ;ROM BIOS diskette services
                 POP      AX                    ;Get it back
                 CMP      AH,03h                ;Was it a write protect?
                 JE       RecovErr              ;Yes, go handle
                 CMP      AH,80h                ;Was it time out?
                 JNE      DE_Exit               ;No, so exit
RecovErr:        MOV      Recoverable,TRUE      ;Recoverable error

DE_Exit:         RET
DoError          ENDP


; ----------------------------------------------------------------
; Convert a binary value in AX into a two-byte ASCII number in AX
; Will handle numbers from 0 to 99
; ----------------------------------------------------------------


ToAsc            PROC     USES BX
                 MOV      BL,10
                 DIV      BL
                 ADD      AX,'00'
                 RET
ToAsc            ENDP


; ----------------------------------------------------------------
; Write the boot sector to the disk
; ----------------------------------------------------------------


WriteBoot        PROC     USES AX BX CX DX ES
                 MOV      BX,SEG BootSector     ;Point to boot sector
                 MOV      ES,BX
                 MOV      AL,SecPerClust
                 MOV      ES:SecClus,AL
                 MOV      AH,0
                 MOV      AL,DIRSectors
                 MOV      CL,16                 ;16 directory entries per sector
                 MUL      CL                    ;AX = maximum directory entries
                 MOV      ES:RDEntries,AX
                 MOV      AH,0
```

```
                    MOV     AL,TtlSectors
                    MOV     ES:SecTrack,AX
                    SHL     AL,1                    ;2 heads
                    MUL     TtlTracks               ;Now have total sectors on disk
                    MOV     ES:TSect,AX
                    MOV     AL,FATid
                    MOV     ES:MediaID,AL
                    MOV     AL,FATSectors
                    SHR     AL,1                    ;Only need sectors in one FAT
                    MOV     AH,0
                    MOV     ES:SecFAT,AX

                    MOV     AL,1                    ;Only 1 sector
                    MOV     CH,0                    ;Track 0
                    MOV     CL,1                    ;Sector 1
                    MOV     DH,0                    ;Side 0
                    MOV     DL,CurDisk              ;This disk
                    MOV     BX,0                    ;ES:0 is buffer
                    MOV     AH,3                    ;Write sector
                    INT     13h                     ;BIOS services
                    RET
WriteBoot           ENDP


; -------------------------------------------------------------
; Write the FAT to the disk
; -------------------------------------------------------------

WriteFAT            PROC    USES AX BX CX DX DI ES DS
                    MOV     AL,FATSectors
                    MOV     AH,0
                    MOV     BL,32                   ;Paragraphs per 512 bytes
                    MUL     BL                      ;AX now contains paragraphs needed
                    MOV     BX,AX
                    MOV     AH,48h                  ;Allocate memory
                    INT     21h                     ;DOS services
                    MOV     ES,AX                   ;Put in proper place
                    MOV     BL,FATid
                    MOV     CH,FATSectors           ;Clear this many words
                    MOV     CL,0
                    MOV     DI,0
                    MOV     AX,0                    ;Want to clear memory area
                    REP     STOSW                   ;Store 0s in memory
```

```
            MOV     AX,0FFFFh
            MOV     ES:[0],BL           ;Store FAT ID
            MOV     ES:[1],AX           ;Store filler
            MOV     AH,FATSectors       ;This many sectors in total FAT
            MOV     AL,0                ;AX now has pointer to start of second FAT
            MOV     DI,AX
            MOV     AX,0FFFFh
            MOV     ES:[DI],BL          ;Store FAT ID
            INC     DI
            MOV     ES:[DI],AX          ;Store filler

            MOV     AL,CurDisk          ;Write to this disk
            MOV     CH,0
            MOV     CL,FATSectors       ;This many sectors in FAT
            MOV     DH,0
            MOV     DL,1                ;Start at sector 1
            PUSH    DS
            PUSH    ES
            POP     DS                  ;Block must be at DS:BX
            MOV     BX,0
            INT     26h                 ;Absolute disk write
            POP     AX                  ;Get rid of flags
            POP     DS                  ;Get back data segment

            MOV     AH,49h              ;Release memory block
            INT     21h                 ;DOS services

            RET
WriteFAT    ENDP


; ---------------------------------------------------------------
; Write the directory to the disk
; ---------------------------------------------------------------

WriteDIR    PROC    USES AX BX CX DX DI ES DS
            MOV     AL,DIRSectors
            MOV     AH,0
            MOV     BL,32               ;Paragraphs per 512 bytes
            MUL     BL                  ;AX now contains paragraphs needed
            MOV     BX,AX
            MOV     AH,48h              ;Allocate memory
            INT     21h                 ;DOS services
            MOV     ES,AX               ;Put in proper place
            MOV     CH,DIRSectors       ;Clear this many words
```

```
            MOV     CL,0
            MOV     DI,0
            MOV     AX,0            ;Want to clear memory area
            REP     STOSW           ;Store 0s in memory

            MOV     AL,CurDisk      ;Write to this disk
            MOV     CH,0
            MOV     CL,DIRSectors   ;This many sectors in FAT
            MOV     DH,0
            MOV     DL,FATSectors   ;Allow for sectors in FAT
            INC     DL              ;Point to first sector of DIR
            PUSH    DS
            PUSH    ES
            POP     DS              ;Block must be at DS:BX
            MOV     BX,0
            INT     26h             ;Absolute disk write
            POP     AX              ;Get rid of flags
            POP     DS              ;Get back data segment

            MOV     AH,49h          ;Release memory block
            INT     21h             ;DOS services

            RET
WriteDIR    ENDP


; --------------------------------------------------------------
; The following routine is the actual code that will be written
; to disk for the boot sector.
; --------------------------------------------------------------


BSect       SEGMENT PARA PRIVATE
            ASSUME CS:BSect, DS:BSect
            ORG     0               ;Boot sector will be here

BootSector: JMP     SHORT BootCode
            NOP


; Note that the following information, between here and BootCode, is the BPB
; used by DOS. This info is compatible with DOS 5, but will also work with
; earlier DOS versions.

            DB      'UAL3E  '
            DW      512             ;Bytes per sector
```

```
SecClus      DB      00                ;Sectors per cluster
             DW      0001              ;Reserved sectors (boot sector only)
             DB      02                ;Number of FATs
RDEntries    DW      0000              ;Root directory entries
TSect        DW      0000              ;Total sectors
MediaID      DB      00                ;Media or FAT ID byte
SecFAT       DW      0000              ;Sectors per FAT
SecTrack     DW      0000              ;Sectors per track
             DW      0002              ;Heads
             DD      00000000          ;Hidden sectors
             DD      00000000          ;Huge sectors (if TSect = 0)
             DB      00                ;Drive number, if a hard disk
             DB      00                ;Reserved
             DB      29h               ;Extended boot signature
             DD      00000000          ;Volume serial number
             DB      11 DUP (' ')      ;Volume label goes here
             DB      'FAT12   '        ;File type

BootCode:    MOV     AX,7C0h           ;Standard loading place for
             MOV     DS,AX             ;   boot sector
             MOV     ES,AX


             MOV     AH,0Fh            ;Get current display mode
             INT     10h               ;BIOS services


             MOV     SI,OFFSET BootMsg
MsgLoop:     MOV     AL,[SI]           ;Get next character
             CMP     AL,0              ;End of string?
             JE      MsgDone           ;Yes, so end
             MOV     AH,0Eh            ;Write text in teletype mode
             INT     10h               ;BIOS services
             INC     SI
             JMP     SHORT MsgLoop


MsgDone:     MOV     AH,0              ;Read keyboard character
             INT     16h               ;BIOS services
             MOV     AL,13             ;Process a carriage return
             MOV     AH,0Eh
             INT     10h
             MOV     AL,10             ;Process a line feed
             MOV     AH,0Eh
             INT     10h
             INT     19h               ;Do a warm boot
```

```
BootMsg         DB      13,10,13,10
                DB      '                     This disk was formatted with a'
                DB      ' program from',13,10
                DB      '                Using Assembly Language, 3rd Edition,'
                DB      ' by Allen L. Wyatt.',13,10
                DB      13,10
                DB      '                     This is a non-system disk.  Remove'
                DB      ' this disk',13,10
                DB      '                      and press any key to reboot your'
                DB      ' system.',13,10
                DB      13,10, 39 DUP (' '), 0

                ORG     510
                DB      55h                    ;Boot sector has to end with
                DB      0AAh                   ;   these bytes, in this order

BSect           ENDS

                END
```

Most of this routine is fairly straightforward, based on the discussions earlier in this chapter.

The loop beginning with FmtLoop is used to step through the individual tracks on the disk. The coding before this loop sets up the variables needed in the rest of the program by transferring information from predefined data tables into the final data area, based on variables passed from the C program.

The real formatting, however, takes place in the subroutine FmtTrack. Here the track address fields are set up and both sides of a single track are formatted. If an error is detected during formatting, up to three retries are performed before returning to the C program with an error.

Notice the routines WriteFAT and WriteDIR, which simply request a block of memory from DOS, zero out the memory area, and write the block to disk. In the case of WriteFAT, the necessary FAT ID is written at the beginning of each copy of the FAT.

The final major routine, WriteBoot, may take some additional explanation. Its purpose is to write the boot sector from the end of the program in the BSect segment to side 0, track 0, sector 1 of the disk. This is the standard location for the boot sector.

Before the boot sector can be written to disk, however, a few variables must be filled in the BPB section of the sector. This special area is used by DOS, and many utility programs, to determine the characteristics of the disk. When your system is booting, and a disk formatted with this routine is in drive A, the programming code included in BSect is executed. An informational message is displayed and the user is prompted to press a key to reboot.

Note that this routine will not do several things. First, it will not format 1.44M disks. Second, it will not mark bad sectors in the FAT. If a bad sector or track is detected, the routine exits with an error. Finally, because of space limitations and the complexity of the proper routines, the routine will not handle critical errors. The major type of critical error that can occur during formatting is that the user leaves the drive gate open.

The Controlling Program

The formatting routine in the preceding section was designed to be called from a C program. The major purpose of this controlling program is to request input from the user, make sure that it is within bounds, and pass the request to the subroutine. The following C program does each of these things:

```c
/* File:     FMT.C
 * Author:   Allen L. Wyatt
 * Date:     10/25/91
 *
 * Purpose:  Program to format a disk
 */

#include <stdio.h>

extern short DiskFmt(short, short);

void main()
{ unsigned short DType=0, Drive, Result;
  char Disk=' ';
  char Temp;

  while (Disk!='A' && Disk!='B')
    { printf("\nDrive A or B?: ");
      Disk=(getche() & 0x5F);
    }

  printf("\n\nPlease select the type of disk to format in drive %c:\n",Disk);
  printf("   1. 360K disk in a 360K drive\n");
  printf("   2. 360K disk in a 1.2M drive\n");
  printf("   3. 1.2M disk in a 1.2M drive\n");
  printf("   4. 720K disk in a 720K drive\n");
  printf("   5. 720K disk in a 1.44M drive\n");
  printf("   6. Cancel operation and exit program\n");
```

```c
while (DType<1 || DType>6)
   { printf("\nPlease select by number: ");
     Temp = getche();
     DType = atoi(&Temp);
   }
printf("\n\n");

if (DType!=6)
   { Drive=0;
     if (Disk=='B') Drive=1;
     Result=DiskFmt(Drive,DType);
     printf("\r");
     switch (Result)
        { case 0:
             printf("Formatting complete\n");
             break;
          case 1:
             printf("Invalid request\n");
             break;
          case 2:
             printf("Bad sector address mark\n");
             break;
          case 3:
             printf("Write-protect error\n");
             break;
          case 4:
             printf("Bad sector or sector not found\n");
             break;
          case 8:
             printf("DMA overrun\n");
             break;
          case 9:
             printf("DMA error\n");
             break;
          case 10:
             printf("Bad CRC on disk read\n");
             break;
          case 20:
             printf("Controller error\n");
             break;
          case 40:
             printf("Seek failure\n");
             break;
```

```
        case 80:
           printf("Timeout\n");
           break;
        default:
           printf("Unknown error: %u\n",Result);
      }
   }
}
```

This program simply asks the user which disk to format, the one in drive A or the one in drive B, and then determines the type of disk and drive being used. Then this information is passed to the DiskFmt routine, where the real work is done.

Summary

Working with disks can sometimes be viewed as a necessary evil of programming. Most disk interaction takes place through the facilities of a high-level language. Some disk operations, such as formatting a disk, cannot be accomplished except by using assembly language routines.

This chapter has discussed, in detail, how to format disks. You saw how BIOS accomplishes this, as well as the development of a full program to illustrate the process. If you master such a complex topic as disk formatting, you have reached a major milestone in assembly language programming. You have attained a level of competency that will enable you to accomplish virtually any assembly language task.

Part IV

Reference

20

Accessing BIOS Services

B IOS (Basic Input/Output System) is the lowest software level for communicating with hardware. Because the BIOS software usually is contained in the computer's read-only memory (ROM), BIOS is often referred to as ROM-BIOS.

The BIOS contains a series of functions that are easily accessible to an outside program—such as one you may develop. These functions, which are nothing more than callable subroutines, are invoked through software interrupts. Interrupts are generated by the assembly language instruction INT, which causes the microprocessor to use an address fetched from an interrupt table in low memory as the address for this special type of subroutine.

Specifically, INT pushes the flag(s) register on the stack and then resets the interrupt and trap flags. The full return address (CS:IP) is placed on the stack and then the desired interrupt vector (address) is retrieved from the interrupt table and placed in CS:IP. Execution of the interrupt then continues until an IRET instruction is encountered, at which point the return address is popped from the stack and placed in CS:IP. The flags register is then restored from the stack, and program execution continues from the point at which the interrupt was invoked.

Notice that the number of the interrupt being invoked determines which interrupt address is fetched from the interrupt table. Thus, the full syntax for calling an interrupt is

INT *XX*

where *XX* represents the number of the appropriate interrupt.

This chapter covers the BIOS interrupt services, listing in detail the different BIOS interrupt numbers and the tasks they perform. (Chapter 21 covers the DOS interrupt services.)

As you may recall, Chapter 18 describes how to access the computer's hardware ports directly. Ordinarily, BIOS does most of this direct accessing. The concept of allowing BIOS to perform hardware interfacing, instead of performing the interfacing in your software, is readily justifiable. Although the chips that make up the computer hardware (or their related port address) may change or vary from one computer to another, the BIOS interfaces should not change. Any given BIOS function should produce identical results, regardless of which computer you're using. The way BIOS performs a task will differ, depending on the hardware. But because of the insulation provided by BIOS, this difference does not affect you, the programmer.

The universality of the BIOS applies only to the world of IBM microcomputers or close clones. Some computers that are purported to be IBM-compatible are not. And there are different levels of compatibility; some computers are hardware-compatible, some are DOS-compatible, and others are BIOS-compatible. The BIOS services listed in this chapter should work on any machine that is BIOS-compatible with the IBM.

The interface layer that BIOS introduces between the hardware and software levels has definite benefits. The primary benefit should be immediately apparent— software development time is greatly enhanced, so programmers can develop software more efficiently. Because of the BIOS, you don't have to develop a different interface for every possible hardware combination. Other benefits include the security of knowing that your software will work on a variety of hardware configurations.

The BIOS Service Categories

The services offered by BIOS can be divided into several broad categories. Generally, these categories are determined by the I/O devices supported by the BIOS functions. Some categories, however, contain BIOS functions that deal with the internal workings of the computer rather than an external peripheral.

The BIOS function categories include

❑ Video services

❑ Keyboard services

❑ Disk services

❑ Printer services

❏ Communications services

❏ Date/time services

❏ Cassette tape services

❏ System services

This section's descriptions of services apply to all IBM-compatible BIOS versions except as noted in the individual write-ups. I can't verify each and every clone design and BIOS, however; it's possible that your own system's services may vary from these descriptions. If you are using a PS/2, note that significant additions were made to the video BIOS service, and that the service originally used as a tape-cassette interface was changed extensively when the PS/2 line was introduced.

The BIOS Services

The rest of this chapter is designed as a convenient reference. Each BIOS function call is described in detail, with the following information listed:

❏ **Function name.** A name based on the BIOS function names selected and listed by IBM in various technical documentation. Where appropriate, names have been modified or expanded to more accurately reflect the true purpose of the service.

❏ **Category.** The general classification of the function.

❏ **Registers on entry.** BIOS function parameters generally are passed through registers. The expected register settings are detailed here.

❏ **Registers on return.** Knowing how registers are affected by interrupts is important for proper operation of software. Because BIOS functions frequently return values through registers, such information is detailed here. For most BIOS operations, all registers (except the AX and flags registers) remain intact.

❏ **Memory areas affected.** Some BIOS functions modify memory. Any affected memory is detailed here.

❏ **Syntax for calling.** A coding section that shows the proper method for calling the interrupt.

❏ **Description.** Details of the purpose, benefits, and special considerations of the function.

The functions are arranged in ascending numerical order. Each function can be identified by the primary interrupt number and a service number. (Each service number is specified by the contents of the AH register.) In this notation scheme, any BIOS service can be denoted by a hexadecimal number pair, *II/SS*, in which *II* is the interrupt number and *SS* is the service number. For example, the service used to set video mode, service 10/0, has an interrupt number of 10h, and a service number (specified through AH) of 0.

Print Screen (Interrupt 5)

Category: Printer services

Registers on Entry: Not significant

Registers on Return: Unchanged

Memory Affected: None

Syntax:

```
INT     5h          ;BIOS print screen interrupt
```

Description: To invoke this BIOS interrupt, press PrtSc (to access PrtSc, you may need to press the Shift key). The interrupt causes the ASCII contents of the video screen to be sent to the printer.

Because most programs do not need a verbatim copy of the screen being sent to the printer, this interrupt normally is not called by a user program. However, the interrupt is designed for this type of use, and there is no problem in calling it from software control. The effect is the same as if the user had pressed the PrtSc key.

By changing the vector for this interrupt, you can create a custom version of the print-screen service or disable it completely. For information on changing an interrupt vector, see DOS service 21/25 (Chapter 21).

When you call this interrupt, the contents of the registers are not significant; they remain unchanged on return. This routine does not change the position of the video cursor.

The status of this operation, which is contained in the single byte at memory address 50:0, is 1 while printing is in progress. The status is 0 if the print operation was successful, and 0FFH if an error occurred during the last print-screen operation.

Set Video Mode (Interrupt 10h, service 0)

Category: Video services

Registers on Entry:

AH: 0
AL: Desired video mode

Registers on Return: Unchanged

Memory Affected: Ordinarily, the video memory area for the desired mode is cleared unless the high-order bit of AL is set and an Enhanced Graphics Adapter card is in use.

Syntax:

```
MOV     AH,0            ;Specify service 0
MOV     AL,3            ;80x25 color, TEXT (CGA display adapter)
INT     10h             ;BIOS video interrupt
```

Description: This service is used to set a specific video mode. The acceptable modes will vary, depending on the type of display adapter installed in the computer. Table 20.1 shows the possible settings for video modes.

Normally, setting the video mode causes the video buffer to be cleared. If you are using an EGA or VGA card, however, you can add the value 128 to any video-mode value to indicate that the video-display memory should not be cleared. Adding 128 is equivalent to setting the high-order bit of AL.

As new types of display adapters become available, the list of video modes listed in table 20.1 probably will change or grow. Depending on the amount of RAM available to the display adapter, the colors available with the EGA or VGA card in the different video modes will vary.

If you use a mode that is not supported by the display adapter you are using, the results can be unpredictable, although the usual result is that no characters are displayed.

Table 20.1. *Video mode settings for BIOS service 10/0.*

Mode Number	Mode Type	Display Adapter	Pixel Resolution	Characters	Colors
0	Text	CGA	320 x 200	40 x 25	16(gray)
		EGA	320 x 350	40 x 25	16(gray)
		MCGA	320 x 400	40 x 25	16
		VGA	360 x 400	40 x 25	16
1	Text	CGA	320 x 200	40 x 25	16
		EGA	320 x 350	40 x 25	16/64
		MCGA	320 x 400	40 x 25	16
		VGA	360 x 400	40 x 25	16
2	Text	CGA	640 x 200	80 x 25	16(gray)
		EGA	640 x 350	80 x 25	16(gray)
		MCGA	640 x 400	80 x 25	16
		VGA	720 x 400	80 x 25	16
3	Text	CGA	640 x 200	80 x 25	16
		EGA	640 x 350	80 x 25	16/64
		MCGA	640 x 400	80 x 25	16
		VGA	720 x 400	80 x 25	16
4	Graph	CGA/EGA/ MCGA/VGA	320 x 200	40 x 25	4
5	Graph	CGA/EGA/	320 x 200	40 x 25	4(gray)
		MCGA/VGA	320 x 200	40 x 25	4
6	Graph	CGA/EGA/ MCGA/VGA	640 x 200	80 x 25	2
7	Text	MDA/EGA	720 x 350	80 x 25	Mono
		VGA	720 x 400	80 x 25	Mono
8	Graph	PCjr	160 x 200	20 x 25	16
9	Graph	PCjr	320 x 200	40 x 25	16
10	Graph	PCjr	640 x 200	80 x 25	4
13	Graph	CGA/EGA/VGA	320 x 200	40 x 25	16
14	Graph	CGA/EGA/VGA	640 x 200	80 x 25	16
15	Graph	EGA/VGA	640 x 350	80 x 25	Mono
16	Graph	EGA/VGA	640 x 350	80 x 25	16
17	Graph	MCGA/VGA	640 x 480	80 x 30	2
18	Graph	VGA	640 x 480	80 x 30	16
19	Graph	MCGA/VGA	320 x 200	40 x 25	256

Set Cursor Size (Interrupt 10h, service 1)

Category: Video services

Registers on Entry:

AH: 1
CH: Beginning scan line of cursor
CL: Ending scan line of cursor

Registers on Return: Unchanged

Memory Affected: None

Syntax:

```
MOV    AH,1              ;Specify service 1
MOV    CH,0              ;Start on scan line 0
MOV    CL,7              ;End on scan line 7
INT    10h              ;BIOS video interrupt
```

Description: Depending on the type of display adapter used, the number of scan lines used by a text character can vary. The MDA and EGA adapters use characters 14 pixels high. The CGA uses a character box 8 pixels high. Each of these pixels corresponds to a *scan line* (the horizontal path traced by the electron beam that paints a character on the video monitor).

This service allows you to specify where in the character box the cursor should start and end. These positions, which are the beginning and ending scan lines, can vary from 0 to 7 lines (for the CGA) or from 0 to 13 lines (for the MDA and EGA). Within the valid numeric range, you can specify any combination of beginning and ending scan lines. If the beginning scan line is greater than the ending scan line, the cursor will wrap around the bottom of the character box, resulting in an apparent two-part cursor. A normal cursor occupies only the bottom one or two scan lines in the character box.

With the MCGA and VGA cards, this service operates a bit differently than with EGA, CGA, or MDA. You usually can treat these cards as you treat the EGA, provided that you are using the normal 80 x 25 text screens; if you change display sizes, however, you must also change cursor sizes, using the character height in pixels (stored in the BIOS RAM area at address 0:0485h, or returned by service 11) to determine the ending stop line. The start value can be the same (for a single-line cursor) or 0 (for a block).

Set Cursor Position (Interrupt 10h, service 2)

Category: Video services

Registers on Entry:

AH: 2
BH: Video page number
DH: Cursor row
DL: Cursor column

Registers on Return: Unchanged

Memory Affected: None

Syntax:

```
MOV     AH,2                ;Specify service 2
MOV     DH,0                ;Place cursor at top left
MOV     DL,0                ;  corner of screen (0,0)
MOV     BH,0                ;Primary text page
INT     10h                 ;BIOS video interrupt
```

Description: This service, which sets the position of the video cursor, is based on a screen-coordinate system. Generally, the cursor row, stored in DH, can vary from 0 to 24. The cursor column, stored in DL, normally varies from 0 to 79. The exact range of positions depends on the type of display adapter you are using and the current video mode, however.

If you are using graphics mode, the video page number stored in BH should be set for 0. In text modes, which can accommodate more than one video page, the number usually varies from 0 to 3. If you are operating in 40-column mode, the video page number can vary from 0 to 7. The cursor position for each video page is independent of the other pages.

Read Cursor Position and Size (Interrupt 10h, service 3)

Category: Video services

Registers on Entry:

AH: 3
BH: Video page number

Registers on Return:

BH: Video page number
CH: Beginning scan line of cursor
CL: Ending scan line of cursor
DH: Cursor row
DL: Cursor column

Memory Affected: None

Syntax:

```
MOV     AH,3                ;Specify service 3
MOV     BH,0                ;Primary text page
INT     10h                 ;BIOS video interrupt
MOV     CUR_SIZE,CX         ;Save current cursor size
MOV     CUR_POSITION,DX     ;Save current position
```

Description: Use this service to determine the cursor's current status. Be sure to save the values so that, after manipulation, the program can restore the cursor condition.

If you are using graphics mode, the video page number stored in BH should be set for 0. In text modes, which can accommodate more than one video page, the video page number usually varies from 0 to 3. If you are operating in 40-column mode, the video page can vary from 0 to 7. The cursor position for each video page is independent of the other pages.

In this service (which is the opposite of services 10/1 and 10/2) the cursor size and position for a desired video page number are returned in CX and DX.

Ordinarily, the scan lines returned in CH and CL will vary from 0 to 7 (for the CGA adapter) or from 0 to 13 (for the MDA and EGA adapters). For additional information on scan-line designations, refer to service 10/1.

The cursor row returned in DH normally varies from 0 to 24, and the cursor column returned in DL varies either from 0 to 39 or from 0 to 79, depending on which video mode currently is set.

Read Light Pen Position (Interrupt 10h, service 4)

Category: Video services

Registers on Entry:

AH: 4

Registers on Return:

AH: Light pen trigger status
BX: Pixel column
CX: Raster line (pixel row)
DH: Light pen row
DL: Light pen column

Memory Affected: None

Syntax:

```
MOV     AH,4                ;Specify service 4
INT     10h                 ;BIOS video interrupt
```

Description: If you have a light pen attached to your computer, this service allows you to determine the status of the light pen. Even though the hardware for using a light pen exists on the MDA, its use effectively is defeated by the long retention time of the phosphor used in monochrome monitors.

On return from this interrupt, you should check the value in AH. If the value is 0, the light pen has not been triggered. Because the other values will be meaningless, do not attempt further analysis and action based on the light pen's status.

If the value in AH is 1, the light pen has been triggered and two sets of coordinates (pixel and text) are returned. The video mode you are using determines which set of coordinates you should use: the pixel coordinates are appropriate for graphics screens; the text coordinates, for text screens.

The register pair CX:BX contains the set of pixel coordinates. CX is the *raster line*, or vertical pixel position, which varies from 0 to 199 or, for some EGA modes, from 0 to 349. BX (the horizontal pixel position) can vary from 0 to 319 or from 0 to 639, depending on the resolution of the video adapter used in the computer.

The accuracy of the pixel coordinates returned by this BIOS service varies. Because the vertical (raster line) coordinate is always a multiple of 2, only even lines are returned, even if an odd-number line triggered the pen. Similarly, if the video mode currently allows for a horizontal resolution of 320 pixels, the horizontal coordinate returned is a multiple of 2. If the horizontal resolution is 640 pixels, the horizontal coordinate is a multiple of 4. Thus, this BIOS function precludes use of a light pen for precise graphics work.

If you are working in text mode, you will want to use the other set of light-pen coordinates: the row (DH) and column (DL) coordinates. The row coordinate normally varies from 0 to 24; the column coordinate varies either from 0 to 39, or from 0 to 80, depending on the video adapter. The coordinate for the upper left corner of the display area is 0,0.

Select Active Display Page (Interrupt 10h, service 5)

Category: Video services

Registers on Entry:

AH: 5
AL: Desired display page

Registers on Return: Unchanged

Memory Affected: This service determines which area of video memory is displayed.

Syntax:

```
MOV    AH,5              ;Specify service 5
MOV    AL,1              ;Want page 1 video
INT    10h               ;BIOS video interrupt
```

Description: Depending on the current display mode and the video adapter you are using, you can use multiple, independent display pages. This BIOS service allows you to specify which video page is to be active, or displayed.

The desired display page is specified in AL. This value will vary within a range determined by the current display mode and the type of adapter you are using (see table 20.2). The video-mode numbers indicated in table 20.2 correlate directly to those shown in table 20.1.

Table 20.2. *Video display pages for various display modes and video adapters.*

Mode Number	Display Adapter	Page Range
0	All	0-7
1	All	0-7
2	CGA	0-3
	EGA/MCGA/VGA	0-7
3	CGA	0-3
	EGA/MCGA/VGA	0-7
7	MDA	0
	CGA/EGA/VGA	0-7
13	EGA/VGA	0-7
14	EGA/VGA	0-3
15	EGA/VGA	0-1
16	EGA/VGA	0-1

Notice that you can set the active display page only if you are operating in text mode. The contents of the different display pages are not modified if you switch between pages.

<hr>

Scroll Window Up (Interrupt 10h, service 6)

Category: Video services

Registers on Entry:

AH: 6
AL: Number of lines to scroll
BH: Display attribute for blank lines
CH: Row for upper left corner of window
CL: Column for upper left corner of window
DH: Row for lower right corner of window
DL: Column for lower right corner of window

Registers on Return: Unchanged

Memory Affected: This service modifies the desired video-buffer area of the active display page.

Syntax:

```
MOV     AH,6            ;Specify service 6
MOV     AL,3            ;Want to scroll 3 lines
MOV     BH,7            ;Normal white-on-black
MOV     CH,5            ;Upper left = 5,5
MOV     CL,5
MOV     DH,15           ;Lower right = 15,74
MOV     DL,74
INT     10h             ;BIOS video interrupt
```

Description: Use this service (which is the opposite of service 10/7) to selectively scroll up portions of the text screen. Only the currently active text display page is affected. The number of lines to scroll, contained in AL, is set for the desired value. If this value is set to 0, or to a value greater than the height of the specified window, the entire window area is cleared. (Using a value 1 greater than the window height will clear the window area more quickly than if you use zero, because the routine loops until AL decrements to zero regardless of its value at entry.)

CX and DX should contain the upper left and lower right coordinates for the window, respectively. The high byte of each register is the row, normally in the range of 0 to 24. The low byte is the column, normally either 0 to 39 or 0 to 79, depending on the current display mode. If the rectangle specified is inverted so that the value in CX is greater than the value in DX, the results will be unpredictable.

The information scrolled off the top of the window is lost. The blank lines scrolled on the bottom of the window consist of spaces with the character attribute specified by the byte value in BH. Table 20.3 lists the character attributes available for a CGA or EGA video adapter; other values may be available, depending on which video adapter card you use.

Table 20.3. *Character attribute byte values.*

Foreground	Background	Hex Value	Decimal Value
Black	Black	00h	0
Blue	Black	01h	1
Green	Black	02h	2
Cyan	Black	03h	3
Red	Black	04h	4
Magenta	Black	05h	5
Brown	Black	06h	6
White	Black	07h	7
Gray	Black	08h	8
Light blue	Black	09h	9
Light green	Black	0Ah	10
Light cyan	Black	0Bh	11
Light red	Black	0Ch	12
Light magenta	Black	0Dh	13
Yellow	Black	0Eh	14
Bright white	Black	0Fh	15
Black	Blue	10h	16
Blue	Blue	11h	17
Green	Blue	12h	18
Cyan	Blue	13h	19
Red	Blue	14h	20
Magenta	Blue	15h	21
Brown	Blue	16h	22
White	Blue	17h	23
Gray	Blue	18h	24

continues

Table 20.3. continued

Foreground	Background	Hex Value	Decimal Value
Light blue	Blue	19h	25
Light green	Blue	1Ah	26
Light cyan	Blue	1Bh	27
Light red	Blue	1Ch	28
Light magenta	Blue	1Dh	29
Yellow	Blue	1Eh	30
Bright white	Blue	1Fh	31
Black	Green	20h	32
Blue	Green	21h	33
Green	Green	22h	34
Cyan	Green	23h	35
Red	Green	24h	36
Magenta	Green	25h	37
Brown	Green	26h	38
White	Green	27h	39
Gray	Green	28h	40
Light blue	Green	29h	41
Light green	Green	2Ah	42
Light cyan	Green	2Bh	43
Light red	Green	2Ch	44
Light magenta	Green	2Dh	45
Yellow	Green	2Eh	46
Bright white	Green	2Fh	47
Black	Cyan	30h	48
Blue	Cyan	31h	49
Green	Cyan	32h	50
Cyan	Cyan	33h	51
Red	Cyan	34h	52
Magenta	Cyan	35h	53
Brown	Cyan	36h	54
White	Cyan	37h	55
Gray	Cyan	38h	56

Foreground	Background	Hex Value	Decimal Value
Light blue	Cyan	39h	57
Light green	Cyan	3Ah	58
Light cyan	Cyan	3Bh	59
Light red	Cyan	3Ch	60
Light magenta	Cyan	3Dh	61
Yellow	Cyan	3Eh	62
Bright white	Cyan	3Fh	63
Black	Red	40h	64
Blue	Red	41h	65
Green	Red	42h	66
Cyan	Red	43h	67
Red	Red	44h	68
Magenta	Red	45h	69
Brown	Red	46h	70
White	Red	47h	71
Gray	Red	48h	72
Light blue	Red	49h	73
Light green	Red	4Ah	74
Light cyan	Red	4Bh	75
Light red	Red	4Ch	76
Light magenta	Red	4Dh	77
Yellow	Red	4Eh	78
Bright white	Red	4Fh	79
Black	Magenta	50h	80
Blue	Magenta	51h	81
Green	Magenta	52h	82
Cyan	Magenta	53h	83
Red	Magenta	54h	84
Magenta	Magenta	55h	85
Brown	Magenta	56h	86
White	Magenta	57h	87
Gray	Magenta	58h	88
Light blue	Magenta	59h	89

continues

Table 20.3. continued

Foreground	Background	Hex Value	Decimal Value
Light green	Magenta	5Ah	90
Light cyan	Magenta	5Bh	91
Light red	Magenta	5Ch	92
Light magenta	Magenta	5Dh	93
Yellow	Magenta	5Eh	94
Bright white	Magenta	5Fh	95
Black	Brown	60h	96
Blue	Brown	61h	97
Green	Brown	62h	98
Cyan	Brown	63h	99
Red	Brown	64h	100
Magenta	Brown	65h	101
Brown	Brown	66h	102
White	Brown	67h	103
Gray	Brown	68h	104
Light blue	Brown	69h	105
Light green	Brown	6Ah	106
Light cyan	Brown	6Bh	107
Light red	Brown	6Ch	108
Light magenta	Brown	6Dh	109
Yellow	Brown	6Eh	110
Bright white	Brown	6Fh	111
Black	White	70h	112
Blue	White	71h	113
Green	White	72h	114
Cyan	White	73h	115
Red	White	74h	116
Magenta	White	75h	117
Brown	White	76h	118
White	White	77h	119
Gray	White	78h	120
Light blue	White	79h	121

Foreground	Background	Hex Value	Decimal Value
Light green	White	7Ah	122
Light cyan	White	7Bh	123
Light red	White	7Ch	124
Light magenta	White	7Dh	125
Yellow	White	7Eh	126
Bright white	White	7Fh	127

Scroll Window Down (Interrupt 10h, service 7)

Category: Video services

Registers on Entry:

AH: 7
AL: Number of lines to scroll
BH: Display attribute for blank lines
CH: Row for upper left corner of window
CL: Column for upper left corner of window
DH: Row for lower right corner of window
DL: Column for lower right corner of window

Registers on Return: Unchanged

Memory Affected: This service modifies the desired video-buffer area of the active display page.

Syntax:

```
MOV     AH,7            ;Specify service 7
MOV     AL,5            ;Want to scroll 5 lines
MOV     BH,7            ;Normal white-on-black
MOV     CH,10           ;Upper left = 10,5
MOV     CL,5
MOV     DH,20           ;Lower right = 20,74
MOV     DL,74
INT     10h             ;BIOS video interrupt
```

Description: Use this service, which is the opposite of service 10/6, to selectively scroll down portions of the text screen. Only the currently active text-display page is affected. The number of lines to scroll, contained in AL, is set for the desired value. If this value is set to 0, or to a value greater than the height of the specified window, the entire window area is cleared. (Using a value 1 greater than the window height will clear the window area more quickly than using zero, because the routine loops until AL decrements to zero, regardless of its value at entry.)

CX and DX should contain the upper left and lower right coordinates for the window, respectively. The high byte of each register is the row, normally in the range of 0 to 24. The low byte is the column, normally either 0 to 39 or 0 to 79, depending on the current display mode. If the rectangle specified is inverted so that the value in CX is greater than that in DX, the results will be unpredictable.

The information scrolled off the bottom of the window is lost, and the blank lines scrolled on the top of the window consist of spaces with the character attribute specified by the value in BH. (Some of the possible video attributes are listed in table 20.3.)

Read Character and Attribute (Interrupt 10h, service 8)

Category: Video services

Registers on Entry:

AH: 8
BH: Video page number

Registers on Return:

AH: Attribute byte
AL: ASCII character code

Memory Affected: None

Syntax:

```
; POSITION CURSOR AT DESIRED LOCATION PRIOR TO USING THIS SERVICE
; (SEE SERVICE 10/2)
MOV    AH,2              ;Specify service 2
MOV    DH,0              ;Place cursor at top left
MOV    DL,0              ;  corner of screen (0,0)
MOV    BH,0              ;Primary text page
INT    10h               ;BIOS video interrupt


; NOW USE SERVICE 10/8 TO READ THE CHARACTER/ATTRIBUTE WORD
```

```
MOV    AH,8                   ;Specify service 8
MOV    BH,0                   ;Primary text page
INT    10h                    ;BIOS video interrupt
```

Description: Because this service reads (from any display page) the character and attribute at the cursor's current position, you are not limited to the currently visible display page.

This service works in both text and graphics modes, although the character attribute has significance only in text mode. In text mode, the value returned in AH represents the character's video attribute (refer to table 20.3). In graphics mode, the color of the character is returned in AH. NULLL (ASCII 0) is returned in AL if the character at the cursor's current position (in graphics mode) does not match any valid ASCII character.

Write Character and Attribute (Interrupt 10h, service 9)

Category: Video services

Registers on Entry:

AH: 9
AL: ASCII character code
BH: Video page number
BL: Video attribute of character in AL
CX: Number of character/attribute words to display

Registers on Return: Unchanged

Memory Affected: This service modifies the desired area of the active display page's video buffer.

Syntax:

```
MOV    AH,9                   ;Specify service 9
MOV    AL,'-'                 ;Want to display a dash
MOV    BH,0                   ;Primary text page
MOV    BL,0Eh                 ;Yellow on black attribute
MOV    CX,50h                 ;Print 80 characters
INT    10h                    ;BIOS video interrupt
```

Description: This service displays a specific number of characters at the cursor's current position on any valid video page.

The character in AL is displayed with the video attribute specified in BL, which is valid only for text modes. (For a list of possible video attributes, refer to table 20.3.)

Pg. 485

In graphics modes, the color of the character (foreground) should be specified in BL. If bit 7 of BL is set to 1, then the color in BL is XORed with the background color where the character is to be displayed. If the same character (AL) is displayed at the same position with the same color (BL) and bit 7 of BL set, the character will be erased and the background will remain undisturbed.

The character displayed by this service can be displayed on any valid video page, not just on the currently visible one. By using this service and service 10/0Ah, you can create a page of text on a background (not displayed) page, and then display the entire page at once through service 10/5.

This service can be used to display any number of characters from 1 through 65,536. Setting the value in CX to 0 signifies 65,536 characters, the ultimate number of character repetitions. In text mode, if the number being displayed extends beyond the right margin, the characters progress from line to line. In graphics mode, however, no line wrap occurs; only those characters on the current line are displayed.

Even though this service displays a specified number of characters at the current cursor position, the cursor position does not advance. To subsequently change the cursor position, use service 10/2.

Write Character (Interrupt 10h, service 0Ah)

Category: Video services

Registers on Entry:

AH: 0Ah
AL: ASCII character code
BH: Video page number
BL: Color of character in AL (in graphics modes only)
CX: Number of character/attribute words to display

Registers on Return: Unchanged

Memory Affected: This service modifies the desired area of the active display page's video buffer.

Syntax:

```
MOV     AH,0Ah              ;Specify service 0Ah
MOV     AL,'*'              ;Want to display an asterisk
MOV     BH,0                ;Primary text page
MOV     CX,1                ;Print only 1 character
INT     10h                 ;BIOS video interrupt
```

Description: This service is effectively the same as service 10/9, but uses the existing video attribute values. In graphics modes, the color of the character (foreground) should be specified in BL. If bit 7 of BL is set to 1, the color in BL is XORed with the background color where the character will be displayed. If the same character (AL) is displayed at the same position with the same color (BL) and bit 7 of BL set, the character will be erased, and the background will remain undisturbed.

The character can be displayed on any valid video page (not just on the currently visible video page). Using this service and service 10/9, you can create a page of text on a background (not displayed) page, and then display the entire page at once through service 10/5.

This service can be used to display any number of characters from 1 through 65,536. Setting the value in CX to 0 signifies 65,536 characters, the ultimate number of character repetitions. In text mode, if the number being displayed extends beyond the right margin, the characters progress from line to line. In graphics mode, however, no line wrap occurs; only the characters on the current line are displayed.

Even though this service displays a specified number of characters at the current cursor position, the cursor position does not advance. To subsequently change the cursor position, use service 10/2.

Set Color Palette (Interrupt 10h, service 0Bh)

Category: Video services

Registers on Entry:

AH: 0Bh
BH: Palette ID
BL: Palette ID color value

Registers on Return: Unchanged

Memory Affected: None

Syntax:

```
MOV     AH,0Bh              ;Specify service 0Bh
MOV     BH,1                ;Setting palette
MOV     BL,0                ;Green/red/brown palette
INT     10h                 ;BIOS video interrupt
```

Description: This service, which is used primarily to set the color palette used by medium-resolution graphics services, has significance only in a few video modes, most notably mode 4. (For more information on video modes, see the service 10/0 description.)

This service does not affect the video memory; it only changes the way the 6845 CRT Controller chip on the CGA board interprets and displays pixel values already in video memory.

If BH contains 0, the value of BL is used as both the background and border colors. If BH contains a 1, the value in BL specifies which color palette to use; BL can be set to any value, but only the contents of the low bit are significant. This bit value determines one or the other of the following palettes:

Value	Palette
0	Green, red, and brown
1	Cyan, magenta, and white

Notice the colors for palette 0. The technical specifications for the CGA card and the 6845 CRT Controller show that these are the proper colors, although the system BIOS reference in the *IBM Technical Reference* manual states that the colors for this palette are green, red, and yellow.

A palette specifies the display colors to be used for various bit combinations. Changing the palette changes the screen display immediately. Rapidly using this service and alternately changing the palette can result in a flashing screen. The pixel bit determination is as follows:

Pixel Value	Palette 0 Color	Palette 1 Color
00	Background	Background
01	Green	Cyan
10	Red	Magenta
11	Brown	White

You can use this service also to set the border color in text mode. In text mode, if BH is 0, the value in BL is used as the border color.

Write Pixel Dot (Interrupt 10h, service 0Ch)

Category: Video services

Registers on Entry:

AH: 0Ch
AL: Pixel value
CX: Pixel column
DX: Raster line (pixel row)

Registers on Return: Unchanged

Memory Affected: This service modifies the desired area of the active display page's video buffer.

Syntax:

```
MOV     AH,0Ch          ;Specify service 0Ch
MOV     AL,11b          ;Pixel value to use
MOV     CX,A0h          ;Position at 100,160
MOV     DX,64h
INT     10h             ;BIOS video interrupt
```

Description: This general-purpose graphics plotting service (the opposite of service 10/0Dh) works in either medium- or high-resolution graphics modes, although the effects in each are different.

In medium-resolution graphics modes on the CGA, the contents of AL can vary from 0 to 3. The display effect of these pixel values depends on the color palette in use (see service 10/0Bh). The results of the various settings of AL are

Pixel Value	Palette 0 Color	Palette 1 Color
00	Background	Background
01	Green	Cyan
10	Red	Magenta
11	Brown	White

In high-resolution graphics modes on the CGA, the value of AL can vary between 0 and 1. These values correspond to whether the pixel is off (black) or on (white).

If the high-order bit of AL is set (1), the pixel color is XORed with the pixel's current contents. Because of the behavior of XORing values, this capability provides a quick way to display a pixel and then to erase it by again writing the same pixel value to the location. If the high-order bit of AL is set (0), the pixel value is written to the pixel location.

The register pair DX:CX contains the pixel's plotting coordinates. DX is the *raster line*, or vertical pixel position; its value can range from 0 to 199, or from 0 to 349 for some EGA video modes. The value of CX (the horizontal pixel position) can range either from 0 to 319 (medium-resolution) or from 0 to 639 (high-resolution). Coordinates are numbered from top to bottom and from left to right; 0,0 is the top left screen corner, and either 199,319 or 199,639 is the bottom right corner, depending on the resolution of the video mode. If you specify coordinates outside the legal range for the current graphics mode, the results can be unpredictable.

Read Pixel Dot (Interrupt 10h, service 0Dh)

Category: Video services

Registers on Entry:

AH: 0Dh
CX: Pixel column
DX: Raster line (pixel row)

Registers on Return:

AL: Pixel value
CX: Pixel column
DX: Raster line (pixel row)

Memory Affected: None

Syntax:

```
MOV     AH,0Dh              ;Specify service 0Dh
MOV     CX,A0h              ;Want pixel value at
MOV     DX,64h              ; coordinate 100,160
INT     10h                 ;BIOS video interrupt
```

Description: This service (the opposite of 10/0Ch) is used in either medium- or high-resolution graphics modes to determine the pixel value of the pixel at any given screen location.

The desired pixel coordinates are specified in the register pair DX:CX. DX is the *raster line*, or vertical pixel position; its value can range from 0 to 199, or from 0 to 349 for some EGA video modes. The value of CX (the horizontal pixel position) can range either from 0 to 319 (medium-resolution) or from 0 to 639 (high-resolution). Notice that this horizontal resolution is in a 16-bit register but that the other coordinate is in an 8-bit register. Coordinates are numbered from top to bottom and from left to right; 0,0 is the top left screen corner, and either 199,319, 199,639, or 349,639 is the bottom right corner, depending on the resolution of the video mode. If you specify coordinates outside the legal range for the current graphics mode, the results can be unpredictable.

The pixel value returned in AL depends on the current video mode. In medium-resolution graphics modes on the CGA, the value of AL can vary from 0 to 3. In high-resolution graphics modes on the CGA, the value of AL can vary between 0 and 1. (For more information about pixel values, see the description for service 10/0Ch.)

TTY Character Output (Interrupt 10h, service 0Eh)

Category: Video services

Registers on Entry:

AH: 0Eh
AL: ASCII character code
BH: Video page number
BL: Character color (graphics foreground)

Registers on Return: Unchanged

Memory Affected: This service modifies the desired area of the active display page's video buffer.

Syntax:

```
MOV     AH,0Eh              ;Specify service 0Eh
MOV     AL,'.'              ;Output a period
MOV     BH,0                ;Primary video page
INT     10h                 ;BIOS video interrupt
```

Description: This service is similar to service 10/9, except that the output is in *Teletype* mode (a limited amount of character processing is performed on the output). The ASCII codes for bell (07), backspace (08), linefeed (10), and carriage return (13) are all intercepted and translated to the appropriate actions. Line wrap and scrolling are performed if the printed characters exceed the right display margin or the bottom display line.

Because the ASCII value of the character to be output is loaded in AL, and the video page number is loaded in BH, this output service can be used for display pages other than the current one. By using this service and service 10/0Ah, you can create a page of text on a background (not displayed) page, and then display the entire page at once through service 10/5. If output is to a background page, the processing of the bell character (ASCII 07) will still result in the familiar "beep."

The foreground color, which is specified in BL, has significance only in graphics modes. Notice that the syntax example for this service does not specify BL. In text mode, the current video attributes for the screen location are used. With this service, you cannot specify a video attribute other than the current one.

You can use this service, which advances the cursor position, to display multiple characters in series. With this service, you do not have to set the cursor position before displaying each character.

Get Current Video State (Interrupt 10h, service 0Fh)

Category: Video services

Registers on Entry:

AH: 0Fh

Registers on Return:

AH: Screen width
AL: Display mode
BH: Active display page

Memory Affected: None

Syntax:

```
MOV     AH,0Fh              ;Specify service 0Fh
INT     10h                 ;BIOS video interrupt
MOV     COLUMNS,AH          ;Save number of columns
MOV     MODE,AL             ;Save display mode
MOV     PAGE,BH             ;Save display page
```

Description: This service, which is used to determine the computer's current video state, returns three pieces of information: the width in columns of the display screen (AH), the current video-display mode (AL), and the current video-display page (BH). Table 20.1 (service 10/0) lists possible video-mode settings.

EGA/VGA Palette Registers (Interrupt 10h, service 10h)

Category: Video services

Registers on Entry:

AH: 10h

AL: 00h, Set palette register
BH: Color value
BL: Palette register to set

AL: 01h, Set border color register
BH: Color value

AL: 02h, Set all registers and border
DX: Offset address of 17-byte color list
ES: Segment address of 17-byte color list

AL: 03h, Toggle blink/intensity (EGA only)
BL: Blink/intensity bit
      00h = Enable intensity
      01h = Enable blinking

AL: 07h, Read palette register (PS/2 only)
BL: Palette register to read (0-15)

AL: 08h, Read overscan register (PS/2 only)

AL: 09h, Read palette registers and border (PS/2 only)
DX: Offset address of 17-byte table for values
ES: Segment address of 17-byte table for values

AL: 10h, Set individual color register
BX: Color register to set
CH: Green value to set
CL: Blue value to set
DH: Red value to set

AL: 12h, Set block of color registers
BX: First color register to set
CX: Number of color registers to set
DX: Offset address of color values
ES: Segment address of color values

AL: 13h, Select color page
BL: 00h, Select paging mode
BH: Paging mode
      00h = 4 register blocks of 64 registers
      01h = 16 register blocks of 16 registers

AL: 13h, Select color page
BL: 01h, Select page
BH: Page number
　　　　　　　　00-03h = 64 register blocks
　　　　　　　　00-0Fh = 16 register blocks

AL: 15h, Read color register (PS/2 only)
BX: Color register to read

AL: 17h, Read block of color registers
BX: First color register to read
CX: Number of color registers to read
DX: Offset address of buffer to hold color values
ES: Segment address of buffer to hold color values

AL: 1Ah, Read color page state

AL: 1Bh, Sum color values to gray shades
BX: First color register to sum
CX: Number of color registers to sum

Registers on Return:

Subfunctions 07h-08h
　　　　　BH: Value read

Subfunction 09h
　　　　　DX: Offset address of 17-byte table
　　　　　ES: Segment address of 17-byte table

Subfunction 15h
　　　　　CH: Green value read
　　　　　CL: Blue value read
　　　　　DH: Red value read

Subfunction 17h
　　　　　DX: Offset address of color table
　　　　　ES: Segment address of color table

Subfunction 1Ah
　　　　　BL: Current paging mode
　　　　　CX: Current page

Memory Affected: Varies by subfunction

Syntax: Varies by subfunction

Description: On the MCGA, EGA, and VGA display systems, this function controls the correspondence of colors to pixel values. Although listed as reserved in the IBM Personal Computer AT BIOS, this function is an extension to the BIOS, applicable to EGA/VGA display systems. Some subfunctions, designated by the contents of AL when calling this function, are not available on the PS/2 Model 30 system. These include subfunctions 01h, 02h, 07h, 08h, 09h, 13h, and 1Ah.

EGA/VGA Character Generator (Interrupt 10h, service 11h)

Category: Video services

Registers on Entry:

AH:	11h
AL:	00h, User alpha load
BH:	Number of bytes per character
BL:	Block to load
CX:	Count to store
DX:	Character offset into table
BP:	Offset address of user table
ES:	Segment address of user table
AL:	01h, ROM monochrome set
BL:	Block to load
AL:	02h, ROM 8*8 double dot
BL:	Block to load
AL:	03h, Set block specifier
BL:	Character-generator block selection
AL:	10h, User alpha load
BH:	Number of bytes per character
BL:	Block to load
CX:	Count to store
DX:	Character offset into table
BP:	Offset address of user table
ES:	Segment address of user table
AL:	11h, ROM monochrome set
BL:	Block to load
AL:	12h, ROM 8*8 double dot
BL:	Block to load
AL:	20h, Set user graphics characters pointer at 1Fh
BP:	Offset address of user table
ES:	Segment address of user table

AL: 21h, Set user graphics characters pointer at 43h
BL: Row specifier
CX: Bytes per character
BP: Offset address of user table
ES: Segment address of user table

AL: 22h, ROM 8*14 set
BL: Row specifier

AL: 23h, ROM 8*8 double dot
BL: Row specifier

AL: 30h, System information
BH: Font pointer

Registers on Return: Varies by subfunction

Memory Affected: Varies by subfunction

Syntax: Varies by subfunction

Description: This service, which contains 14 subfunctions, supports the character-generator functions of the EGA, MCGA, and VGA, enabling a program to set up its own character-generator tables. The service also makes changing the number of rows displayed easy to do. Some subfunctions, designated by the contents of AL when this service is called, are not available on the PS/2 Model 30 system. These include subfunctions 01h, 10h, 11h, 12h, and 22h.

Subfunctions 11h, 12h, and 14h are particularly useful because they reprogram the CRT controller to display more than 25 rows of text. The exact number displayed varies between EGA and VGA; for a VGA, the number depends on how many scan lines were chosen (service 10/12).

Alternate Video Select (Interrupt 10h, service 12h)

Category: Video services

Registers on Entry:

AH: 12h

BL: 10h, Return EGA information

BL: 20h, Select alternate print-screen routine

BL: 30h, Select number of scan lines
AL: 00h = 200 lines
           01h = 350 lines
           02h = 400 lines

BL: 31h, Load palette when setting mode
AL: 00h = enable
        01h = disable

BL: 32h, Video on/off
AL: 00h = enable
        01h = disable

BL: 33h, Sum color to gray scale
AL: 00h = enable
        01h = disable

BL: 34h, Cursor emulation on/off
AL: 00h = enable
        01h = disable

Registers on Return:

Subfunction 10h (setting in BL):

BH: BIOS video mode (0 color/1 mono)
BL: Size of EGA RAM (0=64K to 3=256K)

In all cases, AL = 12h if service was valid.

Memory Affected: None

Syntax:

```
MOV     AX,1202h      ;Service 10/12, set 400 scan lines
MOV     BL,30h
INT     10h           ;BIOS video services interrupt
```

Description: This service and its various subfunctions are effective only for the EGA, MCGA, and VGA adapters.

Write String (Interrupt 10h, service 13h)

Category: Video services

Registers on Entry:

AH: 13h
AL: Mode
BH: Video page number
BL: Character attribute (depending on AL)
CX: Length of string
DH: Cursor row where string is to be displayed
DL: Cursor column where string is to be displayed

BP: Offset address of string
ES: Segment address of string

Registers on Return: Unchanged

Memory Affected: This service modifies the desired area of the active display page's video buffer.

Syntax:

```
MOV     BH,0                     ;Primary video page
MOV     BL,07h                   ;Normal attributes
MOV     DH,5                     ;Display string at
MOV     DL,5                     ;  coordinates 5,5
PUSH    DS                       ;Make ES same as DS
POP     ES
MOV     BP,OFFSET ES:MSG_1 ;Point to message offset
MOV     CX,10h                   ;Standard string length
MOV     AH,13h                   ;Specify service 13h
INT     10h                      ;BIOS video interrupt
```

Description: *This service is available only on PC XTs with BIOS dates of 1/10/86 or later, on the Personal Computer AT, and on machines in the PS/2 family.* Use this service, which is a logical extension of the BIOS character-display functions, to display an entire string on any video page.

The mode specified in AL determines how BIOS will treat the string to be displayed. Table 20.4 lists this service's four modes.

Table 20.4. Modes for service 10/13.

Mode	Cursor	Attribute	String Composition (C=character, A=attribute)
0	Not moved	In BL	CCCCCCC...CC
1	Moved	In BL	CCCCCCC...CC
2	Not moved	In string	CACACACA...CA
3	Moved	In string	CACACACA...CA

Notice that the display attributes can be specified either in BL or in the string, depending on the contents of AL. If you are using mode 2 or 3, the contents of BL are not significant. The mode also determines whether the cursor is moved when the string is displayed.

The string's address is specified in ES:BP. CX contains the length of the string. The service displays the string until CX reaches 0. Do not use a length of 0. If you do, 65,536 characters will be displayed, and the effects of displaying this number of characters probably will be undesirable.

Because this service makes limited use of BIOS service 10/0E, some character processing is performed on the individual string characters. The ASCII codes for bell (07), backspace (08), linefeed (10), and carriage return (13) are all intercepted and directed to service 10/0E, where they are translated to the appropriate actions. Line wrap and scrolling are performed if the printed characters exceed the right display margin or the bottom display line. If the string character is not a bell, backspace, linefeed, or carriage return, it is displayed by service 10/9.

Although this service is neither particularly fast nor efficient, it is convenient. The routines in Chapter 17, "Video Memory," result in faster displays but entail more work for the programmer. Only you can decide which to use.

Get Equipment Status (Interrupt 11h)

Category: System services

Registers on Entry: Not significant

Registers on Return:

AX: Equipment status

Memory Affected: None

Syntax:

```
INT    11h                ;Invoke BIOS interrupt
```

Description: Use this rudimentary service, which returns a minimal amount of information, to determine what equipment is attached to the computer. The equipment status word is set up during the booting process and does not change. The meaning of each bit in the returned word is shown in table 20.5.

Table 20.5. *Bit meanings for equipment status word returned by interrupt 11.*

Bits FEDCBA98	76543210	Meaning of Bits
xx		Number of printers attached
x		Not used
0		Game adapter not installed
1		Game adapter installed
xxx		Number of serial cards attached
x		Not used
	00	1 disk drive attached (if bit 0=1)
	01	2 disk drives attached (if bit 0=1)
	10	3 disk drives attached (if bit 0=1)
	11	4 disk drives attached (if bit 0=1)
	01	Initial video mode—40 x 25 BW/color card
	10	Initial video mode—80 x 25 BW/color card
	11	Initial video mode—80 x 25 BW/mono card
	00	16K system board RAM
	01	32K system board RAM
	10	48K system board RAM
	11	64K system board RAM
	1	Math coprocessor installed
	0	No disk drives installed (bits 6-7 insignificant)
	1	Disk drives installed (bits 6-7 significant)

Depending on the computer you are using, certain portions of this equipment status word may not be significant. If you are using an IBM Personal Computer AT, for example, the value of bits 2 and 3 have no meaning. These bits are relics of the days when 64K of RAM was considered as much as anyone could possibly want in a microcomputer.

You can see that the register contents on entry are not significant and that AX is the only register changed on return.

Get Memory Size (Interrupt 12h)

Category: System services

Registers on Entry: Not significant

Registers on Return:

AX: Memory blocks

Memory Affected: None

Syntax:

```
INT     12h                 ;Invoke BIOS interrupt
```

Description: Use this service to return the number of contiguous 1K blocks of memory installed in the computer. The memory size, which is determined when you power-up the computer, is returned in AX.

Notice that the number of contiguous memory blocks is returned. If the power-on self test (POST) determines that defective RAM chips are installed in the computer, the value returned by this interrupt will be equal to the number of 1K blocks counted before the defective memory area was encountered.

On entry of this interrupt, the register contents are not significant. AX is the only register changed on return.

The method used to determine available memory depends on the system, but usually consists of an attempt to read and write to a memory block. As soon as the write/read cycle fails, the end of memory is assumed to have been reached.

When there is more than 640K of memory, service 15/88 must be called to determine extended-memory size.

On PS/2 systems, this interrupt returns a maximum amount of memory of up to 640K, minus the amount of memory set aside for the extended BIOS data area (EBDA). The EBDA may be as little as 1K. (See service 15/C1 for more information.)

Reset Disk Drives (Interrupt 13h, service 0)

Category: Disk services

Registers on Entry:

AH: 0

DL: Drive number (0 based)
             bit 7 = 0 for a diskette

Registers on Return: Unchanged

Memory Affected: None

Syntax:

```
MOV     AH,0            ;Specify service 0
MOV     DL,82h          ;for drive C
INT     13h             ;BIOS disk interrupt
```

Description: Use this service to reset the disk drive controller. (The service works on the NEC series of floppy disk drive controllers that IBM specifies as standard equipment; in most implementations, it performs the same function for any hard disk drive controllers present.)

Calling this service has no apparent effect on the disk drives. The recalibrate command is sent directly to the floppy drive controller in use, and a reset flag is set to recalibrate all the drives the next time they are used. This recalibration retracts the read/write head to track 0, causing the familiar "grinding" sound often heard after a disk error. The read/write head is forced to track 0 and then must seek out the desired track.

Used primarily in routines that handle critical errors on disks, this service forces the controller to recalibrate itself on the subsequent operation. If a critical error occurs, the service is necessary for reliable disk operation; it forces the disk controller to make no assumptions about its position or condition—assumptions that may be wrong because of the critical-error condition.

Get Floppy Disk Status (Interrupt 13h, service 1)

Category: Disk services

Registers on Entry:

AH: 1
DL: Drive number (0 based)
            bit 7 = 0 for a diskette

Registers on Return:

AH: Status byte

Memory Affected: None

Syntax:

```
MOV     AH,1              ;Specify service 1
MOV     DL,82h            ;for drive C
INT     13h               ;BIOS disk interrupt
```

Description: This service returns the status of the disk drive controller. The status, which is set after each disk operation (such as reading, writing, or formatting), is returned in AH. The meaning of each bit in the returned status byte is shown in table 20.6.

Table 20.6. Meaning of the status byte returned by service 13/1.

Bits 76543210	Hex	Decimal	Meaning of Bits
1	80	128	Time out—drive did not respond
1	40	64	Seek failure—couldn't move to requested track
1	20	32	Controller malfunction
1	10	16	Bad CRC detected on disk read
1 1	9	9	DMA error—64K boundary crossed
1	8	8	DMA overrun
1	4	4	Bad sector/sector not found
11	3	3	Write protect error
1	2	2	Bad sector ID (address) mark
1	1	1	Bad command

Read Disk Sectors (Interrupt 13h, service 2)

Category: Disk services

Registers on Entry:

AH: 2
AL: Number of sectors
BX: Offset address of data buffer
CH: Track
CL: Sector

DH: Head (side) number

DL: Drive number

ES: Segment address of data buffer

Registers on Return:

AH: Return code

Memory Affected: RAM buffer area specified by address starting at ES:BX is overwritten by sectors requested from disk.

Syntax:

```
MOV     AL,1                    ;Reading 1 sector
MOV     CH,TRACK                ;Specify track
MOV     CL,SECTOR               ;  and sector
MOV     DH,SIDE                 ;Specify side
MOV     DL,DRIVE                ;Specify drive
PUSH    DS                      ;Point ES to proper
POP     ES                      ;  segment address
MOV     BX,OFFSET ES:BUFFER     ;Offset of buffer area
MOV     AH,2                    ;Specify service 2
INT     13h                     ;BIOS disk interrupt
```

Description: Use this service to control reading from the disk. This service is the opposite of service 13/3, which controls writing to the disk.

To use this service, you must specify the precise physical location on the disk at which you want to begin reading. The drive is specified in DL (A=0, B=1, C=2, etc., or bit 7 is set if the drive is a hard disk). The side, or head, is specified in DH and can be 0 or 1. CH and CL contain the track and sector, respectively. These values will vary depending on the type of disk drive in use. The number of sectors to be read is specified in AL.

The final registers to be set up specify which RAM area will be used as a buffer for the sectors that are read. This address is specified in ES:BX. You need to know the size of each disk sector ahead of time because this information determines how large the RAM buffer should be. For instance, if each disk sector contains 512 bytes, and you are going to read 4 sectors, the length of your buffer should be 2K, or 2,048 bytes.

This service checks parameters only on the requested drive number (DL); all other passed parameters are not checked for validity. If you pass invalid parameters, the results are unpredictable. Table 20.7 shows some typical parameter ranges for this service.

Table 20.7. Parameter ranges for service 13/2, using a 360K disk.

Parameter	Register	Valid Range
# of sectors	AL	1 through 9
Track	CH	0 through 39
Sector	CL	1 through 9
Head (side)	DH	0 or 1
Drive	DL	0=A, 1=B, 2=C, etc.

On return from this service, the carry flag signifies whether an error occurred. If the carry flag is not set, AH will contain a zero (0). If the carry flag is set, AH will contain the disk-status byte described under service 13/1 (refer to table 20.6). If an error occurs during reading, use service 13/0 to reset the disk system before you attempt another read.

Note: In this service and service 13/3, a particularly confusing error may occur. DMA boundary error (AH=9) means that an illegal boundary was crossed when the information was placed into RAM. Direct Memory Access (DMA) is used by the disk-service routines to place information into RAM. If a memory offset address ending in three zeros (ES:1000, ES:2000, ES:3000, etc.) falls in the middle of the area being overlaid by a sector, this error will occur. You must calculate and read a much smaller chunk so that this type of memory boundary corresponds with a sector boundary. I don't know why this happens; it simply is frustrating as heck to a programmer.

Write Disk Sectors (Interrupt 13h, service 3)

Category: Disk services

Registers on Entry:

AH:	3
AL:	Number of sectors
BX:	Offset address of data buffer
CH:	Track
CL:	Sector
DH:	Head (side) number
DL:	Drive number
ES:	Segment address of data buffer

Registers on Return:

AH: Return code

Memory Affected: None

Syntax:

```
MOV     AL,9                    ;Write entire track
MOV     CH,TRACK                ;Specify track
MOV     CL,SECTOR               ;  and sector
MOV     DH,SIDE                 ;Specify side
MOV     DL,DRIVE              ,  ;Specify drive
PUSH    DS                      ;Point ES to proper
POP     ES                      ;  segment address
MOV     BX,OFFSET ES:BUFFER     ;Offset of buffer area
MOV     AH,3                    ;Specify service 3
INT     13h                     ;BIOS disk interrupt
```

Description: This service, which controls writing to the disk, is the opposite of service 13/2, which controls reading from the disk.

To use this service, you must specify (in ES:BX) which RAM area will be used as the buffer for the sectors written. This buffer area must contain all the information you want written to the disk. You must know the size of the sectors being written on the disk because this service calculates, based on the sector size and the number of sectors to write (AH), the amount of RAM to read and subsequently write. The preceding example requires a buffer of 4,068 bytes (4.5K), assuming that each sector requires 512 bytes.

By setting up the other registers, you determine the precise physical location on the disk at which you wish to begin writing. The drive is specified in DL (A=0, B=1, C=2, etc., or bit 7 is set if the drive is a hard disk). The side, or head, is specified in DH, which can be 0 or 1. CH and CL contain the track and sector, respectively. (These values will vary, depending on the type of disk drive in use.) In AL, specify the number of sectors to be written.

This service checks parameters only on the requested drive number (DL); all other passed parameters are not checked for validity. If you pass invalid parameters, the results are unpredictable and may result in errors or damaged disks. (Some typical parameter ranges for this service are listed in table 20.7.)

On return from this service, the carry flag signifies whether an error occurred. If the carry flag is not set, AH contains a zero (0). If the carry flag is set, AH contains the disk status byte as detailed in service 13/1 (refer to table 20.6). If an error occurs during the writing operation, use service 13/0 to reset the disk system before you attempt another write operation.

Note: In this service and service 13/2, a particularly confusing error may occur. `DMA boundary error (AH=9)` means that an illegal boundary was crossed when the information was placed into RAM. Direct Memory Access (DMA) is used by the disk-service routines to place information into RAM. This error will occur if a memory offset address ending in three zeros (ES:1000, ES:2000, ES:3000, etc.) is crossed before this service completes reading an entire sector of information. You must calculate and reread so that this type of memory boundary corresponds with a sector boundary.

Verify Disk Sectors (Interrupt 13h, service 4)

Category: Disk services

Registers on Entry:

AH: 4
AL: Number of sectors
CH: Track
CL: Sector
DH: Head (side) number
DL: Drive number

Registers on Return:

AH: Return code

Memory Affected: None

Syntax:

```
MOV     AL,9            ;Verify entire track
MOV     CH,TRACK        ;Specify track
MOV     CL,SECTOR       ;  and sector
MOV     DH,SIDE         ;Specify side
MOV     DL,DRIVE        ;Specify drive
MOV     AH,4            ;Specify service 4
INT     13h             ;BIOS disk interrupt
```

Description: Use this service to verify the address fields of the specified disk sectors. No data is transferred to or from the disk during this operation. Disk verification, which takes place on the disk, does not (as some people believe) involve verification of the data on the disk against the data in memory. Notice that this function has no buffer specification. This function does not read or write a disk; rather, it causes the system to read the data in the designated sector or sectors and to check its computed *cyclic redundancy check* (CRC) against data stored on the disk.

The CRC is a sophisticated checksum that detects a high percentage of any errors that may occur. When a sector is written to disk, an original CRC is calculated and written along with the sector data. The verification service reads the sector, recalculates the CRC, and compares the recalculated CRC with the original CRC. If they agree, there is a high probability that the data is correct; if they disagree, an error condition is generated.

You set up the registers to determine the precise physical location on the disk at which you wish to begin verification. The drive is specified in DL (A=0, B=1, C=2, etc.). The side, or head, is specified in DH and can be 0 or 1. CH and CL contain the track and sector, respectively. These values will vary, depending on the type of disk drive in use. Specify in AL the number of sectors to be verified.

This service checks parameters only on the requested drive number (DL); all other passed parameters are not checked for validity. If you pass invalid parameters, the results are unpredictable and may result in errors or damaged disks. (For some typical parameter ranges for this service, refer to table 20.7.)

On return from this service, the carry flag signifies whether an error occurred. If the carry flag is not set, AH contains a zero (0). If the carry flag is set, AH contains the disk-status bits as detailed in service 13/1 (refer to table 20.6). If an error occurs during the writing operation, use service 13/0 to reset the disk system before attempting another read, write, or verify operation.

Format Disk Track (Interrupt 13h, service 5)

Category: Disk services

Registers on Entry:

AH:	5
BX:	Offset address of track address fields
CH:	Track
DH:	Head (side) number
DL:	Drive number
ES:	Segment address of track address fields

Registers on Return:

AH: Return code

Memory Affected: None

Syntax:

```
MOV     CH,TRACK                ;Specify track
MOV     DH,SIDE                 ;Specify side
```

```
MOV      DL,DRIVE                   ;Specify drive
PUSH     DS                         ;Point ES to proper
POP      ES                         ;  segment address
MOV      BX,OFFSET ES:ADR_FIELD     ;Offset of address fields
MOV      AH,5                       ;Specify service 5
INT      13h                        ;BIOS disk interrupt
```

Description: Use this service to format a specific track on a disk. To format an entire disk, you must "step through" each track, invoking this service for each track.

For more detailed information on the use of this service, refer to Chapter 19.

Format Cylinder and Set Bad Sector Flags (Interrupt 13h, service 6)

Category: Disk services

Registers on Entry:

AH: 6
AL: Interleave value
CH: Cylinder (track) number
DH: Head (side) number
DL: Drive number

Registers on Return:

AH: Return code

Memory Affected: None

Syntax:

```
MOV      AL,1            ;1 to 1 interleave
MOV      CH,TRACK        ;Specify track
MOV      DH,SIDE         ;Specify side
MOV      DL,DRIVE        ;Specify drive
MOV      AH,6            ;Specify service 6
INT      13h             ;BIOS disk interrupt
```

Description: When hard disks were introduced for use with the XT and AT computer families, this BIOS service was added to allow formatting of a single track (cylinder) of a hard disk. The value loaded in DL indicates the disk drive to format. This should be a zero-based number, with the high bit (bit 7) set; thus, the first fixed disk is indicated as 80h, the second as 81h.

On return from this service, the carry flag signifies whether an error occurred. If the carry flag is not set, AH contains a zero (0). If the carry flag is set, AH contains the disk status bits as detailed in service 13/1 (refer to table 20.6).

Format Drive from Specified Cylinder (Interrupt 13h, service 7)

Category: Disk services

Registers on Entry:

AH: 7
AL: Interleave value
CH: Cylinder (track) number
DL: Drive number

Registers on Return:

AH: Return code

Memory Affected: None

Syntax:

```
MOV     AL,1            ;1 to 1 interleave
MOV     CH,TRACK        ;Specify track
MOV     DL,DRIVE        ;Specify drive
MOV     AH,7            ;Specify service 7
INT     13h             ;BIOS disk interrupt
```

Description: When hard disks were introduced for use with the XT and AT computer families, this BIOS service was added to allow formatting of the entire fixed disk, beginning with the cylinder (track) indicated in CH. The value loaded in DL indicates the disk drive to format. This should be a zero-based number, with the high bit (bit 7) set; thus, the first fixed disk is indicated as 80h, the second as 81h.

On return from this service, the carry flag signifies whether an error occurred. If the carry flag is not set, AH contains a zero (0). If the carry flag is set, AH contains the disk status bits as detailed in service 13/1 (refer to table 20.6).

Return Drive Parameters (Interrupt 13h, service 8)

Category: Disk services

Registers on Entry:

AH: 8

DL: Drive number (0 based)
        bit 7 is set if fixed disk

Registers on Return:

CH: Number of tracks/side
CL: Number of sectors/track
DH: Number of sides
DL: Number of consecutive drives attached

Memory Affected: None

Syntax:

```
MOV     DL,80h              ;Use first hard disk drive
MOV     AH,8                ;Specify service 8
INT     13h                 ;BIOS disk interrupt
```

Description: Use this service to retrieve disk parameters for a disk drive. *(This service is available only on the IBM Personal Computer AT and PS/2.)*

Notice that when you call this service, you will specify the disk drive number in DL (80h for the first fixed disk, 81h for the second, etc.). These numbers do not correspond to the standard BIOS disk-numbering scheme. If you attempt the service with any out-of-range *fixed* disk drive numbers (those below 80h), an error will be returned.

On return from this service, the carry flag signifies whether an error occurred. If the carry flag is not set, AH contains a zero (0). If the carry flag is set, AH contains the disk-status bits as detailed in service 13/1 (refer to table 20.6).

Initialize Fixed Disk Table (Interrupt 13h, service 9)

Category: Disk services

Registers on Entry:

AH: 9
DL: Fixed disk drive number

Registers on Return: Unchanged

Memory Affected: None

Syntax:

```
MOV     DL,80h          ;Use first disk drive
MOV     AH,9            ;Specify service 9
INT     13h            ;BIOS disk interrupt
```

Description: Use this service to initialize the fixed disk parameter tables for a specific drive. *(This service is available only on the IBM Personal Computer AT and PS/2 and works only with fixed disks.)*

Notice that when you call this service, you will specify the fixed disk drive number in DL (80h for the first fixed disk, 81h for the second, etc.). These numbers do not correspond to the standard BIOS disk-numbering scheme. If you attempt the service with any out-of-range fixed disk drive numbers (those below 80h), an error will be returned.

On return from this service, the carry flag signifies whether an error occurred. If the carry flag is not set, AH contains a zero (0). If the carry flag is set, AH contains the disk-status byte as detailed in service 13/1 (refer to table 20.6).

The fixed disk parameter tables for as many as two fixed disks are contained in RAM at the memory addresses pointed to by interrupt vectors 41h and 46h.

Read Long Sectors (Interrupt 13h, service 0Ah)

Category: Disk services

Registers on Entry:

AH: 0Ah
AL: Number of sectors
BX: Offset address of data buffer
CH: Track
CL: Sector
DH: Head (side) number
DL: Fixed disk drive number
ES: Segment address of data buffer

Registers on Return:

AH: Return code

Memory Affected: RAM data buffer starting at memory address ES:BX is overwritten by sectors requested from the fixed disk.

Syntax:

```
MOV     AL,1                    ;Reading 1 sector
MOV     CH,LOW_TRACK            ;Specify low-order track
MOV     CL,HIGH_TRACK           ;Specify high-order track
MOV     BL,6                    ;Want to shift 6 bits
SHL     CL,BL                   ;  left, place in bits 6/7
OR      CL,SECTOR               ;Place sector in bits 0-5
MOV     DH,SIDE                 ;Specify side
MOV     DL,80h                  ;Use first disk drive
PUSH    DS                      ;Point ES to proper
POP     ES                      ;  segment address
MOV     BX,OFFSET ES:BUFFER     ;Offset of buffer area
MOV     AH,0Ah                  ;Specify service 0Ah
INT     13h                     ;BIOS disk interrupt
```

Description: Use this service to control reading long sectors from the IBM Personal Computer AT's 20M fixed disk drive. (This service, *which is available only on the IBM Personal Computer AT and works only with fixed disks*, is the opposite of service 13/0B, which controls writing long sectors to the fixed disk.) A *long sector* consists of a regular sector of data and four bytes of error-correction information used to verify the information read from the fixed disk.

To use this service, you must specify the precise physical location on the fixed disk at which you want to begin reading. In DL, specify the fixed disk drive number (80h for the first fixed disk, 81h for the second, etc.). These numbers do not correspond to the standard BIOS disk-numbering scheme. If you attempt the service with any out-of-range fixed disk drive numbers (those below 80h), an error will be returned.

In DH, specify the side, or head, which may vary from 0 to 15. CH and CL contain the track and sector, respectively. These values, which will vary depending on what size fixed disk is used, are normally in the range specified in table 20.8. Track (CH) and sector (CL) information in the table are encoded according to the description for this service.

Table 20.8. *Parameter ranges for service 13/A on an IBM Personal Computer AT.*

Parameter	Register	Valid Range
# of sectors	AL	1-121
Track	CH/CL	0-1023
Sector	CL	1-17
Head (side)	DH	0-15
Drive	DL	80=first, 81=second, etc.

As you can see, the track range (CH) can be greater than 255, the largest number that can be contained in a single byte. Actually, the track is specified as a 10-bit number, with the two high-order bits stored in bits 7 and 6 of CL. The sector specification is stored in bits 0 through 5 of CL.

The final registers to be set up specify which RAM area will be used as a buffer for the sectors that are read. This address is specified in ES:BX. To determine the size of the RAM buffer, you must know ahead of time how large each disk sector is. For instance, if each disk sector contains 512 bytes, and you are going to read four sectors, your buffer should be 2,048 bytes (2K) long.

This service checks parameters on the requested drive number (DL) only; all other passed parameters are not checked for validity. If you pass invalid parameters, the results are unpredictable.

On return from this service, the carry flag signifies whether an error occurred. If the carry flag is not set, AH will contain a zero (0). If the carry flag is set, AH will contain the disk-status bits as detailed in service 13/1 (refer to table 20.6). If an error occurs during the reading operation, use service 13/0, with the fixed disk drive number in DL, to reset the fixed disk system before you attempt another read operation.

Note: In this service, a particularly confusing error may occur. DMA boundary error (AH=9) means that an illegal boundary was crossed when the information was placed into RAM. Direct Memory Access (DMA) is used by the disk-service routines to place information into RAM. This error will occur if a memory offset address ending in three zeros (ES:1000, ES:2000, ES:3000, etc.) falls in the middle of the area being overlaid by a sector. You must calculate and reread so that this type of memory boundary corresponds with a sector boundary. I don't know why this happens, but it is frustrating as all get out to a programmer. (This error-code consideration also applies to services 13/2, 13/3, and 13/0Bh.)

Write Long Sectors (Interrupt 13h, service 0Bh)

Category: Disk services

Registers on Entry:

AH: 0Bh
AL: Number of sectors
BX: Offset address of data buffer
CH: Track
CL: Sector
DH: Head (side) number
DL: Fixed disk drive number
ES: Segment address of data buffer

Registers on Return:

AH: Return code

Memory Affected: None

Syntax:

```
MOV     AL,17               ;Writing entire track
MOV     CH,LOW_TRACK        ;Specify low-order track
MOV     CL,HIGH_TRACK       ;Specify high-order track
MOV     BL,6                ;Want to shift 6 bits
SHL     CL,BL               ;  left, place in bits 6/7
OR      CL,SECTOR           ;Place sector in bits 0-5
MOV     DH,SIDE             ;Specify side
MOV     DL,80h              ;Use first disk drive
PUSH    DS                  ;Point ES to proper
POP     ES                  ;  segment address
MOV     BX,OFFSET ES:BUFFER ;Offset of buffer area
MOV     AH,0Bh              ;Specify service 0Bh
INT     13h                 ;BIOS disk interrupt
```

Description: This service, which controls writing long sectors to the IBM Personal Computer AT 20M fixed disk drive, *is available only on the IBM Personal Computer AT and works only with fixed disks*. (It is the opposite of service 13/0Ah, which controls reading long sectors from the fixed disk.) A long sector consists of a regular sector of data and four bytes of error-correction information, which is used to verify the information read from the fixed disk.

To use this service, you must specify (in ES:BX) which RAM area is used as the buffer for the sectors written. The area should be initialized with the desired data in the right amount. Because this service calculates the amount of RAM to read and subsequently write, based on the number of sectors to write (AH) and the sector size, you must know the size of the sectors being written on the disk. Assuming that each sector requires 512 bytes, the example shown in the syntax section requires a buffer of 8,704 bytes (8.5K).

You set up other registers to determine the precise physical location on the fixed disk at which you wish to begin writing. Specify the fixed disk drive number in DL (80h for the first fixed disk, 81h for the second, etc.). These numbers do not correspond to the standard BIOS disk-numbering scheme. If you attempt the service with any out-of-range fixed disk drive numbers (those below 80h), an error will be returned.

The side, or head, is specified in DH and may vary from 0 to 15. CH and CL contain the track and sector, respectively. These values, which will vary depending on the size of fixed disk used, are normally in the range specified in table 20.8 (refer to service 13/0Ah).

The track range (CH) can be greater than 255, the largest number that can be contained in a single byte. Actually, the track is specified as a 10-bit number, with the two high-order bits stored in bits 7 and 6 of CL. The sector specification is stored in bits 0 through 5 of CL.

This service checks parameters on the requested drive number (DL) only; all other passed parameters are not checked for validity. If you pass invalid parameters, the results are unpredictable.

On return from this service, the carry flag signifies whether an error occurred. If the carry flag is not set, AH contains a zero (0). If the carry flag is set, AH contains the disk-status bits as detailed in service 13/1 (refer to table 20.6). If an error occurs during the reading operation, use service 13/0, with the fixed disk drive number in DL, to reset the fixed disk system before you attempt another write operation.

Note: In this service (and services 13/2, 13/3, and 13/0Ah) a particularly confusing error may occur. DMA boundary error (AH=9) means that an illegal boundary was crossed as the information was read from the RAM buffer. Direct Memory Access (DMA) is used by the disk service routines to place information into RAM. This error will occur if a memory offset address ending in three zeros (ES:1000, ES:2000, ES:3000, etc.) is crossed before this service completes reading an entire sector of information. You must calculate and reread so that this type of memory boundary corresponds with a sector boundary.

Seek Cylinder (Interrupt 13h, service 0Ch)

Category: Disk services

Registers on Entry:

AH: 0Ch
CH: Low-order track
CL: High-order track
DH: Head (side) number
DL: Fixed disk drive number

Registers on Return:

AH: Return code

Memory Affected: None

Syntax:

```
MOV    CH,LOW_TRACK      ;Specify low-order track
MOV    CL,HIGH_TRACK     ;Specify high-order track
MOV    BL,6              ;Want to shift 6 bits
SHL    CL,BL             ;  left, place in bits 6/7
MOV    DH,SIDE           ;Specify side
MOV    DL,80h            ;Use first disk drive
MOV    AH,0Ch            ;Specify service 0Ch
INT    13h               ;BIOS disk interrupt
```

Description: Use this service to move the read/write heads of the fixed disk drive to a specific track (cylinder). *This service is available only on the IBM Personal Computer AT and works only with fixed disks.*

To use this service, you must specify the fixed disk drive number (80h for the first fixed disk, 81h for the second, etc.) in DL. These numbers do not correspond to the standard BIOS disk numbering scheme. If you attempt the service with any out-of-range fixed disk drive numbers (those below 80h), an error will be returned.

The side, or head, is specified in DH and may vary from 0 to 15. CH and CL contain the track and sector, respectively. These values, which will vary depending on the size of fixed disk used, are normally in the range specified in table 20.8 (refer to service 13/0Ah).

The track range (CH) can be greater than 255, the largest number that can be contained in a single byte. Actually, the track is specified as a 10-bit number, with the two high-order bits stored in bits 7 and 6 of CL.

This service checks parameters on the requested drive number only (DL); all other passed parameters are not checked for validity. If you pass invalid parameters, the results are unpredictable.

On return from this service, the carry flag signifies whether an error occurred. If the carry flag is not set, AH contains a zero (0). If the carry flag is set, AH contains the disk status byte as detailed in service 13/1 (refer to table 20.6).

Alternate Reset (Interrupt 13h, service 0Dh)

Category: Disk services

Registers on Entry:

AH: 0Dh
DL: Fixed disk drive number

Registers on Return:

AH: Return code

Memory Affected: None

Syntax:

```
MOV    DL,80h        ;Use first disk drive
MOV    AH,0Dh        ;Specify service Dh
INT    13h           ;BIOS disk interrupt
```

Description: This service, *which is available only on the IBM Personal Computer AT*, resets the fixed disk drive.

The IBM Personal Computer AT BIOS shows that, after compensating for the fixed disk drive specification, this service is hard-coded to the same routine address as service 13/0; there is absolutely no difference between the two services. This service apparently was included for future expansion—for the day when identical reset routines could not be used for both fixed and floppy disks.

To use this service, you must specify the fixed disk drive number (80h for the first fixed disk, 81h for the second, etc.) in DL. These numbers do not correspond to the standard BIOS disk-numbering scheme. If you attempt the service with any out-of-range fixed disk drive numbers (those below 80h), an error will be returned.

When this service is called, its effect on the fixed disk drive is not apparent. The recalibrate command is sent directly to the fixed disk controller, and a reset flag is set to recalibrate the drive the next time it is used. (This recalibration consists primarily of retracting the read/write head to track 0.)

Used primarily in routines that handle critical errors, this service forces the controller to recalibrate itself on the subsequent operation. If a critical error occurs, this service is necessary for reliable operation of the fixed disk. The service forces the controller to make no assumptions about its position or condition—assumptions that may be wrong because of the previously experienced critical-error condition.

On return from this service, the carry flag signifies whether an error occurred. If the carry flag is not set, AH will contain a zero (0). If the carry flag is set, AH contains the disk status byte as detailed in service 13/1 (refer to table 20.6).

Unused (Interrupt 13H, services Eh, Fh)

These services, which are listed as unused in the IBM Personal Computer AT BIOS, more than likely will be used as peripherals as capabilities are added.

Read DASD Type (Interrupt 13h, service 15h)

Category: Disk services

Registers on Entry:

AH: 15h
DL: Drive number

Registers on Return:

AH: Return code

CX: High byte—number of fixed disk sectors
DX: Low byte—number of fixed disk sectors

Memory Affected: None

Syntax:

```
MOV    DL,0         ;Use drive A:
MOV    AH,15h       ;Specify service 15h
INT    13h          ;BIOS disk interrupt
```

Description: This service, *which is available only on the PC XT (BIOS dated 1/10/86 or later), PC XT 286, IBM Personal Computer AT, or PS/2 line*, is used to determine the Direct Access Storage Device (DASD) type of a given disk drive.

DL can contain either a normal BIOS disk drive number (0=A, 1=B, 2=C, etc.) or a fixed disk drive number (80h for the first fixed disk, 81h for the second, etc.).

On return from this service, the carry flag signifies whether an error occurred. If the carry flag is set, AH contains the disk status byte as detailed in service 13/1 (refer to table 20.6). If an error occurs, use service 13/0 to reset the disk system before you attempt to use this service again.

If the carry flag is clear, the return code in AH indicates the DASD type of the drive. Table 20.9 lists the possible return codes and their meanings.

Table 20.9. DASD types for service 13/15.

Code	Meaning
0	The drive requested (DL) is not present
1	Drive present, cannot detect disk change
2	Drive present, can detect disk change
3	Fixed disk

If the return code indicates a DASD type of 3 (fixed disk), the register pair CX:DX will indicate the number of sectors on the fixed disk.

Read Disk-Change Line Status (Interrupt 13h, service 16h)

Category: Disk services

Registers on Entry:

AH: 16h
DL: Drive number

Registers on Return:

AH: Return code

Memory Affected: None

Syntax:

```
MOV    DL,0         ;Use drive A:
MOV    AH,16h       ;Specify service 16h
INT    13h          ;BIOS disk interrupt
```

Description: Use this service, *which is available only on the PC XT (BIOS dated 1/10/86 or later), PC XT 286, IBM Personal Computer AT, or PS/2 line*, to determine whether the disk in a drive has been changed.

The result code in AH will be either a zero (0) or a 6. A 0 means that the disk has not been changed; a 6 means that it has. If the disk has not been changed, the carry flag will be clear; if the disk has been changed, the carry flag will be set.

The use of the carry flag can have strange consequences in this service. The carry flag is set not only if an error has occurred but also if the disk has been changed. Because having two uses for the carry flag can be confusing, be sure to check the contents of AH for the true result code. If AH is 0, and the carry flag is set, you know that an error has occurred. AH can then be assumed to contain the disk status byte as detailed in service 13/1 (refer to table 20.6).

Even if no disk is in the drive, this service works and does not generate an error. The drive is activated and checked; if no disk is present, a result of 6 is returned. If this service is called several times with no intervening disk access, the same result code is returned repetitively. For instance, if you request a disk's directory and then invoke this service, a result code of 0 is returned. If you then change the disk, a result code of 6 is generated. If you leave the same disk in the drive and again call this service, a result code of 6 is again returned. A result code of 0, indicating that no change has occurred, is returned only after the disk has been read.

Set DASD Type for Format (Interrupt 13h, service 17h)

Category: Disk services

Registers on Entry:

AH: 17h
AL: DASD format type
DL: Drive number

Registers on Return: Unchanged

Memory Affected: None

Syntax:

```
MOV    AL,3          ;Set DASD for 1.2M
MOV    DL,0          ;Set drive A:
MOV    AH,17h        ;Specify service 17h
INT    13h           ;BIOS disk interrupt
```

Description: Use this service with service 13/5 to format a disk. You must use this service, *which is available only on the PC XT (BIOS dated 1/10/86 or later), PC XT 286, IBM Personal Computer AT, or PS/2 line,* to specify not only the type of disk to format but also the type of drive in which that disk will be formatted.

The DASD format type specified in AL can be a number from 1 to 3 (see table 20.10).

Table 20.10. DASD format types for service 13/17.

Type	Meaning
1	Formatting a 320/360K disk in a 320/360K drive
2	Formatting a 320/360K disk in a 1.2M drive
3	Formatting a 1.2M disk in a 1.2M drive
4	Formatting a 720K disk in either a 720K or 1.44M drive

For more information on the proper use of this service, see the discussion and sample routines for service 13/5.

Set Media Type for Format (Interrupt 13h, service 18h)

Category: Disk services

Registers on Entry:

AH: 18h
CH: Number of tracks
CL: Sectors per track
DL: Drive number (zero based)

Registers on Return:

DI: Offset address of 11-byte parameter table
ES: Segment address of 11-byte parameter table

Memory Affected: None

Syntax:

```
MOV    CH,39         ;Set for 40 tracks
MOV    CL,9          ;Set 9 sectors
MOV    DL,0          ;Set drive A:
```

```
MOV     AH,18h        ;Specify service 18h
INT     13h           ;BIOS disk interrupt
```

Description: This service, *which is available only on the PC XT (BIOS dated 1/10/ 86 or later), PC XT 286, IBM Personal Computer AT, or PS/2 line,* specifies to the formatting routines the number of tracks and sectors per track to be placed on the media. Normally, you will not use this service; it makes possible the creation of nonstandard track layouts.

Park Heads (Interrupt 13h, service 19h)

Category: Disk services

Registers on Entry:

AH: 19h
DL: Drive number, zero-based and HD-coded

Registers on Return: Not significant

Memory Affected: None

Syntax:

```
MOV     DL,80h        ;First fixed drive (C:)
MOV     AH,19h        ;Request park heads service
INT     13h           ;BIOS disk service interrupt
```

Description: This service, *which is available only on the PC XT (BIOS dated 1/10/86 or later), PC XT 286, IBM Personal Computer AT, or PS/2 line*, moves the heads of the specified fixed disk drive to a "safe" storage position.

Format ESDI Unit (Interrupt 13h, service 1Ah)

Category: Disk services

Registers on Entry:

AH: 1Ah
AL: 0 = no defect table
        < > 0 = use defect table
ES: Segment address of defect table
BX: Offset address of defect table
CL: modifier bits:

Bits	
76543210	*Meaning*
1	Ignore primary defect map
1	Ignore secondary defect map
1	Update secondary defect map
1	Perform extended surface analysis
1	Turn periodic interrupts ON
xxx	Reserved

DL: Drive number (zero based)

Registers on Return: Not significant

Memory Affected: None

Description: This service, *which is available only on the PS/2 line models 50, 60, and 80*, reformats an ESDI disk unit. You should never need to use it.

Initialize Communications Port (Interrupt 14h, service 0)

Category: Communications services

Registers on Entry:

AH: 0
AL: Initialization parameter
DX: Communications port

Registers on Return:

AH: Line status
AL: Modem status

Memory Affected: None

Syntax:

```
MOV    AL,10000011b        ;Set for 1200/N/8/1
MOV    DX,0                ;Set COM1:
MOV    AH,0                ;Specify service 0
INT    14h                 ;BIOS comm. interrupt
```

Description: This service is used to initialize the communications (RS-232) port specified in DX. The contents of DX can vary from 0 to 3 (corresponding to COM1:, COM2:, COM3:, and COM4:).

In AL, you specify how the communications port should be initialized. This service allows you to set the baud rate, parity, data length, and stop bits. Specify these settings through the bits of register AL, according to the coding scheme shown in table 20.11.

Table 20.11. *Meaning of AL bits for service 14/0.*

Bits 76543210	*Meaning*
000	110 baud
001	150 baud
010	300 baud
011	600 baud
100	1200 baud
101	2400 baud
110	4800 baud
111	9600 baud
00	No parity
01	Odd parity
10	No parity
11	Even parity
0	1 stopbit
1	2 stopbits
10	7-bit data length
11	8-bit data length

This service returns two values, which correspond to the asynchronous chip's line status (AH) and modem status (AL) registers. These return values, which indicate the status and condition of the asynchronous communications adapter, are the same as those returned in service 14/3. The meaning of each bit of the line status register is shown in table 20.12; table 20.13 lists the meaning of the modem status register.

Table 20.12. *The line status register bit meanings.*

Bits 76543210	Meaning
1	Time-out error
1	Transfer shift register (TSR) empty
1	Transfer holding register (THR) empty
1	Break interrupt detected
1	Framing error
1	Parity error
1	Overrun error
1	Data ready

Table 20.13. *The modem status register bit meanings.*

Bits 76543210	Meaning
1	Receive line-signal detect
1	Ring indicator
1	Data set ready (DSR)
1	Clear to send (CTS)
1	Delta receive line-signal detect
1	Trailing-edge ring detector
1	Delta data-set ready (DDSR)
1	Delta clear to send (DCTS)

Note that the value in AH, which corresponds to the line status register, has an added bit. Although the meaning of bit 7 in the line status register ordinarily is undefined, BIOS uses this bit to signal that an excessive amount of time has passed since a character has been received.

This book does not attempt to explain the purpose, use, and interpretation of each bit in these registers. Many books on asynchronous communications are available.

Transmit Character (Interrupt 14h, service 1)

Category: Communications services

Registers on Entry:

AH: 1
AL: ASCII character
DX: Communications port

Registers on Return:

AH: Return code

Memory Affected: None

Syntax:

```
MOV    AL,'T'          ;Send the letter 'T'
MOV    DX,0            ;Set COM1:
MOV    AH,1            ;Specify service 1
INT    14h            ;BIOS comm. interrupt
```

Description: This service sends a character to the communications (RS-232) port specified in DX. The contents of DX can vary from 0 to 3 (corresponding to COM1:, COM2:, COM3:, and COM4:). Before calling this service for the first time, make sure that service 14/0 has been used to initialize the communications port.

The character to be sent should be loaded in AL. The transmission was successful if the high-order bit of AH is clear (AH < 80h) on return. Table 20.12 shows the balance of the bits in AH after a successful transmission.

If the transmission was unsuccessful, the high-order bit will be set (AH > 7Fh) and the balance of AH will appear as in table 20.12.

Receive Character (Interrupt 14h, service 2)

Category: Communications services

Registers on Entry:

AH: 2
DX: Communications port

Registers on Return:

AH: Return code

Memory Affected: None

Syntax:

```
MOV    DX,0        ;Set COM1:
MOV    AH,2        ;Specify service 2
INT    14h         ;BIOS comm. interrupt
```

Description: This service is used to receive a character from the communications (RS-232) port specified in DX. The contents of DX can vary from 0 to 3 (corresponding to COM1:, COM2:, COM3:, and COM4:). Before calling this service for the first time, make sure that you have used service 14/0 to initialize the communications port.

Because this service waits for a character, other computer processing is suspended until the character is received or until the communications port returns an error.

On return, AH contains a return code. In this return code, which is analogous to the line control register's return values of service 14/3, only the error bits are used (refer to table 20.12).

If you set AL to 0 before calling this service, you can quickly test whether a character was received. Because most receiving software discards NULLL characters (ASCII value of 0), no action need be taken even if a nulll character is received; your routine can continue to wait for an incoming character.

Get Communications Port Status (Interrupt 14h, service 3)

Category: Communications services

Registers on Entry:

AH: 3
DX: Communications port

Registers on Return:

AH: Line status
AL: Modem status

Memory Affected: None

Syntax:

```
MOV    DX,0        ;Set COM1:
MOV    AH,3        ;Specify service 3
INT    14h         ;BIOS comm. interrupt
```

Description: Use this service to check the status of the communications line and the modem. The communications (RS-232) port is specified in DX. The contents of DX can vary from 0 to 3 (corresponding to COM1:, COM2:, COM3:, and COM4:).

This service returns two values, which correspond to the asynchronous chip's line status (AH) and modem status (AL) registers. The meaning of each line status register bit is shown in table 20.12; that of each modem status register bit, in table 20.13.

Notice that the value in AH, which corresponds to the line status register, has an added bit. Although the meaning of bit 7 in the line status register is undefined, BIOS uses this bit to signal that too much time has passed since a character has been received.

This book does not attempt to explain the purpose, use, and interpretation of each bit in these registers. Many books on asynchronous communications are available.

Extended Communications Port Initialization (Interrupt 14h, service 4)

Category: Communications services

Registers on Entry:

AH: 04h
AL: 00h = no break
        01h = break
BH: 00h = no parity
        01h = odd parity
        02h = even parity
        03h = mark parity
        04h = space parity
BL: 00h = one stop bit
        01h = two stop bits
CH: 00h = 5 data bits
        01h = 6 data bits
        02h = 7 data bits
        03h = 8 data bits

CL: 00h = 110 BPS
        01h = 150 BPS
        02h = 300 BPS
        03h = 600 BPS
        04h = 1200 BPS
        05h = 2400 BPS
        06h = 4800 BPS
        07h = 9600 BPS
        08h = 19200 BPS

DX: Serial port (0=COM1, etc.)

Registers on Return:

AH: Port status (table 20.12)

AL: Modem status (table 20.13)

Memory Affected: None

Syntax:

```
MOV    AH,04h     ;extended initialization function
MOV    AL,0       ;no break
MOV    BH,2       ;even parity
MOV    BL,0       ;1 stop bit
MOV    CH,2       ;7 data bits
MOV    CL,4       ;1200 BPS
MOV    DX,0       ;COM1
INT    14h        ;communications service
```

Description: This service, *available only on the PS/2 line*, greatly simplifies the initialization of the communications ports.

Extended Communications Port Control (Interrupt 14h, service 5)

Category: Communications services

Registers on Entry:

AH: 05h

AL: 00h, Read modem control register
        01h, Write modem control register

BL: New MCR content if AL=01h

DX: Serial port (0 = COM1, etc.)

Registers on Return:

AH: Port status (table 20.12)
AL: Modem status (table 20.13)
BL: Modem control register (see Chapter 18):

Bits 76543210	*Meaning*
1	Data terminal ready (DTR)
1	Request to send (RTS)
1	User 1
1	User 2
1	Loopback test
xxx	Reserved

Memory Affected: None

Syntax:

```
MOV     AH,05h      ;extended MCR control function
MOV     AL,0        ;read MCR
MOV     DX,0        ;COM1
INT     14h         ;communications service
```

Description: This service, *available only on the PS/2 line*, greatly simplifies modem control through the communications ports.

Turn On Cassette Motor (Interrupt 15h, service 0)

Category: Cassette services

Registers on Entry:

AH: 0

Registers on Return:

AH: Return code

Memory Affected: None

Syntax:

```
MOV     AH,0        ;Specify service 0
INT     15h         ;BIOS cassette interrupt
```

Description: This service (the opposite of service 15/1) turns on the cassette motor. Because this service works only on older models of the PC, using it on the IBM PC XT or Personal Computer AT causes the return of an 86h in AH and sets the carry flag.

Turn Off Cassette Motor (Interrupt 15h, service 1)

Category: Cassette services

Registers on Entry:

AH: 1

Registers on Return:

AH: Return code

Memory Affected: None

Syntax:

```
MOV    AH,1        ;Specify service 1
INT    15h         ;BIOS cassette interrupt
```

Description: This service (the opposite of service 15/0) turns off the cassette motor. Because this service works only on older models of the PC, using it on the IBM PC XT or Personal Computer AT causes the return of an 86h in AH and sets the carry flag.

Read Data Blocks from Cassette (Interrupt 15h, service 2)

Category: Cassette services

Registers on Entry:

AH: 2
BX: Offset address of data buffer
CX: Number of bytes to read
ES: Segment address of data buffer

Registers on Return:

AH: Return code
DX: Number of bytes read

Memory Affected: RAM buffer area specified by address starting at ES:BX is overwritten with bytes requested from cassette.

Syntax:

```
MOV     CX,NUM_BYTES            ;Read this many bytes
PUSH    DS                      ;Point ES to proper
POP     ES                      ;  segment address
MOV     BX,OFFSET ES:BUFFER     ;Offset of buffer area
MOV     AH,2                    ;Specify service 2
INT     15h                     ;BIOS cassette interrupt
```

Description: This service reads data from the cassette-tape port. Because this service works only on older models of the PC, using it on the IBM PC XT or Personal Computer AT causes the return of an 86h in AH and sets the carry flag.

Information is read from the cassette in 256-byte blocks, but only the number of bytes requested in CX are transferred to the memory address pointed to by ES:BX.

On completion, DX is set to the number of bytes actually read. If no error occurred, the carry flag is clear; if an error occurred, the carry flag is set and AH will contain an error code. The error codes shown in table 20.14 are valid only if the carry flag is set.

Table 20.14. Error codes returned in AH for service 15/2.

Code	Meaning
0h	Invalid command
1h	CRC error
2h	Data transitions lost
3h	No data located on tape
86h	No cassette port available

Write Data Blocks to Cassette (Interrupt 15h, service 3)

Category: Cassette services

Registers on Entry:

AH: 3
BX: Offset address of data buffer
CX: Number of bytes to write
ES: Segment address of data buffer

Registers on Return:

AH: Return code

Memory Affected: None

Syntax:

```
MOV    CX,NUM_BYTES            ;Write this many bytes
PUSH   DS                      ;Point ES to proper
POP    ES                      ;  segment address
MOV    BX,OFFSET ES:BUFFER     ;Offset of buffer area
MOV    AH,3                    ;Specify service 3
INT    15h                     ;BIOS cassette interrupt
```

Description: This service writes data to the cassette-tape port. Because this service works only on older models of the PC, using it on the IBM PC XT or Personal Computer AT causes the return of an 86h in AH and sets the carry flag.

Information is written to the cassette in 256-byte blocks, but only the number of bytes indicated in CX are transferred from the memory address pointed to by ES:BX.

If an error is detected when this service is invoked, the carry flag is set and AH will contain an error code (see table 20.15). These error codes, which are valid only if the carry flag is set, indicate only syntactical errors. Neither of the errors returned indicates that information was written improperly to the cassette.

Table 20.15. Error codes returned in AH for service 15/3.

Code	Meaning
0h	Invalid command
86h	No cassette port available

ESDI Format Hook (Interrupt 15h, service 0Fh)

Category: PS/2 services

Registers on Entry:

AH: 0Fh
AL: 01h = Surface analysis
        02h = Formatting
        Other values reserved

Registers on Return:

Carry flag set if formatting is to stop
AH: 86h if service not available

Memory Affected: None

Description: This service, *available only on the PS/2 line*, is called by the ESDI format service after each cylinder is formatted or analyzed. If you want to perform some action at that time, you can set the INT 15h vector to your own routine, trap the condition of AH=0Fh, and chain on to the existing BIOS code for all other conditions. Most programmers will never use this service.

If called on older PC models, this service sets the carry flag and returns 86h in AH (or 80h on original PC and PCjr models) to indicate that the service is invalid on the model.

On return from this service, the carry flag signifies one of two things: If the carry flag is set and AH contains 86h, the service is not available; if AH contains some other value, formatting is to stop.

Keyboard Intercept Hook (Interrupt 15h, service 4Fh)

Category: PS/2 services

Registers on Entry:

AH: 4Fh
AL: Keyboard scan code

Registers on Return:

AL: New scan code if changed, original code otherwise

Memory Affected: None

Description: This service, *available only on the PS/2 line (except Model 30)*, is called by the BIOS routine that services INT 09h whenever a scan code is received from the keyboard. If you want to provide special processing, you can intercept this service to do so. Normally, this service is never called by a programmer.

If called on older PC models, this service sets the carry flag and returns 86h in AH (or 80h on original PC and PCjr models) to indicate that the service is invalid on the model.

Device Open (Interrupt 15h, service 80h)

Category: PS/2 services

Registers on Entry:

AH: 80h
BX: Device ID code
CX: Process ID code

Registers on Return:

AH: Return code

Memory Affected: None

Syntax:

```
MOV     BX,DEVID            ;device affected
MOV     CX,PROCID           ;process owning device
MOV     AH,80h              ;service code
INT     15h                 ;BIOS extension interrupt
```

Description: This service, available only on systems dated since 11/08/82, is part of the networking and multitasking interface; as such, its use is beyond the scope of this book.

If called on older PC models, this service sets the carry flag and returns 86h in AH (or 80h on original PC and PCjr models) to indicate that the service is invalid on the model.

Device Close (Interrupt 15h, service 81h)

Category: PS/2 services

Registers on Entry:

AH: 81h
BX: Device ID code
CX: Process ID code

Registers on Return:

AH: Return code

Memory Affected: None

Syntax:

```
MOV     BX,DEVID         ;device affected
MOV     CX,PROCID        ;process owning device
MOV     AH,81h           ;service code
INT     15h              ;BIOS extension interrupt
```

Description: This service, available only on systems dated since 11/08/82, is part of the networking and multitasking interface; its use is beyond the scope of this book.

If called on older PC models, this service sets the carry flag and returns 86h in AH (or 80h on original PC and PCjr models) to indicate that the service is invalid on the model.

Terminate Program (Interrupt 15h, service 82h)

Category: PS/2 services

Registers on Entry:

AH: 82h
BX: Process ID code

Registers on Return:

AH: Return code

Memory Affected: None

Syntax:

```
MOV     BX,PROCID        ;process to terminate
MOV     AH,82h           ;service code
INT     15h              ;BIOS extension interrupt
```

Description: This service, available only on systems dated since 11/08/82, is part of the networking and multitasking interface; its use is beyond the scope of this book.

If called on older PC models, this service sets the carry flag and returns 86h in AH (or 80h on original PC and PCjr models) to indicate that the service is invalid on the model.

Event Wait (Interrupt 15h, service 83h)

Category: PS/2 services

Registers on Entry:

AH:	83h
AL:	00h = Set interval
	01h = Cancel interval already set (PS/2 only)
BX:	Offset address of byte to set when time expires
CX:	High-order value of microseconds until posting
DX:	Low-order value of microseconds until posting
ES:	Segment address of byte to set when type expires

Registers on Return:

AH:	Return code

Memory Affected: High-order bit of byte addressed by ES:BX is set as soon as possible after the requested time interval expires. Maximum time that can be set is approximately 70 minutes (2^{32} microseconds).

Syntax:

```
MOV     AH,83h                  ;service code
MOV     AL,00h                  ;set an interval
MOV     BX,OFFSET RByte
PUSH    DS
POP     ES
MOV     CX,0                    ;high word of time count
MOV     DX,10000                ;wait 1/100 second
INT     15h                     ;BIOS extension interrupt
```

Description: This service, available only on systems dated since 11/08/82, is part of the networking and multitasking interface; its use is beyond the scope of this book.

If called on older PC models, this service sets the carry flag and returns 86h in AH (or 80h on original PC and PCjr models) to indicate that the service is invalid for the model.

Joystick Support (Interrupt 15h, service 84h)

Category: Miscellaneous services

Registers on Entry:

AH: 84h
DX: 00h = Read switches
        01h = Read joystick position

Registers on Return:

If reading switches (DX=0):
        AL = Switch settings (bits 4-7)
If reading position (DX=1):
        AX = A(X) value
        BX = A(Y) value
        CX = B(X) value
        DX = B(Y) value

Memory Affected: None

Syntax:

```
MOV     AH,84h      ;joystick service
MOV     DX,1        ;read position
INT     15h         ;BIOS extension interrupt
```

Description: With this service, which is available on all IBM PC and PS/2 systems released since 1983, you can read either the joystick switch settings (called with AL=0) or the joystick position.

If called on older PC models, this service sets the carry flag and returns 86h in AH (or 80h on original PC and PCjr models) to indicate that the service is invalid for the model.

SysRq Key Pressed (Interrupt 15h, service 85h)

Category: Miscellaneous services

Registers on Entry:

AH: 85h
AL: 00h = SysRq key pressed
        01h = SysRq key released

Registers on Return:

AH: Return code

Memory Affected: None

Description: This service, *available only on IBM PC and PS/2 systems released since 1983*, is meaningful only when the keyboard includes the SysRq key (84-key and later designs). BIOS calls the service when INT 09h detects either a press or release of the SysRq key. Normally, programmers never call this service.

To provide special action when the key is pressed, your program must replace the existing INT 15h service routine with a new one that traps the condition AH=85h and passes control on to the original routine for all other cases. Your routine can then determine whether the key was pressed or released by testing the content of the AL register. Be sure to remove your special routine before returning to DOS.

On return from this service, the carry flag signifies whether an error occurred. If the carry flag is set and AH contains 86h, this service is not available.

Delay (Interrupt 15h, service 86h)

Category: Miscellaneous services

Registers on Entry:

AH: 86h
CX: High-order value of delay time in microseconds
DX: Low-order value of delay time in microseconds

Registers on Return:

AH: Return code

Memory Affected: None

Syntax:

```
MOV     AH,86h      ;delay service
MOV     CX,0        ;high 16 bits of value
MOV     DX,10000    ;wait 1/100 second
INT     15h         ;BIOS extension interrupt
```

Description: This service, *which is available only on the IBM Personal Computer AT and PS/2 lines*, pauses a specified length of time before returning to its caller. The service is intended for system use only, not for general application.

If called on older PC models, the service sets the carry flag and returns 86h in AH (or 80h on original PC and PCjr models) to indicate that service is invalid on the model.

Move Block to/from Extended Memory (Interrupt 15h, service 87h)

Category: Miscellaneous services

Registers on Entry:

AH: 87h
CX: Number of words to move
ES: Segment address of GDT (see table 20.16)
SI: Offset address of GDT (see table 20.16)

Registers on Return:

AH: Return code

Memory Affected: As described by GDT values

Syntax:

```
MOV     AH, 87h           ;move block
MOV     CX, 40            ;80 bytes
MOV     ES, SEG GDT       ;set table address
MOV     SI, OFFSET GDT
INT     15h               ;BIOS extension interrupt
```

Description: This service, *available only on the IBM Personal Computer AT and PS/2 lines*, moves data to or from extended memory as described by the global descriptor table (GDT) (see table 20.16). This service cannot transfer more than 64K bytes of data at one call.

***Table 20.16.** Format of global descriptor table.*

Offset	Description
00h	Dummy, set to zero
08h	GDT data-segment location, set to zero
10h	Source GDT, points to 8-byte GDT for source memory block
18h	Target GDT, points to 8-byte GDT for target memory block
20h	Pointer to BIOS code segment, initially zero
28h	Pointer to BIOS stack segment, initially zero
	Source/target GDT layouts
00h	Segment limit
02h	24-bit segment physical address
05h	Data access rights (set to 93h)
06h	Reserved word, must be zero

If called on older PC models, this service sets the carry flag and returns 86h in AH (or 80h on original PC and PCjr models) to indicate that the service is invalid on the model.

Size Extended Memory (Interrupt 15h, service 88h)

Category: Miscellaneous services

Registers on Entry:

AH: 88h

Registers on Return:

AX: Number of contiguous 1K blocks of RAM above 100000h

Memory Affected: None

Syntax:

```
MOV     AH,88h          ;get extended RAM size service
INT     15h             ;BIOS extension interrupt
```

Description: This service, *available only on the IBM Personal Computer AT and PS/2 lines*, returns the amount of "extended" memory available above the normal 1M limit. The service is meaningful only for machines equipped with the 80286 (or later) CPU chip.

If called on older PC models, this service sets the carry flag and returns 86h in AH (or 80h on original PC and PCjr models) to indicate that the service is invalid on the model.

Protected Mode Switch (Interrupt 15h, service 89h)

Category: Miscellaneous services

Registers on Entry:

AH: 89h
BL: IRQ0 vector offset
BH: IRQ8 vector offset

CX: Offset into protected-mode CS to jump to
ES: Segment address of GDT (see table 20.16)
SI: Offset address of GDT (see table 20.16)

Registers on Return:

AH: Return code

Memory Affected: None

Description: This service, *available only on the IBM Personal Computer AT and PS/2 lines*, switches the CPU into protected-mode operation so that you can access directly the full 16M address range. The service is meaningful only for machines equipped with the 80286 or later CPU chip.

You are not likely to use this service with any DOS programs you write because DOS cannot use protected-mode operation.

If called on older PC models, this service sets the carry flag and returns 86h in AH (or 80h on original PC and PCjr models) to indicate that the service is invalid on the model.

Get System Configuration (Interrupt 15h, service C0h)

Category: PS/2 services

Registers on Entry:

AH: C0h

Registers on Return:

BX: Offset address of system-configuration table
ES: Segment address of system-configuration table

Memory Affected: None

Syntax:

```
MOV    AH,C0h      ;request get configuration service
INT    15h         ;BIOS extension interrupt
```

Description: This service, which is available only on PC and PS/2 models dated after 01/10/84, returns a pointer to the system descriptor table. Table 20.17 shows the layout of this area; tables 20.18 and 20.19 provide more detail.

Table 20.17. *System descriptor table.*

Offset	Meaning
00h	Byte count of subsequent data (minimum 8)
02h	Model byte (see table 20.19 for meaning)
03h	Submodel byte (see table 20.19 for meaning)
04h	BIOS revision level (00 = first release)
05h	Feature information (see table 20.18 for meaning)
06-09h	Reserved

Table 20.18. *Feature information byte.*

Bits 76543210	Hex	Decimal	Meaning of Bits
1	80	128	DMA channel 3 used by hard disk BIOS
1	40	64	Second interrupt chip present
1	20	32	Real-time clock present
1	10	16	Keyboard intercept called by INT 09h
1	8	8	Wait for external event is supported
1	4	4	Extended BIOS data area allocated
1	2	2	Micro channel architecture
0			PC bus I/O channel
x			Reserved

Table 20.19. *System model identification.*

Computer Type	Model Byte (offset 02h)	Submodel (offset 03h)	BIOS Revision (offset 04h)	BIOS Date
PC	FFh			
PC XT	FEh			
PC XT	FBh	00h	01h	1/10/86
PC XT	FBh	00h	02h	5/09/86
PCjr	FDh			
AT	FCh			
AT	FCh	00h	01h	6/10/85
AT, COMPAQ 286	FCh	01h	00h	11/15/85
PC XT 286	FCh	02h	00h	
PC Convertible	F9h	00h	00h	
PS/2 Model 30	FAh	00h	00h	
PS/2 Model 50	FCh	04h	00h	
PS/2 Model 60	FCh	05h	00h	
PS/2 Model 80	F8h	00h	00h	

If called on older PC models, this service sets the carry flag and returns 86h in AH (or 80h on original PC and PCjr models) to indicate that the service is invalid on the model.

Get Extended BIOS Address (Interrupt 15h, service C1h)

Category: PS/2 services

Registers on Entry:

AH: C1h

Registers on Return:

AH: Return code
ES: Extended BIOS Data Area's segment address

Memory Affected: None

Syntax:

```
MOV    AH,C1h      ;request service
INT    15h         ;BIOS extension interrupt
```

Description: This service, available only on the PS/2 line, sets the ES register to point to the Extended BIOS Data Area's segment address; it is meaningful only if the feature-information byte (refer to table 20.18) of service 15/C0 indicates that such an area has been allocated.

If called on older PC models, this service sets the carry flag and returns 86h in AH (or 80h on original PC and PCjr models) to indicate that the service is invalid on the model.

Pointing Device Interface (Interrupt 15h, service C2h)

Category: PS/2 services

Registers on Entry:

AH: C2h
AL: 00h = Enable/disable device
       01h = Reset device
       02h = Set sampling rate for device
       03h = Set resolution of device
       04h = Read device type
       05h = Initialize device interface
       06h = Indicate extended commands for device
       07h = Initialize FAR call device
BH: 00h = Enable (if AL=0)
       01h = Disable (if AL=0)

Registers on Return:

AH: Return code

Memory Affected: None

Syntax:

```
MOV    AL,00h      ;enable/disable subfunction
MOV    BH,00h      ;enable pointing device
MOV    AH,C2h      ;request service
INT    15h         ;BIOS extension interrupt
```

Description: This service, *available only on the PS/2 line*, need never be called by your programs; the standard mouse interface of INT 33h uses this service, if applicable, so that your programs can communicate with pointing devices by using the INT 33h interface.

If called on older PC models, this service sets the carry flag and returns 86h in AH (or 80h on original PC and PCjr models) to indicate that the service is invalid with the model.

Watchdog Timer (Interrupt 15h, service C3h)

Category: PS/2 services

Registers on Entry:

AH: C3

AL: 00h = Disable timer
        01h = Enable timer

BX: Timer count (1-255)

Registers on Return: Unchanged

Memory Affected: None

Syntax:

```
MOV     BX,182      ;set alarm for 182 ticks (approx 10 sec)
MOV     AH,C3h      ;request service
MOV     AL,01h      ;enable timer
INT     15h         ;BIOS extension interrupt
; .
; .     do something that must complete within 10 seconds
; .
MOV     AH,C3h      ;request service
MOV     AL,00h      ;disable timer
INT     15h         ;BIOS extension interrupt
```

Description: This service, *available only on the PS/2 line*, sets a "watchdog" alarm based on the 18.2-tick/second main timer cycle. If you call this service to enable the timer with a count from 1 to 255 in the BX register and fail to call the service again before the count reaches zero, a nonmaskable interrupt (INT 02h) is generated. The count decrements by one at each timer tick.

If called on older PC models, this service sets the carry flag and returns 86h in AH (or 80h on original PC and PCjr models) to indicate that the service is invalid on the model.

Programmable Option Select (Interrupt 15h, service C4h)

Category: PS/2 services

Registers on Entry:

AH: C4h

AL: 00h = Return base POS register address
        01h = Enable slot for setup
        02h = Enable adapter

Registers on Return:

DL: Base POS register port address (if AL=0)
BL: Slot number (if AL=1)

Memory Affected: None

Syntax:

```
MOV     AL,00h      ;get address to DL
MOV     AH,C4h      ;request service
INT     15h         ;BIOS extension interrupt
```

Description: This service, *available only on the PS/2 line*, eliminates the need to set DIP switches. Instead, programmable registers accessed by this service establish options for the various plug-in boards.

Note: Using this service improperly can cause physical damage to some plug-in boards. Be sure that you know exactly what your program is doing, and why, before attempting to use this service.

If called on older PC models, this service sets the carry flag and returns 86h in AH (or 80h on original PC and PCjr models) to indicate that the service is invalid on the model.

Read Keyboard Character (Interrupt 16h, service 0)

Category: Keyboard services

Registers on Entry:

AH: 0

Registers on Return:

AH: Keyboard scan code
AL: ASCII value of keystroke

Memory Affected: None

Syntax:

```
MOV     AH,0                ;Specify service 0
INT     16h                 ;BIOS keyboard interrupt
MOV     SCAN_CODE,AH        ;Store scan code
MOV     ASCII_KEY,AL        ;Store ASCII value
```

Description: This service, which is similar to service 16/1, examines the keyboard buffer to determine whether a keystroke is available. If no keystroke is available, the service waits until a key is pressed; otherwise, the service returns the ASCII value of the keystroke in AL and the scan code value in AH.

Several keys or key combinations on a standard IBM PC keyboard do not have a corresponding ASCII value. If these keys are pressed, this service returns a 0 (zero) in AL; the value in AH still represents the appropriate scan-code value. (For a list of keyboard scan codes and ASCII values, see Appendix B.)

You cannot use this service to return a scan code for every possible keystroke on the keyboard. It does not return scan codes for some keys (such as the Shift, Ctrl, and Alt keys) that cause modification to the key(s) which follow. When these keys alone are pressed, no scan code is returned. However, key combinations such as Alt-T or Ctrl-A cause scan code/ASCII combinations to be returned.

Some keys (such as SysRq, PrtSc, and Ctrl-Alt-Del) also cause an interrupt to occur. This service does not trap and return these keys.

Through this service, any ASCII value from 0 to 255 can be derived by combining the Alt key with the numeric keypad. For example, holding down the Alt key while pressing 153 on the keypad, and then releasing the Alt key, causes 0 to be returned in AH (scan code) and 153 to be returned in AL (ASCII value). Pressing a keypad number larger than 255 while holding down the Alt key causes the value returned in AL to be the modulo of that number divided by 256. For example, if you use the preceding Alt-key procedure but press 8529 on the keypad, a value of 81 (the remainder when 8,529 is divided by 256) is returned in AL.

Read Keyboard Status (Interrupt 16h, service 1)

Category: Keyboard services

Registers on Entry:

AH: 1

Registers on Return:

AH: Keyboard scan code
AL: ASCII value of keypress

Memory Affected: None

Syntax:

```
        MOV    AH,1              ;Specify service 1
        INT    16h               ;BIOS keyboard interrupt
        JZ     NO_KEY            ;No key available
        MOV    SCAN_CODE,AH      ;Store scan code
        MOV    ASCII_KEY,AL      ;Store ASCII value
NO_KEY:
```

Description: This service, which is similar to service 16/0, examines the keyboard buffer to determine whether a keystroke is available. If a key is available, the zero flag is cleared, the ASCII value of the keystroke is returned in AL, and the scan code value is returned in AH. If no keystroke is waiting, the zero flag is set on return; the contents of AH and AL are not significant.

Several keys or key combinations on a standard IBM PC keyboard do not have a corresponding ASCII value. If these keys are pressed, this service returns a 0 (zero) in AL; the value in AH still represents the appropriate scan-code value. (For a list of keyboard scan codes and ASCII values, see Appendix B.)

You cannot use this service to return a scan code for every possible keystroke on the keyboard. It does not return scan codes for some keys (such as the Shift, Ctrl, and Alt keys) that cause modification to the key(s) which follow. When these keys alone are pressed, no scan code is returned. However, key combinations such as Alt-T or Ctrl-A cause scan code/ASCII combinations to be returned.

Some keys (such as SysRq, PrtSc, and Ctrl-Alt-Del) also cause an interrupt to occur. This service does not trap and return these keys.

Through this service, any ASCII value from 0 to 255 can be derived by combining the Alt key with the numeric keypad. For example, holding down the Alt key while pressing 153 on the keypad, and then releasing the Alt key, causes 0 to be returned in AH (scan code) and 153 to be returned in AL (ASCII value). Pressing a keypad number larger than 255 while holding down the Alt key causes the value returned in AL to be the modulo of that number divided by 256. For example, if you use the preceding Alt-key procedure but press 8529 on the keypad, a value of 81 (the remainder when 8,529 is divided by 256) is returned in AL.

Read Keyboard Shift Status (Interrupt 16h, service 2)

Category: Keyboard services

Registers on Entry:

AH: 2

Registers on Return:

AL: Shift status (table 20.20)

Memory Affected: None

Syntax:

```
MOV    AH,2         ;Specify service 2
INT    16h          ;BIOS keyboard interrupt
```

Description: This service returns (in AL) the keyboard's current shift status. Each bit of the returned value represents the state of a specific keyboard Shift key (see table 20.20).

Table 20.20. Keyboard shift-status values returned by service 16/2.

Bits 76543210	Hex	Decimal	Meaning of Bits
1	80	128	Insert on
1	40	64	Caps Lock on
1	20	32	Num Lock on
1	10	16	Scroll Lock on
1	8	8	Alt key down
1	4	4	Ctrl key down
1	2	2	Left Shift key down
1	1	1	Right Shift key down

Your programs can use this function to check for exotic key combinations that serve as a signal to perform a certain task. For instance, you may want to minimize the possibility of accidentally exiting your program. Instead of using the Esc key (which is easy to press accidentally) to exit the program, you can set up your program so that the user can exit only by pressing the Ctrl-Alt-Left Shift key combination. This combination is unlikely to be entered by accident.

The BIOS controls the setting of this status byte through the keyboard interrupt. Whenever someone presses the Ins, Shift, Ctrl, Alt, Num Lock, or Scroll Lock key, BIOS changes the appropriate bits in the keyboard status byte and resumes waiting for another key to be pressed.

Adjust Repeat Rate (Interrupt 16h, service 03h)

Category: Extended keyboard services

Registers on Entry:

AH: 03h

AL: 00h = Restore default values (PCjr only)
         01h = Increase initial delay (PCjr only)
         02h = Cut repeat rate in half (PCjr only)
         03h = Do both 01 and 02 (PCjr only)
         04h = turn off keyboard repeat (PCjr only)
         05h = Set repeat rate and delay (Personal Computer AT and PS/2 only)

BH: Repeat delay (0-3 x 250 ms; Personal Computer AT and PS/2 only)

BL: Repeat rate (0-31, lower values are faster; Personal Computer AT and PS/2 only)

Registers on Return: Not significant

Memory Affected: None

Syntax:

```
MOV     AH,03h          ;request service
MOV     AL,05h          ;for AT
MOV     BX,0307h        ;delay=750 ms, rate code=7
INT     16h             ;BIOS keyboard interrupt
```

Description: This service, *available only on the PCjr and on the IBM Personal Computer AT and PS/2 lines*, modifies both the initial delay before repeats begin, and the repeat rate, of the keyboard.

Key-Click Control (Interrupt 16h, service 04h)

Category: Extended keyboard services

Registers on Entry:

AH: 04h
AL: 00h = Silent
        01h = Click sounds

Registers on Return: Not significant

Memory Affected: None

Syntax:

```
MOV     AH,04h          ;request service
MOV     AL,00h          ;be quiet!
INT     16h             ;BIOS keyboard interrupt
```

Description: This service, *available only on the PCjr*, silences or reenables the built-in key-click generator. The service has no effect on other models, but generates no error code.

Write to Keyboard Buffer (Interrupt 16h, service 05h)

Category: Extended keyboard services

Registers on Entry:

AH: 05h
CH: Scan code to write
CL: ASCII code to write

Registers on Return:

AL = 01h if buffer full

Memory Affected: None

Syntax:

```
        MOV     CX,0FFFFh       ;write test codes
        MOV     AH,05h          ;into keyboard buffer
        INT     16h             ;BIOS keyboard interrupt
        MOV     CX,16           ;set loop count
GET_CODES: MOV   AH,10h          ;read test codes back
        INT     16h             ;BIOS keyboard interrupt
        CMP     AX,0FFFFh       ;test to see if test code came back
        JE      HAVE_101        ;found it, enhanced KB present
        LOOP    GET_CODES       ;else keep looking until buffer empty
        JMP     NO_101          ;enhanced KB not present
```

Description: This service, *available only on the IBM Personal Computer AT and PS/2 lines*, is meaningful only when the enhanced 101-key keyboard is being used, because older designs lack buffers into which the service can write.

The syntax example shows a method for using this service (together with service 16/10) to determine whether the enhanced 101-key keyboard is installed.

Get Extended Keystroke (Interrupt 16h, service 10h)

Category: Extended keyboard services

Registers on Entry:

AH: 10h

Registers on Return: Same as for service 16/0

Memory Affected: None

Syntax:

```
MOV     AH,10h          ;request service
INT     16h             ;BIOS keyboard interrupt
```

Description: This service, *available only on the IBM Personal Computer AT and PS/2 lines*, operates exactly like service 16/0; unlike service 16/0, however, this service also recognizes and can distinguish between the keys added to the 101-key keyboard.

Check Extended Keyboard Status
(Interrupt 16h, service 11h)

Category: Extended keyboard services

Registers on Entry:

AH: 11h

Registers on Return: Same as for service 16/1

Memory Affected: None

Syntax:

```
MOV     AH,11h      ;request service
INT     16h         ;BIOS keyboard interrupt
```

Description: This service, *available only on the IBM Personal Computer AT and PS/2 lines*, operates exactly like service 16/1; unlike service 16/1, however, this service also recognizes and can respond to the keys added to the 101-key keyboard.

Get Extended Keyboard Status Flags
(Interrupt 16h, service 12h)

Category: Extended keyboard services

Registers on Entry:

AH: 12h

Registers on Return: Same as for service 16/2

Memory Affected: None

Syntax:

```
MOV     AH,12h      ;request service
INT     16h         ;BIOS keyboard interrupt
```

Description: This service, *available only on the IBM Personal Computer AT and PS/2 lines*, operates exactly like service 16/2; unlike service 16/2, however, this service also recognizes the keys added to the 101-key keyboard, and can respond to them.

Print Character (Interrupt 17h, service 0)

Category: Printer services

Registers on Entry:

AH: 0
AL: Character to print
DX: Printer to be used

Registers on Return:

AH: Printer status (table 20.21)

Memory Affected: None

Syntax:

```
MOV    AL,'*'        ;Print an asterisk
MOV    DX,0          ;Use first printer
MOV    AH,0          ;Specify service 0
INT    17h           ;BIOS printer interrupt
```

Description: This service outputs a character to a printer port. The character to be printed is loaded in AL; the printer to use is designated in DX. A printer designation of 0 to 2 is valid (0 corresponds to LPT1:, 1 to LPT2:, and 2 to LPT3:).

The value this service returns in AH is the printer status byte. (Services 17/1 and 17/2 also return the printer status byte in AH.) Table 20.21 lists the meaning of the bits in this returned byte.

Table 20.21. *Meaning of bits returned in AH for services 17/0, 17/1, and 17/2.*

Bits 76543210	*Meaning of Bits*
1	Printer not busy
0	Printer busy
1	Printer acknowledgment
1	Out of paper
1	Printer selected
1	I/O error
??	Unused
1	Time-out

Initialize Printer (Interrupt 17h, service 1)

Category: Printer services

Registers on Entry:

AH: 1
DX: Printer to be used

Registers on Return:

AH: Printer status

Memory Affected: None

Syntax:

```
MOV    DX,0        ;Use first printer
MOV    AH,1        ;Specify service 1
INT    17h         ;BIOS printer interrupt
```

Description: The outputs from this service initialize the IBM- or EPSON-compatible printer connected to the port specified in DX. A printer designation of 0 to 2 is valid (0 corresponds to LPT1:, 1 to LPT2:, and 2 to LPT3:).

Two values (08h and 0Ch) are output to initialize the printer. The printer interprets these values as a command to perform a reset. *Note that this series works only on IBM- and EPSON-compatible printers.* Other printers may not understand this series and may produce unwanted results.

The value this service returns in AH is the printer status byte. (Refer to table 20.21 for the meaning of the bits in this returned byte.)

Get Printer Status (Interrupt 17h, service 2)

Category: Printer services

Registers on Entry:

AH: 2
DX: Printer to be used

Registers on Return:

AH: Printer status

Memory Affected: None

Syntax:

```
MOV    DX,0        ;Use first printer
MOV    AH,2        ;Specify service 2
INT    17h         ;BIOS printer interrupt
```

Description: This service retrieves the status of the printer specified in DX. A printer designation of 0 to 2 is valid (0 corresponds to LPT1:, 1 to LPT2:, and 2 to LPT3:).

The value this service returns in AH is the printer status byte. (Refer to table 20.21 for the meaning of the bits in this returned byte.)

Boot Process Failure (Interrupt 18h)

Category: System services

Registers on Entry: Not significant

Registers on Return: Not significant

Memory Affected: None

Syntax:

```
INT    18h         ;Boot failure routine
```

Description: This interrupt is used when booting the computer. If the process of loading DOS from a disk drive fails, then this interrupt is executed. On older IBM PCs, it resulted in ROM BASIC being loaded. On newer machines and PC clones, it generally results in display of a message indicating that the boot process failed.

Warm Boot (Interrupt 19h)

Category: System services

Registers on Entry: Not significant

Registers on Return: Not applicable (no return)

Memory Affected: Contents of memory after invocation reflect normal memory conditions after a warm-booting procedure. The contents of any given free memory area are unpredictable.

Syntax:

```
INT    19h          ;BIOS warm boot
```

Description: This interrupt, which performs a warm reboot of the computer system, is functionally the same as pressing Ctrl-Alt-Del.

There are differences between this method and the other methods of starting the computer system, however. This interrupt does not go through the power-on self test (POST) procedures, nor does it reset the equipment status word in memory (refer to Interrupt 11h).

Get Clock Counter (Interrupt 1Ah, service 0)

Category: Date/time services

Registers on Entry:

AH: 0

Registers on Return:

AL: Midnight flag
CX: Clock count high-order word
DX: Clock count low-order word

Memory Affected: None

Syntax:

```
MOV    AH,0          ;Specify service 0
INT    1Ah           ;BIOS date/time interrupt
```

Description: This service retrieves the current value of the system software clock counter. This value is a double word register that is incremented approximately 18.2065 times per second, starting from 0 (midnight). Midnight is assumed when the value of the counter reaches 1800B0h or when the counter has been incremented 1,573,040 times. Dividing this counter value by 18.2065 indicates that this clock count represents 86,399.9121 seconds (a fairly accurate representation of a full day, because there are 86,400 seconds in a 24-hour period).

AL is set to 1 if midnight has been passed since the last read of the clock. If midnight has not been passed, AL is set to 0 (zero). Invoking this service always causes the midnight flag to be reset to 0.

Set Clock Counter (Interrupt 1Ah, service 1)

Category: Date/time services

Registers on Entry:

AH: 1
CX: Clock count high-order word
DX: Clock count low-order word

Registers on Return: Unchanged

Memory Affected: None

Syntax:

```
MOV    CX,HIGH_COUNT          ;Clock high-order word
MOV    DX,LOW_COUNT           ;Clock low-order word
MOV    AH,1                   ;Specify service 1
INT    1Ah                    ;BIOS date/time interrupt
```

Description: This service sets the current value of the system software clock counter. This value is a double word register that is incremented approximately .2065 times per second, starting from 0 (midnight).

To determine the proper settings for any given time of day, simply determine the number of seconds since midnight and then multiply this number by 18.2065. For instance, the clock value for 14:22:17.39 (military time) would be determined as follows:

14 hours =	14 * 60 * 60	=	50400	seconds
22 minutes =	22 * 60	=	1320	seconds
17.39 seconds =	17.39	=	17.39	seconds
Total:			51737.39	seconds
Clock ticks per second =			18.2065	ticks
Ticks represented:			941956.7910	ticks

Because fractional ticks cannot be represented, the number of ticks is rounded to 941,957 (0E5F85h). CX is loaded with 0Eh; DX, with 5F85h.

Be careful. Because this service performs no range checks on the values you specify in CX and DX, you can inadvertently specify an invalid time without any indication from BIOS that you have done so. (An invalid time is any value greater than 1800B0h, the number of ticks in a full 24-hour period.)

Read Real-Time Clock (Interrupt 1Ah, service 2)

Category: Date/time services

Registers on Entry:

AH: 2

Registers on Return:

CH: Hours (BCD)
CL: Minutes (BCD)
DH: Seconds (BCD)

Memory Affected: None

Syntax:

```
MOV     AH,2            ;Specify service 2
INT     1Ah             ;BIOS date/time interrupt
MOV     HOUR,CH         ;Save current hour
MOV     MINUTE,CL       ;Save current minute
MOV     SECOND,DH       ;Save current second
```

Description: This service, *which is available only on the IBM Personal Computer AT*, retrieves the value of the real-time clock. Remember that the values returned in CH, CL, and DH are in *binary coded decimal* (BCD) and that you must make allowances for subsequent calculations that use these return values.

If the clock is not functioning, the carry flag is set on return; otherwise, the carry flag is clear.

Set Real-Time Clock (Interrupt 1Ah, service 3)

Category: Date/time services

Registers on Entry:

AH: 3
CH: Hours (BCD)
CL: Minutes (BCD)
DH: Seconds (BCD)
DL: Daylight saving time

Registers on Return: Unchanged

Memory Affected: None

Syntax:

```
MOV     CH,HOUR                 ;Get current hour
MOV     CL,MINUTE               ;Get current minute
MOV     DH,SECOND               ;Get current second
MOV     DL,0                    ;Normal time
MOV     AH,3                    ;Specify service 3
INT     1Ah                     ;BIOS date/time interrupt
```

Description: This service, *which is available only on the IBM Personal Computer AT*, sets the real-time clock. Remember that the values specified in CH, CL, and DH should be in *binary coded decimal* (BCD).

DL should be set to indicate whether the time being set is daylight saving time. If DL is 0 (zero), standard time is indicated; if DL is 1, daylight saving time is indicated.

Read Date from Real-Time Clock (Interrupt 1Ah, service 4)

Category: Date/time services

Registers on Entry:

AH: 4

Registers on Return:

CH: Century (BCD)
CL: Year (BCD)
DH: Month (BCD)
DL: Day (BCD)

Memory Affected: None

Syntax:

```
MOV     AH,4        ;Specify service 4
INT     1Ah         ;BIOS date/time interrupt
```

Description: This service, *which is available only on the IBM Personal Computer AT*, retrieves the date from the real-time clock. Remember that all values returned are in *binary coded decimal* (BCD) and that you must make allowances for subsequent calculations which use these return values.

For instance, if the date is July 1, 1987, the value returned in CH is 19h, the value in CL is 87h, the value in DH is 07h, and the value in DL is 01h.

If the clock is not functioning, the carry flag is set on return; otherwise, the carry flag is clear.

Set Date of Real-Time Clock (Interrupt 1Ah, service 5)

Category: Date/time services

Registers on Entry:

AH: 5
CH: Century (BCD, 19 or 20)
CL: Year (BCD)
DH: Month (BCD)
DL: Day (BCD)

Registers on Return: Unchanged

Memory Affected: None

Syntax:

```
MOV   CX,1986h    ;Year in BCD
MOV   DH,12h      ;December (BCD)
MOV   DL,25h      ;Day in BCD
MOV   AH,5        ;Specify service 5
INT   1Ah         ;BIOS date/time interrupt
```

Description: This service, *which is available only on the IBM Personal Computer AT*, sets the date of the real-time clock. Remember that all values used by this service should be in *binary coded decimal* (BCD).

Because no range checking is performed on the registers for this service, all range checking should be performed by the user program.

Set Alarm (Interrupt 1Ah, service 6)

Category: Date/time services

Registers on Entry:

AH: 6
CH: Hours (BCD)
CL: Minutes (BCD)
DH: Seconds (BCD)

Registers on Return: Unchanged

Memory Affected: None

Syntax:

```
MOV    CH,01h        ;1 hour
MOV    CL,30h        ;30 minutes (BCD)
MOV    DH,0          ;0 seconds
MOV    AH,6          ;Specify service 6
INT    1Ah           ;BIOS date/time interrupt
```

Description: This service, *which is available only on the IBM Personal Computer AT*, sets the BIOS alarm function. Remember that all values used by this service are expected to be in *binary coded decimal* (BCD). The time specified in the registers (CH, CL, DH) is the elapsed time before the alarm will occur. In the preceding syntax example, the alarm will occur 1 hour, 30 minutes, 0 seconds from the time the service is invoked.

The BIOS alarm function simply generates an interrupt signal after the appropriate period of time has elapsed. The address of the routine you want to perform should be vectored to Interrupt 4Ah.

Because no range checking is performed on the registers for this service, all range checking should be performed by the user program.

If the clock is not functioning or if the alarm is already enabled, the carry flag is set on return; otherwise, the carry flag is clear. To reset the alarm to another time, you must first disable the alarm by invoking service 1A/7; then reset the alarm.

Disable Alarm (Interrupt 1Ah, service 7)

Category: Date/time services

Registers on Entry:

AH: 7

Registers on Return: Unchanged

Memory Affected: None

Syntax:

```
MOV    AH,7          ;Specify service 7
INT    1Ah           ;BIOS date/time interrupt
```

Description: This service, *which is available only on the IBM Personal Computer AT*, disables an alarm interrupt enabled through service 1A/6. This service must be called before the alarm can be reset.

Read Alarm (Interrupt 1Ah, service 9)

Category: Date/time services

Registers on Entry:

AH: 9

Registers on Return:

CH: BCD hours
CL: BCD minutes
DH: BCD seconds
DL: Alarm status:
                     00 = Not enabled
                     01 = Enabled, no power on
                     02 = Enabled, will power system on when alarm triggers

Memory Affected: None

Syntax:

```
MOV     AH,9        ;Specify service 9
INT     1Ah         ;BIOS date/time interrupt
```

Description: This service, *which is available only on the PC Convertible and the PS/2 Model 30*, reports the setting and status of the alarm interrupt enabled through service 1A/6.

Get Day Count (Interrupt 1Ah, service 0Ah)

Category: Date/time services

Registers on Entry:

AH: 0Ah

Registers on Return:

CX: Total count of days since 01/01/80

Memory Affected: None

Syntax:

```
MOV    AH,0Ah        ;Specify service 0Ah
INT    1Ah           ;BIOS date/time interrupt
```

Description: This service, *which is available only on the PC XT with BIOS dated 01/10/86 or later and on the PS/2 line*, reports the number of days that have elapsed since January 1, 1980 (the internal storage format for the date functions).

Set Day Count (Interrupt 1Ah, service 0Bh)

Category: Date/time services

Registers on Entry:

AH: 0Bh
CX: Total count of days since 01/01/80

Registers on Return: Not significant

Memory Affected: None

Syntax:

```
MOV    AH,0Bh        ;Specify service 0Ah
MOV    CX,1761       ;day count for Jan. 1, 1984
INT    1Ah           ;BIOS date/time interrupt
```

Description: This service, *which is available only on the PC XT with BIOS dated 01/10/86 or later and on the PS/2 line*, sets into memory the value in CX as the number of days that have elapsed since January 1, 1980 (the internal storage format for the date functions).

Control-Break Handler (Interrupt 1Bh)

Category: Custom service

Registers on Entry: Not known

Registers on Return: Unchanged

Memory Affected: None

Description: This service is called automatically from INT 09h if the Ctrl-Break keystroke combination is detected and response is enabled. DOS normally points this interrupt to a routine that treats it much the same as a Ctrl-C interrupt. If you want to control all break processing in your program, you can change the service for this interrupt to one of your own choosing. If you do, however, be sure to save the original address and restore it before your program finishes.

CHAPTER 21

The DOS Services

D OS, an acronym for *Disk Operating System*, can apply to either MS-DOS (distributed by Microsoft) or PC DOS (distributed by IBM). Because both operating systems are effectively the same, with the same assembly language function calls available through both, this book refers to either dialect as DOS.

DOS, like BIOS, contains a series of functions that is accessible to outside programs. You invoke these functions (callable subroutines) through the use of software *interrupts*, which are generated through the INT assembly language instruction. INT causes the microprocessor to use an address from an interrupt table in low memory as the address for this special type of subroutine.

Specifically, INT pushes the flags register on the stack and then resets the interrupt and trap flags. The full return address (CS:IP) is placed on the stack, at which point the desired interrupt vector (address) is retrieved from the interrupt table and placed in CS:IP. Execution of the interrupt then continues until an IRET instruction is encountered. At this point, the return address is popped from the stack and placed in CS:IP. The flags register is then restored from the stack, and program execution continues from the point at which the interrupt was invoked.

Notice that the interrupt address is fetched from the interrupt table, based on the number of the interrupt being invoked. The full syntax for calling an interrupt is

INT *XX*

where *XX* is replaced by the number of the appropriate interrupt.

Chapter 20 detailed many BIOS functions that are callable through various interrupts. This chapter provides the same kind of information for DOS services. All the documented DOS services are included in this chapter; the undocumented ones are not. Undocumented DOS services are the ones that are not published in official Microsoft or IBM technical documents. They usually are discovered by individual programmers painstakingly disassembling DOS. Since there is disagreement over what some of these unofficial services do, they are not covered here. Many other books that cover them are available.

The DOS Service Categories

The interrupts and services offered by DOS can be divided into several broad categories, usually specified by the function's task classification. The DOS function categories include

❑ I/O services

❑ Printer services

❑ Disk services

❑ System services

❑ Network services

❑ Date/time services

Some of these categories may look familiar to readers who have referred to Chapter 20. Although the categories are similar to the BIOS services, the operations may vary considerably. The largest categories of DOS services are, understandably, the disk and system services. Table 21.1 lists the DOS services covered in this chapter, sorted by category.

The services are arranged in ascending numerical order. Each service can be identified by the primary interrupt number and an individual service number which is specified by the contents of the AH register when the interrupt is invoked. In this notation scheme, any DOS service can be denoted by a hexadecimal number pair, *II/SS*, where *II* is the interrupt number and *SS* is the service number. For instance, the service used to remove a subdirectory, service 21/3A, has an interrupt number of 21h, and a service number (specified through register AH) of 3Ah.

Other services may be specified as *II/SS/FF*, where the appended *FF* indicates the function number. For instance, the service used to read from a block device, service 21/44/04, has an interrupt number of 21h, a service number (specified through register AH) of 44h, and a function number (specified through register AL) of 04h.

Table 21.1. *DOS services list, sorted by category.*

I/O Services

II	SS	Service Name
21	01	Character Input with Echo
21	02	Output Character
21	03	Auxiliary Input
21	04	Auxiliary Output
21	06	Direct Console I/O
21	07	Direct Character Input without Echo
21	08	Character Input without Echo
21	09	Output Character String
21	0A	Buffered Input
21	0B	Check for Character Waiting
21	0C	Clear Buffer and Get Input

Printer Services

II	SS	Service Name
21	05	Printer Output

Disk Services

II	SS	Service Name
21	0D	Reset Disk
21	0E	Set Default Drive
21	0F	Open File, Using FCB
21	10	Close File, Using FCB
21	11	Search for First File-name Match, Using FCB
21	12	Search for Next File-name Match, Using FCB
21	13	Delete File, Using FCB
21	14	Sequential Read, Using FCB
21	15	Sequential Write, Using FCB
21	16	Create File, Using FCB
21	17	Rename File, Using FCB
21	19	Get Current Drive

continues

Table 21.1. continued

II	SS	Service Name
21	1A	Set Disk Transfer Area (DTA)
21	1B	Get FAT Information for Default Drive
21	1C	Get FAT Information for Drive
21	1F	Get Default Disk Parameter Block
21	21	Random Read, Using FCB
21	22	Random Write, Using FCB
21	23	Get File Size, Using FCB
21	24	Set Random Record Field in FCB
21	27	Read Random Record(s), Using FCB
21	28	Write Random Record(s), Using FCB
21	29	Parse File Name, Using FCB
21	2E	Set Verify Flag
21	2F	Get Disk Transfer Area
21	32	Get Disk Parameter Block
21	36	Get Disk Free Space
21	39	Create Subdirectory
21	3A	Remove Subdirectory
21	3B	Set Directory
21	3C	Create File
21	3D	Open File
21	3E	Close File
21	3F	Read File
21	40	Write File
21	41	Delete File
21	42	Move File Pointer
21	43	Get/Set File Attributes
21	45	Duplicate File Handle
21	46	Force Handle Duplication
21	47	Get Directory Path
21	4E	Search for First File-Name Match
21	4F	Search for Next File-Name Match
21	56	Rename File

II	SS	Service Name
21	57	Get/Set File Date and Time
21	5A	Create Temporary File
21	5B	Create File
21	5C	File Access Control
21	68	Flush Buffer
21	6C	Extended Open/Create File
25		Absolute Disk Read
26		Absolute Disk Write

System Services

II	SS	FF	Service Name
20			Terminate Program
21	00		Terminate Program
21	25		Set Interrupt Vector
21	26		Create Program Segment Prefix (PSP)
21	30		Get DOS Version Number
21	31		Terminate and Stay Resident
21	33	00	Get Ctrl-Break Flag
21	33	01	Set Ctrl-Break Flag
21	33	05	Get Boot Drive Code
21	33	06	Get DOS Version Number
21	34		Get Address of InDOS Flag
21	35		Get Interrupt Vector
21	38		Get/Set Country-Dependent Information
21	44	00	Get Device Information
21	44	01	Set Device Information
21	44	02	Character Device Read
21	44	03	Character Device Write
21	44	04	Block Device Read
21	44	05	Block Device Write
21	44	06	Get Input Status
21	44	07	Get Output Status

continues

Table 21.1. continued

II	SS	FF	Service Name
21	44	08	Block Device Changeable?
21	44	0B	Set Sharing Retry Count
21	44	0C	Handle Generic Code-Page Switching
21	44	0D	Generic IOCTL Block Device Request
21	44	0E	Get Logical Device Map
21	44	0F	Set Logical Device Map
21	44	10	Query Handle
21	44	11	Query Drive
21	48		Allocate Memory
21	49		Free Allocated Memory
21	4A		Change Memory-Block Allocation
21	4B	00	Load Program
21	4B	03	Load Overlay
21	4B	05	Set Execution State
21	4C		Process Terminate
21	4D		Get Return Code of a Subprocess
21	50		Set PSP Address
21	51		Get PSP Address
21	54		Get Verify Setting
21	58	00	Get Allocation Strategy
21	58	01	Set Allocation Strategy
21	58	02	Get High-Memory Link Status
21	58	03	Set High-Memory Link Status
21	59		Get Extended Error Information
21	5D	0A	Set Extended Error Values
21	62		Get Program Segment Prefix (PSP) Address
21	65	01	Get Extended Country Information
21	65	02	Get Uppercase Table
21	65	04	Get Filename Uppercase Table
21	65	05	Get Invalid Filename Character Table
21	65	06	Get Sort Sequence Table

21	65	07	Get Double-Byte Character Set
21	65	20	Convert Character
21	65	21	Convert String
21	65	22	Convert ASCIIZ String
21	66		Get/Set Global Code Page
21	67		Change Handle Count
27			Terminate and Stay Resident
2F			Multiplex Interrupt

Network Services

II	SS	FF	Service Name
21	44	09	Logical Device Local/Remote Determination
21	44	0A	Handle Local/Remote Determination
21	5E	00	Get Machine Name
21	5E	02	Set Printer Setup
21	5E	03	Get Printer Setup
21	5F	02	Get Redirection List Entry
21	5F	03	Redirect Device
21	5F	04	Cancel Redirection

Date/Time Services

II	SS	Service Name
21	2A	Get System Date
21	2B	Set System Date
21	2C	Get System Time
21	2D	Set Time

The number of DOS services available to you depends on which version of DOS you are using. The services explained in this chapter work with DOS versions up through 5.0. Earlier versions of DOS may not include all the functions detailed, although I have tried to indicate these cases in the individual service descriptions. If you have questions, consult your DOS technical manual.

The DOS Services

The rest of this chapter forms a convenient reference section. Each DOS service is described in detail in an organized manner. The following information is provided for each service:

❏ **Service name.** This name is based on the DOS function names selected by IBM or Microsoft and listed in various technical documentation. Where appropriate, the name has been modified or expanded to reflect more accurately the purpose of the service.

❏ **Service category.** The general classification of the service, as previously listed.

❏ **Registers on entry.** DOS service parameters generally are passed through registers. The expected register settings are given here.

❏ **Registers on return.** For proper operation of software, you must know how registers are affected by interrupts. Frequently, DOS functions return values through registers. Such information is detailed here.

❏ **Memory areas affected.** Some DOS functions modify memory based on the desired service. Any affected memory is given.

❏ **Syntax for calling.** A coding section shows the proper method for calling the interrupt.

❏ **Description.** The purpose, benefits, and special considerations of the service are given in this section.

Table 21.2 lists the interrupts and services detailed in this chapter, sorted in ascending numeric order.

Table 21.2. DOS services, listed in numeric order.

II	SS	FF	Service Name
20			Terminate Program
21	00		Terminate Program
21	01		Character Input with Echo
21	02		Output Character
21	03		Auxiliary Input
21	04		Auxiliary Output
21	05		Printer Output
21	06		Direct Console I/O

II	SS	FF	Service Name
21	07		Direct Character Input without Echo
21	08		Character Input without Echo
21	09		Output Character String
21	0A		Buffered Input
21	0B		Check for Character Waiting
21	0C		Clear Buffer and Get Input
21	0D		Reset Disk
21	0E		Set Default Drive
21	0F		Open File, Using FCB
21	10		Close File, Using FCB
21	11		Search for First File-Name Match, Using FCB
21	12		Search for Next File-Name Match, Using FCB
21	13		Delete File, Using FCB
21	14		Sequential Read, Using FCB
21	15		Sequential Write, Using FCB
21	16		Create File, Using FCB
21	17		Rename File, Using FCB
21	19		Get Current Drive
21	1A		Set Disk Transfer Area (DTA)
21	1B		Get FAT Information for Default Drive
21	1C		Get FAT Information for Drive
21	1F		Get Default Disk Parameter Block
21	21		Random Read, Using FCB
21	22		Random Write, Using FCB
21	23		Get File Size, Using FCB
21	24		Set Random Record Field in FCB
21	25		Set Interrupt Vector
21	26		Create Program Segment Prefix (PSP)
21	27		Read Random Record(s), Using FCB
21	28		Write Random Record(s), Using FCB
21	29		Parse File Name, Using FCB

continues

Table 21.2. *continued*

II	SS	FF	Service Name
21	2A		Get System Date
21	2B		Set System Date
21	2C		Get System Time
21	2D		Set Time
21	2E		Set Verify Flag
21	2F		Get Disk Transfer Area
21	30		Get DOS Version Number
21	31		Terminate and Stay Resident
21	32		Get Disk Parameter Block
21	33	00	Get Ctrl-Break Flag
21	33	01	Set Ctrl-Break Flag
21	33	05	Get Boot Drive Code
21	33	06	Get DOS Version Number
21	34		Get Address of InDOS Flag
21	35		Get Interrupt Vector
21	36		Get Disk Free Space
21	38		Get/Set Country-Dependent Information
21	39		Create Subdirectory
21	3A		Remove Subdirectory
21	3B		Set Directory
21	3C		Create File
21	3D		Open File
21	3E		Close File
21	3F		Read File
21	40		Write File
21	41		Delete File
21	42		Move File Pointer
21	43		Get/Set File Attributes
21	44	00	Get Device Information
21	44	01	Set Device Information
21	44	02	Character Device Read

II	SS	FF	Service Name
21	44	03	Character Device Write
21	44	04	Block Device Read
21	44	05	Block Device Write
21	44	06	Get Input Status
21	44	07	Get Output Status
21	44	08	Block Device Changeable?
21	44	09	Logical Device Local/Remote Determination
21	44	0A	Handle Local/Remote Determination
21	44	0B	Set Sharing Retry Count
21	44	0C	Handle Generic Code-Page Switching
21	44	0D	Generic IOCTL Block-Device Request
21	44	0E	Get Logical Device Map
21	44	0F	Set Logical Device Map
21	44	10	Query Handle
21	44	11	Query Drive
21	45		Duplicate File Handle
21	46		Force Handle Duplication
21	47		Get Directory Path
21	48		Allocate Memory
21	49		Free Allocated Memory
21	4A		Change Memory-Block Allocation
21	4B	00	Load Program
21	4B	03	Load Overlay
21	4B	05	Set Execution State
21	4C		Process Terminate
21	4D		Get Return Code of a Subprocess
21	4E		Search for First File-Name Match
21	4F		Search for Next File-Name Match
21	50		Set PSP Address
21	51		Get PSP Address
21	54		Get Verify Setting
21	56		Rename File

continues

Table 21.2. *continued*

II	SS	FF	Service Name
21	57		Get/Set File Date and Time
21	58	00	Get Allocation Strategy
21	58	01	Set Allocation Strategy
21	58	02	Get High-Memory Link Status
21	58	03	Set High-Memory Link Status
21	59		Get Extended Error Information
21	5A		Create Temporary File
21	5B		Create File
21	5C		File Access Control
21	5D	0A	Set Extended Error Values
21	5E	00	Get Machine Name
21	5E	02	Set Printer Setup
21	5E	03	Get Printer Setup
21	5F	02	Get Redirection List Entry
21	5F	03	Redirect Device
21	5F	04	Cancel Redirection
21	62		Get Program Segment Prefix (PSP) Address
21	65	01	Get Extended Country Information
21	65	02	Get Uppercase Table
21	65	04	Get Filename Uppercase Table
21	65	05	Get Invalid Filename Character Table
21	65	06	Get Sort Sequence Table
21	65	07	Get Double-Byte Character Set
21	65	20	Convert Character
21	65	21	Convert String
21	65	22	Convert ASCIIZ String
21	66		Get/Set Global Code Page
21	67		Change Handle Count
21	68		Flush Buffer
21	6C		Extended Open/Create File
22			Terminate Address

23	Ctrl-Break Handler Address
24	Critical Error Handler Address
25	Absolute Disk Read
26	Absolute Disk Write
27	Terminate and Stay Resident
2F	Multiplex Interrupt

Terminate Program (Interrupt 20h)

Category: System services

Registers on Entry: Not significant

Registers on Return: Unspecified (does not return)

Memory Affected: None

Syntax:

```
INT   20h    ;Terminate program
```

Description: You can use this interrupt to terminate a program and return control to DOS. Internally, DOS restores several critical vector addresses (Ctrl-C and critical-error handlers), flushes the file buffers, and transfers control to the termination handler address. This interrupt is equivalent to service 21/0.

This service does not allow you to pass a return code to DOS or to a parent program. For that capability, see services 21/31 and 21/4C.

Terminate Program (Interrupt 21h, service 0)

Category: System services

Registers on Entry:

AH: 0
CS: Segment address of program's PSP

Registers on Return: Unspecified (does not return)

Memory Affected: None

Syntax:

```
MOV   AH,0
INT   21h     ;DOS services interrupt
```

Description: You can use this service to terminate a program and return control to DOS. Internally, DOS restores several critical vector addresses (Ctrl-C and critical-error handlers), flushes the file buffers, and transfers control to the termination handler address. This service is equivalent to issuing an INT 20h.

AH is the only functional register you need to load before calling this service. Because CS, in all likelihood, will not have changed since the program began, CS should already be set to the proper value.

This service does not allow you to pass a return code to DOS or to a parent program. For that capability, see services 21/31 and 21/4C.

Character Input with Echo (Interrupt 21h, service 1)

Category: I/O services

Registers on Entry:

AH: 1

Registers on Return:

AL: Character

Memory Affected: The appropriate areas of video memory are altered to reflect the displayed (echoed) character.

Syntax:

```
MOV   AH,1
INT   21h     ;DOS services interrupt
```

Description: Originally, this service was designed to fetch a character from the keyboard and display that character on the video monitor. Intermediate versions of DOS, however, have modified this service so that I/O redirection is possible. If the standard input device or console has been redirected, this service fetches a character from the specified device. Regardless of the device, the character is echoed to the video monitor.

Even though this service waits for a character to be returned by the keyboard (or redirected I/O device), the service differs significantly from the BIOS keyboard routines in that only one character code is returned in AL. If an extended ASCII code is generated by the keyboard (such as codes generated by the function keys or cursor-control keys), interrupt 21h, service 1 returns a zero in AL. If you invoke the service again, it returns the scan code in AL.

Output Character (Interrupt 21h, service 2)

Category: I/O services

Registers on Entry:

AH: 2
DL: Character (ASCII value)

Registers on Return: Unchanged

Memory Affected: If I/O has not been redirected, the appropriate areas of video memory are altered to reflect the displayed character.

Syntax:

```
MOV    DL,'*'      ;Output an asterisk
MOV    AH,2
INT    21h         ;DOS services interrupt
```

Description: Originally, this service was designed to output a character to the video monitor. Intermediate versions of DOS, however, have modified this service so that I/O redirection is possible. If the standard output device has been redirected, this service sends a character to the specified device.

Auxiliary Input (Interrupt 21h, service 3)

Category: I/O services

Registers on Entry:

AH: 3

Registers on Return:

AL: Character

Memory Affected: None

Syntax:

```
MOV    AH,3
INT    21h             ;DOS services interrupt
```

Description: This service returns a character from the standard auxiliary device, which, if not redirected, is set to be COM1:.

This service is a poor way to read the communications port. More precise and error-free communication is possible through the BIOS communications functions (services 14/0–14/2) or, better yet, through a custom interrupt-driven communications interface. (Such an interface, however, is beyond the scope of this book.)

Auxiliary Output (Interrupt 21h, service 4)

Category: I/O services

Registers on Entry:

AH: 4
DL: Character (ASCII value)

Registers on Return: Unchanged

Memory Affected: None

Syntax:

```
MOV    DL,'_'              ;Output an underscore
MOV    AH,4
INT    21h                 ;DOS services interrupt
```

Description: This service sends a character to the standard auxiliary device, which, if not redirected, is set to COM1:.

This service is a poor way to control the communications port. More precise and error-free communication is possible through the BIOS communications functions (services 14/0–14/2), or better yet through a custom interrupt-driven communications interface. (Such an interface, however, is beyond the scope of this book.)

Printer Output (Interrupt 21h, service 5)

Category: Printer services

Registers on Entry:

AH: 5
DL: Character (ASCII value)

Registers on Return: Unchanged

Memory Affected: None

Syntax:

```
MOV    DL,'_'              ;Print an underscore
MOV    AH,5
INT    21h                 ;DOS services interrupt
```

Description: This service sends a character to the standard list device. Unless redirected, this device is LPT1:.

Direct Console I/O (Interrupt 21h, service 6)

Category: I/O services

Registers on Entry:

AH: 6
DL: Character (ASCII value) or input flag

Registers on Return:

AL: Input character

Memory Affected: If the service is outputting a character to the video monitor, the appropriate video memory areas are changed to reflect the character being displayed.

Syntax:

```
INP_LOOP:      MOV    DL,0FFh           ;Want to input
               MOV    AH,6
               INT    21h               ;DOS services interrupt
               JZ     NO_CHAR           ;No character ready
               CMP    AL,0              ;Was it extended ASCII?
               JNE    GOT_CHAR          ;No, treat as character
               MOV    EXTEND_FLAG,1     ;Yes, so set appropriately
               JMP    INP_LOOP          ;Get scan code
GOT_CHAR:      MOV    CHAR,AL           ;Store character
```

Description: You can use this service for character input or output, depending on the contents of DL. If DL is a value between 0 and 254 (0FEh), the contents of DL are sent to the console (unless redirected, the video screen). If DL contains 255 (0FFh), input is fetched from the console (unless redirected, the keyboard).

When you request input through this service, the zero flag is set on return to indicate the presence of a character. Zero in AL means that a key generating an extended ASCII code has been pressed, and this service should be invoked again to retrieve the scan code.

Direct Character Input without Echo (Interrupt 21h, service 7)

Category: I/O services

Registers on Entry:

AH: 7

Registers on Return:

AL: Character

Memory Affected: None

Syntax:

```
MOV    AH,7
INT    21h            ;DOS services interrupt
```

Description: Originally, this service was designed simply to fetch a character from the keyboard. Intermediate versions of DOS, however, have modified this service so that I/O redirection is possible. If the standard input device or console has been redirected, this service fetches a character from the specified device.

Even though this service waits for a character to be returned by the keyboard (or redirected I/O device), the service differs significantly from the BIOS keyboard routines in that only one character code is returned in AL. If the keyboard generates an extended ASCII code (such as codes generated by the function keys or cursor-control keys), this service returns a 0 in AL. A second invocation returns the scan code in AL.

Character Input without Echo (Interrupt 21h, service 8)

Category: I/O services

Registers on Entry:

AH: 8

Registers on Return:

AL: Character

Memory Affected: None

Syntax:

```
MOV     AH,8
INT     21h              ;DOS services interrupt
```

Description: Originally, this service was designed simply to fetch a character from the keyboard. Intermediate versions of DOS, however, have modified this service so that I/O redirection is possible. If the standard input device or console has been redirected, this service fetches a character from the specified device.

Even though this service waits for a character to be returned by the keyboard (or redirected I/O device), the service differs significantly from the BIOS keyboard routines in that only one character code is returned in AL. If the keyboard generates an extended ASCII code (such as codes generated by the function keys or cursor-control keys), this service returns a 0 in AL. A second invocation returns the scan code in AL.

This service differs from 21/7 in that it performs some interpretation on the characters received. For instance, if Ctrl-C and Ctrl-Break are received, they are translated and acted on by this service.

Output Character String (Interrupt 21h, service 9)

Category: I/O services

Registers on Entry:

AH: 9
DX: Offset address of string
DS: Segment address of string

Registers on Return: Unchanged

Memory Affected: If output is directed to the video display, the contents of the video memory buffers are changed appropriately to reflect the characters displayed.

Syntax:

```
PUSH    CS                        ;Code segment and
POP     DS                        ;  data segment are same
MOV     DX,OFFSET MSG_1           ;Offset address of string
MOV     AH,9
INT     21h                       ;DOS services interrupt
```

Description: This service displays (or outputs) a string on the standard output device. If I/O has been redirected, the string is sent to the specified device.

Each character of the string at DS:DX—up to (but not including) the first occurrence of a dollar sign (ASCII 36)—is displayed by this service. Because of this strange convention (a carryover from CP/M), you cannot display the dollar sign when you are using this service.

Buffered Input (Interrupt 21h, service 0Ah)

Category: I/O services

Registers on Entry:

AH: 0Ah
DX: Offset address of buffer
DS: Segment address of buffer

Registers on Return: Unchanged

Memory Affected: The memory area beginning at DS:DX is overlaid with characters input from the standard input device.

Syntax:

```
PUSH    CS                  ;Code segment and
POP     DS                  ;  data segment are same
MOV     DX,OFFSET BUFFER    ;Offset address of buffer
MOV     AH,0Ah
INT     21h                 ;DOS services interrupt
```

Description: This service allows the input of a specified number of characters from the standard input device. You can change the device, which originally is the keyboard, through I/O redirection.

The input characters are stored at the buffer specified by DS:DX. The value of the first byte of this buffer must indicate the maximum number of characters the buffer can contain. DOS sets the value of the second byte to indicate the number of characters this service returns. Therefore, if your maximum input length is 80 characters, you should set aside 82 bytes for the buffer.

This service does not return until you press Enter. If the buffer is filled before the service detects the carriage return, the extra characters are ignored and the bell sounds with each extra keypress. Remember that each extended ASCII character (function keys, and so on) occupies two bytes in the buffer area.

Check for Character Waiting (Interrupt 21h, service 0Bh)

Category: I/O services

Registers on Entry:

AH: 0Bh

Registers on Return:

AL: Waiting flag

Memory Affected: None

Syntax:

```
KEY_LOOP:      MOV     AH,0Bh
               INT     21h          ;DOS services interrupt
               CMP     AL,0         ;Was there a keypress?
               JE      KEY_LOOP     ;No, continue to wait
```

Description: This service simply checks the status of the standard input device (usually the keyboard) to determine whether a character is available for input. If a character is available, AL equals FFh. If no character is available, AL equals 0.

Clear Buffer and Get Input (Interrupt 21h, service 0Ch)

Category: I/O services

Registers on Entry:

AH: 0Ch
AL: Desired input service
DX: Offset address of buffer
DS: Segment address of buffer

Registers on Return:

AL: Character (ASCII value)

Memory Affected: If AL is loaded with 0Ah, the memory area beginning at DS:DX is overlaid with characters input from the standard input device. Otherwise, memory is not affected.

Syntax:

```
PUSH    CS                      ;Code segment and
POP     DS                      ;  data segment are same
MOV     DX,OFFSET BUFFER        ;Offset address of buffer
MOV     AL,0Ah                  ;Want input service 0Ah
MOV     AH,0Ch
INT     21h                     ;DOS services interrupt
```

Description: This compound service forms a gateway to input services 21/1, 21/6, 21/7, 21/8, and 21/A. You invoke any of these input services by loading the desired service number (1, 6, 7, 8, Ah) into AL. After the type-ahead buffer is cleared, the specified service is invoked.

If AL is set to 0Ah, DS:DX must point to a buffer that is constructed in the fashion described under service 21/A. If AL is set to one of the other services, the contents of DS:DX are not significant.

If AL is set to 1, 6, 7, or 8, on return AL contains the ASCII value of the character fetched. The other characteristics of these DOS services are maintained. Please refer to the appropriate service descriptions for additional information.

Reset Disk (Interrupt 21h, service 0Dh)

Category: Disk services

Registers on Entry:

AH: 0Dh

Registers on Return: Unchanged

Memory Affected: None

Syntax:

```
MOV     AH,0Dh
INT     21h             ;DOS services interrupt
```

Description: This service flushes the DOS disk buffers. If a DOS file buffer contains information to be written to a disk file, that information is written to disk. The service does not close the files.

This service does not change the default drive and has no physical effect on the disk drives or their controllers.

Set Default Drive (Interrupt 21h, service 0Eh)

Category: Disk services

Registers on Entry:

AH: 0Eh
DL: Drive wanted

Registers on Return:

AL: Logical drives

Memory Affected: None

Syntax:

```
MOV    DL,2          ;Set for drive C:
MOV    AH,0Eh
INT    21h           ;DOS services interrupt
```

Description: This service has two purposes: (1) to set the default drive designation by specifying the desired drive in DL, where 0=A, 1=B, 2=C, etc.; (2) to find out how many logical disk drives are connected to the computer.

Logical disk drives include RAM disks, disk emulators, and multisegmented hard disk drives. For instance, if you have two floppy drives (A: and B:), a 40M hard disk partitioned to two disks (C: and D:), and a RAM disk (E:), this service returns a value of 5 in AL even though only three physical drives are connected to the computer.

Clearly, knowing how many logical drives are connected to a computer without actually changing the default disk drive may be beneficial. You can get this information by determining the current default drive (through service 21/19) and then using that information to call this service. The following code segment performs this task:

```
MOV    AH,19h
INT    21h           ;DOS services interrupt
MOV    CUR_DRIVE,AL  ;Store current drive (0-?)
MOV    DL,AL         ;Set for default drive
MOV    AH,0Eh
INT    21h           ;DOS services interrupt
MOV    NUM_DRIVES,AL ;Store number of drives
```

For more information about service 21/19, refer to the description for that service.

Open File, Using FCB (Interrupt 21h, service 0Fh)

Category: Disk services

Registers on Entry:

AH: 0Fh
DX: Offset address of FCB
DS: Segment address of FCB

Registers on Return:

AL: Status byte

Memory Affected: If the service opens the file successfully, DOS fills in the FCB area specified by DS:DX to reflect the status of the file opened.

Syntax:

```
PUSH    CS                      ;Code segment and
POP     DS                      ;  data segment are same
MOV     DX,OFFSET FCB_1         ;Offset address of FCB
MOV     AH,0Fh
INT     21h                     ;DOS services interrupt
```

Description: This service opens a disk file, based on a *file control block,* or FCB. The FCB is a block of information that is set initially by the programmer and then completed by DOS. The FCB consists of 44 bytes constructed in the following manner:

```
FCB_PRE       DB      0FFh              ;Extension flag
              DB      5 DUP(0)          ;Unused
              DB      00                ;File attribute
FCB_1         DB      00                ;Set for default drive
FILE_ROOT     DB      'FILENAME'        ;File name root
FILE_EXT      DB      'EXT'             ;File name extension
BLOCK_NUM     DW      0000              ;Current block number
REC_SIZE      DW      0000              ;Record size
FILE_SIZE     DD      00000000          ;File size
FILE_DATE     DW      0000              ;File date
FILE_TIME     DW      0000              ;File time
              DB      8 DUP(0)          ;DOS work area
REC_NUM       DB      00                ;Current record number
RANDOM_REC    DD      00000000          ;Random record number
```

    The offset address of FCB_1 is the address you specify in DS:DX when you invoke this service. If you are using an extended FCB, use the offset address of FCB_PRE. To call this service, the values for FCB_1 (the drive designator), FILE_ROOT, and FILE_EXT must be specified. Notice that the drive designator is different from the normal method for DOS and BIOS drive designation: 0 represents the default drive, and 1=A, 2=B, 3=C, etc.

If the open operation is successful, DOS returns a 0 in AL and sets FCB_1 to reflect the drive number (1=A, 2=B, 3=C, etc.). DOS also sets BLOCK_NUM to 0; REC_SIZE to 80h; and FILE_SIZE, FILE_DATE, and FILE_TIME to the equivalent of the directory entry for the file. If the open operation is unsuccessful, DOS returns FFh in AL, and the FCB is not filled in.

Notice that this service allows you to use only FCBs. Because FCB file encoding does not allow for path names, any file operations must be performed in the current disk subdirectory. With floppy disks, this limitation may not be a problem, but with fixed disks the limitation can be serious. Refer to service 21/3D for a file-opening method that does not have this limitation.

Close File, Using FCB (Interrupt 21h, service 10h)

Category: Disk services

Registers on Entry:

AH: 10h
DX: Offset address of FCB
DS: Segment address of FCB

Registers on Return:

AL: Status byte

Memory Affected: None

Syntax:

```
PUSH    CS                      ;Code segment and
POP     DS                      ;  data segment are same
MOV     DX,OFFSET FCB_1         ;Offset address of FCB
MOV     AH,10h
INT     21h                     ;DOS services interrupt
```

Description: This service closes a disk file, based on a file control block, or FCB. The FCB consists of 44 bytes constructed in the following manner:

```
FCB_PRE        DB     0FFh                  ;Extension flag
               DB     5 DUP(0)              ;Unused
               DB     00                    ;File attribute
FCB_1          DB     00                    ;Set for default drive
```

```
FILE_ROOT     DB     'FILENAME'          ;File name root
FILE_EXT      DB     'EXT'               ;File name extension
BLOCK_NUM     DW     0000                ;Current block number
REC_SIZE      DW     0000                ;Record size
FILE_SIZE     DD     00000000            ;File size
FILE_DATE     DW     0000                ;File date
FILE_TIME     DW     0000                ;File time
              DB     8 DUP(0)            ;DOS work area
REC_NUM       DB     00                  ;Current record number
RANDOM_REC    DD     00000000            ;Random record number
```

The offset address of FCB_1 is the address you specify in DS:DX when you invoke this service. If you are using an extended FCB, use the offset address of FCB_PRE. To call this service, you must specify the values for FCB_1 (the drive designator), FILE_ROOT, and FILE_EXT. Notice that the drive designator is different from the normal method for DOS and BIOS drive designation. In this instance, 0 represents the default drive, and 1=A, 2=B, 3=C, etc.

If the close operation is successful, DOS returns a 0 in AL; if the operation is unsuccessful, AL contains FFh.

Notice that this service allows you to use only FCBs. Because FCB file encoding does not allow for path names, any file operations must be performed in the current disk subdirectory. With floppy disks, this limitation may not be a problem, but with fixed disks the limitation can be serious. (Service 21/3E, another method of closing files, does not have this limitation.)

Search for First File-Name Match, Using FCB (Interrupt 21h, service 11h)

Category: Disk services

Registers on Entry:

AH: 11h
DX: Offset address of FCB
DS: Segment address of FCB

Registers on Return:

AL: Status byte

Memory Affected: If a file-name match is located, DOS fills in the memory area specified as the disk transfer area (DTA) so that it reflects a completed FCB for the file. DOS alters the original FCB area to allow subsequent searching with service 21/12.

Syntax:

```
PUSH   CS                      ;Code segment and
POP    DS                      ;  data segment are same
MOV    DX,OFFSET FCB_1         ;Offset address of FCB
MOV    AH,11h
INT    21h                     ;DOS services interrupt
```

Description: This service locates a file with a specified name in the current directory of a disk drive, based on a file control block, or FCB. The FCB consists of 44 bytes constructed in the following manner:

```
FCB_PRE        DB     0FFh                ;Extension flag
               DB     5 DUP(0)            ;Unused
FILE_ATTR      DB     00                  ;File attribute
FCB_1          DB     00                  ;Set for default drive
FILE_ROOT      DB     'FILENAME'          ;File name root
FILE_EXT       DB     '???'               ;File name extension
BLOCK_NUM      DW     0000                ;Current block number
REC_SIZE       DW     0000                ;Record size
FILE_SIZE      DD     00000000            ;File size
FILE_DATE      DW     0000                ;File date
FILE_TIME      DW     0000                ;File time
               DB     8 DUP(0)            ;DOS work area
REC_NUM        DB     00                  ;Current record number
RANDOM_REC     DD     00000000            ;Random record number
```

The offset address of FCB_1 is the address you specify in DS:DX when you invoke this service. If you are using an extended FCB, you should use the offset address of FCB_PRE. To call the service, you must specify the values for FCB_1 (the drive designator), FILE_ROOT, and FILE_EXT. Notice that the drive designator is different from the normal method for DOS and BIOS drive designation. In this instance, 0 represents the default drive, and 1=A, 2=B, 3=C, etc.

One useful feature of this service is that you can use the question mark (?) as a wild card in the file-name specification of the FCB. In the sample FCB, any file with the name FILENAME and any extension constitutes a match.

If you are searching for non-normal files (that is, hidden, system, etc.), you must use an extended FCB, which is the sample portion beginning with FCB_PRE. FCB_PRE is set to FFh, signaling that the FCB extension is active. You set the FILE_ATTR file attribute to specify the combination of file attributes you want to search for. Table 21.3 shows possible settings of this byte.

Table 21.3. *Extended FCB attribute byte settings for service 21/11.*

Value	Types of Files Searched
0	Normal files
2	Normal and hidden files
4	Normal and system files
6	Normal, system, and hidden files
8	Volume labels only
16	Directory files

If the search is successful, DOS returns a 0 in AL and constructs a full FCB (either normal or extended) at the DTA location specified through service 21/1A. If the search is unsuccessful, AL contains FFh; the DTA remains undisturbed.

Notice that this service allows you to use only FCBs. Because FCB file encoding does not allow for path names, any file operations must be performed in the current disk subdirectory. With floppy disks, this limitation may not be a problem, but with fixed disks the limitation can be serious. Refer to service 21/4E, another method of searching for files, which does not have this limitation.

Search for Next File-Name Match, Using FCB (Interrupt 21h, service 12h)

Category: Disk services

Registers on Entry:

AH: 12h
DX: Offset address of FCB
DS: Segment address of FCB

Registers on Return:

AL: Status byte

Memory Affected: If a file-name match is located, DOS fills in the memory area specified as the DTA so that it reflects a completed FCB for the file. DOS alters the original FCB area to allow subsequent searching with service 21/12.

Syntax:

```
PUSH    CS                      ;Code segment and
POP     DS                      ;  data segment are same
MOV     DX,OFFSET FCB_1         ;Offset address of FCB
MOV     AH,12h
INT     21h                     ;DOS services interrupt
```

Description: Use this service to locate (in the current directory of a disk drive) a file with a specified name, based on a file control block, or FCB. Before you invoke this service, you must set the FCB by a call to service 21/11. If the FCB is not set, the results can be unpredictable. For more information, see the description for service 21/11.

Because any given directory must contain unique file names, this service is useless if the file specification for which you are searching does not contain the question-mark wild card (?).

Delete File, Using FCB (Interrupt 21h, service 13h)

Category: Disk services

Registers on Entry:

AH: 13h
DX: Offset address of FCB
DS: Segment address of FCB

Registers on Return:

AL: Status byte

Memory Affected: None

Syntax:

```
PUSH    CS                      ;Code segment and
POP     DS                      ;  data segment are same
MOV     DX,OFFSET FCB_1         ;Offset address of FCB
MOV     AH,13h
INT     21h                     ;DOS services interrupt
```

Description: Use this service to delete files by means of a file control block, or FCB. The FCB consists of 44 bytes constructed in the following manner:

```
FCB_PRE      DB    0FFh               ;Extension flag
             DB    5 DUP(0)           ;Unused
FILE_ATTR    DB    00                 ;File attribute
FCB_1        DB    00                 ;Set for default drive
FILE_ROOT    DB    'FILENAME'         ;File name root
FILE_EXT     DB    '???'              ;File name extension
BLOCK_NUM    DW    0000               ;Current block number
REC_SIZE     DW    0000               ;Record size
FILE_SIZE    DD    00000000           ;File size
FILE_DATE    DW    0000               ;File date
FILE_TIME    DW    0000               ;File time
             DB    8 DUP(0)           ;DOS work area
REC_NUM      DB    00                 ;Current record number
RANDOM_REC   DD    00000000           ;Random record number
```

When you invoke this service, specify the offset address of FCB_1 in DS:DX. If you are using an extended FCB, use the offset address of FCB_PRE. To call this service, you must specify the values for FCB_1 (the drive designator), FILE_ROOT, and FILE_EXT. Notice that the drive designator is different from the normal method for DOS and BIOS drive designation. In this instance, 0 represents the default drive, and 1=A, 2=B, 3=C, etc.

A useful feature of this service is that you can use the question mark (?) as a wild card in the file-name specification of the FCB. In the sample FCB, any file with the name FILENAME and any extension is deleted.

Notice that this service allows you to use only FCBs. Because FCB file encoding does not allow for path names, any files deleted must reside in the current disk subdirectory. With floppy disks, this limitation may not be a problem, but with fixed disks, the limitation can be serious. Refer to service 21/41, a method of deleting files that does not have this limitation.

Sequential Read, Using FCB (Interrupt 21h, service 14h)

Category: Disk services

Registers on Entry:

AH: 14h
DX: Offset address of FCB
DS: Segment address of FCB

Registers on Return:

AL: Status byte

Memory Affected: The memory area designated as DTA is overwritten with information read from the disk.

Syntax:

```
PUSH    CS                          ;Code segment and
POP     DS                          ;  data segment are same
MOV     DX,OFFSET FCB_1             ;Offset address of FCB
MOV     AH,14h
INT     21h                         ;DOS services interrupt
```

Description: This service is used to read a block of information from a file that has been opened to the DTA. You designate the block size through the file control block, or FCB. The FCB consists of 44 bytes constructed in the following manner:

```
FCB_PRE         DB      0FFh                ;Extension flag
                DB      5 DUP(0)            ;Unused
FILE_ATTR       DB      00                  ;File attribute
FCB_1           DB      00                  ;Set for default drive
FILE_ROOT       DB      'FILENAME'          ;File name root
FILE_EXT        DB      'DAT'               ;File name extension
BLOCK_NUM       DW      0000                ;Current block number
REC_SIZE        DW      0000                ;Record size
FILE_SIZE       DD      00000000            ;File size
FILE_DATE       DW      0000                ;File date
FILE_TIME       DW      0000                ;File time
                DB      8 DUP(0)            ;DOS work area
REC_NUM         DB      00                  ;Current record number
RANDOM_REC      DD      00000000            ;Random record number
```

When you invoke this service, specify the offset address of FCB_1 in DS:DX. If you are using an extended FCB, use the offset address of FCB_PRE. Before you open the file, set the values for FCB_1 (the drive designator), FILE_ROOT, and FILE_EXT. Specify the size of the block to be read in the REC_SIZE field. The values in BLOCK_NUM and REC_NUM designate where in the file the read is to begin; these fields are incremented automatically after a successful read.

When the service is completed, the value of AL indicates the status of the operation. If AL is 0, the read was successful. If AL is 1, no data was read because the end-of-file was encountered by a previous read command. If AL is 2, the DTA crossed a *segment boundary* (a memory address ending in 000), and an error was generated. If AL is 3, the end-of-file was reached during the read and the service could not read the entire block (the partial block was read and placed in the DTA area).

Sequential Write, Using FCB (Interrupt 21h, service 15h)

Category: Disk services

Registers on Entry:

AH:	15h
DX:	Offset address of FCB
DS:	Segment address of FCB

Registers on Return:

AL: Status byte

Memory Affected: None

Syntax:

```
PUSH    CS                      ;Code segment and
POP     DS                      ;  data segment are same
MOV     DX,OFFSET FCB_1         ;Offset address of FCB
MOV     AH,15h
INT     21h                     ;DOS services interrupt
```

Description: This service is used to write a block of information from the DTA to an open file. You designate the block size through the file control block, or FCB. The FCB consists of 44 bytes constructed in the following manner:

```
FCB_PRE      DB     0FFh            ;Extension flag
             DB     5 DUP(0)        ;Unused
FILE_ATTR    DB     00              ;File attribute
FCB_1        DB     00              ;Set for default drive
FILE_ROOT    DB     'FILENAME'      ;File name root
FILE_EXT     DB     'DAT'           ;File name extension
BLOCK_NUM    DW     0000            ;Current block number
REC_SIZE     DW     0000            ;Record size
FILE_SIZE    DD     00000000        ;File size
FILE_DATE    DW     0000            ;File date
FILE_TIME    DW     0000            ;File time
             DB     8 DUP(0)        ;DOS work area
REC_NUM      DB     00              ;Current record number
RANDOM_REC   DD     00000000        ;Random record number
```

You specify the offset address of FCB_1 in DS:DX when you invoke this service. If you are using an extended FCB, you should use the offset address of FCB_PRE. You should set the values for FCB_1 (the drive designator), FILE_ROOT, and FILE_EXT before you open the file. You specify the size of the block to be written in the REC_SIZE field. The values in BLOCK_NUM and REC_NUM designate where in the file the writing is to begin. After a successful write, these fields are incremented automatically.

When the service is completed, the value of AL indicates the status of the operation. If AL is 0, the write was successful. If AL is 1, a disk-full error was detected during the write. If AL is 2, the DTA crossed a segment boundary (a memory address ending in 000), and an error was generated.

Create File, Using FCB (Interrupt 21h, service 16h)

Category: Disk services

Registers on Entry:

AH: 16h
DX: Offset address of FCB
DS: Segment address of FCB

Registers on Return:

AL: Status byte

Memory Affected: If the file is created successfully, DOS fills in the FCB area (specified by DS:DX) to reflect the status of the file.

Syntax:

```
PUSH    CS                      ;Code segment and
POP     DS                      ;  data segment are same
MOV     DX,OFFSET FCB_1         ;Offset address of FCB
MOV     AH,16h
INT     21h                     ;DOS services interrupt
```

Description: This service uses the information in the file control block, or FCB, to create or truncate a disk file. This FCB is a block of information that the programmer initially sets and DOS subsequently completes. The FCB consists of 44 bytes constructed in the following manner:

```
FCB_PRE       DB      0FFh            ;Extension flag
              DB      5 DUP(0)        ;Unused
              DB      00              ;File attribute
FCB_1         DB      00              ;Set for default drive
FILE_ROOT     DB      'FILENAME'      ;File name root
FILE_EXT      DB      'EXT'           ;File name extension
BLOCK_NUM     DW      0000            ;Current block number
REC_SIZE      DW      0000            ;Record size
FILE_SIZE     DD      00000000        ;File size
FILE_DATE     DW      0000            ;File date
```

```
FILE_TIME     DW    0000        ;File time
              DB    8 DUP(0)    ;DOS work area
REC_NUM       DB    00          ;Current record number
RANDOM_REC    DD    00000000    ;Random record number
```

You specify the offset address of FCB_1 in DS:DX when you invoke this service. If you are using an extended FCB, you should use the offset address of FCB_PRE. To call this service, you must specify the values for FCB_1 (the drive designator), FILE_ROOT, and FILE_EXT. Notice that the drive designator is different from the normal method for DOS and BIOS drive designation. In this instance, 0 represents the default drive, and 1=A, 2=B, 3=C, etc.

If you use the FCB extension area, you can specify the attribute of the file being created. In the example, the extended FCB begins with the area shown as FCB_PRE. FCB_PRE is set to FFh, signaling that the FCB extension is active. The FILE_ATTR file attribute is set to specify the file attribute for the new file.

If the file name specified in the FCB already exists in the current directory, the file is opened and its length is truncated to 0.

If the file is created successfully, DOS returns a 0 in AL. In addition, the service sets FCB_1 to reflect the drive number (1=A, 2=B, 3=C, etc.), and sets BLOCK_NUM to 0, REC_SIZE to 80h, and FILE_SIZE, FILE_DATE, and FILE_TIME to their appropriate values for the new file. If the open operation is unsuccessful, DOS returns FFh in AL and does not fill in the FCB.

When this service is completed, the specified file is left open. You do not need to open the file, but you must remember to close it.

Notice that this service allows you to use only FCBs. Because FCB file encoding does not allow for path names, any file operations must be performed in the current disk subdirectory. With floppy disks, this limitation may not be a problem, but with fixed disks the limitation can be serious. Refer to service 21/3C; this method of creating files does not have this limitation.

Rename File, Using FCB (Interrupt 21h, service 17h)

Category: Disk services

Registers on Entry:

AH: 17h
DX: Offset address of modified FCB
DS: Segment address of modified FCB

Registers on Return:

AL: Status byte

Memory Affected: None

Syntax:

```
PUSH    CS                      ;Code segment and
POP     DS                      ;  data segment are same
MOV     DX,OFFSET FCB_1         ;Offset address of FCB
MOV     AH,17h
INT     21h                     ;DOS services interrupt
```

Description: This service uses information contained in a modified file control block, or FCB, to rename a file in the current directory. This modified FCB consists of 44 bytes constructed in the following manner:

```
MOD_FCB     DB      00          ;Set for default drive
OLD_ROOT    DB      'OLD_FILE'  ;Original file root
OLD_EXT     DB      'EXT'       ;Original file extension
            DB      5 DUP(0)    ;DOS work area
NEW_ROOT    DB      'NEW_FILE'  ;New file root
NEW_EXT     DB      'EXT'       ;New file extension
            DB      16 DUP(0)   ;DOS work area
```

You specify the offset address of MOD_FCB in DS:DX when you invoke this service. To call this service, you must specify the values for MOD_FCB (the drive designator), OLD_ROOT, and OLD_EXT. Notice that the drive designator is different from the normal method for DOS and BIOS drive designation. In this instance, 0 represents the default drive, and 1=A, 2=B, 3=C, etc.

If the renaming operation is successful, DOS returns a 0 in AL. If the operation is unsuccessful, DOS returns FFh in AL.

This service does not allow you to rename files outside the current directory. With floppy disks, this limitation may not be a problem, but with fixed disks the limitation can be serious. Refer to service 21/56; this method of creating files does not have this limitation.

Get Current Drive (Interrupt 21h, service 19h)

Category: Disk services

Registers on Entry:

AH: 19h

Registers on Return:

AL: Drive code

Memory Affected: None

Syntax:

```
MOV     AH,19h
INT     21h                 ;DOS services interrupt
MOV     CUR_DRIVE,AL        ;Store drive designator
```

Description: This service is used to determine the current default disk drive. The service has no calling parameters, and the returned value in AL is a drive code in which 0=A, 1=B, 2=C, etc.

Generally, the default disk drive is the drive from which the computer was booted or the drive last set with service 21/0E.

Set Disk Transfer Area (DTA) (Interrupt 21h, service 1Ah)

Category: Disk services

Registers on Entry:

AH: 1Ah
DX: Offset address of DTA
DS: Segment address of DTA

Registers on Return: Unchanged

Memory Affected: None

Syntax:

```
PUSH    CS                  ;Code segment and
POP     DS                  ;  data segment are same
MOV     DX,OFFSET DTA_1     ;Offset address of DTA
MOV     AH,1Ah
INT     21h                 ;DOS services interrupt
```

Description: When DOS works with file control blocks (FCBs), DOS transfers information to and from the disk through a block of memory called the *disk transfer area* (DTA).

Normally, this DTA is set as a 128-byte memory area at offset 80h in the program segment prefix (PSP). You can, however, set aside for the DTA an area of memory in your program. If the size of the blocks you will be reading and writing is larger than 128 bytes, you need to specify your own DTA through this service.

Get FAT (File Allocation Table) Information for Default Drive (Interrupt 21h, service 1Bh)

Category: Disk services

Registers on Entry:

AH: 1Bh

Registers on Return:

AL: Sectors per cluster
BX: Offset address of FAT ID byte
CX: Bytes per sector
DX: Clusters per disk
DS: Segment address of FAT ID byte

Memory Affected: None

Syntax:

```
MOV    AH,1Bh
INT    21h              ;DOS services interrupt
```

Description: This service returns basic information about the disk in the default drive. The information includes the number of bytes per sector (CX), the number of sectors per cluster (AL), the number of clusters per disk (DX), and the address of the File Allocation Table identification (ID) byte (DS:BX).

Once you know this information, deriving other valuable information is easy. For instance, to determine the byte capacity of the disk, you simply multiply CX by AL by DX.

The File Allocation Table (FAT) identification byte to which DS:BX points indicates the type of disk in use. Actually, this byte indicates only how the disk was formatted. Table 21.4 shows some possible values for the FAT ID byte.

Table 21.4. *Some possible FAT ID byte values.*

Value	Disk Characteristics
F0	High density, 18 sectors/track (1.44M)
F0	High density, 36 sectors/track (2.88M)
F0	Unknown identity
F8	Fixed disk
F9	Double sided, 9 sectors/track (720K)
F9	Double sided, 15 sectors/track (1.2M)

continues

Table 21.4. *continued*

Value	Disk Characteristics
FC	Single sided, 9 sectors/track (180K)
FD	Double sided, 9 sectors/track (360K)
FE	Single sided, 8 sectors/track (160K)
FF	Double sided, 8 sectors/track (320K)

Get FAT Information for Drive (Interrupt 21h, service 1Ch)

Category: Disk services

Registers on Entry:

AH: 1Ch
DL: Drive code

Registers on Return:

AL: Sectors per cluster
BX: Offset address of FAT ID byte
CX: Bytes per sector
DX: Clusters per disk
DS: Segment address of FAT ID byte

Memory Affected: None

Syntax:

```
MOV   DL,0          ;Drive A:
MOV   AH,1Ch
INT   21h           ;DOS services interrupt
```

Description: This service returns basic information about the disk in the drive specified by DL. The drive number is specified as A=0, B=1, C=2, etc.

The information returned by this service is identical to that for service 21/1B. This information includes the number of bytes per sector (CX), the number of sectors per cluster (AL), the number of clusters per disk (DX), and the address of the File Allocation Table ID byte (DS:BX).

Once you know this information, deriving other valuable information is easy. For instance, to determine the byte capacity of the disk, you simply multiply CX by AL by DX.

The FAT ID byte to which DS:BX points indicates the type of disk in use. Actually, this byte indicates only how the disk was formatted. (Refer to table 21.4 for some possible values for the FAT ID byte.)

Get Default Disk Parameter Block
(Interrupt 21h, service 1Fh)

Category: Disk services

Registers on Entry:

AH: 1Fh

Registers on Return:

AL: Error status
BX: Offset address of disk parameter block
DS: Segment address of disk parameter block

Memory Affected: None

Syntax:

```
MOV     AH,1Fh
INT     21h         ;DOS services interrupt
CMP     AL,0FFh      ;was there an error?
JE      ERROR       ;yes, go handle
```

Description: This service is used to return the address of the disk parameter block (DPB). Shown in table 21.5, this parameter table is used by DOS to determine basic information about the disk in the default drive. The structure of the DPB differs, according to which version of DOS you are using.

Table 21.5. *The disk parameter block (DPB)*

Offset Byte	Field Length	Meaning
Basic Structure for All Versions of DOS		
00h	Byte	Drive number (0 = A, 1 = B, etc.)
01h	Byte	Device-driver unit number
02h	Word	Bytes per sector
04h	Byte	Sectors per cluster, minus 1
05h	Byte	Sectors per cluster, as power of 2

continues

Table 21.5. *continued*

Offset Byte	Field Length	Meaning
06h	Word	Beginning sector for first FAT
08h	Byte	Number of FAT copies
09h	Word	Number of root directory entries
0Bh	Word	Beginning sector of first data cluster
0Dh	Word	Clusters on drive, plus 1
Additional Structure for DOS 2 or 3 Only		
0Fh	Byte	Sectors per FAT
10h	Word	Beginning sector for root directory
12h	Double word	Device-driver address
16h	Byte	Media descriptor byte
17h	Byte	Disk parameter block access flag (0FFh indicates need to rebuild)
18h	Double word	Address of next device parameter block
Additional Structure for DOS 2 Only		
1Ch	Word	Starting cluster number for current directory
1Eh	64 bytes	ASCIIZ of current directory path
Additional Structure for DOS 3 Only		
1Ch	Word	Last cluster number allocated
1Eh	Word	Purpose unknown; normally FFFFh
Additional Structure for DOS 4 and 5		
0Fh	Word	Sectors per FAT
11h	Word	Beginning sector for root directory
13h	Double word	Device-driver address
17h	Byte	Media descriptor byte
18h	Byte	Disk parameter block access flag (0FFh indicates need to rebuild)
19h	Double word	Address of next device parameter block
1Dh	Word	Last cluster number allocated
1Fh	Word	Number of free clusters

On return, if AL contains 0, no error occurred; if AL contains FFH, an error occurred.

Random Read, Using FCB (Interrupt 21h, service 21h)

Category: Disk services

Registers on Entry:

AH: 21h
DX: Offset address of FCB
DS: Segment address of FCB

Registers on Return:

AL: Status byte

Memory Affected: The memory area designated as DTA is overwritten with information read from the disk.

Syntax:

```
PUSH   CS                      ;Code segment and
POP    DS                      ;  data segment are same
MOV    DX,OFFSET FCB_1         ;Offset address of FCB
MOV    AH,21h
INT    21h                     ;DOS services interrupt
```

Description: This service is used to read a data record from an open file and place the information in the DTA. You designate the record size through the file control block, or FCB. The FCB consists of 44 bytes constructed in the following manner:

```
FCB_PRE       DB    0FFh            ;Extension flag
              DB    5 DUP(0)        ;Unused
FILE_ATTR     DB    00              ;File attribute
FCB_1         DB    00              ;Set for default drive
FILE_ROOT     DB    'FILENAME'      ;File name root
FILE_EXT      DB    'DAT'           ;File name extension
BLOCK_NUM     DW    0000            ;Current block number
REC_SIZE      DW    0000            ;Record size
FILE_SIZE     DD    00000000        ;File size
FILE_DATE     DW    0000            ;File date
FILE_TIME     DW    0000            ;File time
              DB    8 DUP(0)        ;DOS work area
REC_NUM       DB    00              ;Current record number
RANDOM_REC    DD    00000000        ;Random record number
```

You specify the offset address of FCB_1 in DS:DX when you invoke this service. If you are using an extended FCB, you should use the offset address of FCB_PRE. You should set the values for FCB_1 (the drive designator), FILE_ROOT, and FILE_EXT before the file is opened. You specify the file's record size in the REC_SIZE field. The area set aside as the DTA should be as large as a record. The values in REC_SIZE and RANDOM_REC specify where the file read is to begin. After a successful read, the values in BLOCK_NUM and REC_NUM are updated to the proper values. RANDOM_REC, which is not incremented by this service, remains the same as before the invocation.

When the service is completed, the value of AL indicates the status of the operation. If AL is 0, the read was successful. If AL is 1, no data was read because the end-of-file was encountered by a previous read command. If AL is 2, the DTA crossed a *segment boundary* (a memory address ending in 000), and an error was generated. If AL is 3, the end-of-file was reached during the read and the service could not read the entire block (the partial block was read and placed in the DTA area).

Random Write, Using FCB (Interrupt 21h, service 22h)

Category: Disk services

Registers on Entry:

AH: 22h
DX: Offset address of FCB
DS: Segment address of FCB

Registers on Return:

AL: Status byte

Memory Affected: Certain FCB values are modified.

Syntax:

```
PUSH   CS                      ;Code segment and
POP    DS                      ;  data segment are same
MOV    DX,OFFSET FCB_1         ;Offset address of FCB
MOV    AH,22h
INT    21h                     ;DOS services interrupt
```

Description: This service is used to write a data record to a previously opened file. The information to be written is contained in the DTA. The record size is designated through the file control block, or FCB. The FCB consists of 44 bytes constructed in the following manner:

```
FCB_PRE       DB    0FFh          ;Extension flag
              DB    5 DUP(0)      ;Unused
FILE_ATTR     DB    00            ;File attribute
FCB_1         DB    00            ;Set for default drive
FILE_ROOT     DB    'FILENAME'    ;File name root
FILE_EXT      DB    'DAT'         ;File name extension
BLOCK_NUM     DW    0000          ;Current block number
REC_SIZE      DW    0000          ;Record size
FILE_SIZE     DD    00000000      ;File size
FILE_DATE     DW    0000          ;File date
FILE_TIME     DW    0000          ;File time
              DB    8 DUP(0)      ;DOS work area
REC_NUM       DB    00            ;Current record number
RANDOM_REC    DD    00000000      ;Random record number
```

You specify the offset address of FCB_1 in DS:DX when you invoke this service. If you are using an extended FCB, you should use the offset address of FCB_PRE. You should set the values for FCB_1 (the drive designator), FILE_ROOT, and FILE_EXT before the file is opened. You specify the file's record size in the REC_SIZE field. This size is the number of bytes that will be written by this service. The values in REC_SIZE and RANDOM_REC specify the location in the file at which writing is to begin. After a successful write, the values in BLOCK_NUM and REC_NUM are updated. RANDOM_REC, which is not incremented by this service, remains the same as before the invocation.

When this service is completed, the value of AL indicates the status of the operation. If AL is 0, the write was successful. If AL is 1, a disk-full error was detected during the write. If AL is 2, the DTA crossed a segment boundary (a memory address ending in 000), and an error was generated.

Get File Size, Using FCB (Interrupt 21h, service 23h)

Category: Disk services

Registers on Entry:

AH: 23h
DX: Offset address of FCB
DS: Segment address of FCB

Registers on Return:

AL: Status byte

Memory Affected: Certain FCB values are modified.

Syntax:

```
PUSH    CS                      ;Code segment and
POP     DS                      ;  data segment are same
MOV     DX,OFFSET FCB_1         ;Offset address of FCB
MOV     AH,23h
INT     21h                     ;DOS services interrupt
CMP     AL,0FFh                 ;Was the file found?
JE      FILE_ERR                ;No, so handle error
```

Description: This service searches for a specific file name in the current directory and returns the number of records in that file. You specify the file name to be used in the file control block, or FCB. The FCB consists of 44 bytes constructed in the following manner:

```
FCB_PRE       DB      0FFh            ;Extension flag
              DB      5 DUP(0)        ;Unused
FILE_ATTR     DB      00              ;File attribute
FCB_1         DB      00              ;Set for default drive
FILE_ROOT     DB      'FILENAME'      ;File name root
FILE_EXT      DB      'DAT'           ;File name extension
BLOCK_NUM     DW      0000            ;Current block number
REC_SIZE      DW      0000            ;Record size
FILE_SIZE     DD      00000000        ;File size
FILE_DATE     DW      0000            ;File date
FILE_TIME     DW      0000            ;File time
              DB      8 DUP(0)        ;DOS work area
REC_NUM       DB      00              ;Current record number
RANDOM_REC    DD      00000000        ;Random record number
```

You specify the offset address of FCB_1 in DS:DX when you invoke this service. If you are using an extended FCB, you should use the offset address of FCB_PRE. To use this service, you should set the values for FCB_1 (the drive designator), FILE_ROOT, and FILE_EXT. The value in REC_SIZE indicates the record size in the file and has a direct bearing on the returned value. If this field is set to 1, the value returned by this service is equal to the number of bytes in the file.

On return, the value of AL indicates the status of the operation. If AL is 0, the file was located, and the value in RANDOM_REC indicates the number of records (of size REC_SIZE) in the file. If AL is FFh, the requested file could not be located, and the FCB values are not significant.

Set Random Record Field in FCB
(Interrupt 21h, service 24h)

Category: Disk services

Registers on Entry:

AH: 24h
DX: Offset address of FCB
DS: Segment address of FCB

Registers on Return: Unchanged

Memory Affected: Certain FCB values are modified.

Syntax:

```
PUSH    CS                      ;Code segment and
POP     DS                      ;  data segment are same
MOV     DX,OFFSET FCB_1         ;Offset address of FCB
MOV     AH,24h
INT     21h                     ;DOS services interrupt
```

Description: This service modifies the contents of the random record field in the file control block (FCB) of an open file. The FCB is a 44-byte area constructed as follows:

```
FCB_PRE       DB      0FFh            ;Extension flag
              DB      5 DUP(0)        ;Unused
FILE_ATTR     DB      00              ;File attribute
FCB_1         DB      00              ;Set for default drive
FILE_ROOT     DB      'FILENAME'      ;File name root
FILE_EXT      DB      'DAT'           ;File name extension
BLOCK_NUM     DW      0000            ;Current block number
REC_SIZE      DW      0000            ;Record size
FILE_SIZE     DD      00000000        ;File size
FILE_DATE     DW      0000            ;File date
FILE_TIME     DW      0000            ;File time
              DB      8 DUP(0)        ;DOS work area
REC_NUM       DB      00              ;Current record number
RANDOM_REC    DD      00000000        ;Random record number
```

You specify the offset address of FCB_1 in DS:DX when you invoke this service. If you are using an extended FCB, you should use the offset address of FCB_PRE. Before you call the service, set the values for FCB_1 (the drive designator), FILE_ROOT, and FILE_EXT for the open file. Also set the values in REC_SIZE, REC_NUM, and BLOCK_NUM before calling this service. These values are used to compute the value in RANDOM_REC.

Set Interrupt Vector (Interrupt 21h, service 25h)

Category: System services

Registers on Entry:

AH: 25h
AL: Interrupt number
DX: Offset address of new interrupt handler
DS: Segment address of new interrupt handler

Registers on Return: Unchanged

Memory Affected: The values in the interrupt vector table in low memory are altered.

Syntax:

```
PUSH    DS                      ;Save current data segment
MOV     AL,5                    ;Print-screen interrupt
PUSH    CS                      ;Code segment and
POP     DS                      ;  data segment are same
MOV     DX,OFFSET PS_HANDLER    ;Offset address of handler
MOV     AH,25h
INT     21h                     ;DOS services interrupt
POP     DS                      ;Restore data segment
```

Description: This service provides a uniform method for altering the interrupt vector table in low memory. Such a method is useful if you want to alter or replace the way the system currently handles interrupts.

An important consideration is that, once changed, the old interrupt vector is lost. You can use service 21/35 to determine the current vector so that you can save the vector before changing it. Then, on program completion, you can reset the vector to the original value.

Create Program Segment Prefix (PSP) (Interrupt 21h, service 26h)

Category: System services

Registers on Entry:

AH: 26h
DX: Segment address of new PSP

Registers on Return: Unchanged

Memory Affected: The 256 bytes of memory at the desired segment address are altered.

Syntax:

```
MOV     DX,OFFSET CS:PROG_END    ;Point to end of program
MOV     AH,26h
INT     21h                      ;DOS services interrupt
```

Description: This service, which is used to facilitate overlays and subprograms to the current program, copies the current PSP contents to the desired paragraph and then sets the PSP vector contents to match the contents of the interrupt vector table.

The current DOS technical reference manuals (those supplied with DOS versions released since version 3.0) recommend that this service not be used; instead, they recommend using service 21/4B.

Read Random Record(s), Using FCB (Interrupt 21h, service 27h)

Category: Disk services

Registers on Entry:

AH: 27h
CX: Number of records to read
DX: Offset address of FCB
DS: Segment address of FCB

Registers on Return:

AL: Status byte
CX: Number of records read

Memory Affected: The memory designated by DTA is overlaid with information read from the disk.

Syntax:

```
PUSH    CS                  ;Code segment and
POP     DS                  ;  data segment are same
MOV     DX,OFFSET FCB_1     ;Offset address of FCB
MOV     CX,8                ;Read 8 records
MOV     AH,27h
INT     21h                 ;DOS services interrupt
```

Description: This service is used to read a specified number of data records from a previously opened file and to place the information in the DTA. You specify the number of records to read in CX. Designate the record size through the file control block, or FCB. The FCB consists of 44 bytes constructed in the following manner:

```
FCB_PRE      DB    0FFh          ;Extension flag
             DB    5 DUP(0)      ;Unused
FILE_ATTR    DB    00            ;File attribute
FCB_1        DB    00            ;Set for default drive
FILE_ROOT    DB    'FILENAME'    ;File name root
FILE_EXT     DB    'DAT'         ;File name extension
BLOCK_NUM    DW    0000          ;Current block number
REC_SIZE     DW    0000          ;Record size
FILE_SIZE    DD    00000000      ;File size
FILE_DATE    DW    0000          ;File date
FILE_TIME    DW    0000          ;File time
             DB    8 DUP(0)      ;DOS work area
REC_NUM      DB    00            ;Current record number
RANDOM_REC   DD    00000000      ;Random record number
```

You specify the offset address of FCB_1 in DS:DX when you invoke this service. If you are using an extended FCB, you should use the offset address of FCB_PRE. You set the values for FCB_1 (the drive designator), FILE_ROOT, and FILE_EXT before the file is opened. You specify the file's record size in the REC_SIZE field. The area set aside as the DTA should be large enough to contain the number of records being requested. The values in REC_SIZE and RANDOM_REC specify the location in the file at which the read is to begin. After a successful read, the service updates the values in BLOCK_NUM, REC_NUM, and RANDOM_REC.

When this service is completed, the value of AL indicates the status of the operation. If AL is 0, the read was successful. If AL is 1, no data was read because the end-of-file was already reached. If AL is 2, the DTA crossed a segment boundary (a memory address ending in 000) and an error was generated. If AL is 3, the end-of-file was reached during the read; the service could not read an entire block (the partial block is still read and placed in the DTA area). CX contains the number of records read.

Write Random Record(s), Using FCB (Interrupt 21h, service 28h)

Category: Disk services

Registers on Entry:

AH: 28h
CX: Number of records to write

DX: Offset address of FCB
DS: Segment address of FCB

Registers on Return:

AL: Status byte
CX: Number of records written

Memory Affected: Certain FCB values are modified.

Syntax:

```
PUSH    CS                      ;Code segment and
POP     DS                      ;  data segment are same
MOV     DX,OFFSET FCB_1         ;Offset address of FCB
MOV     CX,8                    ;Write 8 records
MOV     AH,28h
INT     21h                     ;DOS services interrupt
```

Description: This service is used to write a specific number of data records to a previously opened file. The information to be written is contained in the DTA. You specify the number of records to be written in CX. You designate the record size through the file control block, or FCB. The FCB consists of 44 bytes constructed in the following manner:

```
FCB_PRE         DB      0FFh            ;Extension flag
                DB      5 DUP(0)        ;Unused
FILE_ATTR       DB      00              ;File attribute
FCB_1           DB      00              ;Set for default drive
FILE_ROOT       DB      'FILENAME'      ;File name root
FILE_EXT        DB      'DAT'           ;File name extension
BLOCK_NUM       DW      0000            ;Current block number
REC_SIZE        DW      0000            ;Record size
FILE_SIZE       DD      00000000        ;File size
FILE_DATE       DW      0000            ;File date
FILE_TIME       DW      0000            ;File time
                DB      8 DUP(0)        ;DOS work area
REC_NUM         DB      00              ;Current record number
RANDOM_REC      DD      00000000        ;Random record number
```

You specify the offset address of FCB_1 DS:DX when you invoke this service. If you are using an extended FCB, you should use the offset address of FCB_PRE. You set the values for FCB_1 (the drive designator), FILE_ROOT, and FILE_EXT before the file is opened. Specify the file's record size in the REC_SIZE field. The values in REC_SIZE and RANDOM_REC specify the location in the file at which writing is to begin. After a successful write, the service updates the values in BLOCK_NUM, REC_NUM, and RANDOM_REC.

When this service is completed, the value of AL indicates the status of the operation. If AL is 0, the write was successful. If AL is 1, a disk-full error was detected during the write. If AL is 2, the DTA crossed a segment boundary (a memory address ending in 000), and an error was generated. CX contains the number of records written.

Parse File Name, Using FCB (Interrupt 21h, service 29h)

Category: Disk services

Registers on Entry:

AH: 29h
AL: Parsing control byte
SI: Offset address of string to be parsed
DI: Offset address of FCB
DS: Segment address of string to be parsed
ES: Segment address of FCB

Registers on Return:

AL: Status byte
SI: Offset address of first character following parsed string
DI: Offset address of FCB
DS: Segment address of first character following parsed string
ES: Segment address of FCB

Memory Affected: Certain values in the FCB are altered.

Syntax:

```
PUSH   DS                    ;Save data segment
PUSH   ES                    ;Save extra segment
MOV    AX,CS                 ;Code, data, and extra
MOV    DS,AX                 ;  segments are all
MOV    ES,AX                 ;  the same
MOV    SI,OFFSET INPUT       ;Offset address of string
MOV    DI,OFFSET FCB_1       ;Offset address of FCB
MOV    AL,00001111b          ;Set proper parse control
MOV    AH,29h
INT    21h                   ;DOS services interrupt
POP    ES                    ;Restore extra segment
POP    DS                    ;Restore data segment
```

Description: This service is used to parse (translate) a text string to pick out a valid drive designator, file name, and file extension. The service parses for simple drive and file-name designations only, not for path names.

DS:SI points to the text string to be parsed, and ES:DI points to the memory area that will hold the constructed FCB. This area should be at least 44 bytes in length.

The four low-order bits of AL control how the text string is parsed. Table 21.6 details the meanings of the bit settings.

Table 21.6. Bit settings for AL register, service 21/29.

Bits 76543210	Meaning
0000	Reserved—must be set to 0.
0	File extension in FCB is set either to parsed value or to blanks.
1	File extension in FCB is set only if a valid extension is detected in the text string.
0	File name in FCB is set either to parsed value or to blanks.
1	File name in FCB is set only if a valid file name exists in the text string.
0	Drive ID byte is set either to parsed value or to 0.
1	Drive ID byte is set only if a valid drive designator is parsed in the text string.
0	Leading separators are not ignored; parsing stops when one is encountered.
1	Leading separators are ignored.

This service correctly translates wild-card characters (* and ?) to the appropriate FCB values.

On return, AL indicates the parsing status. If AL=0, no wild-card characters were located in the text string. If AL=1, the text string contained wild-card characters. If AL=FFh, the drive specifier was invalid. In all instances, ES:DI points to the first byte of the new FCB.

Get System Date (Interrupt 21h, service 2Ah)

Category: Date/time services

Registers on Entry:

AH: 2Ah

Registers on Return:

AL: Day of week (0-6)
CX: Year (1980-2099)
DH: Month (1-12)
DL: Day (1-31)

Memory Affected: None

Syntax:

```
MOV    AH,2Ah
INT    21h                    ;DOS services interrupt
```

Description: This service, which returns the system date, returns the month (DH), day (DL), and year (CX), along with the day of the week for this date. The day of the week is returned in AL as 0=Sunday, 1=Monday, 2=Tuesday, etc.

Set System Date (Interrupt 21h, service 2Bh)

Category: Date/time services

Registers on Entry:

AH: 2Bh
CX: Year (1980-2099)
DH: Month (1-12)
DL: Day (1-31)

Registers on Return:

AL: Status byte

Memory Affected: None

Syntax:

```
            MOV    DH,MONTH        ;Get current month
            MOV    DL,DAY          ;Get current day
```

```
            MOV    CX,YEAR           ;Get current year
            CMP    CX,100            ;Does CX include century?
            JA     OK_GO             ;Yes, so continue
            ADD    CX,1900           ;No, so adjust
OK_GO:      MOV    AH,2Bh
            INT    21h               ;DOS services interrupt
            CMP    AL,0              ;Was there an error?
            JNE    DATE_ERROR        ;Yes, go handle
```

Description: This service allows the DOS date (system software clock) to be set but does not set the real-time hardware clock on the IBM Personal Computer AT or compatibles.

To use this service, you must load a valid month, day, and year into DH, DL, and CX, respectively. On return, AL contains either a 0 (indicating that the date was valid and has been set) or FFh (indicating that the specified date is invalid).

Get System Time (Interrupt 21h, service 2Ch)

Category: Date/time services

Registers on Entry:

AH: 2Ch

Registers on Return:

CH: Hour (0-23)
CL: Minute (0-59)
DH: Second (0-59)
DL: Hundredths of a second (0-99)

Memory Affected: None

Syntax:

```
MOV    AH,2Ch
INT    21h               ;DOS services interrupt
```

Description: This service converts the value of the computer's system-software clock counter to values that humans readily understand: hours (CH), minutes (CL), seconds (DH), and hundredths of seconds (DL). The hours (CH), which are returned in military time, range from 0 to 23.

Set Time (Interrupt 21h, service 2Dh)

Category: Date/time services

Registers on Entry:

AH: 2Dh
CH: Hour (0-23)
CL: Minute (0-59)
DH: Second (0-59)
DL: Hundredths of a second (0-99)

Registers on Return:

AL: Status byte

Memory Affected: None

Syntax:

```
MOV    CH,HOUR            ;Get current hour
MOV    CL,MINUTE          ;Get current minute
MOV    DH,SECOND          ;Get current second
MOV    DL,0               ;Hundredths doesn't matter
MOV    AH,2Dh
INT    21h                ;DOS services interrupt
CMP    AL,0               ;Was there an error?
JNE    TIME_ERROR         ;Yes, go handle
```

Description: This service converts a specified time to the corresponding number of clock ticks and stores the resulting value in the computer's software clock counter. This service does not reset the real-time clock on the IBM Personal Computer AT or compatibles.

This service determines, through a series of multiplications, the number of clock ticks represented by the specified time. The entered values are converted to a total number of seconds, which then is multiplied by 18.2065 (the approximate number of clock ticks per second). For example, if you are setting the time to 14:22:17.39 (military time), the computer goes through conversions similar to the following:

14 hours =	14 * 60 * 60	=	50400.	seconds
22 minutes =	22 * 60	=	1320.	seconds
17.39 seconds =	17. 39	=	17.39	seconds
Total:			51737.39	seconds
Clock ticks per second =			18.2065	ticks
Ticks represented:			941956.7910	ticks

Because fractional ticks cannot be represented, the total number is rounded to 941,957 ticks. The system software clock is then set to this value. The same type of process sets the system clock with the BIOS date/time services (refer to Chapter 20, service 1A/4). As a programmer, you can easily see the added value of some of these DOS services.

On return, AL contains either a 0 (indicating that the time was valid and has been set) or FFh (indicating that the specified time is invalid).

Set Verify Flag (Interrupt 21h, service 2Eh)

Category: Disk services

Registers on Entry:

AH: 2Eh
AL: Verify setting
DL: 0

Registers on Return: Unchanged

Memory Affected: None

Syntax:

```
MOV     AL,1            ;Set verify on
MOV     DL,0
MOV     AH,2Eh
INT     21h             ;DOS services interrupt
```

Description: This service sets the system flag that determines whether DOS performs a verify operation after each disk write to ensure that information has been recorded accurately. In most applications, the reliability of DOS operations is such that you safely can leave the verify flag set off (the default setting).

The setting of DL is not important if you are working with DOS 3.0 or later versions; for earlier versions, however, DL must be set to 0. This is an undocumented necessity; no reason is given for this setting.

If you are working with a network system, verification is not supported; the setting has no meaning.

Get Disk Transfer Area (Interrupt 21h, service 2Fh)

Category: Disk services

Registers on Entry:

AH: 2Fh

Registers on Return:

BX: Offset address of DTA
ES: Segment address of DTA

Memory Affected: None

Syntax:

```
MOV    AH,2Fh
INT    21h              ;DOS services interrupt
```

Description: This service returns the address of the current DOS disk transfer area (DTA). DOS uses this area to transfer information between the computer and the disk. The address is returned in ES:BX.

Note that all services with numbers lower than 2Fh are available in all distributed versions of DOS. This service and all that follow it (numerically, up to service 58h) became available only with the release of DOS 2, however.

Get DOS Version Number (Interrupt 21h, service 30h)

Category: System services

Registers on Entry:

AH: 30h
AL: 0

Registers on Return:

AL: Major version number
AH: Minor version number
BL: High-order 8 bits of 24-bit user serial number
BH: OEM serial number
CX: Low-order 16 bits of 24-bit user serial number

Memory Affected: None

Syntax:

```
MOV     AH,30h
MOV     AL,0
INT     21h             ;DOS services interrupt
CMP     AL,2            ;At least version 2.0?
JB      DOS_BAD         ;No, so exit early
```

Description: This service determines the version number of the DOS that is operating within the computer (the DOS used during booting). If the DOS 5 SETVER command has been used, this service returns the value set by that command.

The major purpose of this service is to allow programs to determine whether the proper version of DOS is in use for certain functions and services. AL contains the major version number (2 or 3). If AL contains 0, the DOS version is earlier than 2.0. The minor version number returned in AH is the number to the right of the decimal point (to two decimal places). Depending on the OEM that distributed the version of DOS, BH will contain an OEM-specific serial number, and BL:CX will contain a 24-bit user serial number.

Terminate and Stay Resident (Interrupt 21h, service 31h)

Category: System services

Registers on Entry:

AH: 31h
AL: Return code
DX: Memory paragraphs to reserve

Registers on Return: Indeterminable (does not return)

Memory Affected: The available free memory is decreased by the number of paragraphs specified in DX.

Syntax:

```
MOV     AL,0            ;Return code of 0
MOV     DX,100h         ;Reserve 4K of info
MOV     AH,31h
INT     21h             ;DOS services interrupt
```

Description: This service is used to exit a program, leaving all or part of the program's memory intact. The service is used by a wide variety of TSR (terminate-and-stay-resident) programs such as SideKick, ProKey, etc.

The return code you specify in AL when you invoke this service is passed to the parent program or to DOS. From DOS-command level, the return code is available through the ERRORLEVEL batch command; from programs, the return code can be determined through service 21/4D.

The number of paragraphs requested in DX are reserved by DOS and unavailable to other programs. The buffers of any files opened prior to invoking this service are flushed, but the files are left open.

Get Disk Parameter Block (Interrupt 21h, service 32h)

Category: Disk services

Registers on Entry:

AH: 32h
DL: Drive number

Registers on Return:

AL: Error code
BX: Offset address of disk parameter block
DS: Segment address of disk parameter block

Memory Affected: None

Syntax:

```
MOV     AH,1Fh
MOV     DL,3            ;get info for drive C
INT     21h             ;DOS services interrupt
CMP     AL,0FFh         ;was it an invalid drive?
JE      ERROR           ;yes, go handle
```

Description: This service is used to return the address of the disk parameter block (DPB). This parameter table is used by DOS to determine basic information about the disk in the default drive. The structure of the DPB differs, according to which version of DOS you are using. The various DPB structures are detailed in table 21.5 (refer to service 21/1F).

On calling this service, the drive number is specified in DL (0=default, 1=A, 2=B, 3=C, and so on). If called with DL=0, this service is identical to service 21/1F.

Get Ctrl-Break Flag (Interrupt 21h, service 33h, function 00h)

Category: System services

Registers on Entry:

AH: 33h
AL: 00h

Registers on Return:

DL: Ctrl-Break flag setting

Memory Affected: None

Syntax:

```
MOV    AL,0            ;Getting flag
MOV    AH,33h
INT    21h             ;DOS services interrupt
```

Description: This service gets the flag that controls how often DOS checks whether the Ctrl-Break key combination has been pressed. On return, DL contains 0 or 1, depending on whether the flag is off or on.

Set Ctrl-Break Flag (Interrupt 21h, service 33h, function 01h)

Category: System services

Registers on Entry:

AH: 33h
AL: 01h
DL: Ctrl-Break flag setting

Registers on Return: Unchanged

Memory Affected: None

Syntax:

```
MOV    AL,1              ;Setting flag
MOV    DL,0              ;Turn off Ctrl-Break check
MOV    AH,33h
INT    21h               ;DOS services interrupt
```

Description: This service sets the flag that controls how often DOS checks whether the Ctrl-Break key combination has been pressed. Other documentation for this service implies that this flag turns Ctrl-Break checking on or off completely. Not true; this flag controls only the frequency of checking. Even with this flag set to off, checking is performed during certain DOS operations, such as performing video output.

To set the Ctrl-Break flag, load AL with 1 and DL with the desired state of the flag. If DL is 0, Ctrl-Break checking is at the minimum. If DL is 1, checking is more frequent during virtually every DOS operation.

Get Boot Drive Code (Interrupt 21h, service 33h, function 05h)

Category: System services

Registers on Entry:

AH: 33h
AL: 05h

Registers on Return:

DL: Boot drive code

Memory Affected: None

Syntax:

```
MOV    AL,5
MOV    AH,33h
INT    21h               ;DOS services interrupt
```

Description: Added in DOS 4, this function returns in the DL register a code indicating the drive from which the system was booted (1=A, 2=B, 3=C, and so on). This information is stored in the DOS kernel area each time the system initializes itself.

Get DOS Version Number (Interrupt 21h, service 33h, function 06h)

Category: System services

Registers on Entry:

AH: 33h
AL: 06h

Registers on Return:

BL: Major version number
BH: Minor version number
DL: Revision number
DH: DOS memory flags

Memory Affected: None

Syntax:

```
MOV     AH,33h
MOV     AL,6
INT     21h             ;DOS services interrupt
CMP     BL,2            ;At least version 2.0?
JB      DOS_BAD         ;No, so exit early
```

Description: This service is similar to service 21/30. It is used to determine the version number of the DOS operating in the computer (the DOS used during booting). The difference between the two functions is that this one returns a bit more information and is not fooled by the DOS 5 SETVER command. All comments for service 21/30 apply to this service also.

The DOS memory flags returned in DH indicate where in memory DOS is loaded. If bit 3 is set, DOS is in ROM. If bit 4 is set, DOS is loaded in the high-memory area.

Get Address of InDOS Flag (Interrupt 21h, service 34h)

Category: System services

Registers on Entry:

AH: 34h

Registers on Return:

BX: Offset address of InDOS flag
ES: Segment address of InDOS flag

Memory Affected: None

Syntax:

```
MOV    AH,34h
INT    21h                 ;DOS services interrupt
MOV    AL,ES:[BX]          ;get value of InDOS flag
```

Description: The InDOS flag is used to determine whether DOS currently is executing an Interrupt 21h service. If the memory address pointed to by ES:BX is nonzero, a DOS service is in process.

The purpose of this service is to determine when DOS service requests can be issued safely in TSR (terminate-and-stay-resident) programs.

Get Interrupt Vector (Interrupt 21h, service 35h)

Category: System services

Registers on Entry:

AH: 35h
AL: Interrupt number

Registers on Return:

BX: Offset address of interrupt handler
ES: Segment address of interrupt handler

Memory Affected: None

Syntax:

```
PUSH   ES                  ;Save registers
PUSH   BX
MOV    AL,5                ;Print-screen interrupt
MOV    AH,35h
INT    21h                 ;DOS services interrupt
MOV    I5_SEG_OLD,ES       ;Store old segment
MOV    I5_OFF_OLD,BX       ;Store old offset
POP    BX                  ;Restore registers
POP    ES
```

Description: This service allows a uniform method for retrieving the address of an interrupt handler from the interrupt vector table in low memory. This service is used to determine current values so that they can be saved before changing; then service 21/25 can be used to alter the vector.

Get Disk Free Space (Interrupt 21h, service 36h)

Category: Disk services

Registers on Entry:

AH: 36h
DL: Drive code

Registers on Return:

AX: Sectors per cluster
BX: Available clusters
CX: Bytes per sector
DX: Clusters per drive

Memory Affected: None

Syntax:

```
MOV     AH,36h
INT     21h                 ;DOS services interrupt
CMP     AX,0FFFFh           ;Was there an error?
JE      ERROR               ;Yes, so go handle
PUSH    AX                  ;Save sectors/cluster
MUL     DX                  ;AX=sectors/drive
MUL     CX                  ;DX:AX=bytes/drive
MOV     BPD_HI,DX           ;Save high word
MOV     BPD_LO,AX           ;Save low word
POP     AX                  ;Get back sectors/cluster
MUL     BX                  ;AX=free sectors/drive
MUL     CX                  ;DX:AX=free bytes/drive
MOV     FBPD_HI,DX          ;Save high word
MOV     FBPD_LO,AX          ;Save low word
```

Description: This service returns basic information about space on the disk in the drive specified by DL. Notice that the drive code is different from the normal method for DOS and BIOS drive designation. In this instance, 0 represents the default drive, and 1=A, 2=B, 3=C, etc.

On return from this service, the calling program checks AX to determine whether an error has occurred. If AX contains FFFFh, the drive code is invalid and the balance of the registers is undefined.

If AX does not indicate an error, the information this service returns is similar to that provided by services 21/1B and 21/1C. This information includes the number of bytes per sector (CX), the number of sectors per cluster (AX), the number of clusters per disk (DX), and the number of free clusters on the disk (BX).

Once you know this information, deriving other valuable information is easy. For instance, to determine the byte capacity of the disk, you simply multiply CX by AX by DX.

Get/Set Country-Dependent Information (Interrupt 21h, service 38h)

Category: System services

Registers on Entry:

AH: 38h
AL: Country specifier
BX: Country specifier
DS: Segment address of information block
DX: Offset address of information block

Registers on Return: Unchanged

AX: Error code
BX: Country specifier
DS: Segment address of information block
DX: Offset address of information block

Memory Affected: If country information is retrieved, the memory block to which DS:DX points is overwritten with the country-dependent information.

Syntax:

```
MOV    AL,0                    ;Info for current country
PUSH   CS                      ;Code segment and
POP    DS                      ;  data segment are same
MOV    DX,OFFSET INFO_BLOCK    ;Offset address of block
MOV    AH,38h
INT    21h                     ;DOS services interrupt
```

Description: This powerful service allows you to retrieve or set a great deal of system information. The purposes and function of this service have changed over the course of several different versions of DOS. The description here conforms with the function of the service according to DOS 3.0.

DOS uses the country information governed by this service to control elements such as the display of dates and numbers. This service allows a program great flexibility in handling display formats, flexibility that is particularly useful if the software is being used for a market other than the United States. Because most computers sold in the United States come configured for this country, however, this service may have little value for programmers whose sole market is the United States.

To get country-dependent information, simply load DS:DX with the segment:offset address of the 34-byte memory block that will be used to store the retrieved information. Load AL with the country code to be retrieved, as indicated in table 21.7.

Table 21.7. Country codes.

Country	Code
Currently installed	0
United States	1
Canadian-French	2
Latin America	3
Netherlands	31
Belgium	32
France	33
Spain	34
Hungary	36
Yugoslavia	38
Italy	39
Switzerland	41
Czechoslovakia	42
United Kingdom	44
Denmark	45
Sweden	46
Norway	47
Poland	48

continues

Table 21.7. continued

Country	Code
Germany	49
Brazil	55
Australia	61
Portugal	351
Finland	358
Israel	972

If the country code is greater than 255 (as it is for Portugal, Finland, and Israel), you enter FFh in AL and set BX to the country-code value. If AL is less than FFh, the contents of BX are not significant. Notice that if AL is 0, the country information table reflects the current country's information. If a different country is selected, that country's information is returned with no effect on the currently configured country.

On return, the carry flag indicates whether an error has occurred. If the carry flag is set, AX contains the error code, which can be handled through service 21/59. If the carry is clear, DS:DX points to the information table.

The following code segment illustrates a typical pattern for setting up the information table area. The code segment details the fields of the returned information:

```
COUNTRY_TABLE   EQU     THIS BYTE
DATE_FORMAT     DW      0000        ;Numeric code
CURRENCY_SYM    DB      5 DUP(0)    ;ASCIIZ--zero terminated
THOUSANDS_SEP   DB      00          ;ASCIIZ--zero terminated
                DB      00          ;  this byte will be nul
DECIMAL_SEP     DB      00          ;ASCIIZ--zero terminated
                DB      00          ;  this byte will be nul
DATE_SEP        DB      00          ;ASCIIZ--zero terminated
                DB      00          ;  this byte will be nul
TIME_SEP        DB      00          ;ASCIIZ--zero terminated
                DB      00          ;  this byte will be nul
CURRENCY_FMT    DB      00          ;Numeric code
CURRENCY_SD     DB      00          ;Sig. decimals in currency
TIME_FMT        DB      00          ;0=normal, 1=military
MAP_CALL        DD      00000000    ;Map call address
DATALIST_SEP    DB      00          ;ASCIIZ--zero terminated
                DB      00          ;  this byte will be nul
                DB      5 DUP(0)    ;Reserved area
```

To use this code segment, load DS:DX with the segment:offset of COUNTRY_TABLE before calling this service. On return, the information table is filled in and individual fields can be addressed by field name.

DATE_FMT is a numeric code indicating the format to be used to display the date. Table 21.8 gives the possible values for this field. Notice also that this field is one word long, which may indicate significant expansion in future versions of DOS.

Table 21.8. *Date-format codes and their meanings.*

Code	Date Format	Country Affiliation
0	mm dd yy	United States
1	dd mm yy	Europe
2	yy mm dd	Japan and the Far East

Now, refer again to the code segment. CURRENCY_SYM is a null-terminated string that indicates the currency symbol for the country. This symbol can be no more than four characters long because the last character has a value of 0 (thus the designation *null-terminated*, or *ASCIIZ* string).

THOUSANDS_SEP, DECIMAL_SEP, DATE_SEP, TIME_SEP, and DATALIST_SEP also are ASCIIZ strings. They indicate, respectively, the characters to be used to separate thousands in number displays, to indicate the decimal point, to separate date components, to separate time components, and to separate items in a data list. Each field is two bytes long, with the second byte set to nul. Why the writers of DOS felt that a single-byte string needed to be set up as an ASCIIZ string is a mystery.

CURRENCY_FMT is a numeric code indicating the format to be used to display the currency. Table 21.9 gives the possible values for this field.

Table 21.9. *Currency format codes and their meanings.*

Code	Meaning
0	Currency symbol immediately precedes currency value
1	Currency symbol immediately follows currency value
2	Currency symbol and space immediately precede currency value
3	Currency symbol and space immediately follow currency value
4	Currency symbol replaces decimal separator

CURRENCY_SD indicates the number of significant decimal places in the country's currency displays.

Bit 0 of TIME_FMT indicates how the hours of a time display are handled. If bit 0 is 0, a 12-hour clock is used. If bit 0 is 1, a military (or 24-hour) clock is used.

MAP_CALL is the full segment:offset address of a DOS subroutine that converts foreign ASCII lowercase characters to their uppercase equivalents. This routine is intended for ASCII codes with values greater than 7Fh. The original ASCII code is specified in AL; then this routine is called, and the converted ASCII code is returned in AL.

This service returns the country code in BX as well as the information in the country table. This code is meaningful only if you invoked the service with AL set to 0. In this way, you can determine the country for which the computer is configured.

To set country-dependent information, simply load DX with FFFFh, the signal that informs DOS that the country-dependent information is being set. You load AL with the country code (refer to table 21.7) to be retrieved. If the country code is greater than 255 (as for Finland and Israel), you enter FFh in AL and set BX to the country-code value. If AL is less than FFh, the contents of BX are not significant.

On return, the carry flag indicates whether an error has occurred. If the carry flag is set, AX contains the error code, which can be handled through service 21/59. If the carry is clear, no error has occurred and the contents of AX are not significant.

Create Subdirectory (Interrupt 21h, service 39h)

Category: Disk services

Registers on Entry:

AH: 39h
DX: Offset address of path name
DS: Segment address of path name

Registers on Return:

AX: Error code

Memory Affected: None

Syntax:

```
PUSH    CS                      ;Code segment and
POP     DS                      ;  data segment are same
MOV     DX,OFFSET PATH_NAME     ;Offset address of path
MOV     AH,39h
INT     21h                     ;DOS services interrupt
JC      ERROR                   ;Carry set, handle error
```

Description: This service (the opposite of service 21/3A) allows the creation of a subdirectory. The result is the same as the result of using the DOS MKDIR, or MD, command. On entry, DS:DX points to an ASCIIZ (null-terminated ASCII) string that contains the name of the directory.

On return, if the carry flag is set, an error has occurred and the error code is in AX. Service 21/59 can be used to get detailed error information. If the carry flag is not set, the operation was successful and AX is undefined.

Remove Subdirectory (Interrupt 21h, service 3Ah)

Category: Disk services

Registers on Entry:

AH: 3Ah
DX: Offset address of path name
DS: Segment address of path name

Registers on Return:

AX: Error code

Memory Affected: None

Syntax:

```
PUSH    CS                      ;Code segment and
POP     DS                      ;  data segment are same
MOV     DX,OFFSET PATH_NAME     ;Offset address of path
MOV     AH,3Ah
INT     21h                     ;DOS services interrupt
JC      ERROR                   ;Carry set, handle error
```

Description: This service (the opposite of service 21/39) is used to remove existing subdirectories. The result is the same as the result of using the DOS RMDIR, or RD, command. On entry, DS:DX points to an ASCIIZ (null-terminated ASCII) string that contains the name of the directory.

On return, if the carry flag is set, an error has occurred and the error code is in AX. Service 21/59 can be used to get detailed error information. If the carry flag is not set, the operation was successful and AX is undefined.

Set Directory (Interrupt 21h, service 3Bh)

Category: Disk services

Registers on Entry:

AH: 3Bh
DX: Offset address of path name
DS: Segment address of path name

Registers on Return:

AX: Error code

Memory Affected: None

Syntax:

```
PUSH    CS                      ;Code segment and
POP     DS                      ;  data segment are same
MOV     DX,OFFSET PATH_NAME     ;Offset address of path
MOV     AH,3Bh
INT     21h                     ;DOS services interrupt
JC      ERROR                   ;Carry set, handle error
```

Description: This service is used to change the default directory setting. The result is the same as that of using the DOS CHDIR, or CD, command. On entry, DS:DX points to an ASCIIZ (null-terminated ASCII) string that contains the name of the directory.

On return, if the carry flag is set, an error has occurred and the error code is in AX. Service 21/59 can be used to get detailed error information. If the carry flag is not set, the operation was successful and AX is undefined.

Create File (Interrupt 21h, service 3Ch)

Category: Disk services

Registers on Entry:

AH: 3Ch
CX: File attribute

DX: Offset address of path name
DS: Segment address of path name

Registers on Return:

AX: Return code

Memory Affected: None

Syntax:

```
PUSH   CS                    ;Code segment and
POP    DS                    ;  data segment are same
MOV    DX,OFFSET PATH_NAME   ;Offset address of path
MOV    CX,0                  ;File attribute is normal
MOV    AH,3Ch
INT    21h                   ;DOS services interrupt
JC     ERROR                 ;Carry set, handle error
MOV    FILE_HANDLE,AX        ;Store returned handle
```

Description: This service is used to create or truncate a disk file. On entry, DS:DX points to an ASCIIZ (null-terminated ASCII) string that contains the full name of the file, including any applicable path name. CX is set equal to the desired attribute for the file.

This service is identical to service 21/5B except that if the file name specified in the ASCIIZ string already exists, the file is opened and its length is truncated to 0.

On return, if the carry flag is set, an error has occurred and the error code is in AX. Service 21/59 can be used to get detailed error information. If the carry flag is not set, the operation was successful and AX contains the file handle for the newly opened file. This number (file handle) can be used in many other DOS file operations.

When this service is completed, the specified file is left open. You do not need to open the file but you must remember to close it.

Open File (Interrupt 21h, service 3Dh)

Category: Disk services

Registers on Entry:

AH: 3Dh
AL: Open code
DX: Offset address of path name
DS: Segment address of path name

Registers on Return:

AX: File handle or error code

Memory Affected: None

Syntax:

```
PUSH    CS                      ;Code segment and
POP     DS                      ;  data segment are same
MOV     DX,OFFSET PATH_NAME     ;Offset address of path
MOV     AL,11000010b            ;Set proper open mode
MOV     AH,3Dh
INT     21h                     ;DOS services interrupt
JC      ERROR                   ;Carry set, handle error
MOV     FILE_HANDLE,AX          ;Save file handle
```

Description: This service opens a disk file. On entry, DS:DX points to an ASCIIZ (null-terminated ASCII) string that contains the full name of the file, including any applicable path name. AL is set to equal the mode to be used for the open file. Each bit in AL has significance. Table 21.10 gives detailed information.

Table 21.10. *Open-mode bit settings for service 21/3D.*

Bits 76543210	Meaning
0	File is inherited by a child process
1	File is not inherited by a child process
000	Sharing mode—allow compatible access
001	Sharing mode—exclusive access
010	Sharing mode—deny others write access
011	Sharing mode—deny others read access
100	Sharing mode—allow others full access
0	Reserved—set to 0
000	Open for read access
001	Open for write access
010	Open for read/write access

On return, if the carry flag is set, an error has occurred and the error code is in AX. Service 21/59 can be used to get detailed error information. If the carry flag is not set, the operation was successful and AX contains the file handle for the newly opened file. This number (file handle) can be used in many other DOS file operations.

Close File (Interrupt 21h, service 3Eh)

Category: Disk services

Registers on Entry:

AH: 3Eh
BX: File handle

Registers on Return:

AX: Error code

Memory Affected: None

Syntax:

```
MOV     BX,FILE_HANDLE          ;Get file handle
MOV     AH,3Eh
INT     21h                     ;DOS services interrupt
JC      ERROR                   ;Carry set, handle error
```

Description: This service closes a previously opened file. The file handle must be loaded in BX.

On return, if the carry flag is set, an error has occurred and the error code is in AX. Service 21/59 can be used to get detailed error information. If the carry flag is not set, the operation was successful.

Read File (Interrupt 21h, service 3Fh)

Category: Disk services

Registers on Entry:

AH: 3Fh
BX: File handle
CX: Bytes to read
DX: Offset address for buffer
DS: Segment address for buffer

Registers on Return:

AX: Return code

Memory Affected: The memory area specified by DS:DX is overlaid with information read from the disk or other device, using a handle.

Syntax:

```
MOV     BX,FILE_HANDLE          ;Get file handle
PUSH    CS                      ;Code segment and
POP     DS                      ;  data segment are same
MOV     DX,OFFSET BUFFER        ;Offset address of buffer
MOV     CX,1000h                ;Read 4K of info
MOV     AH,3Fh
INT     21h                     ;DOS services interrupt
JC      ERROR                   ;Carry set, handle error
```

Description: This service reads information from a disk file or other device that can be assigned a file handle. The file handle is specified in BX, with DS:DX pointing to the input buffer. CX is set to the number of bytes to be read.

Information is read from the file, based on the value of the file pointer. If the file has just been opened, reading starts at the beginning of the file. Subsequent reads begin at the point at which the last read ended.

On return, if the carry flag is set, an error has occurred and the error code is in AX. Service 21/59 can be used to get detailed error information. If the carry flag is not set, the operation was successful and AX contains the number of bytes read.

Write File (Interrupt 21h, service 40h)

Category: Disk services

Registers on Entry:

AH: 40h
BX: File handle
CX: Bytes to write
DX: Offset address for buffer
DS: Segment address for buffer

Registers on Return:

AX: Return code

Memory Affected: None

Syntax:

```
MOV     BX,FILE_HANDLE          ;Get file handle
PUSH    CS                      ;Code segment and
POP     DS                      ;  data segment are same
MOV     DX,OFFSET BUFFER        ;Offset address of buffer
MOV     CX,1000h                ;Write 4K of info
```

```
PUSH    CX                          ;Save for later reference
MOV     AH,40h
INT     21h                         ;DOS services interrupt
JC      ERROR                       ;Carry set, handle error
POP     CX                          ;Get original bytes back
CMP     AX,CX                       ;Are they the same?
JNE     ERROR                       ;No, go handle
```

Description: This service writes information to a disk file or other device that can be assigned a file handle. The file handle is specified in BX, with DS:DX pointing to the buffer area. CX is set to the number of bytes to be copied from the buffer to the disk.

Writing is done based on the value of the file pointer. If the file has just been opened, writing begins at the front of the file. Subsequent writes begin at the point at which the last write ended.

On return, if the carry flag is set, an error has occurred and the error code is in AX. Service 21/59 can be used to get detailed error information. If the carry flag is not set, the operation was successful and AX contains the number of bytes written. If AX does not equal the number of bytes that should have been written, an error (such as the disk being full) has occurred, even though the carry flag is not set.

Delete File (Interrupt 21h, service 41h)

Category: Disk services

Registers on Entry:

AH: 41h
DX: Offset address of path name
DS: Segment address of path name

Registers on Return:

AX: Error code

Memory Affected: None

Syntax:

```
PUSH    CS                          ;Code segment and
POP     DS                          ;  data segment are same
MOV     DX,OFFSET PATH_NAME         ;Offset address of path
MOV     AH,41h
INT     21h                         ;DOS services interrupt
JC      ERROR                       ;Carry set, handle error
```

Description: This service deletes a disk file. On entry, DS:DX points to an ASCIIZ (null-terminated ASCII) string that contains the full name of the file, including any applicable path name. Wild cards cannot be used in the file designation. If the file being deleted has a read-only attribute, this service returns an error.

On return, if the carry flag is set, an error has occurred and the error code is in AX. Service 21/59 can be used to get detailed error information. If the carry flag is not set, the operation was successful.

Move File Pointer (Interrupt 21h, service 42h)

Category: Disk services

Registers on Entry:

AH:	42h
AL:	Movement code
BX:	File handle
CX:	High-order word of distance to move
DX:	Low-order word of distance to move

Registers on Return:

AX:	Low-order word of new pointer location or error code
DX:	High-order word of new pointer location

Memory Affected: None

Syntax:

```
MOV     BX,FILE_HANDLE          ;Get file handle
MOV     AL,0                    ;Relative to start of file
MOV     CX,DIST_HIGH            ;Distance to move
MOV     DX,DIST_LOW             ;
MOV     AH,42h
INT     21h                     ;DOS services interrupt
JC      ERROR                   ;Carry set, handle error
```

Description: This service causes the file pointer to move to a new location. The file handle is specified in BX, and the distance to move (in bytes) is specified in CX:DX. A movement code is specified in AL (see table 21.11).

Table 21.11. *Movement code for service 21/42.*

Value	Meaning
0	Move relative to beginning of file
1	Move relative to current pointer location
2	Move relative to end of file

If the offset specified in CX:DX is large enough, you can move the file pointer past the beginning or the end of the file. Doing so does not generate an immediate error but does cause an error when reading or writing is attempted later.

On return, if the carry flag is set, an error has occurred and the error code is in AX. Service 21/59 can be used to get detailed error information. If the carry flag is not set, the operation was successful and DX:AX contains the new file-pointer value.

Get/Set File Attributes (Interrupt 21h, service 43h)

Category: Disk services

Registers on Entry:

AH: 43h
AL: Function code
CX: Desired attributes
DX: Offset address of path name
DS: Segment address of path name

Registers on Return:

AX: Error code
CX: Current attributes

Memory Affected: None

Syntax:

```
MOV    AL,0                     ;Get current attributes
PUSH   CS                       ;Code segment and
POP    DS                       ;  data segment are same
MOV    DX,OFFSET PATH_NAME      ;Offset address of PATH
MOV    AH,43h
INT    21h                      ;DOS services interrupt
JC     ERROR                    ;Go handle error
```

Description: This service enables you to determine or set a file's attributes. The desired function is specified in AL. If AL=0, the file attributes are retrieved; if AL=1, the file attributes are set.

DS:DX should point to an ASCIIZ (null-terminated ASCII) string that contains the full name of the file, including any applicable path name. Wild cards cannot be used in the file designation. If you are setting the file attribute (AL=1), place the desired value in CX. Because the file attribute is only one byte long, the new setting is placed in CL, and CH is set to 0. Table 21.12 shows the possible file-attribute settings. In this table, a 1 in a bit position indicated by an *x* means that the attribute is selected; a 0 means that the attribute is not selected.

Table 21.12. *Bit settings for file attributes, service 21/43.*

Bit 76543210	Meaning
00	Reserved—set to 0
x	Archive
0	Subdirectory—set to 0 for this service
0	Volume label—set to 0 for this service
x	System
x	Hidden
x	Read-only

You cannot change the volume-label or subdirectory bits of the file attribute byte. If you attempt to do so, or if these bits are not set to 0, an error is generated. If you are retrieving the file attributes (AL=0), the contents of CX are not significant.

On return, if the carry flag is set, an error has occurred and the error code is in AX. Service 21/59 can be used to get detailed error information. If the carry flag is not set, the operation was successful. If you were retrieving the file attribute, CX contains the requested information.

Get Device Information (Interrupt 21h, service 44h, function 00h)

Category: System services

Registers on Entry:

AH: 44h
AL: 00h
BX: Device handle

Registers on Return:

DX: Device information

Memory Affected: None

Syntax:

```
MOV     AL,0
MOV     BX,DEVICE_HANDLE        ;Use this handle
MOV     AH,44h
INT     21h                     ;DOS services interrupt
```

Description: This function retrieves information about the device or file represented by a file handle. On calling, AL should contain 0 and BX should contain the device handle. On return, DX contains the requested information (see table 21.13).

Table 21.13. *Device information returned by function 21/44/0.*

Bits FEDCBA98 76543210	Meaning
?	Reserved
0	Control strings not allowed for services 21/44/2, 21/44/3, 21/44/4, and 21/44/5. This bit is significant only if bit 7 is 1.
1	Control strings acceptable for services 21/44/2, 21/44/3, 21/44/4, and 21/44/5. This bit is significant only if bit 7 is 1.
??????	Reserved
0	This channel is a disk file.
1	This channel is a device.
0	File has not been written to (if device is a file)
1	File has been written to (if device is a file)
xxxxx	Drive number (if device is a file)
0	End-of-file returned if device is read
1	End-of-file not returned if device is read

continues

Table 21.13. *continued*

Bits FEDCBA98 76543210	*Meaning*
0	Using ASCII mode
1	Using binary mode
0	Not a special device
1	Special device
0	Not a clock device
1	Clock device
0	Normal device
1	Null device
0	Not console output device
1	Console output device
0	Not console input device
1	Console input device

This function is not supported on network devices.

Set Device Information (Interrupt 21h, service 44h, function 01h)

Category: System services

Registers on Entry:

AH: 44h
AL: 01h
BX: Device handle
DH: 0
DL: Device information

Registers on Return: Unchanged

Memory Affected: None

Syntax:

```
MOV     AL,1
MOV     DH,0                    ;Must be set to 0
MOV     DL,DEVICE_INFO          ;Desired configuration
MOV     BX,DEVICE_HANDLE        ;For this device
MOV     AH,44h
INT     21h                     ;DOS services interrupt
```

Description: This function is used to set information about the device. On calling, AL should contain 1, BX should contain the device handle, and DL should contain the device information (see table 21.14). DH must be set to 0.

Table 21.14. Device information for function 21/44/1.

Bits 76543210	*Meaning*
1	Must be set to 1; indicates this channel is a device.
0	End-of-file returned if device is read
1	End-of-file not returned if device is read
0	Using ASCII mode
1	Using binary mode
0	Not a special device
1	Special device
0	Not a clock device
1	Clock device
0	Normal device
1	Null device
0	Not console output device
1	Console output device
0	Not console input device
1	Console input device

This function is not supported on network devices.

Character Device Read (Interrupt 21h, service 44h, function 02h)

Category: System services

Registers on Entry:

AH: 44h
AL: 02h
BX: Device handle
CX: Bytes to read
DX: Offset address of buffer
DS: Segment address of buffer

Registers on Return:

AX: Bytes read

Memory Affected: The buffer area at DS:DX is overwritten with information read from the device driver.

Syntax:

```
PUSH    CS                      ;Code segment and
POP     DS                      ;  data segment are same
MOV     DX,OFFSET BUFFER        ;Address of input buffer
MOV     AL,2
MOV     BX,DEVICE_HANDLE        ;Want this device
MOV     CX,NUM_BYTES            ;Read this many bytes
MOV     AH,44h
INT     21h                     ;DOS services interrupt
```

Description: This function reads a control string from the device. The buffer specified by DS:DX stores the information from device BX. Only CX bytes are read from the device.

For this function to be usable, bit 14 of the device-information word (as returned in the DX register through service 21/44/0) must be 1. (Refer to table 21.13 for the makeup of the device-information word.) This service is not supported on network devices.

Character Device Write (Interrupt 21h, service 44h, function 03h)

Category: System services

Registers on Entry:

AH: 44h
AL: 03h
BX: Device handle
CX: Bytes to write
DX: Offset address of buffer
DS: Segment address of buffer

Registers on Return:

AX: Bytes written

Memory Affected: None

Syntax:

```
PUSH    CS                      ;Code segment and
POP     DS                      ;  data segment are same
MOV     DX,OFFSET BUFFER        ;Address of input buffer
MOV     BX,DEVICE_HANDLE        ;Want this device
MOV     CX,NUM_BYTES            ;Write this many bytes
PUSH    CX                      ;Store for later check
MOV     AL,3
MOV     AH,44h
INT     21h                     ;DOS services interrupt
POP     CX                      ;Get back original number
CMP     AX,CX                   ;Was everything written?
JNE     ERROR                   ;No, go handle
```

Description: This function writes a control string to a device. CX bytes of information stored at the buffer address specified by DS:DX are written to device BX.

For this function to be usable, bit 14 of the device-information word (as returned in the DX register through service 21/44/0) must be 1. (Refer to table 21.13 for the makeup of the device-information word.) This service is not supported on network devices.

Block Device Read (Interrupt 21h, service 44h, function 04h)

Category: System services

Registers on Entry:

AH: 44h
AL: 04h
BL: Drive number
CX: Bytes to read
DX: Offset address of buffer
DS: Segment address of buffer

Registers on Return:

AX: Bytes read

Memory Affected: The buffer area at DS:DX is overwritten with information read from the drive.

Syntax:

```
PUSH    CS                      ;Code segment and
POP     DS                      ;  data segment are same
MOV     DX,OFFSET BUFFER        ;Address of input buffer
MOV     AL,4
MOV     BL,DRIVE                ;Want this drive
MOV     CX,NUM_BYTES            ;Read this many bytes
MOV     AH,44h
INT     21h                     ;DOS services interrupt
```

Description: This function reads a control string from a block device, typically a disk drive. BL is used to specify which drive to use, where 0=default, 1=A, 2=B, 3=C, etc. The information is stored at the buffer specified by DS:DX. Only CX bytes are read.

For this function to be usable, bit 14 of the device-information word (as returned in the DX register through service 21/44/0) must be 1. (Refer to table 21.13 for the makeup of the device-information word.) This service is not supported on network devices.

Block Device Write (Interrupt 21h, service 44h, function 05h)

Category: System services

Registers on Entry:

AH: 44h
AL: 05h
BL: Drive number
CX: Bytes to write
DX: Offset address of buffer
DS: Segment address of buffer

Registers on Return:

AX: Bytes written

Memory Affected: None

Syntax:

```
PUSH    CS                      ;Code segment and
POP     DS                      ;  data segment are same
MOV     DX,OFFSET BUFFER        ;Address of input buffer
MOV     BL,DRIVE                ;Want this drive
MOV     CX,NUM_BYTES            ;Write this many bytes
PUSH    CX                      ;Store for later check
MOV     AL,5
MOV     AH,44h
INT     21h                     ;DOS services interrupt
POP     CX                      ;Get back original number
CMP     AX,CX                   ;Was everything written?
JNE     ERROR                   ;No, go handle
```

Description: This function writes a control string to a block device, typically a disk drive. BL is used to specify which drive to use, where 0=default, 1=A, 2=B, 3=C, etc. CX bytes of information stored at the buffer address specified by DS:DX are written.

For this function to be usable, bit 14 of the device-information word (as returned in the DX register through service 21/44/0) must be 1. (Refer to table 21.13 for the makeup of the device-information word.) This service is not supported on network devices.

Get Input Status (Interrupt 21h, service 44h, function 06h)

Category: System services

Registers on Entry:

AH: 44h
AL: 06h
BX: Device handle

Registers on Return:

AL: Status

Memory Affected: None

Syntax:

```
MOV    BX,DEVICE_HANDLE       ;Use this device
MOV    AL,6
MOV    AH,44h
INT    21h                    ;DOS services interrupt
```

Description: This service determines whether the device is ready for input. If the device is ready, AL returns 0Fh. If the device is not ready, AL returns 0.

If the device specified in BX is a file, AL always returns FFh until the end-of-file is reached, at which point AL is equal to 0.

This function is not supported on network devices.

Get Output Status (Interrupt 21h, service 44h, function 07h)

Category: System services

Registers on Entry:

AH: 44h
AL: 07h
BX: Device handle

Registers on Return:

AL: Status

Memory Affected: None

Syntax:

```
MOV    BX,DEVICE_HANDLE      ;Use this device
MOV    AL,7
MOV    AH,44h
INT    21h                   ;DOS services interrupt
```

Description: This service determines whether the device is ready for output. If the device is ready, AL returns 0Fh. If the device is not ready, AL returns 0.

If the device specified in BX is a file, AL always returns FFh until the end-of-file is reached, at which point AL is equal to 0.

This function is not supported on network devices.

Block Device Changeable? (Interrupt 21h, service 44h, function 08h)

Category: System services

Registers on Entry:

AH: 44h
AL: 08h
BL: Drive number

Registers on Return:

AX: Status

Memory Affected: None

Syntax:

```
MOV    BL,0       ;Check on default drive
MOV    AL,8
MOV    AH,44h
INT    21h        ;DOS services interrupt
CMP    AX,1       ;Is it fixed?
JE     FIXED      ;Yes, so treat accordingly
```

Description: This function (not available before DOS version 3.0) enables your program to determine whether the block device (typically a disk drive) supports removable media. BL is used to specify which drive to check (0=default, 1=A, 2=B, 3=C, and so on).

On return, AX is equal to 0 if removable media is supported, and equal to 1 if the media is not removable (fixed disk). If AX is equal to 0Fh, the value specified in BL is an invalid drive.

This function is not supported on network devices.

Logical Device Local/Remote Determination (Interrupt 21h, service 44h, function 09h)

Category: Network services

Registers on Entry:

AH: 44h
AL: 09h
BL: Drive number

Registers on Return:

DX: Status

Memory Affected: None

Syntax:

```
MOV   BL,0          ;Check on default drive
MOV   AL,9
MOV   AH,44h
INT   21h           ;DOS services interrupt
```

Description: This function (not available before DOS version 3.1) is used in a networking environment to determine whether the block device (usually a disk drive) specified in BL is local or remote. BL is used to specify which drive to check (0=default, 1=A, 2=B, 3=C, and so on).

On return, bit 12 of DX is set if the device is remote. If the device is local or if redirection is paused, bit 12 is clear. If bit 12 is clear, the bits in DX will have the meaning listed in table 21.15.

Table 21.15. *Status value returned by service 21/44/09.*

Bits `FEDCBA98 76543210`	Meaning
`0`	Drive is not substituted
`1`	Drive is substituted for another drive
` 0`	Drive may not work with services 44/04 and 44/05
` 1`	Drive will work with services 44/04 and 44/05
`  0`	Media descriptor byte in FAT not required
`  1`	Media descriptor byte in FAT required
`   0`	Unused; set to 0
`    0`	Drive may not work with service 44/08
`    1`	Drive will work with service 44/08
`     0`	Unused; set to 0
`      0`	Drive is local
`      1`	Drive is local, but shared by other network computers
`       0`	Unused; set to 0
`         0`	Drive may not work with service 44/11
`         1`	Drive will work with service 44/11
`          0`	Drive may not work with services 44/0D, 44/0E, and 44/0F
`          1`	Drive will work with services 44/0D, 44/0E, and 44/0F
`           0`	Unused; set to 0
`            0`	Unused; set to 0
`             0`	Unused; set to 0
`              0`	Unused; set to 0
`               0`	Drive uses 16-bit sector addressing
`               1`	Drive uses 32-bit sector addressing
`                0`	Unused; set to 0

Handle Local/Remote Determination
(Interrupt 21h, service 44h, function 0Ah)

Category: Network services

Registers on Entry:

AH: 44h
AL: 0Ah
BX: File handle

Registers on Return:

DX: Status

Memory Affected: None

Syntax:

```
MOV     BX,FILE_HANDLE          ;Checking this file
MOV     AL,0Ah
MOV     AH,44h
INT     21h                     ;DOS services interrupt
```

Description: This function (not available before DOS version 3.1) is used in a networking environment to determine whether a given file handle (specified in BX) represents a local file or a remote one.

On return, bit 15 of DX is set if the device is remote. If the device is local, bit 15 is clear. The meaning of the rest of the bits depends on whether the handle refers to a file or not. Table 21.16 shows the bit meanings returned in DX if the handle represents a file; table 21.17 indicates the bit meanings if it is not a file.

Table 21.16. *Device information returned by function 21/44/0A, if device is a file (bit 7 is set).*

Bits FEDCBA98 76543210	Meaning
0	Local file
1	Remote file
0	Date/time is set when file is closed.
1	Date/time is not set when file is closed.
?	Reserved
0	Inheritable
1	Not inheritable

Bits		Meaning
FEDCBA98	76543210	
??????		Reserved
0		This device is a disk file.
0		File has been written to
1		File has not been written to
	xxxxxx	Drive number (if device is a file)

Table 21.17. *Device information returned by function 21/44/0A, if device is not a file (bit 7 is clear).*

Bits		Meaning
FEDCBA98	76543210	
0		Local device
1		Remote device
?		Reserved
1		Named pipe
0		Inheritable
1		Not inheritable
1		Network spooler
???		Reserved
	1	This channel is a device.
	0	End-of-file returned if device is read
	1	End-of-file not returned if device is read
	0	Using ASCII mode
	1	Using binary mode
	0	Not a special device
	1	Special device
	0	Not a clock device
	1	Clock device
	0	Normal device
	1	Null device
	0	Not console output device
	1	Console output device
	0	Not console input device
	1	Console input device

Set Sharing Retry Count (Interrupt 21h, service 44h, function 0Bh)

Category: System services

Registers on Entry:

AH: 44h
AL: 0Bh
CX: Delay loop counter
DX: Retries

Registers on Return:

AX: Error code

Memory Affected: None

Syntax:

```
MOV     CX,3            ;3 delay loops
MOV     DX,8            ;8 retries
MOV     AL,0Bh
MOV     AH,44h
INT     21h             ;DOS services interrupt
JC      ERROR           ;Error, go handle
```

Description: This function (not available before DOS version 3.0) is used in a networking environment to specify the number of attempts at file access and the delay between retries. If a file is locked or if a sharing conflict exists, DOS attempts to access the file three times, with one delay loop between attempts, before returning an error.

On return, the carry flag indicates an error if one has occurred. If the carry flag is set, AX contains the error code, which can be handled through service 21/59.

Handle Generic Code-Page Switching (Interrupt 21h, service 44h, function 0Ch)

Category: System services

Registers on Entry:

AH: 44h
AL: 0Ch
BX: Device handle

CH: Major subfunction code
CL: Minor subfunction code
DX: Offset address of parameter block
DS: Segment address of parameter block

Registers on Return:

AX: Error code

Memory Affected: This function can have various effects on memory, depending on the major and minor subfunctions requested.

Syntax:

```
PUSH    CS                          ;Code segment and
POP     DS                          ;  data segment are same
MOV     DX,OFFSET PARM_BLOCK        ;Address of parameter block
MOV     BX,DEVICE_HANDLE            ;Device handle in use
MOV     CH,MAJOR                    ;Major subfunction desired
MOV     CL,MINOR                    ;Minor subfunction desired
MOV     AL,0Ch
MOV     AH,44h
INT     21h                         ;DOS services interrupt
```

Description: This service (not available in this form before DOS 3.3) allows device-driver support for subfunctions that enable code-page switching. You specify the device handle in BX, a major subfunction code in CH, and a minor code in CL. Currently, the service has four major codes and five minor codes, for a total of 20 possible combinations of major/minor codes. Each minor code requires a different set of parameters, which are passed through a parameter block pointed to by DS:DX.

On return, the carry flag indicates an error if one has occurred. If the carry flag is set, AX contains the error code, which can be handled through service 21/59.

Because of the detail and complexity involved with this function, its discussion is best left to another publication. Detailed information about this function, its subfunctions, and the parameter setup is beyond the scope of this book.

Generic IOCTL Block Device Request (Interrupt 21h, service 44h, function 0Dh)

Category: System services

Registers on Entry:

AH: 44h
AL: 0Dh
BL: Drive number
CH: Major subfunction code
CL: Minor subfunction code
DX: Offset address of parameter block
DS: Segment address of parameter block

Registers on Return:

AX: Error code

Memory Affected: This function can have various effects on memory, depending on the major and minor subfunctions requested.

Syntax:

```
PUSH   CS                      ;Code segment and
POP    DS                      ;  data segment are same
MOV    DX,OFFSET PARM_BLOCK    ;Address of parameter block
MOV    BL,0                    ;Check on default drive
MOV    CH,8                    ;Always 8
MOV    CL,MINOR                ;Minor subfunction desired
MOV    AL,0Dh
MOV    AH,44h
INT    21h                     ;DOS services interrupt
```

Description: IOCTL is a contraction for input-output control. This service (not available before DOS version 3.2) allows uniform device support for a number of block device functions—typically, disk drive functions. The drive number is specified in BL (0=default, 1=A, 2=B, 3=C, and so on).

A major subfunction code is specified in CH, which is always 8 (as of DOS 3.3). A minor subfunction code is specified in CL. Table 21.18 details the minor codes possible.

Table 21.18. Minor subfunction codes (CL) for service 21/44/0D.

Value	Meaning
40h	Set device parameters
41h	Write logical device track
42h	Format and verify logical device track
46h	Set media ID
60h	Get device parameters

Value	Meaning
61h	Read logical device track
62h	Verify logical device track
66h	Get media ID
68h	Sense media type

Each minor code requires a different set of parameters, which are passed through a parameter block pointed to by DS:DX.

On return, the carry flag indicates whether an error has occurred. If the carry flag is set, AX contains the error code, which can be handled through service 21/59.

Because of the detail and complexity involved with this function, its discussion is best left to another publication. Detailed information about this function, its subfunctions, and the parameter setup is beyond the scope of this book.

Get Logical Device Map (Interrupt 21h, service 44h, function 0Eh)

Category: System services

Registers on Entry:

AH: 44h
AL: 0Eh
BL: Drive number

Registers on Return:

AX: Return code

Memory Affected: None

Syntax:

```
MOV    BL,0            ;Use default drive
MOV    AL,0Eh
MOV    AH,44h
INT    21h             ;DOS services interrupt
```

Description: This function (not available before DOS version 3.2) determines whether a block device (typically, a disk drive) has more than one logical drive assigned to it. Use BL to specify which drive to check (0=default, 1=A, 2=B, 3=C, and so on).

On return, the carry flag indicates whether an error has occurred. If the carry flag is set, AX contains the error code, which can be handled through service 21/59. If the carry flag is not set, AL contains the result code. If AL is 0, only one logical drive is assigned to the block device. If AL contains another number, that number represents the drive letter last used to reference the device. In this case, 1=A, 2=B, 3=C, etc.

Set Logical Device Map (Interrupt 21h, service 44h, function 0Fh)

Category: System services

Registers on Entry:

AH: 44h
AL: 0Fh
BL: Drive number

Registers on Return:

AX: Return code

Memory Affected: None

Syntax:

```
MOV    BL,0             ;Use default drive
MOV    AL,0Fh
MOV    AH,44h
INT    21h              ;DOS services interrupt
```

Description: This function (not available before DOS version 3.2) assigns a logical drive letter to a block device (typically a disk drive). Use BL to specify the drive letter (1=A, 2=B, 3=C, and so on). You use this function when more than one logical drive letter can be assigned to a single physical block device. An example is a system with a single floppy drive. Even though the system has only one block device (the floppy drive), that device can be addressed logically as two devices (drives A: and B:). This function causes DOS to view the system as either A: or B: in subsequent I/O functions.

On return, the carry flag indicates whether an error has occurred. If the carry flag is set, AX contains the error code, which can be handled through service 21/59.

Query Handle (Interrupt 21h, service 44h, function 10h)

Category: System services

Registers on Entry:

AH: 44h
AL: 10h
BX: Handle number
CL: Minor subfunction code
CH: Category

Registers on Return:

AX: Error code (if carry flag set)

Memory Affected: None

Syntax:

```
MOV    BX,Device_Handle    ;Use default drive
MOV    CL,65h              ;Function checking: Get iteration
MOV    CH,01h              ;Serial device
MOV    AL,10h
MOV    AH,44h
INT    21h                 ;DOS services interrupt
```

Description: This function is used to determine whether a specific device supports IOCTL services. IOCTL is a contraction for input-output control. CL should contain the category number (1=serial device, 2=console, 3=parallel printer), and CH should contain the Interrupt 21/44/0C subfunction to check (45h or 65h).

On return, the carry flag will be clear if IOCTL is supported; otherwise, it will be set. If the carry flag is set, AX contains the error code, which can be handled through service 21/59.

Query Drive (Interrupt 21h, service 44h, function 11h)

Category: System services

Registers on Entry:

AH: 44h
AL: 11h
BL: Drive number
CL: Minor subfunction code
CH: 08h

Registers on Return:

AX: Error code (if carry flag set)

Memory Affected: None

Syntax:

```
MOV    BX,Device_Handle    ;Use default drive
MOV    CL,65h              ;Function checking: Get iteration
MOV    CH,68h              ;Sense media type
MOV    AL,11h
MOV    AH,44h
INT    21h                 ;DOS services interrupt
```

Description: This function is used to test whether a specific drive can support IOCTL services. IOCTL is an acronym for *input-output control*. When using this service, CL should be loaded with an Interrupt 21/44/01 subfunction to test. Table 21.19 lists valid values for CL.

Table 21.19. Minor subfunction codes (CL) for service 21/44/11.

Value	Meaning
40h	Set device parameters
41h	Write logical device track
42h	Format and verify logical device track
46h	Set media ID
60h	Get device parameters
61h	Read logical device track
62h	Verify logical device track
66h	Get media ID
68h	Sense media type

On return, the carry flag will be clear if IOCTL is supported; otherwise, the carry flag will be set. If the carry flag is set, AX contains the error code, which can be handled through service 21/59.

Duplicate File Handle (Interrupt 21h, service 45h)

Category: Disk services

Registers on Entry:

AH: 45h
BX: File handle

Registers on Return:

AX: Return code

Memory Affected: None

Syntax:

```
MOV     BX,FILE_HANDLE_1        ;Use current file handle
MOV     AH,45h
INT     21h                     ;DOS services interrupt
JC      ERROR                   ;Go handle error
MOV     FILE_HANDLE_2,AX        ;Save new handle
```

Description: This service, which duplicates a file handle, results in two handles that point to the same file at the same file position.

There is no clear need or use for this function; you simply can use two different handles to refer to a single file. These handles operate in tandem, not independently, because any change you make to the file pointer by using one of the handles is reflected in the other handle. The most common use for this function is with service 21/46, where you duplicate a handle before reassigning it. This use allows redirection later.

On return, the carry flag indicates whether an error has occurred. If the carry flag is set, AX contains the error code, which can be handled through service 21/59.

Force Handle Duplication (Interrupt 21h, service 46h)

Category: Disk services

Registers on Entry:

AH: 46h
BX: File handle
CX: File handle to be forced

Registers on Return:

AX: Error code

Memory Affected: None

Syntax:

```
MOV     BX,FILE_HANDLE          ;Original handle
MOV     CX,4                    ;Standard printer handle
MOV     AH,46h
INT     21h                     ;DOS services interrupt
JC      ERROR                   ;Branch if error
```

Description: This service forces one file handle to point to the same device (file, for example) as another handle. In the syntax example, BX represents an open file. CX is loaded with the standard printer handle, and through this service, handle 4 is made to point to the open file. Anything sent to handle 4 (normally sent to the printer) is sent to the open file.

On return, the carry flag indicates whether an error has occurred. If the carry flag is set, AX contains the error code, which can be handled through service 21/59.

Get Directory Path (Interrupt 21h, service 47h)

Category: Disk services

Registers on Entry:

AH: 47h
DL: Drive number
SI: Offset address of buffer area
DS: Segment address of buffer area

Registers on Return: Unchanged

AX: Error code
SI: Offset address of buffer area
DS: Segment address of buffer area

Memory Affected: The memory area pointed to by DS:SI is overwritten with the requested directory information.

Syntax:

```
PUSH    CS                      ;Code segment and
POP     DS                      ;  data segment are same
MOV     SI,OFFSET DIR_BUFFER    ;Address of 64-byte buffer
```

```
MOV     DL,0                    ;Use default drive
MOV     AH,47h
INT     21h                     ;DOS services interrupt
```

Description: This service determines the ASCIIZ-string path for the current directory of the drive specified in DL, where 0=default, 1=A, 2=B, 3=C, etc.

The returned string is not the complete path name because the drive designator and root-directory backslash are not returned. These characters can be added to the beginning of the string, however, to create a complete path for the directory. Because an ASCIIZ string is returned, the returned string ends with an ASCII 0 (nul).

Because path names can be up to 64 bytes long, a good practice is to make sure that the buffer area to which DS:SI points is 64 bytes long.

On return, the carry flag indicates whether an error has occurred. If the carry flag is set, AX contains the error code, which can be handled through service 21/59. If the carry flag is not set, the address to which DS:SI points is the start of the returned ASCIIZ string.

Allocate Memory (Interrupt 21h, service 48h)

Category: System services

Registers on Entry:

AH: 48h
BX: Paragraphs to allocate

Registers on Return:

AX: Return code
BX: Maximum paragraphs available

Memory Affected: Although the contents of the requested memory are not changed, the amount of free memory is reduced by the requested number of paragraphs.

Syntax:

```
MOV     BX,100h                 ;Request 4K block of memory
MOV     AH,48h
INT     21h                     ;DOS services interrupt
JC      ERROR                   ;Branch if error
MOV     BLOCK_SEG,AX            ;Save segment address
```

Description: This service is used to set aside blocks of memory for program use. You specify the number of contiguous paragraphs required in BX.

On return, the carry flag indicates whether an error has occurred. If the carry flag is set, AX contains the error code, which can be handled through service 21/59. If an error has occurred, BX contains the maximum number of contiguous paragraphs available.

If the carry flag is not set, AX points to the paragraph or segment address where the memory block begins. This memory block must later be freed (before program completion) through service 21/49.

Free Allocated Memory (Interrupt 21h, service 49h)

Category: System services

Registers on Entry:

AH: 49h
ES: Segment address of memory block

Registers on Return:

AX: Error code

Memory Affected: Although the contents of the requested memory are not changed, the amount of free memory is increased by the size of the block being relinquished.

Syntax:

```
PUSH    ES                      ;Save current segment
MOV     ES,BLOCK_SEG            ;Set to segment to free
MOV     AH,49h
INT     21h                     ;DOS services interrupt
POP     ES                      ;Get register back
JC      ERROR                   ;Branch if error
MOV     BLOCK_SEG,0             ;Zero out variable
```

Description: This service frees memory blocks allocated through service 21/48. You specify the segment address of the block in ES.

On return, the carry flag indicates whether an error has occurred. If the carry flag is set, AX contains the error code, which can be handled through service 21/59.

Change Memory-Block Allocation (Interrupt 21h, service 4Ah)

Category: System services

Registers on Entry:

AH: 4Ah
BX: Total paragraphs to allocate
ES: Segment address of memory block

Registers on Return:

AX: Error code
BX: Maximum paragraphs available

Memory Affected: Although the contents of the requested memory are not changed, the amount of free memory is reduced by the difference between the number of paragraphs already allocated to the block and the requested number of paragraphs.

Syntax:

```
MOV     BX,200h             ;Change to 8K block
MOV     AH,4Ah
INT     21h                 ;DOS services interrupt
JC      ERROR               ;Branch if error
MOV     BLOCK_SEG,AX        ;Save segment address
```

Description: This service changes the size of a memory block previously allocated through service 21/48. You specify the segment address of the existing block in ES.

On return, the carry flag indicates whether an error has occurred. If the carry flag is set, AX contains the error code, which can be handled through service 21/59. If an error has occurred and an increase in block size was requested, BX contains the maximum number of contiguous paragraphs available; the original block allocation is not changed, however.

Load Program (Interrupt 21h, service 4Bh, function 00h)

Category: System services

Registers on Entry:

AH: 4Bh
AL: 00h

BX: Offset address of parameter block
DX: Offset address of path name
DS: Segment address of path name
ES: Segment address of parameter block

Registers on Return:

AX: Error code

Memory Affected: The desired file, if located, is loaded into memory, overwriting previous memory contents.

Syntax:

```
MOV     AX,CS                   ;Code segment is same as
MOV     DS,AX                   ; data segment and
MOV     ES,AX                   ;  extra segment
MOV     DX,OFFSET FILE_PATH     ;Offset address of path
MOV     BX,OFFSET LOAD_PARMS    ;Offset address of parameters
MOV     AL,0                    ;Load only
MOV     AH,4Bh
INT     21h                     ;DOS services interrupt
```

Description: This service allows a disk file to be loaded. DS:DX should point to an ASCIIZ (null-terminated ASCII) string that contains the full name of the file, including any applicable path name. Wild cards cannot be used in the file designation.

ES:BX should point to a parameter block that provides necessary information for loading the file. The parameter block is organized as follows:

```
LOAD_PARMS    DW    SEG ENV_STRING     ;Environment string segment
              DW    OFFSET CMD_LINE    ;Offset of default command
              DW    SEG CMD_LINE       ;Segment of default command
              DW    OFFSET FCB_1       ;Offset of default FCB 1
              DW    SEG FCB_1          ;Segment of default FCB 1
              DW    OFFSET FCB_2       ;Offset of default FCB 2
              DW    SEG FCB_2          ;Segment of default FCB 2
              DW    OFFSET CODE_ADR    ;Offset of starting code address
              DW    SEG CODE_ADR       ;Segment of starting code address
              DW    OFFSET ST_ADR      ;Offset of stack address
              DW    SET ST_ADR         ;Segment of stack address
```

The loaded file or program is called a *child* of the original program, which is referred to as the *parent*. All open files (except files with their inheritance bit set) are available for the child program. Because this service destroys all registers, remember to save all registers before using this service and restore them after returning.

On return, the carry flag indicates whether an error has occurred. If the carry flag is set, AX contains the error code, which can be handled through service 21/59.

Load Overlay (Interrupt 21h, service 4Bh, function 03h)

Category: System services

Registers on Entry:

AH: 4Bh
AL: 03h
BX: Offset address of parameter block
DX: Offset address of path name
DS: Segment address of path name
ES: Segment address of parameter block

Registers on Return:

AX: Error code

Memory Affected: If located, the desired file is loaded into memory, overwriting the current program area.

Syntax:

```
MOV     AX,CS                       ;Code segment is same as
MOV     DS,AX                       ;   data segment and
MOV     ES,AX                       ;   extra segment
MOV     DX,OFFSET FILE_PATH         ;Offset address of path
MOV     BX,OFFSET OVERLAY_PARMS     ;Offset address of parameters
MOV     AL,03h                      ;Load an overlay
MOV     AH,4Bh
INT     21h                         ;DOS services interrupt
```

Description: This service enables a disk file to be loaded as an overlay (placed over the current program in memory), starting at the memory address indicated in the parameter block.

DS:DX should point to an ASCIIZ (null-terminated ASCII) string that contains the full name of the file, including any applicable path name. Wild cards cannot be used in the file designation.

ES:BX should point to a parameter block that provides necessary information for loading the file. The two possible parameter blocks are organized as follows:

```
OVERLAY_PARMS   DW     SEG LOAD_POINT   ;Segment of loading point
                DW     0000             ;Relocation factor for file
```

Because this service destroys all registers, remember to save all registers before using this service and restore them after returning. On return, the carry flag indicates whether an error has occurred. If the carry flag is set, AX contains the error code, which can be handled through service 21/59.

Set Execution State (Interrupt 21h, service 4Bh, function 05h)

Category: System services

Registers on Entry:

AH: 4Bh
AL: 05h
DX: Offset address of parameter block
DS: Segment address of parameter block

Registers on Return: Unchanged

Memory Affected: None

Syntax:

```
MOV     AX,CS                   ;Code segment is same as
MOV     DS,AX                   ; data segment
MOV     DX,OFFSET EXEC_STATE    ;Offset address of parameters
MOV     AL,05h                  ;Load and execute
MOV     AH,4Bh
INT     21h                     ;DOS services interrupt
```

Description: This service prepares DOS to transfer control to a new program, either a child or an overlay. Included in this preparation is setting the DOS version number used by the new program (as in the DOS 5 SETVER command).

DS:DX should point to a parameter block that provides necessary information for the preparation. The parameter block is organized as follows:

```
EXEC_STATE      DW      0                   ;Reserved; must be 0
                DW      TYPE_FLAGS          ;Type flags for new program
                DW      OFFSET PROG_NAME    ;Offset of ASCIIZ for program name
                DW      SEG PROG_NAME       ;Segment of ASCIIZ for program name
                DW      SEG NEW_PSP         ;Segment of new PSP for program
                DD      PROG_START          ;CS:IP address of new program
                DW      PROG_SIZE           ;Size of program and PSP in bytes
```

This function should be called immediately before control is transferred to the child or overlay program. The TYPE_FLAGS parameter in the parameter block specifies the type of program to which execution will be transferred (1=EXE program, 2=overlay program).

Process Terminate (Interrupt 21h, service 4Ch)

Category: System services

Registers on Entry:

AH: 4Ch
AL: Return code

Registers on Return: Undefined (does not return)

Memory Affected: Although not altered, the memory area used by the program is made available to future programs.

Syntax:

```
MOV     AL,RETURN_CODE          ;Return code to pass
MOV     AH,4Ch
INT     21h                     ;DOS services interrupt
```

Description: This service terminates a program and returns control to either a parent program or DOS. This service allows passing a return code to the parent or to DOS. If the program invoking this service is a child program, the return code is retrievable (by the parent program) through service 21/4D. If control is returned to DOS, the return code is available through the ERRORLEVEL batch-file command.

Get Return Code of a Subprocess (Interrupt 21h, service 4Dh)

Category: System services

Registers on Entry:

AH: 4Dh

Registers on Return:

AX: Return code

Memory Affected: None

Syntax:

```
MOV     AH,4Dh
INT     21h                     ;DOS services interrupt
```

Description: This service retrieves the return code that a child program passes through service 21/4C. A reliable return code can be retrieved only once.

The returned value, in AX, is divided into two parts. AL contains the value passed by the child program, and AH contains one of the values shown in table 21.20.

Table 21.20. *AH return codes for service 21/4D.*

Value	Meaning
0	Normal
1	Ctrl-Break
2	Critical error
3	Terminate and stay resident (TSR)

Search for First File-Name Match (Interrupt 21h, service 4Eh)

Category: Disk services

Registers on Entry:

AH: 4Eh
CX: File attribute
DX: Offset address of file name
DS: Segment address of file name

Registers on Return:

AX: Error code

Memory Affected: If the service locates a file-name match, DOS fills the memory area specified as the DTA with 43 bytes of file information.

Syntax:

```
PUSH    CS                      ;Code segment and
POP     DS                      ;  data segment are same
MOV     DX,OFFSET PATH_NAME     ;Offset address of path
MOV     AH,4Eh
INT     21h                     ;DOS services interrupt
JC      ERROR                   ;Branch if error
```

Description: This service locates a file with a specified file name. DS:DX should point to an ASCIIZ (null-terminated ASCII) string that contains the full name of the file, including any applicable path name. Wild cards can be used in the file designation.

You place the desired file-attribute value in CX. Actually, because the file attribute is only one byte long, you should place the new setting in CL, and set CH to 0. Table 21.21 shows bit meanings of the file-attribute byte. In this table, a *1* in a bit position indicated by an *x* means that the attribute is selected; a *0* means that the attribute is not selected.

Table 21.21. *Bit settings for file attribute, service 21/43.*

Bits 76543210	*Meaning*
00	Reserved—set to 0
0	Archive—does not apply to this service
x	Subdirectory
x	Volume label
x	System
x	Hidden
0	Read-only—does not apply to this service

DOS follows a peculiar logic when searching for files with matching attributes. If CX is set to 0, DOS locates normal files (files with no special attributes). Selecting an attribute byte with any combination of subdirectory, system, or hidden bits set results in those files and normal files being selected. If the volume-label bit is set, only files with a volume-label attribute match.

On return, the carry flag indicates whether an error has occurred. If the carry flag is set, AX contains the error code, which can be handled through service 21/59. If the carry flag is not set, the service fills in the DTA with 43 bytes of information about the located file. This information is detailed as follows:

```
           DB     21 DUP(0)       ;Reserved--used by DOS
FILE_ATTR  DB     00              ;File attribute
FILE_TIME  DW     0000            ;File time
FILE_DATE  DW     0000            ;File date
FILE_SIZE  DD     00000000        ;File size
FILE_NAME  DB     13 DUP(0)       ;ASCIIZ of file name
```

The file name returned in FILE_NAME is left-justified, with a period between the root and extension.

Search for Next File-Name Match (Interrupt 21h, service 4Fh)

Category: Disk services

Registers on Entry:

AH: 4Fh

Registers on Return:

AX: Error code

Memory Affected: If the service locates a file-name match, DOS fills in the memory area specified as the DTA with 43 bytes of file information.

Syntax:

```
MOV     AH,4Fh
INT     21h             ;DOS services interrupt
JC      ERROR           ;Branch if error
```

Description: This service locates the next file with a specified file name. Before you invoke this service, the DTA must be set by a call to service 21/4E. Otherwise, the results can be unpredictable. For more information, see the description for service 21/4E.

Because any given directory must contain unique file names, this service is useless if the file specification for which you are searching does not contain the question-mark (?) wild card.

Set PSP Address (Interrupt 21h, service 50h)

Category: System services

Registers on Entry:

AH: 50h
BX: Segment address of new PSP

Registers on Return: None

Memory Affected: None

Syntax:

```
MOV     BX,SEG NEW_PSP
MOV     AH,50h
INT     21h                     ;DOS services interrupt
```

Description: This service allows you to define the address of a new program segment prefix (PSP) for the currently executing program. If you do not specify a valid segment address for a PSP in the BX register, the results of using this service are unpredictable.

Get PSP Address (Interrupt 21h, service 51h)

Category: System services

Registers on Entry:

AH: 51h

Registers on Return:

BX: Segment address of current PSP

Memory Affected: None

Syntax:

```
MOV    AH,51h
INT    21h                  ;DOS services interrupt
MOV    PSP_SEG,BX           ;Store the segment address
```

Description: This service allows you to determine the segment address of the program segment prefix (PSP) for the currently executing program.

Get Verify Setting (Interrupt 21h, service 54h)

Category: System services

Registers on Entry:

AH: 54h

Registers on Return:

AL: Verify flag

Memory Affected: None

Syntax:

```
MOV    AH,54h
INT    21h                  ;DOS services interrupt
```

Description: This service returns the system flag that specifies whether DOS verifies, after each disk write, that the information has been recorded accurately. The return value in AL signifies the state of the verify flag. If AL=0, the verify flag is off. If AL=1, the verify flag is on.

If you are working with a network system, verification is not supported; therefore, the return value has no meaning.

Rename File (Interrupt 21h, service 56h)

Category: Disk services

Registers on Entry:

AH: 56h
DX: Offset address of old file name
DI: Offset address of new file name
DS: Segment address of old file name
ES: Segment address of new file name

Registers on Return:

AX: Error code

Memory Affected: None

Syntax:

```
MOV    AX,CS               ;Code segment is same as
MOV    DS,AX               ;  data segment and
MOV    ES,AX               ;  extra segment
MOV    DX,OFFSET OLD_FILE  ;Offset address of old file
MOV    DI,OFFSET NEW_FILE  ;Offset address of new file
MOV    AH,56h
INT    21h                 ;DOS services interrupt
```

Description: This service allows you to rename files, using ASCIIZ strings. DS:DX should point to an ASCIIZ (null-terminated ASCII) string that contains the full name of the old file, including any applicable path name. ES:DI should point to a similar string for the new file.

Because the directory paths for the files may differ, you can rename files across directories. The only restriction is that both files must reside on the same drive.

On return, the carry flag indicates whether an error has occurred. If the carry flag is set, AX contains the error code, which can be handled through service 21/59.

Get/Set File Date and Time (Interrupt 21h, service 57h)

Category: Disk services

Registers on Entry:

AH: 57h
AL: Function code
BX: File handle
CX: New file time
DX: New file date

Registers on Return:

AX: Error code
CX: File time
DX: File date

Memory Affected: None

Syntax:

```
MOV     AL,0                    ;Get file date and time
MOV     BX,FILE_HANDLE          ;Use this handle
MOV     AH,57h
INT     21h                     ;DOS services interrupt
```

Description: This service allows you to retrieve or set the date and time for an open file, based on the function code in AL. If AL=0, the service retrieves the file date and time; if AL=1, the service sets the file date and time.

If you are setting the file date and time, specify the time in CX and the date in DX.

On return, the carry flag indicates whether an error has occurred. If the carry flag is set, AX contains the error code, which can be handled through service 21/59. If the carry flag is clear and AL=0, CX and DX reflect, on return, the file time and date, respectively.

Get Allocation Strategy (Interrupt 21h, service 58h, function 00h)

Category: System services

Registers on Entry:

AH: 58h
AL: 00h

Registers on Return:

AX: Strategy code

Memory Affected: None

Syntax:

```
MOV    AL,0                      ;Get strategy code
MOV    AH,58h
INT    21h                       ;DOS services interrupt
MOV    STRATEGY,AX               ;Store for later use
```

Description: This function is used to determine which of several memory-allocation strategies DOS is using. The value returned in AX can be one of those shown in table 21.22.

Table 21.22. *AX return codes for service 21/58/00.*

Value	Strategy Meaning
00h	Search conventional memory for the first available memory block (default strategy)
01h	Search conventional memory for the first contiguous block that is large enough
02h	Search conventional memory for the last available block
40h	Search high memory for the first available memory block
41h	Search high memory for the first contiguous block that is large enough
42h	Search high memory for the last available block
80h	Search high memory for the first available memory block, then look in conventional memory
81h	Search high memory for the first contiguous block that is large enough, then look in conventional memory
82h	Search high memory for the last available block, then look in conventional memory

Set Allocation Strategy (Interrupt 21h, service 58h, function 01h)

Category: System services

Registers on Entry:

AH: 58h
AL: 01h
BX: Strategy code

Registers on Return:

AX: Error code

Memory Affected: None

Syntax:

```
MOV     STRATEGY,BX             ;Store for later use
MOV     AL,1                    ;Set strategy code
MOV     AH,58h
INT     21h                     ;DOS services interrupt
JC      STRAT_ERR               ;Error occurred
```

Description: This function is used to set the memory-allocation strategy DOS should use. The strategy specified can be any of those shown in table 21.22 (see service 21/58/00).

On return, the carry flag indicates whether an error has occurred. If the carry flag is set, AX contains the error code, which can be handled through service 21/59.

Get High-Memory Link Status (Interrupt 21h, service 58h, function 02h)

Category: System services

Registers on Entry:

AH: 58h
AL: 02h

Registers on Return:

AL: Link code

Memory Affected: None

Syntax:

```
MOV    AL,2               ;Get link status code
MOV    AH,58h
INT    21h                ;DOS services interrupt
```

Description: In DOS 5, DOS can be directed to use the high-memory area. This function tests whether that area is available for use. On return, if the carry flag is clear, AL will contain the link code. If AL=1, the high-memory area is available; if AL=0, that area is not available.

   If the carry flag is set on return, an error has occurred. If the carry flag is set, AX contains the error code, which can be handled through service 21/59.

Set High-Memory Link Status (Interrupt 21h, service 58h, function 03h)

Category: System services

Registers on Entry:

AH: 58h
AL: 03h
BL: Link code

Registers on Return:

AX: Error code

Memory Affected: None

Syntax:

```
MOV    BL,0               ;Unlink high memory
MOV    AL,3               ;Set link status code
MOV    AH,58h
INT    21h                ;DOS services interrupt
```

Description: In DOS 5, DOS can be directed to use the high-memory area. This function sets whether that area can be used. If BL is set to 1, the high-memory area is linked; if BL is set to 0, it is unlinked.

   On return, the carry flag indicates whether an error has occurred. If the carry flag is set, AX contains the error code, which can be handled through service 21/59.

Get Extended-Error Information
(Interrupt 21h, service 59h)

Category: System services

Registers on Entry:

AH: 59h
BX: 0

Registers on Return:

AX: Extended-error code
BH: Error class
BL: Suggested remedy
CH: Locus

Memory Affected: None

Syntax:

```
ERROR:      PUSH    AX              ;Store all registers
            PUSH    BX
            PUSH    CX
            PUSH    DX
            PUSH    DI
            PUSH    SI
            PUSH    ES
            PUSH    DS
            MOV     BX,0
            MOV     AH,59h
            INT     21h             ;DOS services interrupt
            MOV     ERROR_CODE,AX   ;Store returned values
            MOV     ERROR_CLASS,BH
            MOV     ACTION,BL
            MOV     LOCUS,CH
            POP     DS              ;Restore all registers
            POP     ES
            POP     SI
            POP     DI
            POP     DX
            POP     CX
            POP     BX
            POP     AX
```

Description: This service, not available before DOS version 3.0, returns detailed information on system errors that have occurred. The service is used for DOS service calls that use the carry flag to signify an error.

The *error code* is the general system error code. The *classes* provide further information about the error classification. The suggested *actions* provide remedies that DOS "thinks" are appropriate for the type of error and the circumstances of its occurrence. The *locus* is the general hardware area where the error occurred.

Because this service destroys virtually all registers, you should save all the registers if you need their contents.

The error code returned in AX is one of the values shown in table 21.23. The possible error classes returned in BH are shown in table 21.24; possible suggested actions returned in BL are shown in table 21.25; and table 21.26 details the locus returned in CH.

Table 21.23. *Possible extended-error codes returned in AX for service 21/59.*

Value	Meaning
1	Invalid function
2	File not found
3	Path not found
4	Too many file handles open
5	Access denied
6	Invalid handle
7	Memory control blocks destroyed
8	Insufficient memory
9	Invalid memory-block address
10	Invalid environment
11	Invalid format
12	Invalid access code
13	Invalid data
14	Reserved
15	Invalid drive
16	Attempt to remove current directory
17	Not same device
18	No more files
19	Disk write-protected
20	Unknown unit
21	Drive not ready
22	Unknown command
23	CRC error

Value	Meaning
24	Bad request structure length
25	Seek error
26	Unknown media type
27	Sector not found
28	Out of paper
29	Write fault
30	Read fault
31	General failure
32	Sharing violation
33	Lock violation
34	Invalid disk
35	FCB unavailable
36	Sharing buffer overflow
37	Code page mismatched
38	End of file (using handles)
39	Disk full (using handles)
40	Reserved
41	Reserved
42	Reserved
43	Reserved
44	Reserved
45	Reserved
46	Reserved
47	Reserved
48	Reserved
49	Reserved
50	Network request not supported
51	Remote computer not listening
52	Duplicate name on network
53	Network name not found
54	Network busy
55	Network device no longer exists
56	NetBIOS command limit exceeded
57	Network adapter error

continues

Table 21.23. *continued*

Value	Meaning
58	Incorrect network response
59	Unexpected network error
60	Incompatible remote adapter
61	Print queue full
62	Not enough space for print file
63	Print file deleted
64	Network name deleted
65	Network access denied
66	Network device type incorrect
67	Network name not found
68	Network name limit exceeded
69	NetBIOS session limit exceeded
70	Temporarily paused
71	Network request not accepted
72	Print or disk redirection is paused
73	Reserved
74	Reserved
75	Reserved
76	Reserved
77	Reserved
78	Reserved
79	Reserved
80	File exists
81	Duplicate FCB
82	Cannot make directory entry
83	Fail on INT 24
84	Too many redirections
85	Duplicate redirection
86	Invalid password
87	Invalid parameter
88	Network data fault
89	Function not supported by network
90	Required system component not installed

Table 21.24. *Possible error classes returned in BH for service 21/59.*

Value	Meaning
1	Out of resource
2	Temporary situation
3	Authorization
4	Internal system error
5	Hardware failure
6	System failure
7	Application program error
8	File or item not found
9	Bad file or item format
10	Locked file or item
11	Media problem
12	File or item already exists
13	Unknown

Table 21.25. *Possible suggested actions returned in BL for service 21/59.*

Value	Meaning
1	Retry immediately
2	Delay then retry
3	Reconsider user input
4	Abort with cleanup
5	Immediate exit without cleanup
6	Ignore the error
7	Retry after action taken

Table 21.26. *Possible locus values returned in CH for service 21/59.*

Value	Meaning
1	Unknown
2	Block device
3	Network
4	Serial device
5	Memory

Create Temporary File (Interrupt 21h, service 5Ah)

Category: Disk services

Registers on Entry:

AH: 5Ah
CX: File attribute
DX: Offset address of path name
DS: Segment address of path name

Registers on Return:

AX: Return code
DX: Offset address of completed path name
DS: Segment address of completed path name

Memory Affected: The file name of the unique file created is appended to the ASCIIZ string specified by DS:DX.

Syntax:

```
PUSH    CS                      ;Code segment and
POP     DS                      ;  data segment are same
MOV     DX,OFFSET PATH_NAME     ;Offset address of path
MOV     CX,0                    ;Normal file
MOV     AH,5Ah
INT     21h                     ;DOS services interrupt
JC      ERROR                   ;Branch if error
MOV     FILE_HANDLE,AX          ;Store returned handle
```

Description: This service, not available before DOS version 3.0, causes a file with a unique file name to be created in the specified directory. DS:DX should point to an ASCIIZ (null-terminated ASCII) string which contains the path name of the directory that will contain the file. This path name should end with a backslash.

You should place the file attribute in CX. Actually, because the file attribute is only one byte long, place the new setting in CL, and set CH to 0. Table 21.27 shows the possible file-attribute settings. In this table, a *1* in a bit position indicated by an *x* means that the attribute is selected; a *0* means that the attribute is not selected.

Table 21.27. *Bit settings for file attribute, service 21/43.*

Bits 76543210	*Meaning*
00	Reserved—set to 0
x	Archive
0	Subdirectory—set to 0 for this service
0	Volume label—set to 0 for this service
x	System
x	Hidden
x	Read-only

This service is helpful for programs that need temporary files for program purposes. The service generates a unique file name and opens the file for read/write operations. The file stays open until you close it and is not deleted unless you delete it.

On return, the carry flag indicates whether an error has occurred. If the carry flag is set, AX contains the error code, which can be handled through service 21/59. If the carry flag is clear, AX contains the file handle for the newly created file, and DS:DX points to an ASCIIZ string that represents the full path name of the created file.

Create File (Interrupt 21h, service 5Bh)

Category: Disk services

Registers on Entry:

AH: 5Bh
CX: File attribute
DX: Offset address of path name
DS: Segment address of path name

Registers on Return:

AX: Return code

Memory Affected: None

Syntax:

```
PUSH    CS                      ;Code segment and
POP     DS                      ;  data segment are same
MOV     DX,OFFSET PATH_NAME     ;Offset address of path
MOV     CX,0                    ;File attribute is normal
MOV     AH,5Bh
INT     21h                     ;DOS services interrupt
JC      ERROR                   ;Carry set, handle error
MOV     FILE_HANDLE,AX          ;Store returned handle
```

Description: This service, not available before DOS version 3.0, creates a disk file. On entry, DS:DX points to an ASCIIZ (null-terminated ASCII) string that contains the full name of the file, including any applicable path name. You set CX to equal the desired attribute for the file.

This service is identical to service 21/3C except that if the file name specified in the ASCIIZ string already exists, an error code is returned.

On return, if the carry flag is set, an error has occurred and the error code is in AX. Service 21/59 can be used to get detailed error information. If the carry flag is not set, the operation was successful, and AX contains the file handle for the newly opened file. This number (file handle) can be used in many other DOS file operations.

When this service is completed, the specified file is left open. You do not need to open the file, but you must remember to close it.

File Access Control (Interrupt 21h, service 5Ch)

Category: Disk services

Registers on Entry:

AH: 5Ch
AL: Function code
BX: File handle
CX: Region offset high
DX: Region offset low
DI: Region length low
SI: Region length high

Registers on Return:

AX: Error code

Memory Affected: None

Syntax:

```
MOV     AL,0                    ;Lock region
MOV     BX,FILE_HANDLE          ;Use this file
MOV     CX,PTR_HIGH             ;Offset into file
MOV     DX,PTR_LOW
MOV     SI,0                    ;Only lock 1 record
MOV     DI,REC_LEN
MOV     AH,5Ch
INT     21h                     ;DOS services interrupt
JC      ERROR                   ;Branch if error
```

Description: This service, not available before DOS version 3.0, provides a simple access-limitation convention for files. The user can lock or unlock regions of a file, thereby limiting or expanding access to the file contents. This service is most useful in networked or multitasking environments.

AL should contain either a 0 or a 1. AL=0 means to lock the file specified in BX; AL=1 means to unlock the file. CX:DX contains a byte offset into the file that specifies the start of the region to be locked. SI:DI contains the length of the region to be locked.

On return, if the carry flag is set, an error has occurred and the error code is in AX. Service 21/59 can be used to get detailed error information.

Before exiting a program, be sure to remember to unlock any regions that have been locked. Failure to do so can have unpredictable results.

Set Extended-Error Values (Interrupt 21h, service 5Dh, function 0Ah)

Category: System services

Registers on Entry:

AH: 5Dh
AL: 0Ah
DS: Segment address of parameter table
SI: Offset address of parameter table

Registers on Return: None

Memory Affected: None

Syntax:

```
MOV     AX,SEG ERR_TABLE        ;Segment of error table
MOV     DS,AX
MOV     SI,OFFSET ERR_TABLE     ;Offset of error table
MOV     AL,0Ah
MOV     AH,5Dh
INT     21h                     ;DOS services interrupt
```

Description: This service, not available before DOS version 3.0, provides a simple access-limitation convention for files. The user can lock or unlock regions of a file, thereby limiting or expanding access to the file contents. This service is most useful in networked or multitasking environments.

```
ERR_TABLE    DW ERR_CODE      ;Error code (AX value)
             DB CLASS_CODE    ;Error class code (BH value)
             DB ACT_CODE      ;Action code (BL value)
             DW LOC_CODE      ;Location code (CX value)
             DW VAL_DX        ;Value of DX register
             DW VAL_SI        ;Value of SI register
             DW VAL_DI        ;Value of DI register
             DW VAL_ES        ;Value of ES register
             DW 0             ;Reserved
             DW COMP_ID       ;Computer system ID (0=local)
             DW PROC_ID       ;Process ID (0=local)
```

Description: This service is used to set the extended-error information that will be returned the next time service 21/59 is used (assuming that service 21/59 is called before another system error occurs).

Get Machine Name (Interrupt 21h, service 5Eh, function 00h)

Category: Network services

Registers on Entry:

AH: 5Eh
AL: 0
DX: Offset address of buffer
DS: Segment address of buffer

Registers on Return:

AX: Error code
CH: Indicator flag
CL: NetBIOS number
DX: Offset address of buffer
DS: Segment address of buffer

Memory Affected: The memory area specified by DS:DX is overwritten with the returned string.

Syntax:

```
MOV    AL,0                ;Get machine name
PUSH   CS                  ;Code segment and
POP    DS                  ;  data segment are same
MOV    DX,OFFSET BUFFER    ;Offset address of buffer
MOV    AH,5Eh
INT    21h                 ;DOS services interrupt
JC     ERROR               ;Branch if error
```

Description: You use this function, not available before DOS version 3.1, when you are working under local area network (LAN) software. This function returns a 15-byte string indicating the name of the computer on which the software is operating. The string is padded with spaces and is null-terminated, rendering 16 bytes in total.

On return, if the carry flag is set, an error has occurred and the error code is in AX. Service 21/59 can be used to get detailed error information.

If the carry is clear, CH contains a flag to indicate whether the name is actually returned. If CH is 0, no name has been defined for this computer. If CH < > 0, DS:DX defines and points to the name. CL then contains the NetBIOS number for the name at DS:DX.

Set Printer Setup (Interrupt 21h, service 5Eh, function 02h)

Category: Network services

Registers on Entry:

AH: 5Eh
AL: 02h
BX: Redirection list index
CX: Setup string length
SI: Offset address of buffer
DS: Segment address of buffer

Registers on Return:

AX: Error code

Memory Affected: None

Syntax:

```
MOV    AL,2                    ;Set printer setup
PUSH   CS                      ;Code segment and
POP    DS                      ;  data segment are same
MOV    SI,OFFSET SETUP_STR     ;Offset of setup string
MOV    CX,SETUP_LENGTH         ;Length of setup string
MOV    BX,INDEX                ;Redirection list
MOV    AH,5Eh
INT    21h                     ;DOS services interrupt
JC     ERROR                   ;Branch if error
```

Description: You use this service, not available before DOS version 3.1, when you are operating under local area network (LAN) software. This service allows you to specify a string to precede all files sent from the local node to a network printer. The purpose of the string is to allow the printer to be set up according to individual node requirements. DS:SI points to the string, which can be up to 64 bytes long (length specified in CX). BX contains the redirection-list index pointer, which is determined through service 21/5F/2.

On return, if the carry flag is set, an error has occurred and the error code is in AX. Service 21/59 can be used to get detailed error information.

Get Printer Setup (Interrupt 21h, service 5Eh, function 03h)

Category: Network services

Registers on Entry:

AH: 5Eh
AL: 03h
BX: Redirection list index
DI: Offset address of buffer
ES: Segment address of buffer

Registers on Return:

AX: Error code
CX: Setup string length
DI: Offset address of buffer
ES: Segment address of buffer

Memory Affected: The memory area specified by ES:DI is overwritten with the requested network information.

Syntax:

```
MOV     AL,3                    ;Get printer setup
PUSH    CS                      ;Code segment and
POP     ES                      ;  extra segment are same
MOV     DI,OFFSET SETUP_STR     ;Offset of setup string
MOV     BX,INDEX                ;Redirection list
MOV     AH,5Eh
INT     21h                     ;DOS services interrupt
JC      ERROR                   ;Branch if error
```

Description: You use this service, not available before DOS version 3.1, when you are operating under local area network (LAN) software. This service returns the printer setup string specified with service 21/5E/2. The returned value, which is stored at the buffer specified by ES:DI, may be up to 64 bytes long. Be sure that you set aside a large enough buffer area. BX contains the redirection-list index pointer, which is determined through service 21/5F/2.

On return, if the carry flag is set, an error has occurred and the error code is in AX. Service 21/59 can be used to get detailed error information. If the carry flag is not set, the buffer area to which ES:DI points contains the printer setup string, with CX set to the string length.

Get Redirection List Entry (Interrupt 21h, service 5Fh, function 02h)

Category: Network services

Registers on Entry:

AH: 5Fh
AL: 02h
BX: Redirection list index
DI: Offset address of network name buffer
SI: Offset address of local name buffer
DS: Segment address of local name buffer
ES: Segment address of network name buffer

Registers on Return:

AX: Error code
BH: Device status
BL: Device type
CX: Parameter value

DI: Offset address of network name buffer
SI: Offset address of local name buffer
DS: Segment address of local name buffer
ES: Segment address of network name buffer

Memory Affected: The buffers to which DS:SI and ES:DI point are overwritten with the requested network information.

Syntax:

```
MOV    AX,CS               ;Code segment is same as
MOV    DS,AX               ;  data segment and
MOV    ES,AX               ;   extra segment
MOV    SI,OFFSET LOCAL_BUF ;Offset address of buffer
MOV    DI,OFFSET NET_BUF   ;Offset address of buffer
MOV    BX,1                ;Start with this entry
MOV    AL,2                ;Get list entry
MOV    AH,5Fh
INT    21h                 ;DOS services interrupt
JC     ERROR               ;Branch if error
```

Description: You use this service, not available before DOS version 3.1, when you are operating under local area network (LAN) software. This service returns an entry from the redirection list, which is set up by service 21/5F/3. The buffers to which DS:SI and ES:DI point should each be 128 bytes long.

On return, if the carry flag is set, an error has occurred and the error code is in AX. Service 21/59 can be used to get detailed error information. If the carry flag is not set, DS:SI and ES:DI point to ASCIIZ strings of the requested information; BH, BL, and CX all contain additional device information. This function destroys DX and BP.

Redirect Device (Interrupt 21h, service 5Fh, function 03h)

Category: Network services

Registers on Entry:

AH: 5Fh
AL: 03h
BL: Device type
CX: Caller value
DI: Offset address of network path
SI: Offset address of device name
DS: Segment address of device name
ES: Segment address of network path

Registers on Return:

AX: Error code

Memory Affected: None

Syntax:

```
MOV    AX,CS               ;Code segment is same as
MOV    DS,AX               ;   data segment and
MOV    ES,AX               ;   extra segment
MOV    SI,OFFSET DEVICE    ;Offset of device name
MOV    DI,OFFSET NET_PATH  ;Offset of network path
MOV    AL,3                ;Redirect
MOV    AH,5Fh
INT    21h                 ;DOS services interrupt
JC     ERROR               ;Branch if error
```

Description: You use this service, not available before DOS version 3.1, when you are operating under local area network (LAN) software. The service allows you to add devices to the network redirection list. DS:SI and ES:DI both specify ASCIIZ strings.

On return, if the carry flag is set, an error has occurred and the error code is in AX. Service 21/59 can be used to get detailed error information.

Cancel Redirection (Interrupt 21h, service 5Fh, function 04h)

Category: Network services

Registers on Entry:

AH: 5Fh
AL: 04h
SI: Offset address of device name/path
DS: Segment address of device name/path

Registers on Return:

AX: Error code

Memory Affected: None

Syntax:

```
PUSH   CS                      ;Code segment and
POP    DS                      ;  data segment are same
MOV    SI,OFFSET DEVICE        ;Offset of device name
MOV    AL,4                    ;Get list entry
MOV    AH,5Fh
INT    21h                     ;DOS services interrupt
JC     ERROR                   ;Branch if error
```

Description: You use this service, not available before DOS version 3.1, when you are operating under local area network (LAN) software. The service allows for deleting devices from the network redirection list. DS:SI specifies an ASCIIZ string.

On return, if the carry flag is set, an error has occurred and the error code is in AX. Service 21/59 can be used to get detailed error information.

Get Program Segment Prefix (PSP) Address (Interrupt 21h, service 62h)

Category: System services

Registers on Entry:

AH: 62h

Registers on Return:

BX: PSP segment address

Memory Affected: None

Syntax:

```
MOV    AH,62h
INT    21h                     ;DOS services interrupt
```

Description: This service, not available before DOS version 3.0, returns the program segment prefix (PSP) address for the current program. The PSP segment address is returned in BX.

This service is not supported in DOS 5. Use service 21/51 instead.

Get Extended Country Information (Interrupt 21h, service 65h, function 01h)

Category: System services

Registers on Entry:

AH: 65h
AL: 01h
BX: Code page
CX: Length of information to return
DX: Country ID
DI: Offset address of buffer
ES: Segment address of buffer

Registers on Return:

AX: Error code
DI: Offset address of buffer
ES: Segment address of buffer

Memory Affected: The buffer area to which ES:DI points is overlaid with the requested country information.

Syntax:

```
MOV     AL,1                    ;Want country info
MOV     BX,-1                   ;Use current console device
MOV     DX,-1                   ;Use current country
MOV     CX,41                   ;Want all the information
PUSH    CS                      ;Code segment and
POP     ES                      ;  Extra segment are same
MOV     DI,OFFSET BUFFER        ;Offset address of buffer
MOV     AH,65h
INT     21h                     ;DOS services interrupt
```

Description: This service, not available before DOS version 3.3, returns information similar to that provided by service 21/38. With service 63/64, you specify the information to be returned in AL and the destination in ES:DI. Because the amount of information is specified in CX, only part of the information can be retrieved.

  The code page is specified in BX and the country code in DX. Tables 21.28 and 21.29 detail the valid values for these parameters.

Table 21.28. *Valid code-page values.*

Country	Code
Currently installed	−1
United States	437
Multilingual	850
Slavic	852
Portuguese	860
Canadian-French	863
Nordic	865

Table 21.29. *Country codes.*

Country	Code
Currently installed	−1
United States	1
Canadian-French	2
Latin America	3
Netherlands	31
Belgium	32
France	33
Spain	34
Hungary	36
Yugoslavia	38
Italy	39
Switzerland	41
Czechoslovakia	42
United Kingdom	44
Denmark	45
Sweden	46
Norway	47
Poland	48
Germany	49
Brazil	55

Country	Code
Australia	61
Portugal	351
Finland	358
Israel	972

If the country code (DX) or the code page (BX) is invalid, an error is generated and returned in AX.

To limit the amount of information returned, place a value of at least 5 bytes in CX.

Table 21.30 details the information returned at ES:DI by each possible value for AL. Notice the similarities to information returned by service 21/38.

Table 21.30. *Information returned for service 21/65/01.*

Bytes	Purpose
1	Information specifier (1)
2	Size
2	Country ID
2	Code page
2	Date format
5	Currency symbol
2	Thousands separator
2	Decimal separator
2	Date separator
2	Time separator
1	Currency format
1	Currency decimal digits
1	Time format
4	Case mapping-call address
2	Data-list separator
10	Null bytes

Get Uppercase Table (Interrupt 21h, service 65h, function 02h)

Category: System services

Registers on Entry:

AH: 65h
AL: 02h
BX: Code page
CX: 05h
DX: Country ID
DI: Offset address of buffer
ES: Segment address of buffer

Registers on Return:

AX: Error code
DI: Offset address of buffer
ES: Segment address of buffer

Memory Affected: The buffer area to which ES:DI points is overlaid with the requested information.

Syntax:

```
MOV    AL,2                ;Get mapping table address
MOV    BX,-1               ;Use current console device
MOV    DX,-1               ;Use current country
MOV    CX,5                ;Table is only 5 bytes
PUSH   CS                  ;Code segment and
POP    ES                  ;  Extra segment are same
MOV    DI,OFFSET BUFFER    ;Offset address of buffer
MOV    AH,65h
INT    21h                 ;DOS services interrupt
```

Description: This service is used to determine the address of the uppercase mapping table used by DOS for ASCII characters with a value greater than 127. The code page is specified in BX and the country code in DX. Tables 21.28 and 21.29 detail the valid values for these parameters (refer to service 21/65/01).

If the country code (DX) or the code page (BX) is invalid, an error is generated and returned in AX.

Table 21.31 details the information returned, beginning at ES:DI.

Table 21.31. *Information returned for service 21/65 if AL=2.*

Bytes	Purpose
1	Information specifier (2)
4	32-bit uppercase table address

Get Filename Uppercase Table (Interrupt 21h, service 65h, function 04h)

Category: System services

Registers on Entry:

AH:	65h
AL:	04h
BX:	Code page
CX:	05h
DX:	Country ID
DI:	Offset address of buffer
ES:	Segment address of buffer

Registers on Return:

AX:	Error code
DI:	Offset address of buffer
ES:	Segment address of buffer

Memory Affected: The buffer area to which ES:DI points is overlaid with the requested information.

Syntax:

```
MOV    AL,4                    ;Want filename mapping
MOV    BX,-1                   ;Use current console device
MOV    DX,-1                   ;Use current country
MOV    CX,5                    ;Table is only 5 bytes
PUSH   CS                      ;Code segment and
POP    ES                      ;  Extra segment are same
MOV    DI,OFFSET BUFFER        ;Offset address of buffer
MOV    AH,65h
INT    21h                     ;DOS services interrupt
```

Description: This service is used to determine the address of the uppercase mapping table used by DOS for ASCII characters with a value greater than 127, when those ASCII characters appear in file names. It differs in this way from service 21/65/02.

The code page is specified in BX and the country code in DX. Tables 21.28 and 21.29 detail the valid values for these parameters (refer to service 21/65/01). If either the country code (DX) or the code page (BX) is invalid, an error is generated and returned in AX.

Table 21.32 details the information returned beginning at ES:DI.

Table 21.32. *Information returned for service 21/65/04.*

Bytes	Purpose
1	Information specifier (4)
4	Filename uppercase table address

Get Invalid Filename Character Table (Interrupt 21h, service 65h, function 05h)

Category: System services

Registers on Entry:

AH:	65h
AL:	05h
BX:	Code page
CX:	05h
DX:	Country ID
DI:	Offset address of buffer
ES:	Segment address of buffer

Registers on Return:

AX:	Error code
DI:	Offset address of buffer
ES:	Segment address of buffer

Memory Affected: The buffer area to which ES:DI points is overlaid with the requested information.

Syntax:

```
MOV      AL,5                 ;Get invalid filename char table
MOV      BX,-1                ;Use current console device
MOV      DX,-1                ;Use current country
MOV      CX,5                 ;Table is only 5 bytes
PUSH     CS                   ;Code segment and
POP      ES                   ;  Extra segment are same
MOV      DI,OFFSET BUFFER     ;Offset address of buffer
MOV      AH,65h
INT      21h                  ;DOS services interrupt
```

Description: This service returns an address which points to a table in memory that DOS uses to determine which ASCII characters are invalid for use in a file name. The code page is specified in BX and the country code in DX. Tables 21.28 and 21.29 detail the valid values for these parameters (refer to service 21/65/01). If the country code (DX) or the code page (BX) is invalid, an error is generated and returned in AX.

Table 21.33 details the information returned, beginning at ES:DI.

Table 21.33. *Information returned for service 21/65/05.*

Bytes	Purpose
1	Information specifier (5)
4	Invalid file-name character table address

Get Sort Sequence Table (Interrupt 21h, service 65h, function 06h)

Category: System services

Registers on Entry:

AH:	65h
AL:	06h
BX:	Code page
CX:	05h
DX:	Country ID
DI:	Offset address of buffer
ES:	Segment address of buffer

Registers on Return:

AX: Error code
DI: Offset address of buffer
ES: Segment address of buffer

Memory Affected: The buffer area to which ES:DI points is overlaid with the requested information.

Syntax:

```
MOV    AL,6                  ;Want sorting order table
MOV    BX,-1                 ;Use current console device
MOV    DX,-1                 ;Use current country
MOV    CX,5                  ;Table is only 5 bytes
PUSH   CS                    ;Code segment and
POP    ES                    ;  Extra segment are same
MOV    DI,OFFSET BUFFER      ;Offset address of buffer
MOV    AH,65h
INT    21h                   ;DOS services interrupt
```

Description: This service returns an address which points to a 256-byte table in memory that DOS uses to determine the order in which ASCII characters are sorted. The code page is specified in BX and the country code in DX. Tables 21.28 and 21.29 detail the valid values for these parameters (refer to service 21/65/01). If the country code (DX) or the code page (BX) is invalid, an error is generated and returned in AX.

Table 21.34 details the information returned, beginning at ES:DI.

Table 21.34. Information returned for service 21/65/06.

Bytes	Purpose
1	Information specifier (6)
4	Sorting-order table address

Get Double-Byte Character Set (Interrupt 21h, service 65h, function 07h)

Category: System services

Registers on Entry:

AH: 65h
AL: 07h
BX: Code page
CX: 05h
DX: Country ID
DI: Offset address of buffer
ES: Segment address of buffer

Registers on Return:

AX: Error code
DI: Offset address of buffer
ES: Segment address of buffer

Memory Affected: The buffer area to which ES:DI points is overlaid with the requested information.

Syntax:

```
MOV     AL,7                        ;Want double-byte character set
MOV     BX,-1                       ;Use current console device
MOV     DX,-1                       ;Use current country
MOV     CX,5                        ;Table is only 5 bytes
PUSH    CS                          ;Code segment and
POP     ES                          ;  Extra segment are same
MOV     DI,OFFSET BUFFER            ;Offset address of buffer
MOV     AH,65h
INT     21h                         ;DOS services interrupt
```

Description: This service returns an address that points to a table specifying valid ranges for lead-in bytes for a double-byte character set. The code page is specified in BX and the country code in DX. Tables 21.28 and 21.29 detail the valid values for these parameters (refer to service 21/65/01). If the country code (DX) or the code page (BX) is invalid, an error is generated and returned in AX.

Table 21.35 details the information returned, beginning at ES:DI.

Table 21.35. Information returned for service 21/65/07.

Bytes	Purpose
1	Information specifier (7)
4	Double-byte character-set table address

Convert Character (Interrupt 21h, service 65h, function 20h)

Category: System services

Registers on Entry:

AH: 65h
AL: 20h
DL: Character to convert

Registers on Return:

AX: Error code
DL: Converted character

Memory Affected: None

Syntax:

```
MOV    AL,20h
MOV    DL,ORIG_CHAR          ;Get the character to convert
MOV    AH,65h
INT    21h                   ;DOS services interrupt
```

Description: This service converts a character to its uppercase equivalent, using the uppercase conversion table (see service 21/65/04).

On return, if the carry flag is set, an error has occurred and the error code is in AX. Service 21/59 can be used to get detailed error information.

Convert String (Interrupt 21h, service 65h, function 21h)

Category: System services

Registers on Entry:

AH: 65h
AL: 21h
CX: String length
DX: Offset address of string to convert
DS: Segment address of string to convert

Registers on Return:

AX: Error code

Memory Affected: None

Syntax:

```
PUSH    CS              ;Code segment and
POP     DS              ;  data segment are same
MOV     DX,OFFSET STRING    ;Offset address of string to convert
MOV     CX.STRING_LEN       ;Get length of string
MOV     AL,21h
MOV     AH,65h
INT     21h             ;DOS services interrupt
```

Description: This service converts an entire string of characters to its uppercase equivalent by using the uppercase conversion table (refer to service 21/65/04). The length of the string is specified in CX.

On return, if the carry flag is set, an error has occurred and the error code is in AX. Service 21/59 can be used to get detailed error information.

Convert ASCIIZ String (Interrupt 21h, service 65h, function 22h)

Category: System services

Registers on Entry:

AH: 65h
AL: 22h
DX: Offset address of string to convert
DS: Segment address of string to convert

Registers on Return:

AX: Error code

Memory Affected: None

Syntax:

```
PUSH    CS              ;Code segment and
POP     DS              ;  data segment are same
MOV     DX,OFFSET STRING    ;Offset address of string to convert
MOV     AL,22h
MOV     AH,65h
INT     21h             ;DOS services interrupt
```

Description: This service converts an entire string of characters to its uppercase equivalent, using the uppercase conversion table (refer to service 21/65/04). The string pointed to by DS:DX must be terminated with a null character.

On return, if the carry flag is set, an error has occurred and the error code is in AX. Service 21/59 can be used to get detailed error information.

Get/Set Global Code Page (Interrupt 21h, service 66h)

Category: System services

Registers on Entry:

AH: 66h
AL: Function code
BX: Code page

Registers on Return:

AX: Error code
BX: Code page
DX: Boot code page

Memory Affected: None

Syntax:

```
MOV     AL,1            ;Get global code page
MOV     AH,66h
INT     21h             ;DOS services interrupt
JC      ERROR           ;Branch if error
```

Description: This service, not available before DOS version 3.3, retrieves or changes the code page for the currently selected country information. If AL=1, the code page is retrieved. If AL=2, the code page is set.

If you are retrieving the code page (AL=1), the contents of BX are not significant when calling this service. BX and DX return the requested information.

If you are setting the code page (AL=2), you specify the desired code page in BX. The only return value when you set the code page is the error code in AX (if the carry flag is set).

On return, if the carry flag is set, an error has occurred and the error code is in AX. Service 21/59 can be used to get detailed error information.

Change Handle Count (Interrupt 21h, service 67h)

Category: System services

Registers on Entry:

AH: 67h
BX: Number of handles

Registers on Return:

AX: Error code

Memory Affected: None

Syntax:

```
MOV     BX,50               ;Want 50 handles
MOV     AH,67h
INT     21h                 ;DOS services interrupt
```

Description: This service, not available before DOS version 3.3, allows you to specify the number of file handles available to DOS. You specify this number, which must be between 20 and 65,535, in BX. The number can be larger than 255, which is the maximum number of file handles definable in the CONFIG.SYS file.

On return, if the carry flag is set, an error has occurred and the error code is in AX. Service 21/59 can be used to get detailed error information.

Flush Buffer (Interrupt 21h, service 68h)

Category: Disk services

Registers on Entry:

AH: 68h
BX: File handle

Registers on Return:

AX: Error code

Memory Affected: None

Syntax:

```
MOV     BX,FILE_HANDLE          ;Use this file
MOV     AH,68h
INT     21h                     ;DOS services interrupt
JC      ERROR                   ;Branch if error
```

Description: With this service, not available before DOS version 3.0, the file buffer of the specified file (BX) is written to disk.

On return, if the carry flag is set, an error has occurred and the error code is in AX. Service 21/59 can be used to get detailed error information.

This was the highest-numbered service provided with any of the version 3.x releases of DOS. All services with higher numbers first appeared at version 4.0 or later.

Extended Open/Create File (Interrupt 21h, service 6Ch)

Category: Disk services

Registers on Entry:

AH: 6Ch
AL: 00h (required)
BX: Access mode (table 21.36)
CX: File attributes (table 21.37)
DX: Action flags (table 21.38)

Registers on Return:

AX: File handle
CX: Action taken:
      00 = file existed and was opened
      01 = did not exist, was created
      02 = existed, was replaced

Memory Affected: None

Syntax:

```
MOV     AX,6C00h
MOV     BX,0            ;read only, compatible, DOS defaults
MOV     CX,0            ;open as normal file
MOV     DX,1            ;fail if file does not exist
INT     21h            ;DOS services interrupt
JC      ERROR          ;bail out on error
MOV     MY_HANDLE,AX    ;save handle to refer to file
```

Description: This function, not available before DOS version 4.0, combines functions previously provided by services 21/3C, 21/3D, and 21/5B into a single, multipurpose facility that opens and creates files.

On return, if the carry flag is set, an error has occurred and the error code is in AX. Service 21/59 can be used to get detailed error information.

The values available for registers upon entry to service 21/6C (the access modes in BX, the file attributes in CX, and the action codes in DX) are listed in tables 21.36, 21.37, and 21.38, respectively.

***Table 21.36.** Access modes for service 21/6C (in BX).*

FEDCBA98 76543210	*Meaning*
x	Not used
1	Immediate writes
0	Buffered writes
1	Return error only
0	Use INT 24h handler
xxxxx	Not used
1	Child does not get handles
0	Child inherits handles
100	Deny none
011	Deny read sharing
010	Deny write sharing
001	Deny all sharing
000	Compatibility mode
x	Not used
010	Read/Write access
001	Write-only access
000	Read-only access

Table 21.37. *File attributes for service 21/6C (in CX).*

FEDCBA98 76543210	Meaning
xxxxxxxx xx	Not used
1	Modified (archive bit)
0	Not modified
x	Not used
1	Volume label
0	Not volume label
1	System file
0	Normal user file
1	Hidden
0	Visible
1	Read only
0	Read/write

Table 21.38. *Action flags for service 21/6C (in DX).*

FEDCBA98 76543210	Meaning
xxxxxxxx	Not used
1xxx	Not used
01xx	Not used
001x	Not used
0001	Create file if it does not exist
0000	Fail if file does not exist
1xxx	Not used
01xx	Not used
0011	Not used
0010	Replace if file exists
0001	Open if file exists
0000	Fail if file exists

Terminate Address (Interrupt 22h)

Description: This is not a serviceable interrupt but rather a vector to the termination handler for DOS. Control passes to this address when a program ends.

Ctrl-Break Handler Address (Interrupt 23h)

Description: This is not a serviceable interrupt but rather a vector to the address of the routine that receives control from DOS when a Ctrl-Break key combination is detected.

Critical-Error Handler Address (Interrupt 24h)

Description: This is not a serviceable interrupt but rather a vector to the address of the routine that receives control from DOS when a critical error is detected.

Absolute Disk Read (Interrupt 25h)

Category: Disk services

Registers on Entry:

AL: Drive number
BX: Offset address of buffer (or parameter block if CX=−1)
CX: Sectors to read (-1 indicates extended format for DOS 4)
DX: Logical starting sector
DS: Segment address of buffer (or parameter block if CX=−1)

Registers on Return:

AX: Return code

Memory Affected: The buffer area specified by DS:BX (or by the parameter block pointed to, if extended format is used) is overlaid with information read from the disk.

Syntax:

```
MOV    AL,2                   ;Drive C:
MOV    DX,0                   ;Starting with sector 0
MOV    CX,3                   ;Read 3 sectors
MOV    BX,OFFSET DS:BUFFER    ;Offset of buffer area
INT    25h                    ;Read sectors
POP    DX                     ;Clean up stack
JC     ERROR                  ;Branch if error
```

Description: This interrupt, which allows DOS to read any sector from the disk, is the opposite of interrupt 26h (and similar to BIOS service 13/2).

To use this service, you must specify the precise physical location on the disk at which you want to begin reading. Specify the drive in AL, where A=0, B=1, C=2, etc. DX is the logical starting sector. (All sectors on the disk are numbered logically in sequential order, starting with 0.) CX is the number of sectors to read. The final registers to be set up specify which RAM area will be used as a buffer for the sectors that are read. This address is specified in DS:BX.

With the introduction of DOS version 4, an extended format capable of dealing with 32-bit logical sector numbers was added to this interrupt. If CX is set to -1 rather than to a positive value, DS:BX is a far pointer to a 10-byte parameter block with the following information:

Offset	Length	Contents
00h	Double word	Logical sector number, zero based
04h	Word	Number of sectors to transfer
06h	Double word	Far pointer to data buffer

On return, if the carry flag is set, an error has occurred and the error code is in AX. You must realize that on return from this interrupt, the flags are still on the stack. They must be removed from the stack before the program continues.

Absolute Disk Write (Interrupt 26h)

Category: Disk services

Registers on Entry:

AL: Drive number
BX: Offset address of buffer (or parameter block if CX=−1)

CX: Sectors to write (-1 indicates extended format)
DX: Logical starting sector
DS: Segment address of buffer (or parameter block if CX=−1)

Registers on Return:

AX: Return code

Memory Affected: None

Syntax:

```
MOV    AL,2                  ;Drive C:
MOV    DX,0                  ;Starting with sector 0
MOV    CX,3                  ;Write 3 sectors
MOV    BX,OFFSET DS:BUFFER   ;Offset of buffer area
INT    26h                   ;Write sectors
POP    DX                    ;Clean up stack
JC     ERROR                 ;Branch if error
```

Description: This interrupt, which is the opposite of interrupt 25h (and similar to BIOS service 13/3), allows DOS to write any sector to the disk.

To use this service, you must specify the precise physical location on the disk at which you want to begin writing. You specify the drive in AL, where A=0, B=1, C=2, etc. DX is the logical starting sector. (All sectors on the disk are numbered logically in sequential order, starting with 0.) CX is the number of sectors to write. The final registers to be set up specify the RAM area from which to take the information to be written. This address is specified in DS:BX.

With the introduction of DOS version 4, an extended format capable of dealing with 32-bit logical sector numbers was added to this interrupt. If CX is set to -1 rather than to a positive value, DS:BX is a far pointer to a 10-byte parameter block with the following information:

Offset	Length	Contents
00h	Double word	Logical sector number, zero based
04h	Word	Number of sectors to transfer
06h	Double word	Far pointer to data buffer

On return, if the carry flag is set, an error has occurred and the error code is in AX. You must realize that on return from this interrupt, the flags are still on the stack. They must be removed from the stack before the program continues.

Terminate and Stay Resident (Interrupt 27h)

Category: System services

Registers on Entry:

DX: Pointer to last byte of program

Registers on Return: Unknown (does not return)

Memory Affected: None

Syntax:

```
MOV    DX,OFFSET CS:END_BYTE   ;Point to end of program
INT    27h                     ;TSR
```

Description: This interrupt, which is similar to the preferred TSR service of 21/31, allows the program to exit to DOS without freeing the program memory space.

Because only one register is used to point to the program end point, the maximum usable program size for this interrupt is clearly 64K. Any files created or opened by the program remain open after this interrupt is invoked.

Multiplex Interrupt (Interrupt 2Fh)

Category: System services

Registers on Entry: Varies

Registers on Return: Varies

Memory Affected: Varies

Description: This interrupt allows user-defined routines to share the space set aside for special DOS programs such as PRINT, ASSIGN, and SHARE.

The use and function of this interrupt are beyond the scope of this book. For more information, please refer to the DOS *Technical Reference Manual*.

Processor Instruction Set

The heart of your computer is the microprocessor. In the IBM PC or PS/2 and compatibles, this is usually the Intel family of microprocessors. Your system may contain a numeric coprocessor, which Intel refers to as a *Numeric Processing Extension*, or NPX. The numeric coprocessor is used to aid in advanced mathematic operations.

The instruction sets for both Intel microprocessors and NPXs are covered in this chapter. These include the following:

❏ 8086/8088   ❏ 8087

❏ 80286   ❏ 80287

❏ 80386   ❏ 80387

❏ 80486

Notice that there is no corresponding NPX for the 80486 microprocessor. The 80486 includes all of the capabilities of the 80387 NPX; these collective advanced mathematic operations are handled in the 80486 by the *floating point unit*, or FPU.

Programming Models

Intel describes the instruction sets of its processors in terms of a *programming model*, which defines all parts of the processor that are visible to the programmer; those portions of the device that cannot be affected directly by the program are omitted. To use the instructions, it is helpful to know the corresponding programming model. Let's look at the programming model for each chip, first the microprocessors and then the NPXs.

8086/8088

The 8086 and 8088 processors are identical internally, although the 8086 has a full 16-bit data bus and the 8088 has an 8-bit bus automatically multiplexed to perform 16-bit transfers.

The programming model for these processors consists of the register set described in Chapter 1.

80286

The 80286 processor added several special-purpose registers to the 8086 programming model. These include the following:

Register	Use
GDT	Global descriptor table
LDT	Local descriptor table
IDT	Interrupt descriptor table
MSW	Machine status word
TASK	Task register

Typically, you will never need to use these registers. They are used only when programming for *protected mode* operation, a condition in which DOS cannot operate. All DOS operations run in *real mode*, the other operating mode of the 80286.

Two of the descriptor table registers, GDT and LDT, make it possible to access 16M of memory address space rather than the 1M limit of the 8086/8088 designs, but this capability is available only when operating in protected mode. If programmed for compatibility with DOS, the 80286 is little more than a faster version of the 8086/8088 programming model.

80386

Unlike its 8-bit and 16-bit predecessors, the 80386 is a 32-bit microprocessor. The registers in the 80386 reflect this enlarged structure. The 80386 still uses the same general-purpose registers as the 8086/8088 and the 80286 (AX, BX, CX, and DX), but the registers' full 32-bit counterparts are addressed by using the E (extended) prefix. EAX, EBX, ECX, and EDX are 32-bit general-purpose registers. Without the E, only the lower 16 bits of each register are accessed. Using the traditional AL, AH, BL, BH, CL, CH, DL, or DH gives you access to 8-bit chunks of the lower 16 bits of the registers.

This use of the E prefix to denote 32-bit register size also applies to other microprocessor registers, such as BP, SI, DI, and SP, which become EBP, ESI, EDI, and ESP, respectively.

The other segment registers—CS, DS, SS, and ES—are intact as implemented in earlier Intel microprocessors. These registers are still 16 bits wide. They are joined, however, by two additional segment registers (also 16 bits wide): the FS and GS registers, which operate the same as the ES register.

As in earlier microprocessors, the 80386 uses a flags register, but it is also 32 bits wide. This flags register is examined later in this chapter.

80486

Like the 80386, the 80486 is a 32-bit microprocessor, but contains many more internal functions than any previous member of the Intel microprocessor family.

In addition to adding six more instructions to the set, the 80486 design moved the NPX functions onto the main chip. Thus, there is no 80487; all functions previously handled by an NPX were assumed by the FPU portion of the 80486. The chip also contains an 8K cache memory and a built-in *memory management unit* (MMU).

Despite these significant changes in design, the chip retains full compatibility with the 80386 and 80387 operations, and three of the six added instructions deal with strictly system-level programming. For all programming purposes, the 80486 processor is just a faster version of a combined 80386 and 80387.

8087

The first generation Intel NPX is truly that—an extension to the functionality of the main microprocessor. The 8087 appears virtually transparent to programmers. The instruction and register sets of the 8086/8088 simply seem to be expanded.

No special assembler directives are needed to use the 8087 mnemonic instructions with either MASM or TASM. The assembler's default instruction set can translate properly the 8086/8088 and 8087 source code. You may want to study Chapters 5 and 6, however, to learn about assembler options.

In design philosophy, the 8087 is a bit different from the 8086/8088. It uses a floating stack for all operations, whereas the 8086/8088 uses general-purpose registers. The 8087 uses 8 internal stack registers, each of which is 80 bits wide. These stack registers are numbered 0 through 7, with most operations able to address the registers directly as ST, ST(1), ST(2), ST(3), and so on, through ST(7).

In addition to this stack-oriented design, the 8087 uses several other registers to reflect the condition of its stack and to control NPX operation. The status word and control word are described later in this chapter.

80287

The function and operation of the 80287 are similar to those of the 8087. This second-generation NPX can operate at levels demanded by the 80286, the microprocessor with which it should be paired. Several mnemonic instructions were added to take advantage of the expanded capabilities of the 80286.

The design structure of the 80287 is virtually equivalent to that of the 8087. The 80287 changes the definition of several bits in the control word, but otherwise nothing changes.

80387

As you might expect, the 80387 is the numeric processor extension for the 80386 microprocessor. The 80387 added only a few new commands not present in the 80287 and defined one additional bit in the status word. All other operations and structure remain the same as for the earlier generations of NPXs.

Instruction Sets

The NPX functions, because they are an extension of the instructions offered by the microprocessor, are considered an integral part of the overall instruction set of the Intel family.

The overall instruction set can be divided according to the purpose of the individual instruction. The nine general classifications of instructions (six for CPUs and three more for numeric coprocessors) are as follows:

- ❏ Data transfer
- ❏ Arithmetic
- ❏ Numeric transcendental
- ❏ Numeric constant
- ❏ Bit manipulation
- ❏ Numeric comparison
- ❏ String manipulation
- ❏ Control transfer
- ❏ Flag and processor control

Let's take a look at the processing instructions in each area.

Data-Transfer Instructions

This group of instructions is used to move data. The movement can be between registers, between registers and memory, or between memory locations. The following 86 instructions are included:

BSWAP	FST	INSW	LGDT
FBLD	FSTP	LAHF	LGS
FBSTP	FXCH	LAR	LIDT
FILD	IN	LDS	LLDT
FIST	INS	LEA	LMSW
FISTP	INSB	LES	LSL
FLD	INSD	LFS	LSS

LTR	PUSHA	SETNA	SETP
MOV	PUHAD	SETNAE	SETPE
MOVSX	PUSHF	SETNB	SETPO
MOVZX	PUSHFD	SETNBE	SETS
OUT	SAHF	SETNC	SETZ
OUTS	SETA	SETNE	SGDT
OUTSB	SETAE	SETNG	SIDT
OUTSD	SETB	SETNGE	SLDT
OUTSW	SETBE	SETNL	SMSW
POP	SETC	SETNLE	STR
POPA	SETE	SETNO	XADO
POPAD	SETG	SETNP	XCHG
POPF	SETGE	SETNS	XLAT
POPFD	SETL	SETNZ	
PUSH	SETLE	SETO	

Not all of these instructions are available on all microprocessors or NPXs. Later, this chapter specifies which instructions work on which chips. You can also refer to the detailed instructions at the end of the chapter for more information.

Arithmetic Instructions

This classification of instruction includes the simplest of mathematic operations. These instructions are used for operations like conversions, BCD math, integer math, and simple floating-point math. Included in this grouping are the following 49 instructions:

AAA	CWD	FDIV	FMUL	FSUBRP
AAD	CWDE	FDIVP	FMULP	FXTRACT
AAM	DAA	FDIVR	FPREM	IDIV
AAS	DAS	FDIVRP	FPREM1	IMUL
ADC	DEC	FIADD	FRNDINT	INC
ADD	DIV	FIDIV	FSCALE	MUL
CBW	FABS	FIDIVR	FSQRT	NEG
CDQ	FADD	FIMUL	FSUB	SBB
CMP	FADDP	FISUB	FSUBP	SUB
CMPXCHG	FCHS	FISUBR	FSUBR	

Numeric Transcendental Instructions

This group of instructions is performed only by the NPX/FPU chips. It includes instructions that implement basic calculations for the following common functions:

- ❏ Trigonometric
- ❏ Inverse trigonometric
- ❏ Hyperbolic
- ❏ Inverse hyperbolic
- ❏ Logarithmic
- ❏ Exponential

These tasks can be time consuming. The eight instructions that make up this group are the following:

F2XM1	FPATAN	FSIN	FYL2X
FCOS	FPTAN	FSINCOS	FYL2XP1

Numeric Constant Instructions

This instruction group operates only on the NPX/FPU chips. It results in common mathematic constants being pushed on the stack (as used within the NPX/FPU). Because they are specialized and do not actually transfer data, these instructions are categorized separately from the data-transfer instructions. The top stack register simply is set to be a constant value predefined by the instruction used.

The seven instructions in this group are

FLD1	FLDLG2	FLDPI
FLDL2E	FLDLN2	FLDZ
FLDL2T		

Bit-Manipulation Instructions

These instructions do just what they say: they manipulate the bits in individual registers. The result of this (besides changed register values for some instructions) is that the flags register is changed to reflect the outcome of the operation. Program execution can then be modified based upon the outcome. The 22 instructions in this grouping are

AND	BTC	RCL	SAL	SHR
ARPL	BTR	RCR	SAR	SHRD
BSF	BTS	ROL	SHL	TEST
BSR	NOT	ROR	SHLD	XOR
BT	OR			

Numeric Comparison Instructions

The NPX/FPU uses these instructions to set flags in the status-word register. As with other instructions, the results of these instructions can alter program execution. These 10 instructions are the following:

| FCOM | FCOMPP | FICOMP | FUCOM | FUCOMPP |
| FCOMP | FICOM | FTST | FUCOMP | FXAM |

String-Manipulation Instructions

This instruction group operates on strings in memory. These strings are simply instructions that manipulate contiguous blocks of memory; they are not strings in the same sense as the term is used in high-level languages. When combined with repetition instructions, which are included in this instruction group, string-manipulation instructions are powerful for moving or comparing large blocks of information. This group contains the following 20 instructions:

CMPSB	LODSD	MOVSW	REPNZ	SCASW
CMPSD	LODSW	REP	REPZ	STOSB
CMPSW	MOVSB	REPE	SCASB	STOSD
LODSB	MOVSD	REPNE	SCASD	STOSW

Control-Transfer Instructions

These instructions are used to change the order in which a program is executed. They directly affect the program counter, loading a different memory address into this register. After the instruction is encountered, program execution continues from a different location.

Many of these instructions are conditional; that is, they take effect after matching a condition determined by the instruction. Usually the condition pertains to flags in the flags register or status word. These 43 instructions are the following:

CALL	JCXZ	JNAE	JNO	LOOP
INT	JE	JNB	JNP	LOOPE
INTO	JECXZ	JNBE	JNS	LOOPNE
IRET	JG	JNC	JNZ	LOOPNZJPE
JA	JGE	JNE	JO	LOOPZ
JAE	JL	JNG	JP	JPO
JB	JLE	JNGE	JS	RET
JBE	JMP	JNL	JZ	
JC	JNA	JNLE		

Flag- and Processor-Control Instructions

This final instruction group contains instructions that directly affect the flags register, status word, or control word. Included in this group are the following 46 instructions:

BOUND	FDISI	FNENI	FSETPM	LOCK
CLC	FENI	FNINIT	FSTCW	NOP
CLD	FFREE	FNOP	FSTENV	STC
CLI	FINCSTP	FNSAVE	FSTSW	STD
CLTS	FINIT	FNSTCW	FWAIT	STI
CMC	FLDCW	FNSTENV	HLT	VERR
ENTER	FLDENV	FNSTSW	INVD	VERW
ESC	FNCLEX	FRSTOR	INVLPG	WAIT
FCLEX	FNDISI	FSAVE	LEAVE	WBINVD
FDECSTP				

The Complete Instruction Set

Now that you know which instructions fall within each group, let's take a quick look at the entire Intel family instruction set along with the chips that use the instructions. Table 22.1 details this information. Even more detailed information is available later in this chapter.

Table 22.1. *Instructions for the Intel family.*

Instruction	Meaning	88	286	386	486	87	287	387
				Chips				
AAA	ASCII adjust for addition	X	X	X	X			
AAD	ASCII adjust for division	X	X	X	X			
AAM	ASCII adjust for multiplication	X	X	X	X			
AAS	ASCII adjust for subtraction	X	X	X	X			
ADC	Add with carry	X	X	X	X			
ADD	Add	X	X	X	X			
AND	Logical AND	X	X	X	X			
ARPL	Adjust RPL field of selector		X	X	X			
BOUND	Check array index against bounds		X	X	X			
BSF	Bit scan forward			X	X			
BSR	Bit scan reverse			X	X			
BSWAP	Swap 32-bit byte order				X			
BT	Bit test			X	X			
BTC	Bit test and complement			X	X			
BTR	Bit test and reset			X	X			
BTS	Bit test and set			X	X			
CALL	Perform subroutine	X	X	X	X			
CBW	Convert byte to word	X	X	X	X			
CDQ	Convert doubleword to quadword			X	X			
CLC	Clear carry flag	X	X	X	X			
CLD	Clear direction flag	X	X	X	X			
CLI	Clear interrupt flag	X	X	X	X			
CLTS	Clear task switched flag		X	X	X			
CMC	Complement carry flag	X	X	X	X			
CMP	Compare	X	X	X	X			
CMPSB	Compare strings by byte	X	X	X	X			
CMPSD	Compare strings by doubleword			X	X			
CMPSW	Compare strings by word	X	X	X	X			
CMPXCHG	Atomic compare/exchange				X			
CWD	Convert word to doubleword	X	X	X	X			

					Chips			
Instruction	Meaning	88	286	386	486	87	287	387
CWDE	Convert word to extended doubleword			X	X			
DAA	Decimal adjust for addition	X	X	X	X			
DAS	Decimal adjust for subtraction	X	X	X	X			
DEC	Decrement	X	X	X	X			
DIV	Divide	X	X	X	X			
ENTER	Make stack frame		X	X	X			
ESC	Escape	X	X	X	X			
F2XM1	2^x-1					X	X	X	X
FABS	Absolute value					X	X	X	X
FADD	Add real					X	X	X	X
FADDP	Add real and POP					X	X	X	X
FBLD	BCD load					X	X	X	X
FBSTP	BCD store and POP					X	X	X	X
FCHS	Change sign					X	X	X	X
FCLEX	Clear exceptions with WAIT					X	X	X	X
FCOM	Compare real					X	X	X	X
FCOMP	Compare real and POP					X	X	X	X
FCOMPP	Compare real and POP twice					X	X	X	X
FCOS	Cosine					X			X
FDECSTP	Decrement stack pointer					X	X	X	X
FDISI	Disable interrupts with WAIT					X			
FDIV	Divide real					X	X	X	X
FDIVP	Divide real and POP					X	X	X	X
FDIVR	Divide real reversed					X	X	X	X
FDIVRP	Divide real reversed and POP					X	X	X	X
FENI	Enable interrupts with WAIT					X			
FFREE	Free register					X	X	X	X
FIADD	Integer add					X	X	X	X
FICOM	Integer compare					X	X	X	X
FICOMP	Integer compare and POP					X	X	X	X

continues

Table 22.1. *continued*

Instruction	Meaning	88	286	386	486	87	287	387
FIDIV	Integer divide				X	X	X	X
FIDIVR	Integer divide reversed				X	X	X	X
FILD	Integer load				X	X	X	X
FIMUL	Integer multiply				X	X	X	X
FINCSTP	Increment stack pointer				X	X	X	X
FINIT	Initialize processor with WAIT				X	X	X	X
FIST	Integer store				X	X	X	X
FISTP	Integer store and POP				X	X	X	X
FISUB	Integer subtract				X	X	X	X
FISUBR	Integer subtract reversed				X	X	X	X
FLD	Load real				X	X	X	X
FLD1	Load 1.0				X	X	X	X
FLDCW	Load control word				X	X	X	X
FLDENV	Load environment				X	X	X	X
FLDL2E	Load $\log_2 e$				X	X	X	X
FLDL2T	Load $\log_2 10$				X	X	X	X
FLDLG2	Load $\log_{10} 2$				X	X	X	X
FLDLN2	Load $\log_e 2$				X	X	X	X
FLDPI	Load π				X	X	X	X
FLDZ	Load 0.0				X	X	X	X
FMUL	Multiply real				X	X	X	X
FMULP	Multiply real and POP				X	X	X	X
FNCLEX	Clear exceptions				X	X	X	X
FNDISI	Disable interrupts					X		
FNENI	Enable interrupts					X		
FNINIT	Initialize processor				X	X	X	X
FNOP	No operation				X	X	X	X
FNSAVE	Save state				X	X	X	X
FNSTCW	Store control word				X	X	X	X
FNSTENV	Store environment				X	X	X	X

Instruction	Meaning	88	286	386	486	87	287	38
				Chips				
FNSTSW	Store status word				X	X	X	X
FPATAN	Partial arctangent				X	X	X	X
FPREM	Partial remainder				X	X	X	X
FPREM1	IEEE partial remainder				X			X
FPTAN	Partial tangent				X	X	X	X
FRNDINT	Round to integer				X	X	X	X
FRSTOR	Restore state				X	X	X	X
FSAVE	Save state with WAIT				X	X	X	X
FSCALE	Scale				X	X	X	X
FSETPM	Set protected mode						X	
FSIN	Sine				X			X
FSINCOS	Sine and cosine				X			X
FSQRT	Square root				X	X	X	X
FST	Store real				X	X	X	X
FSTCW	Store control word with WAIT				X	X	X	X
FSTENV	Store environment with WAIT				X	X	X	X
FSTP	Store Real and POP				X	X	X	X
FSTSW	Store status word with WAIT				X	X	X	X
FSUB	Subtract real				X	X	X	X
FSUBP	Subtract real and POP				X	X	X	X
FSUBR	Subtract real reversed				X	X	X	X
FSUBRP	Subtract real reversed and POP				X	X	X	X
FTST	Test				X	X	X	X
FUCOM	Unordered compare				X			X
FUCOMP	Unordered compare and POP				X			X
FUCOMPP	Unordered compare and POP twice				X			X
FWAIT	CPU wait				X	X	X	X
FXAM	Examine				X	X	X	X
FXCH	Exchange registers				X	X	X	X
FXTRACT	Extract exponent and significand				X	X	X	X
FYL2X	$Y*\log_2 X$				X	X	X	X

continues

Table 22.1. *continued*

Instruction	Meaning	88	286	386	486	87	287	387
					Chips			
FYL2XP1	Y*log$_2$(X+1)					X	X	X	X
HLT	Halt	X	X	X	X			
IDIV	Integer divide	X	X	X	X			
IMUL	Integer multiply	X	X	X	X			
IN	Input from port	X	X	X	X			
INC	Increment	X	X	X	X			
INS	Input string from port		X	X	X			
INSB	Input string byte from port		X	X	X			
INSD	Input string doubleword from port			X	X			
INSW	Input string word from port		X	X	X			
INT	Software interrupt	X	X	X	X			
INTO	Interrupt on overflow	X	X	X	X			
INVD	Invalidate full cache				X			
INVLPG	Invalidate TLB entry				X			
IRET	Return from interrupt	X	X	X	X			
JA	Jump if above	X	X	X	X			
JAE	Jump if above or equal	X	X	X	X			
JB	Jump if below	X	X	X	X			
JBE	Jump if below or equal	X	X	X	X			
JC	Jump on carry	X	X	X	X			
JCXZ	Jump if CX=0	X	X	X	X			
JE	Jump if equal	X	X	X	X			
JECXZ	Jump if ECX=0			X	X			
JG	Jump if greater	X	X	X	X			
JGE	Jump if greater or equal	X	X	X	X			
JL	Jump if less	X	X	X	X			
JLE	Jump if less or equal	X	X	X	X			
JMP	Jump	X	X	X	X			
JNA	Jump if not above	X	X	X	X			
JNAE	Jump if not above or equal	X	X	X	X			

Instruction	Meaning	Chips						
		88	286	386	486	87	287	387
JNB	Jump if not below	X	X	X	X			
JNBE	Jump if not below or equal	X	X	X	X			
JNC	Jump on no carry	X	X	X	X			
JNE	Jump if not equal	X	X	X	X			
JNG	Jump if not greater	X	X	X	X			
JNGE	Jump if not greater or equal	X	X	X	X			
JNL	Jump if not less	X	X	X	X			
JNLE	Jump if not less or equal	X	X	X	X			
JNO	Jump on no overflow	X	X	X	X			
JNP	Jump on no parity	X	X	X	X			
JNS	Jump on not sign	X	X	X	X			
JNZ	Jump on not zero	X	X	X	X			
JO	Jump on overflow	X	X	X	X			
JP	Jump on parity	X	X	X	X			
JPE	Jump on parity even	X	X	X	X			
JPO	Jump on parity odd	X	X	X	X			
JS	Jump on sign	X	X	X	X			
JZ	Jump on zero	X	X	X	X			
LAHF	Load AH with flags	X	X	X	X			
LAR	Load access-rights byte		X	X	X			
LDS	Load DS register	X	X	X	X			
LEA	Load effective address	X	X	X	X			
LEAVE	High-level procedure exit		X	X	X			
LES	Load ES register	X	X	X	X			
LFS	Load FS register			X	X			
LGDT	Load GDT register		X	X	X			
LGS	Load GS register			X	X			
LIDT	Load IDT register		X	X	X			
LLDT	Load LDT register		X	X	X			
LMSW	Load machine status word		X	X	X			
LOCK	Lock bus	X	X	X	X			

continues

Table 22.1. *continued*

Instruction	Meaning	Chips						
		88	286	386	486	87	287	387
LODSB	Load byte from string to AL	X	X	X	X			
LODSD	Load doubleword from string to EAX			X	X			
LODSW	Load word from string to AX	X	X	X	X			
LOOP	Loop	X	X	X	X			
LOOPE	Loop while equal	X	X	X	X			
LOOPNE	Loop while not equal	X	X	X	X			
LOOPNZ	Loop while not zero	X	X	X	X			
LOOPZ	Loop while zero	X	X	X	X			
LSL	Load segment limit		X	X	X			
LSS	Load SS register			X	X			
LTR	Load task register		X	X	X			
MOV	Move	X	X	X	X			
MOVSB	Move string byte-by-byte	X	X	X	X			
MOVSD	Move string doubleword-by-doubleword			X	X			
MOVSW	Move string word-by-word	X	X	X	X			
MOVSX	Move with sign extended			X	X			
MOVZX	Move with zero extended			X	X			
MUL	Multiply	X	X	X	X			
NEG	Negate	X	X	X	X			
NOP	No operation	X	X	X	X			
NOT	Logical NOT	X	X	X	X			
OR	Logical OR	X	X	X	X			
OUT	Output to port	X	X	X	X			
OUTS	Output string to port		X	X	X			
OUTSB	Output string byte to port		X	X	X			
OUTSD	Output string doubleword to port			X	X			
OUTSW	Output string word to port		X	X	X			
POP	Remove data from stack	X	X	X	X			

Instruction	Meaning	Chips						
		88	286	386	486	87	287	387
POPA	POP all general registers		X	X	X			
POPAD	POP all general doubleword registers			X	X			
POPF	Remove flags from stack	X	X	X	X			
POPFD	Remove extended flags from stack			X	X			
PUSH	Place data on stack	X	X	X	X			
PUSHA	Push all general registers		X	X	X			
PUSHAD	Push all general doubleword registers			X	X			
PUSHF	Place flags on stack	X	X	X	X			
PUSHFD	Place extended flags on stack			X	X			
RCL	Rotate left through carry	X	X	X	X			
RCR	Rotate right through carry	X	X	X	X			
REP	Repeat	X	X	X	X			
REPE	Repeat if equal	X	X	X	X			
REPNE	Repeat if not equal	X	X	X	X			
REPNZ	Repeat if not zero	X	X	X	X			
REPZ	Repeat if zero	X	X	X	X			
RET	Return from subroutine	X	X	X	X			
ROL	Rotate left	X	X	X	X			
ROR	Rotate right	X	X	X	X			
SAHF	Store AH into flags register	X	X	X	X			
SAL	Arithmetic shift left	X	X	X	X			
SAR	Arithmetic shift right	X	X	X	X			
SBB	Subtract with carry	X	X	X	X			
SCASB	Scan string for byte	X	X	X	X			
SCASD	Scan string for doubleword			X	X			
SCASW	Scan string for word	X	X	X	X			
SETA	Set byte if above			X	X			
SETAE	Set byte if above or equal			X	X			
SETB	Set byte if below			X	X			
SETBE	Set byte if below or equal			X	X			

continues

Table 22.1. *continued*

Instruction	Meaning	88	286	Chips 386	486	87	287	387
SETC	Set byte on carry			X	X			
SETE	Set byte if equal			X	X			
SETG	Set byte if greater			X	X			
SETGE	Set byte if greater or equal			X	X			
SETL	Set byte if less			X	X			
SETLE	Set byte if less or equal			X	X			
SETNA	Set byte if not above			X	X			
SETNAE	Set byte if not above or equal			X	X			
SETNB	Set byte if not below			X	X			
SETNBE	Set byte if not below or equal			X	X			
SETNC	Set byte on no carry			X	X			
SETNE	Set byte if not equal			X	X			
SETNG	Set byte if not greater			X	X			
SETNGE	Set byte if not greater or equal			X	X			
SETNL	Set byte if not less			X	X			
SETNLE	Set byte if not less or equal			X	X			
SETNO	Set byte on no overflow			X	X			
SETNP	Set byte on no priority			X	X			
SETNS	Set byte on not sign			X	X			
SETNZ	Set byte if not zero			X	X			
SETO	Set byte on overflow			X	X			
SETP	Set byte on parity			X	X			
SETPE	Set byte on parity even			X	X			
SETPO	Set byte on parity odd			X	X			
SETS	Set byte on sign			X	X			
SETZ	Set byte if zero			X	X			
SGDT	Store GDT register		X	X	X			
SHL	Shift left	X	X	X	X			
SHLD	Shift left, double precision			X	X			
SHR	Shift right	X	X	X	X			

Instruction	Meaning	88	286	Chips 386	486	87	287	387
SHRD	Shift right, double precision			X	X			
SIDT	Store IDT register		X	X	X			
SLDT	Store LDT register		X	X	X			
SMSW	Store machine status word		X	X	X			
STC	Set carry flag	X	X	X	X			
STD	Set direction flag	X	X	X	X			
STI	Set interrupt flag	X	X	X	X			
STOSB	Store byte in AL at string	X	X	X	X			
STOSD	Store doubleword in EAX at string			X	X			
STOSW	Store word in AX at string	X	X	X	X			
STR	Store task register		X	X	X			
SUB	Subtract	X	X	X	X			
TEST	Test bits	X	X	X	X			
VERR	Verify segment for reading		X	X	X			
VERW	Verify segment for writing		X	X	X			
WAIT	Wait	X	X	X	X			
WBINVD	Invalidate cache and write back				X			
XADD	Exchange and add to memory				X			
XCHG	Exchange	X	X	X	X			
XLAT	Translate	X	X	X	X			
XOR	Logical XOR	X	X	X	X			

Specialized Registers: Flags, Control, and Status

Most instructions either control or change the status of the bits in any of several specialized registers used by the microprocessor or the NPX/FPU. These specialized registers include the following:

❏ Flags register

❏ Control word

❏ Status word

The flags register applies to the microprocessors, and the status and control words apply to the NPX/FPU. Which bits are affected by each instruction depends on the instruction and results of the instruction.

The Flags Register

Each of the Intel microprocessors uses a flags register to indicate the status of operations. These flags can be tested to control program execution, or they can be set to control certain tasks performed by the microprocessor.

The size of the flags register depends on the microprocessor. For instance, the 8086/8088 and 80286 use a 16-bit flags register, but the 80386 and 80486 both use 32-bit flags registers. However, not every bit is always used. Table 22.2 details how each bit is used by each microprocessor.

Table 22.2. *The flags register.*

| Bits | Code | Use | Microprocessor | | | |
			88	286	386	486
0	CF	Carry	X	X	X	X
2	PF	Parity	X	X	X	X
4	AF	Auxiliary carry	X	X	X	X
6	ZF	Zero	X	X	X	X
7	SF	Sign	X	X	X	X
8	TF	Trap	X	X	X	X
9	IF	Interrupt	X	X	X	X
10	DF	Direction	X	X	X	X
11	OF	Overflow	X	X	X	X
12-13	IOPL	I/O privilege level		X	X	X
14	NT	Nested task		X	X	X
16	RF	Resume			X	X
17	VM	Virtual mode			X	X
18	AC	Alignment check enabled				X

Notice that although the 8086/8088 defines only 9 bits, Intel found it necessary to define more bits with each succeeding generation of microprocessor: the 80286 uses 11, the 80386 uses 13, and the 80486 uses 14 bits. All other bits in the flags register remain reserved and undefined by Intel. Table 22.3 details which instructions affect which bits in the flags register. Instructions that have no effect on the flags are omitted from this table.

Table 22.3. How instructions affect the flags register.

Instruction	Meaning	0 CF	2 PF	4 AF	6 ZF	7 SF	8 TF	9 IF	10 DF	11 OF	12/13 IOPL	14 NT	16 RF	17 VM	18 AC
AAA	ASCII adjust for addition	X	?	X	?	?				?					
AAD	ASCII adjust for division	?	X	?	X	X				?					
AAM	ASCII adjust for multiplication	?	X	?	X	X				?					
AAS	ASCII adjust for subtraction	X	?	X	?	?				?					
ADC	Add with carry	X	X	X	X	X				X					
ADD	Add	X	X	X	X	X				X					
AND	Logical AND	X	X	?	X	X				X					
ARPL	Adjust RPL field of selector				X										
BSF	Bit scan forward				X										
BSR	Bit scan reverse				X										
BT	Bit test	X													
BTC	Bit test and complement	X													
BTR	Bit test and reset	X													
BTS	Bit test and set	X													
CLC	Clear carry flag	X													
CLD	Clear direction flag								X						
CLI	Clear interrupt flag							X							
CMC	Complement carry flag	X													

continues

Table 22.3. continued

Instruction	Meaning	Flags													
		0 CF	2 PF	4 AF	6 ZF	7 SF	8 TF	9 IF	10 DF	11 OF	12/13 IOPL	14 NT	16 RF	17 VM	18 AC
CMP	Compare	X	X	X	X	X				X					
CMPSB	Compare strings by byte	X	X	X	X	X				X					
CMPSD	Compare strings by doubleword	X	X	X	X	X				X					
CMPSW	Compare strings by word	X	X	X	X	X				X					
CMPXCHG	Compare and Exchange	X	X	X	X	X				X					
DAA	Decimal adjust for addition	X	X	X	X	X				?					
DAS	Decimal adjust for subtraction	X	X	X	X	X				?					
DEC	Decrement		X	X	X	X				X					
DIV	Divide	?	?	?	?	?				?					
IDIV	Integer divide	?	?	?	?	?				?					
IMUL	Integer multiply	X	?	?	?	?				X					
INC	Increment		X	X	X	X				X					
INT	Software interrupt						X	X							
IRET	Return from interrupt	X	X	X	X	X	X	X	X	X	X	X	X	X	X
MUL	Multiply	X	?	?	?	?				X					
NEG	Negate	X	X	X	X	X				X					

continues

Instruction	Meaning						Flags									
		0 CF	2 PF	4 AF	6 ZF	7 SF	8 TF	9 IF	10 DF	11 OF	12/13 IOPL	14 NT	16 RF	17 VM	18 AC
OR	Logical OR	X	X	?	X	X				X					
POPF	Remove flags from stack	X	X	X	X	X	X	X	X	X	X	X			
POPFD	Remove extended flags from stack	X	X	X	X	X	X	X	X	X	X	X			
RCL	Rotate left through carry	X								X					
RCR	Rotate right through carry	X								X					
ROL	Rotate left	X								X					
ROR	Rotate right	X								X					
SAHF	Store AH into flags register	X	X	X	X	X									
SAL	Arithmetic shift left	X	X	?	X	X				X					
SAR	Arithmetic shift right	X	X	?	X	X				X					
SBB	Subtract with carry	X	X	X	X	X				X					
SCASB	Scan string for byte	X	X	X	X	X				X					
SCASD	Scan string for doubleword	X	X	X	X	X				X					
SCASW	Scan string for word	X	X	X	X	X				X					
SHL	Shift left	X	X	?	X	X				X					
SHLD	Shift left double precision	X	X	?	X	X				?					

Table 22.3. *continued*

Instruction	Meaning	Flags													
		0 CF	2 PF	4 AF	6 ZF	7 SF	8 TF	9 IF	10 DF	11 OF	12/13 IOPL	14 NT	16 RF	17 VM	18 AC
SHR	Shift right	X	X	?	X	X				X					
SHRD	Shift right double precision	X	X	?	X	X				?					
STC	Set carry flag	X													
STD	Set direction flag								X						
STI	Set interrupt flag							X							
SUB	Subtract	X	X	X	X	X				X					
TEST	Test bits	X	X	?	X	X				X					
VERR	Verify a segment for reading				X										
VERW	Verify a segment for writing				X										
XADD	Exchange and add to memory	X	X	X	X	X				X					
XOR	Logical exclusive-or	X	X	?	X	X				X					

The Control Word

All the Intel NPX chips (including the FPU on the 80486) use a *control word* to govern how the chip works. Each of the 16 bits in this word has a different use. Table 22.4 details how each bit is used in each type of NPX or FPU.

Table 22.4. *The NPX/FPU control word.*

Bits	Code	Use	NPX/FPU 87	287	387	486
0	IM	Invalid operation	X	X	X	X
1	DM	Denormalized operand	X	X	X	X
2	ZM	Zero divide	X	X	X	X
3	OM	Overflow	X	X	X	X
4	UM	Underflow	X	X	X	X
5	PM	Precision	X	X	X	X
6		Reserved				
7	IEM	Interrupt enable mask	X			
		0 = Enabled				
		1 = Disabled				
8-9	PC	Precision control	X	X	X	X
		00 = 24 bits	X	X	X	X
		01 = Reserved	X	X	X	X
		10 = 53 bits	X	X	X	X
		11 = 64 bits	X	X	X	X
10-11	RC	Rounding control	X	X	X	X
		00 = Nearest or even				
		01 = Down				
		10 = Up				
		11 = Truncate				
12	IC	Infinity control	X	X		
		0 = Projective				
		1 = Affine				
13-15		Reserved				

To change the values in this word, you must construct it in memory and then use specific mnemonic instructions to direct it to be stored in the NPX/FPU. These instructions are covered later in this section.

The Status Word

The NPX/FPU family uses a *status word* to describe the current condition of the coprocessor. This 16-bit register contains a series of bits that reflect the result of recent numeric operations. The first 6 bits (0 through 5) are exception flags; they are set when an exception occurs. Compare these flags to the similar flags in the NPX/FPU control word that govern whether exceptions for the individual conditions are trapped.

Table 22.5 defines the status word and how it is used among the members of the NPX/FPU family.

Notice the different use of bits across generations of NPX/FPU. In particular, the use of bits 6 and 7 has changed. For the 8087 and 80287, bit 6 was considered reserved; it was defined starting with the 80387. The designation and use of bit 7 changed entirely from the 8087 to the 80287.

Regardless of how the NPX/FPU uses it, the status word cannot be examined directly. To analyze the status word, you must first transfer it to memory.

The bits of the 8087, 80287, 80387, and 80486 numeric processor status words are affected by various instructions, as shown in table 22.6. Because bits 6 and 7 of the status word are defined differently from one model of numeric processor to the next, there are two columns for bit 7.

Table 22.5. *The NPX/FPU status word.*

Status Word Bits	Code	Use	NPX/FPU 87	287	387	486
0	IE	Invalid operation	X	X	X	X
1	DE	Denormalized operand	X	X	X	X
2	ZE	Zero divide	X	X	X	X
3	OE	Overflow	X	X	X	X
4	UE	Underflow	X	X	X	X
5	PE	Precision	X	X	X	X
6	SF	Stack flag			X	X
7	IR	Interrupt request	X			
7	ES	Error summary status		X	X	X
8	C0	Condition code 0	X	X	X	X
9	C1	Condition code 1	X	X	X	X
10	C2	Condition code 2	X	X	X	X
11-13	ST	Stack-top pointer	X	X	X	X
14	C3	Condition code 3	X	X	X	X
15	B	Busy signal	X	X	X	X

Table 22.6. *How instructions affect the status word.*

Instruction	Meaning	0 IE	1 DE	2 ZE	3 OE	4 UE	5 PE	6 SF	7 IR	7 ES	8 C0	9 C1	10 C2	11/13 ST	14 C3	15 B
F2XM1	2^x-1					X	X									
FABS	Absolute value	X														
FADD	Add real	X	X		X	X	X									
FADDP	Add real and POP	X	X		X	X	X									
FBLD	BCD load	X														
FBSTP	BCD store and POP	X														
FCHS	Change sign	X														
FCLEX	Clear exceptions with WAIT	X	X	X	X	X	X		X							X
FCOM	Compare real	X	X								X		X		X	
FCOMP	Compare real and POP	X	X								X		X		X	
FCOMPP	Compare real and POP twice	X	X								X		X		X	
FCOS	Cosine	X	X			X	X									
FDECSTP	Decrement stack pointer													X		
FDIV	Divide real	X	X	X	X	X	X									
FDIVP	Divide real and POP	X	X	X	X	X	X									
FDIVR	Divide real reversed	X	X	X	X	X	X									
FDIVRP	Divide real reversed and POP	X	X	X	X	X	X									
FIADD	Integer add	X	X		X		X									
FICOM	Integer compare	X	X								X		X		X	
FICOMP	Integer compare and POP	X	X								X		X		X	

Status Word Bits

continues

Instruction	Meaning	Status Word Bits													
		0 IE	1 DE	2 ZE	3 OE	4 UE	5 PE	6 SF	7 IR	8 C0	9 C1	10 C2	11/13 ST	14 C3	15 B
FIDIV	Integer divide	X	X	X	X	X	X								
FIDIVR	Integer divide reversed	X	X	X	X	X	X								
FILD	Integer load	X													
FIMUL	Integer multiply	X	X		X		X								
FINCSTP	Increment stack pointer												X		
FIST	Integer store	X					X								
FISTP	Integer store and POP	X			X		X								
FISUB	Integer subtract	X	X		X		X								
FISUBR	Integer subtract reversed	X	X		X		X								
FLD	Load real	X	X												
FLD1	Load 1.0	X													
FLDENV	Load environment	X	X	X	X	X	X	X	X	X	X	X	X	X	X
FLDL2E	Load $\log_2 e$	X													
FLDL2T	Load $\log_2 10$	X													
FLDLG2	Load $\log_{10} 2$	X													
FLDLN2	Load $\log_e 2$	X													
FLDPI	Load π	X													
FLDZ	Load 0.0	X			X	X									
FMUL	Multiply real	X	X		X	X	X								

Table 22.6. continued

Status Word Bits

Instruction	Meaning	0 IE	1 DE	2 ZE	3 OE	4 UE	5 PE	6 SF	7 IR	7 ES	8 C0	9 C1	10 C2	11/13 ST	14 C3	15 B
FMULP	Multiply real and POP	X	X		X	X	X									
FNCLEX	Clear exceptions	X	X	X	X	X	X		X							X
FPATAN	Partial arctangent	X	X			X	X									
FPREM	Partial remainder	X	X			X					X	X	X		X	
FPREM1	Partial remainder, IEEE version	X	X			X					X	X	X		X	
FPTAN	Partial tangent	X					X									
FRNDINT	Round to integer	X					X									
FRSTOR	Restore state	X	X	X	X	X	X	X	X	X	X	X	X	X	X	
FSCALE	Scale	X			X	X	X									
FSIN	Sine	X	X			X	X									
FSINCOS	Sine and cosine	X	X			X	X									
FSQRT	Square root	X	X				X									
FST	Store real	X			X	X	X									
FSTP	Store real and POP	X			X	X	X									
FSUB	Subtract real	X	X		X	X	X									
FSUBP	Subtract real and POP	X	X		X	X	X									
FSUBR	Subtract real reversed	X	X		X	X	X									
FSUBRP	Subtract real reversed and POP	X	X		X	X	X									

Status Word Bits

Instruction	Meaning	0 IE	1 DE	2 ZE	3 OE	4 UE	5 PE	6 SF	7 IR	ES	8 C0	9 C1	10 C2	11/13 ST	14 C3	15 B
FTST	Test	X	X								X		X		X	
FUCOM	Unordered compare	X	X								X		X		X	
FUCOMP	Unordered compare and POP	X	X								X		X		X	
FUCOMPP	Unordered compare and POP twice	X	X								X		X		X	
FXAM	Examine										X	X	X		X	
FXCH	Exchange registers	X														
FXTRACT	Extract exponent and significand	X														
FYL2X	Y*log$_2$X						X									
FYL2XP1	Y*log$_2$(X+1)						X									

Detailed Instruction Information

In the remainder of this chapter, each member of the Intel instruction set is described in detail. The following information is given for each instruction:

❏ **Instruction name.** This name is based on the standard mnemonic code designed by Intel.

❏ **Applicable processors.** This paragraph lists the processors that perform the instruction.

❏ **Instruction category.** The general classification for the instruction is provided.

❏ **Flags affected.** The majority of the instructions change the status of the bits in the flags register (or the status word, in the case of numeric processor instructions). The individual flags affected are listed in this section.

❏ **Coding examples.** Brief examples of the use of the instruction are given.

❏ **Description.** A narrative description of each instruction is provided.

The instructions are arranged in ascending alphabetical order.

AAA: ASCII Adjust for Addition

Applicable processors: 8086/8088, 80286, 80386, 80486

Category: Arithmetic instructions

Flags affected: AF, CF, OF (undefined), PF (undefined), SF (undefined), ZF (undefined)

Coding example:

AAA

Description: AAA changes the contents of AL to a valid unpacked decimal number with the high-order nibble zeroed.

AAD: ASCII Adjust for Division

Applicable processors: 8086/8088, 80286, 80386, 80486

Category: Arithmetic instructions

Flags affected: AF (undefined), CF (undefined), OF (undefined), PF, SF, ZF

Coding example:

AAD

Description: AAD multiplies the contents of AH by 10, adds the result to the contents of AL, and places the result in AL. The instruction then sets AH to 0. You use this instruction before you divide unpacked decimal numbers.

AAM: ASCII Adjust for Multiplication

Applicable processors: 8086/8088, 80286, 80386, 80486

Category: Arithmetic instructions

Flags affected: AF (undefined), CF (undefined), OF (undefined), PF, SF, ZF

Coding example:

AAM

Description: After multiplying two unpacked decimal numbers, you use AAM to correct the result to an unpacked decimal number. For the instruction to work properly, each number multiplied must have had its high-order nibbles set to 0.

AAS: ASCII Adjust for Subtraction

Applicable processors: 8086/8088, 80286, 80386, 80486

Category: Arithmetic instructions

Flags affected: AF, CF, OF (undefined), PF (undefined), SF (undefined), ZF (undefined)

Coding example:

AAS

Description: AAS corrects the result of a previous unpacked decimal subtraction so that the value in AL is a true unpacked decimal number.

ADC: Add with Carry

Applicable processors: 8086/8088, 80286, 80386, 80486

Category: Arithmetic instructions

Flags affected: AF, CF, OF, PF, SF, ZF

Coding examples:

```
ADC        AX,BX           ;AX=AX+BX+CF
ADC        AX,TEMP         ;AX=AX+TEMP+CF
ADC        SUM,BX          ;SUM=SUM+BX+CF
ADC        CL,10           ;CL=CL+10+CF
ADC        AX,TEMP[BX]     ;Indirect address example
```

Description: ADC adds the contents of the source operand to (and stores the result in) the destination operand. If the carry flag is set, the result changes in increments of 1. In this routine, the values being added are assumed to be binary.

ADD: Add

Applicable processors: 8086/8088, 80286, 80386, 80486

Category: Arithmetic instructions

Flags affected: AF, CF, OF, PF, SF, ZF

Coding examples:

```
ADD        AX,BX           ;AX=AX+BX
ADD        AX,TEMP         ;AX=AX+TEMP
ADD        SUM,BX          ;SUM=SUM+BX
ADD        CL,10           ;CL=CL+10
ADD        AX,TEMP[BX]     ;Indirect address example
```

Description: ADD adds the contents of the source operand to (and stores the result in) the destination operand. In this routine the values being added are assumed to be binary.

AND: Logical AND on Bits

Applicable processors: 8086/8088, 80286, 80386, 80486

Category: Bit-manipulation instructions

Flags affected: AF (undefined), CF, OF, PF, SF, ZF

Coding examples:

```
AND     AX,BX           ;Using two 16-bit registers
AND     AX,TEMP         ;TEMP must be a word
AND     SUM,BX          ;SUM must be a word
AND     CL,00001111b    ;Zero high nibble
AND     AX,TEMP[BX]     ;Indirect address example
```

Description: This instruction performs a logical AND of the operands and stores the result in the destination operand. Each bit of the resultant byte or word is set to 1 only if the corresponding bit of each operand is set to 1.

ARPL: Adjust RPL Field of Selector

Applicable processors: 80286, 80386, 80486

Category: Bit-manipulation instructions

Flags affected: ZF

Coding examples:

```
ARPL    SELECTOR,AX
ARPL    AX,CX
```

Description: ARPL compares the RPL bits (bits 0 and 1) of the first operand with those of the second. If the RPL bits of the first operand are less than those of the second, the two bits of the first operand are set equal to the two bits of the second, and the zero flag is set. Otherwise, the zero flag is cleared. This instruction is used only in operating system software, not in applications software.

BOUND: Check Array Index against Bounds

Applicable processors: 80286, 80386, 80486

Category: Flag- and processor-control instructions

Flags affected: None

Coding example:

```
BOUND    BX,LIMITS
```

Description: BOUND determines whether the signed value in the first operand falls between the two boundaries specified by the second operand. The word at the second operand is assumed to be the lower boundary, and the following word is assumed to be the upper boundary. An interrupt 5 occurs if the value in the first operand is less than the lower limit or greater than the upper limit.

BSF: Bit Scan Forward

Applicable processors: 80386, 80486

Category: Bit-manipulation instructions

Flags affected: ZF

Coding examples:

```
BSF      EAX,TEMP
BSF      CX,BX
```

Description: BSF scans the bits of the second operand (starting with bit 0) to see whether any are set. If all bits are clear (second operand is 0), the first operand is not changed, and the zero flag is set. If any bit is set, the zero flag is cleared, and the first operand is set equal to the bit number of the bit that is set.

BSR: Bit Scan Reverse

Applicable processors: 80386, 80486

Category: Bit-manipulation instructions

Flags affected: ZF

Coding examples:

```
BSR      EAX,TEMP
BSR      CX,BX
```

Description: BSR scans the bits of the second operand (starting with the high-order bit) to see whether any are set. If all bits are clear (second operand is 0), the first operand is not changed, and the zero flag is set. If any bit is set, the zero flag is cleared, and the first operand is set equal to the bit number of the bit that is set.

BSWAP: Swap 32-Bit Byte Order

Applicable processors: 80486

Category: Data-transfer instructions

Flags affected: None

Coding examples:

```
BSWAP          EAX
BSWAP          EDX
```

Description: This instruction uses an extended (32-bit) register as an operand. It reverses the byte order in the register. Byte 0 is swapped with byte 3, and byte 1 is swapped with byte 2.

BT: Bit Test

Applicable processors: 80386, 80486

Category: Bit-manipulation instructions

Flags affected: CF

Coding examples:

```
BT    TEMP,EAX
BT    BX,CX
BT    TEMP,3                 ;Test 3rd bit
```

Description: BT uses the value of the second operand as a bit index into the value of the first operand. The bit at the indexed position of the first operand is copied into the carry flag.

BTC: Bit Test and Complement

Applicable processors: 80386, 80486

Category: Bit-manipulation instructions

Flags affected: CF

Coding examples:

```
BTC        TEMP,EAX
BTC        BX,CX
BTC        TEMP,3          ;Opposite of 3rd bit
```

Description: BTC uses the value of the second operand as a bit index into the value of the first operand. The opposite value of the bit at the indexed position of the first operand is copied into the carry flag.

BTR: Bit Test and Reset

Applicable processors: 80386, 80486

Category: Bit-manipulation instructions

Flags affected: CF

Coding examples:

```
BTR        TEMP,EAX
BTR        BX,CX
BTR        TEMP,3          ;Value of 3rd bit
```

Description: BTR uses the value of the second operand as a bit index into the value of the first operand. The bit at the indexed position of the first operand is copied into the carry flag, and then the original bit value is cleared.

BTS: Bit Test and Set

Applicable processors: 80386, 80486

Category: Bit-manipulation instructions

Flags affected: CF

Coding examples:

```
BTS        TEMP,EAX
BTS        BX,CX
BTS        TEMP,3          ;Value of 3rd bit
```

Description: BTS uses the value of the second operand as a bit index into the value of the first operand. The bit at the indexed position of the first operand is copied into the carry flag, and then the original bit value is set.

CALL: Perform Subroutine

Applicable processors: 8086/8088, 80286, 80386, 80486

Category: Control-transfer instructions

Flags affected: None

Coding examples:

```
CALL    WHIZ_BANG    ;WHIZ_BANG is a subroutine
CALL    [BX]         ;Perform subroutine with address at [BX]
CALL    AX           ;Subroutine address in AX
```

Description: CALL does the following:

❏ Pushes offset address of following instruction on the stack

❏ If procedure being called is declared as FAR, pushes segment address of following instruction on the stack

❏ Loads IP with the offset address of the procedure being called

❏ If procedure being called is declared as FAR, loads CS with the segment address of the procedure being called

Execution then continues at the newly loaded CS:IP address until a RET instruction is encountered.

CBW: Convert Byte to Word

Applicable processors: 8086/8088, 80286, 80386, 80486

Category: Arithmetic instructions

Flags affected: None

Coding example:

```
CBW
```

Description: CBW converts the byte value in AL to a word value in AX by extending the high-order bit value of AL through all bits of AH.

CDQ: Convert Doubleword to Quadword

Applicable processors: 80386, 80486

Category: Arithmetic instructions

Flags affected: None

Coding example:

```
CDQ
```

Description: CDQ converts the doubleword value in EAX to a quadword value in EDX:EAX by extending the high-order bit value of EAX through all bits of EDX.

CLC: Clear Carry Flag

Applicable processors: 8086/8088, 80286, 80386, 80486

Category: Flag- and processor-control instructions

Flags affected: CF

Coding example:

```
CLC
```

Description: CLC clears the flags register's carry flag by setting it to 0.

CLD: Clear Direction Flag

Applicable processors: 8086/8088, 80286, 80386, 80486

Category: Flag and processor-control instructions

Flags affected: DF

Coding example:

```
CLD
```

Description: CLD clears the direction flag of the flags register by setting the flag to 0.

CLI: Clear Interrupt Flag

Applicable processors: 8086/8088, 80286, 80386, 80486

Category: Flag- and processor-control instructions

Flags affected: IF

Coding example:

```
CLI
```

Description: CLI clears the interrupt flag of the flags register by setting the flag to 0. While the interrupt flag is cleared, the CPU recognizes no maskable interrupts.

CLTS: Clear Task-Switched Flag

Applicable processors: 80286, 80386, 80486

Category: Flag- and processor-control instructions

Flags affected: None

Coding example:

```
CLTS
```

Description: CLTS clears the task-switched flag of the machine status word (MSW). This instruction is used only in operating system software, not in applications software.

CMC: Complement Carry Flag

Applicable processors: 8086/8088, 80286, 80386, 80486

Category: Flag- and processor-control instructions

Flags affected: CF

Coding example:

```
CMC
```

Description: CMC switches the carry flag of the flags register to the opposite of the flag's current setting.

CMP: Compare

Applicable processors: 8086/8088, 80286, 80386, 80486

Category: Arithmetic instructions

Flags affected: AF, CF, OF, PF, SF, ZF

Coding examples:

```
CMP  AX,BX          ;Compare two 16-bit registers
CMP  AX,TEMP        ;TEMP must be a word
CMP  SUM,EBX        ;SUM must be a doubleword
CMP  CL,3           ;Compare to constant
CMP  AX,TEMP[BX]    ;Indirect address example
```

Description: CMP is considered an arithmetic instruction because the source operand is subtracted from the destination operand. The result is not stored anywhere, however; it is used for setting the flags. You can use subsequent testing of the flags for program control.

CMPSB: Compare Strings, Byte-for-Byte

Applicable processors: 8086/8088, 80286, 80386, 80486

Category: String-manipulation instructions

Flags affected: AF, CF, OF, PF, SF, ZF

Coding examples:

```
CMPSB           ;Compare strings
REPE CMPSB      ;Repeat a comparison loop
```

Description: CMPSB compares strings, byte-by-byte. DI and SI change in increments or decrements of 1, depending on the setting of the direction flag. Ordinarily, this instruction is used with the REPE, REPNE, REPNZ, or REPZ instructions to repeat the comparison for a maximum of CX number of bytes. Intel lists this command as CMPS, but the assembler makes the byte (CMPSB) and word (CMPSW) distinctions. This instruction affects only the flags; no changes are made to the operands.

CMPSD: Compare Strings, Doubleword-for-Doubleword

Applicable processors: 80386, 80486

Category: String-manipulation instructions

Flags affected: AF, CF, OF, PF, SF, ZF

Coding examples:

```
CMPSD           ;Compare strings
REPE CMPSD      ;Repeat a comparison loop
```

Description: CMPSD compares strings, doubleword-for-doubleword. EDI and ESI change in increments or decrements of four, depending on the setting of the direction flag. Usually, this instruction is used with REPE, REPNE, REPNZ, or REPZ instructions to repeat the comparison for the number of times specified in ECX. This instruction affects only the flags; no changes are made to the operands.

CMPSW: Compare Strings, Word-for-Word

Applicable processors: 8086/8088, 80286, 80386, 80486

Category: String-manipulation instructions

Flags affected: AF, CF, OF, PF, SF, ZF

Coding examples:

```
CMPSW           ;Compare strings
REPE CMPSW      ;Repeat a comparison loop
```

Description: CMPSW compares strings, word-for-word. DI and SI change in increments or decrements of two, depending on the setting of the direction flag. Ordinarily, this instruction is used along with REPE, REPNE, REPNZ, or REPZ instructions to repeat the comparison for the number of times specified in CX. Intel lists this command as CMPS, but the assembler makes the byte (CMPSB) and word (CMPSW) distinctions. This instruction affects only the flags; no changes are made to the operands.

CMPXCHG: Compare and Exchange

Applicable processors: 80486

Category: Arithmetic instructions

Flags affected: AF, CF, OF, PF, SF, ZF

Coding example:

```
CMPXCHG    ECX,EBX,EAX

CMPXCHG    CL,CH,AL
```

Description: As you can see from the coding examples, this instruction uses three operands, all three of which must be the same size. They are (in order) the source, destination, and accumulator operands. This instruction tests the destination against the accumulator—if they are equal, the value of the source is loaded into the destination; if they are unequal, nothing is changed (except ZF is cleared).

CWD: Convert Word to Doubleword

Applicable processors: 8086/8088, 80286, 80386, 80486

Category: Arithmetic instructions

Flags affected: None

Coding example:

```
CWD
```

Description: CWD converts the word value in AX to a doubleword value in DX:AX by extending the high-order bit value of AX through all bits of DX.

CWDE: Convert Word to Extended Doubleword

Applicable processors: 80386, 80486

Category: Arithmetic instructions

Flags affected: None

Coding example:

```
CWDE
```

Description: CWDE converts the word value in AX to a doubleword value in EAX by extending the high-order bit value of AX through the remaining bits of EAX.

DAA: Decimal Adjust for Addition

Applicable processors: 8086/8088, 80286, 80386, 80486

Category: Arithmetic instructions

Flags affected: AF, CF, OF (undefined for all processors through 80286, not affected beginning with 80386), PF, SF, ZF

Coding example:

DAA

Description: DAA corrects the result (AL) of a previous binary-coded decimal (BCD) addition operation.

DAS: Decimal Adjust for Subtraction

Applicable processors: 8086/8088, 80286, 80386, 80486

Category: Arithmetic instructions

Flags affected: AF, CF, OF (undefined for all processors through 80286, not affected beginning with 80386), PF, SF, ZF

Coding example:

DAS

Description: DAS corrects the result (AL) of a previous binary-coded decimal (BCD) subtraction operation.

DEC: Decrement

Applicable processors: 8086/8088, 80286, 80386, 80486

Category: Arithmetic instructions

Flags affected: AF, OF, PF, SF, ZF

Coding examples:

```
DEC     AX
DEC     ECX
DEC     SUM
DEC     CL
DEC     TEMP[SI]
```

Description: DEC changes, in decrements of 1, the contents of the operand. The operand is assumed to be an unsigned binary value.

DIV: Divide

Applicable processors: 8086/8088, 80286, 80386, 80486

Category: Arithmetic instructions

Flags affected: AF (undefined), CF (undefined), OF (undefined), PF (undefined), SF (undefined), ZF (undefined)

Coding examples:

```
DIV     BX              ;AX=DX:AX/BX
DIV     WORD_TEMP       ;AX=DX:AX/WORD_TEMP
DIV     BYTE_SUM        ;AL=AX/BYTE_SUM
DIV     DWORD_SUM       ;EAX=EDX:EAX/DWORD_SUM
DIV     WORD_TBL[BX]    ;Indirect address example
```

Description: If the operand is a byte value, DIV divides the contents of AX by the contents of the operand and stores the result in AL and the remainder in AH. If the operand is a word value, DIV divides the contents of DX:AX by the contents of the operand and stores the result in AX and the remainder in DX.

For the 80386 and 80486, if the operand is a doubleword value, DIV divides the contents of EDX:EAX by the contents of the operand and stores the result in EAX and the remainder in EDX.

This instruction treats numbers as unsigned binary values.

ENTER: Make Stack Frame for Procedure Parameters

Applicable processors: 80286, 80386, 80486

Category: Flag- and processor-control instructions

Flags affected: None

Coding examples:

```
ENTER    PPTR,3
ENTER    DS:BX,0
```

Description: ENTER modifies the stack appropriately for entry to a high-level language procedure. The first operand specifies the number of bytes of storage to be allocated on the stack; the second operand specifies the nesting level of the routine. The effects of this instruction are undone by the LEAVE instruction.

ESC: Escape

Applicable processors: 8086/8088, 80286, 80386, 80486

Category: Flag- and processor-control instructions

Flags affected: None

Coding examples:

```
ESC      6,TEMP
ESC      15,CL
```

Description: ESC provides a means for coprocessors (such as the NPX/FPU) to access data in the microprocessor data stream. When this instruction is encountered, it causes the microprocessor to place the operand on the data bus and perform a NOP internally.

F2XM1: 2^x-1

Applicable processors: 8087, 80287, 80387, 80486

Category: Transcendental instruction

Status affected: PE, UE

Coding example:

```
F2XM1
```

Description: F2XM1 calculates $Y=2^x-1$, where X is the top stack element (ST). The result (Y) replaces X as the top stack element (ST). This instruction performs no validation checking of the input value. The program ensures that $0<=X<=0.5$.

FABS: Absolute Value

Applicable processors: 8087, 80287, 80387, 80486

Category: Arithmetic instruction

Status affected: IE

Coding example:

```
FABS
```

Description: FABS changes the top stack element (ST) to its absolute value.

FADD: Add Real

Applicable processors: 8087, 80287, 80387, 80486

Category: Arithmetic instruction

Status affected: DE, IE, OE, PE, UE

Coding examples:

```
FADD       TEMP              ;ST=ST+TEMP
FADD       TEMP,ST(3)        ;TEMP=TEMP+ST(3)
```

Description: FADD adds two numbers together and stores them at the destination operand. If no destination operand is given (only one operand is specified), ST is the assumed destination.

FADDP: Add Real and POP

Applicable processors: 8087, 80287, 80387, 80486

Category: Arithmetic instruction

Status affected: DE, IE, OE, PE, UE

Coding examples:

```
FADDP       TEMP            ;ST=ST+TEMP
FADDP       TEMP,ST(3)      ;TEMP=TEMP+ST(3)
```

Description: FADDP adds two numbers together, stores them at the destination operand, and pops the stack. If no destination operand is given (only one operand is specified), ST is the assumed destination.

FBLD: BCD Load

Applicable processors: 8087, 80287, 80387, 80486

Category: Data-transfer instruction

Status affected: IE

Coding example:

```
FBLD        TEMP
```

Description: FBLD converts the BCD number at the operand address to a temporary real and pushes it on the stack.

FBSTP: BCD Store and POP

Applicable processors: 8087, 80287, 80387, 80486

Category: Data-transfer instruction

Status affected: IE

Coding example:

```
FBSTP       TEMP
```

Description: FBSTP converts the top stack element (ST) to a BCD integer, stores it at the operand address, and pops the stack.

FCHS: Change Sign

Applicable processors: 8087, 80287, 80387, 80486

Category: Arithmetic instruction

Status affected: IE

Coding example:

```
FCHS
```

Description: FCHS changes the sign of the top stack element (ST).

FCLEX: Clear Exceptions with WAIT

Applicable processors: 8087, 80287, 80387, 80486

Category: Flag- and processor-control instructions

Status affected: B, DE, IE, IR, OE, PE, UE, ZE

Coding example:

```
FCLEX
```

Description: FCLEX clears the exception flags, interrupt request, and busy flags of the NPX/FPU status word. A CPU wait prefix precedes this instruction. See also FNCLEX.

FCOM: Compare Real

Applicable processors: 8087, 80287, 80387, 80486

Category: Comparison instruction

Status affected: C0, C2, C3, DE, IE

Coding examples:

```
FCOM                 ;Compare ST to ST(1)
FCOM     ST(4)       ;Compare ST to ST(4)
FCOM     TEMP        ;Compare ST to memory
```

Description: The top stack element (ST) is compared to the second stack element (ST(1)) or another specified operand. Condition codes are affected accordingly.

FCOMP: Compare Real and POP

Applicable processors: 8087, 80287, 80387, 80486

Category: Comparison instruction

Status affected: C0, C2, C3, DE, IE

Coding examples:

```
FCOMP               ;Compare ST to ST(1)
FCOMP     ST(4)     ;Compare ST to ST(4)
FCOMP     TEMP      ;Compare ST to memory
```

Description: The top stack element (ST) is compared to the second stack element (ST(1)) or another specified operand; the stack is then popped. Condition codes are affected accordingly.

FCOMPP: Compare Real and POP Twice

Applicable processors: 8087, 80287, 80387, 80486

Category: Comparison instruction

Status affected: C0, C2, C3, DE, IE

Coding example:

```
FCOMPP              ;Compare ST to ST(1)
```

Description: The top stack element (ST) is compared to the second stack element (ST(1)) and the stack is popped twice. Condition codes are affected accordingly.

FCOS: Cosine

Applicable processors: 80387, 80486

Category: Transcendental instruction

Status affected: DE, IE, PE, UE

Coding example:

```
FCOS        ;Replace value in radians with cosine
```

Description: The top stack element (ST) is replaced with its cosine, considering the element to be an angle in radians. Condition codes are affected accordingly.

FDECSTP: Decrement Stack Pointer

Applicable processors: 8087, 80287, 80387, 80486

Category: Flag- and processor-control instructions

Status affected: ST

Coding example:

```
FDECSTP
```

Description: FDECSTP decrements the stack pointer of the NPX/FPU status word.

FDISI: Disable Interrupts with WAIT

Applicable processors: 8087

Category: Flag- and processor-control instructions

Status affected: None

Coding example:

```
FDISI
```

Description: FDISI sets the interrupt-enable mask of the 8087 control word, thus preventing the 8087 from initiating an interrupt. A CPU wait prefix precedes this instruction. See also FNDISI.

FDIV: Divide Real

Applicable processors: 8087, 80287, 80387, 80486

Category: Arithmetic instruction

Status affected: DE, IE, OE, PE, UE, ZE

Coding examples:

```
FDIV       TEMP             ;ST=TEMP/ST
FDIV       TEMP,ST(3)       ;TEMP=ST(3)/TEMP
```

Description: FDIV divides the destination by the source operand and stores the result at the destination operand. If no destination operand is given (only one operand is specified), ST is the assumed destination.

FDIVP: Divide Real and POP

Applicable processors: 8087, 80287, 80387, 80486

Category: Arithmetic instruction

Status affected: DE, IE, OE, PE, UE, ZE

Coding examples:

```
FDIVP     TEMP              ;ST=TEMP/ST
FDIVP     TEMP,ST(3)        ;TEMP=ST(3)/TEMP
```

Description: FDIVP divides the destination by the source operand, stores the result at the destination operand, and pops the stack. If no destination operand is given (only one operand is specified), ST is the assumed destination.

FDIVR: Divide Real Reversed

Applicable processors: 8087, 80287, 80387, 80486

Category: Arithmetic instruction

Status affected: DE, IE, OE, PE, UE, ZE

Coding examples:

```
FDIVR     TEMP              ;ST=ST/TEMP
FDIVR     TEMP,ST(3)        ;TEMP=TEMP/ST(3)
```

Description: FDIVR divides the source by the destination operand and stores the result at the destination operand. If no destination operand is given (only one operand is specified), ST is the assumed destination.

FDIVRP: Divide Real Reversed and POP

Applicable processors: 8087, 80287, 80387, 80486

Category: Arithmetic instruction

Status affected: DE, IE, OE, PE, UE, ZE

Coding examples:

```
FDIVRP    TEMP              ;ST=ST/TEMP
FDIVRP    TEMP,ST(3)        ;TEMP=TEMP/ST(3)
```

Description: FDIVRP divides the source by the destination operand, stores the result at the destination operand, and pops the stack. If no destination operand is given (only one operand is specified), ST is the assumed destination.

FENI: Enable Interrupts with WAIT

Applicable processors: 8087

Category: Flag- and processor-control instructions

Status affected: None

Coding example:

```
FENI
```

Description: FENI clears the interrupt-enable mask of the 8087 control word, so that the 8087 can initiate interrupts. A CPU wait prefix precedes this instruction. See also FNENI.

FFREE: Free Register

Applicable processors: 8087, 80287, 80387, 80486

Category: Flag- and processor-control instructions

Status affected: None

Coding example:

```
FFREE    ST(3)
```

Description: FFREE changes the tag for the specified stack register to indicate that the stack register is empty.

FIADD: Integer Add

Applicable processors: 8087, 80287, 80387, 80486

Category: Arithmetic instruction

Status affected: DE, IE, OE, PE

Coding examples:

```
FIADD     TEMP          ;ST=ST+TEMP
FIADD     TEMP,ST(3)    ;TEMP=TEMP+ST(3)
```

Description: FIADD adds two numbers together as integers and stores them at the destination operand. If no destination operand is given (only one operand is specified), ST is the assumed destination.

FICOM: Integer Compare

Applicable processors: 8087, 80287, 80387, 80486

Category: Comparison instruction

Status affected: C0, C2, C3, DE, IE

Coding example:

```
FICOM     TEMP_INT      ;Compare memory to ST
```

Description: FICOM converts the operand (assumed to be an integer) to a temporary real and compares it to the top stack element (ST). Condition codes are set accordingly.

FICOMP: Integer Compare and POP

Applicable processors: 8087, 80287, 80387, 80486

Category: Comparison instruction

Status affected: C0, C2, C3, DE, IE

Coding example:

```
FICOMP    TEMP_INT      ;Compare memory to ST
```

Description: FICOMP converts the operand (assumed to be an integer) to a temporary real, compares it to the top stack element (ST), and then pops the stack. Condition codes are set accordingly.

FIDIV: Integer Divide

Applicable processors: 8087, 80287, 80387, 80486

Category: Arithmetic instruction

Status affected: DE, IE, OE, PE, UE, ZE

Coding examples:

```
FIDIV      TEMP              ;ST=TEMP/ST
FIDIV      TEMP,ST(3)        ;TEMP=ST(3)/TEMP
```

Description: FIDIV divides the destination by the source operand, as integers, and stores the result at the destination operand. If no destination operand is given (only one operand is specified), ST is the assumed destination.

FIDIVR: Integer Divide Reversed

Applicable processors: 8087, 80287, 80387, 80486

Category: Arithmetic instruction

Status affected: DE, IE, OE, PE, UE, ZE

Coding examples:

```
FIDIVR     TEMP              ;ST=ST/TEMP
FIDIVR     TEMP,ST(3)        ;TEMP=TEMP/ST(3)
```

Description: FIDIVR divides the destination by the source operand, as integers, and stores the result at the destination operand. If no destination operand is given (only one operand is specified), ST is the assumed destination.

FILD: Integer Load

Applicable processors: 8087, 80287, 80387, 80486

Category: Data-transfer instruction

Status affected: IE

Coding example:

```
FILD       TEMP
```

Description: FILD converts the binary integer number at the operand address to a temporary real and pushes it on the stack.

FIMUL: Integer Multiply

Applicable processors: 8087, 80287, 80387, 80486

Category: Arithmetic instruction

Status affected: DE, IE, OE, PE

Coding examples:

```
FIMUL      TEMP              ;ST=ST*TEMP
FIMUL      TEMP,ST(3)        ;TEMP=TEMP*ST(3)
```

Description: FIMUL multiplies the source by the destination operand, as integers, and stores the result at the destination operand. If no destination operand is given (only one operand is specified), ST is the assumed destination.

FINCSTP: Increment Stack Pointer

Applicable processors: 8087, 80287, 80387, 80486

Category: Flag- and processor-control instructions

Status affected: ST

Coding example:

```
FINCSTP
```

Description: FINCSTP increments the stack pointer of the NPX/FPU status word.

FINIT: Initialize Processor with WAIT

Applicable processors: 8087, 80287, 80387, 80486

Category: Flag- and processor-control instructions

Status affected: None

Coding example:

```
FINIT
```

Description: FINIT initializes the NPX/FPU. This action is functionally equivalent to performing a hardware RESET. A CPU wait prefix precedes this instruction. See also FNINIT.

FIST: Integer Store

Applicable processors: 8087, 80287, 80387, 80486

Category: Data-transfer instruction

Status affected: IE, PE

Coding example:

```
FIST    TEMP
```

Description: FIST rounds the top stack element (ST) to a binary integer number and stores it at the operand address.

FISTP: Integer Store and POP

Applicable processors: 8087, 80287, 80387, 80486

Category: Data-transfer instruction

Status affected: IE, PE

Coding example:

```
FISTP    TEMP
```

Description: FISTP rounds the top stack element (ST) to a binary integer number, stores it at the operand address, and pops ST from the stack.

FISUB: Integer Subtract

Applicable processors: 8087, 80287, 80387, 80486

Category: Arithmetic instruction

Status affected: DE, IE, OE, PE

Coding examples:

```
FISUB     TEMP            ;ST=ST-TEMP
FISUB     TEMP,ST(3)      ;TEMP=TEMP-ST(3)
```

Description: FISUB subtracts the source from the destination operand, as integers, and stores the result at the destination operand. If no destination operand is given (only one operand is specified), ST is the assumed destination.

FISUBR: Integer Subtract Reversed

Applicable processors: 8087, 80287, 80387, 80486

Category: Arithmetic instruction

Status affected: DE, IE, OE, PE

Coding examples:

```
FISUBR    TEMP            ;ST=TEMP-ST
FISUBR    TEMP,ST(3)      ;TEMP=ST(3)-TEMP
```

Description: FISUBR subtracts the destination from the source operand, as integers, and stores the result at the destination operand. If no destination operand is given (only one operand is specified), ST is assumed to be the destination.

FLD: Load Real

Applicable processors: 8087, 80287, 80387, 80486

Category: Data-transfer instruction

Status affected: DE, IE

Coding examples:

```
FLD       ST(3)
FLD       TEMP
```

Description: FLD pushes the value of the source operand on the stack.

FLD1: Load 1.0

Applicable processors: 8087, 80287, 80387, 80486

Category: Constant instruction

Status affected: IE

Coding example:

```
FLD1
```

Description: FLD1 pushes the value +1.0 on the stack. This value becomes ST.

FLDCW: Load Control Word

Applicable processors: 8087, 80287, 80387, 80486

Category: Flag- and processor-control instructions

Status affected: None

Coding example:

```
FLDCW     MEM_CW          ;Transfer control word
```

Description: FLDCW loads the NPX/FPU control word with the word value pointed to by the source operand.

FLDENV: Load Environment

Applicable processors: 8087, 80287, 80387, 80486

Category: Flag- and processor-control instructions

Status affected: B, C0, C1, C2, C3, DE, ES, IE, IR, OE, PE, SF, ST, UE, ZE

Coding example:

```
FLDENV    SAVE_AREA
```

Description: FLDENV restores all environment variables of the NPX/FPU from the 14-word memory location specified by the operand.

FLDL2E: Load $\log_2 e$

Applicable processors: 8087, 80287, 80387, 80486

Category: Constant instruction

Status affected: IE

Coding example:

FLDL2E

Description: FLDL2E pushes the value of $\log_2 e$ on the stack. This value becomes ST.

FLDL2T: Load $\log_2 10$

Applicable processors: 8087, 80287, 80387, 80486

Category: Constant instruction

Status affected: IE

Coding example:

FLDL2T

Description: FLDL2T pushes the value of $\log_2 10$ on the stack. This value becomes ST.

FLDLG2: Load $\log_{10} 2$

Applicable processors: 8087, 80287, 80387, 80486

Category: Constant instruction

Status affected: IE

Coding example:

FLDLG2

Description: FLDLG2 pushes the value of $\log_{10} 2$ on the stack. This value becomes ST.

FLDLN2: Load log$_e$2

Applicable processors: 8087, 80287, 80387, 80486

Category: Constant instruction

Status affected: IE

Coding example:

FLDLN2

Description: FLDLN2 pushes the value of log$_e$2 on the stack. This value becomes ST.

FLDPI: Load π

Applicable processors: 8087, 80287, 80387, 80486

Category: Constant instruction

Status affected: IE

Coding example:

FLDPI

Description: FLDPI pushes the value of π on the stack. This value becomes ST.

FLDZ: Load 0.0

Applicable processors: 8087, 80287, 80387, 80486

Category: Constant instruction

Status affected: IE

Coding example:

FLDZ

Description: FLDZ pushes the value 0.0 on the stack. This value becomes ST.

FMUL: Multiply Real

Applicable processors: 8087, 80287, 80387, 80486

Category: Arithmetic instruction

Status affected: DE, IE, OE, PE, UE

Coding examples:

```
FMUL        TEMP             ;ST=ST*TEMP
FMUL        TEMP,ST(3)       ;TEMP=TEMP*ST(3)
```

Description: FMUL multiplies the source by the destination operand and stores the result at the destination operand. If no destination operand is given (only one operand is specified), ST is the assumed destination.

FMULP: Multiply Real and POP

Applicable processors: 8087, 80287, 80387, 80486

Category: Arithmetic instruction

Status affected: DE, IE, OE, PE, UE

Coding examples:

```
FMULP       TEMP             ;ST=ST*TEMP
FMULP       TEMP,ST(3)       ;TEMP=TEMP*ST(3)
```

Description: FMULP multiplies the source by the destination operand, stores the result at the destination operand, and pops the stack. If no destination operand is given (only one operand is specified), ST is the assumed destination.

FNCLEX: Clear Exceptions

Applicable processors: 8087, 80287, 80387, 80486

Category: Flag- and processor-control instructions

Status affected: B, DE, IE, IR, OE, PE, UE, ZE

Coding example:

FNCLEX

Description: FNCLEX clears the exception flags, interrupt request, and busy flags of the NPX/FPU status word. This instruction is not preceded by a CPU wait prefix. See also FCLEX.

FNDISI: Disable Interrupts

Applicable processors: 8087

Category: Flag- and processor-control instructions

Status affected: None

Coding example:

FNDISI

Description: FNDISI sets the interrupt-enable mask of the 8087 control word, thus preventing the 8087 from initiating an interrupt. This instruction is not preceded by a CPU wait prefix. See also FDISI.

FNENI: Enable Interrupts

Applicable processors: 8087

Category: Flag- and processor-control instructions

Status affected: None

Coding example:

FNENI

Description: FNENI clears the interrupt-enable mask of the 8087 control word so that the 8087 can initiate interrupts. This instruction is not preceded by a CPU wait prefix. See also FENI.

FNINIT: Initialize Processor

Applicable processors: 8087, 80287, 80387, 80486

Category: Flag- and processor-control instructions

Status affected: None

Coding example:

```
FNINIT
```

Description: FNINIT initializes the NPX/FPU. This action is functionally equivalent to performing a hardware RESET. This instruction is not preceded by a CPU wait prefix. See also FINIT.

FNOP: No Operation

Applicable processors: 8087, 80287, 80387, 80486

Category: Flag- and processor-control instructions

Status affected: None

Coding example:

```
FNOP
```

Description: FNOP does nothing but take time and space; the NPX/FPU performs no operation.

FNSAVE: Save State

Applicable processors: 8087, 80287, 80387, 80486

Category: Flag- and processor-control instructions

Status affected: None

Coding example:

```
FNSAVE    SAVE_AREA
```

Description: FNSAVE saves, at the memory location specified by the operand, all registers and environment variables of the NPX/FPU. This save requires 94 words of memory. After the save, the NPX/FPU is initialized as though the FINIT or FNINIT instructions had been issued. This instruction (FNSAVE) is not preceded by a CPU wait prefix. See also FSAVE.

FNSTCW: Store Control Word

Applicable processors: 8087, 80287, 80387, 80486

Category: Flag- and processor-control instructions

Status affected: None

Coding example:

```
FNSTCW    MEM_CW    ;Transfer control word
```

Description: FNSTCW copies the NPX/FPU control word to the word value pointed to by the source operand. This instruction is not preceded by a CPU wait prefix. See also FSTCW.

FNSTENV: Store Environment

Applicable processors: 8087, 80287, 80387, 80486

Category: Flag- and processor-control instructions

Status affected: None

Coding example:

```
FNSTENV    SAVE_AREA
```

Description: FNSTENV saves, at the memory location specified by the operand, all environment variables of the NPX/FPU. This save requires 14 words of memory. After the save, this instruction sets the exception masks of the NPX/FPU control word. This instruction is not preceded by a CPU wait prefix. See also FSTENV.

FNSTSW: Store Status Word

Applicable processors: 8087, 80287, 80387, 80486

Category: Flag- and processor-control instructions

Status affected: None

Coding example:

```
FNSTSW    MEM_SW    ;Transfer status word
```

Description: FNSTSW copies the NPX/FPU status word to the word value pointed to by the source operand. This instruction is not preceded by a CPU wait prefix. See also FSTSW.

FPATAN: Partial Arctangent

Applicable processors: 8087, 80287, 80387, 80486

Category: Transcendental instruction

Status affected: PE, UE

Coding example:

FPATAN

Description: FPATAN computes θARCTAN(Y/X), where X is the top stack element (ST), and Y is the second stack element (ST(1)). Both stack elements are popped; the result (0) is pushed on the stack and becomes ST. This instruction performs no validation checking of the input value. The program ensures that $0<Y<X<\infty$.

FPREM: Partial Remainder

Applicable processors: 8087, 80287, 80387, 80486

Category: Arithmetic instruction

Status affected: C0, C1, C3, DE, IE, UE

Coding example:

FPREM

Description: FPREM calculates the modulo of the two top stack elements. By successively subtracting ST(1) from ST, this instruction calculates an exact remainder and remains in ST.

FPREM1: Partial Remainder, IEEE version

Applicable processors: 80387, 80486

Category: Arithmetic instruction

Status affected: C0, C1, C2, C3, DE, IE, UE

Coding example:

FPREM1

Description: FPREM1 calculates the modulo of the two top stack elements. Formula used is $ST = ST - (ST(1) * quotient)$, where *quotient* is the integer nearest the exact value ST/ST(1). If two integers are equally close, the even one is used. This formula is the only difference between FPREM1 and FPREM.

FPTAN: Partial Tangent

Applicable processors: 8087, 80287, 80387, 80486

Category: Transcendental instruction

Status affected: IE, PE

Coding example:

FPTAN

Description: FPTAN computes $Y/X = TAN(\theta)$, where θ is the top stack element (ST). The top stack element is replaced by the computed Y, and the computed X is pushed on the stack. Thus, at the end of this operation, $ST(1) = Y$ and $ST = X$. This instruction performs no validation checking of the input value. The program ensures that $0 <= \theta <= \pi 4$.

FRNDINT: Round to Integer

Applicable processors: 8087, 80287, 80387, 80486

Category: Arithmetic instruction

Status affected: IE, PE

Coding example:

FRNDINT

Description: FRNDINT rounds the number in the top stack element (ST) to an integer.

FRSTOR: Restore State

Applicable processors: 8087, 80287, 80387, 80486

Category: Flag- and processor-control instructions

Status affected: B, C0, C1, C2, C3, DE, ES, IE, IR, OE, PE, SF, ST, UE, ZE

Coding example:

FRSTOR   SAVE_AREA

Description: FRSTOR restores all registers and environment variables of the NPX/FPU from the 94-word memory location specified by the operand.

FSAVE: Save State with WAIT

Applicable processors: 8087, 80287, 80387, 80486

Category: Flag- and processor-control instructions

Status affected: None

Coding example:

FSAVE   SAVE_AREA

Description: FSAVE saves, at the memory location specified by the operand, all registers and environment variables of the NPX/FPU. This save requires 94 words of memory. After the save, the NPX/FPU is initialized as though the FINIT or FNINIT instructions had been issued. This instruction (FSAVE) is preceded by a CPU wait prefix. See also FNSAVE.

FSCALE: Scale

Applicable processors: 8087, 80287, 80387, 80486

Category: Arithmetic instruction

Status affected: IE, OE, UE

Coding example:

```
FSCALE
```

Description: FSCALE calculates X=X*2Y, where X is the value of the top stack element (ST), and Y is the value of the second stack element (ST(1)).

FSETPM: Set Protected Mode

Applicable processors: 80287

Category: Flag- and processor-control instructions

Status affected: None

Coding example:

```
FSETPM
```

Description: FSETPM causes the 80287 to operate in protected mode. Ordinarily, operation mode is of no concern to programmers of applications software created in real mode.

FSIN: Sine

Applicable processors: 80387, 80486

Category: Transcendental instruction

Status affected: DE, IE, PE, UE

Coding example:

```
FSIN    ;Replace value in radians with sine
```

Description: The top stack element (ST) is replaced with its sine, considering the element to be an angle in radians. Condition codes are affected accordingly.

FSINCOS: Sine and Cosine

Applicable processors: 80387, 80486

Category: Transcendental instruction

Status affected: DE, IE, PE, UE

Coding example:

```
FSINCOS    ;Replace value in radians with sine and cosine
```

Description: The top stack element (ST) is replaced with its sine, considering the element to be an angle in radians, and then the cosine is calculated and pushed onto the stack. Condition codes are affected accordingly.

FSQRT: Square Root

Applicable processors: 8087, 80287, 80387, 80486

Category: Arithmetic instruction

Status affected: DE, IE, PE

Coding example:

```
FSQRT
```

Description: FSQRT calculates the square root of the top stack element (ST) and stores it as the new ST. The old ST is lost.

FST: Store Real

Applicable processors: 8087, 80287, 80387, 80486

Category: Data-transfer instruction

Status affected: IE, OE, PE, UE

Coding examples:

```
FST        ST(3)
FST        TEMP
```

Description: FST copies the value of the top stack element (ST) to the operand or operand address.

FSTCW: Store Control Word with WAIT

Applicable processors: 8087, 80287, 80387, 80486

Category: Flag- and processor-control instructions

Status affected: None

Coding example:

```
FSTCW    MEM_CW    ;Transfer control word
```

Description: FSTCW copies the NPX/FPU control word to the word value pointed to by the source operand. A CPU wait prefix precedes this instruction. See also FNSTCW.

FSTENV: Store Environment with WAIT

Applicable processors: 8087, 80287, 80387, 80486

Category: Flag- and processor-control instructions

Status affected: None

Coding example:

```
FSTENV    SAVE_AREA
```

Description: FSTENV saves, at the memory location specified by the operand, all environment variables of the NPX/FPU. This save requires 14 words of memory. After the save, this instruction sets the exception masks of the NPX/FPU control word. A CPU wait prefix precedes this instruction. See also FNSTENV.

FSTP: Store Real and POP

Applicable processors: 8087, 80287, 80387, 80486

Category: Data-transfer instruction

Status affected: IE, OE, PE, UE

Coding examples:

```
FSTP    ST(3)
FSTP    TEMP
```

Description: FSTP copies the value of the top stack element (ST) to the operand or operand address and pops the stack.

FSTSW: Store Status Word with WAIT

Applicable processors: 8087, 80287, 80387, 80486

Category: Flag- and processor-control instructions

Status affected: None

Coding example:

```
FSTSW     MEM_SW     ;Transfer status word
```

Description: FSTSW copies the NPX/FPU status word to the word value pointed to by the source operand. A CPU wait prefix precedes this instruction. See also FNSTSW.

FSUB: Subtract Real

Applicable processors: 8087, 80287, 80387, 80486

Category: Arithmetic instruction

Status affected: DE, IE, OE, PE, UE

Coding examples:

```
FSUB      TEMP           ;ST=ST-TEMP
FSUB      TEMP,ST(3)     ;TEMP=TEMP-ST(3)
```

Description: FSUB subtracts the source from the destination operand, and stores the result at the destination operand. If no destination operand is given (only one operand is specified), ST is the assumed destination.

FSUBP: Subtract Real and POP

Applicable processors: 8087, 80287, 80387, 80486

Category: Arithmetic instruction

Status affected: DE, IE, OE, PE, UE

Coding examples:

```
FSUBP     TEMP           ;ST=ST-TEMP
FSUBP     TEMP,ST(3)     ;TEMP=TEMP-ST(3)
```

Description: FSUBP subtracts the source from the destination operand, stores the result at the destination operand, and pops the stack. If no destination operand is given (only one operand is specified), ST is the assumed destination.

FSUBR: Subtract Real Reversed

Applicable processors: 8087, 80287, 80387, 80486

Category: Arithmetic instruction

Status affected: DE, IE, OE, PE, UE

Coding examples:

```
FSUBR      TEMP              ;ST=TEMP-ST
FSUBR      TEMP,ST(3)        ;TEMP=ST(3)-TEMP
```

Description: FSUBR subtracts the destination from the source operand and stores the result at the destination operand. If no destination operand is given (only one operand is specified), ST is the assumed destination.

FSUBRP: Subtract Real Reversed and POP

Applicable processors: 8087, 80287, 80387, 80486

Category: Arithmetic instruction

Status affected: DE, IE, OE, PE, UE

Coding examples:

```
FSUBRP     TEMP              ;ST=TEMP-ST
FSUBRP     TEMP,ST(3)        ;TEMP=ST(3)-TEMP
```

Description: FSUBRP subtracts the destination from the source operand, stores the result at the destination operand, and pops the stack. If no destination operand is given (only one operand is specified), ST is the assumed destination.

FTST: Test

Applicable processors: 8087, 80287, 80387, 80486

Category: Comparison instruction

Status affected: C0, C2, C3, DE, IE

Coding example:

```
FTST
```

Description: FTST compares the top stack element (ST) to zero and sets the condition codes accordingly.

FUCOM: Unordered Compare

Applicable processors: 80387, 80486

Category: Comparison instruction

Status affected: C0, C2, C3, DE, IE

Coding example:

```
FUCOM              ;default comparison
FUCOM     ST(2)    ;compare top and ST(2)
```

Description: FUCOM compares the specified source with the top stack element (ST). If no operand is specified, FUCOM compares ST and ST(1). This instruction differs from FCOM in that FUCOM does not cause an invalid operation exception if one of the operands is a NaN. Condition codes are affected accordingly.

FUCOMP: Unordered Compare and POP

Applicable processors: 80387, 80486

Category: Comparison instruction

Status affected: C0, C2, C3, DE, IE

Coding example:

```
FUCOMP             ;default comparison
FUCOMP    ST(2)    ;compare top and ST(2)
```

Description: FUCOMP compares the specified source with the top stack element (ST). If no operand is specified, FUCOMP compares ST and ST(1). This instruction differs from FCOM in that FUCOMP does not cause an invalid operation exception if one of the operands is a NaN. Condition codes are affected accordingly. The stack is then popped one time.

FUCOMPP: Unordered Compare and POP Twice

Applicable processors: 80387, 80486

Category: Comparison instruction

Status affected: C0, C2, C3, DE, IE

Coding example:

```
FUCOMPP     ;compare ST and ST(1)
```

Description: FUCOMPP compares the specified source with the top stack element (ST). If no operand is specified, FUCOMPP compares ST and ST(1). This instruction differs from FCOM in that FUCOMPP does not cause an invalid operation exception if one of the operands is a NaN. Condition codes are affected accordingly. The stack is then popped twice.

FWAIT: CPU Wait

Applicable processors: 8087, 80287, 80387, 80486

Category: Flag- and processor-control instructions

Status affected: None

Coding example:

```
FWAIT
```

Description: FWAIT is effectively the same as the WAIT command. This instruction enables the synchronization of the microprocessor and the NPX/FPU. FWAIT causes the microprocessor to suspend operation until it receives a signal indicating that the NPX/FPU has completed the last operation.

FXAM: Examine

Applicable processors: 8087, 80287, 80387, 80486

Category: Comparison instruction

Status affected: C0, C1, C2, C3

Coding example:

```
FXAM
```

Description: FXAM examines the top stack element (ST) and reports (in the condition codes) the condition, or attributes, of the value.

FXCH: Exchange Registers

Applicable processors: 8087, 80287, 80387, 80486

Category: Data-transfer instruction

Status affected: IE

Coding examples:

```
FXCH      ST(3)
FXCH      TEMP
```

Description: FXCH switches the value of the top stack element (ST) with the value of the operand.

FXTRACT: Extract Exponent and Significand

Applicable processors: 8087, 80287, 80387, 80486

Category: Arithmetic instruction

Status affected: IE

Coding example:

```
FXTRACT
```

Description: FXTRACT removes the top stack element (ST) and converts it to two numbers: the exponent and significand of the original number. The exponent is pushed on the stack, followed by the significand, which results in ST=significand and ST(1)=exponent.

FYL2X: Y*$\log_2$X

Applicable processors: 8087, 80287, 80387, 80486

Category: Transcendental instruction

Status affected: PE

Coding example:

FYL2X

Description: FYL2X calculates $Z=Y*LOG_2 X$, where X is the top stack element (ST), and Y is the second stack element (ST(1)). Both stack elements are popped, and the result (Z) is pushed on the stack and becomes the new ST. This instruction performs no validation checking of the input value. The program ensures that $0<X<\infty$ and $-\infty<Y<+\infty$.

FYL2XP1: $Y*log_2(X+1)$

Applicable processors: 8087, 80287, 80387, 80486

Category: Transcendental instruction

Status affected: PE

Coding example:

FYL2XP1

Description: FYL2XP1 calculates $Z=Y*LOG_2(X=1)$, where X is the top stack element (ST), and Y is the second stack element (ST(1)). Both stack elements are popped, and the result (Z) is pushed on the stack and becomes the new ST. This instruction performs no validation checking of the input value. The program ensures that $0<|X|<(1-(\sqrt{2}/2))$ and $-\infty<Y<+\infty$.

HLT: Halt

Applicable processors: 8086/8088, 80286, 80386, 80486

Category: Flag- and processor-control instructions

Flags affected: None

Coding example:

HLT

Description: HLT causes the microprocessor to stop execution and leaves the CS:IP registers pointing to the instruction following the HLT. This halt condition is terminated only after the system receives an interrupt or after the RESET line is activated.

IDIV: Integer Divide

Applicable processors: 8086/8088, 80286, 80386, 80486

Category: Arithmetic instructions

Flags affected: AF (undefined), CF (undefined), OF (undefined), PF (undefined), SF (undefined), ZF (undefined)

Coding examples:

```
IDIV       BX                ;AX=DX:AX/BX
IDIV       WORD_TEMP         ;AX=DX:AX/WORD_TEMP
IDIV       BYTE_SUM          ;AL=AX/BYTE_SUM
IDIV       DWORD_SUM         ;EAX=EDX:EAX/DWORD_SUM
IDIV       WORD_TBL[BX]      ;Indirect address example
```

Description: If the operand is a byte value, IDIV divides the contents of AX by the contents of the operand and stores the result in AL and the remainder in AH. If the operand is a word value, IDIV divides the contents of DX:AX by the contents of the operand and stores the result in AX and the remainder in DX.

On the 80386 and 80486, if the operand is a doubleword value, IDIV divides the contents of EDX:EAX by the contents of the operand, and stores the result in EAX and the remainder in EDX.

This instruction treats numbers as signed binary values.

IMUL: Integer Multiply

Applicable processors: 8086/8088, 80286, 80386, 80486

Category: Arithmetic instructions

Flags affected: AF (undefined), CF, OF, PF (undefined), SF (undefined), ZF (undefined)

Coding examples:

```
IMUL       BX                ;DX:AX=AX*BX
IMUL       WORD_TEMP         ;DX:AX=AX*WORD_TEMP
IMUL       BYTE_SUM          ;AX=AL*BYTE_SUM
IMUL       WORD_TBL[BX]      ;Indirect address example
IMUL       ECX,DWORD_TEMP,10 ;ECX=DWORD_TEMP*10
```

Description: The results of this operation depend on the number of operands specified. Processors other than the 80386 and 80486 require exactly one operand for this instruction.

If only one operand is given, it is multiplied by AL, AX, or EAX. If the operand is a byte value, IMUL multiplies the contents of AL by the contents of the operand and stores the result in AX. If the operand is a word value, IMUL multiplies the contents of AX by the contents of the operand and stores the result in DX:AX.

If two operands are given, IMUL multiplies the first operand by the second one and stores the result in the first operand. Both operands must be of equal size.

If three operands are given and the third operand is an immediate value, IMUL multiplies the second operand by the third one and stores the result in the first operand.

This instruction treats numbers as signed binary values.

IN: Input from Port

Applicable processors: 8086/8088, 80286, 80386, 80486

Category: Data-transfer instructions

Flags affected: None

Coding examples:

```
IN      AL,64h
IN      AX,DX
IN      EAX,DX
```

Description: IN loads a byte, word, or doubleword to AL, AX, or EAX, respectively, from the specified hardware I/O port address. A port number less than 256 may be specified as a constant or as a variable in the DX register. A port number greater than 255, however, *must* be specified in the DX register.

INC: Increment

Applicable processors: 8086/8088, 80286, 80386, 80486

Category: Arithmetic instructions

Flags affected: AF, OF, PF, SF, ZF

Coding examples:

```
INC     AX
INC     SUM
INC     CL
INC     EDI
INC     TEMP[SI]
```

Description: INC changes, by increments of 1, the contents of the operand. The operand is assumed to be an unsigned binary value.

INS: Input String from Port

Applicable processors: 80286, 80386, 80486

Category: Data-transfer instructions

Flags affected: None

Coding examples:

```
INS     CX,DX      ;Load word
INS     BL,DX      ;Load byte
INS     EAX,DX     ;Load doubleword
```

Description: INS loads a byte, word, or doubleword from the specified hardware I/O port address (indicated by the value in DX) to the destination operand. The size of the destination operand determines whether a byte, word, or doubleword is transferred. If the destination operand is an offset address, that address is relative to the ES register. No segment override is possible.

INSB: Input String Byte from Port

Applicable processors: 80286, 80386, 80486

Category: Data-transfer instructions

Flags affected: None

Coding example:

```
INSB
```

Description: Upon receiving a byte from the hardware I/O port address specified in DX, INSB loads that byte to the address specified by ES:[DI]. The port number can range from 0 to 65,535. After the transfer, DI changes in an increment or decrement of 1, depending on the setting of the direction flag.

INSD: Input String Doubleword from Port

Applicable processors: 80386, 80486

Category: Data-transfer instructions

Flags affected: None

Coding example:

```
INSD
```

Description: INSD loads a doubleword from the hardware I/O port address specified in DX to the address specified by ES:[EDI]. After the transfer, EDI changes in increments or decrements of four, depending on the setting of the direction flag.

INSW: Input String Word from Port

Applicable processors: 80286, 80386, 80486

Category: Data-transfer instructions

Flags affected: None

Coding example:

```
INSW
```

Description: INSW loads a word from the hardware I/O port address specified in DX to the address specified by ES:[DI]. The port number can range from 0 to 65,535. After the transfer, DI changes in increments or decrements of two, depending on the setting of the direction flag.

INT: Software Interrupt

Applicable processors: 8086/8088, 80286, 80386, 80486

Category: Control-transfer instructions

Flags affected: IF, TF

Coding examples:

```
INT         10h
INT         13h
```

Description: INT initiates a software interrupt of the CPU, and starts the following functions:

- ❏ Pushing the flags on the stack
- ❏ Clearing the TF and IF flags
- ❏ Pushing the value of CS on the stack
- ❏ Loading CS with the segment address of the interrupt being invoked (this segment address is found at the calculated address in the interrupt vector table)
- ❏ Pushing the value of IP on the stack
- ❏ Loading IP with the offset address of the interrupt being invoked (this offset address is found at the calculated address in the interrupt vector table)

Execution then continues at the newly loaded CS:IP address until an IRET instruction is encountered.

INTO: Interrupt on Overflow

Applicable processors: 8086/8088, 80286, 80386, 80486

Category: Control-transfer instructions

Flags affected: None

Coding example:

```
INTO
```

Description: If the overflow flag (OF) is set, INTO executes an interrupt 4 and control proceeds as though an INT 4 had been issued. Be aware that, in this case, the flags register is affected as described for the INT instruction.

INVD: Invalidate Data Cache

Applicable processors: 80486

Category: Processor-control instructions

Flags affected: None

Coding example:

```
INVD
```

Description: This instruction causes the information in the on-chip cache to be flushed. It also causes a special-function bus cycle to be issued, which can be used as an indicator to external caches (those on the 80486) to flush as well.

INVLPG: Invalidate TLB Entry If Present

Applicable processors: 80486

Category: Processor-control instructions

Flags affected: None

Coding example:

```
INVLPG          TLB_LOC
```

Description: This instruction is used to invalidate an entry in the cache used for table entries (the TLB). If the address of the operand is a valid entry in the TLB (one that has not previously been invalidated), it is marked as invalid.

IRET: Return from Interrupt

Applicable processors: 8086/8088, 80286, 80386, 80486

Category: Control-transfer instructions

Flags affected: AC, AF, CF, DF, IF, IOPL, NT, OF, PF, RF, SF, TF, VM, ZF

Coding example:

```
IRET
```

Description: IRET terminates an interrupt procedure and, by popping the values of IP, CS, and the flags register from the stack, returns control to the point at which the interrupt occurred.

JA: Jump If Above

Applicable processors: 8086/8088, 80286, 80386, 80486

Category: Control-transfer instructions

Flags affected: None

Coding example:

```
JA   NEXT_STEP
```

Description: JA causes program execution to branch to the operand address if the carry and zero flags are both clear. This instruction is functionally the same as JNBE.

JAE: Jump If Above or Equal

Applicable processors: 8086/8088, 80286, 80386, 80486

Category: Control-transfer instructions

Flags affected: None

Coding example:

```
JAE  NEXT_STEP
```

Description: JAE causes program execution to branch to the operand address if the carry flag is clear. This instruction is functionally the same as JNB or JNC.

JB: Jump If Below

Applicable processors: 8086/8088, 80286, 80386, 80486

Category: Control-transfer instructions

Flags affected: None

Coding example:

```
JB   NEXT_STEP
```

Description: JB causes program execution to branch to the operand address if the carry flag is set. This instruction is functionally the same as JC or JNAE.

JBE: Jump If Below or Equal

Applicable processors: 8086/8088, 80286, 80386, 80486

Category: Control-transfer instructions

Flags affected: None

Coding example:

```
JBE   NEXT_STEP
```

Description: JBE causes program execution to branch to the operand address if either the carry or zero flag is set. This instruction is functionally the same as JNA.

JC: Jump on Carry

Applicable processors: 8086/8088, 80286, 80386, 80486

Category: Control-transfer instructions

Flags affected: None

Coding example:

```
JC    NEXT_STEP
```

Description: JC causes program execution to branch to the operand address if the carry flag is set. This instruction is functionally the same as JB or JNAE.

JCXZ: Jump If CX=0

Applicable processors: 8086/8088, 80286, 80386, 80486

Category: Control-transfer instructions

Flags affected: None

Coding example:

```
JCXZ     SKIP_LOOP
```

Description: JCXZ causes program execution to branch to the operand address if the value of CX is 0.

JE: Jump If Equal

Applicable processors: 8086/8088, 80286, 80386, 80486

Category: Control-transfer instructions

Flags affected: None

Coding example:

```
JE    NEXT_STEP
```

Description: JE causes program execution to branch to the operand address if the zero flag is set. This instruction is functionally the same as JZ.

JECXZ: Jump If ECX=0

Applicable processors: 80386, 80486

Category: Control-transfer instructions

Flags affected: None

Coding example:

```
JECXZ    SKIP_LOOP
```

Description: JECXZ causes program execution to branch to the operand address if the value of ECX is 0. Although functionally the same as JCXZ, JECXZ works with the 32-bit ECX register.

JG: Jump If Greater

Applicable processors: 8086/8088, 80286, 80386, 80486

Category: Control-transfer instructions

Flags affected: None

Coding example:

```
JG    NEXT_STEP
```

Description: JG causes program execution to branch to the operand address if the sign flag equals the overflow flag or if the zero flag is clear. This instruction is functionally the same as JNLE.

JGE: Jump If Greater or Equal

Applicable processors: 8086/8088, 80286, 80386, 80486

Category: Control-transfer instructions

Flags affected: None

Coding example:

```
JGE      NEXT_STEP
```

Description: JGE causes program execution to branch to the operand address if the sign flag equals the overflow flag. This instruction is functionally the same as JNL.

JL: Jump If Less

Applicable processors: 8086/8088, 80286, 80386, 80486

Category: Control-transfer instructions

Flags affected: None

Coding example:

```
JL   NEXT_STEP
```

Description: JL causes program execution to branch to the operand address if the sign flag does not equal the overflow flag. This instruction is functionally the same as JNGE.

JLE: Jump If Less or Equal

Applicable processors: 8086/8088, 80286, 80386, 80486

Category: Control-transfer instructions

Flags affected: None

Coding example:

```
JLE      NEXT_STEP
```

Description: JLE causes program execution to branch to the operand address if the sign flag does not equal the overflow flag or if the zero flag is set. This instruction is functionally the same as JNG.

JMP: Jump

Applicable processors: 8086/8088, 80286, 80386, 80486

Category: Control-transfer instructions

Flags affected: None

Coding examples:

```
JMP       EXIT_CODE
JMP       [BX]            ;Jump to address at [BX]
JMP       AX              ;Jump to address in AX
```

Description: JMP initiates program execution at the designated operand address, affecting the CS and IP registers as necessary to cause this unconditional branch.

JNA: Jump If Not Above

Applicable processors: 8086/8088, 80286, 80386, 80486

Category: Control-transfer instructions

Flags affected: None

Coding example:

```
JNA       NEXT_STEP
```

Description: JNA causes program execution to branch to the operand address if either the carry or zero flag is set. This instruction is functionally the same as JBE.

JNAE: Jump If Not Above or Equal

Applicable processors: 8086/8088, 80286, 80386, 80486

Category: Control-transfer instructions

Flags affected: None

Coding example:

```
JNAE      NEXT_STEP
```

Description: JNAE causes program execution to branch to the operand address if the carry flag is set. This instruction is functionally the same as JB or JC.

JNB: Jump If Not Below

Applicable processors: 8086/8088, 80286, 80386, 80486

Category: Control-transfer instructions

Flags affected: None

Coding example:

```
JNB       NEXT_STEP
```

Description: JNB causes program execution to branch to the operand address if the carry flag is clear. This instruction is functionally the same as JAE or JNC.

JNBE: Jump If Not Below or Equal

Applicable processors: 8086/8088, 80286, 80386, 80486

Category: Control-transfer instructions

Flags affected: None

Coding example:

```
JNBE      NEXT_STEP
```

Description: JNBE causes program execution to branch to the operand address if both the carry and zero flags are clear. This instruction is functionally the same as JA.

JNC: Jump on No Carry

Applicable processors: 8086/8088, 80286, 80386, 80486

Category: Control-transfer instructions

Flags affected: None

Coding example:

```
JNC       NEXT_STEP
```

Description: JNC causes program execution to branch to the operand address if the carry flag is clear. This instruction is functionally the same as JAE or JNB.

JNE: Jump If Not Equal

Applicable processors: 8086/8088, 80286, 80386, 80486

Category: Control-transfer instructions

Flags affected: None

Coding example:

```
JNE       NEXT_STEP
```

Description: JNE causes program execution to branch to the operand address if the zero flag is clear. This instruction is functionally the same as JNZ.

JNG: Jump If Not Greater

Applicable processors: 8086/8088, 80286, 80386, 80486

Category: Control-transfer instructions

Flags affected: None

Coding example:

```
JNG       NEXT_STEP
```

Description: JNG causes program execution to branch to the operand address if the sign flag does not equal the overflow flag or if the zero flag is set. This instruction is functionally the same as JLE.

JNGE: Jump If Not Greater or Equal

Applicable processors: 8086/8088, 80286, 80386, 80486

Category: Control-transfer instructions

Flags affected: None

Coding example:

```
JNGE      NEXT_STEP
```

Description: JNGE causes program execution to branch to the operand address if the sign flag does not equal the overflow flag. This instruction is functionally the same as JL.

JNL: Jump If Not Less

Applicable processors: 8086/8088, 80286, 80386, 80486

Category: Control-transfer instructions

Flags affected: None

Coding example:

```
JNL       NEXT_STEP
```

Description: JNL causes program execution to branch to the operand address if the sign flag equals the overflow flag. This instruction is functionally the same as JGE.

JNLE: Jump If Not Less or Equal

Applicable processors: 8086/8088, 80286, 80386, 80486

Category: Control-transfer instructions

Flags affected: None

Coding example:

```
JNLE      NEXT_STEP
```

Description: JNLE causes program execution to branch to the operand address if the sign flag equals the overflow flag or the zero flag is clear. This instruction is functionally the same as JG.

JNO: Jump on No Overflow

Applicable processors: 8086/8088, 80286, 80386, 80486

Category: Control-transfer instructions

Flags affected: None

Coding example:

```
JNO       NEXT_STEP
```

Description: JNO causes program execution to branch to the operand address if the overflow flag is clear.

JNP: Jump on No Parity

Applicable processors: 8086/8088, 80286, 80386, 80486

Category: Control-transfer instructions

Flags affected: None

Coding example:

```
JNP      NEXT_STEP
```

Description: JNP causes program execution to branch to the operand address if the parity flag is clear. This instruction is functionally the same as JPO.

JNS: Jump on Not Sign

Applicable processors: 8086/8088, 80286, 80386, 80486

Category: Control-transfer instructions

Flags affected: None

Coding example:

```
JNS      NEXT_STEP
```

Description: JNS causes program execution to branch to the operand address if the sign flag is clear.

JNZ: Jump on Not Zero

Applicable processors: 8086/8088, 80286, 80386, 80486

Category: Control-transfer instructions

Flags affected: None

Coding example:

```
JNZ      NEXT_STEP
```

Description: JNZ causes program execution to branch to the operand address if the zero flag is clear. This instruction is functionally the same as JNE.

JO: Jump on Overflow

Applicable processors: 8086/8088, 80286, 80386, 80486

Category: Control-transfer instructions

Flags affected: None

Coding example:

```
JO   NEXT_STEP
```

Description: JO causes program execution to branch to the operand address if the overflow flag is set.

JP: Jump on Parity

Applicable processors: 8086/8088, 80286, 80386, 80486

Category: Control-transfer instructions

Flags affected: None

Coding example:

```
JP   NEXT_STEP
```

Description: JP causes program execution to branch to the operand address if the parity flag is set. This instruction is functionally the same as JPE.

JPE: Jump on Parity Even

Applicable processors: 8086/8088, 80286, 80386, 80486

Category: Control-transfer instructions

Flags affected: None

Coding example:

```
JPE        NEXT_STEP
```

Description: JPE causes program execution to branch to the operand address if the parity flag is set. This instruction is functionally the same as JP.

JPO: Jump on Parity Odd

Applicable processors: 8086/8088, 80286, 80386, 80486

Category: Control-transfer instructions

Flags affected: None

Coding example:

```
JPO      NEXT_STEP
```

Description: JPO causes program execution to branch to the operand address if the parity flag is clear. This instruction is functionally the same as JNP.

JS: Jump on Sign

Applicable processors: 8086/8088, 80286, 80386, 80486

Category: Control-transfer instructions

Flags affected: None

Coding example:

```
JS    NEXT_STEP
```

Description: JS causes program execution to branch to the operand address if the sign flag is set.

JZ: Jump on Zero

Applicable processors: 8086/8088, 80286, 80386, 80486

Category: Control-transfer instructions

Flags affected: None

Coding example:

```
JZ    NEXT_STEP
```

Description: JZ causes program execution to branch to the operand address if the zero flag is set. This instruction is functionally the same as JE.

LAHF: Load AH Register with Flags

Applicable processors: 8086/8088, 80286, 80386, 80486

Category: Data-transfer instructions

Flags affected: None

Coding example:

```
LAHF
```

Description: LAHF copies the low-order byte of the flags register to AH. After execution of this instruction, bits 7, 6, 4, 2, and 1 of AH are equal to SF, ZF, AF, PF, and CF, respectively.

LAR: Load Access-Rights Byte

Applicable processors: 80286, 80386, 80486

Category: Data-transfer instructions

Flags affected: ZF

Coding example:

```
LAR        AX,SELECT
```

Description: Based on the selection in the second operand, the high byte of the destination register is overwritten by the value of the access-rights byte, and the low byte is zeroed. The loading is done only if the descriptor is visible at the current privilege level and at the selector RPL. The zero flag is set if the loading operation is successful.

LDS: Load DS Register

Applicable processors: 8086/8088, 80286, 80386, 80486

Category: Data-transfer instructions

Flags affected: None

Coding example:

```
LDS        SI,SOURCE_BUFFER
```

Description: LDS performs two distinct operations: it loads DS with the segment address of the source operand and loads the destination operand with the offset address of the source operand.

LEA: Load Effective Address

Applicable processors: 8086/8088, 80286, 80386, 80486

Category: Data-transfer instructions

Flags affected: None

Coding example:

```
LEA        AX,MESSAGE_1
```

Description: LEA transfers the offset address of the source operand to the destination operand. The destination operand must be a general word register.

LEAVE: High-Level Procedure Exit

Applicable processors: 80286, 80386, 80486

Category: Flag- and processor-control instructions

Flags affected: None

Coding example:

```
LEAVE
```

Description: LEAVE undoes the changes performed by the ENTER instruction. This instruction is used for exiting high-level-language subroutines.

LES: Load ES Register

Applicable processors: 8086/8088, 80286, 80386, 80486

Category: Data-transfer instructions

Flags affected: None

Coding example:

```
LES      DI,DEST_BUFFER
```

Description: LES performs two distinct operations: it loads ES with the segment address of the source operand and loads the destination operand with the offset address of the source operand.

LFS: Load FS Register

Applicable processors: 80386, 80486

Category: Data-transfer instructions

Flags affected: None

Coding example:

```
LFS      DI,DEST_BUFFER
```

Description: LFS performs two distinct operations: it loads FS with the segment address of the source operand and then loads the destination operand with the offset address of the source operand.

LGDT: Load GDT Register

Applicable processors: 80286, 80386, 80486

Category: Data-transfer instructions

Flags affected: None

Coding example:

```
LGDT     TEMP[BX]
```

Description: LGDT loads the six bytes associated with the global descriptor table (GDT) from the memory address specified in the operand. This instruction is for use in protected-mode operating system software; it is not used in applications software.

LGS: Load GS Register

Applicable processors: 80386, 80486

Category: Data-transfer instructions

Flags affected: None

Coding example:

```
LGS     DI,DEST_BUFFER
```

Description: LGS performs two distinct operations: it loads GS with the segment address of the source operand and then loads the destination operand with the offset address of the source operand.

LIDT: Load IDT Register

Applicable processors: 80286, 80386, 80486

Category: Data-transfer instructions

Flags affected: None

Coding example:

```
LIDT    TEMP[BX]
```

Description: LIDT loads the six bytes associated with the interrupt descriptor table (IDT) from the memory address specified in the operand. This instruction is for use in protected-mode operating system software; it is not used in applications software.

LLDT: Load LDT Register

Applicable processors: 80286, 80386, 80486

Category: Data-transfer instructions

Flags affected: None

Coding example:

```
LLDT    AX
```

Description: Based on the selector specified in the operand, LLDT transfers the valid global descriptor table entry to the local descriptor table (LDT). This instruction is used in protected-mode operating system software but not used in applications software.

LMSW: Load Machine Status Word

Applicable processors: 80286, 80386, 80486

Category: Data-transfer instructions

Flags affected: None

Coding example:

```
LMSW    AX
```

Description: LMSW copies the value of the operand to the machine status word. This instruction is for use in operating system software only, not in applications software.

LOCK: Lock Bus

Applicable processors: 8086/8088, 80286, 80386, 80486

Category: Flag- and processor-control instructions

Flags affected: None

Coding example:

```
LOCK XLAT
```

Description: LOCK prohibits interference from any other coprocessors during the execution of the next instruction issued. LOCK is a prefix to be used with other operations.

LODSB: Load a Byte from String into AL

Applicable processors: 8086/8088, 80286, 80386, 80486

Category: String-manipulation instructions

Flags affected: None

Coding example:

```
LODSB
```

Description: LODSB loads AL with the contents of the address pointed to by SI. SI then changes in increments or decrements of 1, depending on the setting of the direction flag. Intel lists this command as LODS; however, the assembler distinguishes between byte (LODSB) and word (LODSW).

LODSD: Load a Doubleword from String into EAX

Applicable processors: 80386, 80486

Category: String-manipulation instructions

Flags affected: None

Coding example:

```
LODSD
```

Description: LODSD loads EAX with the contents of the address pointed to by ESI. ESI then changes in increments or decrements of four, depending on the setting of the direction flag.

LODSW: Load a Word from String into AX

Applicable processors: 8086/8088, 80286, 80386, 80486

Category: String-manipulation instructions

Flags affected: None

Coding example:

```
LODSW
```

Description: LODSW loads AX with the contents of the address pointed to by SI. SI then changes in increments or decrements of two, depending on the setting of the direction flag. Intel lists this command as LODS; however, the assembler distinguishes between byte (LODSB) and word (LODSW).

LOOP: Loop

Applicable processors: 8086/8088, 80286, 80386, 80486

Category: Control-transfer instructions

Flags affected: None

Coding example:

```
LOOP       PRINT_LOOP
```

Description: This instruction causes program execution to branch to the address of the destination operand, based on the contents of CX. If CX does not equal 0, CX changes in decrements of 1, and the branch occurs. If CX is 0, no decrements or branching occurs, and execution proceeds to the next instruction.

LOOPE: Loop While Equal

Applicable processors: 8086/8088, 80286, 80386, 80486

Category: Control-transfer instructions

Flags affected: None

Coding example:

```
LOOPE     TEST_LOOP
```

Description: Based on the contents of CX and the zero flag, program execution branches to the address of the destination operand. If CX does not equal 0 and the zero flag is set, CX changes in decrements of 1, and the branch occurs. If CX is 0 or the zero flag is clear, no decrements or branching occurs, and execution proceeds to the next instruction. This instruction is functionally equivalent to LOOPZ.

LOOPNE: Loop While Not Equal

Applicable processors: 8086/8088, 80286, 80386, 80486

Category: Control-transfer instructions

Flags affected: None

Coding example:

```
LOOPNE TEST_LOOP
```

Description: Based on the contents of CX and the zero flag, program execution branches to the address of the destination operand. If CX does not equal 0 and the zero flag is clear, CX changes in decrements of 1, and the branch occurs. If CX is 0 or the zero flag is set, no decrements or branching occurs, and execution proceeds to the next instruction. This instruction is functionally equivalent to LOOPNZ.

LOOPNZ: Loop While Not Zero

Applicable processors: 8086/8088, 80286, 80386, 80486

Category: Control-transfer instructions

Flags affected: None

Coding example:

```
LOOPNZ TEST_LOOP
```

Description: Based on the contents of CX and the zero flag, program execution branches to the address of the destination operand. If CX does not equal 0 and the zero flag is clear, CX changes in decrements of 1, and the branch occurs. If CX is 0 or the zero flag is set, no decrements or branching occurs, and execution proceeds to the next instruction. This instruction is functionally equivalent to LOOPNE.

LOOPZ: Loop While Zero

Applicable processors: 8086/8088, 80286, 80386, 80486

Category: Control-transfer instructions

Flags affected: None

Coding example:

```
LOOPZ   TEST_LOOP
```

Description: Based on the contents of CX and the zero flag, program execution branches to the address of the destination operand. If CX does not equal 0 and the zero flag is set, CX changes in decrements of 1, and the branch occurs. If CX is 0 or the zero flag is clear, no decrements or branching occur, and execution proceeds to the next instruction. This instruction is functionally equivalent to LOOPE.

LSL: Load Segment Limit

Applicable processors: 80286, 80386, 80486

Category: Data-transfer instructions

Flags affected: ZF

Coding example:

```
LSL     AX,SELECTOR
```

Description: Based on the selector specified in the source operand, LSL loads the descriptor's limit field into the target operand (register). The descriptor denoted by the selector must be visible. If the loading is successful, the zero flag is set; otherwise, it is cleared.

LSS: Load SS Register

Applicable processors: 80386, 80486

Category: Data-transfer instructions

Flags affected: None

Coding example:

```
LSS     DI,DEST_BUFFER
```

Description: LSS performs two distinct operations: it loads SS with the segment address of the source operand and then loads the destination operand with the offset address of the source operand.

LTR: Load Task Register

Applicable processors: 80286, 80386, 80486

Category: Data-transfer instructions

Flags affected: None

Coding examples:

```
LTR     DX
LTR     TEMP[BX]
```

Description: LTR loads the task register from the value of the source operand. This instruction is for use in operating system software only and is not used in applications software.

MOV: Move

Applicable processors: 8086/8088, 80286, 80386, 80486

Category: Data-transfer instructions

Flags affected: None

Coding examples:

```
MOV       AX,BX           ;AX=BX
MOV       EAX,TEMP        ;EAX=TEMP (doubleword)
MOV       SUM,BX          ;SUM=BX (SUM is a word)
MOV       CL,57           ;CL=57
MOV       DECIMAL,10      ;DECIMAL=10
MOV       AX,TEMP[BX]     ;Indirect address example
```

Description: MOV copies the contents of the source operand to the destination operand. When the source operand is not an immediate value, both operands must be of equal length. If the source or destination operand is a doubleword register, the other register can be a special register, such as CR0, CR2, CR3, DR0, DR1, DR2, DR3, DR6, DR7, TR6, or TR7.

MOVSB: Move String, Byte-by-Byte

Applicable processors: 8086/8088, 80286, 80386, 80486

Category: String-manipulation instructions

Flags affected: None

Coding examples:

```
MOVSB
REP MOVSB       ;Repeat a move loop
```

Description: MOVSB moves strings, byte-by-byte. The values of SI and DI change in increments or decrements of 1, depending on the setting of the direction flag. Usually, this instruction is used with the REP instruction to repeat the move for a maximum of CX bytes. Intel lists this command as MOVS; however, the assembler makes the byte/word distinctions.

MOVSD: Move String, Doubleword-by-Doubleword

Applicable processors: 80386, 80486

Category: String-manipulation instructions

Flags affected: None

Coding examples:

```
MOVSD
REP MOVSD       ;Repeat a move loop
```

Description: MOVSD moves strings, doubleword-by-doubleword. The values of ESI and EDI change in increments or decrements of four, depending on the setting of the direction flag. Usually, this instruction is used with the REP instruction to repeat the move for a maximum of ECX words.

MOVSW: Move String, Word-by-Word

Applicable processors: 8086/8088, 80286, 80386, 80486

Category: String-manipulation instructions

Flags affected: None

Coding examples:

```
MOVSW
REP MOVSW       ;Repeat a move loop
```

Description: MOVSW moves strings, word-by-word. The values of SI and DI change in increments or decrements of two, depending on the setting of the direction flag. Usually, this instruction is used with the REP instruction to repeat the move for a maximum number of CX words. Intel lists this command as MOVS; however, the assembler makes the byte/word distinctions.

MOVSX: Move with Sign Extended

Applicable processors: 80386, 80486

Category: Data-transfer instructions

Flags affected: None

Coding examples:

```
MOVSX    EAX,BX    ;EAX=BX
MOVSX    EAX,TEMP  ;EAX=TEMP (TEMP is a word)
MOVSX    CX,AL     ;CX=AL
```

Description: MOVSX moves the source operand to the destination operand and extends the high-order bit to the balance of the bits in the destination operand. The source operand must be smaller than the destination operand.

MOVZX: Move with Zero Extended

Applicable processors: 80386, 80486

Category: Data-transfer instructions

Flags affected: None

Coding examples:

```
MOVZX    EAX,BX    ;EAX=BX
MOVZX    EAX,TEMP  ;EAX=TEMP (TEMP is a word)
MOVZX    CX,AL     ;CX=AL
```

Description: MOVZX moves the source operand to the destination operand and clears the remaining bits in the destination operand. The source operand must be smaller than the destination operand.

MUL: Multiply

Applicable processors: 8086/8088, 80286, 80386, 80486

Category: Arithmetic instructions

Flags affected: AF (undefined), CF, OF, PF (undefined), SF (undefined), ZF (undefined)

Coding examples:

```
MUL    BX              ;DX:AX=AX*BX
MUL    ECX             ;EDX:EAX=EAX*ECX
MUL    WORD_TEMP       ;DX:AX=AX*WORD_TEMP
MUL    BYTE_SUM        ;AX=AL*BYTE_SUM
MUL    WORD_TBL[BX]    ;Indirect address example
```

Description: If the operand is a byte value, MUL multiplies the contents of AL by the contents of the operand and stores the result in AX. If the operand is a word value, MUL multiplies the contents of AX by the contents of the operand and stores the result in DX:AX. If the operand is a doubleword value, MUL multiplies the contents of EAX by the contents of the operand and stores the result in EDX:EAX. This instruction treats numbers as unsigned binary values.

NEG: Negate

Applicable processors: 8086/8088, 80286, 80386, 80486

Category: Arithmetic instructions

Flags affected: AF, CF, OF, PF, SF, ZF

Coding examples:

```
NEG      TEMP
NEG      CL
NEG      EAX
```

Description: NEG calculates the two's complement of the destination operand and stores the result in the destination operand. This calculation is effectively the same as subtracting the destination operand from zero.

NOP: No Operation

Applicable processors: 8086/8088, 80286, 80386, 80486

Category: Flag- and processor-control instructions

Flags affected: None

Coding example:

```
NOP
```

Description: NOP simply takes space and time. It causes the CPU to do nothing. The instruction is used primarily when patching executable files, to block out instructions already in place.

NOT: Logical NOT

Applicable processors: 8086/8088, 80286, 80386, 80486

Category: Bit-manipulation instructions

Flags affected: None

Coding examples:

```
NOT       CL
NOT       BYTE_SUM        ;Use byte value
NOT       WORD_SUM        ;Use word value
NOT       DWORD_SUM       ;Use doubleword value
NOT       AX
NOT       EBX
```

Description: NOT inverts the bits in the destination operand (0 becomes 1, and 1 becomes 0) and stores the inverted bits in the destination operand.

OR: Logical OR

Applicable processors: 8086/8088, 80286, 80386, 80486

Category: Bit-manipulation instructions

Flags affected: AF (undefined), CF, OF, PF, SF, ZF

Coding examples:

```
OR        AL,BL
OR        AL,10000000b
OR        EAX,0FFFFh
OR        DX,TEMP
OR        AX,CX
```

Description: OR performs a logical OR of the operands and stores the result in the destination operand. Each bit of the resultant byte or word is set to 1 if either or both of the corresponding bits of each operand are set to 1.

OUT: Output to Port

Applicable processors: 8086/8088, 80286, 80386, 80486

Category: Data-transfer instructions

Flags affected: None

Coding examples:

```
OUT     64h,AL
OUT     DX,AX
OUT     DX,EAX
```

Description: OUT sends a byte (AL), word (AX), or doubleword (EAX) to the specified hardware I/O port address. A port number lower than 256 may be specified as a constant or as a variable in the DX register. A port number higher than 255, however, *must* be specified in the DX register.

OUTS: Output String to Port

Applicable processors: 80286, 80386, 80486

Category: Data-transfer instructions

Flags affected: None

Coding examples:

```
OUTS    DX,CX       ;Output word
OUTS    DX,BL       ;Output byte
```

Description: OUTS sends a byte or a word (length is specified by the size of the source operand) to the hardware I/O port address specified in DX. The port number can range from 0 to 65,535.

OUTSB: Output String Byte to Port

Applicable processors: 80286, 80386, 80486

Category: Data-transfer instructions

Flags affected: None

Coding example:

```
OUTSB
```

Description: OUTSB sends a byte from the address specified by DS:[SI] to the hardware I/O port address specified in DX. The port number can range from 0 to 65,535. After the transfer, DI changes in an increment or decrement of 1, depending on the setting of the direction flag.

OUTSD: Output String Doubleword to Port

Applicable processors: 80386, 80486

Category: Data-transfer instructions

Flags affected: None

Coding example:

```
OUTSD
```

Description: OUTSD sends a word from the address specified by DS:[ESI] to the hardware I/O port address specified in DX. After the transfer, DI changes in increments or decrements of four, depending on the setting of the direction flag.

OUTSW: Output String Word to Port

Applicable processors: 80286, 80386, 80486

Category: Data-transfer instructions

Flags affected: None

Coding example:

```
OUTSW
```

Description: OUTSW sends a word from the address specified by DS:[SI] to the hardware I/O port address specified in DX. The port number can range from 0 to 65,535. After the transfer, DI changes in increments or decrements of two, depending on the setting of the direction flag.

POP: Remove Data from Stack

Applicable processors: 8086/8088, 80286, 80386, 80486

Category: Data-transfer instructions

Flags affected: None

Coding examples:

```
POP        AX
POP        DS
POP        GS
POP        HOLD_REG
```

Description: POP removes from the stack a word or a doubleword (depending on the size of the operand) and places that word or doubleword in the desired destination operand.

POPA: POP All General Registers

Applicable processors: 80286, 80386, 80486

Category: Data-transfer instructions

Flags affected: None

Coding example:

```
POPA
```

Description: POPA removes the general-purpose registers and loads them from the stack in this order: DI, SI, BP, SP, BX, DX, CX, AX. The SP register is discarded when it is popped.

POPAD: POP All General Doubleword Registers

Applicable processors: 80386, 80486

Category: Data-transfer instructions

Flags affected: None

Coding example:

```
POPAD
```

Description: POPAD removes and loads the general-purpose registers from the stack in this order: EDI, ESI, EBP, ESP, EBX, EDX, ECX, EAX. The ESP register is discarded when it is popped.

POPF: Remove Flags from Stack

Applicable processors: 8086/8088, 80286, 80386, 80486

Category: Data-transfer instructions

Flags affected: AC, AF, CF, DF, IF, IOPL, NT, OF, PF, SF, TF, ZF

Coding example:

```
POPF
```

Description: POPF removes a word from the stack and places the word in the flags register.

POPFD: Remove Extended Flags from Stack

Applicable processors: 80386, 80486

Category: Data-transfer instructions

Flags affected: AF, CF, DF, IF, IOPL, NT, OF, PF, SF, TF, ZF

Coding example:

```
POPFD
```

Description: POPFD removes a doubleword from the stack and places that doubleword in the extended flags register.

PUSH: Place Data on Stack

Applicable processors: 8086/8088, 80286, 80386, 80486

Category: Data-transfer instructions

Flags affected: None

Coding examples:

```
PUSH      AX
PUSH      EBX
PUSH      DS
PUSH      HOLD_REG
PUSH      50h                 ;Will not work on 8086/8088
```

Description: PUSH places a copy of the operand's value on the stack. For the 8086/8088, only the values of registers (byte or word) can be pushed. For all other microprocessors, immediate values also can be pushed.

PUSHA: Push All General Registers

Applicable processors: 80286, 80386, 80486

Category: Data-transfer instructions

Flags affected: None

Coding example:

```
PUSHA
```

Description: The general-purpose registers are pushed on the stack in this order: AX, CX, DX, BX, SP, BP, SI, DI. The SP value pushed is the value existing before this instruction is executed.

PUSHAD: Push All General Doubleword Registers

Applicable processors: 80386, 80486

Category: Data-transfer instructions

Flags affected: None

Coding example:

```
PUSHAD
```

Description: PUSHAD pushes the general-purpose doubleword registers on the stack in this order: EAX, ECX, EDX, EBX, ESP, EBP, ESI, EDI. The ESP value pushed is the value existing before this instruction is executed.

PUSHF: Place Flags on Stack

Applicable processors: 8086/8088, 80286, 80386, 80486

Category: Data-transfer instructions

Flags affected: None

Coding example:

PUSHF

Description: PUSHF places a copy of the flags register on the stack.

PUSHFD: Place Extended Flags on Stack

Applicable processors: 80386, 80486

Category: Data-transfer instructions

Flags affected: None

Coding example:

PUSHFD

Description: PUSHFD places a copy of the extended flags register on the stack.

RCL: Rotate Left through Carry

Applicable processors: 8086/8088, 80286, 80386, 80486

Category: Bit-manipulation instructions

Flags affected: CF, OF

Coding examples:

```
RCL       AX,1
RCL       BL,3
RCL       EDX,16
RCL       TEMP,CL
```

Description: RCL rotates all bits in the destination operand to the left by the number of places specified in the source operand. The rotation is performed through the carry flag in an order that rotates the most significant bit of the destination operand to the carry flag and rotates the carry flag to the least significant bit of the destination operand.

RCR: Rotate Right through Carry

Applicable processors: 8086/8088, 80286, 80386, 80486

Category: Bit-manipulation instructions

Flags affected: CF, OF

Coding examples:

```
RCR      AX,1
RCR      BL,3
RCR      EDX,16
RCR      TEMP,CL
```

Description: RCR rotates all bits in the destination operand to the right by the number of places specified in the source operand. The rotation is performed through the carry flag in an order that rotates the least significant bit of the destination operand to the carry flag and rotates the carry flag to the most significant bit of the destination operand.

REP: Repeat

Applicable processors: 8086/8088, 80286, 80386, 80486

Category: String-manipulation instructions

Flags affected: None

Coding example:

```
REP MOVSB
```

Description: REP causes string-manipulation instructions to be repeated the number of iterations specified in CX (if working with byte or word operands) or ECX (if working with doubleword operands).

REPE: Repeat If Equal

Applicable processors: 8086/8088, 80286, 80386, 80486

Category: String-manipulation instructions

Flags affected: None

Coding example:

```
REPE CMPSW
```

Description: REPE causes string-manipulation instructions to be repeated the number of iterations specified in CX (if working with byte or word operands) or ECX (if working with doubleword operands). When used with CMPSB, CMPSW, SCASB, or SCASW, this instruction repeats only while the zero flag is set. REPE is functionally equivalent to REPZ.

REPNE: Repeat If Not Equal

Applicable processors: 8086/8088, 80286, 80386, 80486

Category: String-manipulation instructions

Flags affected: None

Coding example:

```
REPNE CMPSW
```

Description: REPNE causes string-manipulation instructions to be repeated the number of iterations specified in CX (if working with byte or word operands) or ECX (if working with doubleword operands). When used with CMPSB, CMPSW, SCASB, or SCASW, this instruction repeats only while the zero flag is clear. This instruction is functionally equivalent to REPNZ.

REPNZ: Repeat If Not Zero

Applicable processors: 8086/8088, 80286, 80386, 80486

Category: String-manipulation instructions

Flags affected: None

Coding example:

```
REPNZ CMPSW
```

Description: REPNZ causes string-manipulation instructions to be repeated the number of iterations specified in CX (if working with byte or word operands) or ECX (if working with doubleword operands). When used with CMPSB, CMPSW, SCASB, or SCASW, this instruction repeats only while the zero flag is clear. REPNZ is functionally equivalent to REPNE.

REPZ: Repeat If Zero

Applicable processors: 8086/8088, 80286, 80386, 80486

Category: String-manipulation instructions

Flags affected: None

Coding example:

```
REPZ CMPSW
```

Description: REPZ causes string-manipulation instructions to be repeated the number of iterations specified in CX (if working with byte or word operands) or ECX (if working with doubleword operands). When used with CMPSB, CMPSW, SCASB, or SCASW, this instruction repeats only while the zero flag is set. REPZ is functionally equivalent to REPE.

RET: Return from Subroutine

Applicable processors: 8086/8088, 80286, 80386, 80486

Category: Control-transfer instructions

Flags affected: None

Coding examples:

```
RET
RET         2
```

Description: By popping IP from the stack, RET transfers program control back to the point at which a CALL was issued. If the CALL was to a FAR procedure, both CS:IP are popped from the stack.

If the RET has a specified return value (2, in the coding example), the stack is adjusted by that number of bytes. The coding example shows that a word is discarded from the stack after either IP or CS:IP is popped.

ROL: Rotate Left

Applicable processors: 8086/8088, 80286, 80386, 80486

Category: Bit-manipulation instructions

Flags affected: CF, OF

Coding examples:

```
ROL       AX,1
ROL       BL,3
ROL       DX,16
ROL       TEMP,CL
```

Description: ROL rotates all bits in the destination operand to the left by the number of places specified in the source operand.

ROR: Rotate Right

Applicable processors: 8086/8088, 80286, 80386, 80486

Category: Bit-manipulation instructions

Flags affected: CF, OF

Coding examples:

```
ROR       AX,1
ROR       BL,3
ROR       DX,16
ROR       TEMP,CL
```

Description: ROR rotates all bits in the destination operand to the right by the number of places specified in the source operand.

SAHF: Store AH into Flags Register

Applicable processors: 8086/8088, 80286, 80386, 80486

Category: Data-transfer instructions

Flags affected: AF, CF, PF, SF, ZF

Coding example:

```
SAHF
```

Description: SAHF copies the contents of AH to the low-order byte of the flags register. After execution of this instruction, SF, ZF, AF, PF, and CF are equal to bits 7, 6, 4, 2, and 1 of AH, respectively.

SAL: Arithmetic Shift Left

Applicable processors: 8086/8088, 80286, 80386, 80486

Category: Bit-manipulation instructions

Flags affected: AF (undefined for all processors through 80286, not affected beginning with 80386), CF, OF, PF, SF, ZF

Coding examples:

```
SAL      AX,1
SAL      BL,3
SAL      DX,16
SAL      TEMP,CL
```

Description: SAL shifts all bits in the destination operand to the left by the number of places specified in the source operand. High-order bits are lost and low-order bits are cleared.

SAR: Arithmetic Shift Right

Applicable processors: 8086/8088, 80286, 80386, 80486

Category: Bit-manipulation instructions

Flags affected: AF (undefined for all processors through 80286, not affected beginning with 80386), CF, OF, PF, SF, ZF

Coding examples:

```
SAR      AX,1
SAR      BL,3
SAR      DX,16
SAR      TEMP,CL
```

Description: SAR shifts all bits in the destination operand to the right by the number of places specified in the source operand. Low-order bits are lost and high-order bits are set equal to the existing high-order bit.

SBB: Subtract with Carry

Applicable processors: 8086/8088, 80286, 80386, 80486

Category: Arithmetic instructions

Flags affected: AF, CF, OF, PF, SF, ZF

Coding examples:

```
SBB      AX,BX          ;AX=AX-BX-CF
SBB      AX,TEMP        ;AX=AX-TEMP-CF
SBB      SUM,EBX        ;SUM=SUM-EBX-CF
SBB      CL,10          ;CL=CL-10-CF
SBB      AX,TEMP[BX]    ;Indirect address example
```

Description: SBB subtracts the contents of the source operand from (and stores the result in) the destination operand. If the carry flag is set, the result changes in a decrement of 1. In this instruction, the values being added are assumed to be binary.

SCASB: Scan String for Byte

Applicable processors: 8086/8088, 80286, 80386, 80486

Category: String-manipulation instructions

Flags affected: AF, CF, OF, PF, SF, ZF

Coding examples:

```
SCASB
REPNZ SCASB     ;Repeat a scan loop
```

Description: SCASB subtracts the destination-operand string byte (pointed to by DI) from the value of AL. The result is not stored, but the flags are updated. Then the value of DI changes in increments or decrements of 1, depending on the setting of the direction flag. Usually, this instruction is used with the REPE, REPNE, REPNZ, or REPZ instructions to repeat the scan for a maximum of CX bytes, or until SCASB finds a match or difference. Intel lists this command as SCAS; however, the assembler makes the byte/word distinctions.

SCASD: Scan String for Doubleword

Applicable processors: 80386, 80486

Category: String-manipulation instructions

Flags affected: AF, CF, OF, PF, SF, ZF

Coding examples:

```
SCASD
REPNZ SCASD    ;Repeat a scan loop
```

Description: SCASD subtracts the destination-operand string word (pointed to by EDI) from the value of EAX. The result is not stored, but the flags are updated. Then the value of EDI changes in increments or decrements of four, depending on the setting of the direction flag. Usually, this instruction is used with the REPE, REPNE, REPNZ, or REPZ instructions to repeat the scan for a maximum of CX bytes or until a match or difference is found.

SCASW: Scan String for Word

Applicable processors: 8086/8088, 80286, 80386, 80486

Category: String-manipulation instructions

Flags affected: AF, CF, OF, PF, SF, ZF

Coding examples:

```
SCASW
REPNZ SCASW    ;Repeat a scan loop
```

Description: SCASW subtracts the destination-operand string word (pointed to by DI) from the value of AX. The result is not stored, but the flags are updated. Then the value of DI changes in increments or decrements of two, depending on the setting of the direction flag. Usually, this instruction is used with the REPE, REPNE, REPNZ, or REPZ instructions to repeat the scan for a maximum of CX bytes, or until SCASW finds a match or difference. Intel lists this command as SCAS; however, the assembler makes the byte/word distinctions.

SETA: Set Byte If Above

Applicable processors: 80386, 80486

Category: Data-transfer instructions

Flags affected: None

Coding example:

```
SETA    CL
```

Description: SETA stores a 1 in the operand if the carry and zero flags are both clear. If this condition is not met, a zero is stored in the operand. The operand must be a byte-length register or memory location. This instruction is functionally the same as SETNBE.

SETAE: Set Byte If Above or Equal

Applicable processors: 80386, 80486

Category: Data-transfer instructions

Flags affected: None

Coding example:

```
SETAE  CL
```

Description: SETAE stores a 1 in the operand if the carry flag is clear. If this condition is not met, a zero is stored in the operand. The operand must be a byte-length register or memory location. This instruction is functionally the same as SETNB or SETNC.

SETB: Set Byte If Below

Applicable processors: 80386, 80486

Category: Data-transfer instructions

Flags affected: None

Coding example:

```
SETB   CL
```

Description: SETB stores a 1 in the operand if the carry flag is set. If this condition is not met, a zero is stored in the operand. The operand must be a byte-length register or memory location. This instruction is functionally the same as SETC or SETNAE.

SETBE: Set Byte If Below or Equal

Applicable processors: 80386, 80486

Category: Data-transfer instructions

Flags affected: None

Coding example:

```
SETBE   CL
```

Description: SETBE stores a 1 in the operand if either the carry or zero flag is set. If this condition is not met, a zero is stored in the operand. The operand must be a byte-length register or memory location. This instruction is functionally the same as SETNA.

SETC: Set Byte on Carry

Applicable processors: 80386, 80486

Category: Data-transfer instructions

Flags affected: None

Coding example:

```
SETC   CL
```

Description: SETC stores a 1 in the operand if the carry flag is set. If this condition is not met, a zero is stored in the operand. The operand must be a byte-length register or memory location. This instruction is functionally the same as SETB or SETNAE.

SETE: Set Byte If Equal

Applicable processors: 80386, 80486

Category: Data-transfer instructions

Flags affected: None

Coding example:

```
SETE   CL
```

Description: SETE stores a 1 in the operand if the zero flag is set. If this condition is not met, a zero is stored in the operand. The operand must be a byte-length register or memory location. This instruction is functionally the same as SETZ.

SETG: Set Byte If Greater

Applicable processors: 80386, 80486

Category: Data-transfer instructions

Flags affected: None

Coding example:

```
SETG    CL
```

Description: SETG stores a 1 in the operand if the sign flag equals the overflow flag or if the zero flag is clear. If neither condition is met, a zero is stored in the operand. The operand must be a byte-length register or memory location. This instruction is functionally the same as SETNLE.

SETGE: Set Byte If Greater or Equal

Applicable processors: 80386, 80486

Category: Data-transfer instructions

Flags affected: None

Coding example:

```
SETGE   CL
```

Description: SETGE stores a 1 in the operand if the sign flag equals the overflow flag. If this condition is not met, a zero is stored in the operand. The operand must be a byte-length register or memory location. This instruction is functionally the same as SETNL.

SETL: Set Byte If Less

Applicable processors: 80386, 80486

Category: Data-transfer instructions

Flags affected: None

Coding example:

```
SETL    CL
```

Description: SETL stores a 1 in the operand if the sign flag does not equal the overflow flag. If this condition is not met, a zero is stored in the operand. The operand must be a byte-length register or memory location. This instruction is functionally the same as SETNGE.

SETLE: Set Byte If Less or Equal

Applicable processors: 80386, 80486

Category: Data-transfer instructions

Flags affected: None

Coding example:

```
SETLE   CL
```

Description: SETLE stores a 1 in the operand if the sign flag does not equal the overflow flag or if the zero flag is set. If neither condition is met, a zero is stored in the operand. The operand must be a byte-length register or memory location. This instruction is functionally the same as SETNG.

SETNA: Set Byte If Not Above

Applicable processors: 80386, 80486

Category: Data-transfer instructions

Flags affected: None

Coding example:

```
SETNA   CL
```

Description: SETNA stores a 1 in the operand if either the carry or zero flag is set. If neither condition is met, a zero is stored in the operand. The operand must be a byte-length register or memory location. This instruction is functionally the same as SETBE.

SETNAE: Set Byte If Not Above or Equal

Applicable processors: 80386, 80486

Category: Data-transfer instructions

Flags affected: None

Coding example:

```
SETNAE CL
```

Description: SETNAE stores a 1 in the operand if the carry flag is set. If this condition is not met, a zero is stored in the operand. The operand must be a byte-length register or memory location. This instruction is functionally the same as SETB or SETC.

SETNB: Set Byte If Not Below

Applicable processors: 80386, 80486

Category: Data-transfer instructions

Flags affected: None

Coding example:

```
SETNB  CL
```

Description: SETNB stores a 1 in the operand if the carry flag is clear. If this condition is not met, a zero is stored in the operand. The operand must be a byte-length register or memory location. This instruction is functionally the same as SETAE or SETNC.

SETNBE: Set Byte If Not Below or Equal

Applicable processors: 80386, 80486

Category: Data-transfer instructions

Flags affected: None

Coding example:

```
SETNBE CL
```

Description: SETNBE stores a 1 in the operand if both the carry and zero flags are clear. If this condition is not met, a zero is stored in the operand. The operand must be a byte-length register or memory location. This instruction is functionally the same as SETA.

SETNC: Set Byte on No Carry

Applicable processors: 80386, 80486

Category: Data-transfer instructions

Flags affected: None

Coding example:

```
SETNC   CL
```

Description: SETNC stores a 1 in the operand if the carry flag is clear. If this condition is not met, a zero is stored in the operand. The operand must be a byte-length register or memory location. This instruction is functionally the same as SETAE or SETNB.

SETNE: Set Byte If Not Equal

Applicable processors: 80386, 80486

Category: Data-transfer instructions

Flags affected: None

Coding example:

```
SETNE   CL
```

Description: SETNE stores a 1 in the operand if the zero flag is clear. If this condition is not met, a zero is stored in the operand. The operand must be a byte-length register or memory location. This instruction is functionally the same as SETNZ.

SETNG: Set Byte If Not Greater

Applicable processors: 80386, 80486

Category: Data-transfer instructions

Flags affected: None

Coding example:

```
SETNG   CL
```

Description: SETNG stores a 1 in the operand if the sign flag does not equal the overflow flag or the zero flag is set. If neither condition is met, a zero is stored in the operand. The operand must be a byte-length register or memory location. This instruction is functionally the same as SETLE.

SETNGE: Set Byte If Not Greater or Equal

Applicable processors: 80386, 80486

Category: Data-transfer instructions

Flags affected: None

Coding example:

```
SETNGE CL
```

Description: SETNGE stores a 1 in the operand if the sign flag does not equal the overflow flag. If this condition is not met, a zero is stored in the operand. The operand must be a byte-length register or memory location. This instruction is functionally the same as SETL.

SETNL: Set Byte If Not Less

Applicable processors: 80386, 80486

Category: Data-transfer instructions

Flags affected: None

Coding example:

```
SETNL  CL
```

Description: SETNL stores a 1 in the operand if the sign flag equals the overflow flag. If this condition is not met, a zero is stored in the operand. The operand must be a byte-length register or memory location. This instruction is functionally the same as SETGE.

SETNLE: Set Byte If Not Less or Equal

Applicable processors: 80386, 80486

Category: Data-transfer instructions

Flags affected: None

Coding example:

```
SETNLE CL
```

Description: SETNLE stores a 1 in the operand if the sign flag equals the overflow flag or the zero flag is clear. If neither condition is met, a zero is stored in the operand. The operand must be a byte-length register or memory location. This instruction is functionally the same as SETG.

SETNO: Set Byte on No Overflow

Applicable processors: 80386, 80486

Category: Data-transfer instructions

Flags affected: None

Coding example:

```
SETNO  CL
```

Description: SETNO stores a 1 in the operand if the overflow flag is clear. If this condition is not met, a zero is stored in the operand. The operand must be a byte-length register or memory location.

SETNP: Set Byte on No Parity

Applicable processors: 80386, 80486

Category: Data-transfer instructions

Flags affected: None

Coding example:

```
SETNP  CL
```

Description: SETNP stores a 1 in the operand if the parity flag is clear. If this condition is not met, a zero is stored in the operand. The operand must be a byte-length register or memory location. This instruction is functionally the same as SETPO.

SETNS: Set Byte on Not Sign

Applicable processors: 80386, 80486

Category: Data-transfer instructions

Flags affected: None

Coding example:

```
SETNS   CL
```

Description: SETNS stores a 1 in the operand if the sign flag is clear. If this condition is not met, a zero is stored in the operand. The operand must be a byte-length register or memory location.

SETNZ: Set Byte If Not Zero

Applicable processors: 80386, 80486

Category: Data-transfer instructions

Flags affected: None

Coding example:

```
SETNZ   CL
```

Description: SETNZ stores a 1 in the operand if the zero flag is clear. If this condition is not met, a zero is stored in the operand. The operand must be a byte-length register or memory location. This instruction is functionally the same as SETNE.

SETO: Set Byte on Overflow

Applicable processors: 80386, 80486

Category: Data-transfer instructions

Flags affected: None

Coding example:

SETO   CL

Description: SETO stores a 1 in the operand if the overflow flag is set. If this condition is not met, a zero is stored in the operand. The operand must be a byte-length register or memory location.

SETP: Set Byte on Parity

Applicable processors: 80386, 80486

Category: Data-transfer instructions

Flags affected: None

Coding example:

SETP   CL

Description: SETP stores a 1 in the operand if the parity flag is set. If this condition is not met, a zero is stored in the operand. The operand must be a byte-length register or memory location. This instruction is functionally the same as SETPE.

SETPE: Set Byte on Parity Even

Applicable processors: 80386, 80486

Category: Data-transfer instructions

Flags affected: None

Coding example:

SETPE   CL

Description: SETPE stores a 1 in the operand if the parity flag is set. If this condition is not met, a zero is stored in the operand. The operand must be a byte-length register or memory location. This instruction is functionally the same as SETP.

SETPO: Set Byte on Parity Odd

Applicable processors: 80386, 80486

Category: Data-transfer instructions

Flags affected: None

Coding example:

```
SETPO   CL
```

Description: SETPO stores a 1 in the operand if the parity flag is clear. If this condition is not met, a zero is stored in the operand. The operand must be a byte-length register or memory location. This instruction is functionally the same as SETNP.

SETS: Set Byte on Sign

Applicable processors: 80386, 80486

Category: Data-transfer instructions

Flags affected: None

Coding example:

```
SETS    CL
```

Description: SETS stores a 1 in the operand if the sign flag is set. If this condition is not met, a zero is stored in the operand. The operand must be a byte-length register or memory location.

SETZ: Set Byte If Zero

Applicable processors: 80386, 80486

Category: Data-transfer instructions

Flags affected: None

Coding example:

```
SETZ    CL
```

Description: SETZ stores a 1 in the operand if the zero flag is set. If this condition is not met, a zero is stored in the operand. The operand must be a byte-length register or memory location. This instruction is functionally the same as SETE.

SGDT: Store GDT Register

Applicable processors: 80286, 80386, 80486

Category: Data-transfer instructions

Flags affected: None

Coding example:

```
SGDT    TEMP[BX]
```

Description: SGDT transfers the six bytes of the global descriptor table to the memory address specified in the operand. This instruction is used in protected-mode operating system software but not in applications software.

SHL: Shift Left

Applicable processors: 8086/8088, 80286, 80386, 80486

Category: Bit-manipulation instructions

Flags affected: AF (undefined for all processors through 80286, not affected beginning with 80386), CF, OF, PF, SF, ZF

Coding examples:

```
SHL     AX,1
SHL     BL,3
SHL     DX,16
SHL     TEMP,CL
```

Description: SHL shifts all bits in the destination operand to the left by the number of places specified in the source operand. High-order bits are lost and low-order bits are cleared.

SHLD: Shift Left, Double Precision

Applicable processors: 80386, 80486

Category: Bit-manipulation instructions

Flags affected: AF (undefined), CF, OF (undefined), PF, SF, ZF

Coding examples:

```
SHLD        AX,BX,4
SHLD        DWORD_TEMP,EAX,16
```

Description: SHLD shifts all bits in the first operand to the left by the number of places specified in the third operand. High-order bits are lost; low-order bits are copied from the second operand, starting with the second operand's low-order bit. The result is stored in the first operand.

SHR: Shift Right

Applicable processors: 8086/8088, 80286, 80386, 80486

Category: Bit-manipulation instructions

Flags affected: AF (undefined for all processors through 80286, not affected beginning with 80386), CF, OF, PF, SF, ZF

Coding examples:

```
SHR         AX,1
SHR         BL,3
SHR         DX,16
SHR         TEMP,CL
```

Description: SHR shifts all bits in the destination operand to the right by the number of places specified in the source operand. Low-order bits are lost and high-order bits are cleared.

SHRD: Shift Right, Double Precision

Applicable processors: 80386, 80486

Category: Bit-manipulation instructions

Flags affected: AF (undefined), CF, OF (undefined), PF, SF, ZF

Coding examples:

```
SHRD      AX,BX,4
SHRD      DWORD_TEMP,EAX,16
```

Description: SHRD shifts all bits in the first operand to the right by the number of places specified in the third operand. Low-order bits are lost; high-order bits are copied from the second operand, starting with the second operand's high-order bit. The result is stored in the first operand.

SIDT: Store Interrupt Descriptor Table Register

Applicable processors: 80286, 80386, 80486

Category: Data-transfer instructions

Flags affected: None

Coding example:

```
SIDT      TEMP[BX]
```

Description: SIDT transfers the six bytes of the interrupt descriptor table to the memory address specified in the operand. This instruction is used in protected-mode operating system software but not in applications software.

SLDT: Store Local Descriptor Table Register

Applicable processors: 80286, 80386, 80486

Category: Data-transfer instructions

Flags affected: None

Coding examples:

```
SLDT      AX
SLDT      LDT_TEMP
```

Description: SLDT copies the contents of the local descriptor table to the two bytes of the operand. This instruction is used in protected-mode operating system software but not in applications software.

SMSW: Store Machine Status Word

Applicable processors: 80286, 80386, 80486

Category: Data-transfer instructions

Flags affected: None

Coding examples:

```
SMSW      AX
SMSW      MSW_TEMP
```

Description: SMSW copies the value of machine status word to the operand. This instruction is used in operating system software only, not in applications software.

STC: Set Carry Flag

Applicable processors: 8086/8088, 80286, 80386, 80486

Category: Flag- and processor-control instructions

Flags affected: CF

Coding example:

```
STC
```

Description: STC sets the carry flag regardless of the flag's present condition.

STD: Set Direction Flag

Applicable processors: 8086/8088, 80286, 80386, 80486

Category: Flag- and processor-control instructions

Flags affected: DF

Coding example:

```
STD
```

Description: STD sets the direction flag regardless of the flag's present condition. This setting affects the string instructions.

STI: Set Interrupt Flag

Applicable processors: 8086/8088, 80286, 80386, 80486

Category: Flag- and processor-control instructions

Flags affected: IF

Coding example:

```
STI
```

Description: STI sets the interrupt flag regardless of the flag's present condition. While this flag is set, the CPU responds to maskable interrupts.

STOSB: Store Byte in AL at String

Applicable processors: 8086/8088, 80286, 80386, 80486

Category: String-manipulation instructions

Flags affected: None

Coding example:

```
STOSB
```

Description: STOSB copies the contents of AL to the byte address pointed to by DI. DI then changes in increments or decrements of 1, depending on the setting of the direction flag. Intel lists this command as STOS; however, the assembler makes the byte/word distinctions.

STOSD: Store Doubleword in EAX at String

Applicable processors: 80386, 80486

Category: String-manipulation instructions

Flags affected: None

Coding example:

```
STOSD
```

Description: STOSD copies the contents of EAX to the word address pointed to by EDI. DI then changes in increments or decrements of four, depending on the setting of the direction flag.

STOSW: Store Word in AX at String

Applicable processors: 8086/8088, 80286, 80386, 80486

Category: String-manipulation instructions

Flags affected: None

Coding example:

```
STOSW
```

Description: STOSW copies the contents of AX to the word address pointed to by DI. DI then changes in increments or decrements of two, depending on the setting of the direction flag. Intel lists this command as STOS; however, the assembler makes the byte/word distinctions.

STR: Store Task Register

Applicable processors: 80286, 80386, 80486

Category: Data-transfer instructions

Flags affected: None

Coding examples:

```
STR        AX
STR        MSW_TEMP
```

Description: STR copies the value of the task register to the operand. This instruction is used in operating system software only; it is not used in applications software.

SUB: Subtract

Applicable processors: 8086/8088, 80286, 80386, 80486

Category: Arithmetic instructions

Flags affected: AF, CF, OF, PF, SF, ZF

Coding examples:

```
SUB        AX,BX          ;AX=AX-BX
SUB        AX,TEMP        ;AX=AX-TEMP
SUB        SUM,EBX        ;SUM=SUM-EBX
SUB        CL,10          ;CL=CL-10
SUB        AX,TEMP[BX]    ;Indirect address example
```

Description: SUB subtracts the contents of the source operand from (and stores the result in) the destination operand. In this instruction, the values being added are assumed to be binary.

TEST: Test Bits

Applicable processors: 8086/8088, 80286, 80386, 80486

Category: Bit-manipulation instructions

Flags affected: AF (undefined for all processors through 80286, not affected beginning with 80386), CF, OF, PF, SF, ZF

Coding examples:

```
TEST       AX,BX          ;
TEST       AX,TEMP        ;TEMP must be a word
TEST       SUM,EBX        ;SUM must be a doubleword
TEST       CL,00001111b   ;
TEST       AX,TEMP[BX]    ;Indirect address example
```

Description: TEST performs a logical AND of the operands, but the result is not stored. Only the flags are affected. Each bit of the resultant byte or word is set to 1 only if the corresponding bit of each operand is set to 1.

VERR: Verify a Segment for Reading

Applicable processors: 80286, 80386, 80486

Category: Flag- and processor-control instructions

Flags affected: ZF

Coding examples:

```
VERR       TEMP
VERR       AX
```

Description: VERR determines whether the selector specified in the operand is visible at the current privilege level and is readable. The zero flag is set if the selector is accessible.

VERW: Verify a Segment for Writing

Applicable processors: 80286, 80386, 80486

Category: Flag- and processor-control instructions

Flags affected: ZF

Coding examples:

```
VERW      TEMP
VERW      AX
```

Description: VERW determines whether the selector specified in the operand is visible at the current privilege level and can be written. The zero flag is set if the selector is accessible.

WAIT: Wait

Applicable processors: 8086/8088, 80286, 80386, 80486

Category: Flag- and processor-control instructions

Flags affected: None

Coding example:

```
WAIT
```

Description: WAIT causes the CPU to wait for an external interrupt on the TEST line before continuing.

WBINVD: Invalidate Cache and Write Back

Applicable processors: 80486

Category: Processor-control instructions

Flags affected: None

Coding examples:

```
WBINVD
```

Description: This instruction is similar to the INVD instruction. It results in the internal (on-chip) data cache being flushed, but the special-function bus cycles that follow are different. Two of the bus cycles are issued: the first is an instruction to external caches to write their information back to main memory; the second instructs the caches to flush their contents (same as INVD).

XADD: Exchange and Add to Memory

Applicable processors: 80486

Category: Data-transfer instructions

Flags affected: AF, CF, OF, PF, SF, ZF

Coding examples:

```
XADD          EAX,EBX
```

Description: Exchanges the values in the two operands before doing an addition. Functionally equivalent to exchanging and adding with multiple instructions.

XCHG: Exchange

Applicable processors: 8086/8088, 80286, 80386, 80486

Category: Data-transfer instructions

Flags affected: None

Coding examples:

```
XCHG      AX,BX                 ;Swap AX with BX
XCHG      EAX,DWORD_TEMP        ;Swap EAX with DWORD_TEMP
XCHG      CL,CH                 ;Swap CL with CH
XCHG      AX,TEMP               ;Swap AX with TEMP (word)
```

Description: XCHG swaps the contents of the source and destination operands. The operands must be of equal length.

XLAT: Translate

Applicable processors: 8086/8088, 80286, 80386, 80486

Category: Data-transfer instructions

Flags affected: None

Coding example:

```
XLAT
```

Description: Assuming that the offset address of a 256-byte translation table is contained in BX, this instruction uses the value in AL as a zero-based offset into the table, and subsequently loads AL with the byte value at that calculated offset. This instruction is helpful for translation tables.

XOR: Logical Exclusive-Or

Applicable processors: 8086/8088, 80286, 80386, 80486

Category: Bit-manipulation instructions

Flags affected: AF (undefined), CF, OF, PF, SF, ZF

Coding examples:

```
XOR     AX,BX           ;
XOR     EAX,TEMP        ;TEMP must be a doubleword
XOR     SUM,BX          ;SUM must be a word
XOR     CL,00001111b
XOR     AX,TEMP[BX]     ;Indirect address example
```

Description: XOR performs a logical XOR of the operands and stores the result in the destination operand. Each bit of the resultant byte or word is set to 1 only if the corresponding bit of each operand contains opposite values.

Assembler Directives

A ssembler directives are mentioned and used throughout this book. In fact, doing any assembly language programming without using at least a few directives is difficult, if not impossible.

The basic mnemonic language used by assemblers cannot be expanded; it is set by the microprocessor for which the assembler was written. To make the language more versatile, assembler-writers have taken to expanding the language by adding directives and have expanded or extended instructions.

The range of directives available is quite impressive. Many of them you will use daily, whereas others you may use only once in a while. In Chapter 3, "Choosing and Using Your Assembler," you learned about directives—what they are and how they are used in a general sense. This chapter is a comprehensive reference to all the directives available with both MASM and TASM.

This chapter does not cover the additional or extended instructions that are available with some assemblers. For instance, Turbo Assembler 3.0 has modified the way in which some instructions, such as PUSH and POP, operate. These are considered *extended instructions*, since they expand the basic capabilities of existing mnemonics.

Additional instructions, on the other hand, are instructions that do not fall clearly into the directive category, but add to the basic instruction set. During assembly, they generally expand into a series of instructions that accomplish a discrete task. Examples are the smart flag instructions available with Turbo Assembler 3.0.

Directive Categories

In this reference, each directive is categorized into one of the following general categories:

❏ Processor specification
❏ Global control
❏ Simplified segment control
❏ Complete segment control
❏ Procedures and code labels
❏ Scope and visibility
❏ Data allocation
❏ Complex data types
❏ Control flow
❏ Macros and repeat blocks
❏ Conditional assembly
❏ Conditional error
❏ Listing control
❏ String control
❏ Miscellaneous

Note that the listing-control group encompasses the most directives. Note also that a great many of these directives simply offer duplicate ways to accomplish the same task. (In effect, they are synonyms of each other.)

Let's look at each of these categories. Note that some directives appear in more than one category because they perform more than one task, depending on the context in which they are used.

Processor Specification

This group of directives is used to specify the processor for which you want the assembler to generate code. Different directives control the processor, the numeric coprocessor, and the type of instructions (protected-mode, etc.) that can be generated for each processor. The directives are as follows:

.186	.386C	.8086	P286P	P486
.286	.386P	.8087	P287	P486N
.286C	.387	.NO87	P386	P8086
.286P	.486	P186	P386N	P8087
.287	.486C	P286	P386P	PNO87
.386	.486P	P286N	P387	

Global Control

These directives affect the way in which the assembler views and interprets the source code that follows. Some set different operating modes, others may affect the amount and type of optimization done. The directives are

ALIGN	.MSFLOAT	NOSMART	.RADIX
EMUL	MULTERRS	NOWARN	RADIX
IDEAL	NAME	OPTION	SMALLSTACK
JUMPS	NOEMUL	POPCONTEXT	SMART
LARGESTACK	NOJUMPS	PUSHCONTEXT	VERSION
MASM	NOMASM51	QUIRKS	WARN
MASM51	NOMULTERRS		

Simplified Segment Control

Simplified segment control is a great aid in developing assembly language programs. With these directives, you can leave many of the details of segment grouping and ordering to the assembler and linker:

ASSUME	.DATA	.FARDATA	.STARTUP
.CODE	.DATA?	FARDATA	STARTUPCODE
CODESEG	DATASEG	.FARDATA?	UDATASEG
.CONST	.EXIT	.MODEL	UFARDATA
CONST	EXITCODE	MODEL	

Complete Segment Control

These are the directives to use when you want complete control over the way segments are handled by the assembler and linker. Use of these directives has decreased dramatically since the advent of the simplified segment-control directives.

.ALPHA	DOSSEG	ORG	SEQ
ALPHA	END	SEGMENT	.STACK
ASSUME	ENDS	.SEQ	STACK
.DOSSEG	GROUP		

Procedures and Code Labels

These directives are used in the definition and use of procedures, and labels (symbolic names) in those procedures:

ARG	LABEL	NOLOCALS	PROTO
ENDP	LOCAL	PROC	USES
INVOKE	LOCALS		

Scope and Visibility

Scope has to do with how accessible a label is to other modules, and visibility has to do with whether certain labels can be located by the current module. These directives control both these items:

COMM	EXTRN	INCLUDE	PUBLICDLL
EXTERN	GLOBAL	INCLUDELIB	PUBLIC
EXTERNDEF			

Data Allocation

These directives cause the assembler to allocate memory in the OBJ file for your data:

BYTE	DT	QWORD	SDWORD
DB	DW	REAL4	SWORD
DD	DWORD	REAL8	TBYTE
DF	DQ	REAL10	WORD
DP	FWORD	SBYTE	

Complex Data Types

Relatively new to assembly language programming is the concept of complex data types. These include user-defined pointers, structures, unions, tables, and records. The directives follow:

ALIGN	EVEN	STRUC	TBLPTR
ENDS	EVENDATA	STRUCT	TYPEDEF
ENUM	RECORD	TABLE	UNION

Control Flow

In the past, assembly language programmers have had to write their own control structures, generally to handle looping. Because this can be confusing to many programmers who are used to the ways in which this is done in high-level languages, this group of directives was created.

.BREAK	.ELSEIF	.IF	.UNTILCXZ
.CONTINUE	.ENDIF	.REPEAT	.WHILE
.ELSE	.ENDW	.UNTIL	

Macros and Repeat Blocks

Macros have long been a part of the collection of tools available to assembly language programmers. Theoretically, macros make programming easier. Unless the macros are well documented, however, the job of maintaining the code can be difficult later.

ENDM	GOTO	MACRO	REPT
EXITM	IRP	PURGE	TEXTEQU
FOR	IRPC	REPEAT	WHILE
FORC	LOCAL		

Conditional Assembly

Conditional assembly directives allow you to control which portions of your source code are assembled, based on flags and other control statements you devise.

ELSE	IF1	IFDIF	IFIDNI
ELSEIF	IF2	IFDIFI	IFNB
ENDIF	IFB	IFE	IFNDEF
IF	IFDEF	IFIDN	

Conditional Error

This category of directives is similar to the conditional assembly directives, in that they control how the assembler does its work, based on a detected condition during the assembly process. This group of directives allows you to control when errors are generated. Typically, these directives are used in macros to ensure that the user passes the proper parameters.

.ERR	.ERRDIFI	ERRIFB	ERRIFIDNI
ERR	.ERRE	ERRIFDEF	ERRIFNB
.ERR1	.ERRIDN	ERRIFDIF	ERRIFNDEF
.ERR2	.ERRIDNI	ERRIFDIFI	.ERRNB
.ERRB	ERRIF	ERRIFE	.ERRNDEF
.ERRDEF	ERRIF1	ERRIFIDN	.ERRNZ
.ERRDIF	ERRIF2		

Listing Control

The largest of the directive groups, these directives affect how the listing file is generated. It includes directives that change the appearance of the information printed, as well as what is and is not included in the listing.

%BIN	%LIST	%NOLIST	.SFCOND
%CONDS	.LIST	.NOLIST	SUBTITLE
%CREF	.LISTALL	.NOLISTIF	%SUBTTL
.CREF	.LISTIF	.NOLISTMACRO	SUBTTL
%CREFALL	.LISTMACRO	%NOMACS	$SYMS
%CREFREF	.LISTMACROALL	%NOSYMS	%TABLSIZE
%CREFUREF	%MACS	%NOTRUNC	%TEXT
%CTLS	%NEWPAGE	PAGE	.TFCOND
%DEPTH	%NOCONDS	$PAGESIZE	%TITLE
%INCL	%NOCREF	%PCNT	TITLE
.LALL	.NOCREF	%POPLCTL	%TRUNC
.LFCOND	%NOCTLS	%PUSHLCTL	.XALL
%LINUM	%NOINCL	.SALL	.XCREF
			.XLIST

String Control

This is the least-populated group. It consists of the following four directives, which manipulate strings assigned to text macros:

```
CATSTR
INSTR
SIZESTR
SUBSTR
```

Miscellaneous

The six "left-over" directives in this category do not fit in the other groups:

=	ECHO
COMMENT	EQU
DISPLAY	%OUT

Detailed Directive Information

In the remainder of this chapter, each directive available with TASM and MASM is described in detail. The following information is given for each instruction:

❏ **Directive name.** This name is based on the names provided by Microsoft and/or Borland.

❏ **Applicable assemblers.** This paragraph lists the assembler versions that perform the directive.

❏ **Directive category.** The general classification for the directive is provided.

❏ **Syntax.** A quick notation of the proper and full way in which the directive can be used.

❏ **Description.** A narrative description of each directive is provided.

❏ **Example.** If it would be instructive, a brief example or two of the use of the directive. If the syntax of the directive is too simple to warrant an example, none is given.

=: Assign a Value to a Label

Applicable assemblers: Microsoft Quick Assembler 2.51, MASM 5.1, MASM 6.0, TASM 2.0, TASM 3.0

Directive category: Miscellaneous

Syntax:

```
label = value
```

Description: This is one of the most used directives in any assembler, although people rarely stop to think of it as a directive. The equal sign is used to assign a value to a user-designated label. It is similar in purpose and function to the EQU directive. Using the equal sign does not result in storage space (memory area) being assigned in a program; it just assigns a value to a label. This label can then be used in place of the value later in the program. Use of the equal-sign directive increases program clarity and maintainability.

The expression following the equal sign must be equivalent, in some way, to an integer value: it can be a number, a formula that can be resolved to a number, up to four text characters (whatever can be stored in a register or extended register on the processor), or an address.

The difference between the equal sign and the EQU directive is that values defined with the equal sign can be changed in a program. After a value is set with EQU, it cannot be changed.

Examples:

```
Mono          = 0B000h        ;Mono video buffer start
Color         = 0B800h        ;Color video buffer start
MaxRows       = 25 * 80       ;Regular screen size
Affirmative   = 'Y'           ;Acceptable keypress
TableStart    = THIS BYTE     ;Table starts here
```

.186: Enable 80186 Programming

Applicable assemblers: Microsoft Quick Assembler 2.51, MASM 5.1, MASM 6.0, TASM 2.0, TASM 3.0

Directive category: Processor specification

Syntax:

```
.186
```

Description: Both MASM and TASM allow you to program for specific microprocessors. The default processor is the 8086. This directive causes the assembler to handle instructions compatible with the 80186 microprocessor.

If you are using TASM, this directive is equivalent to the P186 directive.

.286: Enable 80286 Programming

Applicable assemblers: Microsoft Quick Assembler 2.51, MASM 5.1, MASM 6.0, TASM 2.0, TASM 3.0

Directive category: Processor specification

Syntax:

.286

Description: Both MASM and TASM allow you to program for specific microprocessors. The default processor is the 8086. This directive causes the assembler to handle instructions compatible with the 80286 microprocessor.

If you are using TASM, this directive is equivalent to the P286N directive.

.286C: Enable 80286 Nonprotected-Mode Programming

Applicable assemblers: Microsoft Quick Assembler 2.51, TASM 2.0, TASM 3.0

Directive category: Processor specification

Syntax:

.286C

Description: This directive is functionally equivalent to the .286 directive, and the opposite of the .286P directive. With it, you can program for the 80286 processor, but the assembler makes sure that you use no instructions that require protected mode.

If you are using TASM, this directive is equivalent to the P286N directive.

.286P: Enable 80286 Protected-Mode Programming

Applicable assemblers: MASM 6.0, TASM 2.0, TASM 3.0

Directive category: Processor specification

Syntax:

.286P

Description: Both MASM and TASM allow you to program for specific micro-processors. The default processor is the 8086. This directive causes the assembler to handle instructions compatible with the 80286 microprocessor. The difference between this and the .286 directive is that when this directive is used, you can program for protected-mode operations.

If you are using TASM, this directive is equivalent to the P286P directive.

.287: Enable 80287 Programming

Applicable assemblers: Microsoft Quick Assembler 2.51, MASM 5.1, MASM 6.0, TASM 2.0, TASM 3.0

Directive category: Processor specification

Syntax:

.287

Description: Both MASM and TASM allow you to take advantage of numeric coprocessors in your programs. By default, the assembler allows you to code for the 8087 NPX. This directive causes the assembler to handle instructions compatible with the 80287 numeric coprocessor.

If you are using TASM, this directive is equivalent to the P287 directive.

.386: Enable 80386 Programming

Applicable assemblers: MASM 5.1, MASM 6.0, TASM 2.0, TASM 3.0

Directive category: Processor specification

Syntax:

.386

Description: Both MASM and TASM allow you to program for specific micro-processors. The default processor is the 8086. This directive causes the assembler to handle instructions compatible with the 80386 microprocessor, including instructions that use the expanded register set of the 80386.

If you are using TASM, this directive is equivalent to the P386N directive.

.386C: Enable 80386 Nonprotected-Mode Programming

Applicable assemblers: TASM 2.0, TASM 3.0

Directive category: Processor specification

Syntax:

```
.386C
```

Description: This directive is functionally equivalent to the `.386` directive, and the opposite of the `.386P` directive. With it, you can program for the 80386 processor, but the assembler makes sure that you use no instructions that require protected mode.

If you are using TASM, this directive is equivalent to the P386N directive.

.386P: Enable 80386 Protected-Mode Programming

Applicable assemblers: MASM 6.0, TASM 2.0, TASM 3.0

Directive category: Processor specification

Syntax:

```
.386P
```

Description: Both MASM and TASM allow you to program for specific microprocessors. The default processor is the 8086. This directive causes the assembler to handle instructions compatible with the 80386 microprocessor. The difference between this and the `.386` directive is that when this directive is used, you can program for protected-mode operations.

If you are using TASM, this directive is equivalent to the P386P directive.

.387: Enable 80387 Programming

Applicable assemblers: MASM 6.0, TASM 2.0, TASM 3.0

Directive category: Processor specification

Syntax:

```
.387
```

Description: Both MASM and TASM allow you to take advantage of numeric coprocessors in your programs. By default, the assembler allows you to code for the 8087 NPX. This directive causes the assembler to handle instructions compatible with the 80387 numeric coprocessor.

If you are using TASM, this directive is equivalent to the P387 directive.

.486: Enable 80486 Programming

Applicable assemblers: MASM 6.0, TASM 3.0

Directive category: Processor specification

Syntax:

`.486`

Description: Both MASM and TASM allow you to program for specific microprocessors. The default processor is the 8086. This directive causes the assembler to handle instructions compatible with the 80486 microprocessor. This includes instructions that use the expanded register set of the 80486.

You should note that the .486 directive enables the use of instructions designed to take advantage of the NPX built into the 80486. If your code is designed to ultimately run on the 80486 SX chip, make sure that you do not use instructions which require the NPX. Even though the assembler will allow them (after this directive is executed), the resulting code will not run on the 80486 SX.

If you are using TASM, this directive is equivalent to the P486N directive.

.486C: Enable 80486 Nonprotected-Mode Programming

Applicable assemblers: TASM 3.0

Directive category: Processor specification

Syntax:

`.486C`

Description: This directive is functionally equivalent to the .486 directive, and the opposite of the .486P directive. With it, you can program for the 80486 processor (including instructions that use the expanded register set of the 80486), but the assembler makes sure that you use no instructions which require protected mode.

Note that the .486 directive enables the use of instructions designed to take advantage of the NPX built into the 80486. If your code is designed to ultimately run on the 80486 SX chip, make sure that you do not use instructions which require the NPX. Even though the assembler will allow them (after this directive is executed), the resulting code will not run on the 80486 SX.

If you are using TASM, this directive is equivalent to the P486N directive.

.486P: Enable 80486 Protected-Mode Programming

Applicable assemblers: MASM 6.0, TASM 3.0

Directive category: Processor specification

Syntax:

.486P

Description: Both MASM and TASM allow you to program for specific microprocessors. The default processor is the 8086. This directive causes the assembler to handle instructions compatible with the 80486 microprocessor. This includes instructions that use the expanded register set of the 80486. The difference between this and the .486 directive is that when this directive is used, you can program for protected-mode operations.

Note that this directive enables the use of instructions designed to take advantage of the NPX built into the 80486. If your code is designed to ultimately run on the 80486 SX chip, make sure that you do not use instructions which require the NPX. Even though the assembler will allow them (after this directive is executed), the resulting code will not run on the 80486 SX.

.8086: Enable 8086 Programming

Applicable assemblers: Microsoft Quick Assembler 2.51, MASM 5.1, MASM 6.0, TASM 2.0, TASM 3.0

Directive category: Processor specification

Syntax:

.8086

Description: This is the default programming paradigm for both MASM and TASM. Although you can use other directives to enable various levels of processor compatibility, this directive can be used to make absolutely sure that your program will work with all members of the 80x86 family.

A typical use of this directive is when you have been programming for a different level of compatibility (80286 or higher) and you want to make sure that the code being written will assemble into a final finished program that will then be able to run on an older processor. Using this directive helps ensure that, by enforcing which instructions are allowed to be used.

If you are using TASM, this directive is equivalent to the P8086 directive.

.8087: Enable 8087 Programming

Applicable assemblers: Microsoft Quick Assembler 2.51, MASM 5.1, MASM 6.0, TASM 2.0, TASM 3.0

Directive category: Processor specification

Syntax:

```
.8087
```

Description: This is the default programming capability of both MASM and TASM. You can use this directive to state explicity in your program that you are programming for the 8087 numeric coprocessor, but use of the directive is not mandatory.

If you are using TASM, this directive is equivalent to the P8087 directive.

ALIGN: Adjust the Assembler Location Counter

Applicable assemblers: Microsoft Quick Assembler 2.51, MASM 5.1, MASM 6.0, TASM 2.0, TASM 3.0

Directive category: Global control, complex data types

Syntax:

```
ALIGN boundary
```

Description: ALIGN is used to designate where the assembler should place the assembled information immediately following the directive. For instance, you may need to have data placed at a specific word, doubleword, or paragraph boundary. This directive is used to accomplish the task.

The argument used with ALIGN can be either a power-of-two number or an align type such as WORD, DWORD, PARA, or PAGE. Using ALIGN WORD or ALIGN 2 is the same as using the EVEN or EVENDATA directives. EVENDATA is available only if you are using TASM.

Examples:

```
ALIGN   WORD            ;Align to word boundary
ALIGN   PARA            ;Align to paragraph boundary
ALIGN   4               ;Align to doubleword boundary
```

.ALPHA: Place Segments in Alphabetic Order

Applicable assemblers: Microsoft Quick Assembler 2.51, MASM 5.1, MASM 6.0, TASM 2.0, TASM 3.0

Directive category: Complete segment control

Syntax:

```
.ALPHA
```

Description: Normally, the assembler places segments in the OBJ file in the order in which they occur in the source file. You can override this, however, with the .ALPHA directive. Typically, you would use this directive only if there were a specific need to do so. For example, early versions of MASM (1.0, 2.0, and 3.0) put segments in alphabetical order by default; if you are working with source code developed for early versions of MASM, you may need to use this directive to ensure compatibility.

You can affect the ordering of segments with the .DOSSEG, DOSSEG, .SEQ, and SEQ directives also.

ARG: Specify Arguments Passed on the Stack

Applicable assemblers: MASM 5.1, TASM 2.0, TASM 3.0

Directive category: Procedures and code labels

Syntax:

```
ARG argument[, argument] ... [=label] [RETURNS
    argument[, argument] ...]
```

where each argument has the following construction:

label [[*arraysize*]] [:[*debugsize*] [*type*][:*count*]]

Description: This directive can be used to specify arguments being passed from a high-level language. Each argument has, at minimum, a label name and a type, such as WORD or DWORD. In the syntax for the directive, the label following the equal sign can be used with the RET instruction at the end of the routine to clean up the stack (if necessary); the assembler automatically assigns the collective length of the arguments to this label.

In effect, the ARG directive, like the EQU statement, is a way of specifying rigid equates that point onto the stack. For instance, each argument specified with the ARG directive is treated by the assembler as an offset on the stack. Thus, the statement

ARG First, Second, Third:WORD

may be functionally equivalent, later in the program, to

```
First  EQU     [BP+4]
Second EQU     [BP+6]
Third  EQU     [BP+8]
```

Every time the assembler subsequently encounters the label, it substitutes the pointer onto the stack. Clearly, the EQU values used depend on the programming model (see .MODEL) being used by the assembler.

This directive is not available in MASM 6.0. With MASM 6.0, you specify arguments in the PROC declaration at the beginning of the subroutine.

ASSUME: Assign Segment Registers

Applicable assemblers: Microsoft Quick Assembler 2.51, MASM 5.1, MASM 6.0, TASM 2.0, TASM 3.0

Directive category: Simplified segment control, complete segment control

Syntax:

ASSUME [*segmentreg*:]*name* [, *segmentreg*:*name*] ...

Description: This directive is used to specify which user-defined segment names should be associated with which segment registers. The segmentreg can be CS, DS, ES, SS, FS, or GS. The name can be any user-defined segment name, or the special name NOTHING. If the name is not NOTHING, segmentreg is required. The name must also correspond to a name declared using a GROUP or SEGMENT directive.

Examples:

```
ASSUME  CS:CODESEG, DS:DATASEG, ES:NOTHING
ASSUME  CS:CODESEG, DS:CODESEG
ASSUME  NOTHING
```

%BIN: Set Listing-File Object-Code Field Width

Applicable assemblers: MASM 5.1, TASM 2.0, TASM 3.0

Directive category: Listing control

Syntax:

```
%BIN width
```

Description: When you have requested a listing file (LST file) during assembly, this directive controls the width of the object-code field. The default value is 20 characters wide, but you can set it to any reasonable value.

.BREAK: Terminate a .REPEAT or .WHILE Loop

Applicable assemblers: MASM 6.0

Directive category: Control flow

Syntax:

```
.BREAK [.IF condition]
```

Description: When you are using the .REPEAT or .WHILE directives to control program flow, you can use the .BREAK directive to terminate control of the loop. This directive is another example of the way in which MASM is mutating toward high-level language coding and constructs. In this case, .BREAK functions in the same manner as the BREAK statement in C.

The condition used by the loop must resolve to either true or false. It can be complex in nature (testing for two or more conditions) and may contain any of the following operators:

Operator	Meaning
==	Equal
!=	Not equal
>	Greater than
>=	Greater than or equal to
<	Less than
<=	Less than or equal to
&	Bit test
&&	Logical AND
||	Logical OR
!	Logical NOT

You also can test automatically the condition of flags by using the following specialized flag-name operators:

Operator	Sample Use
CARRY?	.BREAK .IF (CARRY?)
OVERFLOW?	.BREAK .IF (OVERFLOW?)
PARITY?	.BREAK .IF (PARITY?)
SIGN?	.BREAK .IF (SIGN?)
ZERO?	.BREAK .IF (ZERO?)

Example:

```
.REPEAT                 ;Wait for the Enter key to be pressed
MOV     AH,7            ;Direct character input without echo
INT     21h             ;DOS services
.BREAK  .IF AL == 27    ;Jump out if Esc was pressed
.UNTIL  (AL == 13)      ;Keep going until Enter is pressed
```

BYTE: Allocate a Byte of Storage Space

Applicable assemblers: MASM 6.0

Directive category: Data allocation

Syntax:

[*label*] BYTE *expression*[, *expression*]

Description: This directive is equivalent to the DB directive. It is used to allocate memory in the executable file for data storage. The label is a user-defined name you can use later to refer symbolically to the stored information. Each expression must be one of the following:

❏ A number between –128 and 255

❏ A formula resolving to a number between –128 and 255

❏ Text characters

❏ A question mark (used to hold space but not initialize the data area)

In addition, you can use the DUP operator to specify multiple occurrences of the data in the expression.

If the data allocated by the BYTE directive is actually longer than a single byte, the label refers only to the first byte of the allocated data.

If you are working explicitly with signed data, you can use the SBYTE directive also.

Examples:

```
ValidKeys   BYTE    'YyNy'
ULCol       BYTE    00
BoxSize     BYTE    5 * 7
Buffer      BYTE    2048 DUP(?)
Stack       BTYE    128 DUP('STACK    ')
```

CATSTR: Concatenate Strings

Applicable assemblers: Microsoft Quick Assembler 2.51, MASM 5.1, MASM 6.0, TASM 2.0, TASM 3.0

Directive category: String control

Syntax:

label CATSTR string[, string] ...

Description: This directive, which is used to make string building easier, can be used also to convert numbers to ASCII text. This conversion takes place during assembly, not at run-time.

The label is a user-defined name you can use later to refer symbolically to the new string. Each string can be any of the following:

❏ A string enclosed in angle brackets (<>)

❏ An existing text macro

❏ A percent sign followed by a number to be included in the text string

It is important that you realize that the resulting string is not stored in the executable file; rather, it is used by the assembler for later substitutions. In this way, CATSTR is functionally equivalent to the TEXTEQU directive (available only in MASM 6.0).

Examples:

```
BoxSize     BYTE    5 * 7
BoxMessage  CATSTR  <The size of the box is >, %BoxSize, < units.>
```

.CODE: Define Beginning of Program Code

Applicable assemblers: Microsoft Quick Assembler 2.51, MASM 6.0, TASM 2.0, TASM 3.0

Directive category: Simplified segment control

Syntax:

```
.CODE [name]
```

Description: If you are using simplified segment directives, you will be using the .CODE directive, which is used to inform the assembler that the information immediately following should be placed in the code segment. You must use the .MODEL directive before using .CODE.

If you are using the medium, large, or huge memory model, you can use an optional name with .CODE; otherwise, the name is ignored. If you do not provide a name, the assembler creates one automatically from the module name. Later, the linker uses this name to concatenate and order segments.

CODESEG: Define Beginning of Program Code

Applicable assemblers: TASM 2.0, TASM 3.0

Directive category: Simplified segment control

Syntax:

```
CODESEG [name]
```

Description: This directive is the same as the .CODE directive, but is meant to be used in ideal mode only. CODESEG is used to inform the assembler that the information immediately following should be placed in the code segment. You must use the .MODEL directive before using CODESEG.

If you are using the medium, large, or huge memory model, you can use an optional name with CODESEG; otherwise the name is ignored. If you do not provide a name, the assembler creates one automatically from the module name. Later, the linker uses this name to concatenate and order segments.

COMM: Define a Communal Variable

Applicable assemblers: Microsoft Quick Assembler 2.51, MASM 5.1, MASM 6.0, TASM 2.0, TASM 3.0

Directive category: Scope and visibility

Syntax:

COMM vardef[, vardef] ...

where each vardef has the following construction:

[language] [distance] label[[arraysize]]:type[:count]

Description: Communal variables are used for compatibility with some high-level languages. They are similar in nature to external variables declared with EXTERN but, once set, they cannot be changed. Because the memory space for communal variables is not assigned until the executable file is loaded, using them can reduce the file size of your programs.

In each variable definition, the language can be one of the following, depending on your assembler:

Language	MASM	TASM
BASIC	X	X
C	X	X
CPP		X
FORTRAN	X	X
NOLANGUAGE		X
Pascal	X	X
Prolog		X
STDCALL	X	
SYSCALL	X	

The distance can be either NEAR or FAR, and the type can be one of the standard data sizes such as BYTE, WORD, or DWORD.

COMMENT: Define the Start of a Comment Block

Applicable assemblers: Microsoft Quick Assembler 2.51, MASM 5.1, MASM 6.0, TASM 2.0, TASM 3.0

Directive category: Miscellaneous

Syntax:

COMMENT *char*

Description: This directive is invaluable for use in defining comment blocks in your program. It is used extensively at the start of each assembly language program in this book.

The char is the character the assembler will use to define the limits of the beginning and end of the comment block. The assembler ignores everything between char and the second occurrence of char, treating them as comments. It is important to use a character that will not be used in the comment block itself.

Example:

```
Comment ¦
*********************************************************************

File:     CEX1.ASM
Author:   Allen L. Wyatt
Date:     8/26/91

Purpose:  Subroutine designed to turn the cursor on and off.

Format:   curon()
          curoff()


*********************************************************************¦
```

%CONDS: List All Conditional Statements
Applicable assemblers: TASM 2.0, TASM 3.0

Directive category: Listing control

Syntax:

%CONDS

Description: Instructs the assembler to include all conditional code in the listing file, whether it is included in the OBJ file or not. This directive is the same as the .LFCOND directive.

.CONST: Define Beginning of Constant Data

Applicable assemblers: Microsoft Quick Assembler 2.51, MASM 5.1, MASM 6.0, TASM 2.0, TASM 3.0

Directive category: Simplified segment control

Syntax:

.CONST

Description: This is one of several available simplified data-segment directives. The others include .DATA, .DATA?, .FARDATA, and .FARDATA?. If you are using TASM, you can also use CONST, DATASEG, and FARDATA.

This directive is used to delineate data that will not change during program execution. It is not a necessary segment in stand-alone programs, but may be necessary for compatibility with some high-level languages.

CONST: Define Beginning of Constant Data

Applicable assemblers: TASM 2.0, TASM 3.0

Directive category: Simplified segment control

Syntax:

CONST

Description: This is one of several available simplified data-segment directives. The others include .CONST, .DATA, .DATA?, DATASEG, .FARDATA, .FARDATA?, and FARDATA.

This directive is used to delineate data that will not change during program execution. It is not a necessary segment in stand-alone programs, but may be necessary for compatibility with some high-level languages.

.CONTINUE: Modify Execution of a .REPEAT or .WHILE Loop

Applicable assemblers: MASM 6.0

Directive category: Control flow

Syntax:

```
.CONTINUE [.IF condition]
```

Description: When you are using the `.REPEAT` or `.WHILE` directives to control program flow, you can use the `.CONTINUE` directive to modify how program execution occurs in the loop. This directive is another example of the way in which MASM is mutating toward high-level language coding and constructs. In this case, `.CONTINUE` functions in the same way as the `CONTINUE` statement in C. It causes program control to be transferred to the end of the loop.

The `condition` used by the loop must resolve to either true or false. It can be complex in nature (testing for two or more conditions), and may contain any of the following operators:

Operator	Meaning
==	Equal
!=	Not equal
>	Greater than
>=	Greater than or equal to
<	Less than
<=	Less than or equal to
&	Bit test
&&	Logical AND
||	Logical OR
!	Logical NOT

You can also test automatically the condition of flags by using the following specialized flag-name operators:

Operator	Sample Use
CARRY?	.CONTINUE .IF (CARRY?)
OVERFLOW?	.CONTINUE .IF (OVERFLOW?)
PARITY?	.CONTINUE .IF (PARITY?)
SIGN?	.CONTINUE .IF (SIGN?)
ZERO?	.CONTINUE .IF (ZERO?)

Example:

```
MOV       AL,0              ;Start out with clean slate
MOV       CX,0              ;Got no characters so far
.WHILE    (AL != 13)        ;Keep going until Enter is pressed
MOV       AH,7              ;Direct character input without echo
INT       21h               ;DOS services
.BREAK    .IF AL == 27      ;Jump out if Esc was pressed
.CONTINUE .IF (AL '0') ¦¦ (AL > '9') ;Only want digits
PUSH      AX                ;Save character for later
MOV       DL,AL             ;Get ready to output character
MOV       AH,2              ;Output character
INT       21h               ;DOS services
INC       CX                ;Character count
.BREAK    .IF CX == 4       ;Only get up to 4 characters
.ENDW
```

.CREF: Enable Cross-Referencing

Applicable assemblers: MASM 5.1, MASM 6.0, TASM 2.0, TASM 3.0

Directive category: Listing control

Syntax:

```
.CREF
```

Description: This is the default condition for listing files generated by the assembler. It results in cross-reference information being generated and included at the end of the listing file. If the .NOCREF or %XCREF directives were in effect, cross-referencing information is included only from the line in which .CREF is encountered.

When used with TASM, this directive also causes an XRF (cross-reference) file to be generated.

%CREF: Enable Cross-Referencing

Applicable assemblers: TASM 2.0, TASM 3.0

Directive category: Listing control

Syntax:

%CREF

Description: This is the default condition for listing files generated by the assembler. It results in cross-reference information being generated and included at the end of the listing file. If the %NOCREF, .NOCREF, .XCREF, or %XCREF directives were in effect, cross-referencing information is included only from the line in which .CREF is encountered.

This directive also causes an XRF (cross-reference) file to be generated.

%CREFALL: Cross-Reference All Variables

Applicable assemblers: TASM 2.0, TASM 3.0

Directive category: Listing control

Syntax:

%CREFALL

Description: This is the default condition for listing files created with TASM. It results in cross-referencing all referenced and unreferenced variables, assuming that general cross-referencing has been enabled. This directive undoes the effect of the %CREFREF and %CREFUREF directives.

%CREFREF: Cross-Reference Only Referenced Variables

Applicable assemblers: TASM 2.0, TASM 3.0

Directive category: Listing control

Syntax:

%CREFREF

Description: After this directive is processed, only variables that are referenced as operands are listed in the cross-reference part of the listing file and in the XRF file. Normally, all variables (referenced and unreferenced) are included. This directive is used if you don't want the cross-reference to be cluttered by variables that are defined but never referenced.

The %CREFALL directive undoes the effects of %CREFREF.

%CREFUREF: Cross-Reference Only Unreferenced Variables

Applicable assemblers: TASM 2.0, TASM 3.0

Directive category: Listing control

Syntax:

%CREFUREF

Description: After this directive is processed, only variables that are defined but not referenced are included in the cross-reference part of the listing file and in the XRF file. Normally, all variables (referenced and unreferenced) are included.

The %CREFALL directive undoes the effects of %CREFUREF.

%CTLS: Include Listing-Control Directives in the Listing File

Applicable assemblers: TASM 2.0, TASM 3.0

Directive category: Listing control

Syntax:

%CTLS

Description: Normally, TASM does not include listing-control directives in a generated listing file. This directive causes these types of directives to be included. Since the change takes place after this directive is executed, the line including this directive never appears in a listing file.

.DATA: Define Beginning of Data Segment

Applicable assemblers: Microsoft Quick Assembler 2.51, MASM 5.1, MASM 6.0, TASM 2.0, TASM 3.0

Directive category: Simplified segment control

Syntax:

`.DATA`

Description: This is one of several available simplified data-segment directives. The others include `.CONST`, `.DATA?`, `.FARDATA`, and `.FARDATA?`. If you are using TASM, you can also use `CONST`, `DATASEG`, `FARDATA`, `UDATASEG`, and `UFARDATA`.

This is a simplified segment directive used to inform the assembler that the information immediately following should be placed in the data segment. You must use the `.MODEL` directive before using `.DATA`.

If you are using TASM, this directive is the same as the `DATASEG` directive.

.DATA?: Define Beginning of Uninitialized Data Segment

Applicable assemblers: Microsoft Quick Assembler 2.51, MASM 5.1, MASM 6.0, TASM 2.0, TASM 3.0

Directive category: Simplified segment control

Syntax:

`.DATA?`

Description: This is one of several available simplified data-segment directives. The others include `.CONST`, `.DATA`, `.FARDATA`, and `.FARDATA?`. If you are using TASM, you can also use `CONST`, `DATASEG`, `FARDATA`, `UDATASEG`, and `UFARDATA`.

This is a simplified segment directive used to inform the assembler that the information immediately following should be placed in a special uninitialized data segment. You must use the `.MODEL` directive before using `.DATA?`.

It is not necessary to use this special type of segment, but you may want to use it to group your data. Such grouping may help you better understand the different parts of your program.

If you are using TASM, this directive is the same as the `UDATASEG` directive.

DATASEG: Define Beginning of Data Segment

Applicable assemblers: TASM 2.0, TASM 3.0

Directive category: Simplified segment control

Syntax:

DATASEG

Description: This is one of several simplified data-segment directives available. The others include .CONST, CONST, .DATA, .DATA?, .FARDATA, .FARDATA?, FARDATA, UDATASEG, and UFARDATA. This directive is the same as the .DATA directive, but is designed to be used in ideal mode only.

This is a simplified segment directive used to inform the assembler that the information immediately following should be placed in the data segment. You must use the .MODEL or MODEL directives before using DATASEG.

DB: Allocate a Byte of Storage Space

Applicable assemblers: Microsoft Quick Assembler 2.51, MASM 5.1, MASM 6.0, TASM 2.0, TASM 3.0

Directive category: Data allocation

Syntax:

[*label*] DB *expression*[*, expression*]

Description: This directive is used to allocate memory in the executable file for data storage. The label is a user-defined name you can use later to refer symbolically to the stored information. Each expression must be one of the following:

❏ A number between –128 and 255

❏ A formula resolving to a number between –128 and 255

❏ Text characters

❏ A question mark (used to hold space but not initialize the data area)

In addition, you can use the DUP operator to specify multiple occurrences of the data in the expression.

If the data allocated by the BYTE directive is longer than a single byte, the label refers only to the first byte of the allocated data.

If you are using MASM 6.0, this directive is equivalent to the BYTE directive. If you are working explicitly with signed data, you can use the SBYTE directive also.

Examples:

```
ValidKeys   DB      'YyNy'
ULCol       DB      00
BoxSize     DB      5 * 7
Buffer      DB      2048 DUP(?)
Stack       DB      128 DUP('STACK    ')
```

DD: Allocate a Doubleword of Storage Space

Applicable assemblers: Microsoft Quick Assembler 2.51, MASM 5.1, MASM 6.0, TASM 2.0, TASM 3.0

Directive category: Data allocation

Syntax:

[label] DD *expression[, expression]*

Description: This directive is used to allocate four bytes of memory (a doubleword) for data storage in the executable file. The label is a user-defined name you can use later to refer symbolically to the stored information. Each expression must be one of the following:

❏ A number between –2,147,483,648 and 4,294,967,295

❏ A formula resolving to a number between –2,147,483,648 and 4,294,967,295

❏ A 32-bit floating-point number between $\pm1.18 \times 10^{-38}$ and $\pm3.40 \times 10^{38}$

❏ A far address pointer (segment and offset)

❏ A question mark (used to hold space but not initialize the data area)

In addition, you can use the DUP operator to specify multiple occurrences of the data in the expression.

If the data allocated by the DD directive is longer than a single doubleword, the label refers only to the first doubleword of the allocated data.

If you are using MASM 6.0, this directive is equivalent to the DWORD directive. You can also use the REAL4 directive for floating-point numbers.

Examples:

```
FarAddress   DD      Routine
Values       DD      2.345, 59.682
Counter      DD      0
MemArea      DD      1024 * 64 * 4
Array        DD      12 DUP(?)
```

%DEPTH: Set Listing-File Depth-Field Width

Applicable assemblers: TASM 2.0, TASM 3.0

Directive category: Listing control

Syntax:

%DEPTH *width*

Description: When you have requested a listing file (LST file) during assembly, this directive controls the width of the depth field. This field is used as an indent when INCLUDE files and macros are expanded. The default value is 1 character wide, but you can set it to any reasonable value.

DF: Allocate 6 Bytes of Storage Space

Applicable assemblers: MASM 5.1, MASM 6.0, TASM 2.0, TASM 3.0

Directive category: Data allocation

Syntax:

[*label*] DF *expression*[, *expression*]

Description: This directive is used to allocate 6 bytes of memory for data storage in the executable file. Typically, this data size is used for 48-bit far pointers in the 80386 or 80486 environment. The label is a user-defined name you can use later to refer symbolically to the stored information. Each expression must be one of the following:

❑ A number between –140,737,488,355,328 and 281,474,976,710,655

❑ A formula resolving to a number between –140,737,488,355,328 and 281,474,976,710,655

❏ A 48-bit far address pointer (segment and 32-bit offset)

❏ A question mark (used to hold space but not initialize the data area)

In addition, you can use the DUP operator to specify multiple occurrences of the data in the expression.

If the data allocated by the DF directive is longer than six bytes, the label refers only to the first six bytes of the allocated data.

If you are using MASM 6.0, this directive is equivalent to the FWORD directive. For some assembler versions, this directive is equivalent to the DP directive.

Examples:

```
FarAddress  DF      Routine
Values      DF      2.345, 59.682
Counter     DF      0
MemArea     DF      1024 * 64 * 4
Array       DF      12 DUP(?)
```

DISPLAY: Output a String to the Screen

Applicable assemblers: TASM 2.0, TASM 3.0

Directive category: Miscellaneous

Syntax:

```
DISPLAY "text"
```

Description: This directive is used to display a text string to the video monitor during assembly. It does not result in any code being generated, nor does it take memory in the generated file.

The string to be displayed, text, must be enclosed in quotation marks. You can use this directive to aid in debugging, so that you can see immediately when certain conditional instructions are being assembled.

Similar functions are provided by the ECHO and %OUT directives.

Example:

```
DISPLAY "Now adding debug routines"
```

.DOSSEG: Order Segments in Microsoft High-Level-Language Order

Applicable assemblers: MASM 6.0

Directive category: Complete segment control

Syntax:

```
.DOSSEG
```

Description: This directive causes the linker to order segments in a structured manner defined by Microsoft high-level languages. The directive typically is used in stand-alone programs, and then only in the main module. This directive was introduced with MASM 6.0 so that the instruction would be more consistent with the syntax of the .ALPHA and .SEQ directives.

This directive orders segments as follows:

1. Code segments with the class name CODE.

2. All other code segments.

3. Data segments with the class name BEGDATA.

4. All other data segments except those with the class names BSS or STACK.

5. Data segments with the class name BSS.

6. Data segments with the class name STACK.

You can also affect the ordering of segments with the .ALPHA, ALPHA, .SEQ, and SEQ directives.

This directive is equivalent to the DOSSEG directive.

DOSSEG: Order Segments in Microsoft High-Level-Language Order

Applicable assemblers: Microsoft Quick Assembler 2.51, MASM 5.1, MASM 6.0, TASM 2.0, TASM 3.0

Directive category: Complete segment control

Syntax:

```
DOSSEG
```

Description: This directive causes the linker to order segments in a structured manner defined by Microsoft high-level languages. It is typically used in stand-alone programs, and then only in the main module.

This directive orders segments as follows:

1. Code segments with the class name CODE.

2. All other code segments.

3. Data segments with the class name BEGDATA.

4. All other data segments except those with the class names BSS or STACK.

5. Data segments with the class name BSS.

6. Data segments with the class name STACK.

You can also affect the ordering of segments with the .ALPHA, ALPHA, .SEQ, and SEQ directives.

DP: Allocate 6 Bytes of Storage Space

Applicable assemblers: MASM 5.1, TASM 2.0, TASM 3.0

Directive category: Data allocation

Syntax:

```
[label] DP expression[, expression]
```

Description: This directive is equivalent to the DF directive. It is used to allocate 6 bytes of memory for data storage in the executable file. Typically, this data size is used for 48-bit far pointers in the 80386 or 80486 environment. The label is a user-defined name you can use later to refer symbolically to the stored information. Each expression must be one of the following:

❑ A number between –140,737,488,355,328 and 281,474,976,710,655

❑ A formula resolving to a number between –140,737,488,355,328 and 281,474,976,710,655

❑ A 48-bit far address pointer (segment and 32-bit offset)

❑ A question mark (used to hold space but not initialize the data area)

In addition, you can use the DUP operator to specify multiple occurrences of the data in the expression.

If the data allocated by the DP directive is longer than six bytes, the label refers only to the first six bytes of the allocated data.

This directive is not available with MASM 6.0; you should use FWORD or DF instead.

Examples:

```
FarAddress  DP      Routine
Values      DP      2.345, 59.682
Counter     DP      0
MemArea     DP      1024 * 64 * 4
Array       DP      12 DUP(?)
```

DQ: Allocate a Quadword of Storage Space

Applicable assemblers: Microsoft Quick Assembler 2.51, MASM 5.1, MASM 6.0, TASM 2.0, TASM 3.0

Directive category: Data allocation

Syntax:

[*label*] DQ *expression*[, *expression*]

Description: This directive is used to allocate 8 bytes of memory (a quadword) for data storage in the executable file. Typically, this data size is used for 8-byte integers used with numeric coprocessors. The label is a user-defined name you can use later to refer symbolically to the stored information. Each expression must be one of the following:

❑ A number between -2^{63} and $2^{64}-1$

❑ A formula resolving to a number between -2^{63} and $2^{64}-1$

❑ A 64-bit floating-point number between $\pm 2.23 \times 10^{-308}$ and $\pm 1.79 \times 10^{308}$

❑ A question mark (used to hold space but not initialize the data area)

In addition, you can use the DUP operator to specify multiple occurrences of the data in the expression.

If the data allocated by the DQ directive is longer than a single quadword, the label refers only to the first quadword of the allocated data.

If you are using MASM 6.0, this directive is equivalent to the QWORD directive. You can use the REAL8 directive also for floating-point numbers.

Examples:

```
Values     DQ      12345.6789, 987.6543
MemArea    DQ      1024 * 64 * 4
Array      DQ      12 DUP(?)
```

DT: Allocate 10 Bytes of Storage Space

Applicable assemblers: Microsoft Quick Assembler 2.51, MASM 5.1, MASM 6.0, TASM 2.0, TASM 3.0

Directive category: Data allocation

Syntax:

[*label*] DT *expression*[, *expression*]

Description: This directive is used to allocate 10 bytes of memory for data storage in the executable file. Typically, this data size is used for 10-byte integers or real-number formats used with numeric coprocessors. The label is a user-defined name you can use later to refer symbolically to the stored information. Each expression must be one of the following:

❏ A number between -2^{79} and $2^{80}-1$

❏ A formula resolving to a number between -2^{79} and $2^{80}-1$

❏ A packed decimal number between 0 and $10^{20}-1$

❏ An 80-bit temporary floating-point number between $\pm3.37 \times 10^{-4932}$ and $\pm1.18 \times 10^{4932}$

❏ A question mark (used to hold space but not initialize the data area)

In addition, you can use the DUP operator to specify multiple occurrences of the data in the expression.

If the data allocated by the DT directive is longer than 10 bytes, the label refers only to the first 10 bytes of the allocated data.

If you are using MASM 6.0, this directive is equivalent to the TWORD directive. You can also use the REAL10 directive for floating-point numbers.

Examples:

```
Values     DT      12345.6789, 987.6543
MemArea    DT      1024 * 64 * 4
Array      DT      12 DUP(?)
```

DW: Allocate a Word of Storage Space

Applicable assemblers: Microsoft Quick Assembler 2.51, MASM 5.1, MASM 6.0, TASM 2.0, TASM 3.0

Directive category: Data allocation

Syntax:

[*label*] DW *expression*[, *expression*]

Description: This directive is used to allocate 2 bytes of memory (a word) for data storage in the executable file. The label is a user-defined name you can use later to refer symbolically to the stored information. Each expression must be one of the following:

- ❏ A number between –32,767 and 65,535
- ❏ A formula resolving to a number between –32,767 and 65,535
- ❏ An offset for an address pointer
- ❏ A segment for an address pointer
- ❏ A question mark (used to hold space but not initialize the data area)

In addition, you can use the DUP operator to specify multiple occurrences of the data in the expression.

If the data allocated by the DW directive is longer than a single word, the label refers only to the first word of the allocated data.

If you are using MASM 6.0, this directive is equivalent to the WORD directive. If you are working exclusively with signed data, you can use the SWORD directive.

Examples:

```
Address1     DW      Routine          ;Address1 contains only the offset
Address2     DW      OFFSET Routine   ;Address1 contains only the offset
Address3     DW      SEGMENT Routine  ;Address1 contains only the segment
Counter      DW      0
ScreenSize   DW      80 * 25
Array        DW      12 DUP(?)
```

DWORD: Allocate a Doubleword of Storage Space

Applicable assemblers: MASM 6.0

Directive category: Data allocation

Syntax:

[*label*] DWORD *expression*[, *expression*]

Description: This directive is equivalent to the DD directive. It is used to allocate 4 bytes of memory (a doubleword) for data storage in the executable file. The label is a user-defined name you can use later to refer symbolically to the stored information. Each expression must be one of the following:

❑ A number between –2,147,483,648 and 4,294,967,295

❑ A formula resolving to a number between –2,147,483,648 and 4,294,967,295

❑ A 32-bit floating-point number between $\pm 1.18 \times 10^{-38}$ and $\pm 3.40 \times 10^{38}$

❑ A far address pointer (segment and offset)

❑ A question mark (used to hold space but not initialize the data area)

In addition, you can use the DUP operator to specify multiple occurrences of the data in the expression.

If the data allocated by the DWORD directive is longer than a single doubleword, the label refers only to the first doubleword of the allocated data.

If you are working exclusively with signed numbers, you can use the SDWORD directive. You can use the REAL4 directive also for floating-point numbers.

Examples:

```
FarAddress   DWORD    Routine
Values       DWORD    2.345, 59.682
Counter      DWORD    0
MemArea      DWORD    1024 * 64 * 4
Array        DWORD    12 DUP(?)
```

ECHO: Output a String to the Screen

Applicable assemblers: MASM 6.0

Directive category: Miscellaneous

Syntax:

```
ECHO text
```

Description: This directive is used to display a text string to the video monitor during assembly. It does not result in any code being generated, nor does it take memory in the generated file.

You can use this directive to aid in debugging, so that you can see immediately when certain conditional instructions are being assembled. The DISPLAY and %OUT directives provide similar functions.

Example:

```
ECHO Now adding debug routines
```

.ELSE: Conditional Program Execution

Applicable assemblers: MASM 6.0

Directive category: Control flow

Syntax:

```
.ELSE
```

Description: This directive, in conjunction with the .IF and .ENDIF directives, can be used in assembly language programs to provide the same functionality as their counterparts in high-level languages.

Example:

```
GetKey:     MOV     AH,7                    ;Direct character input without echo
            INT     21h                     ;DOS services
            .IF     (AL >= 'a') ¦¦ (AL <= 'z')
            AND     AL,05Fh                 ;Convert to uppercase
            .ENDIF
            .IF     AL == 'X'
            MOV     BX, OFFSET Exit         ;Address of exit routine
            .ELSEIF AL == 'B'
            MOV     BX, OFFSET Beginning    ;Address warm program start
            .ELSEIF AL == 'F'
            MOV     BX, OFFSET FileOps      ;Address of file operations
            .ELSE
            MOV     BX, OFFSET GetKey       ;Beginning of this routine
            .ENDIF
            JMP     [BX]                    ;Jump to right routine
```

ELSE: Conditional Assembly

Applicable assemblers: Microsoft Quick Assembler 2.51, MASM 5.1, MASM 6.0, TASM 2.0, TASM 3.0

Directive category: Conditional assembly

Syntax:

ELSE

Description: This directive, in conjunction with the IF, ELSEIF, and ENDIF directives, can be used in assembly language programs to control which portions of the code are assembled.

The instructions immediately following the ELSE directive, up to the ENDIF directive, are executed if the expression used in the original IF directive is false. Any preceding ELSEIF directives must also evaluate as false for the instructions following the ELSE directive to be executed.

Example:

```
DemoCount    DW      0
             IF      Demo EQ 1
DemoMessage DB      'This is a bare-bones demo version of the program', 0
             ELSEIF  Demo EQ 2
DemoMessage DB      'This is a deluxe demo version of the program', 0
             ELSE
             %OUT Demo value is not set correctly
             ENDIF
```

.ELSEIF: Conditional Program Execution

Application assemblers: MASM 6.0

Directive category: Control flow

Syntax:

.ELSEIF *condition*

Description: This directive, in conjunction with the .IF and .ENDIF directives, can be used in assembly language programs to provide the same functionality as their counterparts in high-level languages.

The condition used by the .ELSEIF directive must resolve to either true or false. It can be complex (testing for two or more conditions) and may contain any of the following operators:

Operator	Meaning
==	Equal
!=	Not equal
>	Greater than
>=	Greater than or equal to
<	Less than
<=	Less than or equal to
&	Bit test
&&	Logical AND
||	Logical OR
!	Logical NOT

You can also test automatically the condition of flags by using the following specialized flag-name operators:

Operator	Sample Use
CARRY?	.BREAK .IF (CARRY?)
OVERFLOW?	.BREAK .IF (OVERFLOW?)
PARITY?	.BREAK .IF (PARITY?)
SIGN?	.BREAK .IF (SIGN?)
ZERO?	.BREAK .IF (ZERO?)

Example:

```
GetKey:   MOV      AH,7                          ;Direct character input without echo
          INT      21h                           ;DOS services
          .IF      (AL >= 'a') || (AL <= 'z')
          AND      AL,05Fh                       ;Convert to uppercase
          .ENDIF
          .IF      AL == 'X'
          MOV      BX, OFFSET Exit               ;Address of exit routine
          .ELSEIF  AL == 'B'
          MOV      BX, OFFSET Beginning          ;Address warm program start
          .ELSEIF  AL == 'F'
          MOV      BX, OFFSET FileOps            ;Address of file operations
```

```
        .ELSE
        MOV     BX, OFFSET GetKey       ;Beginning of this routine
        .ENDIF
        JMP     [BX]                    ;Jump to right routine
```

ELSEIF: Conditional Assembly

Applicable assemblers: Microsoft Quick Assembler 2.51, MASM 6.0, TASM 2.0, TASM 3.0

Directive category: Conditional assembly

Syntax:

ELSEIF *expression*

Description: This directive, in conjunction with the IF and ENDIF directives, can be used in assembly language programs to control which portions of the code are assembled.

The conditional expression must evaluate to true for the following code to be assembled. If the expression is not true, assembly continues at the next ELSEIF, ELSE, or ENDIF directive.

Example:

```
DemoCount   DW      0
            IF      Demo EQ 1
DemoMessage DB      'This is a bare-bones demo version of the program', 0
            ELSEIF  Demo EQ 2
DemoMessage DB      'This is a deluxe demo version of the program', 0
            ELSE
            %OUT Demo value is not set correctly
            ENDIF
```

EMUL: Use Floating-Point Emulation

Applicable assemblers: TASM 2.0, TASM 3.0

Directive category: Global control

Syntax:

EMUL

Description: Normally, TASM assumes that you have some sort of numeric coprocessor present in your system. This means that during assembly the assembler generates code that can take advantage of the coprocessor. If you include this directive, TASM assumes that you have installed an emulation package which will provide the higher-level math functions normally provided by the NPX.

END: Designate Source-File End

Applicable assemblers: Microsoft Quick Assembler 2.51, MASM 5.1, MASM 6.0, TASM 2.0, TASM 3.0

Directive category: Complete segment control

Syntax:

```
END [address]
```

Description: This directive is designed to be the last statement in your source file. It lets the assembler know that the end of the file has been reached and assembly should stop.

Optionally, you can include an address that designates the address at which you want execution to begin in the program. This address typically is in the form of a label previously assigned to the beginning of the main routine.

.ENDIF: Conditional Program Execution

Applicable assemblers: MASM 6.0

Directive category: Control flow

Syntax:

```
.ENDIF
```

Description: This directive, in conjunction with the .IF directive, can be used in assembly language programs to provide the same functionality as their counterparts in high-level languages.

Example:

```
GetKey:     MOV     AH,7                    ;Direct character input without echo
            INT     21h                     ;DOS services
            .IF     (AL >= 'a') ¦¦ (AL <= 'z')
            AND     AL,05Fh                 ;Convert to uppercase
            .ENDIF
            .IF     AL == 'X'
            MOV     BX, OFFSET Exit         ;Address of exit routine
            .ELSEIF AL == 'B'
            MOV     BX, OFFSET Beginning    ;Address warm program start
          ' .ELSEIF AL == 'F'
            MOV     BX, OFFSET FileOps      ;Address of file operations
            .ELSE
            MOV     BX, OFFSET GetKey       ;Beginning of this routine
            .ENDIF
            JMP     [BX]                    ;Jump to right routine
```

ENDIF: Conditional Assembly

Applicable assemblers: Microsoft Quick Assembler 2.51, MASM 5.1, MASM 6.0, TASM 2.0, TASM 3.0

Directive category: Conditional assembly

Syntax:

ENDIF

Description: This directive, in conjunction with a conditional assembly instruction, can be used in assembly language programs to control which portions of the code are assembled. The ENDIF directive is used to conclude a conditional assembly block begun with one of the following directives:

IF	IFDIFI
IF1	IFE
IF2	IFIDN
IFB	IFIDNI
IFDEF	IFNB
IFDIF	IFNDEF

Example:

```
DemoCount     DW       0
              IF       Demo EQ 1
DemoMessage DB         'This is a bare-bones demo version of the program', 0
              ELSEIF   Demo EQ 2
DemoMessage DB         'This is a deluxe demo version of the program', 0
              ELSE
              %OUT Demo value is not set correctly
              ENDIF
```

ENDM: End a Macro or Loop

Applicable assemblers: Microsoft Quick Assembler 2.51, MASM 5.1, MASM 6.0, TASM 2.0, TASM 3.0

Directive category: Macros and repeat blocks

Syntax:

```
ENDM
```

Description: ENDM can be used in several ways. In a general sense, it simply marks the end of a macro begun with the MACRO directive, or the end of a loop begun with the IRP, IRPC, or REPT directives. If you are using MASM 6.0, it also terminates loops started with the FOR, FORC, REPEAT, and WHILE directives.

ENDP: End a Procedure

Applicable assemblers: Microsoft Quick Assembler 2.51, MASM 5.1, MASM 6.0, TASM 2.0, TASM 3.0

Directive category: Procedures and code labels

Syntax:

```
[label] ENDP
```

or, if using TASM's ideal mode:

```
ENDP [label]
```

Description: Defines the point at which the assembler should consider the procedure closed. Generally, the ENDP directive is used on the line immediately following the RET instruction.

The optional `label` must match the procedure-name label used at the beginning of the procedure.

ENDS: End a Segment or Structure

Applicable assemblers: Microsoft Quick Assembler 2.51, MASM 5.1, MASM 6.0, TASM 2.0, TASM 3.0

Directive category: Complete segment control, complex data types

Syntax:

```
label ENDS
```

or, if using TASM's ideal mode:

```
ENDS [label]
```

Description: Defines the point at which the assembler should consider a segment or structure closed. If ENDS is closing a segment, that segment is one begun with the SEGMENT directive. If you are using simplified segment directives, the ENDS directive is not necessary. The `label` must match the segment-name label used at the beginning of the segment.

When closing a structure or a union, ENDS is used to declare the end of a structure begun with the STRUC directive, or a union begun with the UNION directive. If you are using MASM 6.0, structures can also begin with the STRUCT directive. The `label` must match the label used at the beginning of the structure or union.

.ENDW: End a .WHILE Loop

Applicable assemblers: MASM 6.0

Directive category: Control flow

Syntax:

```
.ENDW
```

Description: This directive is used to mark the end of a loop constructed with the .WHILE directive. These loops function the same as their counterparts in high-level languages.

Example:

```
MOV      AL,0            ;Start out with a clean slate
.WHILE   (AL != 13)      ;Keep going until Enter is pressed
MOV      AH,7            ;Direct character input without echo
INT      21h             ;DOS services
.ENDW
```

ENUM: Define Enumerated Data

Applicable assemblers: TASM 3.0

Directive category: Complex data types

Syntax:

label ENUM [*variable*[, *variable*] ...]

or, if using ideal mode:

ENUM *label* [*variable*[, *variable*] ...]

where each variable has the construction

varlabel[=*value*]

Description: Enumerated data types have long been used by high-level language programmers. The ENUM directive allows you to define enumerated data, which is simply a group of values stored in a nonstandard number of bits. The largest value stored determines how many bits are used.

The label is the symbolic name you want to assign to the data type, and varlabel is the name of each variable in the data type. Optionally, you can assign a value to each varlabel.

If you find your enumerated data definitions becoming quite large, you can use the multiline version of this directive, which simply requires that you place a left brace ({) on the same line as the ENUM directive. Everything encountered up to a right brace (}) is considered part of the definition.

EQU: Assign a Constant Value to a Label

Applicable assemblers: Microsoft Quick Assembler 2.51, MASM 5.1, MASM 6.0, TASM 2.0, TASM 3.0

Directive category: Miscellaneous

Syntax:

label EQU *expression*

Description: This directive is used to assign a constant value to a user-designated label. EQU is similar in purpose and function to the equal-sign directive (=). Using the EQU directive does not result in storage space (memory area) being assigned in a program; it just assigns a value to a label. Then, later in the program, this label can be used in place of the value. Use of the EQU directive makes programs clearer and easier to maintain.

The *expression* to the right of the EQU directive must be equivalent, in some way, to an integer value. It can be a number, a formula that can be resolved to a number, up to four text characters (whatever can be stored in a register or extended register on the processor), or an address.

The difference between the EQU directive and the equal sign is that values defined with EQU are constant, whereas values defined with the equal sign can be changed in a program.

Examples:

```
Mono            EQU   0B000h        ;Mono video buffer start
Color           EQU   0B800h        ;Color video buffer start
MaxRows         EQU   25 * 80       ;Regular screen size
Affirmative     EQU   'Y'           ;Acceptable keypress
TableStart      EQU   THIS BYTE     ;Table starts here
```

.ERR: Force an Error To Occur

Applicable assemblers: Microsoft Quick Assembler 2.51, MASM 5.1, MASM 6.0, TASM 2.0, TASM 3.0

Directive category: Conditional error

Syntax:

.ERR [*<message>*]

Description: Whenever this directive is encountered, the assembler generates an error. Typically, .ERR is used inside conditional assembly blocks, in conjunction with the DISPLAY, ECHO, or %OUT directives, to signify that a certain type of assembly has occurred. If you are using MASM 6.0, you can include an optional error *message*, enclosed in angle brackets (<>), after the .ERR directive. This message will be displayed when the error is generated.

If you are using TASM, you can use the ERR directive also.

ERR: Force an Error To Occur

Applicable assemblers: TASM 2.0, TASM 3.0

Directive category: Conditional error

Syntax:

ERR

Description: This directive is the same as the .ERR directive. Whenever this directive is encountered, the assembler generates an error. Typically, ERR is used inside conditional assembly blocks, in conjunction with the DISPLAY, ECHO, or %OUT directives, to signify that a certain type of assembly has occurred.

.ERR1: Force an Error To Occur on Assembler Pass 1

Applicable assemblers: Microsoft Quick Assembler 2.51, MASM 5.1, TASM 2.0, TASM 3.0

Directive category: Conditional error

Syntax:

.ERR1

Description: This directive is meaningful only in old versions of MASM (earlier than MASM 6.0) and if you are using TASM in multipass mode. MASM 6.0 is a single-pass assembler, as is TASM under normal circumstances.

If this directive is used, it is treated essentially the same as the ERR directive. If you are using TASM, this directive is the same as the ERRIF1 directive.

.ERR2: Force an Error To Occur on Assembler Pass 2

Applicable assemblers: Microsoft Quick Assembler 2.51, MASM 5.1, TASM 2.0, TASM 3.0

Directive category: Conditional error

Syntax:

.ERR2

Description: This directive is meaningful only in old versions of MASM (prior to MASM 6.0) and if you are using TASM in multipass mode. MASM 6.0 is a single-pass assembler, as is TASM under normal circumstances.

Because this directive is obsolete, using it with the newer versions of the assemblers results in an error message being generated. TASM generates a warning message only if functioning in the default single-pass mode.

.ERRB: Generate an Error If Argument Is Blank

Applicable assemblers: Microsoft Quick Assembler 2.51, MASM 5.1, MASM 6.0, TASM 2.0, TASM 3.0

Directive category: Conditional error

Syntax:

```
.ERRB <argument>[, <message>]
```

Description: In macro definitions, this directive is used to test whether an argument was passed to the macro. If one was not passed, an error is forced. The label of the argument to be tested, argument, must be enclosed in angle brackets (<>).

If you are using MASM 6.0, you can include an optional error message, enclosed in angle brackets (<>), after the .ERRB directive. This message will be displayed when the error is generated.

If you are using TASM, you can use the ERRIFB directive also to accomplish this same task.

Example:

```
DOSCall    MACRO   Service
           .ERRB   <Service>            ;Need to have a service argument
           MOV     AH,Service           ;Load service in proper place
           INT     21h                  ;DOS interrupt
           ENDM
```

.ERRDEF: Generate an Error If Symbol Is Defined

Applicable assemblers: Microsoft Quick Assembler 2.51, MASM 5.1, MASM 6.0, TASM 2.0, TASM 3.0

Directive category: Conditional error

Syntax:

`.ERRDEF` *label*[, *<message>*]

Description: When you are working in a large program, remembering whether you already have generated symbols is difficult—particularly if you are using macros. If you already have defined `label`, an error is generated if this directive is encountered.

If you are using MASM 6.0, you can include an optional error `message`, enclosed in angle brackets (< >), after the `.ERRDEF` directive. This message will be displayed when the error is generated.

If you are using TASM, you can use the `ERRIFDEF` directive also to accomplish this same task.

Example:

```
DOSCall   MACRO   Service
          .ERRB   <Service>           ;Need to have a service argument
          .ERRDEF DOSInt              ;Should not have been defined before
DOSInt    =       21h
          MOV     AH,Service          ;Load service in proper place
          INT     DOSInt              ;DOS interrupt
          ENDM
```

.ERRDIF: Generate Error If Strings Are Different

Applicable assemblers: Microsoft Quick Assembler 2.51, MASM 5.1, MASM 6.0, TASM 2.0, TASM 3.0

Directive category: Conditional error

Syntax:

`.ERRDIF` *<string1>*,*<string2>*[, *<message>*]

Description: When you are working with macros, being able to tell whether the arguments being passed to the macro are correct is handy. This directive compares two strings and generates an error if they are different. Both `string1` and `string2` must be enclosed in angle brackets (< >), and either one of them can be an argument name. `.ERRDIF` is sensitive to case—`string1` and `string2` have to match, character for character.

If you are using MASM 6.0, you can include an optional error `message`, enclosed in angle brackets (< >), after the `.ERRDIF` directive. This message will be displayed when the error is generated.

If you are using TASM, you can use the ERRIFDIF directive also to accomplish this same task.

Example:

```
DOSCall    MACRO  Service
           .ERRDIF <Service>,<8>       ;Only allow service 8 so far
           MOV    AH,Service           ;Load service in proper place
           INT    21h                  ;DOS interrupt
           ENDM
```

.ERRDIFI: Generate Error If Strings Are Different (Case Insensitive)

Applicable assemblers: Microsoft Quick Assembler 2.51, MASM 5.1, MASM 6.0, TASM 2.0, TASM 3.0

Directive category: Conditional error

Syntax:

```
.ERRDIFI <string1>,<string2>[, <message>]
```

Description: This directive is essentially the same as .ERRDIF, except that it is not case-sensitive.

When working with macros, being able to tell whether the arguments being passed to the macro are correct is handy. This directive compares two strings and generates an error if they are different. Both string1 and string2 must be enclosed in angle brackets (< >), and either one of them can be an argument name.

If you are using MASM 6.0, you can include an optional error message, enclosed in angle brackets (< >), after the .ERRDIFI directive. This message will be displayed when the error is generated.

If you are using TASM, you can use the ERRIFDIFI directive also to accomplish this same task.

Example:

```
PrtYy      MACRO  Char
           .ERRDIFI <Char>,<Y>         ;Only allow Y or y
           MOV    AH,2                 ;Output character
           MOV    DL,Char              ;Exact character passed
           INT    21h                  ;DOS interrupt
           ENDM
```

.ERRE: Generate Error If False

Applicable assemblers: Microsoft Quick Assembler 2.51, MASM 5.1, MASM 6.0, TASM 2.0, TASM 3.0

Directive category: Conditional error

Syntax:

```
.ERRE expression[, <message>]
```

Description: This directive generates an error if the expression resolves to be false (0). If you are using MASM 6.0, you can include an optional error message, enclosed in angle brackets (<>), after the directive. This message will be displayed when the error is generated.

If you are using TASM, you can use the ERRIFE directive instead of this one.

Example:

```
DOSCall    MACRO   Service
           .ERRE Service           ;Error if argument is 0
           MOV     AH,Service      ;Load service in proper place
           INT     21h             ;DOS interrupt
           ENDM
```

.ERRIDN: Generate Error If Strings Are Identical

Applicable assemblers: Microsoft Quick Assembler 2.51, MASM 5.1, MASM 6.0, TASM 2.0, TASM 3.0

Directive category: Conditional error

Syntax:

```
.ERRIDN <string1>,<string2>[, <message>]
```

Description: When working with macros, being able to tell whether the arguments being passed to the macro are correct is handy. This directive compares two strings and generates an error if they are the same. Thus, you can ensure that certain arguments are not used with your macro. You simply compare a passed argument with the argument you want to exclude, and if they are the same, this directive will generate an error.

Both string1 and string2 must be enclosed in angle brackets (<>), and either one of them can be an argument name. .ERRIDN is sensitive to case—string1 and string2 have to match, character for character.

If you are using MASM 6.0, you can include an optional error `message`, enclosed in angle brackets (<>), after the `.ERRIDN` directive. This message will be displayed when the error is generated.

If you are using TASM, you can use the `ERRIFIDN` directive instead of this one.

Example:

```
DOSCall    MACRO  Service
           .ERRIDN <Service>,<8>     ;Don't allow service 8
           MOV    AH,Service         ;Load service in proper place
           INT    21h                ;DOS interrupt
           ENDM
```

.ERRIDNI: Generate Error If Strings Are Identical (Case Insensitive)

Applicable assemblers: Microsoft Quick Assembler 2.51, MASM 5.1, MASM 6.0, TASM 2.0, TASM 3.0

Directive category: Conditional error

Syntax:

`.ERRIDNI <string1>,<string2>[, <message>]`

Description: This directive is essentially the same as `.ERRIDN`, except that it is case-insensitive.

When working with macros, being able to tell whether the arguments being passed to the macro are correct is handy. This directive compares two strings and generates an error if they are identical, except for case. Thus, you can exclude certain arguments from working with your macro. Both `string1` and `string2` must be enclosed in angle brackets (<>), and either one of them can be an argument name.

If you are using MASM 6.0, you can include an optional error `message`, enclosed in angle brackets (<>), after the `.ERRIDNI` directive. This message will be displayed when the error is generated.

If you are using TASM, you can use the `ERRIFIDNI` directive instead of this one.

Example:

```
DontPrtYy  MACRO  Char
           .ERRIDNI <Char>,<Y>       ;Anything except Y or y
           MOV    AH,2               ;Output character
```

```
        MOV     DL,Char                 ;Exact character passed
        INT     21h                     ;DOS interrupt
        ENDM
```

ERRIF: Generate Error If True

Applicable assemblers: TASM 2.0, TASM 3.0

Directive category: Conditional error

Syntax:

ERRIF *expression*

Description: This directive generates an error if the expression resolves to be true (non 0). ERRIF is the same as the .ERRNZ directive.

Example:

```
DOSCall  MACRO  Service
         ERRIF  Service EQ 8            ;Don't let work for service 8
         MOV    AH,Service             ;Load service in proper place
         INT    21h                    ;DOS interrupt
         ENDM
```

ERRIF1: Force an Error To Occur on Assembler Pass 1

Applicable assemblers: TASM 2.0, TASM 3.0

Directive category: Conditional error

Syntax:

ERRIF1

Description: This directive is the same as the .ERR1 directive. It is meaningful only if you are using TASM in multipass mode. If this directive is used, it is treated essentially the same as the ERR directive.

ERRIF2: Force an Error To Occur on Assembler Pass 2

Applicable assemblers: TASM 2.0, TASM 3.0

Directive category: Conditional error

Syntax:

```
ERRIF2
```

Description: This directive is the same as the .ERR2 directive. It is meaningful only if you are using TASM in multipass mode. If this directive is used when TASM is operating in a single-pass mode, it generates a warning message.

ERRIFB: Generate an Error If Argument Is Blank

Applicable assemblers: TASM 2.0, TASM 3.0

Directive category: Conditional error

Syntax:

```
ERRIFB <argument>
```

Description: This directive is the same as the .ERRB directive. Used in macro definitions, this directive tests whether an argument was passed to the macro. If one was not passed, an error is forced. The label of the argument to be tested, argument, must be enclosed in angle brackets (< >).

Example:

```
DOSCall   MACRO  Service
          ERRIFB <Service>          ;Need to have a service argument
          MOV    AH,Service         ;Load service in proper place
          INT    21h                ;DOS interrupt
          ENDM
```

ERRIFDEF: Generate an Error If Symbol Is Defined

Applicable assemblers: TASM 2.0, TASM 3.0

Directive category: Conditional error

Syntax:

```
ERRIFDEF label
```

Description: This directive is the same as the .ERRDEF directive. When you are working in a large program, remembering whether you already have generated symbols is difficult—particularly if you are using macros. If you have already defined label and this directive is encountered, an error is generated.

Example:

```
DOSCall   MACRO  Service
          ERRIFB <Service>        ;Need to have a service argument
          ERRIFDEF DOSInt         ;Should not have been defined before
DOSInt    =      21h
          MOV    AH,Service       ;Load service in proper place
          INT    DOSInt           ;DOS interrupt
          ENDM
```

ERRIFDIF: Generate Error If Strings Are Different

Applicable assemblers: TASM 2.0, TASM 3.0

Directive category: Conditional error

Syntax:

ERRIFDIF <*string1*>,<*string2*>

Description: This directive is the same as the .ERRDIF directive. When working with macros, being able to tell whether the arguments being passed to the macro are correct is handy. This directive compares two strings and generates an error if they are different. Both string1 and string2 must be enclosed in angle brackets (<>), and either one of them can be an argument name. ERRIFDIF is case-sensitive— string1 and string2 have to match, character for character.

Example:

```
DOSCall   MACRO  Service
          ERRIFDIF <Service>,<8>  ;Only allow service 8 so far
          MOV    AH,Service       ;Load service in proper place
          INT    21h              ;DOS interrupt
          ENDM
```

ERRIFDIFI: Generate Error If Strings Are Different (Case Insensitive)

Applicable assemblers: TASM 2.0, TASM 3.0

Directive category: Conditional error

Syntax:

```
ERRIFDIFI <string1>,<string2>
```

Description: This directive is the same as the .ERRDIFI directive. It is also essentially the same as the ERRIFDIF and .ERRDIF directives, except that it is insensitive to case.

When you work with macros, being able to tell whether the arguments being passed to the macro are correct is handy. This directive compares two strings and generates an error if they are different. Both string1 and string2 must be enclosed in angle brackets (<>), and either one of them can be an argument name.

Example:

```
PrtYy      MACRO  Char
           ERRIFDIFI <Char>,<Y>      ;Only allow Y or y
           MOV    AH,2               ;Output character
           MOV    DL,Char            ;Exact character passed
           INT    21h                ;DOS interrupt
           ENDM
```

ERRIFE: Generate Error If False

Applicable assemblers: TASM 2.0, TASM 3.0

Directive category: Conditional error

Syntax:

```
ERRIFE expression
```

Description: This directive generates an error if the expression resolves to be false (0). It is the same as the .ERRE directive.

Example:

```
DOSCall    MACRO  Service
           ERRIFE Service           ;Error if argument is 0
           MOV    AH,Service        ;Load service in proper place
           INT    21h               ;DOS interrupt
           ENDM
```

ERRIFIDN: Generate Error If Strings Are Identical

Applicable assemblers: TASM 2.0, TASM 3.0

Directive category: Conditional error

Syntax:

```
ERRIFIDN <string1>,<string2>
```

Description: This directive is the same as the `.ERRIDN` directive. When you are working with macros, being able to tell whether the arguments being passed to the macro are correct is handy. This directive compares two strings and generates an error if they are the same. Thus, you can ensure that certain arguments are not used with your macro. You simply compare a passed argument with the argument you want to exclude, and if they are the same, this directive will generate an error.

Both `string1` and `string2` must be enclosed in angle brackets (`<>`), and either one of them can be an argument name. `ERRIFIDN` is sensitive to case—`string1` and `string2` have to match, character for character.

Example:

```
DOSCall    MACRO   Service
           ERRIFIDN <Service>,<8>     ;Don't allow service 8
           MOV     AH,Service         ;Load service in proper place
           INT     21h                ;DOS interrupt
           ENDM
```

ERRIFIDNI: Generate Error If Strings Are Identical (Case Insensitive)

Applicable assemblers: TASM 2.0, TASM 3.0

Directive category: Conditional error

Syntax:

```
ERRIFIDNI <string1>,<string2>
```

Description: This directive is the same as the `.ERRIDNI` directive. It is also essentially the same as the `ERRIFIDN` and `.ERRIDN` directives, except that it is insensitive to case.

When you are working with macros, being able to tell whether the arguments being passed to the macro are correct is handy. This directive compares two strings and generates an error if they are identical, except for case. Thus, you can ensure that certain arguments are not used with your macro. You simply compare a passed argument with the argument you want to exclude, and if they are the same, this directive will generate an error.

Both string1 and string2 must be enclosed in angle brackets (<>), and either one of them can be an argument name.

Example:

```
DontPrtYy    MACRO   Char
             ERRIFIDNI <Char>,<Y>      ;Anything except Y or y
             MOV     AH,2              ;Output character
             MOV     DL,Char           ;Exact character passed
             INT     21h               ;DOS interrupt
             ENDM
```

ERRIFNB: Generate an Error If Argument Is Not Blank

Applicable assemblers: TASM 2.0, TASM 3.0

Directive category: Conditional error

Syntax:

ERRIFNB *<argument>*

Description: This directive is the same as the .ERRNB directive. In macro definitions, this directive is used to test whether an argument was passed to the macro. If one was passed, an error is forced. This is helpful in ensuring that the macro is used correctly. The label of the argument to be tested, argument, must be enclosed in angle brackets (<>).

Example:

```
DOSCall    MACRO   Service, Func
           ERRIFB  <Service>          ;Need to have a service argument
           ERRIFNB <Func>             ;Can't allow functions; haven't coded for yet
           MOV     AH,Service         ;Load service in proper place
           INT     21h                ;DOS interrupt
           ENDM
```

ERRIFNDEF: Generate an Error If Symbol Is Not Defined

Applicable assemblers: TASM 2.0, TASM 3.0

Directive category: Conditional error

Syntax:

ERRIFNDEF *label*

Description: This directive is the same as the .ERRNDEF directive. When you are working in a large program, remembering whether you already have generated symbols is difficult—particularly if you are using macros. If you have not already defined label and this directive is enountered, an error is generated.

Example:

```
DOSCall     MACRO   Service
            ERRIFB <Service>            ;Need to have a service argument
            MOV     AH,Service          ;Load service in proper place
            ERRIFNDEF DOSInt            ;Should have been defined before
            INT     DOSInt              ;DOS interrupt
            ENDM
```

.ERRNB: Generate an Error If Argument Is Not Blank

Applicable assemblers: Microsoft Quick Assembler 2.51, MASM 5.1, MASM 6.0, TASM 2.0, TASM 3.0

Directive category: Conditional error

Syntax:

.ERRNB *<argument>*[, *<message>*]

Description: In macro definitions, this directive is used to test whether an argument was passed to the macro. If one was passed, an error is forced. This is helpful in ensuring that the macro is used correctly. The label of the argument to be tested, argument, must be enclosed in angle brackets (<>).

If you are using MASM 6.0, you can include an optional error message, enclosed in angle brackets (<>), after the .ERRNB directive. This message will be displayed when the error is generated.

If you are using TASM, you can use the ERRIFNB directive instead of this one.

Example:

```
DOSCall     MACRO   Service, Func
            .ERRB   <Service>           ;Need to have a service argument
            .ERRNB  <Func>              ;Can't allow functions; haven't coded for yet
            MOV     AH,Service          ;Load service in proper place
            INT     21h            .    ;DOS interrupt
            ENDM
```

.ERRNDEF: Generate an Error If Symbol Is Not Defined

Applicable assemblers: Microsoft Quick Assembler 2.51, MASM 5.1, MASM 6.0, TASM 2.0, TASM 3.0

Directive category: Conditional error

Syntax:

.ERRNDEF *label*[, *<message>*]

Description: When you are working in a large program, remembering whether you already have generated symbols is difficult—particularly if you are using macros. If you have not already defined label and this directive is encountered, an error is generated.

If you are using MASM 6.0, you can include an optional error message, enclosed in angle brackets (< >), after the .ERRNDEF directive. This message will be displayed when the error is generated.

If you are using TASM, you can use the ERRIFNDEF directive instead of this one.

Example:

```
DOSCall     MACRO   Service
            .ERRB   <Service>           ;Need to have a service argument
            MOV     AH,Service          ;Load service in proper place
            .ERRNDEF DOSInt             ;Should have been defined before
            INT     DOSInt              ;DOS interrupt
            ENDM
```

.ERRNZ: Generate Error If True

Applicable assemblers: Microsoft Quick Assembler 2.51, MASM 5.1, MASM 6.0, TASM 2.0, TASM 3.0

Directive category: Conditional error

Syntax:

.ERRNZ *expression*[, <*message*>]

Description: This directive generates an error if the expression resolves to be true (non 0). If you are using MASM 6.0, you can include an optional error message, enclosed in angle brackets (<>), after the directive. This message will be displayed when the error is generated.

If you are using TASM, you can use the ERRIF directive instead of this one.

Example:

```
DOSCall    MACRO   Service
           .ERRNZ Service EQ 8      ;Don't let work for service 8
           MOV     AH,Service       ;Load service in proper place
           INT     21h              ;DOS interrupt
           ENDM
```

EVEN: Adjust the Assembler Location Counter to an Even Address

Applicable assemblers: Microsoft Quick Assembler 2.51, MASM 5.1, MASM 6.0, TASM 2.0, TASM 3.0

Directive category: Complex data types

Syntax:

EVEN

Description: Using this directive is the same as using the ALIGN WORD or ALIGN 2 directives. EVEN causes the assembler to place the immediately following instruction or data at an address that is divisible by two. To do this, the assembler inserts a NOP instruction or a 0 byte in the output file, if necessary.

EVENDATA: Adjust the Assembler Location Counter to an Even Address

Applicable assemblers: TASM 2.0, TASM 3.0

Directive category: Complex data types

Syntax:

```
EVENDATA
```

Description: If you are using TASM, this directive is intended for use in data segments to align the immediately following data with an even memory address. If necessary, the assembler will place a 0 byte in the output file to accomplish this.

This directive is functionally equivalent to the `ALIGN BYTE` or `ALIGN 2` directives.

.EXIT: Specify Program Exit Point

Applicable assemblers: MASM 6.0, TASM 3.0

Directive category: Simplified segment control

Syntax:

```
.EXIT
```

Description: One of the simplified segment directives available in MASM 6.0, this directive should be used in connection with the `.STARTUP` directive. It allows you to specify the exit point of your program. The assembler then automatically generates code that "cleans up" tasks performed by the code generated by `.STARTUP`.

This directive should only be used once, at the end of the main module.

EXITCODE: Specify Program Exit Point

Applicable assemblers: TASM 3.0

Directive category: Simplified segment control

Syntax:

```
EXITCODE
```

Description: This directive is the same as the .EXIT directive. One of the simplified segment directives, it should be used with the STARTUPCODE directive. EXITCODE allows you to specify the exit point of your program. The assembler then automatically generates code that "cleans up" tasks performed by code generated by STARTUPCODE.

This directive should be used once, at the end of the main module.

EXITM: Exit a Macro Immediately

Applicable assemblers: Microsoft Quick Assembler 2.51, MASM 5.1, MASM 6.0, TASM 2.0, TASM 3.0

Directive category: Macros and repeat blocks

Syntax:

```
EXITM [<exitcode>]
```

Description: At times, when you are working with macros or repeat blocks (using the FOR, REPEAT, WHILE, IRP, FORC, IRPC, and REPT directives), you will want to exit before the macro or block has completed. Typically, this happens because a condition has been detected that makes exiting mandatory. For instance, you may need to exit a FOR block if a predefined variable was set when the assembly was started.

This directive, which allows you to exit a macro or repeat block immediately, normally is used in conjunction with the conditional macro directives. Assembly continues at the instruction immediately following the terminating ENDM directive.

If you are using MASM 6.0 and working with macro functions, you must specify an exitcode, enclosed in angle brackets (<>), for your macro. This code is substituted for the macro function in the line where the macro function was invoked.

EXTERN: Declare a Label as Being Defined in Another Module

Applicable assemblers: MASM 6.0

Directive category: Scope and visibility

Syntax:

```
EXTERN definition[, definition] ...
```

where each occurrence of `definition` has the following construction:

```
[language] label[(altID)]:type
```

Description: It is very common, especially in larger programs, to have data elements or routines that are defined in other modules in other files. The EXTERN directive allows you to declare them so that they can be accounted for correctly when the current module is being assembled. The EXTERN directive is the same as the EXTRN directive.

At a minimum, you need to provide a `label` that represents the name of the variable or routine, along with a `type`, which can be any of the following:

❏ A distance declaration such as NEAR, FAR, or PROC

❏ A size declaration such as BYTE, WORD, DWORD, DATAPTR, CODEPTR, FWORD, PWORD, QWORD, or TBYTE

❏ A structure name

❏ The special type ABS, which imports `label` as a constant (numeric external declarations only)

In each declaration, the optional `language` can be one of the following, depending on your assembler:

Language	MASM	TASM
BASIC	X	X
C	X	X
CPP		X
FORTRAN	X	X
NOLANGUAGE		X
Pascal	X	X
Prolog		X
STDCALL	X	
SYSCALL	X	

Any labels declared external are resolved at link time. Any EXTERN references must have corresponding PUBLIC references in a different module.

EXTERNDEF: MultiUse External Definition

Applicable assemblers: MASM 6.0

Directive category: Scope and visibility

Syntax:

EXTERNDEF *definition*[, *definition*] ...

where each occurrence of definition has the following construction:

[*language*] *label*:*type*

Description: New in MASM 6.0, EXTERNDEF is an extremely powerful directive. It effectively replaces the PUBLIC and EXTRN or EXTERN directives with a single directive. The idea is simple: you create an include file that contains all the declarations which may be external to any particular module in your program. When you include this file in each module, the EXTERNDEF directive alternately acts as either PUBLIC or EXTRN (EXTERN), as necessary. Thus, you no longer have to worry whether your EXTRNs match your PUBLICs, or vice versa. You can make any changes in one place and have them be globally applicable.

Each EXERNDEF declaration requires, at minimum, a label that represents the name of the variable or routine, along with a type, which can be any of the following:

❏ A distance declaration such as NEAR, FAR, or PROC

❏ A size declaration such as BYTE, WORD, DWORD, DATAPTR, CODEPTR, FWORD, PWORD, QWORD, or TBYTE

❏ A structure name

❏ The special type ABS, which imports label as a constant (numeric external declarations only)

In each declaration, the optional language can be BASIC, C, FORTRAN, Pascal, STDCALL, or SYSCALL.

If you are using TASM, you can use the GLOBAL directive instead of EXTERNDEF.

EXTRN: Declare a Label as Being Defined in Another Module

Applicable assemblers: Microsoft Quick Assembler 2.51, MASM 5.1, MASM 6.0, TASM 2.0, TASM 3.0

Directive category: Scope and visibility

Syntax:

EXTRN *definition*[, *definition*] ...

where each occurrence of definition has the following construction if you are using TASM:

[*language*] *label*[[*arraysize*]]:*type*[:*count*]

or the following construction if you are using MASM:

[*language*] *label*[(*altID*)]:*type*

Description: Having data elements or routines that are defined in other modules in other files is very common, especially in larger programs. The EXTRN directive allows you to declare these data elements or routines so that they can be accounted for correctly when the current module is being assembled.

At a minimum, you need to provide a label that represents the name of the variable or routine, along with a type, which can be any of the following:

❏ A distance declaration such as NEAR, FAR, or PROC

❏ A size declaration such as BYTE, WORD, DWORD, DATAPTR, CODEPTR, FWORD, PWORD, QWORD, or TBYTE

❏ A structure name

❏ The special type ABS, which imports label as a constant (numeric external declarations only)

In each declaration, the optional language can be one of the following, depending on your assembler:

Language	*MASM*	*TASM*
BASIC	X	X
C	X	X
CPP		X
FORTRAN	X	X
NOLANGUAGE		X
Pascal	X	X
Prolog		X
STDCALL	X	
SYSCALL	X	

Any labels declared external are resolved at link time. Any EXTRN references must have corresponding PUBLIC references in a different module.

.FARDATA: Define Beginning of Far Data Segment

Applicable assemblers: Microsoft Quick Assembler 2.51, MASM 5.1, MASM 6.0, TASM 2.0, TASM 3.0

Directive category: Simplified segment control

Syntax:

.FARDATA [*label*]

Description: This is one of several simplified data-segment directives available. The others include .CONST, .DATA, .DATA?, and .FARDATA?. If you are using TASM, you can also use CONST, DATASEG, FARDATA, UDATASEG, and UFARDATA.

This simplified segment directive is used to inform the assembler that the information immediately following should be placed in the far data segment. You must use the .MODEL directive before using .FARDATA.

It is not necessary to use this special type of segment, but you may want to use it to group your data. Such grouping may help you understand the different parts of your program better. If you use the optional *label*, it should be a name that guides the way the linker combines different far data segments while linking.

If you are using TASM, this directive is the same as the FARDATA directive.

.FARDATA?: Define Beginning of Uninitialized Far Data Segment

Applicable assemblers: Microsoft Quick Assembler 2.51, MASM 5.1, MASM 6.0, TASM 2.0, TASM 3.0

Directive category: Simplified segment control

Syntax:

.FARDATA? [*label*]

Description: This is one of several simplified data segment directives available. The others include .CONST, .DATA, .DATA?, and .FARDATA. If you are using TASM, you can also use CONST, DATASEG, FARDATA, UDATASEG, and UFARDATA.

This simplified segment directive is used to inform the assembler that the information immediately following should be placed in a special uninitialized far data segment. You must use the .MODEL directive before using .FARDATA?.

It is not necessary to use this special type of segment, but you may want to use it to group your data. Such grouping may help you understand the different parts of your program better. If you use the optional label, it should be a name that guides the way the linker combines different far data segments while linking.

If you are using TASM, this directive is the same as the UFARDATA directive.

FARDATA: Define Beginning of Far Data Segment

Applicable assemblers: TASM 2.0, TASM 3.0

Directive category: Simplified segment control

Syntax:

```
FARDATA [label]
```

Description: This is one of several simplified data-segment directives available. The others include .CONST, CONST, .DATA, .DATA?, DATASEG, .FARDATA, .FARDATA?, UDATASEG, and UFARDATA. This directive is the same as the .FARDATA directive.

This simplified segment directive is used to inform the assembler that the information immediately following should be placed in the far data segment. You must use the .MODEL or MODEL directives before using .FARDATA.

It is not necessary to use this special type of segment, but you may want to use it to group your data. Such grouping may help you understand the different parts of your program better. If you use the optional label, it should be a name that guides the way the linker combines different far data segments while linking.

FOR: Repeat a Block of Instructions, Using an Argument List

Applicable assemblers: MASM 6.0

Directive category: Macros and repeat blocks

Syntax:

```
FOR param, <arg1[, arg2] ... >
```

Description: This directive is the same as the IRP directive. It provides a way for the assembler to repeat a code block a number of times, substituting different variables along the way.

The param represents a replaceable parameter within the code block. Each time param is encountered, it is replaced by an argument from the argument list, which is enclosed in angle brackets (<>). On the first iteration, param is replaced by arg1, the second time with arg2, and so on until each of the arguments has been used or an EXITM directive is encountered.

FORC: Repeat a Block of Instructions, Using a String

Applicable assemblers: MASM 6.0

Directive category: Macros and repeat blocks

Syntax:

```
FORC param, <string>
```

Description: This directive is the same as the IRPC directive. It provides a way for the assembler to repeat a code block a number of times, substituting different variables along the way.

The param represents a replaceable parameter within the code block. Each time param is encountered, it is replaced with a character from the string, which is enclosed in angle brackets (<>). On the first iteration, param is replaced with the first character of string, the second time with the second character, and so on until each character of string (including spaces) has been used or an EXITM directive is encountered.

FWORD: Allocate 6 Bytes of Storage Space

Applicable assemblers: MASM 6.0

Directive category: Data allocation

Syntax:

```
[label] FWORD expression[, expression]
```

Description: This directive is equivalent to the DF directive. It is used to allocate 6 bytes of memory for data storage in the executable file. Typically, this data size is used for 48-bit far pointers in the 80386 or 80486 environment. The label is a user-defined name you can use later to refer symbolically to the stored information. Each expression must be one of the following:

❏ A number between –140,737,488,355,328 and 281,474,976,710,655

❏ A formula resolving to a number between –140,737,488,355,328 and 281,474,976,710,655

❏ A 48-bit far-address pointer (segment and 32-bit offset)

❏ A question mark (used to hold space but not initialize the data area)

In addition, you can use the DUP operator to specify multiple occurrences of the data in the expression.

If the data allocated by the FWORD directive is longer than six bytes, the label refers only to the first six bytes of the allocated data.

Examples:

```
FarAddress   FWORD    Routine
Values       FWORD    2.345, 59.682
Counter      FWORD    0
MemArea      FWORD    1024 * 64 * 4
Array        FWORD    12 DUP(?)
```

GLOBAL: MultiUse Global Definition

Applicable assemblers: TASM 2.0, TASM 3.0

Directive category: Scope and visibility

Syntax:

```
GLOBAL definition[, definition] ...
```

where each occurrence of definition has the following construction:

```
[language] label[[arraysize]]:type[:count]
```

Description: GLOBAL is a very powerful directive. It effectively replaces the PUBLIC and EXTRN directives with a single directive. The idea is simple: you create an include file which contains all the declarations that may be external to any particular module in your program. When you include this file in each module, the GLOBAL directive alternately acts as either PUBLIC or EXTRN, as necessary. Thus, you no longer have to worry whether your EXTRNs match your PUBLICs, or vice versa. You can make any changes in one place and have them be globally applicable.

Each GLOBAL declaration requires, at minimum, a label that represents the name of the variable or routine, along with a type, which can be any of the following:

❏ A distance declaration such as NEAR, FAR, or PROC

❏ A size declaration such as BYTE, WORD, DWORD, DATAPTR, CODEPTR, FWORD, PWORD, QWORD, or TBYTE

❏ A structure name

❏ The special type ABS, which imports label as a constant (numeric external declarations only)

In each declaration, the optional language can be BASIC, C, CPP, FORTRAN, NOLANGUAGE, Pascal, or Prolog.

If you are using MASM 6.0, you can use the EXTERNDEF directive instead of GLOBAL.

GOTO: Transfer Control

Applicable assemblers: MASM 6.0, TASM 3.0

Directive category: Macros and repeat blocks

Syntax:

GOTO *macrolabel*

Description: The GOTO directive, which must be used inside macros or repeat blocks, is used to transfer control. It works just like the GOTO statement in MS-DOS batch files. When GOTO is executed, control is transferred to macrolabel, which is designated by a colon followed by macrolabel.

Example:

```
DOSCall     MACRO   Service
            IFB     <Service>               ;Was there an argument?
            GOTO    BadCall                 ;No, so go handle
            ENDIF
            MOV     AH,Service              ;Load service in proper place
            INT     21h                     ;DOS interrupt
            EXITM
:BadCall    ECHO    Sorry, but you called DOSCall without an argument!
            .ERR
            ENDM
```

GROUP: Specify Common Segment Grouping

Applicable assemblers: Microsoft Quick Assembler 2.51, MASM 5.1, MASM 6.0, TASM 2.0, TASM 3.0

Directive category: Complete segment control

Syntax:

label GROUP *seglabel*[, *seglabel*] ...

or, if you are using TASM in ideal mode:

GROUP *label seglabel*[, *seglabel*] ...

Description: This directive allows you to specify a name for a group (label), and which segments (seglabel) belong to that group. The linker uses this information to determine how to order segments in the executable file.

IDEAL: Enter Ideal Assembly Mode

Applicable assemblers: TASM 2.0, TASM 3.0

Directive category: Global control

Syntax:

IDEAL

Description: Unique to TASM, ideal mode is used to modify the way the assembler operates. In ideal mode, the assembler is less forgiving and more structured in what it will and will not accept in a source code file. Ideal mode is discussed more fully elsewhere in this book.

.IF: Conditional Program Execution

Applicable assemblers: MASM 6.0

Directive category: Control flow

Syntax:

.IF *condition*

Description: This directive, in conjunction with the .ENDIF directive, can be used in assembly language programs to provide the same functionality as their counterparts in high-level languages.

The condition used by the .IF directive must resolve to either true or false. It can be complex (testing for two or more conditions), and may contain any of the following operators:

Operator	Meaning
==	Equal
!=	Not equal
>	Greater than
>=	Greater than or equal to
<	Less than
<=	Less than or equal to
&	Bit test
&&	Logical AND
||	Logical OR
!	Logical NOT

You can also test automatically the condition of flags by using the following specialized flag-name operators:

Operator	Sample Use
CARRY?	.BREAK .IF (CARRY?)
OVERFLOW?	.BREAK .IF (OVERFLOW?)
PARITY?	.BREAK .IF (PARITY?)
SIGN?	.BREAK .IF (SIGN?)
ZERO?	.BREAK .IF (ZERO?)

Example:

```
GetKey:     MOV     AH,7                    ;Direct character input without echo
            INT     21h                     ;DOS services
            .IF     (AL >= 'a') ¦¦ (AL <= 'z')
            AND     AL,05Fh                 ;Convert to uppercase
            .ENDIF
            .IF     AL == 'X'
            MOV     BX, OFFSET Exit         ;Address of exit routine
```

```
        .ELSEIF  AL == 'B'
        MOV      BX, OFFSET Beginning    ;Address warm program start
        .ELSEIF  AL == 'F'
        MOV      BX, OFFSET FileOps      ;Address of file operations
        .ELSE
        MOV      BX, OFFSET GetKey       ;Beginning of this routine
        .ENDIF
        JMP      [BX]                    ;Jump to right routine
```

IF: Conditional Assembly

Applicable assemblers: Microsoft Quick Assembler 2.51, MASM 5.1, MASM 6.0, TASM 2.0, TASM 3.0

Directive category: Conditional assembly

Syntax:

IF *expression*

Description: This directive, in conjunction with the ENDIF directive, can be used in assembly language programs to control which portions of the code are assembled.

The conditional expression must evaluate to true for the following code to be assembled. If the expression is not true, assembly continues at the next ELSEIF, ELSE, or ENDIF directive.

Example:

```
DemoCount   DW       0
            IF       Demo EQ 1
DemoMessage DB       'This is a bare-bones demo version of the program', 0
            ELSEIF   Demo EQ 2
DemoMessage DB       'This is a deluxe demo version of the program', 0
            ELSE
            %OUT Demo value is not set correctly
            ENDIF
```

IF1: Assemble If on Assembler Pass 1

Applicable assemblers: Microsoft Quick Assembler 2.51, MASM 5.1, TASM 2.0, TASM 3.0

Directive category: Conditional assembly

Syntax:

IF1

Description: This directive is meaningful only in old versions of MASM (prior to MASM 6.0) and if you are using TASM in multipass mode. MASM 6.0 is a single-pass assembler, as is TASM, under normal circumstances.

If this directive is used, it is treated essentially the same as the IF directive. The conditional assembly block is terminated with the ENDIF directive.

IF2: Assemble If on Assembler Pass 2

Applicable assemblers: Microsoft Quick Assembler 2.51, MASM 5.1, TASM 2.0, TASM 3.0

Directive category: Conditional assembly

Syntax:

IF2

Description: This directive is meaningful only in old versions of MASM (prior to MASM 6.0) and if you are using TASM in multipass mode. MASM 6.0 is a single-pass assembler, as is TASM, under normal circumstances.

Because this directive is obsolete, using it with MASM 6.0 results in an error message being generated. TASM generates a warning message only if functioning in the default single-pass mode. The conditional assembly block is terminated with the ENDIF directive.

IFB: Assemble If Blank

Applicable assemblers: Microsoft Quick Assembler 2.51, MASM 5.1, MASM 6.0, TASM 2.0, TASM 3.0

Directive category: Conditional assembly

Syntax:

IFB <argument>

Description: This directive is used to start a conditional assembly block. Typically, this directive is used in macros. If the argument, enclosed in angle brackets (<>), is blank, the subsequent instructions are assembled. If not, assembly continues after the next ELSE, ELSEIF, or ENDIF directive.

Example:

```
DOSOut     MACRO  Service
           IFB    <Service>            ;Was argument blank?
           MOV    AH,2                 ;Yes, so use default output
           ELSE
           MOV    AH,Service           ;Load service in proper place
           ENDIF
           INT    21h                  ;DOS interrupt
           ENDM
```

IFDEF: Assemble If Defined

Applicable assemblers: Microsoft Quick Assembler 2.51, MASM 5.1, MASM 6.0, TASM 2.0, TASM 3.0

Directive category: Conditional assembly

Syntax:

```
IFDEF label
```

Description: When you are working in a large program, remembering whether you already have generated symbols is difficult—particularly if you are using macros. If you already have defined label and this directive is encountered, the code immediately following the directive is assembled.

Example:

```
VerMsg     MACRO  Version
           .ERRB  <Version>                ;Need to have a version argument
           IFDEF  Demo
VersionMsg DB     'This is a demo version of the program',0
           ELSE
VersionMsg DB     'This is version &Version of the program',0
           ENDIF
           ENDM
```

IFDIF: Assemble If Strings Are Different

Applicable assemblers: Microsoft Quick Assembler 2.51, MASM 5.1, MASM 6.0, TASM 2.0, TASM 3.0

Directive category: Conditional assembly

Syntax:

```
IFDIF <string1>,<string2>
```

Description: Sometimes being able to assemble different versions of software, based on comparisions, is handy. This directive compares two strings and, if they are different, assembles the following instructions. Both string1 and string2 must be enclosed in angle brackets (<>); either one of them can be an argument name (if in a macro). IFDIF is case-sensitive—string1 and string2 have to match, character for character.

Example:

```
VerMsg      MACRO  Version
            .ERRB  <Version>           ;Need to have a version argument
            IFDIF  <Version>,<9>       ;Is this version 9?
VersionMsg  DB     'This is version &Version of the program',0
            ELSE
VersionMsg  DB     'This is a deluxe version of the program',0
            ENDIF
            ENDM
```

IFDIFI: Assemble If Strings Are Different (Case Insensitive)

Applicable assemblers: Microsoft Quick Assembler 2.51, MASM 5.1, MASM 6.0, TASM 2.0, TASM 3.0

Directive category: Conditional assembly

Syntax:

```
IFDIFI <string1>,<string2>
```

Description: This directive is essentially the same as IFDIF, except that it is insensitive to case.

Sometimes being able to assemble different versions of software, based on comparisions, is handy. This directive compares two strings and, if they are different, assembles the following instructions. Both string1 and string2 must be enclosed in angle brackets (<>); either one of them can be an argument name (if in a macro).

Example:

```
VerMsg      MACRO  Version
            .ERRB  <Version>              ;Need to have a version argument
            IFDIFI <Version>,<Demo>       ;Is this the demo version?
VersionMsg  DB     'This is version &Version of the program',0
            ELSE
VersionMsg  DB     'This is the demo version of the program',0
            ENDIF
            ENDM
```

IFE: Assemble If False

Applicable assemblers: Microsoft Quick Assembler 2.51, MASM 5.1, MASM 6.0, TASM 2.0, TASM 3.0

Directive category: Conditional assembly

Syntax:

```
IFE expression
```

Description: This directive controls whether a block of instructions is assembled, based on whether the expression resolves to be false (0). If the expression is false, the instructions are assembled.

Example:

```
            IFE    BuffSize          ;Is the buffer size specified
BuffSize    EQU    1024              ;No, so set to default
            ENDIF
Buffer      DB     BuffSize DUP (0)
```

IFIDN: Assemble If Strings Are Identical

Applicable assemblers: Microsoft Quick Assembler 2.51, MASM 5.1, MASM 6.0, TASM 2.0, TASM 3.0

Directive category: Conditional assembly

Syntax:

```
IFIDN <string1>,<string2>
```

Description: This directive compares the contents of two strings and, if they are identical, assembles the instructions in the conditional block immediately following the IFIDN directive. Both string1 and string2 must be enclosed in angle brackets (<>); either one of them can be an argument name (if within a macro). IFIDN is case-sensitive—string1 and string2 have to match, character for character.

Example:

```
          IFIDN   <Version>,<9>       ;Is this version 9?
BuffSize  EQU     4096                ;Yes, so use larger buffer size
          ELSE
BuffSize  EQU     1024                ;No, so use standard buffer size
          ENDIF
Buffer    DB      BuffSize DUP (0)
```

IFIDNI: Assemble If Strings Are Identical (Case Insensitive)

Applicable assemblers: Microsoft Quick Assembler 2.51, MASM 5.1, MASM 6.0, TASM 2.0, TASM 3.0

Directive category: Conditional assembly

Syntax:

```
IFIDNI <string1>,<string2>
```

Description: This directive is essentially the same as IFIDN, except that it is not case-sensitive.

This directive compares the contents of two strings and, if they are identical, assembles the instructions in the conditional block immediately following the IFIDNI directive. Both string1 and string2 must be enclosed in angle brackets (<>); either one of them can be an argument name (if within a macro).

Example:

```
          IFIDNI <Version>,<Demo>     ;Is this a demo version?
BuffSize  EQU     512                 ;Yes, so use limited buffer size
          ELSE
```

```
BuffSize     EQU     4096                  ;No, so use standard buffer size
             ENDIF
Buffer       DB      BuffSize DUP (0)
```

IFNB: Assemble If Argument Is Not Blank

Applicable assemblers: Microsoft Quick Assembler 2.51, MASM 5.1, MASM 6.0, TASM 2.0, TASM 3.0

Directive category: Conditional assembly

Syntax:

IFNB <*argument*>

Description: In macro definitions, this directive is used to test whether an argument was passed to the macro. If one was passed, the conditional assembly block is assembled. The label of the argument to be tested, argument, must be enclosed in angle brackets (<>).

Example:

```
VerMsg       MACRO   Version
             IFNB    <Version>            ;Is there a version specified?
VersionMsg   DB      'This is version &Version of the program',0
             ENDIF
             ENDM
```

IFNDEF: Assemble If Not Defined

Applicable assemblers: Microsoft Quick Assembler 2.51, MASM 5.1, MASM 6.0, TASM 2.0, TASM 3.0

Directive category: Conditional assembly

Syntax:

IFNDEF *label*

Description: When you are working in a large program, remembering whether you already have generated symbols is difficult—particularly if you are using macros. If you have not defined label and this directive is encountered, the code immediately following the directive is assembled.

Example:

```
VerMsg      MACRO   Version
            .ERRB   <Version>          ;Need to have a version argument
            IFNDEF Demo
VersionMsg  DB      'This is version &Version of the program',0
            ELSE
VersionMsg  DB      'This is a demo version of the program',0
            ENDIF
            ENDM
```

%INCL: Enable Listing of INCLUDE Files

Applicable assemblers: TASM 2.0, TASM 3.0

Directive category: Listing control

Syntax:

```
%INCL
```

Description: Normally, TASM lists INCLUDE files as they are encountered. The listing of INCLUDE files can be turned off, however, with the %NOINCL directive. Later, if you want to have them listed, you can use the %INCL directive.

INCLUDE: Insert Source Code from Another File

Applicable assemblers: Microsoft Quick Assembler 2.51, MASM 5.1, MASM 6.0, TASM 2.0, TASM 3.0

Directive category: Scope and visibility

Syntax:

```
INCLUDE filename
```

or, if using TASM in ideal mode:

```
INCLUDE "filename"
```

Description: Using INCLUDE files is quite common in assembly language programming. You can place macros and common definitions in a single file, and then include them where necessary in your programs. INCLUDE files can be nested.

When the assembler encounters the INCLUDE directive, it determines whether you have provided a complete file name. If you have not provided an extension for your file name, the extension ASM is assumed. If you have not specified a complete path for the file, the assembler looks for the file in the following places:

❏ In the current directory

❏ In any directories specified on the assembler command line

❏ In any directories specified with the INCLUDE option in the environment

If the assembler still cannot locate the INCLUDE file, an error is generated.

INCLUDELIB: Specify Library for Linker To Use

Applicable assemblers: Microsoft Quick Assembler 2.51, MASM 5.1, MASM 6.0, TASM 2.0, TASM 3.0

Directive category: Scope and visibility

Syntax:

```
INCLUDELIB filename
```

or, if using TASM in ideal mode:

```
INCLUDELIB "filename"
```

Description: If you use several standard libraries, you can use this directive to save time. By using INCLUDELIB, you can specify which libraries the linker should use when linking. You do not have to specify each library every time you link the program.

INSTR: Return a Position of One String in Another

Applicable assemblers: Microsoft Quick Assembler 2.51, TASM 2.0, TASM 3.0

Directive category: String control

Syntax:

```
label INSTR [start, ]fullstring, substring
```

Description: This directive functions much like its counterpart in some high-level languages. When assembled, it resolves to a single number—either the position of substring in fullstring, or 0 if substring cannot be found in fullstring. Optionally, you can provide a start position where searching should begin within fullstring.

For instance, the following statements

```
VerDate     TEXTEQU  '10/13/1991'
Divider1    INSTR    Verdate, </>
Divider2    INSTR    Divider1+1, Verdate, </>
```

result in `Divider1` being equal to 3, and `Divider2` being equal to 6.

INVOKE: Execute a Procedure

Applicable assemblers: MASM 6.0

Directive category: Procedures and code labels

Syntax:

```
INVOKE expression[, argument] ...
```

Description: This directive can be used to execute a procedure. Normally, this is done by the CALL instruction, but INVOKE enables you to specify an argument list to pass (via the stack) to the procedure. The expression can be any procedure label or a specific address pointer. If the arguments being passed by INVOKE are not as wide as those expected by the procedure, the assembler will make sure that the correct code is generated to widen the arguments to the proper width.

IRP: Repeat a Block of Instructions, Using an Argument List

Applicable assemblers: Microsoft Quick Assembler 2.51, MASM 5.1, MASM 6.0, TASM 2.0, TASM 3.0

Directive category: Macros and repeat blocks

Syntax:

```
IRP param, <arg1[, arg2] ... >
```

Description: This directive provides a way for the assembler to repeat a code block several times, substituting different variables along the way.

The param represents a replaceable parameter within the code block. Each time param is encountered, it is replaced by an argument from the argument list, which is enclosed in angle brackets (<>). On the first iteration, param is replaced by arg1, the second time by arg2, and so on until each of the arguments has been used or an EXITM directive is encountered.

If you are using MASM 6.0, you can use the FOR directive instead of IRP.

IRPC: Repeat a Block of Instructions, Using a String

Applicable assemblers: Microsoft Quick Assembler 2.51, MASM 5.1, MASM 6.0, TASM 2.0, TASM 3.0

Directive category: Macros and repeat blocks

Syntax:

```
IRPC param, <string>
```

Description: This directive provides a way for the assembler to repeat a code block a number of times, substituting different variables along the way.

The param represents a replaceable parameter within the code block. Each time param is encountered, it is replaced by a character from the string, which is enclosed in angle brackets (<>). On the first iteration, param is replaced by the first character of string, the second time by the second character, and so on until each character of string (including spaces) has been used or an EXITM directive is encountered.

If you are using MASM 6.0, you can use the FORC directive instead of IRPC.

JUMPS: Enable Jump Stretching

Applicable assemblers: TASM 2.0, TASM 3.0

Directive category: Global control

Syntax:

```
JUMPS
```

Description: After this directive is executed, TASM analyzes every branching operation in your source-code file; if you have specified a short jump that cannot be accomplished, the assembler generates the proper code to allow the jump to occur.

LABEL: Define a Symbol

Applicable assemblers: Microsoft Quick Assembler 2.51, MASM 5.1, MASM 6.0, TASM 2.0, TASM 3.0

Directive category: Procedures and code labels

Syntax:

name LABEL type

or, if using TASM in ideal mode:

LABEL name type

Description: With this directive you can define a specific position in your source file, assigning it a label name. The type can be any of the following:

❏ NEAR, FAR, or PROC

❏ BYTE, WORD, DATAPTR, CODEPTR, DWORD, FWORD, PWORD, QWORD, or TBYTE

❏ A structure name

.LALL: Enable Listing of All Macro Expansions

Applicable assemblers: Microsoft Quick Assembler 2.51, MASM 5.1, MASM 6.0, TASM 2.0, TASM 3.0

Directive category: Listing control

Syntax:

.LALL

Description: This directive is used to reverse the effects of the .XALL directive. Normally, the assembler only expands macros that result in code being generated. After this directive is executed, all macros are expanded, regardless of whether they result in code being generated.

If you are using TASM, this directive is the same as the %MACS directive. If you are using MASM 6.0, this directive is the same as the .LISTMACROALL directive.

LARGESTACK: Specify 32-Bit Stack Pointer

Applicable assemblers: TASM 3.0

Directive category: Global control

Syntax:

LARGESTACK

Description: Normally, the prologue and epilogue code generated automatically by TASM controls the way a procedure uses the stack. If you are using an 80386 or 80486, however, you can use either a 16-bit or 32-bit stack pointer. This directive overrides the default stack size selected with the .MODEL or MODEL directive, and ensures that a 32-bit pointer is used.

.LFCOND: List All Conditional Statements

Applicable assemblers: Microsoft Quick Assembler 2.51, MASM 5.1, MASM 6.0, TASM 2.0, TASM 3.0

Directive category: Listing control

Syntax:

```
.LFCOND
```

Description: Instructs the assembler to include all conditional code in the listing file, whether it is included in the OBJ file or not. If you are using TASM, this directive is the same as the %CONDS directive. Under MASM 6.0, this is the same as the .LISTIF directive.

%LINUM: Set Listing-File Line-Number Field Width

Applicable assemblers: TASM 2.0, TASM 3.0

Directive category: Listing control

Syntax:

```
%LINUM width
```

Description: When you have requeted a listing file (LST file) during assembly, this directive controls the width of the line-number field in the listing. The default value is 4 characters wide, which will handle line numbers up to 9999. If you have larger source files, you will want to make the field wider.

%LIST: Enable Source-Code Listing

Applicable assemblers: TASM 2.0, TASM 3.0

Directive category: Listing control

Syntax:

`%LIST`

Description: The `%LIST` directive is the same as the `.LIST` directive. Executing this directive results in a listing file being generated by the assembler. TASM does this by default, but if you use the `%NOLIST` directive, you can cause TASM not to write the source lines to the file. You can use both `%NOLIST` and `%LIST` to control selectively what goes into the listing file.

.LIST: Enable Source-Code Listing

Applicable assemblers: Microsoft Quick Assembler 2.51, MASM 5.1, MASM 6.0, TASM 2.0, TASM 3.0

Directive category: Listing control

Syntax:

`.LIST`

Description: Executing this directive results in a listing file being generated by the assembler. The assembler normally does this by default, but if you use the `.XLIST`, `.NOLIST`, or `%NOLIST` directives, you can cause the assembler not to write the source lines to the file. You can use both groups (`.XLIST`, `.NOLIST`, and `.LIST`, or `%NOLIST` and `%LIST`) to selectively control what goes into the listing file.

The `%LIST` and `%NOLIST` directives apply only if you are using TASM. The `.NOLIST` directive is available only under MASM 6.0.

.LISTALL: Include Everything in Listing File

Applicable assemblers: MASM 6.0

Directive category: Listing control

Syntax:

`.LISTALL`

Description: This directive results in the most information in your listing file. It will include all source-code lines, all macro expansions, and all conditionals, whether they are false or not.

.LISTIF: List All Conditional Statements

Applicable assemblers: MASM 6.0

Directive category: Listing control

Syntax:

`.LISTIF`

Description: Normally, MASM includes conditional assembly statements in the listing file only if they result in generated code. This directive, however, causes all conditionals to be included. This is the same as the `.LFCOND` directive.

.LISTMACRO: List Only Macros that Generate Code

Applicable assemblers: MASM 6.0

Directive category: Listing control

Syntax:

`.LISTMACRO`

Description: If you use macros a great deal, you probably will use this directive also. It results only in the expansion (listing) of macros that generate code. This directive is the same as the `.XALL` directive.

.LISTMACROALL: Enable Listing of All Macro Expansions

Applicable assemblers: MASM 6.0

Directive category: Listing control

Syntax:

`.LISTMACROALL`

Description: This directive is used to reverse the effects of the `.LISTMACRO` directive. Normally, the assembler expands only macros that result in code being generated. After this directive is executed, all macros are expanded, regardless of whether they result in code being generated.

This directive is the same as the `.LALL` directive.

LOCAL: Define Local Variables

Applicable assemblers: Microsoft Quick Assembler 2.51, MASM 5.1, MASM 6.0, TASM 2.0, TASM 3.0

Directive category: Procedures and code labels, macros and repeat blocks

Syntax:

LOCAL *vardef*[, *vardef*] ... [=*sizelabel*]

where each vardef has the following construction:

label[[*arraysize*]][:*type*][:*count*]

Description: This directive is used to define local variables for use within a procedure or a macro. Space for these variables is allocated on the stack and released when a procedure is finished.

The label is the symbolic name used to reference the variable in the procedure. The optional arraysize, enclosed in brackets ([]), specifies the size of the array referred to by label. The type is a data type such as BYTE, WORD, etc. TASM also allows you to specify a count that indicates how many of the type should be allocated. In this case, the total size allocated for label would be arraysize times count times the width of type.

Notice that no allowance is made for initializing local variables. You must do this manually in your procedure.

The optional sizelabel designates a symbolic name which should be assigned a value equal to the amount of space required by all the local variables. This option is not available in MASM 6.0.

LOCALS: Enable Local Symbols

Applicable assemblers: TASM 2.0, TASM 3.0

Directive category: Procedures and code labels

Syntax:

LOCALS [*prefix*]

Description: This directive allows you to enable the assembler to process local symbols and optionally change the prefix characters assigned to local symbols. Normally, the characters @@ are used to begin local symbols. You can use this directive to change this prefix to any other two characters (such as ::) that the assembler does not reserve for some other use.

To disable local symbols, use the NOLOCALS directive.

MACRO: Define the Start of a Macro

Applicable assemblers: Microsoft Quick Assembler 2.51, MASM 5.1, MASM 6.0, TASM 2.0, TASM 3.0

Directive category: Macros and repeat blocks

Syntax:

label MACRO [*parameter*[, *parameter*] ...]

or, if using TASM in ideal mode:

MACRO *label* [*parameter*[, *parameter*] ...]

Description: Macros can be used to handle automatic code generation or to provide a different name for an operation. The assembler includes an entire macro language, composed of directives, which can be used between the MACRO directive and the ENDM directive.

Example:

```
DOSCall    MACRO   Service, Func
           ERRIFB <Service>            ;Need to have a service argument
           ERRIFNB <Func>             ;Can't allow functions; haven't coded for yet
           MOV    AH,Service           ;Load service in proper place
           INT    21h                  ;DOS interrupt
           ENDM
```

%MACS: Enable Listing of All Macro Expansions

Applicable assemblers: TASM 2.0, TASM 3.0

Directive category: Listing control

Syntax:

%MACS

Description: This directive is the same as the .LALL directive. It is used to reverse the effects of the %NOMACS directive. Normally, the assembler expands only macros that result in code being generated. After this directive is executed, all macros are expanded, regardless of whether they result in code being generated.

MASM: Enable MASM 4.0 Compatibility

Applicable assemblers: TASM 2.0, TASM 3.0

Directive category: Global control

Syntax:

MASM

Description: Some differences between TASM and MASM may cause problems with the way your source code assembles. Use this directive to instruct TASM to operate in a manner compatible with MASM 4.0.

Instead of using this directive, you may want to use the VERSION directive, which is new to TASM 3.0.

MASM51: Enable MASM 5.1 Compatibility

Applicable assemblers: TASM 2.0, TASM 3.0

Directive category: Global control

Syntax:

MASM51

Description: Some capabilities of MASM 5.1 are not in the default configuration of TASM. After this directive is executed, TASM will be able to understand and properly process the following:

❏ SUBSTR, CATSTR, SIZESTR, and INSTR directives

❏ Line continuation with a backslash character (\)

Later, if you want to disable MASM 5.1 compatibility, you can use the NOMASM51 directive.

Instead of using this directive, you may want to use the VERSION directive, which is new to TASM 3.0.

.MODEL: Specify Memory Model

Applicable assemblers: Microsoft Quick Assembler 2.51, MASM 5.1, MASM 6.0, TASM 2.0, TASM 3.0

Directive category: Simplified segment control

Syntax:

.MODEL *memorymodel*[, *language*][, *opsys*][, *modelmod*]

If you are using TASM, the following syntax also can be used:

.MODEL [*modelmod*] *memorymodel* [*label*][,[*langmod*] *language*][, *modelmod*]

Description: This directive allows the assembler to determine how to handle all the other simplified segment directives. Basically, it is here that you define the environment for which you are programming.

Notice that the only required parameter is the memorymodel, which can be any of the following memory models, depending on your assembler. In addition to valid memorymodel, this table indicates the applicable assemblers and assembler assumptions for each memorymodel.

Model	MASM	TASM	Code	Data	CS Group	DS Group	SS Group
TINY	X	X	NEAR	NEAR	DGROUP	DGROUP	DGROUP
SMALL	X	X	NEAR	NEAR	_TEXT	DGROUP	DGROUP
COMPACT	X	X	NEAR	FAR	_TEXT	DGROUP	DGROUP
MEDIUM	X	X	FAR	NEAR	label_TEXT	DGROUP	DGROUP
LARGE	X	X	FAR	FAR	label_TEXT	DGROUP	DGROUP
HUGE	X	X	FAR	FAR	label_TEXT	DGROUP	DGROUP
FLAT	X	X	NEAR	NEAR	FLAT	FLAT	FLAT
TCHUGE		X	FAR	FAR	label_TEXT	NOTHING	NOTHING
TPASCAL		X	NEAR	FAR	CODE	DATA	NOTHING

If you are using TASM, you can also specify an optional label when using the MEDIUM, LARGE, HUGE, or TCHUGE memory models. This label is used in assigning a code segment GROUP name. If you do not provide a label, then the module name is automatically used.

The assembler uses the optional language parameter to set calling, naming, and parameter-passing conventions for procedures and public symbols. This parameter may also determine how the automatic prologue and epilogue code for each procedure is generated. The language can be any one of the following, depending on your assembler:

Language	MASM	TASM
BASIC	X	X
C	X	X
CPP		X
FORTRAN	X	X
NOLANGUAGE		X
Pascal	X	X
Prolog		X
STDCALL	X	
SYSCALL	X	

Notice that if you are using TASM, you can further specify a language modifier, langmod, which can be NORMAL, WINDOWS, ODDNEAR, or ODDFAR. Again, this parameter is used to control the procedure prologue and epilogue generation.

When using MASM 6.0, you can also specify an operating system, opsys, for the memory model. This parameter, which can be either OS_DOS or OS_OS2, controls the way the .STARTUP and .EXIT directives generate their code. If you do not use .STARTUP and .EXIT in your programs, you do not need to specify the opsys parameter.

Finally, modelmod is a model modifier typically used to specify how the stack should be grouped with other GROUPs. The use of this parameter is expanding, however, to control other things (depending on your assembler). The valid modelmod settings are as follows:

Modifier	MASM	TASM	Meaning
NEARSTACK	X	X	Stack segment should be included in DGROUP
FARSTACK	X	X	Stack segment should not be included in DGROUP
USE16		X	Use 16-bit segment addresses for 80386 or 80486
USE32		X	Use 32-bit segment addresses for 80386 or 80486

Notice that if you are using TASM, modelmod can appear either before or after the memorymodel.

If you are using TASM, you can also use the MODEL directive rather than .MODEL.

MODEL: Specify Memory Model

Applicable assemblers: TASM 2.0, TASM 3.0

Directive category: Simplified segment control

Syntax:

```
MODEL [modelmod] memorymodel [label][,[ langmod] language][, modelmod]
```

Description: Applicable only with TASM, this is an alternate method of specifying the memory model. It works exactly as the .MODEL directive does. See the discussion under that directive for more information.

.MSFLOAT: Specify Microsoft Floating-Point Format

Applicable assemblers: Microsoft Quick Assembler 2.51

Directive category: Global control

Syntax:

```
.MSFLOAT
```

Description: Normally, the assembler stores numbers according to the IEEE format. If you use this directive at the beginning of your program, floating-point numbers will be stored in the Microsoft binary format.

MULTERRS: Enable Multiple Error Reporting

Applicable assemblers: TASM 2.0, TASM 3.0

Directive category: Global control

Syntax:

```
MULTERRS
```

Description: Typically, the assembler flags and reports the first error it finds on each source-code line. This directive forces the assembler to evaluate each line and report any additional errors it may find.

The effects of this directive can be reversed with the NOMULTERRS directive.

NAME: Define the Module Name

Applicable assemblers: Microsoft Quick Assembler 2.51, MASM 5.1, MASM 6.0, TASM 2.0, TASM 3.0

Directive category: Global control

Syntax:

```
NAME label
```

Description: This directive allows you to assign a symbolic name to the module being assembled. Normally, the module has the same name as the file name.

Note that this directive has meaning only in TASM ideal mode. It will not generate errors or warnings in TASM's MASM mode, or in any version of MASM. Even though it does not generate an error, it has no effect on the object file created by the assembler.

%NEWPAGE: Advance Listing File to New Page

Applicable assemblers: TASM 2.0, TASM 3.0

Directive category: Listing control

Syntax:

```
%NEWPAGE
```

Description: This is the same as the PAGE directive with no arguments. It results in the listing file jumping to the top of a new page for the next line printed.

.NO87: Disable Numeric Coprocessor Programming

Applicable assemblers: MASM 6.0

Directive category: Processor specification

Syntax:

```
.NO87
```

Description: By default, MASM allows you to program for the 8087 numeric coprocessor. You can also use the .287, .387, .486, or .486P directives to enable varying levels of NPX compatibility. This directive, on the other hand, disallows all programming for a numeric coprocessor. If you know you are programming for an environment where there is no coprocessor chip, you can use this directive if you want to make absolutely sure that there will be no incompatible code in your program.

%NOCONDS: List True Conditional Statements

Applicable assemblers: TASM 2.0, TASM 3.0

Directive category: Listing control

Syntax:

%NOCONDS

Description: This is the same as the .SFCOND directive. It instructs the assembler to include only conditional code (no other kind) in the listing file only if the condition is true. In other words, only code that makes it to the OBJ file will be listed.

%NOCREF: Disable Cross-Referencing

Applicable assemblers: TASM 2.0, TASM 3.0

Directive category: Listing control

Syntax:

%NOCREF [*label*[, *label*] ...]

Description: This directive is similar to the .XCREF directive, but much more versatile. If this directive is executed without any parameters, cross-referencing is turned off completely, both in the listing file and the XRF file. If you include one or more labels, however, only cross-referencing for those labels is affected.

If you are using MASM 6.0, you can use the .NOCREF directive.

.NOCREF: Disable Cross-Referencing

Applicable assemblers: MASM 6.0

Directive category: Listing control

Syntax:

```
.NOCREF [label[, label] ...]
```

Description: This directive is similar to the .XCREF directive, but much more versatile. If this directive is executed without any parameters, cross-referencing is turned off completely. If you include one or more labels, however, only cross-referencing for those labels is affected.

If you are using TASM, you can use the %NOCREF directive.

%NOCTLS: Exclude Listing-Control Directives from the Listing File

Applicable assemblers: TASM 2.0, TASM 3.0

Directive category: Listing control

Syntax:

```
%NOCTLS
```

Description: Normally, TASM does not include listing-control directives in a generated listing file. The %NOCTLS directive restores this default if you have used the %CTLS directive to cause listing-control directives to be included.

NOEMUL: Don't Use Floating-Point Emulator

Applicable assemblers: TASM 2.0, TASM 3.0

Directive category: Global control

Syntax:

```
NOEMUL
```

Description: By default, TASM assumes that you have some sort of numeric coprocessor present in your system. This means that while assembling, the assembler generates code that can take advantage of the coprocessor. If you previously used the EMUL directive and now want to turn off emulation, you can use this directive to do so. Unless you have previously used the EMUL directive, using NOEMUL is unnecessary.

%NOINCL: Disable Listing of INCLUDE Files

Applicable assemblers: TASM 2.0, TASM 3.0

Directive category: Listing control

Syntax:

```
%NOINCL
```

Description: Normally, TASM lists INCLUDE files as they are encountered. The listing of INCLUDE files can be turned off, however, with this directive. Later, if you want to have these files listed, you can use the %INCL directive.

NOJUMPS: Disable Jump Stretching

Applicable assemblers: TASM 2.0, TASM 3.0

Directive category: Global control

Syntax:

```
NOJUMPS
```

Description: *Jump stretching* is the automatic rewriting of your branching instructions to avoid errors caused by trying to short jump too far. TASM normally does not do jump stretching, unless you use the JUMPS directive. NOJUMPS can then later be used to again disable jump stretching.

%NOLIST: Disable Source-Code Listing

Applicable assemblers: TASM 2.0, TASM 3.0

Directive category: Listing control

Syntax:

```
%NOLIST
```

Description: This directive is the same as the .XLIST directive. Use this directive to instruct the assembler to suspend sending listing information to the listing file. Even with this directive in place, however, the assembler will include symbol and cross-reference information in the file.

.NOLIST: Disable Source-Code Listing

Applicable assemblers: MASM 6.0

Directive category: Listing control

Syntax:

`.NOLIST`

Description: Use this directive to instruct the assembler to suspend sending listing information to the listing file. Even with this directive in place, however, the assembler will include symbol and cross-reference information in the file.

This directive is the same as the `.XLIST` directive.

.NOLISTIF: List True Conditional Statements

Applicable assemblers: MASM 6.0

Directive category: Listing control

Syntax:

`.NOLISTIF`

Description: Instructs the assembler to include only conditional code (no other kind) in the listing file only if the condition is true. In other words, only code that makes it to the OBJ file will be listed. This directive is the same as the `.SFCOND` directive.

.NOLISTMACRO: Disable Macro Listing

Applicable assemblers: MASM 6.0

Directive category: Listing control

Syntax:

`.NOLISTMACRO`

Description: Normally, the assembler lists (in the listing file) the macro lines that generate code. If you use this directive, only the macro invocation line is listed. All other macro expansion is not listed, even if it generates code. `.NOLISTMACRO` is the same as the `.SALL` directive.

NOLOCALS: Disable Local Symbols

Applicable assemblers: TASM 2.0, TASM 3.0

Directive category: Procedures and code labels

Syntax:

```
NOLOCALS
```

Description: Normally, TASM treats any symbol that begins with the characters @@ as a local symbol. You can change that with the LOCALS directive, or completely turn off local symbol recognition with this directive.

%NOMACS: List Only Macros that Generate Code

Applicable assemblers: TASM 2.0, TASM 3.0

Directive category: Listing control

Syntax:

```
%NOMACS
```

Description: If you use macros a great deal, you probably will use this directive also. It results in the expansion (listing) only of macros that generate code. It is the same as the .XALL directive.

NOMASM51: Disable MASM 5.1 Compatibility

Applicable assemblers: TASM 2.0, TASM 3.0

Directive category: Global control

Syntax:

```
NOMASM51
```

Description: Normally TASM is not 100% compatibile with MASM 5.1. For instance, TASM does not understand some directives, and the backslash (\) line-continuation character does not work. If you need these capabilities, you can use the MASM51 directive to ensure 100% compatibility. If you later decide you no longer need the compatibility, use the NOMASM51 directive.

NOMULTERRS: Disable Multiple Error Reporting

Applicable assemblers: TASM 2.0, TASM 3.0

Directive category: Global control

Syntax:

NOMULTERRS

Description: This is the default condition for error reporting. Typically, the assembler flags and reports only the first error it finds on each source-code line. The effects of this directive can be reversed with the MULTERRS directive.

NOSMART: Disable Code Optimization

Applicable assemblers: TASM 3.0

Directive category: Global control

Syntax:

NOSMART

Description: If you want to disable any optimization that TASM normally may do, use this directive. To turn on optimization, use the SMART directive. SMART is the normal assembly condition for TASM.

%NOSYMS: Disable Symbol Table in Listing File

Applicable assemblers: TASM 2.0, TASM 3.0

Directive category: Listing control

Syntax:

%NOSYMS

Description: Normally, TASM generates a symbol table when a listing file is generated. If you do not want to include the symbol table, you can use this directive. If you want to start generating the table later, you can use the %SYMS directive.

%NOTRUNC: Control Word-Wrapping in the Listing File

Applicable assemblers: TASM 2.0, TASM 3.0

Directive category: Listing control

Syntax:

```
%NOTRUNC
```

Description: Normally, if the source-code lines or the generated code in the listing file are too long to be listed properly, the code is truncated. This truncation occurs only in the listing file—not in the OBJ file. This directive turns off the truncation and causes the long elements to wrap to the next line in the file. Alternatively, you can use the %BIN and %TEXT directives to change the field widths so that truncation is not necessary.

NOWARN: Disable Warnings

Applicable assemblers: TASM 2.0, TASM 3.0

Directive category: Global control

Syntax:

```
NOWARN [class]
```

Description: Normally, TASM displays warnings as they occur during assembly. Sometimes, however, you may want to turn off some or all of the warning messages. If you provide a warning class, this directive will suppress warning messages in that class. If you provide no parameters, all warning messages are suppressed.

The warning classes are as follows:

Class	Meaning
ALN	Segment alignment
ASS	Assume segment is 16-bit
BRK	Brackets needed
ICG	Inefficient code
LCO	Location-counter overflow
OPI	Unterminated (open) IF condition
OPP	Unclosed (open) procedure

Class	Meaning
OPS	Unclosed (open) segment
OVF	Arithmetic overflow
PDC	Pass-dependent coding
PRO	Incorrect protected-mode memory write
RES	Reserved word infraction
TPI	Illegal Turbo Pascal operation

OPTION: Set Assembler Processing Parameters

Applicable assemblers: MASM 6.0

Directive category: Global control

Syntax:

```
OPTION argument[, argument] ...
```

Description: MASM 6.0 enables you to control, in a global fashion, the way the assembler does its work. When you use the OPTION directive, you specify a series of arguments that define how the assembler should treat your source code from that point forward. Valid arguments are as follows:

Argument	Meaning
CASEMAP:*type*	Defines how MASM treats upper- and lower-case letters in symbols. Valid type arguments are NONE, NOTPUBLIC, and ALL.
DOTNAME	Enables use of periods as leading characters in symbols.
EMULATOR	Assumes that floating-point instructions will be done by an emulator linked to the program.
EPILOGUE:*macro*	Instructs assembler to use the macro named *macro* to generate procedure epilogue code, rather than the regular epilogue.
EXPR16	Sets the expression word size to 16 bits.
EXPR32	Sets the expression word size to 32 bits (the default).

Argument	Meaning
LANGUAGE:*lang*	Sets the default language type. Valid *lang* choices are C, Pascal, FORTRAN, BASIC, SYSCALL, or STDCALL. This argument sets what the default language is if not specified in the .MODEL directive.
LJMP	Enables smart processing of conditional jumps; handled in TASM by the JUMPS directive.
M510	Ensures complete compatibility with MASM 5.10.
NODOTNAME	Disables use of periods as leading characters in symbols.
NOEMULATOR	Generates floating-point instructions to work with numeric coprocessors (the default setting).
NOKEYWORD:<*list*>	Disables individual reserved words. Reserved words in the *list* must be separated by spaces, and the entire list must be enclosed in angle brackets (<>).
NOLJMP	Disables smart processing of conditional jumps; handled in TASM by the NOJUMPS directive.
NOM510	Default operating condition for MASM 6.0; opposite of the M510 argument.
NOOLDMACROS	Handles macros according to new rules for MASM 6.0 (the default setting).
NOOLDSTRUCTS	Treats structure members according to new rules for MASM 6.0 (the default setting).
NOREADONLY	Normal error handling; allows any access of segments (the default condition).
NOSCOPED	Labels inside procedures are available outside the procedure.
NOSIGNEXTEND	Uses non-sign-extended opcodes for AND, OR, and XOR instructions.
OFFSET:*type*	Specifies how offset instructions should be handled. Valid *type* options are SEGMENT, GROUP (the default), and FLAT.
OLDMACROS	Handles macros as was done in MASM 5.10.

Argument	Meaning
OLDSTRUCTS	Treats structure members as in MASM 5.10.
PROC:*visibility*	Sets default procedure visibility (normally PUBLIC) to PUBLIC, PRIVATE, or EXPORT.
PROLOGUE:*macro*	Instructs assembler to use the macro named *macro* to generate procedure prologue code rather than the regular prologue.
READONLY	Generates error if instructions are not read-only. Guarantees that segments will be read-only, which is necessary for OS/2 and code which will be written to and executed from ROM.
SCOPED	Ensures that all labels inside procedures are local to the procedure (the default condition).
SEGMENT:*size*	Sets global default segment *size*. Valid choices are USE16, USE32, or FLAT.

ORG: Specify Starting Segment Address

Applicable assemblers: Microsoft Quick Assembler 2.51, MASM 5.1, MASM 6.0, TASM 2.0, TASM 3.0

Directive category: Complete segment control

Syntax:

```
ORG address
```

Description: If you use the simplified segment directives, you will not need to use the ORG directive. It is intended for use with the nonsimplified versions, and designed to indicate to the assembler and linker where in memory the segment should reside.

%OUT: Output a String to the Screen

Applicable assemblers: Microsoft Quick Assembler 2.51, MASM 5.1, MASM 6.0, TASM 2.0, TASM 3.0

Directive category: Miscellaneous

Syntax:

```
%OUT text
```

Description: This directive is used to display a text string to the video monitor during assembly. It does not result in any code being generated, nor does it take memory in the generated file.

You can use this directive to aid in debugging, so that you can see immediately when certain conditional instructions are being assembled. Similar functions are provided by the DISPLAY and ECHO directives.

Example:

```
%OUT Now adding debug routines
```

P186: Enable 80186 Programming

Applicable assemblers: TASM 2.0, TASM 3.0

Directive category: Processor specification

Syntax:

```
P186
```

Description: This directive is equivalent to the .186 directive. TASM allows you to program for specific microprocessors, the default being the 8086. This directive causes the assembler to handle instructions compatible with the 80186 microprocessor.

P286: Enable 80286 Programming

Applicable assemblers: TASM 2.0, TASM 3.0

Directive category: Processor specification

Syntax:

```
P286
```

Description: This directive is similar to the .286 directive. TASM allows you to program for specific microprocessors, the default being the 8086. This directive causes the assembler to handle instructions compatible with the 80286 microprocessor.

This directive differs from the `.286` directive in that, with this one, you can program for all modes of the 80286, whereas the `.286` directive allows only nonprotected-mode programming.

P286N: Enable 80286 Nonprotected-Mode Programming

Applicable assemblers: TASM 2.0, TASM 3.0

Directive category: Processor specification

Syntax:

P286N

Description: This directive is functionally equivalent to the `.286` and `.286C` directives, and the opposite of the `.286P` and P286P directives. It is also more restrictive than the P286 directive.

With this directive you can program for the 80286 processor, but the assembler makes sure that you use no instructions that require protected mode.

P286P: Enable 80286 Protected-Mode Programming

Applicable assemblers: TASM 2.0, TASM 3.0

Directive category: Processor specification

Syntax:

P286P

Description: This directive is equivalent to the `.286P` directive. TASM allows you to program for specific microprocessors, the default being the 8086. This directive causes the assembler to handle instructions compatible with the 80286 microprocessor, including those instructions that require protected mode.

P287: Enable 80287 Programming

Applicable assemblers: TASM 2.0, TASM 3.0

Directive category: Processor specification

Syntax:

P287

Description: TASM enables you to take advantage of numeric coprocessors in your programs, the default being the 8087 NPX. This directive causes the assembler to handle instructions compatible with the 80287 numeric coprocessor.

If you have used the .286, .286C, .286P, P286, P286N, or P286P directives, using the P287 directive is redundant and unnecessary.

P386: Enable 80386 Programming

Applicable assemblers: TASM 2.0, TASM 3.0

Directive category: Processor specification

Syntax:

P386

Description: This directive is similar to the .386 directive. TASM allows you to program for specific microprocessors, the default being the 8086. This directive causes the assembler to handle instructions compatible with the 80386 micropro- cessor, including instructions that use the expanded register set of the 80386.

This directive differs from the .386 directive in that, with this one, you can program for all modes of the 80386, whereas the .386 directive allows only nonprotected-mode programming.

P386N: Enable 80386 Nonprotected-Mode Programming

Applicable assemblers: TASM 2.0, TASM 3.0

Directive category: Processor specification

Syntax:

P386N

Description: This directive is functionally equivalent to the .386 and .386C direc- tives, and the opposite of the .386P and P386P directives. It is also more restrictive than the P386 directive.

With this directive you can program for the 80386 processor, but the assem- bler makes sure that you use no instructions that require protected mode.

P386P: Enable 80386 Protected-Mode Programming

Applicable assemblers: TASM 2.0, TASM 3.0

Directive category: Processor specification

Syntax:

P386P

Description: This directive is equivalent to the .386P directive. TASM allows you to program for specific microprocessors, the default being the 8086. This directive causes the assembler to handle instructions compatible with the 80386 microprocessor, including those that require protected mode.

P387: Enable 80387 Programming

Applicable assemblers: TASM 2.0, TASM 3.0

Directive category: Processor specification

Syntax:

P387

Description: TASM enables you to take advantage of numeric coprocessors in your programs, the default being the 8087 NPX. This directive causes the assembler to handle instructions compatible with the 80387 numeric coprocessor.

If you have used the .386, .386C, .386P, P386, P386N, or P386P directives, using the P387 directive is redundant and unnecessary.

P486: Enable 80486 Programming

Applicable assemblers: TASM 2.0, TASM 3.0

Directive category: Processor specification

Syntax:

P486

Description: This directive is similar to the .386 directive. TASM allows you to program for specific microprocessors, the default being the 8086. This directive causes the assembler to handle instructions compatible with the 80486 microprocessor, including instructions that use the expanded register set of the 80486.

This directive differs from the .486 directive in that, with this one, you can program for all modes of the 80486, whereas the .486 directive allows only nonprotected-mode programming.

Note that the P486 directive enables the use of instructions designed to take advantage of the NPX built into the 80486. If your code is designed to run ultimately on the 80486 SX chip, make sure not to use instructions that require the NPX. Even though the assembler will allow them (after this directive is executed), the resulting code will not run on the 80486 SX.

P486N: Enable 80486 Nonprotected-Mode Programming

Applicable assemblers: TASM 2.0, TASM 3.0

Directive category: Processor specification

Syntax:

P486N

Description: This directive is functionally equivalent to the .486 and .486C directives, and the opposite of the .486P and P486P directives. It is also more restrictive than the P486 directive.

With this directive you can program for the 80386 processor, but the assembler makes sure that you use no instructions that require protected mode.

Note that the P486N directive enables the use of instructions designed to take advantage of the NPX built into the 80486. If your code is designed to run ultimately on the 80486 SX chip, be sure not to use instructions that require the NPX. Even though the assembler will allow them (after this directive is executed), the resulting code will not run on the 80486 SX.

P8086: Enable 8086 Programming

Applicable assemblers: TASM 2.0, TASM 3.0

Directive category: Processor specification

Syntax:

P8086

Description: This is the default programming paradigm for TASM. This directive is equivalent to the .8086 directive. Although you can use other directives to enable various levels of processor compatibility, this directive can be used to make absolutely sure that your program will work with all members of the 80x86 family.

A typical use of this directive is after you have been programming for a different level of compatibility (80286 or higher) and you want to make sure that your program will still assemble for use with older processors.

P8087: Enable 8087 Programming

Applicable assemblers: TASM 2.0, TASM 3.0

Directive category: Processor specification

Syntax:

P8087

Description: This is the default programming capability of TASM. This directive is equivalent to the .8087 directive. You can use this directive to state explicity in your program that you are programming for the 8087 numeric coprocessor, but use of the directive is not mandatory.

PAGE: Listing-File Page Control

Applicable assemblers: Microsoft Quick Assembler 2.51, MASM 5.1, MASM 6.0, TASM 2.0, TASM 3.0

Directive category: Listing control

Syntax:

PAGE [*rows*][, *columns*]

or

PAGE +

Description: You control the size of the printed page in the listing file with this directive. The optional rows and columns parameters specify how deep and wide to print each page. If PAGE is issued with no parameters, the next line of the listing file is printed at the top of a new page.

If you use a plus sign (+) after the PAGE directive, you not only cause the listing file to jump to the top of a new page, but you also cause the section number to increment and the page number to be reset to 1.

%PAGESIZE: Set Listing-File Page Dimensions

Applicable assemblers: TASM 2.0, TASM 3.0

Directive category: Listing control

Syntax:

```
%PAGESIZE [rows][, columns]
```

Description: You control the size of the printed page in the listing file with this directive. The optional rows and columns parameters specify how deep and wide to print each page. Alternatively, you can use the PAGE directive to do this task.

%PCNT: Set Listing-File Address-Field Width

Applicable assemblers: TASM 2.0, TASM 3.0

Directive category: Listing control

Syntax:

```
%PCNT width
```

Description: When you have requested a listing file (LST file) during assembly, this directive controls the width of the offset address field. The default width is 4 for 16-bit segments and 8 for 32-bit segments, but you can set it to any reasonable value.

PNO87: Disable Numeric-Coprocessor Programming

Applicable assemblers: TASM 2.0, TASM 3.0

Directive category: Processor specification

Syntax:

```
PNO87
```

Description: By default, TASM enables you to program for the 8087 numeric coprocessor. You can use any of the other processor directives to enable varying levels of NPX compatibility. This directive, on the other hand, disallows all programming for a numeric coprocessor. If you know that you are programming for an environment with no coprocessor chip, you can use this directive to make absolutely sure that no incompatible code will be in your program.

POPCONTEXT: Restore Assembler Environment

Applicable assemblers: MASM 6.0

Directive category: Global control

Syntax:

```
POPCONTEXT condition
```

Description: This directive generally is used in macros to restore assembler settings saved with the PUSHCONTEXT directive. The condition can be the following:

Condition	Meaning
ASSUME	Current segment register assumptions
CPU	State of current CPU and processor directives
LISTING	State of listing and cross-reference directives (similar to the %POPCTLS directive for TASM)
RADIX	Current default radix
ALL	All of the above

If you try to restore something that you have not previously saved, or if you attempt to restore more than you previously saved, the assembler generates an error.

%POPLCTL: Restore Listing Controls

Applicable assemblers: TASM 2.0, TASM 3.0

Directive category: Listing control

Syntax:

```
%POPLCTL
```

Description: Using this directive allows you to restore the condition of the %MACS, %LIST, and %INCL directives previously saved with the %PUSHLCTL directive.

If you use MASM 6.0, you can use the POPCONTEXT directive to accomplish this task.

PROC: Start a Procedure

Applicable assemblers: Microsoft Quick Assembler 2.51, MASM 5.1, MASM 6.0, TASM 2.0, TASM 3.0

Directive category: Procedures and code labels

Syntax:

```
label PROC [attributes] [USES reglist][, variable[:type]
    [, variable[:type] ...][, arg1:VARARG]
```

or, if you are using TASM:

```
label PROC [attributes]
```

or, if you are using TASM in ideal mode:

```
PROC label [attributes]
```

where attributes has the following construction:

```
[distance] [[langmod ]language] [visibility] [<prologuearg>]
```

Description: The use of the PROC directive varies widely, depending on how many bells and whistles you include and which assembler you are using. Note, however, that only the label and the PROC directive are required.

The label is the symbolic name you use to refer to the procedure. The distance controls the way the RET at the end of the procedure functions. It can be either NEAR or FAR, and serves to override the default distance defined by the .MODEL or MODEL directives.

The langmod parameter, applicable only in TASM, can be NORMAL, WINDOWS, ODDNEAR, or ODDFAR. The language specification is used to override the default language as defined with the .MODEL or MODEL directive. It can be any one of the following, depending on your assembler:

Language	MASM	TASM
BASIC	X	X
C	X	X
CPP		X
FORTRAN	X	X
NOLANGUAGE		X
Pascal	X	X
Prolog		X
STDCALL	X	
SYSCALL	X	

The visibility, available only with MASM 6.0, can be PRIVATE, PUBLIC, or EXPORT. Also available only with MASM 6.0 is the prologuearg parameter, which controls the way the assembler generates the prologue and epilogue. Valid options here are LOADDS, which assigns and restores the DS register, and FORCEFRAME, which forces MASM to create a stack for the procedure. Notice that the prologuearg options must be enclosed in angle brackets (<>).

If your procedure uses registers whose contents you do not want the routine to modify, you can use the USES keyword and specify a register list, reglist. Registers to be pushed in the prologue and popped in the epilogue should be listed with only one space between them. Note that if you are using TASM, the USES keyword is actually a directive and is handled differently. See the USES directive for more information.

If you are using MASM 6.0, you can specify an argument list on the PROC line. This list consists of the variable name and any valid type specification for the variable, such as BYTE, WORD, etc. Note that this is different from the way arguments were specified before MASM 6.0, and from the way they continue to be specified with TASM. This argument list capability was implemented with the ARG directive, to which you may want to refer for more information.

Also, MASM 6.0 enables you to build procedures for a variable number of arguments. This is done by using the VARARG keyword at the end of the PROC declaration, where arg1 is the name of the first argument. All other arguments are then accessed as offsets from this first one. Note that VARARG is applicable only if you are using the C, SYSCALL, or STDCALL language calling conventions.

PROTO: Declare Procedure Prototype

Applicable assemblers: MASM 6.0

Directive category: Procedures and code labels

Syntax:

```
label PROTO [distance] [language][, variable[:type]
    [, variable[:type] ...][, arg1:VARARG]
```

Description: Prototypes in MASM 6.0 function in the same manner as prototypes in the C language. They are designed so that you can declare what the real procedure will look like, without having to write the actual procedure.

The syntax of the PROTO directive is essentially the same as for the PROC directive. The label is the symbolic name you use to refer to the procedure. The distance controls the way the RET at the end of the procedure functions. It can be either NEAR or FAR, and serves to override the default distance, which is defined by the .MODEL or MODEL directives.

The language specification is used to override the default language as defined with the .MODEL or MODEL directive. The language specification can be BASIC, C, FORTRAN, Pascal, STDCALL, or SYSCALL.

You can specify an argument list with this directive in the same manner that you can with the PROC directive. This list consists of the variable name and any valid type specification for the variable, such as BYTE, WORD, etc.

You can use the VARARG keyword also to signify that the procedure will use a variable number of arguments. This is done with the VARARG keyword at the end of the PROC declaration, where arg1 is the name of the first argument. All other arguments are then accessed as offsets from this first one. Note that VARARG is applicable only if you are using the C, SYSCALL, or STDCALL language calling conventions.

PUBLIC: Declare Symbols as PUBLIC

Applicable assemblers: Microsoft Quick Assembler 2.51, MASM 5.1, MASM 6.0, TASM 2.0, TASM 3.0

Directive category: Scope and visibility

Syntax:

```
PUBLIC [language ]symbol[, [language ]symbol] ...
```

Description: This directive allows you to specify how symbols in your program will be seen by other modules. This specification is necessary at link time, when externals must be resolved.

The language specifier is used to override the default language, which is set with the `.MODEL` or `MODEL` directives. The `language` can be one of the following, depending on your assembler:

Language	MASM	TASM
BASIC	X	X
C	X	X
CPP		X
FORTRAN	X	X
NOLANGUAGE		X
Pascal	X	X
Prolog		X
STDCALL	X	
SYSCALL	X	

The `symbol` is the name of a procedure or some other label that is defined in the module.

PUBLICDLL: Declare Symbols as PUBLIC for Dynamic Link Libraries

Applicable assemblers: TASM 2.0, TASM 3.0

Directive category: Scope and visibility

Syntax:

```
PUBLICDLL [language ]symbol[, [language ]symbol] ...
```

Description: This directive is a special version of the `PUBLIC` directive, for use with OS/2 and Windows dynamic link libraries (DLL). The language specifier is used to override the default language, which is set with the `.MODEL` or `MODEL` directives. Valid choices for `language` are BASIC, C, CPP, FORTRAN, NOLANGUAGE, Pascal, or Prolog. The `symbol` is the name of a procedure or some other label that is defined in the module.

PURGE: Delete Macro Definition

Applicable assemblers: Microsoft Quick Assembler 2.51, MASM 5.1, MASM 6.0, TASM 2.0, TASM 3.0

Directive category: Macros and repeat blocks

Syntax:

```
PURGE label[, label] ...
```

Description: After a macro has been defined, it remains in memory until you use this directive to remove it. PURGE accepts, as label, the name of previously defined macros.

PUSHCONTEXT: Save Assembler Environment

Applicable assemblers: MASM 6.0

Directive category: Global control

Syntax:

```
PUSHCONTEXT condition
```

Description: This directive generally is used inside macros to save current assembler settings temporarily. The condition can be the following:

Condition	Meaning
ASSUME	Current segment register assumptions
CPU	State of current CPU and processor directives
LISTING	State of listing and cross-reference directives (similar to the %PUSHCTLS directive for TASM)
RADIX	Current default radix
ALL	All of the above

The stored settings can be restored by using the POPCONTEXT directive.

%PUSHLCTL: Temporarily Save Listing Controls

Applicable assemblers: TASM 2.0, TASM 3.0

Directive category: Listing control

Syntax:

`%PUSHLCTL`

Description: Using this directive allows you to save the condition of the %MACS, %LIST, and %INCL directives. You can restore them later with the %POPLCTL directive.

If you use MASM 6.0, you can use the PUSHCONTEXT directive to accomplish this task.

QUIRKS: Enable Handling of MASM Quirks

Applicable assemblers: TASM 2.0, TASM 3.0

Directive category: Global control

Syntax:

`QUIRKS`

Description: MASM has some odd behavior that TASM normally will not tolerate. When you use this directive, you are instructing TASM to behave exactly as MASM does, regardless of whether it makes logical sense. If your code takes advantage of some of the documented quirks in MASM, you should rewrite the code so that it will work properly under both assemblers. If you want more information on exactly what the MASM quirks are, you should refer to the Turbo Assembler manual.

QWORD: Allocate a Quadword of Storage Space

Applicable assemblers: MASM 6.0

Directive category: Data allocation

Syntax:

`[label] QWORD expression[, expression]`

Description: This directive is equivalent to the DQ directive. It is used to allocate 8 bytes of memory (a quadword) for data storage in the executable file. Typically, this data size is used for 8-byte integers used with numeric coprocessors. The label is a user-defined name that you can use later to refer symbolically to the stored information. Each expression must be one of the following:

❏ A number between -2^{63} and $2^{64}-1$

❏ A formula resolving to a number between -2^{63} and $2^{64}-1$

❏ A 64-bit floating-point number between $\pm 2.23 \times 10^{-308}$ and $\pm 1.79 \times 10^{308}$

❏ A question mark (used to hold space but not initialize the data area)

In addition, you can use the DUP operator to specify multiple occurrences of the data in the expression.

If the data allocated by the QWORD directive is longer than a single quadword, the label refers only to the first quadword of the allocated data.

You can use the REAL8 directive for floating-point numbers also.

Examples:

```
Values    QWORD    12345.6789, 987.6543
MemArea   QWORD    1024 * 64 * 4
Array     QWORD    12 DUP(?)
```

.RADIX: Specify the Default Radix

Applicable assemblers: Microsoft Quick Assembler 2.51, MASM 5.1, MASM 6.0, TASM 2.0, TASM 3.0

Directive category: Global control

Syntax:

```
.RADIX setting
```

Description: The default radix for the assembler is decimal (all numbers are assumed to be decimal, unless an override radix is used), but this directive allows you to change the radix. Valid settings are 2, 8, 10, and 16.

If you are using TASM, you can use the RADIX directive also.

RADIX: Specify the Default Radix

Applicable assemblers: TASM 2.0, TASM 3.0

Directive category: Global control

Syntax:

RADIX *setting*

Description: This directive is the same as the .RADIX directive. The default radix for the assembler is decimal (all numbers are assumed to be decimal, unless an override radix is used), but this directive allows you to change the radix. Valid settings are 2, 8, 10, and 16.

REAL4: Allocate a Doubleword of Storage Space for a 32-Bit Floating-Point Number

Applicable assemblers: MASM 6.0

Directive category: Data allocation

Syntax:

[*label*] REAL4 *expression*[, *expression*]

Description: This directive allocates 4 bytes of memory (a doubleword) for data storage in the executable file. In this way, it is similar to the DD and DWORD directives. It also assumes that the contents of this memory area will be 32-bit floating-point values.

The label is a user-defined name you can use later to refer symbolically to the stored information. Each expression must be one of the following:

❏ A 32-bit floating-point number between $\pm1.18 \times 10^{-38}$ and $\pm3.40 \times 10^{38}$

❏ An expression that resolves to a 32-bit floating-point number between $\pm1.18 \times 10^{-38}$ and $\pm3.40 \times 10^{38}$

❏ A question mark (used to hold space but not initialize the data area)

In addition, you can use the DUP operator to specify multiple occurrences of the data in the expression.

If the data allocated by the REAL4 directive is longer than a single doubleword, the label refers only to the first doubleword of the allocated data.

There is effectively no difference between floating-point numbers generated with this directive and those generated with DD or DWORD. The practical difference is apparent, however, when you use CodeView to debug your code. If you use the REAL4 directive, CodeView knows how to treat and display the numbers.

Examples:

```
Value1     REAL4    98765.432987
Values     REAL4    2.345, 59.682
Array      REAL4    50 DUP(?)
```

REAL8: Allocate a Quadword of Storage Space for a 64-Bit Floating-Point Number

Applicable assemblers: MASM 6.0

Directive category: Data allocation

Syntax:

```
[label] REAL8 expression[, expression]
```

Description: This directive allocates 8 bytes of memory (a quadword) for data storage in the executable file. In this way, it is similar to the DQ and QWORD directives. It also assumes that the contents of this memory area will be 64-bit floating-point values.

The label is a user-defined name you can use later to refer symbolically to the stored information. Each expression must be one of the following:

❑ A 64-bit floating-point number between $\pm 2.23 \times 10^{-308}$ and $\pm 1.79 \times 10^{308}$

❑ An expression that resolves to a 64-bit floating-point number between $\pm 2.23 \times 10^{-308}$ and $\pm 1.79 \times 10^{308}$

❑ A question mark (used to hold space but not initialize the data area)

In addition, you can use the DUP operator to specify multiple occurrences of the data in the expression.

If the data allocated by the REAL8 directive is longer than a single quadword, the label refers only to the first quadword of the allocated data.

There is effectively no difference between floating-point numbers generated with this directive and those generated with DQ or QWORD. The practical difference is apparent, however, when you use CodeView to debug your code. If you use the REAL8 directive, CodeView knows how to treat and display the numbers.

Examples:

```
Value1    REAL8   13 / 3
Values    REAL8   465825432.345, 508543249.682
Array     REAL8   50 DUP(?)
```

REAL10: Allocate 10 Bytes of Storage Space for an 80-Bit Floating-Point Number

Applicable assemblers: MASM 6.0

Directive category: Data allocation

Syntax:

[*label*] REAL10 *expression*[, *expression*]

Description: This directive allocates 10 bytes of memory for data storage in the executable file. In this way, it is similar to the DT and TWORD directives. It also assumes that the contents of this memory area will be a temporary 80-bit floating-point value.

The label is a user-defined name you can use later to refer symbolically to the stored information. Each expression must be one of the following:

❏ An 80-bit floating-point number between $\pm3.37 \times 10^{-4932}$ and $\pm1.18 \times 10^{4932}$

❏ An expression that resolves to an 80-bit floating-point number between $\pm3.37 \times 10^{-4932}$ and $\pm1.18 \times 10^{4932}$

❏ A question mark (used to hold space but not initialize the data area)

In addition, you can use the DUP operator to specify multiple occurrences of the data in the expression.

If the data allocated by the REAL10 directive is longer than 10 bytes, the label refers only to the first 10 bytes of the allocated data.

There is effectively no difference between floating-point numbers generated with this directive and those generated with DT or TWORD. The practical difference is apparent, however, when you use CodeView to debug your code. If you use the REAL10 directive, CodeView knows how to treat and display the numbers.

Examples:

```
Value1    REAL10   123456789 / 987612345
Values    REAL10   465825432.345, 508543249.682
Array     REAL10   50 DUP(?)
```

RECORD: Define Records

Applicable assemblers: Microsoft Quick Assembler 2.51, MASM 5.1, MASM 6.0, TASM 2.0, TASM 3.0

Directive category: Complex data types

Syntax:

```
label RECORD [field[, field] ...]
```

or, if you are using TASM in ideal mode:

```
RECORD label [field[, field] ...]
```

where each field has the construction:

```
fieldlabel:width[=value]
```

Description: This is a user-defined data type composed of a number of bit fields that collectively add up to a complete record. The `label` is the symbolic name for the record. Each bit field has a symbolic field name, `fieldlabel`, and a `width`, in bits. Optionally, you can assign a `value` to each bit field.

If your record definitions grow quite large, you can use the multiline version of this directive, which simply requires that you place a left brace ({) on the same line as the `RECORD` directive. Everything encountered up to a right brace (}) is considered part of the definition.

.REPEAT: Declare the Beginning of a Controlled Loop

Applicable assemblers: MASM 6.0

Directive category: Control flow

Syntax:

```
.REPEAT
```

Description: This directive is used to eliminate the need for the programmer to determine the best way to construct a repetitive loop. The `.REPEAT` directive, which is similar in construct to the `DO` loop in C or the `REPEAT` loop in Pascal, is a continuing attempt to build higher-level functionality into assembly language.

Loops that use `.REPEAT` can be nested with other loops that use `.REPEAT` or `.WHILE`. These loops also can be terminated normally with the `.UNTIL` or `.UNTILCXZ` directives, or prematurely with the `.BREAK` or `.CONTINUE` directives.

Do not confuse the .REPEAT directive with the REPEAT directive; they have different purposes and actions.

Example:

```
        .REPEAT                 ;Wait for ESC key to be pressed
        MOV     AH,7            ;Direct character input without echo
        INT     21h             ;DOS services
        .UNTIL  (AL == 27)      ;Keep going until ESC is pressed
```

This example is the same as the following nondirective method of coding the loop:

```
InLoop:  MOV    AH,7            ;Direct character input without echo
         INT    21h             ;DOS services
         CMP    AL,27           ;Was ESC key pressed?
         JNE    InLoop          ;No, so do it again
```

REPEAT: Repeat a Block of Instructions

Applicable assemblers: MASM 6.0

Directive category: Macros and repeat blocks

Syntax:

REPEAT *expression*

Description: This directive is the same as the REPT directive. It provides a way for the assembler to repeat a code block several times. Typically, this directive is used in macros.

The expression represents the number of times the code block and/or instructions should be repeated. Every source-code line between the REPT directive and the ENDM or EXITM directives is repeated this number of times.

Example:

```
DataSet    MACRO  Times
           .ERRB  <Times>             ;Need to have an argument
BufrTable  DW     Times DUP (0)
           REPT   Times
           DB     512 DUP (?)
           ENDM
           ENDM
```

REPT: Repeat a Block of Instructions

Applicable assemblers: Microsoft Quick Assembler 2.51, MASM 5.1, MASM 6.0, TASM 2.0, TASM 3.0

Directive category: Macros and repeat blocks

Syntax:

```
REPT expression
```

Description: This directive provides a way for the assembler to repeat a code block several times. Typically, this directive is used in macros.

The expression represents the number of times the code block and/or instructions should be repeated. Every source-code line between the REPT directive and the ENDM or EXITM directives is repeated this number of times.

If you are using MASM 6.0, you can use the REPEAT directive also.

Example:

```
DataSet      MACRO   Times
             .ERRB   <Times>              ;Need to have an argument
BufrTable    DW      Times DUP (0)
             REPT    Times
             DB      512 DUP (?)
             ENDM
             ENDM
```

.SALL: Disable Macro Listing

Applicable assemblers: Microsoft Quick Assembler 2.51, MASM 5.1, MASM 6.0, TASM 2.0, TASM 3.0

Directive category: Listing control

Syntax:

```
.SALL
```

Description: Normally, the assembler lists (in the listing file) the macro lines that generate code. If you use this directive, only the macro invocation line is listed. No other macro expansion is listed, even if it generates code. Under MASM 6.0, this is the same as the .NOLISTMACRO directive.

SBYTE: Allocate a Signed Byte of Storage Space

Applicable assemblers: MASM 6.0

Directive category: Data allocation

Syntax:

```
[label] SBYTE expression[, expression]
```

Description: This directive is similar to the DB and BYTE directives. It is used to allocate memory in the executable file for data storage. The label is a user-defined name you can use later to refer symbolically to the stored information. Each expression must be one of the following:

❑ A number between −128 and 127

❑ A formula resolving to a number between −128 and 127

❑ A question mark (used to hold space but not initialize the data area)

In addition, you can use the DUP operator to specify multiple occurrences of the data in the expression.

If the data allocated by the SBYTE directive is longer than a single byte, the label refers only to the first byte of the allocated data.

Examples:

```
Value1      SBYTE    0
Value2      SBYTE    -83
BoxSize     SBYTE    5 * 7
Array       SBYTE    200 DUP(?)
TruthTable  SBTYE    8 DUP(-128)
```

SDWORD: Allocate a Signed Doubleword of Storage Space

Applicable assemblers: MASM 6.0

Directive category: Data allocation

Syntax:

```
[label] SDWORD expression[, expression]
```

Description: This directive is similar to the DD and DWORD directives. It is used to allocate 4 bytes of memory (a doubleword) for data storage in the executable file. The label is a user-defined name you can use later to refer symbolically to the stored information. Each expression must be one of the following:

❏ A number between −2,147,483,648 and 2,147,483,647

❏ A formula resolving to a number between −2,147,483,648 and 2,147,483,647

❏ A question mark (used to hold space but not initialize the data area)

In addition, you can use the DUP operator to specify multiple occurrences of the data in the expression.

If the data allocated by the SDWORD directive is longer than a single doubleword, the label refers only to the first doubleword of the allocated data.

Examples:

```
Values    SDWORD  -24565, 67845, 0, -99253665
Counter   SDWORD  0
MemArea   SDWORD  1024 * 64 * 4
Array     SDWORD  100 DUP(?)
```

SEGMENT: Define Beginning of a Segment

Applicable assemblers: Microsoft Quick Assembler 2.51, MASM 5.1, MASM 6.0, TASM 2.0, TASM 3.0

Directive category: Complete segment control

Syntax:

label SEGMENT [*align*] [*attributes*] ['*class*']

or, if you are using TASM in ideal mode:

SEGMENT *label* [*align*] [*attributes*] ['*class*']

Description: This is the nonsimplified method of designating the beginning of a segment. Used in conjunction with the ENDS directive, SEGMENT marks what the assembler and linker should include in a specific segment.

The label can be any symbolic name you want the segment to use. The align parameter specifies how the segment should be aligned: BYTE, WORD, DWORD, PARA, or PAGE. If you are using TASM, you can use MEMPAGE as an align type also.

The `attributes` can be a combination of the following:

Attribute	MASM	TASM	Meaning
PRIVATE	X	X	Segment will not be combined with other segments outside this module, even if they have the same name. This is the default attribute.
PUBLIC	X	X	Segment will be combined with other segments (outside this module) with the same name.
MEMORY	X	X	Same as PUBLIC.
COMMON	X	X	Causes segments of the same name to share the same memory space. All such segments begin at the same memory address.
STACK	X		Combines all segments having the same name, and causes the operating system to set SS:00 to the start of this segment and SS:SP to the top of it.
READONLY	X	X	Segment cannot be modified. Assembler will generate an error if it detects information being changed in the segment.
READWRITE		X	Segment can be accessed normally.
EXECONLY		X	Segment contains only executable code. Assembler will generate an error if it detects any other type of access.
EXECREAD		X	Segment can be executed and read from, but not modified. Assembler will generate an error if it detects any other type of access.
VIRTUAL		X	A child segment attached to and enclosed in any other type of segment.
AT *para*	X	X	Specifies that the segment should begin at the specified *para*graph address.
USE16	X	X	Use 16-bit word size (offset addressing) if using an 80386 or 80486.

Attribute	MASM	TASM	Meaning
USE32	X	X	Use 32-bit word size (offset addressing) if using an 80386 or 80486.
FLAT	X	X	Don't use segment:offset notation.

You can specify an optional `class` type, enclosed in single quotation marks (apostrophes), if you want to dictate how the linker should combine this segment with other segments. Segments are ordered first by group and then by name. Segments having the same name but belonging to different groups are never combined.

.SEQ: Place Segments in Sequential Order

Applicable assemblers: Microsoft Quick Assembler 2.51, MASM 5.1, MASM 6.0, TASM 2.0, TASM 3.0

Directive category: Complete segment control

Syntax:

```
.SEQ
```

Description: Normally, both MASM and TASM place segments in the OBJ file in the order in which they are encountered in the source file. Since that is also the purpose of this directive, using `.SEQ` is redundant and unnecessary.

You can affect the ordering of segments with the `.ALPHA`, `ALPHA`, `.DOSSEG`, and `DOSSEG` directives also. If you are using TASM, this directive is equivalent to the `SEQ` directive.

SEQ: Place Segments in Sequential Order

Applicable assemblers: TASM 3.0

Directive category: Complete segment control

Syntax:

```
SEQ
```

Description: Normally, both MASM and TASM place segments in the OBJ file in the order in which they are encountered in the source file. Since that is also the purpose of this directive, using `SEQ` is redundant and unnecessary.

You can affect the ordering of segments with the `.ALPHA`, `ALPHA`, `.DOSSEG`, and `DOSSEG` directives also.

This directive is equivalent to the `.SEQ` directive.

.SFCOND: List True Conditional Statements

Applicable assemblers: Microsoft Quick Assembler 2.51, MASM 5.1, MASM 6.0, TASM 2.0, TASM 3.0

Directive category: Listing control

Syntax:

```
.SFCOND
```

Description: Instructs the assembler to include conditional code in the listing file only if it is a true condition. In other words, only code that makes it to the OBJ file is listed. If you are using TASM, this directive is the same as the `%NOCONDS` directive. Under MASM 6.0, this is the same as the `.NOLISTIF` directive.

SIZESTR: Return the Length of a String

Applicable assemblers: Microsoft Quick Assembler 2.51, MASM 6.0, TASM 2.0, TASM 3.0

Directive category: String control

Syntax:

```
label SIZESTR string
```

Description: This directive functions much like its counterpart in some high-level languages. When assembled, it assigns to the text macro `label` the length of `string`. For instance, the following statements:

```
VerDate    TEXTEQU '10/13/1991'
VDLen      SIZESTR Verdate
```

result in `VDLen` being equal to 10.

SMALLSTACK: Specify 16-Bit Stack Pointer

Applicable assemblers: TASM 3.0

Directive category: Global control

Syntax:

SMALLSTACK

Description: Normally, the prologue and epilogue code generated automatically by TASM controls the way a procedure uses the stack. If you are using an 80386 or 80486, however, it is possible to use either a 16-bit or 32-bit stack pointer. This directive overrides the default stack size selected with the .MODEL or MODEL directive and ensures that a 16-bit pointer is used.

SMART: Enable Code Optimization

Applicable assemblers: TASM 3.0

Directive category: Global control

Syntax:

SMART

Description: TASM normally optimizes code to operate the quickest way possible in the least amount of memory. If you use the NOSMART directive to turn off optimization, you can use this directive later to return to the default.

.STACK: Define Beginning of Stack Segment

Applicable assemblers: Microsoft Quick Assembler 2.51, MASM 5.1, MASM 6.0, TASM 2.0, TASM 3.0

Directive category: Complete segment control

Syntax:

.STACK [*size*]

Description: This directive causes the assembler to create a stack segment of size bytes. If no size is specified, a default stack of 1,024 bytes is created.

Typically, you need to create a stack only if you are writing stand-alone assembly language programs. If you are writing routines for use with high-level languages, the linker allows you to use the same stack used by the high-level language.

Alternatively, if you are using TASM, you can use the STACK directive.

STACK: Define Beginning of Stack Segment

Applicable assemblers: TASM 2.0, TASM 3.0

Directive category: Complete segment control

Syntax:

```
STACK [size]
```

Description: This directive is the same as the .STACK directive. It causes the assembler to create a stack segment of size bytes. If no size is specified, a default stack of 1,024 bytes is created.

Typically, you need to create a stack only if you are writing stand-alone assembly language programs. If you are writing routines for use with high-level languages, the linker allows you to use the same stack used by the high-level language.

.STARTUP: Specify Program Entry Point

Applicable assemblers: Microsoft Quick Assembler 2.51, MASM 5.1, MASM 6.0, TASM 2.0, TASM 3.0

Directive category: Simplified segment control

Syntax:

```
.STARTUP
```

Description: .STARTUP, one of the simplified segment directives, should be used with the .EXIT directive. .STARTUP enables you to specify the entry point of your program. Then the assembler automatically generates code that sets up the environment of your program to be consistent with the environment you specified with the .MODEL directive. When your program is complete, this work is "cleaned up" by the code generated by .EXIT.

Place this directive in the main module of your program, immediately following the .CODE directive.

STARTUPCODE: Specify Program Entry Point

Applicable assemblers: TASM 3.0

Directive category: Simplified segment control

Syntax:

STARTUPCODE

Description: This directive is the same as the .STARTUP directive. One of the simplified segment directives, it should be used with the EXITCODE directive. STARTUPCODE allows you to specify the entry point of your program. Then the assembler automatically generates code that sets up the environment of your program to be consistent with the environment you specified with the .MODEL or MODEL directives. When your program is complete, this work is "cleaned up" by the code generated by EXITCODE.

Place this directive in the main module of your program, immediately following the .CODE directive.

STRUC: Define a Data Structure

Applicable assemblers: Microsoft Quick Assembler 2.51, MASM 5.1, MASM 6.0, TASM 2.0, TASM 3.0

Directive category: Complex data types

Syntax:

label STRUC [*align*][, NONUNIQUE]

or, if you are using TASM in ideal mode:

STRUC *label*

Description: Similar to user-defined data structures in high-level languages, the STRUC directive enables you to specify the beginning of a data structure. The data-definition directives that follow, until the next ENDS directive is encountered, define the *members* of the structure. Members of the structure can be any data-definition directive you want; they do not have to be similar in type. The data structure collectively will be known by the symbolic name label.

If you are using MASM 6.0, you can specify an alignment value, align, which is used to align members of the structure within memory. Valid values are 1, 2, or 4. If you specify align, the amount of space taken by the structure may increase, but so will the speed with which members of the structure can be accessed. This applies only to 16- or 32-bit processors.

Also, the `NONUNIQUE` parameter specifies how stringent the assembler is in allowing subsequent references to members of the structure. If you use this parameter, you must provide a full structure and member name each time you want to reference a member.

Alternatively, if you are using MASM 6.0, you can use the `STRUCT` directive to define data structures.

Example:

```
PayRecord    STRUC
LastName     DB      15 DUP (0)
FirstName    DB      15 DUP (0)
Address      DB      30 DUP (0)
City         DB      25 DUP (0)
State        DB      '  ',0
ZipCode      DB      10 DUP (0)
BasePay      REAL4   0
Commission   REAL4   0
HireMonth    DB      '  -'
HireDay      DB      '  -'
HireYear     DB      '    ',0
             ENDS
```

STRUCT: Define a Data Structure

Applicable assemblers: MASM 6.0

Directive category: Simplified segment control

Syntax:

label STRUCT [*align*][, NONUNIQUE]

Description: This directive, which is the same as the `STRUC` directive, is provided so that the many C programmers using MASM can comfortably spell the directive in their customary way.

Like user-defined data structures in high-level languages, the `STRUCT` directive allows you to specify the beginning of a data structure. The data-definition directives that follow, until the next `ENDS` directive is encountered, define the members of the structure. Members of the structure can be any data-definition directive you want; they do not have to be similar in type. The data structure will be known collectively by the symbolic name `label`.

If you are using MASM 6.0, you can specify an alignment value, `align`, which is used to align members of the structure in memory. Valid values are 1, 2, or 4. If you specify `align`, the amount of space taken by the structure may increase, but so will the speed with which members of the structure can be accessed. (The preceding sentence applies only to 16- or 32-bit processors.)

Also, the `NONUNIQUE` parameter specifies how stringent the assembler is in allowing subsequent references to members of the structure. If you use this parameter, you must provide a full structure and member name each time you want to reference a member.

Example:

```
PayRecord    STRUCT
LastName     DB      15 DUP (0)
FirstName    DB      15 DUP (0)
Address      DB      30 DUP (0)
City         DB      25 DUP (0)
State        DB      '  ',0
ZipCode      DB      10 DUP (0)
BasePay      REAL4   0
Commission   REAL4   0
HireMonth    DB      '  -'
HireDay      DB      '  -'
HireYear     DB      '    ',0
             ENDS
```

SUBSTR: Return a Substring

Applicable assemblers: Microsoft Quick Assembler 2.51, MASM 6.0, TASM 2.0, TASM 3.0

Directive category: String control

Syntax:

label SUBSTR *string, start*[*, end*]

Description: This directive functions much like its counterpart in some high-level languages. When assembled, it defines a text macro, with the name `label`, to be equal to a substring of `string`. You specify the `start` character position in `string`, and optionally specify an end character position. If you do not specify end, `label` will be equal to the part of `string` from `start` to the end of `string`.

For instance, the following statements:

```
VerDate    TEXTEQU   '10/13/1991'
Divider    SUBSTR    Verdate, 3, 1
Year       SUBSTR    Verdate, 7
```

result in Divider being equal to /, and Year being equal to 1991.

SUBTITLE: Specify Listing-File Subtitle

Applicable assemblers: MASM 6.0

Directive category: Listing control

Syntax:

SUBTITLE [*text*]

Description: This directive, which is the same as the SUBTTL directive, is used to specify a subtitle that appears at the top of each page in the listing file. If a subtitle was set previously, the new subtitle will appear at the top of the following listing page. If you use SUBTITLE without a subtitle, no subtitle will be printed from that point forward.

Normally, you use SUBTITLE with other page-control directives to get the effect you want. No subtitle is printed on the first page of a listing file, because the headers for the first page are printed before any of the lines of the source code are analyzed.

SUBTTL: Specify Listing-File Subtitle

Applicable assemblers: Microsoft Quick Assembler 2.51, MASM 5.1, MASM 6.0, TASM 2.0, TASM 3.0

Directive category: Listing control

Syntax:

SUBTTL [*text*]

Description: This directive is used to specify a subtitle that appears at the top of each page in the listing file. If a subtitle was set previously, the new subtitle will appear at the top of the following listing page. If you use SUBTTL without a subtitle, no subtitle will be printed from that point forward.

Normally, you should use SUBTTL with other page-control directives to get the effect you want. No subtitle is printed on the first page of a listing file, because the headers for the first page are printed before any of the lines of the source code are analyzed.

If you are using TASM, you can use the %SUBTTL directive also to set a subtitle. Under MASM 6.0, you can use the SUBTITLE directive.

%SUBTTL: Specify Listing-File Subtitle

Applicable assemblers: TASM 2.0, TASM 3.0

Directive category: Listing control

Syntax:

```
%SUBTTL "text"
```

Description: This directive, identical in function and similar in form to the SUBTTL directive, is used to specify a subtitle that appears at the top of each page in the listing file. If a subtitle was set previously, the new subtitle will appear at the top of the following listing page.

Normally, you use %SUBTTL with other page-control directives to get the effect you want. No subtitle is printed on the first page of a listing file, because the headers for the first page are printed before any of the lines of the source code are analyzed.

SWORD: Allocate a Signed Word of Storage Space

Applicable assemblers: MASM 6.0

Directive category: Data allocation

Syntax:

```
[label] SWORD expression[, expression]
```

Description: This directive is similar to the DW and WORD directives. It is used to allocate 2 bytes of memory (a word) for data storage in the executable file. The label is a user-defined name you can use later to refer symbolically to the stored information. Each expression must be one of the following:

❏ A number between −32,767 and 32,767

❏ A formula resolving to a number between −32,767 and 32,767

❏ A question mark (used to hold space but not initialize the data area)

In addition, you can use the DUP operator to specify multiple occurrences of the data in the expression.

If the data allocated by the SWORD directive is longer than a single word, the label refers only to the first word of the allocated data.

Examples:

```
Value1      SWORD   -5432
Value2      SWORD   2653
Counter     SWORD   0
ScreenSize  SWORD   80 * 25
Array       SWORD   12 DUP(?)
```

%SYMS: Enable Symbol Table in Listing File

Applicable assemblers: TASM 2.0, TASM 3.0

Directive category: Listing control

Syntax:

%SYMS

Description: This directive, which is used to reverse the effects of the %NOSYMS directive, is the normal default condition for a listing file generated by TASM.

TABLE: Define a Method Table

Applicable assemblers: TASM 3.0

Directive category: Complex data types

Syntax:

label TABLE [*member*[, *member*] ...]

or, if using ideal mode:

TABLE *label* [*member*[, *member*] ...]

where each member has the following construction:

[VIRTUAL] *memberlabel* [[*arraysize*]][:*memtype*[:*count*]][=*expression*]

Description: Tables are used with object-oriented programming. They represent method tables in such languages as Turbo Pascal and Borland C++. If you are writing extensive subroutines for use with these languages, you necessarily will get into the use of tables.

The `label` is the symbolic name used for referring to the table; the `memberlabel` is the name by which each member of the table is known. The `memtype` can be any valid data type, including pointers. If you want to initialize any instances of the table members, you can use the `expression` to do so.

If you are working in ideal mode, table member names are local to the table. If you are working in MASM mode, the names are global.

If your table definitions grow quite large, you can use the multiline version of this directive, which simply requires that you place a left brace ({) on the same line as the `TABLE` directive. Everything encountered up to a right brace (}) is considered part of the definition.

%TABSIZE: Set Listing-File Tab-Stop Width

Applicable assemblers: TASM 2.0, TASM 3.0

Directive category: Listing control

Syntax:

```
%TABSIZE width
```

Description: Normally, any listing file generated by the assembler has a tab-stop width of eight characters. You can change the `width` (the number of characters) between tab stops with this directive.

TBLPTR: Force Table-Pointer Inclusion

Applicable assemblers: TASM 3.0

Directive category: Complex data types

Syntax:

```
TBLPTR
```

Description: When working with objects, you may want to locate explicitly the virtual table pointer for a method table. The `TBLPTR` directive enables you to do this.

Typically, TASM automatically provides this information in an object's data structure as necessary. This directive is designed to override the arbitrary nature of the table pointer's inclusion, however. When you include TBLPTR in the object data-structure definition, the pointer is included all the time.

TBYTE: Allocate 10 Bytes of Storage Space

Applicable assemblers: MASM 6.0

Directive category: Data allocation

Syntax:

[*label*] TBYTE *expression*[, *expression*]

Description: This directive is equivalent to the DT directive. It is used to allocate 10 bytes of memory for data storage in the executable file. Typically, this data size is used for 10-byte integers or real number formats used with numeric coprocessors. The label is a user-defined name you can use later to refer symbolically to the stored information. Each expression must be one of the following:

❏ A number between -2^{79} and $2^{80}-1$

❏ A formula resolving to a number between -2^{79} and $2^{80}-1$

❏ A packed decimal number between 0 and $10^{20}-1$

❏ An 80-bit temporary floating-point number between $\pm 3.37 \times 10^{-4932}$ and $\pm 1.18 \times 10^{4932}$

❏ A question mark (used to hold space but not initialize the data area)

In addition, you can use the DUP operator to specify multiple occurrences of the data in the expression.

If the data allocated by the TBYTE directive is longer than 10 bytes, the label refers only to the first 10 bytes of the allocated data.

You can use the REAL10 directive also for floating-point numbers.

Examples:

```
Values     TBYTE    12345.6789, 987.6543
MemArea    TBYTE    1024 * 64 * 4
Array      TBYTE    12 DUP(?)
```

%TEXT: Set Listing-File Source-Field Width

Applicable assemblers: TASM 2.0, TASM 3.0

Directive category: Listing control

Syntax:

`%TEXT width`

Description: When you request a listing file (LST file) during assembly, this directive controls the width of the source-code field. You can set `width` to any reasonable number.

TEXTEQU: Define a Text Macro

Applicable assemblers: MASM 6.0

Directive category: Macros and repeat blocks

Syntax:

`label TEXTEQU value`

Description: This directive is used to assign strings to labels, which are known as *text macros*. The `label` is the name by which you want the string to be known; it is the name of the text macro. The `value` must resolve to a string or be the name of another text macro. Then, when the `label` is used later in your program, the assembler substitutes the text assigned to the name. The string must be enclosed in angle brackets (<>).

Examples:

```
Var1        TEXTEQU <[bp+4]>                 ;Var1 is the text '[bp+4]'
Arg1        TEXTEQU Var1                     ;Now Arg1 == Var1
Number      =       4
Ex4         TEXTEQU <Example > + %Number ;Ex4 is the text 'Example 4'
```

.TFCOND: Switch State of Conditional-Statement Listings

Applicable assemblers: Microsoft Quick Assembler 2.51, MASM 5.1, MASM 6.0, TASM 2.0, TASM 3.0

Directive category: Listing control

Syntax:

```
.TFCOND
```

Description: This directive switches (to the opposite method) the way the assembler handles listing conditional assembly blocks. If they are being listed, executing .TFCOND causes them not to be listed from that point on (and vice versa). You can use the .LFCOND and .SFCOND directives to specify exactly how conditionals should be handled in listings.

TITLE: Specify Listing-File Title

Applicable assemblers: Microsoft Quick Assembler 2.51, MASM 5.1, MASM 6.0, TASM 2.0, TASM 3.0

Directive category: Listing control

Syntax:

```
TITLE text
```

Description: This directive, which can be used only once in your file, is used to specify a title that appears at the top of each page in the listing file.

Normally, you use TITLE with other page-control directives to get the effect you want. No title is printed on the first page of a listing file, because the headers for the first page are printed before any of the lines of the source code are analyzed.

If you are using TASM, you can use the %TITLE directive also to set a title.

%TITLE: Specify Listing-File Title

Applicable assemblers: TASM 2.0, TASM 3.0

Directive category: Listing control

Syntax:

```
%TITLE "text"
```

Description: This directive, which is identical in function and similar in form to the TITLE directive, is used to specify a title that appears at the top of each page in the listing file. This directive can be used only once in your file.

%TRUNC: Control Word-Wrapping in the Listing File

Applicable assemblers: TASM 2.0, TASM 3.0

Directive category: Listing control

Syntax:

%TRUNC

Description: Normally, if the source-code lines or the generated code in the listing file are too long to be listed properly, they are truncated. This truncation occurs only in the listing file—not in the OBJ file. If truncation has been disabled with the %NOTRUNC directive, the %TRUNC directive enables again.

TYPEDEF: Define a Pointer Type

Applicable assemblers: MASM 6.0, TASM 3.0

Directive category: Complex data types

Syntax:

label TYPEDEF [*distance*] PTR *type*

Description: This directive allows you to define your own type of pointers for use in your programs. The label is the name you will use to refer to the defined type. The optional distance, used to override the default distances defined with the .MODEL directive, can be either NEAR or FAR. Finally, type represents any regular data type such as BYTE, WORD, etc.

UDATASEG: Define Beginning of Uninitialized Data Segment

Applicable assemblers: TASM 2.0, TASM 3.0

Directive category: Simplified segment control

Syntax:

UDATASEG

Description: This directive is the same as the .DATA? directive. It is one of several simplified data-segment directives available. The others include .CONST, CONST, .DATA, .DATA?, DATASEG, .FARDATA, FARDATA, .FARDATA?, and UFARDATA.

This simplified segment directive is used to inform the assembler that the information immediately following should be placed in a special uninitialized data segment. You must use the .MODEL or MODEL directives before using UDATASEG.

It is not necessary to use this special type of segment, but you may want to use it to group your data. Such grouping may help you understand the different parts of your program better.

UFARDATA: Define Beginning of Uninitialized Far Data Segment

Applicable assemblers: TASM 2.0, TASM 3.0

Directive category: Simplified segment control

Syntax:

UFARDATA [*label*]

Description: This directive is the same as the .FARDATA? directive. UFARDATA is one of several simplified data-segment directives available. The others include .CONST, CONST, .DATA, .DATA?, DATASEG, .FARDATA, .FARDATA?, FARDATA, and UDATASEG.

This simplified segment directive is used to inform the assembler that the information immediately following should be placed in a special uninitialized far data segment. You must use the .MODEL or MODEL directives before using UFARDATA.

It is not necessary to use this special type of segment, but you may want to use it to group your data. Such grouping may help you understand the different parts of your program better. If you use the optional label, the name should guide the way the linker combines different far data segments while linking.

UNION: Define a Data Union

Applicable assemblers: MASM 6.0, TASM 2.0, TASM 3.0

Directive category: Complex data types

Syntax:

label UNION[, NONUNIQUE]

or, if you are using TASM in ideal mode:

UNION *label*

Description: A *union* is a user-defined data structure in which members of the structure overlap one another. Thus, you can use unions to specify different ways to access the same data.

The UNION directive allows you to specify the beginning of a data union. The data-definition directives that follow, until the next ENDS directive is encountered, define the members of the union. Members of the union can be any data-definition directive you want; they do not have to be similar in type. The data union will be known collectively by the symbolic name label.

In MASM 6.0, the NONUNIQUE parameter specifies how stringent the assembler is in allowing subsequent references to members of the union. If you use this parameter, you must provide a full union and member name each time you want to reference a member.

.UNTIL: End a .REPEAT Loop

Applicable assemblers: MASM 6.0

Directive category: Control flow

Syntax:

```
.UNTIL condition
```

Description: This directive is used to mark the end of a loop constructed with the .REPEAT directive. These loops function like their counterparts in high-level languages.

The condition used by the loop must resolve to either true or false. It can be complex (testing for two or more conditions) and may contain any of the following operators:

Operator	Meaning
==	Equal
!=	Not equal
>	Greater than
>=	Greater than or equal to
<	Less than
<=	Less than or equal to
&	Bit test
&&	Logical AND
||	Logical OR
!	Logical NOT

You can also test automatically the condition of flags by using the following specialized flag-name operators:

Operator	Sample Use
CARRY?	.UNTIL (CARRY?)
OVERFLOW?	.UNTIL (OVERFLOW?)
PARITY?	.UNTIL (PARITY?)
SIGN?	.UNTIL (SIGN?)
ZERO?	.UNTIL (ZERO?)

Example:

```
.REPEAT                   ;Wait for ESC key to be pressed
MOV     AH,7              ;Direct character input without echo
INT     21h               ;DOS services
.UNTIL  (AL == 27)        ;Keep going until ESC is pressed
```

.UNTILCXZ: End a .REPEAT Loop

Applicable assemblers: MASM 6.0

Directive category: Control flow

Syntax:

.UNTILCXZ [*condition*]

Description: This directive is used to mark the end of a loop constructed with the .REPEAT directive. These loops function the same as their counterparts in high-level languages. If used without a condition, the loop repeats until the value in CX is 0. If a condition is included, the loop continues until the condition is true or CX is 0.

The condition used by the loop must resolve to either true or false. It can be complex (testing for two or more conditions) and may contain any of the following operators:

Operator	Meaning
==	Equal
!=	Not equal
>	Greater than
>=	Greater than or equal to

Operator	Meaning
<	Less than
<=	Less than or equal to
&	Bit test
&&	Logical AND
||	Logical OR
!	Logical NOT

You can also test automatically the condition of flags by using the following specialized flag-name operators:

Operator	Sample Use
CARRY?	.UNTILCXZ (CARRY?)
OVERFLOW?	.UNTILCXZ (OVERFLOW?)
PARITY?	.UNTILCXZ (PARITY?)
SIGN?	.UNTILCXZ (SIGN?)
ZERO?	.UNTILCXZ (ZERO?)

Example:

```
MOV     CX,4                ;Want 4 characters
.REPEAT                     ;Loop until 4 are input
MOV     AH,7                ;Direct character input without echo
INT     21h                 ;DOS services
.UNTILCXZ
```

USES: Specify Registers To Save

Applicable assemblers: TASM 2.0, TASM 3.0

Directive category: Procedures and code labels

Syntax:

USES *register*[, *register*] ...

Description: This directive allows you to specify the registers you want saved when a procedure is invoked and restored when the procedure is finished. The registers should be separated by commas.

Note that if you are using MASM, you can specify a register-saving list on the PROC line. Refer to the PROC directive for more information.

VERSION: Specify Version Compatibility

Applicable assemblers: TASM 3.0

Directive category: Global control

Syntax:

```
VERSION versionID
```

Description: Most programmers know that assembler makers change things from one version to another. Sometimes those changes can wreak havoc with your code.

With this directive, you can specify the assembler and version for which you have written your code. The versionID must be one of the following:

ID	Compiler
M400	MASM 4.0
M500	MASM 5.0
M510	MASM 5.1
M520	Quick Assembler
T100	TASM 1.0
T101	TASM 1.01
T200	TASM 2.0
T250	TASM 2.5
T300	TASM 3.0

Using this directive limits the directive and power available with the assembler. It also sets the proper settings for the MASM, MASM51, QUIRKS, and SMART directives.

WARN: Enable Warnings

Applicable assemblers: Microsoft Quick Assembler 2.51, TASM 2.0, TASM 3.0

Directive category: Global control

Syntax:

```
WARN [class]
```

Description: TASM allows you to disable warnings with the NOWARN directive. This directive allows you to enable display of certain warning classes (or all warnings) that may have been suppressed previously.

If you provide a warning class, this directive enables display of warning messages in that class. If you provide no parameters, all warning messages are enabled.

The warning classes are as follows:

Class	Meaning
ALN	Segment alignment
ASS	Assume segment is 16-bit
BRK	Brackets needed
ICG	Inefficient code
LCO	Location counter overflow
OPI	Unterminated (open) IF condition
OPP	Unclosed (open) procedure
OPS	Unclosed (open) segment
OVF	Arithmetic overflow
PDC	Pass-dependent coding
PRO	Incorrect protected-mode memory write
PQK	Assuming constant warning
RES	Reserved word infraction
TPI	Illegal Turbo Pascal operation

.WHILE: Declare the Beginning of a Controlled Loop

Applicable assemblers: MASM 6.0

Directive category: Control flow

Syntax:

```
.WHILE condition
```

Description: This directive is used to construct a loop similar to the WHILE loops in high-level languages. The loop, which may contain any number of statments, is terminated with the .ENDW directive.

The condition used by the loop must resolve to either true or false. It can be complex (testing for two or more conditions) and may contain any of the following operators:

Operator	Meaning
==	Equal
!=	Not equal
>	Greater than
>=	Greater than or equal to
<	Less than
<=	Less than or equal to
&	Bit test
&&	Logical AND
||	Logical OR
!	Logical NOT

You can also test automatically the condition of flags by using the following specialized flag-name operators:

Operator	Sample Use
CARRY?	.WHILE (CARRY?)
OVERFLOW?	.WHILE (OVERFLOW?)
PARITY?	.WHILE (PARITY?)
SIGN?	.WHILE (SIGN?)
ZERO?	.WHILE (ZERO?)

Loops that use .WHILE can be nested with other .WHILE or .REPEAT loops. These loops can be terminated normally with the .ENDW directive, or prematurely with the .BREAK or .CONTINUE directives.

Do not confuse the .WHILE directive with the WHILE directive. They have different purposes and actions.

Example:

```
MOV     AL,0                ;Start with a clean slate
.WHILE  (AL != 13)          ;Keep going until Enter is pressed
MOV     AH,7                ;Direct character input without echo
INT     21h                 ;DOS services
.ENDW
```

The preceding example is the same as the following, nondirective method of coding this loop:

```
        MOV     AL,0            ;Start with a clean slate
InLoop: CMP     AL,13           ;Was Enter pressed?
        JE      OutLoop         ;Yes, so exit
        MOV     AH,7            ;Direct character input without echo
        INT     21h             ;DOS services
        JMP     InLoop          ;Back to the beginning
OutLoop:
```

WHILE: Repeat a Block of Instructions

Applicable assemblers: MASM 6.0, TASM 3.0

Directive category: Macros and repeat blocks

Syntax:

WHILE *expression*

Description: This directive provides a way for the assembler to repeat a code block until a certain expression proves false. Typically, this directive is used in macros. Every source-code line between the WHILE directive and the ENDM or EXITM directives is repeated until WHILE proves to false (0).

Example:

```
Alphabet    EQU     THIS BYTE
            letter = 'A'
            WHILE   letter LE 'Z'
            DB      letter
            letter = letter +1
            ENDM
```

WORD: Allocate a Word of Storage Space

Applicable assemblers: MASM 6.0

Directive category: Data allocation

Syntax:

[*label*] WORD *expression*[, *expression*]

Description: This directive is equivalent to the DW directive. It is used to allocate 2 bytes of memory (a word) for data storage in the executable file. The label is a user-defined name you can use later to refer symbolically to the stored information. Each expression must be one of the following:

❑ A number between –32,767 and 65,535

❑ A formula resolving to a number between –32,767 and 65,535

❑ An offset for an address pointer

❑ A segment for an address pointer

❑ A question mark (used to hold space but not initialize the data area)

In addition, you can use the DUP operator to specify multiple occurrences of the data in the expression.

If the data allocated by the WORD directive is longer than a single word, the label refers only to the first word of the allocated data.

If you are working exclusively with signed data, you can use the SWORD directive also.

Examples:

```
Address1    WORD    Routine         ;Address1 contains only the offset
Address2    WORD    OFFSET Routine  ;Address1 contains only the offset
Address3    WORD    SEGMENT Routine ;Address1 contains only the segment
Counter     WORD    0
ScreenSize  WORD    80 * 25
Array       WORD    12 DUP(?)
```

.XALL: List Only Macros that Generate Code

Applicable assemblers: Microsoft Quick Assembler 2.51, MASM 5.1, MASM 6.0, TASM 2.0, TASM 3.0

Directive category: Listing control

Syntax:

```
.XALL
```

Description: If you use macros a great deal, you probably will use this directive also. It results in the expansion (listing) only of macros that generate code. If you use TASM, this is the same as the %NOMACS directive.

.XCREF: Disable Cross-Referencing

Applicable assemblers: MASM 5.1, MASM 6.0, TASM 2.0, TASM 3.0

Directive category: Listing control

Syntax:

```
.XCREF
```

Description: If this directive is executed, cross-referencing is turned off completely in the listing file. If you are using TASM, it is turned off in the XRF file also.

.XLIST: Disable Source-Code Listing

Applicable assemblers: Microsoft Quick Assembler 2.51, MASM 5.1, MASM 6.0, TASM 2.0, TASM 3.0

Directive category: Listing control

Syntax:

```
.XLIST
```

Description: Use this directive to instruct the assembler to suspend sending listing information to the listing file. Even with this directive in place, however, the assembler will include symbol and cross-reference information in the file.

If you are using TASM, you can use the %NOLIST directive interchangeably with this one. Also, you can use .NOLIST under MASM 6.0.

The ASCII Character Set

Hex	Dec	Screen	Ctrl	Key	Hex	Dec	Screen	Ctrl	Key
00h	0		NUL	^@	1Ah	26	→	SUB	^Z
01h	1	☺	SOH	^A	1Bh	27	←	ESC	^[
02h	2	●	STX	^B	1Ch	28	∟	FS	^\
03h	3	♥	ETX	^C	1Dh	29	↔	GS	^]
04h	4	♦	EOT	^D	1Eh	30	▲	RS	^^
05h	5	♣	ENQ	^E	1Fh	31	▼	US	^_
06h	6	♠	ACK	^F	20h	32			
07h	7	●	BEL	^G	21h	33	!		
08h	8	◘	BS	^H	22h	34	"		
09h	9	○	HT	^I	23h	35	#		
0Ah	10	◙	LF	^J	24h	36	$		
0Bh	11	♂	VT	^K	25h	37	%		
0Ch	12	♀	FF	^L	26h	38	&		
0Dh	13	♪	CR	^M	27h	39	'		
0Eh	14	♫	SO	^N	28h	40	(		
0Fh	15	☼	SI	^O	29h	41	)		
10h	16	►	DLE	^P	2Ah	42	*		
11h	17	◄	DC1	^Q	2Bh	43	+		
12h	18	↕	DC2	^R	2Ch	44	,		
13h	19	‼	DC3	^S	2Dh	45	–		
14h	20	¶	DC4	^T	2Eh	46	.		
15h	21	§	NAK	^U	2Fh	47	/		
16h	22	▬	SYN	^V	30h	48	0		
17h	23	↨	ETB	^W	31h	49	1		
18h	24	↑	CAN	^X	32h	50	2		
19h	25	↓	EM	^Y	33h	51	3		

Hex	Dec	Screen	Hex	Dec	Screen	Hex	Dec	Screen
34h	52	4	62h	98	b	90h	144	É
35h	53	5	63h	99	c	91h	145	æ
36h	54	6	64h	100	d	92h	146	Æ
37h	55	7	65h	101	e	93h	147	ô
38h	56	8	66h	102	f	94h	148	ö
39h	57	9	67h	103	g	95h	149	ò
3Ah	58	:	68h	104	h	96h	150	û
3Bh	59	;	69h	105	i	97h	151	ù
3Ch	60	<	6Ah	106	j	98h	152	ÿ
3Dh	61	=	6Bh	107	k	99h	153	Ö
3Eh	62	>	6Ch	108	l	9Ah	154	Ü
3Fh	63	?	6Dh	109	m	9Bh	155	¢
40h	64	@	6Eh	110	n	9Ch	156	£
41h	65	A	6Fh	111	o	9Dh	157	¥
42h	66	B	70h	112	p	9Eh	158	₧
43h	67	C	71h	113	q	9Fh	159	ƒ
44h	68	D	72h	114	r	A0h	160	á
45h	69	E	73h	115	s	A1h	161	í
46h	70	F	74h	116	t	A2h	162	ó
47h	71	G	75h	117	u	A3h	163	ú
48h	72	H	76h	118	v	A4h	164	ñ
49h	73	I	77h	119	w	A5h	165	Ñ
4Ah	74	J	78h	120	x	A6h	166	ª
4Bh	75	K	79h	121	y	A7h	167	º
4Ch	76	L	7Ah	122	z	A8h	168	¿
4Dh	77	M	7Bh	123	{	A9h	169	⌐
4Eh	78	N	7Ch	124	|	AAh	170	¬
4Fh	79	O	7Dh	125	}	ABh	171	½
50h	80	P	7Eh	126	~	ACh	172	¼
51h	81	Q	7Fh	127	Δ	ADh	173	¡
52h	82	R	80h	128	Ç	AEh	174	«
53h	83	S	81h	129	ü	AFh	175	»
54h	84	T	82h	130	é	B0h	176	░
55h	85	U	83h	131	â	B1h	177	▒
56h	86	V	84h	132	ä	B2h	178	▓
57h	87	W	85h	133	à	B3h	179	│
58h	88	X	86h	134	å	B4h	180	┤
59h	89	Y	87h	135	ç	B5h	181	╡
5Ah	90	Z	88h	136	ê	B6h	182	╢
5Bh	91	[	89h	137	ë	B7h	183	╖
5Ch	92	\	8Ah	138	è	B8h	184	╕
5Dh	93	]	8Bh	139	ï	B9h	185	╣
5Eh	94	^	8Ch	140	î	BAh	186	║
5Fh	95	_	8Dh	141	ì	BBh	187	╗
60h	96	`	8Eh	142	Ä	BCh	188	╝
61h	97	a	8Fh	143	Å	BDh	189	╜

Hex	Dec	Screen	Hex	Dec	Screen	Hex	Dec	Screen
BEh	190	⌐	D4h	212	╘	EAh	234	Ω
BFh	191	╗	D5h	213	╒	EBh	235	δ
C0h	192	╚	D6h	214	╓	ECh	236	∞
C1h	193	⊥	D7h	215	╫	EDh	237	φ
C2h	194	╥	D8h	216	╪	EEh	238	∈
C3h	195	├	D9h	217	╝	EFh	239	∩
C4h	196	─	DAh	218	┌	F0h	240	≡
C5h	197	┼	DBh	219	█	F1h	241	±
C6h	198	╞	DCh	220	▄	F2h	242	≥
C7h	199	╟	DDh	221	▌	F3h	243	≤
C8h	200	╚	DEh	222	▐	F4h	244	⌠
C9h	201	╔	DFh	223	▀	F5h	245	⌡
CAh	202	╩	E0h	224	α	F6h	246	÷
CBh	203	╦	E1h	225	β	F7h	247	≈
CCh	204	╠	E2h	226	Γ	F8h	248	°
CDh	205	═	E3h	227	π	F9h	249	•
CEh	206	╬	E4h	228	Σ	FAh	250	·
CFh	207	╧	E5h	229	σ	FBh	251	√
D0h	208	╨	E6h	230	μ	FCh	252	ⁿ
D1h	209	╤	E7h	231	τ	FDh	253	²
D2h	210	╥	E8h	232	Φ	FEh	254	■
D3h	211	╙	E9h	233	θ	FFh	255	

B

Keyboard Interpretation Tables

This appendix contains two tables that will be useful when you interface to the keyboard, either through BIOS or directly through the hardware port.

BIOS Keyboard Codes

Table B.1 shows the scan code/ASCII value combinations returned through the BIOS keyboard services. The keyboard controller does not return the scan codes directly. Instead, BIOS translates (into the codes shown in this table) the codes it gives to the keyboard controller.

Table B.1. *BIOS keyboard codes.*

Scan Code		ASCII Value		
Decimal	Hex	Decimal	Hex	Keystroke
0	00	0	00	Break
1	01	27	1B	Esc
2	02	49	31	1
		33	21	!
3	03	50	32	2
		64	40	@
		0	00	Ctrl-@

Table B.1. *continued*

Scan Code			ASCII Value		
Decimal	Hex		Decimal	Hex	Keystroke
4	04		51	33	3
			35	23	#
5	05		52	34	4
			36	24	$
6	06		53	35	5
			37	25	%
7	07		54	36	6
			94	5E	^
			30	1E	Ctrl-^
8	08		55	37	7
			38	26	&
9	09		56	38	8
			42	2A	* (Shift-8)
10	0A		57	39	9
			40	28	(
11	0B		48	30	0
			41	29	)
12	0C		45	2D	-
			95	5F	_
			31	1F	Ctrl-_
13	0D		61	3D	=
			43	2B	+
14	0E		8	08	Backspace
			127	7F	Ctrl-Backspace
15	0F		9	09	Tab
			0	00	Back tab
16	10		113	71	q
			81	51	Q
			0	00	Alt-Q
			17	11	Ctrl-Q
17	11		119	77	w
			87	57	W
			0	00	Alt-W
			23	17	Ctrl-W

| Scan Code | | ASCII Value | | |
Decimal	Hex	Decimal	Hex	Keystroke
18	12	101	65	e
		69	45	E
		0	00	Alt-E
		5	05	Ctrl-E
19	13	114	72	r
		82	52	R
		0	00	Alt-R
		18	12	Ctrl-R
20	14	116	74	t
		84	54	T
		0	00	Alt-T
		20	14	Ctrl-T
21	15	121	79	y
		89	59	Y
		0	00	Alt-Y
		25	19	Ctrl-Y
22	16	117	75	u
		85	55	U
		0	00	Alt-U
		21	15	Ctrl-U
23	17	105	69	i
		73	49	I
		0	00	Alt-I
		9	09	Ctrl-I
24	18	111	6F	o
		79	4F	O
		0	00	Alt-O
		15	0F	Ctrl-O
25	19	112	70	p
		80	50	P
		0	00	Alt-P
		16	10	Ctrl-P
26	1A	91	5B	[
		123	7B	{
		27	1B	Ctrl-[
27	1B	93	5D	]
		125	7D	}
		29	1D	Ctrl-]

continues

Table B.1. continued

Scan Code			ASCII Value		
Decimal	Hex		Decimal	Hex	Keystroke
28	1C		13	0D	Enter
30	1E		97	61	a
			65	41	A
			0	00	Alt-A
			1	01	Ctrl-A
31	1F		115	73	s
			83	53	S
			0	00	Alt-S
			19	13	Ctrl-S
32	20		100	64	d
			68	44	D
			0	00	Alt-D
			4	04	Ctrl-D
33	21		102	66	f
			70	46	F
			0	00	Alt-F
			6	06	Ctrl-F
34	22		103	67	g
			71	47	G
			0	00	Alt-G
			7	47	Ctrl-G
35	23		104	68	h
			72	48	H
			0	00	Alt-H
			8	08	Ctrl-H
36	24		106	6A	j
			74	4A	J
			0	00	Alt-J
			10	0A	Ctrl-J
37	25		107	6B	k
			75	4B	K
			0	00	Alt-K
			11	0B	Ctrl-K
38	26		108	6C	l
			76	4C	L
			0	00	Alt-L
			12	0C	Ctrl-L

Scan Code		ASCII Value		
Decimal	Hex	Decimal	Hex	Keystroke
39	27	59	3B	;
		58	3A	:
40	28	39	27	'
		34	22	"
41	29	96	60	` (accent grave)
		126	7E	~
43	2B	92	5C	\
		124	7C	|
		28	1C	Ctrl-\
44	2C	122	7A	z
		90	5A	Z
		0	00	Alt-Z
		26	1A	Ctrl-Z
45	2D	120	78	x
		88	58	X
		0	00	Alt-X
		24	18	Ctrl-X
46	2E	99	63	c
		67	43	C
		0	00	Alt-C
		3	03	Ctrl-C
47	2F	118	76	v
		86	56	V
		0	00	Alt-V
		22	16	Ctrl-V
48	30	98	62	b
		66	42	B
		0	00	Alt-B
		2	02	Ctrl-B
49	31	110	6E	n
		78	4E	N
		0	00	Alt-N
		14	0E	Ctrl-N
50	32	109	6D	m
		77	4D	M
		0	00	Alt-M
		13	0D	Ctrl-M

continues

Table B.1. *continued*

| Scan Code | | ASCII Value | | |
Decimal	Hex	Decimal	Hex	Keystroke
51	33	44	2C	,
		60	3C	<
52	34	46	2E	.
		62	3E	>
53	35	47	2F	/
		63	3F	?
55	37	42	2A	* (next to keypad)
		0	00	Alt-Pause
56	38	0	00	Alt-Break
57	39	32	20	Space
58	3A	0	00	Caps Lock
59	3B	0	00	F1
60	3C	0	00	F2
61	3D	0	00	F3
62	3E	0	00	F4
63	3F	0	00	F5
64	40	0	00	F6
65	41	0	00	F7
66	42	0	00	F8
67	43	0	00	F9
68	44	0	00	F10
69	45	0	00	Num Lock
70	46	0	00	Scroll Lock
71	47	0	00	Home
		55	37	7 (keypad)
72	48	0	00	Up arrow
		56	38	8 (keypad)
73	49	0	00	PgUp
		57	39	9 (keypad)
74	4A	45	2D	– (next to keypad)
75	4B	0	00	Left arrow
		52	34	4 (keypad)
76	4C	0	00	Center key (keypad)
		53	35	5 (keypad)

| Scan Code | | ASCII Value | | |
Decimal	Hex	Decimal	Hex	Keystroke
77	4D	0	00	Right arrow
		54	36	6 (keypad)
78	4E	43	2B	+ (next to keypad)
79	4F	0	00	End
		49	31	1 (keypad)
80	50	0	00	Down arrow
		50	32	2 (keypad)
81	51	0	00	PgDn
		51	33	3 (keypad)
82	52	0	00	Ins
		48	30	0 (keypad)
83	53	0	00	Del
		46	2E	. (keypad)
84	54	0	00	Shift-F1
85	55	0	00	Shift-F2
86	56	0	00	Shift-F3
87	57	0	00	Shift-F4
88	58	0	00	Shift-F5
89	59	0	00	Shift-F6
90	5A	0	00	Shift-F7
91	5B	0	00	Shift-F8
92	5C	0	00	Shift-F9
93	5D	0	00	Shift-F10
94	5E	0	00	Ctrl-F1
95	5F	0	00	Ctrl-F2
96	60	0	00	Ctrl-F3
97	61	0	00	Ctrl-F4
98	62	0	00	Ctrl-F5
99	63	0	00	Ctrl-F6
100	64	0	00	Ctrl-F7
101	65	0	00	Ctrl-F8
102	66	0	00	Ctrl-F9
103	67	0	00	Ctrl-F10

continues

Table B.1. *continued*

| Scan Code | | ASCII Value | | |
Decimal	Hex	Decimal	Hex	Keystroke
104	68	0	00	Alt-F1
105	69	0	00	Alt-F2
106	6A	0	00	Alt-F3
107	6B	0	00	Alt-F4
108	6C	0	00	Alt-F5
109	6D	0	00	Alt-F6
110	6E	0	00	Alt-F7
111	6F	0	00	Alt-F8
112	70	0	00	Alt-F9
113	71	0	00	Alt-F10
114	72	0	00	Ctrl-PrtSc
115	73	0	00	Ctrl-Left arrow
116	74	0	00	Ctrl-Right arrow
117	75	0	00	Ctrl-End
118	76	0	00	Ctrl-PgDn
119	77	0	00	Ctrl-Home
120	78	0	00	Alt-1 (keyboard)
121	79	0	00	Alt-2 (keyboard)
122	7A	0	00	Alt-3 (keyboard)
123	7B	0	00	Alt-4 (keyboard)
124	7C	0	00	Alt-5 (keyboard)
125	7D	0	00	Alt-6 (keyboard)
126	7E	0	00	Alt-7 (keyboard)
127	7F	0	00	Alt-8 (keyboard)
128	80	0	00	Alt-9 (keyboard)
129	81	0	00	Alt-0 (keyboard)
130	82	0	00	Alt-– (keyboard)
131	83	0	00	Alt-= (keyboard)
132	84	0	00	Ctrl-PgUp

Keyboard Controller Codes

Table B.2 shows the key codes returned when you access the keyboard controller through hardware port 60h. Notice that this table is a good deal shorter than table B.1. The keyboard controller does no translation on the Shift, Ctrl, and Alt keys. Each key is given a specific position value, which BIOS translates into the appropriate scan code/ASCII value combination.

Table B.2. *Keyboard controller codes.*

Decimal	Key Code Hex	Key
1	01	Esc
2	02	1
3	03	2
4	04	3
5	05	4
6	06	5
7	07	6
8	08	7
9	09	8
10	0A	9
11	0B	0
12	0C	-
13	0D	=
14	0E	Backspace
15	0F	Tab
16	10	q
17	11	w
18	12	e
19	13	r
20	14	t
21	15	y
22	16	u
23	17	i
24	18	o

continues

Table B.2. *continued*

Decimal	Key Code Hex	Key
25	19	p
26	1A	[
27	1B	]
28	1C	Enter
29	1D	Ctrl
29/69	ID/45	Pause
30	1E	a
31	1F	s
32	20	d
33	21	f
34	22	g
35	23	h
36	24	j
37	25	k
38	26	l
39	27	;
40	28	'
41	29	` (accent grave)
42	2A	Left Shift
42/52	2A/34	PrtSc (enhanced keyboard)
42/71	2A/47	Home (middle, enhanced keyboard)
42/72	2A/48	Up arrow (middle, enhanced keyboard)
42/73	2A/49	PgUp (middle, enhanced keyboard)
42/75	2A/4B	Left arrow (middle, enhanced keyboard)
42/77	2A/4D	Right arrow (middle, enhanced keyboard)
42/79	2A/4F	End (middle, enhanced keyboard)
42/80	2A/50	Down arrow (middle, enhanced keyboard)
42/81	2A/51	PgDn (middle, enhanced keyboard)
42/82	2A/52	Insert (middle, enhanced keyboard)
42/83	2A/53	Del (middle, enhanced keyboard)
43	2B	\

Decimal	Key Code Hex	Key
44	2C	z
45	2D	x
46	2E	c
47	2F	v
48	30	b
49	31	n
50	32	m
51	33	,
52	34	.
53	35	/
54	36	Right Shift
55	37	* (next to keypad)
56	38	Alt
57	39	Space
58	3A	Caps Lock
59	3B	F1
60	3C	F2
61	3D	F3
62	3E	F4
63	3F	F5
64	40	F6
65	41	F7
66	42	F8
67	43	F9
68	44	F10
69	45	Num Lock
70	46	Scroll Lock
71	47	Home (keypad)
72	48	Up arrow (keypad)
73	49	PgUp (keypad)
74	4A	– (next to keypad)
75	4B	Left arrow (keypad)
76	4C	5 (keypad)

continues

Table B.2. *continued*

Decimal	Key Code Hex	Key
77	4D	Right arrow (keypad)
78	4E	+ (next to keypad)
79	4F	End (keypad)
80	50	Down arrow (keypad)
81	51	PgDn (keypad)
82	52	Ins (keypad)
83	53	Del (keypad)
84	54	[Currently unused]
85	55	[Currently unused]
86	56	[Currently unused]
87	57	F11
88	58	F12

Some keys, especially on the enhanced 101-key keyboard, return double values. These values, shown with a slash between the two numbers, are listed according to the first number of the pair.

Each key is designated by the unshifted value shown on the keycap.

Glossary

Align type. An assembly language directive specifying how the start of the segment is to be aligned in memory. The align type is specified on the same line as the segment name. See also *BYTE*, *PAGE*, *PARA*, and *WORD*.

ALU. Arithmetic/Logic Unit, the portion of the CPU that performs arithmetic functions on data. The ALU controls the settings of the bits in the flags register.

ASCII. American Standard Code for Information Interchange.

ASCIIZ. An ASCII string that is terminated with a null character (value of θ). ASCIIZ is used extensively in DOS interrupt services.

Assembler. The software program that translates (assembles) assembly language mnemonics into machine language for direct execution by the computer.

Assembly language. The pseudo-English language, called *source code*, that is written and hopefully readable by humans. Assembly language is not directly executable by a computer.

Assembly. The process of code conversion performed by an assembler. Assembly language source code is translated into machine language through this process.

AT. A segment combine type used generally to prepare a template to be used for accessing fixed-location data. In the format *AT XXXX* (where *XXXX* is a memory address), *AT* signifies that addresses and offsets are to be calculated relative to the specified memory address. See also *Combine type*, *COMMON*, *MEMORY*, *PRIVATE*, *PUBLIC*, and *STACK*.

Auxiliary carry flag. The bit in the flag register that indicates whether the previous decimal operation resulted in a carry out of or borrow into the four low-order bits of the byte.

AX. A general-purpose data register.

Base register. A register containing an address that is used as a base in indirect addressing methods. The base register is usually the BP or BX register.

BCD. Binary Coded Decimal.

Binary. A numbering system based on only two digits. The only valid digits in a binary system are 0 and 1. See also *Bit*.

BIOS. An acronym for Basic Input/Output System—a collection of low-level system functions that enable programs to take advantage of system resources.

Bit. Binary digit, the smallest unit of storage on a computer. Each bit can have a value of 0 or 1, indicating the absence or presence of an electrical signal. See also *Binary*.

BP. The base pointer register.

BX. A general-purpose data register.

Byte. A basic unit of data storage and manipulation. A byte is equivalent to 8 bits and can contain a value ranging from 0 through 255.

BYTE. A segment align type that directs the assembler to place the segment at the next available byte after completing the preceding segment. See also *Align type*, *PAGE*, *PARA*, and *WORD*.

CALL. An assembly language instruction telling the assembler to perform the subroutine.

Carry flag. The bit in the flag register that indicates whether the previous operation resulted in a carry out of or borrow into the high-order bit of the resulting byte or word.

CGA. Color Graphics Adapter.

Class type. An assembler directive indicating how individual segments are to be grouped when linked. Segments having the same class type are loaded contiguously in memory before another class type is begun. The class type is specified on the same line as the segment name and is enclosed by single quotation marks.

Combine type. An optional assembler directive that defines how segments with the same name will be combined.

COMMON. A segment combine type. It causes individual segments of the same name and of the COMMON combine type to begin at a common memory address. All COMMON segments with the same name begin at the same point, with the resulting segment equal in length to the longest individual segment. All addresses and offsets in the resulting segment are relative to a single segment register. See also *AT*, *Combine type*, *MEMORY*, *PRIVATE*, *PUBLIC*, and *STACK*.

Compiler. A program that translates high-level language source code into either machine code or pseudocode. Machine code can be directly executed by a computer, but pseudocode requires a run-time routine to work properly.

Control Word. A 16-bit register used in the NPX/FPU to govern the way the chip works.

CPU. The microprocessor (central processing unit) responsible for operations inside the computer. These operations generally include system timing, logical processing, and logical operations.

CS. The code segment register.

CX. A general-purpose data register, normally used for counting functions.

DASD. Direct access storage device. The term was coined by IBM and is used extensively in their documentation.

Device driver. A program that controls the way DOS communicates with an external device. Typically, device drivers are loaded when DOS is started (booted).

DI. The destination index register.

Direction flag. The bit in the flag register that indicates whether string operations should increment (DF clear) or decrement (DF set) the index registers.

Displacement. An offset from a specified base point.

DMA. Direct memory access; a method of data transfer involving direct access of the RAM buffer area through specialized circuitry. DMA frees the CPU for other operations and results in a more efficient use of computer resources.

DOS. An acronym for Disk Operating System, the program that controls the way your computer functions.

DOS extender. A control program that allows DOS to access and use memory above the historical 640K boundary.

DS. The data segment register.

DTA. A memory area (disk transfer area) used with FCB file operations for the transfer of information to and from the floppy disk. See also Chapter 21, service 21/1A.

DX. A general-purpose data register.

EGA. Enhanced Graphics Adapter.

ENDP. An assembler directive indicating the end of a procedure. See also *PROC*.

EQU. An assembly language directive (equate). See also *Equate*.

Equate. The full-word form of the assembly language directive EQU. Equate assigns to a mnemonic label a value that is later substituted for other occurrences of the label during program assembly. See also *EQU*.

ES. The extra segment register.

Exception. An NPX/FPU term relating to a flag set in the status word register if an operation renders an exceptional result (outside normal bounds).

FAR. A procedure that pushes the full return address (effectively, the contents of CS:IP) on the stack. FAR is assumed to be in a code segment different from the current segment.

FCB. File Control Block.

Flag. An indicator used to control or signal other software or hardware functions.

Flat addressing. A memory configuration scheme in which all of memory is viewed as one contiguous stream of bytes.

FPU. An acronym for *Floating-Point Unit*. This is the equivalent of an 80387 NPX built into the 80486 microprocessor.

FS. An additional "extra" segment register for the 80286 and 80386. Identical in use to the ES register.

Function. A self-contained coding segment designed to do a specific task. A function is sometimes referred to as a procedure or subroutine.

GDT. Global Descriptor Table. Used in protected-mode programming of the 80286, 80386, or 80486 to detail segment register contents and other descriptors for the entire operation of the CPU.

Graphics. A video presentation consisting mostly of pictures and figures rather than letters and numbers. See also *Text*.

Group. A collection of segments that fit into a 64K segment of RAM. At link time, LINK.EXE uses segment group classifications to determine how segments are combined.

GS. An additional "extra" segment register for the 80286 and 80386. Identical in use to the ES register.

Hexadecimal. A numbering system based on 16 elements. Digits are numbered 0 through F, as follows: 0, 1, 2, 3, 4, 5, 6, 7, 8, 9, A, B, C, D, E, F.

HGA. Hercules Graphics Adapter.

IDT. Interrupt Descriptor Table. Used in protected-mode programming of the 80286, 80386, or 80486 to replace the interrupt vectors normally located in low memory on the 8086/8088.

Index register. A register assumed to contain an address for use in indirect addressing modes. Usually, the index register consists of the SI (source index) or DI (destination index) registers.

Instruction Set. The group of mnemonic directions used to control a processor.

Interpreter. A program that translates high-level language source code into machine code which is immediately executed. Programs that use an interpreter run much slower than programs using a compiler.

Interrupt. An event, internal or external to the computer, that causes the CPU to stop what it is doing and begin execution of an interrupt handler. Interrupts generally are used to make the most efficient use of a CPU's time.

Interrupt flag. The bit in the flag register that indicates whether the CPU should handle maskable interrupts. If this flag is set, interrupts are handled. If it is clear, interrupts are ignored.

IOCTL. An acronym for Input/Output Control. A collection of DOS services that provide standardized control of block and character devices. These services are available through Int 21/44.

IP. The instruction pointer register.

LDT. Local Descriptor Table. Used in protected-mode programming of the 80286, 80386, or 80486 to detail segment register contents and other descriptors for a local task.

LIB.EXE. The library-management software distributed by Microsoft and IBM with their assemblers.

Library. A collection of object-code modules saved in a single file. The assembler searches this file during the linking process to resolve external references in the main programs.

Linker. A program that combines object files into their final executable state.

Linking. The process of resolving external references and address references in object code, resulting in machine language instructions that are directly executable by the computer.

Machine language. The series of binary digits a microprocessor executes to perform individual tasks. People seldom (if ever) program in machine language. Instead, they program in assembly language, and an assembler translates their instructions into machine language.

MASM. Macro Assembler, sold and supported by Microsoft.

MCB. Memory Control Block.

MCGA. Multi-Color Graphics Array.

MDA. Monochrome Display Adapter.

MEMORY. A segment combine type that results in all segments with the same name being joined into one segment when linked. All addresses and offsets in the resulting segment relate to a single segment register. See also *AT*, *Combine type*, *COMMON*, *PRIVATE*, *PUBLIC*, and *STACK*.

Memory manager. A control program that allocates, monitors, and otherwise manages the use of memory resources in a computer system.

Memory map. An organized method of depicting the use of an area of computer memory.

MMU. An acronym for *Memory Management Unit*, a specialized section of the 80486.

Monochrome. A single color.

MSW. Machine Status Word.

NaN. An acronym for *Not a Number*. This term is used in conjunction with NPX/FPU chips. It represents a floating-point value that does not represent a numeric or infinite quantity value. NaN is typically generated as the result of a serious error and can contain error information that can indicate the source of the error.

NEAR. An assembly language directive that indicates the type of procedure you are creating. Issued on the same line as the PROC directive, NEAR controls how you call and return from the procedure.

NPX. Numeric Processor Extension. This is the 8087, 80287, or 80387 numeric coprocessor.

Object code. A "halfway step" between source code and executable machine language, object code consists mostly of machine language but is not directly executable by the computer. It must first be linked in order to resolve external references and address references.

Offset. A distance from a given paragraph boundary in memory. The offset usually is given as a number of bytes.

Overflow flag. The bit in the flag register that indicates whether the signed result of the preceding operation can be represented in the result byte or word.

PAGE. A segment align type that directs the assembler, after it completes the preceding segment, to place the segment at the next available hexadecimal address ending in 00. See also *Align type*, *BYTE*, *PARA*, and *WORD*.

PARA. A segment align type that directs the assembler, after it completes the preceding segment, to place the segment at the next available hexadecimal address ending in 0. See also *Align type*, *BYTE*, *PAGE*, and *WORD*.

Parity flag. The bit in the flag register that indicates whether the low-order 8 bits of the result contain an even number (PF set) or odd number (PF clear) of bits equal to 1.

Parse. A process of analyzing information to make logical sense of it. Command lines are parsed by a command parser or command processor. An assembler parses a source-code file to determine what is necessary to create an object file.

Polling. A method of interrogating external devices to see whether they have information for or need information from the CPU.

PRIVATE. A segment combine type that results in the affected segment not being combined with other segments when linked. See also *AT*, *Combine type*, *COMMON*, *MEMORY*, and *STACK*.

PROC. An assembly language directive indicating the start of a procedure. See also *ENDP*.

Procedure. A self-contained coding segment designed to do a specific task, sometimes referred to as a subroutine.

Protected Mode. An alternative operating mode of the 80286, 80386, and 80486 chips. Protected mode causes a different use of the segment registers and memory than real mode.

Pseudo-Op. A type of operation code that is not a direction to the microprocessor but a command for the assembler or linker to follow when producing the executable file.

PSP. Program Segment Prefix.

PUBLIC. A segment combine type that results in all segments with the same name being joined into one segment when linked. All addresses and offsets in the resulting segment relate to a single segment register. See also *AT*, *Combine type*, *COMMON*, *MEMORY*, *PRIVATE*, and *STACK*.

Queue. A list of information (or files) waiting to be processed by a program.

RAM. Random-Access Memory.

Real Mode. The native operating mode of the 8086/8088. Also available as the default operating mode on later Intel CPUs.

Register. The data-holding areas, usually 16 bits long, used by the processor in performing operations.

ROM. Read-Only Memory.

RPL. Requested Privilege Level.

Run-time system. A system manager that oversees proper operation of the language during program execution.

Segment. A particular area of memory, 64K in size.

Segment offset. The value to be added to the result of 16 times the segment value, thereby producing an absolute memory address.

Segment register. Any of the CPU registers designed to contain a segment address. They include the CS, DS, ES, and SS registers.

SI. The source index register.

Sign flag. The bit in the flag register that is set equal to the high-order bit of the result of the last operation.

Significand. The portion of a floating-point number that contains the most significant nonzero bits of the number.

Source code. The assembly language instructions, written by humans, that an assembler translates into object code.

SP. The stack pointer register.

SS. The stack segment register.

Stack. An area of memory set aside for the temporary storage of values in a computing environment. The stack operates in a LIFO fashion. In an 8088-based environment, only whole words (16 bits) can be pushed on and popped from the stack.

STACK. A segment combine type resulting in all segments with this combine type being joined to form one segment when linked. All addresses and offsets in the resulting segment are relative to the stack segment register. The SP register is initialized to the ending address of the segment. This combine type normally is used to define the stack area for a program. See also *AT*, *Combine type*, *COMMON*, *MEMORY*, *PRIVATE*, and *PUBLIC*.

Status Word. A 16-bit register used in the NPX/FPU to indicate the status or result of certain operations.

Subroutine. A self-contained coding segment designed to do a specific task, sometimes referred to as a procedure.

SVGA. Super Video Graphics Array, a nonstandardized type of display adapter based on extensions to the VGA standard.

TASM. Turbo Assembler, sold and supported by Borland International.

Text. A video presentation scheme consisting mostly of letters and numbers. See also *Graphics*.

TLB. Translation Lookaside Buffer, the 80486 on-chip cache for page table entries.

TLIB. Turbo Library utility, sold and supported by Borland International.

Trap flag. The bit in the flag register that indicates a single-step instruction execution mode. If the trap flag is set, a single-step interrupt occurs. The flag is cleared after the assembler executes the next instruction.

VGA. Video Graphics Array, a type of display adapter.

Virtual Mode. An alternative operating mode of the 80386 and 80486 chips under which a protected-mode task can appear to be running in a virtual real-mode 8086 environment.

WAIT. An assembly language instruction (wait).

Word. In general usage, two consecutive bytes (16 bits) of data.

WORD. A segment align type that directs the assembler, after it completes the preceding segment, to place the segment at the next available even address. If the preceding segment ends on an odd address, WORD effectively is equivalent to BYTE. See also *Align type*, *BYTE*, *PAGE*, and *PARA*.

Zero flag. The bit in the flag register that indicates whether the result of the preceding operation is zero. If the result is zero, the flag is set. If the result is not zero, the flag is clear.

Index

A

O

S

How Much is <u>Your</u> Time Worth?

Only you know the answer. But we bet it isn't a productive use of your time to enter the listings in this book. Why not **save time and money** by ordering the companion listing disk?

Order Your Program Disk Today!

You can save hours of tedious, error-prone typing by ordering the companion disk to *Using Assembly Language, 3rd Edition*. The disk contains the **source code for every listing** in the book.

Simply make a copy of this page, enclose payment and shipping information, and send to:

Discovery Computing Inc.
PO Box 88
South Jordan, UT 84065

Item	Disk Size	Format	Copies	Price Each	Amount
UAL3E Code Disk	5.25"	360K	_____	24.95	_____
UAL3E Code Disk	3.5"	720K	_____	24.95	_____

Utah residents add 6.25% sales tax: _____

Subtotal: _____

For COD or non-U.S. orders, add S&H charge of $5.00: _____

Total: _____

Payment method: Check: _____   Money Order: _____   COD: _____

Shipping Information:

Name: _____

Company: _____

Address: _____

_____

City: _____ State: _____ Zip: _____

Phone: _____ (daytime, in case there are questions about your order)

- -

Checks and money orders should be made payable to Discovery Computing Inc. Orders outside the U.S. must pay by international money order in U.S. funds. This offer is made by Discovery Computing Inc., not by Que Corporation or Prentice Hall Computer Publishing.

Directives Supported by Major Assemblers *(continued from inside front cover)*

Directive (Pseudooperation)	MASM 6.0	MASM 5.1	MsQA 2.51	TASM 3.0	TASM 2.0
.LFCOND	✓	✓	✓	✓	✓
%LINUM				✓	✓
%LIST				✓	✓
.LIST	✓	✓	✓	✓	✓
.LISTALL	✓				
.LISTIF	✓				
.LISTMACRO	✓				
.LISTMACROALL	✓				
LOCAL	✓	✓	✓	✓	✓
LOCALS				✓	✓
MACRO	✓	✓	✓	✓	✓
%MACS				✓	✓
MASM				✓	✓
MASM51				✓	✓
.MODEL	✓	✓	✓	✓	✓
MODEL				✓	
.MSFLOAT			✓		
MULTERRS				✓	✓
NAME	✓	✓	✓	✓	✓
%NEWPAGE				✓	✓
.NO87	✓				
%NOCONDS				✓	✓
%NOCREF				✓	✓
.NOCREF	✓				
%NOCTLS				✓	✓
NOEMUL				✓	✓
%NOINCL				✓	✓
NOJUMPS				✓	✓
%NOLIST				✓	✓
.NOLIST	✓				
.NOLISTIF	✓				
.NOLISTMACRO	✓				
NOLOCALS				✓	✓
%NOMACS				✓	✓
NOMASM51				✓	✓
NOMULTERRS				✓	✓
NOSMART				✓	
%NOSYMS				✓	
%NOTRUNC				✓	✓
NOWARN				✓	✓
OPTION	✓				
ORG	✓	✓	✓	✓	✓
%OUT	✓	✓	✓	✓	✓
P186, P286				✓	✓
P286N				✓	✓
P286P				✓	✓
P287, P386				✓	✓
P386N				✓	✓
P386P				✓	✓
P387, P486				✓	✓
P486N				✓	✓
P8086				✓	✓
P8087				✓	✓
PAGE	✓	✓	✓	✓	✓
%PAGESIZE				✓	✓
%PCNT				✓	✓
PNO87				✓	
POPCONTEXT	✓				
%POPLCTL				✓	✓
PROC	✓	✓	✓	✓	✓